# Johann Sebastian Bach's
*Christmas Oratorio*

# Johann Sebastian Bach's
# *Christmas Oratorio*

## *Music, Theology, Culture*

MARKUS RATHEY

**OXFORD**
UNIVERSITY PRESS

# OXFORD
UNIVERSITY PRESS

Oxford University Press is a department of the University of Oxford. It furthers
the University's objective of excellence in research, scholarship, and education
by publishing worldwide. Oxford is a registered trade mark of Oxford University
Press in the UK and certain other countries.

Published in the United States of America by Oxford University Press
198 Madison Avenue, New York, NY 10016, United States of America.

Library of Congress Cataloging-in-Publication Data
Names: Rathey, Markus.
Title: Johann Sebastian Bach's Christmas Oratorio : music, theology, culture/Markus Rathey.
Description: New York : Oxford University Press, [2016] | Includes
bibliographical references and index.
Identifiers: LCCN 2015049008 (print) | LCCN 2015049271 (ebook) |
ISBN 9780190275259 (hardcover : alk. paper) | ISBN 9780190275266 (e-book)
Subjects: LCSH: Bach, Johann Sebastian, 1685–1750. Weihnachts-Oratorium.
Classification: LCC ML410.B13 R287 2016 (print) | LCC ML410.B13 (ebook) | DDC
782.23—dc23
LC record available at http://lccn.loc.gov/2015049008

This volume is published with the generous support of the Lloyd Hibberd Endowment of the
American Musicological Society, funded in part by the National Endowment for the Humanities and the
Andrew W. Mellon Foundation

3 5 7 9 8 6 4 2
Printed by Sheridan Books, Inc., United States of America

*Tell me where is fancy bred/Or in the heart, or in the head?*
William Shakespeare, *The Merchant of Venice*, III, 2

*Perché s'è ver, che nel tuo cor io sia,*
*Entro al tuo sen celata,*
*Non posso da' tuoi lumi esser mirata.*
Claudio Monteverdi, *L'incoronazione di Poppea*, I, 3

*God's love and grace are not just mathematical or mechanical relations,*
*but have their true seat and origin in the movement of the heart of God.*
Karl Barth, *Church Dogmatics* II, 1, 370

# CONTENTS

# ACKNOWLEDGMENTS

My first words of thanks go to my graduate students who have, in several seminars, discussed Bach and his vocal music, the interpretation of Bach sources, the history of the oratorio in the seventeenth and eighteenth centuries, and the religious and devotional landscape in Germany in the eighteenth century. I have learned a lot from the keen eyes of music theorists, conductors, singers, music historians, and theologians. The unique mixture of talents and interests at Yale has left its mark on the multifaceted approach to Bach's *Christmas Oratorio* and is reflected in this book.

I would also like to thank my colleagues at Yale, the School of Music, the Department of Music, the Divinity School, and in particular my colleagues and friends at the Institute of Sacred Music for their encouragement and the valuable advice. It has been inspiring for me as a scholar to prepare performances of Bach's works with my colleagues Marguerite Brooks, Simon Carrington, David Hill, and Masaaki Suzuki. Having one of my favorite Bach-tenors, James Taylor, as a friend and colleague also provided inspiration. His warm voice on the Rilling recording of the oratorio from 2000 accompanied me through the process of writing this book. My colleague Ellen Rosand's book on Monteverdi's *Venetian Trilogy* (2007) encouraged me to bridge the gulf between philology and semantics, between details of the compositional process and the religious and dramatic function of the music.

A large number of friends and colleagues were kind enough to read all or parts of the manuscript at various stages of its development: Danielle Annett, Eric Chafe, Ellen Exner, Bruce Gordon, and Robin Leaver. My thanks go especially to Michael Marissen, who meticulously read the final draft and made numerous suggestions that improved both the style as well as the content of the book. Other colleagues who have lent me their ears and their advice during the genesis of the book were Stephen Crist, Don Franklin, Andreas Glöckner, Michael Maul, Daniel Melamed, Mark Peters, and Thomas Troeger.

Some of my current and former students have aided me in my research: Kathryn Aaron, Blenda Bo Kyung Im, Katharine Arnold Luce; my research assistant, Emily Coakley, meticulously edited the manuscript.

I am grateful to a large number of libraries and archives that provided me access to their holdings and which have patiently responded to my requests for copies, scans, and bibliographic information: the Deutsche Staatsbibliothek Berlin (esp. the Musikabteilung), the Bach Archive Leipzig, the Riemenschneider Bach Institute at Baldwin-Wallace University, the Bibliotheca Albertina Leipzig, the Herzog August Bibliothek Wolfenbüttel, the Universitäts- und Forschungsbibliothek Erfurt/ Gotha, the Sächsische Landesbibliothek Dresden, and especially the libraries at Yale: the Beinecke Library, the Music Library, and the library of the Divinity School.

The research for this book would not have been possible without the financial support of several institutions. First and foremost I have to thank again the Yale Institute of Sacred Music for institutional and financial support, and for granting me a sabbatical in 2012, which allowed me to examine Bach's composition score for the *Christmas Oratorio* and other Bach sources in the Deutsche Staatsbibliothek Berlin. The research in Berlin was also supported through a Scheide Research Grant by the American Bach Society. The Martha Goldsworthy Fellowship by the Riemenschneider Bach Institute allowed me to spend several weeks in Berea, Ohio, and to take advantage of the holdings of the institute. I am grateful to the former director Mel Unger as well as the librarian Sandra Eichenberg.

Suzanne Ryan, Daniel Gibney, and Andrew Maillet at Oxford University Press have supported me in this project and have overseen a smooth and efficient production process. I am grateful for their encouragement and their patience during the final stages of the completion of the book. Mary Sutherland copyedited the manuscript, using her editorial skill to improve it in ways too numerous to count.

This book is dedicated to the memory of my late father, Karl-Heinz Rathey (1934–85) and to my mother, who has supported me on every step of my academic career.

Markus Rathey
New Haven, November 2015

# A NOTE ON TRANSLATIONS

The translations of the texts for Bach's oratorios are based on Michael Marissen, *Bach's Oratorios: The Parallel German-English Texts with Annotations* (Oxford: Oxford University Press, 2008). Translations of texts from Bach's cantatas follow Alfred Dürr, *The Cantatas of J. S. Bach*, trans. Richard D. P. Jones (Oxford: Oxford University Press, 2005). All other translations (especially of theological texts from the seventeenth and eighteenth centuries) are mine unless stated otherwise.

# ABBREVIATIONS

The capitalization of pitches and keys uses italics for individual pitches ($c$–$d$–$e$) and roman type for key areas and chords (C–D–E). Chords (both major and minor) are capitalized whereas pitches appear in lower-case letters (with indication of octaves, like in $c'$); only pitches in the lower octave (C–D–B) are capitalized.

Names of biblical books are spelled out in full (Matthew 1:2–3) when cited in running text; cited in parentheses are the abbreviated forms (Mt 1:2–3):

| | |
|---|---|
| Chr | Chronicles |
| Eph | Ephesians |
| Gal | Galatians |
| Gen | Genesis |
| Isa | Isaiah |
| Jas | James |
| Jn | John |
| Lk | Luke |
| Mk | Mark |
| Mt | Matthew |
| Ps (Pss) | Psalm (Psalms) |
| Sam | Samuel |

| | |
|---|---|
| *BachDok* | *Bach-Dokumente*. Leipzig and Kassel, 1963–72. Complete critical edition of the source material on Bach, with extensive commentaries. Edited under the auspices of the Bach-Archiv Leipzig as a supplement to the *Neue Bach-Ausgabe*. |
| bc | basso continuo. |
| BuxWV | Buxtehude-Werke-Verzeichnis: Georg Karstädt. *Thematisch-systematisches Verzeichnis der musikalischen Werke von Dietrich Buxtehude*, Wiesbaden: Breitkopf & Härtel, 1974. |

BWV      *Bach Werke-Verzeichnis*, Wolfgang Schmieder. *Thematisch-systematisches Verzeichnis der musikalischen Werke Johann Sebastian Bachs*, Leipzig, 1950. Rev. ed. Wiesbaden: Breitkopf & Härtel, 1990.

BWV      *Bach Werke-Verzeichnis: Kleine Ausgabe.* Edited by Alfred Dürr and Yoshitake Kobayashi, Wiesbaden: Breitkopf & Härtel, 1998.

H      Helm Catalogue: E. Eugene Helm. *Thematic Catalogue of the Works of Carl Philipp Emanuel Bach*, New Haven/London: Yale University Press, 1989.

MGG      *Die Musik in Geschichte und Gegenwart: Allgemeine Enzyklopaedie der Musik.*Edited by Friedrich Blume. Kassel: Bärenreiter, 1949f.

NBA I, II /KB      *Neue Bach-Ausgabe: Kritischer Bericht* (critical commentary).

NBA      *Neue Bach-Ausgabe. Johann Sebastian Bach Complete Works.* Edited under the auspices of the Johann-Sebastian-Bach-Institute Göttingen and the Bach-Archiv Leipzig, Kassel and Leipzig, 1954f.

P 32      Abbreviated call number for Bach's autograph score of the Christmas Oratorio in Deutsche Staatsbibliothek Berlin (complete call number: Mus. ms. Bach P 32).

Rit      Ritornello.

TVWV      Telemann Vokal Werke Verzeichnis: Martin Ruhnke. *Georg Philipp Telemann: Thematisches Verzeichnis der Vokalwerke von Georg Philipp Telemann. Frankfurt: Vittorio Klostermann, 1983.*

TWV      Telemann Werke Verzeichnis: Werner Menke. *Thematisch-Systematisches Verzeichnis seiner Werke.* Kassel, Bärenreiter, 1984–1999.

# Johann Sebastian Bach's
## *Christmas Oratorio*

# Prologue

At the bottom of the score for movement 38 in part IV of the *Christmas Oratorio*, hidden in the lower right-hand corner of the page, a keen observer will discover a small drawing by Johann Sebastian Bach. The drawing shows a little heart, with the symbol replacing the German word for "heart" in the text "mein Jesus labet Herz und Brust" (my Jesus refreshes heart and breast) (fig. 1.1). Why would Bach draw a symbol of a heart rather than write the text? It is easy to give a pragmatic explanation for this: Bach simply ran out of room at the end of the page, and the symbol occupied less space in the score than the complete word would have done. A few pages later, in the aria "Ich will nur dir zu Ehren leben" (no. 41), Bach does the same thing. In mm. 19 and 32, the word "Herz" is once more replaced with a heart; and again, space constraints appear to be the primary reason. However, pragmatism alone underestimates the significance of the symbol for eighteenth-century devotion and piety. The composer could easily have abbreviated the word with the initial "H." His copyists, who prepared the performance parts, had access to the libretto and could have inserted the correct word. Instead, Bach repeatedly uses a symbol that is ubiquitous in devotional literature and iconography of his time, and were as omnipresent as symbols such as :-) and @ are in our age of digital communication.

While drawing the heart saved Bach needed space in the score, it is more than just a philological detail. For Bach or any other eighteenth-century beholder, the heart signified much more. The heart symbolized the intimate relationship between the believer and Jesus—the very same idea that is expressed in these movements from part IV of the oratorio. This unassuming little detail taken by itself is not much more than a music historical footnote, so unassuming, in fact, that it was not even mentioned in the critical commentary for the *Neue Bach-Ausgabe*. Yet it directs our attention to the theological framework of the *Christmas Oratorio*, which will be explored in detail in chapter 3 of this book. The heart draws our attention to other aspects of the work as well, specifically the genesis of the oratorio itself and its compositional process. The conventional practice of composing recitatives among eighteenth-century

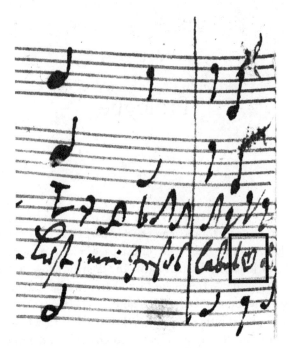

*Figure 1.1* J. S. Bach, BWV 248/38, autograph score (D-B Mus. ms. Bach P 32, fol. 35ᵛ) (bpk, Berlin/Mendelssohn-Archiv, Staatsbibliothek zu Berlin, Stiftung Preussischer Kulturbesitz, Berlin, Germany/Art Resource, NY)

composers like Handel, Hasse, and Bach was to copy the text first and then turn to the composition of the music. This second step was sometimes postponed until a later point in the compositional process after the more demanding movements like arias and choruses had been written. The unevenly spaced handwriting as well as the drawing of the heart in mvt. 38 suggests that the order of events was different in this particular case. It appears that Bach wrote the text *after* the music had already been written. Consequently, words sometimes spill over bar lines or, as in the case of "Herz," do not fit at all. The reason for Bach's unorthodox procedure is the unusual character of the movement. Not only is it an *accompagnato* recitative, but in the second half of the movement the bass is joined in a duet by the soprano who is singing a chorale text. Consequently, the music could not simply follow the text as in a regular recitative; here, Bach had to deal with the composition of the music first. The analysis of this movement in chapter 9 will show how Bach employs a gendered use of voices (soprano and bass) and parallel movements in thirds and sixths to create the impression of a love-duet that musically captures the erotic imagery of the text, and which directly correlates to the use of the little heart.

Bach's autograph score of the *Christmas Oratorio* grants us insight into the compositional process, which in turn will bring into focus important aspects of the music and its relationship with the text. In the second instance of the heart, in the tenor aria mvt. 41 ("Ich will nur dir zu Ehren leben"), the compositional process was different than that in no. 38 but equally interesting. The music was originally composed for the secular cantata *Laßt uns sorgen, laßt uns wachen*, BWV 213. For its use in part IV of the oratorio, Bach's librettist wrote a new text that fit the music. Accordingly, Bach copied the entire movement first and then inserted the text, common procedure in parodies like this. The text-underlay could be challenging if the new text required more space than the music provided, as in the present case. But again, he could have solved the problem differently; instead, he deliberately chose to draw the heart.

Bach's use of the heart symbol challenges us to explore two seemingly disparate sides of the oratorio simultaneously: the theological profile of the piece as well as the philological study of the manuscript source. The polarity and interconnectedness between theology and philology captures the two main foci of this book. This study of Bach's *Christmas Oratorio* explores the genesis of the piece and analyzes the music while paying particular attention to traces of the compositional process, like corrections and revisions and the use of older material in parodies. In several instances, Bach's changes and corrections illuminate his final solutions for compositional problems and help us better understand his musical goals. The paths not taken also help us understand and appreciate the paths he eventually did take. The composition score for the *Christmas Oratorio* serves as a tool that allows us to reconstruct some of the thought processes that led to the final work. We encounter numerous cases in which the changes made during the compositional process highlight certain aspects of the text by emphasizing a word or by heightening the emotive quality of the libretto. In these cases, philology and theology stand in direct conversation with one another. In other instances, though, they simply coexist. Not every compositional revision serves the text and its meaning. Rather, some changes have the purpose of simply increasing the beauty or the syntactic coherence of the music.

This book locates Bach's oratorio not only within his own oeuvre but also in the cultural and religious climate of eighteenth-century Germany. The libretto for the oratorio often echoes common themes, phrases, or motifs from the late seventeenth and early eighteenth centuries. Other authors of church music texts employed similar ideas, but these poets are often forgotten because their texts were either not set to music or composed by those who exist in the shadows of our musical canon. To name but one example of a composer who wrote Christmas cantatas contemporary with Bach—Johann Balthasar Christian Freißlich (1687–1764)—and who today is familiar with his cantatas? The same is true for the large number of sermons from Bach's time. Including these texts in our discussion demonstrates a repertory of common ideas, motifs, and allusions that resonated with the librettist while he drafted the text for the *Christmas Oratorio*, with Bach when he composed the music, and among the listeners when they first heard the piece in Leipzig during the Christmas season 1734/35.

Let us return again to heart drawn into mvt. 38: the heart as a dwelling place of Christ features prominently in countless hymns, sermons, devotional books, and religious images from the seventeenth and early eighteenth centuries. Bach's listeners would not have seen the little symbol in the score, but they would have understood and appreciated its significance as much as they would have been aware of the centrality of this heart-imagery throughout the oratorio. But it is also important to emphasize that music and text do not always convey the same thing. It would be misleading to interpret every detail in Bach's music theologically. Instead, music and theology have to be understood as two separate (yet interconnected) discourses, each following their own paradigms, traditions, and rules. Both have their strengths and weaknesses, capabilities and limitations. The discourses are independent but they also intersect. If music is paired with a religious text, it necessarily and automatically participates in a theological discourse as well. Every decision a composer makes, to highlight certain words or to de-emphasize others, is a statement about the meaning of the text. This statement might seem superficial, but it still reflects and generates a particular understanding of the words. This exegesis exists and is shaped by the cultural environment in which both the music and the words were created. For religious music such as Bach's oratorio, this environment is reflected in theological treatises, hymns, devotional literature, and sermons. Referring to these sources in an interpretation of Bach's music does not imply that he necessarily was familiar with all these texts, but they are a window into the religious culture of his time. The composer probably did not study a theological treatise on the Gospel of Luke before he embarked on setting the Christmas story from Luke 2, yet theological and devotional texts help reconstruct a framework of understanding in which the composer worked and his audience perceived the piece. Musical and theological discourses also intersect on a higher level of meta-discourses, like the perception of reality, of time, and of the divine. These conversations are connected since they unfurled at the same time and at the same place: Leipzig, 1734. They are shaped by the same *Zeitgeist*.[1] Accordingly, these theological and philosophical sources provide a framework in which we are able to analyze the libretto as well as Bach's treatment of the text.

One important detail is missing from this framework. The identity of the author of the libretto is still unknown. Christian Friedrich Henrici (1700–1764), known by his pen name Picander, has often been suggested as the possible author for the libretto of BWV 248. Bach and Picander had collaborated since 1725, and by the

---

[1] A word coined by Johann Gottfried Herder in 1769, two years before he began to collaborate with Johann Sebastian Bach's son Johann Christoph Friedrich Bach in Bückeburg. This is merely a historical coincidence but demonstrates how historical lines sometimes intersect.

early 1730s he was Bach's main librettist. What is unusual, however, is that the libretto was not reprinted in one of Picander's collections with poetry, as is the case with most of the other texts he had written for Bach. While this might speak against him as being the librettist, there are also no internal reasons (theological or poetical) that would rule out his collaboration. We will return briefly to this question in chapter 3 of this book.

While the *Christmas Oratorio* is one of the most frequently performed works by Bach, it has not received much attention by scholars, particularly in the English-speaking world. The only monographic treatment of BWV 248 is Ignace Bossuyt's overview from 2004, which was translated from Dutch.[2] Other books appeared only in German. The two main reasons for this lack of interest are the seemingly simple character of the work and the extensive use of parodies, which seemed to render it esthetically less valuable than the Passions, for instance. In fact, the editor of the *Christmas Oratorio* for the *Bach-Gesellschaft*, Wilhelm Rust, deemed it necessary to defend the piece against possible accusations of esthetic inferiority, due to the inclusion of previously composed material. His argument rests on the assumption that Bach had always intended the parodied movements for the oratorio. In other words, the secular cantatas, in which they appeared first, were only their temporary home (and thus deemed esthetically inferior), while the oratorio was their intended place.[3] The parody problem ("Parodieproblem") has been discussed repeatedly by scholars and commentators. While it is obvious that composers in the eighteenth century did not view the parody technique as esthetically problematic, as soon as the *Christmas Oratorio* was viewed as a part of the canon of Western music, it was then measured against the postulate of originality applied to Beethoven's symphonies, Schubert's songs, and Wagner's operas. The most significant contribution to this question has been made by Ludwig Finscher in an essay from 1969, in which he not only analyzed the technical procedures Bach applied in his parodies but also attributed an esthetic surplus ("ästhetischer Überschuß") to Bach's music. This surfeit transcends the plain relationship between specific texts and music, as well as composition and original function.[4] Accordingly, this book traces Bach's use of parodies in the *Christmas Oratorio* and shows how Bach meticulously plans the use of previously composed material within the work. Bach revises the existing music to fit the new text and he also improves minute details that are independent from the words of the libretto. These revisions are often little different from revisions he would make in newly composed arias and choral movements,

---

[2] Ignace Bossuyt, *Johann Sebastian Bach, Christmas oratorio (BWV 248)*, trans. Stratton Bull (Leuven: Leuven University Press, 2004). The book was originally published in Dutch in 2002 and appeared in an English translation two years later.

[3] Wilhelm Rust, foreword to *Bach-Gesellschaft Edition* (1856), viii.

[4] Ludwig Finscher, "Zum Parodieproblem bei Bach," in *Bach-Interpretationen*, ed. Martin Geck, FS Walter Blankenburg zum 65. Geburtstag (Göttingen: Vandenhoeck & Ruprecht 1969), 94–105.

which make the use of parodies firmly integrated into the compositional process of this oratorio. It is ironic that the *B-Minor Mass,* held in highest esteem by scholars and listeners alike, is even to a larger degree based on parodies. However, the transformation of the musical material in the Mass is more substantive than that seen in the oratorio. Furthermore, the *B-Minor Mass* had already acquired the status of a model composition in the early nineteenth century before critics became aware of the parody relationships.

Much of the work in this book is indebted to contributions by earlier generations of Bach scholars, particularly since the 1950s. The beginning of the second half of the twentieth century saw a quantum leap for Bach studies. The publication of Schmieder's *Bach-Werke-Verzeichnis* (BWV) in 1950 provided a reliable catalogue of Bach's works—and a universal numbering system that is still in place today. The start of the *Neue Bach-Ausgabe* (NBA) in 1954, replacing the *Bach-Gesellschaft Ausgabe* from the nineteenth century, not only helped create new editions that reflected the most advanced state of philological scholarship but also necessitated a new assessment of the sources. This in turn led to the "new chronology." Alfred Dürr's and Georg von Dadelsen's research has revolutionized our knowledge of the chronology and genesis of Bach's Leipzig vocal works. The authors showed that the cantatas were, for the most part, a product of his earlier years in Leipzig and not (as hitherto assumed) the fruit of his more mature years. While the *Christmas Oratorio* was not directly affected by the new chronology (the autograph score is dated in Bach's own hand and its chronology had never been in doubt), it does nuance the contextual understanding of the piece. It is now clear that Bach had turned to the genre of oratorio at a time when his production of cantatas had ebbed. Sacred compositions in the 1730s were an exception for Bach, not the norm any more.

The edition of the oratorio for the *Neue Bach-Ausgabe* was prepared collaboratively by Alfred Dürr and Walter Blankenburg—the former a leading expert of Bach philology of his time, and the latter a musicologist with a keen interest in hymnology and theology. Their different perspectives are reflected in two important and influential books on the oratorio, which are still considered cornerstones of modern scholarship on Bach's *Christmas Oratorio.* Dürr's small study from 1967 focuses almost entirely on the music: the description of the sources, the technical aspects of the parody process, and Bach's use of musical genres.[5] Blankenburg's book, published in 1982, gives a description of the music as well but focuses much more on the theological interpretation of Bach's composition.[6] For the most part Blankenburg

[5] Alfred Dürr, *Johann Sebastian Bach: Weihnachts-Oratorium, BWV 248,* Meisterwerke der Musik 8 (Munich: Fink, 1967).

[6] Walter Blankenburg, *Das Weihnachts-Oratorium von Johann Sebastian Bach* (Munich: Deutscher Taschenbuch-Verlag/Bärenreiter, 1982).

does not consult theological texts from Bach's time, but instead he works under the implicit assumption that the music is charged with religious meaning and that this meaning can be decoded from a modern perspective. His perspective is that of a German Lutheran and thus relies primarily on Luther as a theological source. The approaches of both books are limited. Dürr disregards the cultural and religious context, while Blankenburg takes an anachronistic approach by using a sixteenth-century theologian and his twentieth-century reception as a Rosetta stone for the interpretation of an eighteenth-century composition.

Noteworthy is Günter Jena's book *Brich an, o schönes Morgenlicht* (1997).[7] Written not by a scholar but by a performer, it addresses a general audience and adds some very perceptive observations about the architecture of Bach's music and about the ways he manipulates his musical material. The most recent comprehensive discussion of Bach's *Christmas Oratorio* to date is Meinrad Walter's book from 2006.[8] Like Blankenburg, Walter is mostly interested in the oratorio as a work of religious expression. What differentiates him from his predecessor are a broader knowledge of seventeenth- and eighteenth-century theology and a number of short excurses into Bach's workshop ("Blick in die Werkstatt"), which highlight significant details of Bach's compositional process and of his handwriting. An exclusive treatment of the theological aspects of the oratorio from a historical perspective is Martin Petzoldt's *Bach Kommentar*, which contains commentary on each of the six parts of the *Christmas Oratorio*.[9] Petzoldt provides the first systematic discussion of the theology of the piece. In spite of some methodological shortcomings and a rather narrow source base, Petzoldt's commentary is still an important resource for further scholarship.

Outside of these monographic treatments, the *Christmas Oratorio* has only occasionally received the attention of scholars. Important contributions that have shaped our understanding of the piece are the studies of Bach's parody technique by Werner Neumann (1965) and Ludwig Finscher (1969);[10] Andreas Glöckner's considerations of a model for the last part of the oratorio (2000);[11] and two important

---

[7] Günter Jena, *Brich an, o schönes Morgenlicht: Das Weihnachtsoratorium von Johann Sebastian Bach* (Freiburg, Herder: 1999).

[8] Meinrad Walter, *Johann Sebastian Bach—Weihnachtsoratorium* (Kassel: Bärenreiter, 2006).

[9] Martin Petzoldt, *Bach-Kommentar II: Die geistlichen Kantaten vom 1. Advent bis zum Trinitatisfest,* Schriftenreihe Internationale Bachakademie 14, 2 (Stuttgart/Kassel: Internationale Bachakademie/ Bärenreiter, 2007). While not an independent monograph, the sections on the oratorio comprise ninety-five pages.

[10] Werner Neumann, "Über Ausmaß und Wesen des Bachschen Parodieverfahrens," *Bach-Jahrbuch* 51 (1965): 63–85; Finscher, "Zum Parodieproblem bei Bach," 94–105.

[11] Andreas Glöckner, "Eine Michaeliskantate als Parodievorlage für den sechsten Teil des Bachschen Weihnachts-Oratoriums?," *Bach-Jahrbuch* 86 (2000): 317–26.

articles by the theologian Ernst Koch about the function of the echo aria in part IV (1989) and the significance of the alto voice in the oratorio (1995).[12] Koch replaces Blankenburg's intuitive approach with a more careful evaluation of seventeenth- and eighteenth-century sources. Finally, Christoph Wolff outlines, in a recent article, the ramifications of Bach's oratorio concept, which views the three oratorios for the major feast days (Christmas, Easter, Ascension) as part of a larger, unified oratorio project.[13] Chapter 4 of this book summarizes Wolff's observations and adds some details to his analysis.

The celebration of Christmas as we know it today was born in the nineteenth century. The idea of a family feast that revolved around consumerism and, at the same time, struggled with it developed in the early decades of the nineteenth century and took shape over the following decades. Scholars such as Stephen Nissenbaum, Joe Perry, and Susan K. Roll have analyzed the emergence of the modern feast.[14] A study of the understanding of the feast in Bach's *Christmas Oratorio* therefore has to go back before the Romantic period. The following two chapters demonstrate that Bach himself lived during a time of change. When he was born in 1685, Christmas traditions still retained some of their medieval roots: carnivalesque rituals and misrule were still frequent in the streets of Lutheran cities in Germany toward the latter half of the seventeenth century. Both theologians and secular authorities strove to abolish these traditions. This "war on Christmas" coincided with a general trend of internalizing religiosity. Physical and bodily religious practices (like the Christmas plays we discuss in chapter 2) gave way to an interior spirituality. Christmas became a feast that was no longer celebrated in the streets but was instead contemplated in the human heart. What remained in devotional texts about Christmas were metaphors—like love, marriage, and the heart—which had physical roots but were now confined to the realm of language and symbol. The rocking of a real cradle, once a popular practice in the Christmas rituals all over Europe, was transformed into the image of Jesus inhabiting the cradle of the human heart. Most of these images were much older and rooted in medieval mysticism and Lutheran theology; around 1700, though, these metaphors acquired a new

---

[12] Ernst Koch, "Tröstendes Echo: Zur theologischen Deutung der Echo-Arie im IV. Teil des Weihnachts-Oratoriums von Johann Sebastian Bach," *Bach-Jahrbuch* 75 (1989): 203–11, and "Die Stimme des Heiligen Geistes: Theologische Hintergründe der solistischen Altpartien in der Kirchenmusik Johann Sebastian Bachs," *Bach-Jahrbuch* 81 (1995): 61–81.

[13] Christoph Wolff, "Under the Spell of Opera? Bach's Oratorio Trilogy," in *J. S. Bach and the Oratorio Tradition*, ed. Daniel R. Melamed, Bach Perspectives 8 (Urbana: University of Illinois Press, 2011), 1–12.

[14] Stephen Nissenbaum, *The Battle for Christmas* (New York: Vintage, 1996); Joe Perry, *Christmas in Germany. A Cultural History* (Chapel Hill: University of North Carolina Press, 2010); and Susan K. Roll, *Toward the Origins of Christmas* (Kampen: Kok Pharos, 1995).

function as they replaced external and physical practices. Bach's *Christmas Oratorio* participates in this internalization of religiosity. Chapter 3 outlines this theological understanding of the Christmas feast in Bach's time, and it demonstrates how this theological understanding of Christmas influenced both the libretto as well as the structural framework of Bach's composition. A tripartite temporal framework (past, present, and future)—which is employed by theological treatises—also shapes the ground plan of Bach's oratorio.

In his outline for a sermon preached on Christmas Day 1733, the Leipzig superintendent Salomon Deyling succinctly captured the understanding of Christmas in Leipzig around the time of Bach's composition of the oratorio. It is likely that Bach (and maybe even his librettist) heard the sermon, which occurred exactly one year before the congregation witnessed part I of the oratorio. But even if they had not, Deyling poetically summarizes a conventional view of the feast, which Bach would have encountered throughout his life:

1. **Die Glaubens-Lehre:** GOtt wird ein Mensch, und kommt zu uns auf Erden. Nun können wir gerecht und GOttes Kinder werden.

2. **Die Lebens-Pflicht:** Dein Heiland kömmt zu dir, ist auch dein Hertze rein? Wo Sünd und Unflath ist, will er nicht kehren ein.

3. **Der Glauben-Trost:** GOtt ist mit uns versöhnt. Drum weichet Traurigkeit. Es freu sich jedermann, dem seine Sünd ist leid.[15]

1. **The doctrine of faith:** God becomes man and comes to us on earth. Now we can become justified and God's children.

2. **The duty in life:** Your Savior comes to you, is your heart pure? Where there are sin and misbehavior, he will not enter.

3. **The consolation of faith:** God is reconciled with us. Thus, sadness retreats. Everybody who regrets their sin shall be joyful.

Here, we understand that Christ comes as a child to make mankind children of God. He dwells in the human heart and grants consolation in times of sadness. Chapter 3 explores in more detail these theological ideas and how they were woven into the libretto for the oratorio.

While chapters 2 and 3 provide the cultural and religious context for the oratorio, chapters 4 and 5 will deal with practical issues. As Christoph Wolff has recently shown, Bach worked on a larger oratorio project during the 1730s, which included pieces for Christmas, Easter, Ascension, the revision of the *St. John* and *St. Matthew Passions*, and possibly plans for a Pentecost oratorio as well.[16] Chapter 4 considers

---

[15] Salomon Deyling, *Herrliche Dinge in der Stadt Gottes geprediget* (Leipzig, 1734), 5.
[16] Wolff, "Under the Spell of Opera?," 1–12.

the reasons for Bach's sudden interest in this genre in 1734, and it demonstrates how his own understanding of the genre shaped the peculiar profile of BWV 248. Chapter 5 then delves into more detail by reconstructing the compositional process from the earliest planning stages, the inclusion of parody movements, the order of composition of individual movements within the oratorio, the shaping of musical ideas, and the revision of both smaller and larger details in the music. The work in that chapter would not have been possible without the magisterial study of Bach's compositional process by Robert Marshall (1972).[17] Chapter 5 applies Marshall's general observations to the *Christmas Oratorio* and adds further details to the picture.

The following six chapters deal with each of the six parts of the oratorio individually. Instead of simply proceeding movement by movement, like most of the previous monographs on the oratorio, each chapter focuses on one crucial aspect and analyzes its realization in text and music. Part I of the oratorio explores a set of dichotomies, most of which are already alluded to in Deyling's sermon outline quoted earlier: God and man, heaven and earth, sin and salvation, rich and poor, as well as concepts of time and social status. The first part also introduces the love imagery that dominates the entire oratorio: bride and bridegroom, the beloved, and the heart as the dwelling place of the divine. The three parody movements in part I, the opening chorus and the two arias, provide case studies for Bach's parody technique in the oratorio as a whole.

The second part of the oratorio, which culminates in the angelic hymn "Ehre sei Gott in der Höhe" (May honor be to God on high) can be read and heard as an essay on the meaning of music and sound. Music as a means of communication between earthly and heavenly realms is already present in the harmonious dialogue between angelic and pastoral choruses in the opening sinfonia, and later movements in part II of the oratorio return to this subject repeatedly. This view of music—again deeply rooted in the theology of Bach's time—has ramifications beyond part II as it demonstrates how sound and harmony can aid in the unification of God and men.

This unification, the *unio mystica*, metaphorically taking place in the human heart, as point 2 in Deyling's sermon suggests, is the focus of part III of the oratorio. The physical (external) movement of the shepherds toward the manger is reinterpreted as the spiritual (internal) movement of God toward man. This deliberate embodiment of an external act correlates with the internalization and spiritualization of Christmas during Bach's lifetime. The musical and theological center of part III is the alto aria "Schließe, mein Herze" (no. 31). It is also the only newly composed

---

[17]  Robert Lewis Marshall, *The Compositional Process of J. S. Bach: A Study of the Autograph Scores of the Vocal Works*, 2 vols. (Princeton: Princeton University Press, 1972).

aria in the entire oratorio. Bach's careful work on this particular movement and the numerous changes and revisions reflect its importance within the context of the entire oratorio. As chapter 3 shows, this aria is the turning point in the temporal as well as the structural framework of the *Christmas Oratorio.*

Part IV of the oratorio is an extensive meditation on the meaning of the name of Jesus as the essence of his divine and human nature. The two movements, mentioned at the beginning of this prologue, in which Bach drew a heart instead of writing out the word, appear in this part of the oratorio. The contemplation of the divine name is intrinsically intertwined with the mystical unity symbolized by the heart in eighteenth-century devotional writing. Musical and theological questions also intersect in the famous echo-aria of part IV.

The last two parts of the *Christmas Oratorio* tell the story of the three wise men and their journey to the manger in Bethlehem. As the star is the guide to the newborn child, part V explores the metaphors of light and darkness: light or "enlightenment" becomes a metaphor for the clearer knowledge and understanding of God and God's will. The opening movement for part V is the only large-scale choral movement that was not based on a parody, and this provides another opportunity to study Bach's compositional process in more depth. The final part of the oratorio returns to the juxtaposition of earlier parts, pitting the bridegroom Christ against his adversaries: namely, King Herod, but by extension all such enemies as Satan, death, and sin. This part is characterized in particular by its eschatological outlook, directing one's view from the past (Christ's birth) and the present (Christ's dwelling in the human heart) to the future (Christ's return), thus completing the tripartite temporal structure we explore further in chapter 3.

The *Christmas Oratorio* weaves together two narratives: the birth of Jesus according to the gospels of Luke (parts I–IV) and Matthew (parts V–VI), and the welcoming of Christ into the human heart. This second narrative ranges from the expectation of his coming (parts I–II) to the preparation of the heart (part III) to the notion that he was "already there," as the terzet in part V announces. The turning point of this narrative is the aria "Schließe mein Herze" in part III. Both the special attention Bach pays to this aria and his use of the symbolic hearts in part IV suggest that Bach was keenly aware of this "second narrative" when he composed the oratorio. However, this study makes no attempt to reconstruct Bach's own piety or demonstrate his position as the "fifth evangelist." Given the available sources, this is not possible. What is possible to reconstruct is how the *Christmas Oratorio*, both its music and libretto, fits into the religious landscape of early eighteenth-century Germany.

This book oscillates between musical analysis, source studies, and theology. It is written not only for musicologists but also for readers who are interested in the religious landscape of the early eighteenth century as well as the study of central

European culture at the end of the Baroque era. Given the interdisciplinary nature of the subject, readers from different fields of study will sometimes need patience when the book seems to digress into unfamiliar territory. These tangents are necessary to establish the context of Bach's piece and to show how the *Christmas Oratorio* relates to the views of the Christmas feast in other text genres and disciplines.

# 2

# Redefining Christmas

When Johann Sebastian Bach extended his leave from his duties as organist in 1705/6 by several months in order to study with Dieterich Buxtehude in Lübeck, not only did he enrage his superiors in Arnstadt but he also missed a little spectacle that took place during the Christmas season. Bach had already embarked on his journey when in November 1705 the students from the *prima*, the highest class at the Arnstadt *Lyceum*, petitioned the local consistory to be allowed to perform a *Christ Comodie*, a Christmas play.[1] As they pointed out, the play revived an older tradition. The petition affirms that plays like this had been common in the past, and the pupils assured the authorities that the performance would not give any reason for complaint. The text of the play was attached to the petition, allowing the members of the consistory to confirm that there was no immediate reason for theological or moral concern. Within two days—on November 25, 1705—permission was granted.

The *Christ Comodie* was not a Christmas pageant performed in church or on a public stage, as had been the case with the medieval mystery plays; it was instead an event during which the schoolboys went from house to house in Arnstadt (probably upon invitation) and enacted a dramatic scene in front of parents, children, and any other members of the household present. The play featured several stock characters from the nativity story: angels, shepherds, Mary, Joseph, and the three wise men, along with Moses and John the Baptist. The illustrious cast also included two peasants. While the two peasants do not belong to the biblical Christmas story, they are, as we shall see, essential to the Arnstadt *Christ Comodie*.[2] The characters of

---

[1] See Bernhard Grosse, "Zwei Arnstädter 'Heilige Christ-Komödien,'" in *Programm des Fürstl. Gymnasiums zu Arnstadt* (Arnstadt: Frotscher, 1899), 16.

[2] Even though the peasants are inspired by the shepherds from the biblical nativity story from Luke 2, the author of the play associates them closely with the peasants by rendering their text in the local dialect while the other characters speak High German.

the play do not enact anything even remotely related to the biblical story; instead, their dialogue provided the framework for a catechetical and moral examination. If successful, the children were permitted to receive their Christmas presents. On the off chance that a child failed the exam (a case the text alludes to but never really anticipates) he or she was threatened with corporal punishment by one of the peasants, a shadowy fellow named Knecht Ruprecht.

Ruprecht's character, in name and function as punisher of the children, connects the origins of the Arnstadt play to medieval carnivalesque folk rituals that were originally associated with St. Nicholas's Day (December 6). Ruprecht traditionally served as the sidekick to St. Nicholas, representing the dark counterpart to the children-loving, gift-bearing saint.[3] The Lutheran Reformation had attempted to abolish these folk traditions, replacing St. Nicholas, the bringer of gifts, with the "Christkind" (Christ Child) or "Heilig Christ" (Holy Christ), who brought the gifts on December 24 or 25. Knecht Ruprecht was soon abolished altogether.[4] The traditions, however, proved more resilient than the theological shift. The folk rituals around the Christmas season did not disappear under the pressure of reform.[5] Instead, the folk traditions amalgamated both old and new practices. Now the Heilig Christ or Christkind appeared in person and questioned the children before he handed over the Christmas gifts. In line with the older tradition, the character of the Holy Christ, while initially symbolizing the newborn infant Jesus, was typically played during the seventeenth century by a much older boy or an adult, who frequently wore a long beard (just as St. Nicholas had traditionally done).[6] What changed was not so much the ritual but rather the name of the central character. Even his visual representation remained essentially the same: the Heilige Christ was a visual amalgamation of the Lutheran Christkind and the older St. Nicholas tradition.

The practice of celebrating the end of the year with masks and pageantry was, of course, much older. Dressing up, hiding behind masks, and noisy celebrations were remnants of the medieval tradition of welcoming the winter solstice, rooted in both Germanic rituals and the Roman Saturnalia.[7] The St. Nicholas and Heilig Christ

[3] Cf. Stephen Nissenbaum, *The Battle for Christmas* (New York: Vintage, 1996), 99–100.

[4] See Joe Perry, *Christmas in Germany. A Cultural History* (Chapel Hill: University of North Carolina Press, 2010), 36.

[5] Robert W. Scribner has demonstrated the resilience of some carnivalesque traditions during the Reformation in his article "Reformation, Carnival and the World Turned Upside-Down"; see Scribner, *Popular Culture and Popular Movements in Reformation Germany* (London: Hambledon Press, 1987), 71–102.

[6] Cf. Joe Wheeler and Jim Rosenthal, *St. Nicholas: A Closer Look at Christmas* (Nashville: Thomas Nelson, 2005), 145.

[7] For the pagan roots of some of the Christmas rituals, see the overview by Daniel Miller, ed., "A Theory of Christmas," in *Unwrapping Christmas* (Oxford: Clarendon Press, 2001), 3–37. See also the excellent study by Susan K. Roll, *Toward the Origins of Christmas* (Kampen: Kok Pharos, 1995).

plays, Christmas masks, and New Year's plays can be traced throughout Europe during the early modern period and were frequently a gateway to inappropriate and riotous behavior. Participants hiding behind masks, confident in the anonymity that such props afforded, went noisily from house to house; some got drunk and some even took advantage of the security of the mask to engage in sexual acts with servants of the house.

The main points of the petition in question by the students of Arnstadt, assuring that there was no reason for complaint, allude to these well-known problems. In most German cities and towns, the Christmas plays were prohibited in the 1680s and '90s, and this apparently was the case in Arnstadt as the last evidence of that play in the seventeenth century dates from 1690.[8] Reintroduced in 1705 by approval of the Arnstadt consistory, the "new" play represented a "purified" version without the contested and theologically problematic Heilige Christ. Although this version included a Knecht Ruprecht, he appeared as a rather toothless threat and only mildly punished the children. Earlier sources for comparable Christmas plays from other German cities depict a much scarier and violent Ruprecht. Nonetheless, even with these changes the *Christ Comodie* in Arnstadt seemed to have ignited disorderly conduct and transgressive behavior. Its performance was sanctioned again in 1706 (Bach was now back in Arnstadt and would have witnessed the spectacle) but not in the years following. This, however, did not stop the boys from performing it. In 1713 nine students, plus two others, were arrested by the police during a similar play, and again in 1724 nine boys were taken into custody for inappropriate and riotous behavior during the Christmas season.[9] Folk traditions like this, including the riotous excesses, existed all over Europe in the seventeenth century; theologians and secular authorities vehemently condemned them. Clearly, any holiday or local tradition that produced such a consistent police blotter would be problematic for the community image, no matter how popular it was. In Puritan England (and even more so in the Puritan states in New England) similar Christmas traditions were responsible for abolishing the celebration of Christmas altogether.[10]

Similar plays were enacted almost everywhere in central Germany in the seventeenth and early eighteenth century, and so we can assume that Johann Sebastian Bach was familiar with the Heilig Christ plays even before he moved to Arnstadt. When Bach composed his *Christmas Oratorio* in 1734, the "Heilig Christ plays had long been abolished, at least officially. The discussions about the plays, which went

---

[8]  Grosse, "Zwei Arnstädter 'Heilige Christ-Komödien,'" 16.

[9]  Ibid.

[10]  Stephen Nissenbaum points out that Christmas was "systematically suppressed by Puritans during the colonial period.... It was actually illegal to celebrate Christmas in Massachusetts between 1659 and 1681" (Nissenbaum, *Battle for Christmas*, 3). In 1659, celebrating Christmas was declared a criminal offense in Massachusetts. The reasons for abolishment of the feast resemble

on well into the eighteenth century, are indicative of a shift in the general understanding of Christmas and hold significance for both the theological and musical
concepts of the oratorio. Although the Reformation had attempted to abolish older
traditions, they were still very much alive. In fact, most of the traditions were gradually extirpated only in the last decades of the seventeenth century. The changes that
took place in last third of the seventeenth century are particularly characterized by
an increasing rejection of all external, physical, and corporeal aspects of religiosity
(touching, moving, walking) in favor of an internalized and spiritualized faith.[11] The
coming of Christ and his angels was not to be experienced in a public enactment
but by meditating on the biblical narrative. Corporeality was preserved only on a
linguistic level, in metaphors. An example for metaphorical physicality is the image
of the bride and the bridegroom who are unified in spiritual love, an image that is
frequently present in Christmas songs and Christmas compositions from the early
modern period.

    Leipzig played a central role in the so-called war on Christmas in the years
around 1700. Several important treatises against the Christmas plays originated
there, were written by authors who had received their academic training there, or
were texts printed by Leipzig publishers. In fact, the plays had existed in Leipzig
quite undisturbed until 1680. On December 24, 1676, the rector of Leipzig's
St. Thomas School, Jakob Thomasius (1622–84), wrote the following account in his
diary. It was his first year at the school, and he was obviously not yet familiar with all
the details of his new position:

| | |
|---|---|
| Haben vnsere schulknaben, so hierzu theils vom Thomas-, theils von Niclasküster in vorigen tagen erbethen worden, den heilgen Christ in denen heusern agiret; vnd zwar vnter denenselben auch Hetscher (ein guter discantist) anfangs bestimmet, | Our school boys have, invited by the sextons from St. Thomas and St. Nicholas, acted the Holy Christ in the houses; among the pupils who were originally chosen to do so was also Hetscher (a good discant); however, since the honorable town |

those we find in texts by German critics of the Christmas plays. Both mention the "disorders" that
were associated with the feast. The law from 1659 states that the celebration of Christmas was
abolished "for preventing disorders arising in several places within the jurisdiction, by reason
of some still observing such Festivals as were superstitiously kept in other countries" (*Battle for
Christmas*, 14).

    [11] Material-corporeal elements of religiosity were an important part of folk culture as they
were often more easily accessible to common people; however, these forms of religiosity were also
more difficult to control by the authorities; cf. Richard van Dülmen, "Volksfrömmigkeit und konfessionelles Christentum im 16. und 17. Jahrhundert," *Geschichte und Gesellschaft, Sonderheft* 11
(1986): 22.

weil aber E.E. Rath jüngsthin bey
mir erinnern lassen, das die guten
discantisten, damit sie bey solcher
gelegenheit nicht etwa ihre stimme
verliehren, außgesetzt werden solten,
ist an Hetschers statt Erler verordnet
worden. Den anfang haben sie, so
der Küster zu S. Thomas gebraucht,
der gewohnheit nach im Schulhuse
gemacht da es noch tag gewesen gegen
4. vhr, vnd sich also vnsern (meinen,
Conrectoris, des Sel. Cantoris vnd
Tertii) Kindern präsentiret: *ipsius
S. Christi personam agente M. Röslero
Collaboratore:* vnd wird ihnen
deswegen kein Gratial, außer
mündlicher bedanckung abgestattet.[12]

council has reminded me recently
that the good discantists should not
participate so that they would not
lose their voices, Erler was chosen
instead of Hetscher. As the sexton
from St. Thomas used to do it, they
have started in the school during the
day at about 4 pm and have played
in front of our children (mine, the
deputy director's, the late cantor's,
and the tertii's). The part of Christ
himself was played by the teacher
Magister Rössler. They did not
receive a remuneration but only an
oral "thank you."

The Leipzig plays were supervised by the sextons of the two main churches, St. Thomas and St. Nicholas, which probably guaranteed a more orderly conduct than we have seen in Arnstadt. However, the plays could be strenuous for the boys' voices,[13] so that the discantist Hetscher (who was, according to the list of the four choirs compiled by Thomasius in the same year, member of the second choir), was replaced with the boy Erler, who appears in Thomasius's list as a member of the less proficient third choir.[14] The play, which was a semi-official event,

---

[12] *Acta Nicolaitana et Thomana: Aufzeichungen von Jakob Thomasius während seines Rektorates an der Nicolai- und Thomasschule zu Leipzig (1670–84),* ed. Richard Sachse (Leipzig: Wörner, 1912) 202–3.

[13] David S. Büttner uses the negative impact the performance of the Christmas plays had on the voices of those who had to sing in church during the Christmas times as an argument against the plays: "Und nachdem die Comödianten in Städten gemeiniglich solche Personen sind/die der Vocal-Music beywohnen/kan man leicht schliessen/wie andächtig und geschickt sie hierbey seyn müßen/die weder einen auffgeräumten Kopff noch ausgeräumte Kehle mit bringen/wie sie anders dem Schlaff noch so viel abbrechen und erscheinen wollen," David Siegmund Büttner, *Christ-Larven oder Böß-benahmter Heiliger Christ / nach dem Ursprung und Häßlichkeit meist Historisch beschrieben* (Halle: Waisenhaus, 1702), 81. (And since the participants in these comedies in the cities are normally those who also perform the vocal-music (in church), one can easily conclude how pious and skilled they will be in performing their music. They neither have a clear head nor do they have a clear voice and they show up with not enough sleep.)

[14] *Acta Nicolaitana et Thomana,* 196; regarding the duties and members of the four choirs, see the thorough study by Michael Maul, *"Dero berühmter Chor": Die Leipziger Thomasschule und ihre Kantoren*

was enacted in the presence of the rector and his colleagues, and it involved at least one of the teachers at St. Thomas, Magister Jacob Rössler. Rössler was also leader of the "Singestunden" (choir practice) and must have had considerable musical abilities. Rössler played the part of Jesus in the 1676 performance of the Christmas play—probably an unexpected choice for the role of Christ in a nativity play but fully in line with its character as an amalgamation of the Christ Child and the older St. Nicholas. Even though we can assume that the play contained some musical elements, the description by Thomasius does not suggest that larger portions of the text were sung. Even an extensive recitation of spoken text would have been strenuous to the voices of the boys, in particular considering the freezing temperatures in Leipzig at the end of December.[15] Bernd Baselt, in his study of Schelle's *Actus musicus* is mistaken when he assumes, misinterpreting a description of the play by Schering, that the Christmas play was performed in the two main churches and that the play was interpolated with familiar Christmas tunes.[16] The play was not a nativity play but a typical Heilig Christ play. While the account by Thomasius does not question the practice of the play, it would soon be abolished. The Leipzig chronicler Johann Jacob Vogel states that in the year 1680:

| | |
|---|---|
| Den 21. Dec. ergieng ein Verboth an die Küster / daß die *Larvae Natalitiae*, oder das so genannte Heil. Christ-Spiel nicht allein wegen der Churfürstl. Trauer / sondern auch wegen des besorglichen Schreckens und Furcht unter denen Kindern bey dieser elenden und betrübten-Zeit | On Dec. 21 an order was issued to the sexton prohibiting the *Larvae Natilitiae*, or the so-called Holy Christ Plays, not only because of the time of mourning for the Elector but also because of the worrying fright and fear among the children in this wretched |

1212–1804 (Leipzig: Lehmstedt, 2012). See also Andreas Glöckner, "Bemerkungen zur vokalen und instrumentalen Besetzung von Bachs Leipziger Ensemblewerken," in *Vom Klang der Zeit: Besetzung, Bearbeitung und Aufführungspraxis bei Johann Sebastian Bach. Klaus Hofmann zum 65. Geburtstag*, ed. Ulrich Bartel and Uwe Wolf (Wiesbaden: Breitkopf & Härtel, 2004), 86–96; Andreas Glöckner, "Alumnen und Externe in den Kantoreien der Thomasschule zur Zeit Bachs," *Bach-Jahrbuch* 92 (2006), 9–36; and the short overview in Christoph Wolff, *Johann Sebastian Bach: The Learned Musician* (New York: Norton, 2000), 251–53.

[15] Arnold Schering (*Musikgeschichte Leipzigs II* [Leipzig: Kistner, 1926, 76]) also assumes that music might have been part of the play, albeit without being able to provide evidentiary support: "Ganz ohne Gesang wird es auch dabei nicht abgegangen sein." ("The whole thing might have been done not entirely without music").

[16] Bernd Baselt, "Der 'Actus Musicus auf Weyh-Nachten' des Leiziger Thomaskantors Johann Schelle," in *Wissenschaftliche Zeitschrift der Martin-Luther-Universität Halle-Wittenberg. Gesellschafts- und Sprachwissenschaftliche Reihe* XIV (1965), 341.

solte eingestellet werden. Im
folgenden Jahre darauff ward
dieser Päpstische Greuel gäntzlich
abgeschafft.[17]

and sad time. In the following year,
this papist atrocity was completely
abolished.

The *Larvae Natilitiae* (Nativity masks) was another common name for the Christmas plays in the seventeenth century. The two reasons stated for the eventual discontinuation of the *Larvae Natilitiae* are of different nature. The immediate cause is the official time of mourning that followed the death of Elector Johann Georg II in August 1680. At that time, public plays and musical performances were prohibited. On a more general level, the Roman Catholic roots of the plays as well as the fear and angst of the little children during the "sad times" of the plague, which raged in Leipzig (and other German cities) in 1680/81, that led to the prohibition of the plays. The authorities wanted to spare the children the encounter with the rod-swinging Knecht Ruprecht and his scary entourage.

While the chronicler's account for 1681 does not mention the *Larvae Natilitiae*, Vogel states briefly in 1682: "Den 24. Dec. ließ E.E. Rath den so genandten H. Christ zu agiren verbiethen,"[18] (On Dec. 24 the honorable town council prohibited the performance of the so-called Holy Christ). The abolishment of the plays in Leipzig in the early 1680s was preceded by a request to the local theological faculty, regarding whether the *Larvae Natilitiae* should be continued or abolished. The theologians from the university replied on March 1680:

Halten dannenhero schrifftmäßig
davor, daß so beschaffenes
Heil. Christ-Spiel in Haupt
und Fuß zu verändern, daß
sowol die vornehmste Person,
der vermummte Heil. Christ,
als die unterste, nehmlich der
Knecht Ruprecht, abzuschaffen
seynnd, damit weder *Occasion* zur
Abgötterey noch zu allerhand

We deem it more appropriate to the
scripture to change the Holy Christ-
Play completely, that both the most
noble character, the masked Holy
Christ, and the least noble character,
Knecht Ruprecht, have to be abolished,
so that there is neither an occasion for
heresy nor for disgrace or luxuriance on
these occasions. The characters in the
middle, like angels, S. Peter, or

---

[17] Johann Jacob Vogel, *Leipzigisches Geschicht-Buch, oder Annales, das ist: Jahr- und Tage-Bücher Der Weltberümten Königl. und Churfürstl. Sächsischen Kauff- und Handels-Stadt Leipzig in welchen die meisten merckwürdigsten Geschichte und geschehene Veränderungen . . . enthalten sind* (Leipzig: Lank, 1756), 769.

[18] Ibid., 821.

Schand und Üppigkeit in
Zusammenkünfften gegeben werde.
Die mittel Personen können, als
Engel, S. Petrus, oder von dem Heil.
Christ abgeordnete Diener, die
Kinder *examiniren,* beten zu lassen,
und von Untugenden abzumahnen,
in geziemenden Schrancken wohl
beybehalten, und hierdurch die
Kinder bey Christlicher Weyhnacht-
Freude, die *Agi*renden aber bey den
hergebrachten *Acczidenze* (darum
es sonsten zu thun zu seyn scheinen
will) gelassen werden . . . [19]

the servants of the Holy Christ, can
examine the children and admonish
them to pray and keep them in the
appropriate boundaries. This will
keep the Christian joy of Christmas
and provide, at the same time, the
participants with the money they
usually receive (which seems to be at
the core of the problem) . . .

The decision by the university theologians could not save the Leipzig Christmas
plays; instead of referencing theological reasons, the decree from 1680 used the
plague and the time of mourning as a pretext for the abolition of the tradition.
David Siegmund Büttner (1660–1719), a deacon in Querfurt with close ties to
the Pietists in Halle, quotes from another decision in 1701 by the theological
faculty in Leipzig. The statement by the university was an answer to a request
by an unspecified German city. It was probably not Leipzig (where the tradition
had already been abolished for quite some time), but the reply by the theologians
demonstrates that the tradition was still well known and that it was still perceived
as a problem:

[D]ie Weyh- und Christ-Comödie ist
an und vor sich selbst in seiner Natur
ein sündliches Wesen und schändlicher
Greul der unter wahren Christen nicht
zu dulden. Weiln 1) der Ursprung
dieses Spiels abgöttisch. 2) der zarten
Jugend abgöttische *Impressiones* von
Christo / deßen heiligen Aposteln und
Engeln gemacht werden /—solche
Meynungen hernach 3) Anlaß

The Christmas or Christ-Comedy is
inherently sinful and an abominable
atrocity and it is not acceptable
among true Christians. Because
1) the origins of this play are pagan,
2) the tender youth is presented
with pagan impressions of Christ,
his holy apostles and angels . . . this
3) might give reason to believe that
what the scriptures tell about Christ

---

[19] Alexander Tille, *Die Geschichte der Deutschen Weihnacht* (Leipzig: Ernst Keil's Nachfolger,
1893), 140.

zugedencken geben / als wenn das / was von Christo und seinen Heiligen aus der Schrift gelehret wird / Fabel-Werck wäre etc. etc. 4) Kinder beredet werden/ihre innige Kinder-Gebetgen vor dem vermummten und vermeynten heiligen Christ / Engeln und Aposteln/ ja gar vor dem verlarvten Knecht Ruprecht abgöttisch abzulegen.[20]

and his Saints were fairy-tales as well etc. 4) And because children are talked into performing their faithful children's prayers in front of what only pretends to be Christ and the angels and apostles, yes, even before the person dressed as that pagan Knecht Ruprecht.

The Pietist Büttner's treatise against Christmas plays is based on a general mistrust of rituals and religious traditions. However, his quote regarding the decision of the theological faculty in Leipzig is trustworthy as is reiterates arguments we find in other treatises from Leipzig dating from the late seventeenth century. Johann Gabriel Drechssler (+1677)—one of the most vocal authors in the struggle over the Christmas plays—also had a connection to Leipzig. Drechssler was a teacher in Halle and had received his *magister* degree at the University of Leipzig in 1670 (with a thesis on music in the Old Testament, *De Cithara musica*[21]). He was therefore familiar with the traditions of the Christmas play in Leipzig in the late 1660s and early 1670s. Drechssler had a direct impact on the discussions ca. 1680. His criticism of the plays is echoed by sources for their abolishment: Vogel's chronicle had called the *Larvae Natilitiae* "Päpstische Greuel," and Drechssler points likewise to their roots in "papist" times and writes "Larvae hæ Natilitiae (ita vocabimus) ad nos venerunt ex Papatu." Like Vogel, he also protests that the play scared little children without having a lasting educational value.[22]

Drechssler's treatise was published in Leipzig in several editions, versions, and languages: the first edition, then without Drechssler's name but with the anagram "Chressulder," appeared in 1674 and included a theological treatise in Latin and an abridged version in German, significantly expanding the possible readership (fig. 2.1). His treatise (and the bilingual publication in Latin and German) was met with some criticism, especially that from an unnamed colleague who is quoted in

---

[20] Büttner, *Christ-Larven oder Böß-benahmter Heiliger Christ* (Halle: Waisenhaus, 1702), 104.

[21] Johann Gabriel Drechssler, *De cithara musica* (Leipzig, 1670); with subsequent editions in 1671 and 1712; see Werner Braun, "Aspekte des Klingenden in lutherischen Universitätsschriften zwischen 1600 und 1750," in Ekkehard Ochs et al., *Universität und Musik im Ostseeraum. Greifswalder Beiträge zur Musikwissenschaft* 17 (Berlin: Frank & Timme, 2009), 14.

[22] Johann Gabriel Drechssler, *Christianorum Larvas Natalitias Sancti Christi nomine commendatas, post evolutam originem, confodit Stylo Theologico conscientiosus Christi cultor Chressulder* (Leipzig: Coler, 1674), 7–8, 23, 123.

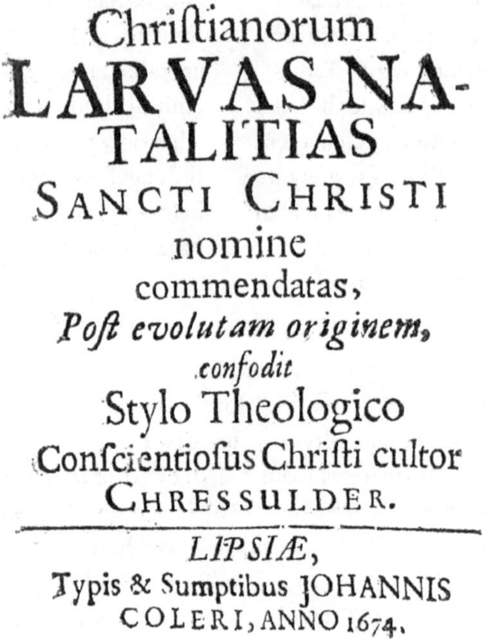

Chriſtianorum
# LARVAS NA-
## TALITIAS
S A N C T I   C H R I S T I
nomine
commendatas,
*Poſt evolutam originem,*
*.confodit*
Stylo Theologico
Conſcientioſus Chriſti cultor
C H R E S S U L D E R.

*LIPSIÆ,*
Typis & Sumptibus JOHANNIS
C O L E R I , ANNO 1674.

*Figure 2.1* Johann Gabriel Drechssler, *Christianorum Larvas Natalitias,* Leipzig 1674 (Universitätsbibliothek Mannheim)

a later edition. Drechssler published a second edition of the treatise in 1677, now including an *Apologia,* a detailed justification of his arguments. This edition likewise appeared under the pseudonym "Chressulder."[23] A third edition of the book (including the *Apologia* and the German version) was printed posthumously in 1683, six years after the author's death and now with his full name.[24] A separate edition of the German translation alone finally appeared in a 1703 issue of the short-lived Leipzig journal *Deliciarum Manipulus.*[25] In his widely published and also

[23] Drechssler, *Christianorum larvas natalitias Sancti Christi nomine commendatas, post evolutam originem, confodit Stylo Theologico conscientiosus Christi cultor: auctius jam prodit, cum Apologia, quam Autor opposuit festinatio quorundam judiciis* (Leipzig: Coler, 1677).

[24] Drechssler, *De Larvis Natalitiis, Earumque Usu & Fine, Tempore, ut vocant, Sancti Christi solitis Cum Apologia* (Leipzig, Weidmann, 1683).

[25] Deliciarum Manipulus, das ist: Annehmliche und rare Discurse von mancherley nützlichen und curiosen Dingen (Leipzig and Dresden: Mieth, 1703), no. 18: "Curiöser Bericht wegen der schändlichen Weyhnacht-Larven so man insgemein Heiligen Christ nennet herausgegeben."

frequently quoted treatise, Drechssler condemns the Christmas plays for being a remnant of Catholicism, as well as continuing superstitions and practices with roots in pagan traditions.[26] The plays were, to Drechssler, a profanation of Christmas Its pagan roots were visible to him in the character of "Knecht Ruprecht."[27] In the German section of his treatise, Drechssler gives a short account of the play and the part of Ruprecht:

Da nehmlich/lange vorher / vermumte Personen mit klingenden Schellen herumb lauffen / sich vor des Heil. Christs Knecht / Sanct Martin oder Niclas ausgeben / die Kinder erschrecken/zum Beten antreiben / und mit etwas wenigen beschencken. Rückt hernach das heilige Weynacht-Fest näher herzu / so nehmen die Irrgeister umb desto mehr überhand: biß endlich den heilgen Abend das gantze himmlische Heer (welches der schwartze Popantz vielleicht außschicket / ) Häuser und Strassen anfüllet. Da führt man das neugebohrne Jesulein / den Heil. Christ / auff / mit Kron / Scepter und Bart gezieret: gleich als ob das liebe Christ-Kindlein in solcher Gestalt wäre auff die Welt gebohren worden. Diesen begleiten die Engel, S. Peter mit dem Schlüssel / andere Apostel / und dann etliche Rupert/oder verdammte Geister.

Long before [Christmas] masked persons run around with jingling bells, pretending to be a servant of the Holy Christ, Saint Martin or Santa Claus, scare the children, admonish them to pray, and give them little gifts. When Christmas draws nearer, the number of crazy spirits increases until finally on Christmas Eve the whole heavenly host (which is probably sent out by the black bogeyman) fills the streets. Then one enacts the newborn Jesus, the Holy Christ [Play], ornate with crown, scepter, and beard, as if the dear Christ-Child had come into that world that way. He is accompanied by angels, S. Peter with the key, other apostles, then several Ruprechts or dammed spirits. Such a holy company is led in front of little

---

[26] Drechssler, *Christianorum Larvas Natalitias* (1674), 7–8, 11–16. The latter had already been dealt with extensively in a book also published in Leipzig, Johannes Praetorius, *Saturnalia, das ist, Eine Compagnie Weihnachts-Fratzen, oder Centner-Lügen und possierliche Positiones . . . Im Jahr: LIeber! antV-Vorte deM Narren naCh seIner Narrheit* (Leipzig: Joh. Wittigau, [1663]).

[27] Drechssler, *Christianorum Larvas Natalitias* (1674), 8, 50–53. Ruprecht was encountered frequently in central-German Christmas plays in the seventeenth century, and his presence in the rituals around Christmas was increasingly a target for criticism; see Karl Hase, *Das geistliche Schauspiel: Geschichtliche Übersicht* (Leipzig: Breitkopf & Härtel, 1858), 119; see also Tille, *Geschichte der Deutschen Weihnacht*, 119 and 128–29.

Solche heilige Compagnie führt man vor die aus Furcht halb-erstorbenen kleiner Kinder. Der Ertz-Bösewicht / Knecht Rupert / fängt an wider sie eine harte Klage zu führen: der Heilige Christ / hefftig entrüstet darüber / bricht auf / will weiter gehen: der Engel Gabriel / gleich wie auch Petrus und andere heilige Gefährten legen eine Vorbitte ein; worauf der H. Christ besänfftiget / reiche Bescherungen lässet aufftragen / und Gnade und Güte den kleinen Abgöttern verspricht. Sie die betrogenen Kinder sind unter des voller Andacht / welche alle auff diese sichtbare Dunst [Gunst] gerichtet. Der H. Christ wird mit Gebet verehret wegen der Bescherungen; die umbstehende Heilige wegen der kräfftigen Vorbitt; der Rupert wegen leichter Begütigung und inhaltender Straffe.[28]

children, who are nearly dead of fear. The arch-villain, Knecht Ruprecht, begins accusing them. The Holy Christ, being upset, leaves and wants to go; however, the angel Gabriel as well as Peter and the other companions intercede and placate the Holy Christ, after which he makes them bring in plenty of gifts and promises mercy and kindness to the little idols. The little children, who were cheated, are meanwhile full of devotion which is directed toward this visible mercy. The Holy Christ is worshipped with prayers because of the gifts; the surrounding saints because of their intercessions; and Ruprecht because of the mercy and only light punishment.

The depiction of Christ, not as a little child as we (and obviously Drechssler) would expect in a Christmas play, but as a grown man, explains why, in the 1676 Leipzig performance described by Thomasius, Christ was played not by one of the boys but by the teacher Jacob Rössler. Drechssler elaborates in a detailed theological argument that the tradition and practice of the *Larvae Natilitiae* contradicted Christian ethics and the Ten Commandments. Even more than the theological problems of the plays themselves, the *Larvae* created an opportunity for ethically questionable misbehavior; the boys often changed the texts and occasionally would even mock both Christ and the listeners:

Der H. Christ kömmt: der H. Christ brummet: der H. Christ hat mir einen Quarck bescheret: der arme H. Christ fiel in Koth: der arme H. Christ ist nicht viel werth: der H. Christ ist ein Mausekopff etc. . . . [29]

The Holy Christ comes; the Holy Christ growls; the Holy Christ has presented me with some rubbish; the Holy Christ fell into the crap; the poor Holy Christ is not worth much; the Holy Christ is a mouse-head . . .

[28] Drechssler, *Christianorum Larvas Natalitias* (1674), 91–93.
[29] Ibid., 115.

In other words, besides being theologically suspect, the Christmas plays were an opportunity for the boys to get out of control, to transgress religious and social boundaries. The *Larvae Natilitiae* with their rituals and practices were indeed occasions for carnivalesque behavior, as it was described by literary theorist Mikhail Bakhtin.[30] Bakhtin differentiates between several forms of folk culture in the Middle Ages and the Renaissance. One form was comprised of *"Ritual spectacles*: carnival pageants, comic shows of the market place."* The Christmas masks in Leipzig greatly resemble these pageants, albeit on a much smaller scale. Bakhtin describes a second form of carnivalesque folk ritual as *"comic verbal compositions*: parodies both oral and written in Latin and in the vernacular."[31] The changes in the texts for the play in Leipzig, and the mocking of both Christ and the city's citizens, fall into this second category.

An essential part of Bakhtin's understanding of carnival (and the carnivalesque) is physiological: the bodily experience of the spectacle.[32] This is one of the aspects that was criticized in Leipzig around 1680. Soon, the physical experience of religiosity should be replaced with purely spiritual piety.[33] With the abolishment of the Christmas plays, the Christmas rituals also lost a participatory element. As Bakhtin points out, "Carnival is not a spectacle seen by the people; they live in it, and everyone participates because its very idea embraces all the people."[34] Finally, that behavior at all times questions (and threatens) the established order and authorities, suspending "hierarchical rank, privileges, norms, and prohibitions."[35] This had to be suspect, even threatening, to the authorities of cities in the second half of the seventeenth century, especially in Leipzig, where they attempted to enforce the social order and increase control over their subjects. The arrests made after the performances of the plays in Arnstadt, in 1713 and 1724, served this very purpose. Certain types of carnivalesque processions had, in fact, already been prohibited in Leipzig earlier in the seventeenth century, but we continuously find orders in the city records against dressing up in public and nightly excursions (mostly of students) until the early eighteenth century.[36]

---

[30] The mocking transformation of the texts for the Christmas plays was a typical element for carnivalesque forms of popular culture as well; see Peter Burke, *Popular Culture in Early Modern Europe* (Aldershot: Scholar Press 1994), 123.

[31] Mikhail Bakhtin, *Rabelais and his World*, trans. Hélène Iswolsky (Bloomington: Indiana University Press, 1984), 5.

[32] Ibid., 19.

[33] See also Van Dülmen, "Volksfrömmigkeit und konfessionelles Christentum," 25–26.

[34] Bakhtin, *Rabelais*, 7.

[35] Cf. Bakhtin, *Rabelais*, 10. See also the perceptive interpretation of carnival traditions in early modern Europe in Burke, *Popular Culture*, 178–204, especially his analysis of Christmas traditions, 193–94.

[36] Cf. Axel Flügel, "'Gott mit uns'—Zur Festkultur im 17. Jahrhundert am Beispiel der Lob- und Dankfeste und Fastnachtsbräuche in Leipzig," in *Feste und Feiern: Zum Wandel städtischer Festkultur in Leipzig*, ed. Karin Keller (Leipzig: Edition Leipzig, 1994), 66–67.

When Thomasius was asked in 1683 whether it was permitted to celebrate the three days of carnival before Lent, he responded negatively—with arguments that closely resemble those given by Drechssler against the *Larvae Natilitiae*.[37]

A direct connection between the Christmas plays and carnivalesque rituals is most vividly drawn in a novel by the famous playwright and poet Christian Weise, a friend of Johann Kuhnau's (Bach's predecessor in Leipzig). In chapter 34 of Weise's novel *Die drei ärgsten Erznarren* (1673) he outlines the contemporary Christmas rituals in satirical exaggeration:

| | |
|---|---|
| Es kam die Zeit, da man die Weyhnacht Feyertage begehen pfleget, da hatten sich an dem vorhergehenden heiligen Abend unterschiedlene Partheyen bunt und rauch unter einander angezogen, und gaben vor, sie wolten den heiligen Christ *agiren*. Einer hatte Flügel, der ander einen Bart, der dritte einen rauchen Peltz. In Summa, es schien als hätten sich die Kerlen in der Fastnacht verirret, und hätten sie anderthalb Monat zu früh angefangen. Der Wirth hatte kleine Kinder, drum bat er alle Gäste, sie möchten doch der *solenität* beywohnen. Aber *Gelanor* hörete so viel Schwachheiten, so viel Zoten und Gotteslästerungen, die absonderlich von denen also genanten Rupperten vorgebracht worden, daß er mitten in während *action* darvon gieng. . . . | It came time when the Christmas holidays are celebrated; on the preceding Christmas Eve all those present dressed in a colorful and wild manner, pretending to enact the Holy Christ. One had wings, another one a beard, the third was wearing a rough fleece. Altogether, it looked as if the lads had lost their way from carnival and had begun a month and a half too early. The innkeeper had little children; therefore, he asked all the guests, to be present at this celebration. But Gelanor heard so much nonsense, so many obscene jokes and blasphemies, which were in particular uttered by the so-called Ruprechts, that he left during the play. . . . Indeed, among the common people such rough and thoughtless sayings are very common, |

[37] Cf. *Acta Nicolaitana et Thomana*, 569, "Ob man auch mit gutem gewissen die hin vnd wieder annoch gewöhnlichen 3. Fastnachtsfeyertage gestatten könne? *Respondebat negative*, weil (1.) selbige nichts anders als *reliquiae Bacchanaliorum*, welche der Teuffel auch endlich vnter die Christenheit eingeführet zu dem ende, damit nicht allein *pia devition de passione Christi* gehindert, sondern auch den leidens Christi gespottet würde. (2.) weil man selbige mit fressen vnd sauffen zubringe, welches auch vnverantwortlich . . . vnd eine todt- vnd himmelschreyende sünde sey; wofür auch diejeigen vor Gottes gericht zu antworten, so dieselben gestatten." (Whether one could, with good conscience, occasionally celebrate the three days of carnival? He gave a negative answer, because (1) they were nothing but remnants of bacchanals which the devil had introduced among Christianity to prohibit them not only from a pious devotion towards the Passion of Christ but also to mock the suffering of Christ; (2) because those days are only spent with scoffing and drinking which would be irresponsible . . . and a mortal sin for which those who allow it have to be held responsible before God's judgment.)

Schwange, darbey die Kinder von Jugend an sich liederlicher und Gottvergessener Reden angewehnen. Ein Schuster, wenn er seinen Kindern ein paar Schuh hinleget, so ist die gemeine Redensart, der heilige Christ habe sie aus dem Laden gestohlen. . . . Doch gesetzt,es wäre ein Nutz darbey, weiß man denn nicht, daß der Nutz kein Nutz ist, wenn er einen grössern Mißbrauch nach sich zeucht. Es ist ein eben thun umb die Furcht und um die Freude, die etwan drey oder vier Tage währet. Ist die Furcht groß, so ist die Verachtung desto grösser, wenn sie hernach den heiligen Christ kennen lernen, da haben sie ein gut *principium* gefast, sie dürffen nicht allem glauben, was die Eltern von der Gottesfurcht vorschwatzen.[38]

and the children already get used to such slovenly and blasphemous talking in their youth. When a cobbler presents his children with a pair of shoes, it is the saying that the Holy Christ had stolen them from his shop. . . . Even if [the play] were somewhat useful, don't the people know that the use is not a use if it leads to even greater misuse? The same is true for the fear and joy [of the children] which only lasts about three or four days. If the fear is great the scorn will be even greater when they afterwards meet the Holy Christ; they will have learned that they should not believe all the babbling of their parents about the fear of God.

Weise's novel has no intention of being a realistic depiction of contemporary practices; instead, exaggeration here is a vehicle for criticism. In spite of its satirical undertone Weise's description corroborates Drechssler's criticism published three years later. Drechssler urges his readers to celebrate Christmas as a day of contemplation of the salvific meaning of Christ's coming instead of carnivalesque rioting[39] with drinking[40] and mischief:

Der H. Abend soll ein Rüsttag und Vorbereitung zur Andacht seyn; Aber er wird zum heydnischen Lauff- und Sauff-Abend. Die Gassen sind voll

Christmas Eve should be a day of preparation for devotion; but it is turned into a pagan running- and drinking-evening. The alleys are full

---

[38] Christian Weise, *Die drei ärgsten Erznarren in der ganzen Welt* (1673; repr., Halle: Niemeyer, 1878), 181–83.

[39] Cf. Drechssler, *Christianorum Larvas Natalitias* (1674), 116–17.

[40] For the relationship between drinking, carnival, and social change in the early modern period, see B. Ann Tlusty, *Bacchus and Civic Order. The Culture of Drink in Early Modern Germany* (Charlottesville: University Press of Virginia, 2001).

| thörichter Irrwische/voll Büberey und | with foolish little rascals, full with |
|---|---|
| Muthwillen. . . . Und das wehrt durch | knavish tricks and mischief. . . . |
| die lieben Nacht.[41] | And that lasts all night. |

Drechssler's treatises, Weise's satirical description, and the regulations of the Leipzig town council in 1680 reflect a larger theological discourse about the proper celebration of Christmas.[42] The Strassburg theologian Johann Conrad Dannhauer (a popular preacher and later a teacher of Pietist theologian Philipp Jacob Spener) had earlier (in 1642) criticized the Catholic tradition of the crèches and the use of Christmas trees.[43] Other contemporary texts have a similar tenor, such as Georg Grabow's *Entdeckung der schädlichen und schändlichen Finsterniß / welche in der Lutherischen Kirche unter den so genannten heiligen Christ enthalten ist* (Berlin: Runge, 1679)[44] or Caspar Sagittarius's treatise *Scribanii Arcularii Dissertation de Abusu Circumforaneae Processionis Circa Ferias Jesu Christi Natalitias* (Jena: Bauhofer, 1674). Attempts to abolish traditional Christmas plays can be found in numerous central German cities in the second half of the seventeenth century, reflecting a more general shift at this time,[45] such as the Thuringian city of Mühlhausen, where the plays were abolished in 1692[46] or in Berlin, where Friedrich Wilhelm I (the "Great Elector") prohibited the performance of similar plays.[47] Even after the official decree of their abolishment, the Christmas plays were still under discussion in Leipzig. In 1699 Carl

---

[41]  Drechssler, *Christianorum Larvas Natalitias* (1674), 118.

[42]  Burke, *Popular Culture in Early Modern Europe*, differentiates between two waves of reform of popular culture. The first phase was the time from ca. 1500 to ca. 1650 (207–22); this phase coincides in our case with the Lutheran reforms of medieval, Catholic folk traditions. The second phase of the reform began in the middle of the seventeenth century and was aimed at, among other things, the abolition of traditions that were rooted in pre-Reformation Catholicism (235). This phase went along with a religious revival that "involved an important shift of emphasis away from the reform of ritual and belief. . . towards inner or moral reform" (239–40.). The reform of Christmas traditions, which began around the middle of the seventeenth century, fall into this second category.

[43]  Quoted in Drechssler, *Christianorum Larvas Natalitias* (1674), 34–35, 75–76.

[44]  See also by Georg Grabow: *Danck-Opffer in welchem zugleich erwiesen/daß das so genante heilge Christ-Spiel/kein gut Werck/oder Mittelding; sondern ein sündliche Wesen/und schädlicher Greuel vor Gott sey* (Leipzig: Krüger, 1683), as well as additional treatises against the plays that appeared in the later 1680s.

[45]  About the discussion regarding the plays in other cities, see Hase, *Das geistliche Schauspiel*, 119–24; Tille, *Geschichte der Deutschen Weihnacht*, 81–147; and Rudolf Heidrich, *Christnachtsfeier und Christnachtsgesänge in der evangelischen Kirche* (Göttingen: Vandenhoeck & Ruprecht, 1907), 9–11.

[46]  See *Badersche Chronik, Die Mühlhäusischen Alterthümer in einer Chronica vorgestellet zum Nützlichen Gebrauch vor die Nachkommen aus vielen Alten Chronicken und einiger Erfahrung zusammen getragen, auch mit vielen Gemählden gezieret von George Andreas Sellmann*, Mühlhausen 1791 (manuscript) (Stadtarchiv Mühlhausen 61/24), 430–31. The tradition in Mühlhausen before 1692 is particulary interesting because it combined a liturgical celebration with the folk tradition of the play.

[47]  Cf. Heidrich, *Christnachtsfeier und Christnachtsgesänge*, 9.

Friedrich Pezold published his philosophical dissertation, *Sancti ut vocant Christi Larvis et munisculis,* submitted at Leipzig University. The author makes extensive use of Drechssler's treatise as a foundation for his rejection of the *Larvae Natilitiae* as "Catholic" and "pagan."[48] Pezold also quotes a short section from a Christmas play, spoken by the scary character of Knecht Ruprecht. It is possible that this represents a version of the text of the play that had been previously used in Leipzig:

| | |
|---|---|
| Ich bin der böse Mann / Der alle Kinder stracks auff einmal fressen kan/Ich Herr Knecht Ruprecht / ich hab auch was zu sagen / Das mir der Heil. Christ zu sagen auffgetragen / Es ist der Heil. Christ mit seinen Engeln draussen / Und will euch nun durch mich die Kolben lassen lausen.[49] | I am the evil man who can wolf down the children all at once; I, Knecht Ruprecht, have something to say as well, which the Holy Christ has told me to say: The Holy Christ is outside with his angels and he wants me to delouse (rather: beat) your heads. |

It is easy to imagine why the town council saw a text like this as possibly threatening to children, in particular during the times of the plague. As historian Tanya Kevorkian has pointed out, the plague epidemic was a formative experience for the religious factions in Leipzig, both for the pietistic movement that was in *statu nascendi* and for Lutheran orthodox theologians.[50] The epidemic triggered a critique of moral and ethical maxims and of consumerism. A new order for funerals, baptisms, and weddings was issued by the town in 1680 and reflected a heightened sensibility for the importance of a Christian (and that meant, socially controlled) life.[51] The order from 1680 criticized, for instance, the singing of motets and hymns in front of the houses of the mourning, and it enforced the rule that modes of dress must reflect social standing. In other words, any kind of overindulgence in music, culture, food, and clothing had to be prohibited. While rules like this were not unusual for the seventeenth century, the plague gave them a new urgency, as the epidemic was widely believed to be a divine punishment for the sinful life that citizens had led in the past.

The *Larvae Natilitiae* were not mentioned in this order by the town in 1680, but the regulations had a similar tenor and goal. The Christmas play represented precisely what was supposed to be prohibited in the aftermath of the plague: overindulgence in social

---

[48] Carl Friedrich Pezold, *Dissertatio Philosophica, De Sancti ut vocant Christi Larvis Et Munusculis . . .* (Leipzig: Brandenburger, 1699), Cap. I, § VIII–XI, , Cap. I, § XI.

[49] Ibid., Cap. I, § XIII.

[50] Tanya Kevorkian, *Baroque Piety: Religion, Society, and Music in Leipzig, 1650–1750* (Aldershot: Ashgate, 2007), 11.

[51] E. E. *Hochweisen Raths der Stadt Leipzig verbesserte Ordnung Wie ein jeder Stand bey Verlöbnissen/ Hochzeiten/Gastereyen/Kindtäuffen und Leich-Begängnissen Ingleichen Kleidungen sich zuverhalten* (Leipzig, 1680).

and cultural pleasures like music and theater, disorderly conduct that was not in line with ethical behavior, and the wearing of clothes that were too lavish or not representative of appropriate social stratification.[52] The abolishment of the Christmas plays was part of the restructuring of the social order in Leipzig on a larger scale. Transgressions—like uncontrolled plays and dressing up as Ruprecht or Heiliger Christ—had to be prohibited. At the same time, the changes in the Christmas traditions also reflected a shift in religiosity away from external rituals (not exclusively the highly problematic ones such as the *Larvae Natilitiae*) toward a spiritual religiosity, and this put a stronger emphasis on the personal relationship between the individual and Christ. It was a shift from a physical religiosity to a spiritual one, focusing—metaphorically speaking—on the presence of Christ in the believer's heart, as contemporary theologians would have put it.[53] We will return to this aspect of Christmas in chapter 3.

A few years after the controversy over the *Larvae Natilitiae*, the town council of Leipzig considered in 1702 prohibiting the *Kindelwiegen*–the rocking of the child in the cradle while singing songs like "In dulci jubilo" or "Josef, lieber Josef mein"[54]—which was also a pre-Reformational tradition that lasted well into the Protestant era.[55] The decision was somewhat related to the one from 1680/82, as it also affected one of the "physical" Christmas rituals.[56] In his "Apologia" from 1677, Drechssler stresses that he rejected just the chaotic and anti-Christian *Larvae* and the abuses of the Christmas plays, but not the quasi-dramatic realizations of the biblical narrative. A critic had asked whether dramatic enactments of the Passion were not an old and

---

[52] Cf. Lieselotte Constanze Eisenbart, *Kleiderordnungen der deutschen Städte zwischen 1350 und 1700: Ein Beitrag zur Kulturgeschichte des deutschen Bürgertums* (Göttingen: Musterschmidt, 1962).

[53] It is interesting to note in this context that in this process of spiritualization the religious metaphors were increasingly charged with erotic (and therefore physical) images from the Song of Songs. Physicality therefore did not disappear but was shifted to a metaphorical level.

[54] Cf. Helmut Loos, *Weihnachten in der Musik: Grundzüge der Geschichte weihnachtlicher Musik* (Bonn: Gudrun Schöder, 1992), 32–34; see also Martin Rössler, *Da Christus geboren ward: Texte, Typen und Themen des deutschen Weihnachtsliedes* (Stuttgart: Calwer, 1981), 87–91.

[55] See Schering, *Musikgeschichte Leipzigs II*, 37–38. The document is a petition of the town council to the Elector of Saxony, recorded on February 13, 1702: "So we have deemed it desirable that the variously mentioned Latin responses, antiphons, psalms, hymns, and collects as well as the so-called Laudes customary at Christmas time, with 'Joseph, lieber Joseph mein' and the rocking of the Christ Child, should not from now on be used in public worship services, but in their place in the churches of this region, appropriate German songs, prayers, and texts throughout should be used." (Leipziger Ratsakten, Tit. VII B 31, fol. 1–3), English trans. Larry D. Cook, "The German Troped Polyphonic Magnificat," vol. I (PhD diss., University of Iowa, 1976), 33–34.

[56] A very different contribution to the "Battle for Christmas" in Leipzig was a theological dissertation by Thomas Ittig, archdeacon at St. Thomas. In *De Ritu festum nativitatis* from 1696, Ittig explains that the celebration of Christmas on December 25 could be traced back only to the fourth century and that in the Orthodox tradition, the feast was celebrated on January 6. Ittig refrains from comments on contemporary practices, but the topic of the dissertation and the critical evaluation of the sources for the celebration of Christmas in December make clear that the feast day was still an important topic in the theological

(if done properly) beneficial tradition: Could not Christmas plays have a similarly positive effect?[57] In his reply Drechssler grants that he has no objections if it is done with the necessary seriousness; he is only criticizing the excess of current traditions and the inclusion of characters and materials that are not appropriate.[58] In fact, he had nothing against dramatic plays (*"omnes actus dramaticos"*), comedies, representations of sacred histories, and sacred musical dialogues (*"dialogos sacros musicos"*). He wanted only to abolish the abuse and criticize the problematic (if not heretic) theological underpinnings of the current plays in order to counteract a profanization of Christmas.[59] In other words, while the carnivalesque excess had to be prohibited in Drechssler's view, accurate and serious adaptations of the biblical narrative were not objectionable. On the contrary, it could be desirable to channel the energy from the excessive *Larvae Natilitiae* to more appropriate plays or sacred musical dialogues.

Once again, the Pietist theologian David S. Büttner argued in a similar vein in his treatise against the Christmas plays printed in 1702. Even though he had certain reservations against highly virtuosic vocal music, echoing frequent Pietist criticism of sacred music,[60] he conceded that musical dialogues based on biblical texts were inherently different from the Christmas *larvae* since performers were not dressed according to their characters and therefore could not be confused with the real biblical characters:

| | |
|---|---|
| Die Music weiß ja von keiner Verkleidung. So wird auch kein Mensch den *Bassist*en vor Christum halten. Ja da in der Kirchen bey Tage mit löblicher Stimme geistliche *Arien* und biblische Sprüche gesungen werden; hört man hingegen des Nachts bey den Christi-Larven das Gebrülle der Ruprechte/ Toben des nachlaufenden Volcks/ und Geläute/von den Karn-Gauln genommen/nebst dem verzogenen Geheule der Hirten/das Ohren und Seele davon weh thun?[61] | In music there is no costuming. Nobody will confuse the bassist with Christ. This is when arias and biblical texts are sung in church during the day with a voice of praise. But what if one hears the braying of the Ruprechts at night during the Christ-Larves [masques], the romping of the people following him, and the chiming of the bell that sounds like it was taken from a carriage horse, as well as the wailing of the shepherds, so that one's ears and soul hurt? |

discourse; see Thomas Ittig, "Dissertatio III. De Ritu festum nativitatis Christi d. 25. Decembr. celebrandi ejusque antiquitate," in Ittig, *Appendix dissertationis de Haeresiarchis . . .* (Leipzig 1696), 386–400, here 400.

[57] Drechssler, "Apologia," in Drechssler, *De Larvis Natalitiis, Earumque Usu & Fine, Tempore, ut vocant, Sancti Christi solitis Cum Apologia* (Leipzig, Weidmann, 1683), 14.

[58] Ibid., 14–15.

[59] Ibid., 15–17.

[60] For the typical criticism of church music by seventeenth-century Pietists, see Joyce L. Irwin, "German Pietists and Church Music in the Baroque Age," *Church History* 54 (1985): 29–40

[61] Büttner, *Anti-Christische Christ-Larven*, 132–33.

Büttner does not see a problem in the musical setting of the biblical narrative, nor in the dialogical representation of different characters in the music. What he criticizes is the "staging," which leads to a suspension of disbelief and therefore to a (heretical) identification of the characters with Christ and his angels.

The shift in the understanding of Christmas in the late seventeenth century is visually represented in the frontispiece of a book by another Pietist theologian, Johann Caspar Schade, published for the first time in Leipzig in 1693.[62] Schade describes the meaning of Christmas in a game of questions and answers, resembling contemporary catechisms and school books. In his preface, the author rejects the tradition of the Christmas *larvae* ("verlarvten Christum"), criticizing in particular disorderly excesses in contemporary folk traditions.[63] The frontispiece can be read as a visualization of how, in Schade's eyes, Christmas should be celebrated (fig. 2.2). The upper right third of the engraving shows a host of angels in the clouds, some of them playing instruments, others probably singing. In the middle of the image, rays of light shine down on three shepherds and their sheep; along one of the rays appears the text "Sihe ich verkündige euch grosse freude etc." (See, I announce to you good news of great joy, etc., Lk 2:10). The upper left third of the engraving depicts another source of light, the star of Bethlehem (Mt 2:2) guiding the wise men. The three Magi bear gifts and are already on their way to the stable which occupies the left side of the lower third of the image. The child Jesus lies in the manger, with Mary and Joseph, as well as one unidentified character, on the very left, adoring him. So far, the image is a faithful depiction of familiar scenes from the biblical narrative. The lower right side of the image depicts what Schade would identify as the appropriate reception of the narrative. In that picture, at the far left, is a teacher surrounded by a group of students. His hands point into the direction of the stable. One of the boys has opened the door and looks at the nativity scene by himself. The *subscriptio* underneath the image explains, "O Kinder freuet euch, Gott selbsten wird ein kind. Schaut was er guths euch bringt. Nur heists wer sucht der find" (O children be delighted, God himself becomes a child. See what good he brings you. But as it is said, only he who seeks will find). The readers are urged to search and inquire about the true meaning of Christmas; this true meaning is, as Schade points out and as the frontispiece suggests, present in the biblical narrative and its proper interpretation.

The general trajectory in the shift in the understanding of Christmas in the later decades of the seventeenth century is the rejection of physical, outwardly religious practices in favor of an internalized, spiritual, yet scripture-based religiosity. Johann Sebastian Bach's *Christmas Oratorio*, standing at the end of this gradual shift, realizes

---

[62] Johann Caspar Schade, *Ein Herrliches Geschenck, oder schöne Christ-Bescherung in einem Einfältigen Gespräch Zwischen Lehrer und Kinder Von der Geburth des lieben Jesus-Kindleins . . . von Einem Kinder Freunde* (Leipzig: Heinichen/Richter, 1693). The first editions appeared anonymously; only the eighteenth-century editions bear Schade's name. The book saw several editions up to 1720.

[63] Ibid.

*Figure 2.2* Johann Caspar Schade, *Ein Herrliches Geschenck* (frontispiece), Leipzig 1693 (Herzog August Bibliothek Wolfenbüttel: Yv 1074.8° Helmst. (1))

this paradigm of nonphysical religiosity in an almost radical fashion as it remains faithful to the characterization of the biblical narrative. This is a different realization in Christmas oratorios by Bach's contemporaries: Johann Mattheson in his Christmas oratorio *Das größte Kind*, from 1720, introduces characters like Mary, Joseph, shepherds, and a "foreigner" who engage in a vivid dialogue.[64] Similarly, in his oratorio *Die Kindheit Jesu*, Bach's son Johann Christoph Friedrich, composes sequences of scenes

---

[64] Cf. Mattheson's autograph score in D-Hs ND VI 140; see also the printed text *Dialogus von der Geburt Christ* from 1707 that served as a model for Mattheson's libretto; see Christine Blanken, Kritischer Bericht, in Reinhard Kaiser, *Weihnachtsoratorium: Dialogus von der Geburt Christi* (Stuttgart: Carus, 2007), 69.

that feature several shepherds, Mary, the angel, and the aging Simeon.[65] Johann Sebastian Bach steers clear of such realistic depictions. He even disregards several opportunities provided by the biblical text to give soliloquies to individual characters, as in recit no. 16 where a part of the announcement of the angel is sung by the evangelist (though the angel had sung in no. 13) or in recit no. 50, where a text spoken by King Herod's theological advisers is again taken over by the evangelist. We will see in a later chapter that this de-dramatization is in concordance with Bach's concept of oratorios in the 1730s. Bach also eliminates the outwardly dramatic character of two parody movements, the duet "Herr, dein Mitleid" (no. 29) and the terzet "Ach, wenn wird die Zeit erscheinen" (no. 51). Both had originated as dramatic dialogues in secular cantatas by Bach but are here reduced to deliver a theological interpretation that transcends the dramatic action of the oratorio. The de-dramatization and spiritualization of the narrative can finally (and most clearly) be seen in the way Bach and his librettist interpret external movement in the biblical story. The use of space had been (and still is) an essential part of folk rituals around Christmas, and still to this day, in the Catholic tradition of the "Sternsinger," children walk from house to house, singing and asking for gifts while leaving a blessing. Even Luther's hymn "Vom Himmel hoch" (From heaven high) encourages the singer (albeit metaphorically) to "go with the shepherds" to the manger.[66] The text of the *Christmas Oratorio* consequently reinterprets the spacial movement of the protagonists as an internalized movement toward Jesus present in the human heart. We see this especially in part V, where the gospel sections about the journey of the wise men are turned "inward" by closely linking them to the search for Jesus in the believer's breast ("seek him in my breast." (no. 45). We will return to this aspect in chapter 10.

## Transforming the Christmas plays

A further exploration of attempts to "rescue" the Christmas plays in the later seventeenth century bring into sharper relief additional characteristics of Bach's oratorio and the traditions on which it stands. An alternative to the *Larvae Natilitiae* was presented by one of the earlier critics of the Christmas plays, the poet and playwright Christian Weise. In his *Reiffe Gedancken* from 1682 Weise sketches a way to circumvent the excess while still maintaining the popular plays; we find references to Weise's model as late as Pezold's Leipzig dissertation from 1699.[67] The text printed in Weise's collection is a

---

[65] Johann Christoph Friedrich Bach, *Die Kindheit Jesu*, ed. Hermann J. Dahmen (Heidelberg: Willy Müller, 1976).

[66] Martin Luther, *Vom Himmel hoch*, stanza 6: "Des laßt uns alle fröhlich sein und mit den Hirten gehn hinein" (Now let us all with songs of cheer, follow the shepherds and draw near).

[67] Pezold, *Dissertatio Philosophica*, Cap. I, § XX.

response to a friend, from 1675, who had requested a suggestion for the performance of the play. In his introduction Weise asserts that it would be better to abolish this tradition altogether, but since the plays were so <u>deeply engrained in the folk rituals around Christmas</u> it would probably be impossible to prohibit them entirely. Instead, one should at least correct the three major abuses and misunderstandings. Like Drechssler does in his treatise, Weise (1) rejects the Catholic components, (2) wants to see the depiction of Christ as a child rather than an old man or adult, and (3) speaks to the moral problems of the current (carnivalesque) form of the play:

Narren herumb lauffen/welche dem jungen liederlichen Volcke wenig Anlaß zu guten Gedancken geben. Und möchts man sich wol verwundern / warum allenthalben in der AdventZeit alle prächtige Musiken / Comoedien / Hochzeiten u.d.g. verboten sind / und gleichwol solche Narrenhändel da tausendmahl mehr *Excesse* vorgehn / so gar frey und ungehindert gelassen werden. Endlich zum dritten kömmt es läppisch heraus / daß man das gebohrene Kindel in einem grauen und häßlichen Barte herein treten läst / gesetzt auch man wolte es nach einer bekandten Gewohnheit **den himmlischen Vater** heissen / so weiß ich nicht / ob sich GOttes heilige Person so leicht verspotten läst. Es ist bekandt / was die vermummten Leute mit den Mägden bißweilen vor Nachtspiele halten: sollen sie nun des himmlischen Vaters so liederlich darbey gedencken / so mag es der Jenige verantworten / der die schöne *Invention* ersonnen oder erhalten hat.[68]

The first abuse is that there are so many apostles and holy men as if one was to adore these people together with the papists. Second, it is outrageous that, at the very time when one should prepare oneself for the devotion of the feast, so many Ruprechts and other carnival-fools are running around, giving the young and slovenly people not many incentives for good thoughts. And one cannot help but wonder why during Advent all the splendid music, comedies, weddings, etc. are prohibited but these foolish activities, during which a thousand times more excess occurs, can freely happen. And thirdly, it is rather ridiculous that the new-born child enters [the houses] with a grey and ugly beard. Even if one wanted to call him according to a known custom **the heavenly father**, I do not know if God's holy person can be mocked that lightly. It is known what kind of nightly games dressed and masked people do with the maids; if this is the way how we should commemorate the heavenly father then he who has invented (or still maintains) these plays has to be held accountable.

---

[68] Christian Weise, *Reiffe Gedancken, das ist, Allerhand Ehren-Lust-Trauer- und Lehr-Gedichte . . . zu Verbesserung der überflüssigen Gedanken herausgegeben* (Leipzig: C. Weidmann, 1682), 366.

Instead of the characters that had formerly populated the plays, Weise proposes a group of five angels, carrying a child wrapped in swaddling clothes (clearly a puppet, not a real baby, and most definitely not a bearded older man) who personifies the newborn Jesus.[69] Weise suggests using five singers, a quartet with doubled discant. The participants do not necessarily need a libretto; well-known Christmas hymns, especially "Vom Himmel hoch, da komm ich her," would do.

| | |
|---|---|
| Darohalben ist meine Meynung/man lasse lauter Engel mit oder ohne Flügel herum gehen / verhülle die Gesichter mit zarten Cammertuche / oder mit güldenen Netzen / und gebe dem vornehmsten Engel ein schön eingewickelt Kind / welches er den Kindern zeigen kan. An statt Rupperts kan zur Noth ein Engel mit einem blossen Schwerdte von Holtze etwas harte drauungen gebrauchen. . . . weil allhier nicht über fünff Personen darbey sind / so mag es auch darbey bleiben / und sind also 2. *Cant. Alt. Ten. Bass.* | Therefore it is my opinion, one should let angels walk around, with or without wings; cover their faces with cambric or golden veils and give the noblest angel a beautifully wrapped child that he can show the children. Instead of Ruprecht an angel with a wooden sword can utter some threats. . . . Since not more than five people should be involved, that should be it; and the [five people] should be 2 cantus, alto, tenor, and bass. |
| Erstlich zwar muß gesungen werden/und kan also nach belieben ein oder etliche Verse aus bekandten Weyhnacht-Liedern / sonderlich / von Himmel hoch da komm ich her etc. ausgelesen werden. | First of all, they indeed have to sing and one can chose one or several verses from well-known Christmas hymns, especially *Vom Himmel hoch.* |
| Wolte man etwas neues haben / wie man unterschiedliche Leute antrifft / welchen die gewöhnlichen Lieder in dergleichen *Actibus* nicht gefallen / so mag es folgender Gestalt angefangen werden.[70] | If one wanted to have something new, as one encounters people who don't like the usual hymns in plays like this, one can also do it in the following way. |

For those who desired a libretto, Weise provides a text. Besides the five soloists the text has sections labeled as "chorus." These sections could have been sung either by the soloists alone or doubled by additional performers. The "angels" go from house

---

[69] This also solves the problem mentioned by Drechssler that Christ was traditionally played by a man and who would then have to be adored by the audience; cf. Drechssler, *Christianorum Larvas Natalitias* (1674), 106.

[70] Weise, *Reiffe Gedancken*, 366–67.

to house, examine the children, and either reward or (if necessary) scold them. The focus of the text, however, is neither on scaring the children nor on entertaining their parents who are watching. The text tries to avoid any kind of carnivalesque excess, but rather emphasizes the soteriological meaning of the Christmas feast and the coming of Christ.[71] There is no evidence that Weise's text was ever set to music, but it is significant that Weise had a musical play in mind when he conceptualized the text. Weise's suggestions could not save the *Larvae Natilitiae*, nor could other texts that tried to reform the plays like a *Heilige Christ-Komödie* from Arnstadt from 1705.[72] The Christmas plays were eventually prohibited in most areas of Germany.[73] Nonetheless, Weise's libretto is interesting as it demands a stronger focus on the biblical Christmas story.

[71] At the very end of the libretto Weise makes a suggestion for the use of instruments to accompany the choir of angels: "Vor der Thüre mag noch ein Weihnacht-Lied gesungen werden. Und wäre so unangenehm nicht / wenn die Engel mit Cymbeln / Schellen und Triangeln unter dem Singen spieleten / denn solche Instrument sind dem [*sic*!] Kindern fremde / und helffen also ihre Einfalt besser bestätigen / als wenn man mit Fiedeln und Pfeiffen auffgezogen kömmt" (A Christmas hymn can be sung in front of the doors. And it would not be unpleasant if the angels played cymbals, little bells and triangles during the singing because such instruments are unknown to the children and they can spark their imagination better than if the angels came with fiddles and fifes). Weise, *Reiffe Gedancken*, 377.

[72] Another attempt of revising the plays was made in 1695 by Friedrich Freise (1668–1721), a teacher in Altenburg. He purges the play from all pagan influences and focuses on the moral and religious bettering of the children; see Friedrich Friese, *Das Danckbarliche Andencken Der heiligen Christ-Nacht / Wolte auff Hohe Vergünstigung Und nach längst eingeführter Gewohnheit ohne Heydnische und Abgöttische Ceremonien Der zarten und in der Gottseeligkeit anzuführenden Jugend In schuldiger Auffwartung und hier entworffenen Action Zu Gemüthe führen die zu Altenburg Anno 1695. Studirende Jugend* (Altenburg: Richter, 1695). Friese's little Christmas play follows the model of Weise's school plays, which were well known in Altenburg; however, there is no evidence that he also knew Weise's suggestion for a "reformed" Christmas play.

[73] We still find traces for similar plays in some German cities throughout the eighteenth century. The Naumburg pastor Johann Martin Schamelius published in 1727 a sermon in which he vehemently criticizes the "Christ-Spiel," which he calls an "Affenspiel" (monkey's game). Like Drechssler before him, he reprimands the participants for breaking several of the Ten Commandments; see Andreas Lindner, *Leben im Spannungsfeld von Orthodoxie, Pietismus und Frühaufklärung: Johann Martin Schamelius, Oberpfarrer in Naumburg* (Gießen: Brunnen, 1998), 266–67, fn. 52; another sermon against the Christmas plays by Schamelius was published in 1717 but is now lost; see Lindner, *Schamelius, List of works, no. 24*. Nevertheless, the Knecht Ruprecht tradition survived in some parts of Germany well into the second half of the eighteenth century. The British author Samuel Taylor Coleridge writes about a visit to the northern German city of Ratzeburg in 1798: Ruprecht, wearing a mask and dressed up "goes around to every house and says, that Jesus Christ his master sent him thither—the parents and elder children receive him with great pomp of reverence, while the little ones are most terribly frightened—He then enquires for the children, and according to the character which he hears from the parent, he gives them the intended present as if they came out of heaven from Jesus Christ." Samuel Taylor Coleridge, "Christmas in Ratzeburg," in *The Friend*, (Burlington, VT: 1831), 322; quoted after Nissenbaum, *Battle for Christmas*, 99–100.

The shift in the understanding of Christmas during the 1680s is reflected in two large-scale compositions in Leipzig, both of which were created only a few years after the decree to abolish the *Larvae Natilitiae*: a setting of the biblical Christmas narrative by Johann Schelle, the cantor at St. Thomas, and a bucolic Christmas scene by Johann Magnus Knüpfer, son of the late Sebastian Knüpfer, Schelle's predecessor. The text for the Christmas scene was written by Paul Thymich, a teacher at St. Thomas school and the first librettist for the opera house in Leipzig. The two Christmas compositions differ significantly; one makes extensive use of the biblical text and hymns; the other is a free poetic rendition of the Christmas story. While Johann Schelle's *Actus Musicus auf Weyh-Nachten* has long been known and studied as a precursor to Bach's *Christmas Oratorio*,[74] the libretto for Knüpfer's *Hirten-Freude* has only recently surfaced.[75] Although both works were composed for Leipzig and were first performed there, their impact reached beyond the Saxon city. There is evidence of performances of Schelle's *Actus Musicus* in Luckau, Lower Lusatia, and in Stettin (Szczecin),[76] and of Knüpfer's *Hirten-Freude* in Jena. While Bach did not model his 1734 *Christmas Oratorio* after these two works, they stand at the beginning of new traditions in Leipzig and elsewhere that were still in place when Bach and his librettist set out to treat the biblical Christmas narrative in an oratorio. The Christmas compositions by Schelle and Thymich/Knüpfer were of a different genre than the prohibited *Larvae Natilitiae* or than Weise's suggested model. Neither piece was intended for the performance in the houses of Leipzig inhabitants but for a "stationary" performance in a church (Schelle) or a public place (Thymich/Knüpfer). However, both participate as quasi-dramatic renditions of the Christmas story in a similar discourse and both reflect in a different way the problems and solutions proffered at this time.

Johann Schelle's *Actus musicus*, probably written in 1683, is a somewhat straightforward setting of the Christmas story from Luke 2, combined with hymn stanzas and occasional instrumental interludes. As Bernd Baselt has demonstrated, Schelle's composition stands in a long tradition of biblical *Historiae* and *Actus musicae* in the seventeenth century and has its predecessor in Heinrich Schütz's *Historia der Freuden- und Gnadenreichen Geburth Gottes und Marien Sohnes, Jesu Christi* (*Weihnachtshistorie*) from 1660/64, as well as a simpler Christmas concerto

---

[74] See, for instance, Bernd Baselt, "Der 'Actus Musicus auf Weyh-Nachten' des Leiziger Thomaskantors Johann Schelle," in *Wissenschaftliche Zeitschrift der Martin-Luther-Universität Halle-Wittenberg: Gesellschafts- und Sprachwissenschaftliche Reihe* XIV (1965), 331–44; Walter Blankenburg, *Das Weihnachts-Oratorium von Johann Sebastian Bach* (Kassel: Bärenreiter, 4th edition, 1999), 26–32; and Howard E. Smither, *A History of the Oratorio 2: The Oratorio in the Baroque Era. Protestant Germany and England* (Chapel Hill: University of North Carolina Press, 1977), 37.

[75] See Markus Rathey, "Die Geistliche Hirten-Freude: Eine Leipziger Weihnachtsmusik im Jahre 1685 und die Transformation weihnachtlicher Bukolik im späten 17. Jahrhundert," *Daphnis: Zeitschrift für Mittlere Deutsche Literatur und Kultur der Frühen Neuzeit (1400–1750)* 40 (2011): 567–606.

[76] Baselt, "Actus Musicus auf Weyh-Nachten," 332.

by Schelle's predecessor Sebastian Knüpfer.[77] Schelle's *Actus musicus* was part of a cycle of gospel compositions performed at St. Thomas and St. Nicholas in 1683/84, which amalgamated the biblical narrative, hymns, and in some cases reflective poetry into an oratorio-like libretto.[78] Schelle's collaborator during the cycle of cantatas in 1683/84 was Paul Thymich, who would soon after write the libretto for Johann Magnus Knüpfer's extraliturgical Christmas play. Thymich did not provide any texts for the *Actus musicus* (at least not in the version we know today), but we can assume that he and Schelle were in an ongoing conversation about these matters.

Leipzig had known larger scale Christmas compositions incorporating a quasi-dramatic component for quite some time.[79] Sebastian Knüpfer served as the Leipzig agent for the distribution of Heinrich Schütz's *Weihnachtshistorie*, and we can assume that the piece was at some point performed in Leipzig as well.[80] Except for the framing movements, *Exordium* and *Conclusio*, Schütz's *Weihnachtshistorie* uses only biblical texts from the gospels of Luke and Matthew. Most of the biblical text is sung in simple cantilation by the tenor. Additionally, Schütz composes eight *intermedia*, featuring sections of the biblical text in concerto-like fashion with instrumental accompaniment. The *intermedia* not only sonically introduce characters such as the angels, the wise men, or King Herod but also provide an opportunity to introduce the traditional rocking of the child in the cradle (Kindelwiegen) into the play. The headline to the first *intermedium* states: "Der Engel zu den Hirten auf dem Felde: Worunter bisweilen des Christkindleins Wiege miteingeführet wird" (The angel [says] to the shepherds in the fields: During which occasionally the cradle of the Christ-child is introduced). Although the use of the cradle is optional, the statement offers that option, reflecting a contemporary tradition and representing a point in the piece where the biblical text is supplemented by a nonbiblical commentary on a performative and physical level.

A piece on a smaller scale was composed by Sebastian Knüpfer himself.[81] The text for Knüpfer's Christmas concerto is a compilation of fragments from different sources: Luther's hymns *Vom Himmel hoch, da komm ich her* and *Vom Himmel kam der Engel Schar*, the German Gloria from Luke 2:14, the fifth stanza of Kaspar

[77] For Knüpfer's piece, see Claudia Theis, "'Vom Himmel hoch, da komm ich her'—Ein Weihnachtskonzert von Sebastian Knüpfer," *Musik und Kirche* 62 (1992): 264–69; and Sebastian Knüpfer, *Vom Himmel hoch, da komm ich her*, ed. Claudia Theis (Kassel: Bärenreiter, 1992).

[78] Cf. *Acta Nicolaitana et Thomana*, 653–55.

[79] For an overview of Christmas compositions by cantors at Leipzig's St. Thomas Church, see Helmut Loos, "Weihnachtsmusiken Leipziger Thomaskantoren des 17. Jahrhunderts," in *Jahrbuch Ständige Konferenz Mitteldeutsche Barockmusik 2002* (Hamburg: Wagner, 2004), 264–71.

[80] Theis, "Vom Himmel hoch," 268.

[81] Claudia Theis has shown that the composition was probably inspired by and modeled on Schütz's *Weihnachtshistorie* (SWV 435); see Theis, "Vom Himmel hoch," 268; Baselt suggests that Schelle's *Actus musicus* was inspired by Schütz's composition as well; see Baselt, "Actus Musicus auf Weyh-Nachten," 331.

Füger's hymn *Wir Christenleut,* and free poetic texts. Knüpfer sonically differentiates the protagonists of his little play by juxtaposing a choir of angels (3 sopranos) against a choir of shepherds (alto, tenor, bass). Knüpfer's concert ends with a double choir, directly juxtaposing the choirs of angels and shepherds, the latter completed with an additional soprano for the tutti sections. Without being an oratorio-like setting of the biblical narrative, like Schütz's or Schelle's pieces, Sebastian Knüpfer's concerto has a clear dramatic element by introducing the angel at the beginning with his announcement of the birth of the child and with the sonic differentiation of the two groups of protagonists. Knüpfer rarely employs the original biblical text; instead, he works with paraphrases and familiar hymn stanzas.

Johann Schelle's *Actus musicus auf Weyh-Nachten* (1683), while also quoting several hymns as well, sticks closely to the original biblical text. The composition for vocal ensemble and instruments stands in the tradition of *historia* compositions in the seventeenth century. At the same time, the piece serves as an amalgamation of a biblical dialogue composition and a chorale cantata: Schelle interpolates into the text from Luke 2 several stanzas from Luther's Christmas hymn *Vom Himmel hoch, da komm ich her.* The composer changes the order of the stanzas (so that they fit seamlessly into the biblical context) but otherwise leaves the hymn texts and the melody intact with the exception of the thirteenth stanza. Additionally, he quotes further hymn tunes in the instrumental parts of the *Actus.* It is important to note—especially within the context of the discussion about Christmas in the late 1670s and early 1680s—that Schelle only employs material that could be considered "liturgical," meaning just biblical texts and hymns. Any kind of free interpretative text is absent.

The *Actus musicus* is divided into three sections, each of which is introduced by an instrumental *Sonata.* The protagonists of the piece are mostly the same as in Knüpfer's little concerto: an angel, sung by a soprano, a choir of angels (for the German Gloria), and a choir of shepherds, who sing the text "Lasset uns nun gehen" (Let us now go). Schelle also introduces a tenor serving as evangelist or narrator, who sings the framing texts in a simple recit style. Schelle adds an additional solo movement (also sung by the soprano), a setting of the thirteenth stanza of the hymn "Vom Himmel hoch"— "Ach mein herzliebes Jesulein." This movement stands out especially because of its soloistic treatment and because the setting abandons the original hymn melody for a freer and in particular, more emotional treatment. The text implores the beloved child Jesus ("Ach mein herzliebes Jesulein") to come into the heart of the believer. The words are treated like free poetry and by neglecting the sixteenth-century melody Schelle composes a virtual outburst of emotion in the context of a rather matter-of-fact presentation of the Christmas story. Schelle's remarkable setting features sigh motifs, sequences, and repetitions to highlight the emotional depth of the text. We will return to the theological context of this emotional outburst in the following chapter.[82]

---

[82] The highly emotional sighs from the Lutheran chorale alternate with lines from another hymn, Kaspar Füger's "Wir Christenleut," which are played as interludes by the trombones. Additional hymns

Schelle's *Actus musicus* is not necessarily a direct reaction to the struggle about Christmas and Christmas plays in Leipzig in the early 1680s. The *Actus musicus* and the *Larvae Natilitiae*, however, correlate with this strife on a theological and socio-logical level: the struggle over the Christmas plays around 1680 has broader implica-tions for the understanding and the celebration of Christmas itself. The critics urged for a biblical understanding of the feast (instead of a play with pagan and "papist" roots) and emphasized the spiritual meaning of Christmas over the corporeal experi-ence (with its processions, masks, costumes, and, in a different context, the rocking of the child). Schelle's *Actus musicus* steers clear of all the problems of the plays: it is focused solely on the presentation of the gospel text, and as liturgical music it would naturally have been performed without masks and costumes. Furthermore, the text for the piece is exclusively based on the Bible and traditional hymns. Schelle's *Actus* avoided any pagan and "papal horror," representing instead a Lutheran orthodox rendition of the Christmas scene, while at the same time satisfying the wish for a dramatic presentation of the text. Instead of inserting free arias Schelle turns a set-ting of that stanza of *Vom Himmel hoch* into a highly expressive aria, emphasizing the emotional connection between Christ and the believer.[83] Schelle does not employ any texts that were outside of the accepted liturgical canon, but the way he treats the chorale stanza is much closer to seventeenth-century love songs than anything else in the *Actus musicus*. The choice of a voice register that often had female connotations (even though sung by a boy) is significant; she sings the aria immediately after the Evangelist has mentioned that Mary kept "all she had seen and heard" in her heart. It would be an oversimplification to interpret the voice here as a personification of Mary. However, the way Schelle structures his composition suggests a typological analogy between Mary and the singer of the hymn stanza by not only featuring the central keyword "Herz" (heart) in both the gospel and hymn texts, but also through the image of female love that is both represented by Mary (as motherly love) and in the words of the hymn, "My most beloved Jesus" (as love for Christ). It is a spiritu-alized form of love that is at the core of the movement, which goes along with the anticorporeal and antiphysical understanding of Christmas in the late seventeenth century: the celebration of Christmas is cleared of its corporeal elements while at the same time the metaphors, borrowed from love and erotic poetry, are spiritualized.

---

quoted in the instrumental parts are "In dulci jubilo" in the two *Sonatae Pastorellae* (Nos. 4 and 13) and the Lutheran hymn "Gelobet seist du, Jesu Christ" (No. 7). The melody quotations provide an addi-tional intertextual layer to the piece without overtly increasing the number of texts sung and thus dis-tracting from the biblical narrative. See also Smither, *History of the Oratorio* 2, 37.

[83] The theological context for this aria is the concept of mystic unity (*unio mystica*), which was conventionally described in contemporary theology with metaphors resembling love poetry, employ-ing the image of the heart as the dwelling pace of the beloved—in this case of Christ; cf. chapter 3, this book; for a general overview, see Isabella van Elferen, *Mystical Love in the German Baroque: Theology, Poetry, Music*. Contextual Bach Studies 2 (Lanham, MD: Scarecrow Press, 2009).

The ban on the *Larvae Natilitiae* in 1680 meant the death of the extraliturgical Christmas play in Leipzig—or so it seemed. The recently surfaced libretto for the performance of a "musical dialogue" by the *Collegium musicum* in Leipzig proves otherwise. According to the title page, the ensemble performed a musical dialogue "after the days of Christmas 1685," called *Geistliche Hirten-Freude*. The phrase "after the days of Christmas" is not entirely clear as it either can mean that the piece was performed after the three main holidays of Christmas (December 25–27) or it can refer to the end of the Christmas season on Epiphany day, which would indicate that the piece would have been performed after January 6, 1686. While the topic of the play might be closer to liturgical readings of the main Christmas holidays, the later date would place it in the time of the New Year's fair in Leipzig, an occasion during which the *Collegium musicum* frequently performed.[84]

The composition for the Christmas piece is lost; it was most likely never printed. The libretto, however, was printed and either sold or distributed at the performance (or performances) in 1685/86. The print mentions neither the librettist nor the name of the composer. We would have to speculate on their identities if the piece had not seen at least one other performance. In 1693 the sacred shepherds' play was performed at the Collegien-Kirche in Jena (the university church of Jena University). The libretto printed for that occasion identifies Paul Thymich as the author of the text and Johann Magnus Knüpfer (1661–1715) as composer of the music (fig. 2.3).

The performance took place during a worship service on the third day of Christmas (December 27) 1693. The print itself is dedicated to the rector and the professors of Jena University. The libretto was then printed a third time (again in 1693) with a dedicatory poem in honor of Johann Georg II of Sachsen-Eisenach and his wife, Sophie Charlotte. The text that is preserved in the three librettos is almost identical; the version for the Leipzig performance differs only in a few orthographic details from the one printed for the performance in Jena.[85] Since Johann Magnus Knüpfer was the organist at the Collegien-Kirche in Jena we can assume that he initiated the performance and the two prints from 1693. He was the son of a former Thomas cantor, Sebastian Knüpfer (1633–76), and had unsuccessfully tried to take over the position

---

[84] The fair would also be the time when the Leipzig opera house, which was founded a few years later in 1693, would put up a new production; cf. Michael Maul, *Barockoper in Leipzig (1693–1720)*, Freiburger Beiträge zur Musikgeschichte 12/1 (Freiburg: Rombach, 2009), 230–34.

[85] The only major differences are the title (the Jena version is called "Geistliches Hirten-Gespräch" while the print from Leipzig has "Weihnachtliches Hirten-Gespäch") and the exchange of "allertreuster Hirte" from the Leipzig version for "allerliebster Hirte" in the Jena version. The latter difference could easily be a mistake and does not represent a significant change. The only known copy of the print dedicated to Johann Georg II was destroyed during the fire in the Anna-Amalia-Bibliothek in Weimar in 2004. Nonetheless, the first three pages exist as a scan and show that the version is almost identical with the one used for the performance at the Collegien-Kirche in the same year. The title page and dedication were exchanged and a dedicatory poem added. There is no reason to presume that the rest of the text, which is now lost, was any different from the other prints.

*6.5*

**P. THIEMICHS**

Geiftliches

**Hirten = Gespräche**

von

der heilsam-und Gnadenreichen Geburt

unsers Herrn und Heilandes

**Jesü Christi**

Zu Vermehrung Christl. Andacht

Bey dem

in der Collegien-Kirche zu Jena

auf den III. Christ-Feyertag

dieses zu Ende lauffenden 169̤ ften Jahres

angestellten

**Gottes = Dienstes**

In ein Musicalisches Singe = Spiel

gebracht

durch

JOH. MAGNVM **Knüpfern** / Lipf.

Not. Publ. Cæfar.

JENA

Zu finden bey Joh. Zach. Nisien.

*Figure 2.3* Paul Thymich, *Geistliches Hirten-Gespräche,* Jena 1693 (version for Collegien-Kirche) (Universität der Künste Berlin, Universitätsbibliothek)

of organist at St. Thomas in 1682; his application to succeed Schelle as cantor at St. Thomas in 1701 was unsuccessful as well.[86] Both times he lost against Johann Kuhnau. From 1690 to 1694 he was organist at the Collegien-Kirche in Jena and served in the same position until 1715 at St. Wenzel in Naumburg.[87] Both Thymich and J. M. Knüpfer can, at least indirectly, be connected to two earlier musical works for Christmas in Leipzig. Knüpfer's father had composed the Christmas concerto discussed earlier, which explored some dramatic possibilities by introducing sonically

[86] See the documentation of his applications in Richard Münnich, "Kuhnaus Leben," *Sammelbände der Internationalen Musikgesellschaft* 3 (1902): 524–25.

[87] Cf. Walter Haacke, "Die Organisten an St. Wenceslai zu Naumburg a.d. Saale im 17. und 18. Jahrhundert," in *Kerygma und Melos: Christhard Mahrenholz 70 Jahre,* ed. Walter Blankenburg

differentiated characters and groups. Also, Thymich was Schelle's librettist for the "oratorio-like" cantata cycle during 1683/84, the time during which Schelle's *Actus musicus* was composed and performed. Thymich had experience with both sacred poetry (through his collaboration with Schelle, among others) and with dramatic music, providing the text for the *dramma per musica* composed by Johann Kuhnau and performed by the students in 1683 in honor of the Saxon Elector.[88]

Thymich's libretto for the *Hirten-Freude* consists of a prologue and eight "Abtheilungen" (sections) narrating and embellishing the Christmas story:


| [Prologue] | Praise of Music |
|---|---|
| 1st section | Lament of the shepherds and hope for the coming of the Savior |
| 2nd section | Message of the Angel; paraphrase of Gloria |
| 3rd section | Shepherds depart for the manger |
| 4th section | Mary and the angel rock the child (Kindelwiegen) |
| 5th section | Shepherds arrive at the manger and adore the child |
| 6th section | Shepherds leave and praise God and Mary |
| 7th section | Shepherds ask Jesus to come to them |
| 8th section | Expanded paraphrase of Gloria, choirs of shepherds and angels |


Each section ends with a choral movement or a four-part ensemble aria; the only exception is the seventh section, which leads directly to section eight, a large-scale choral movement that serves as closing movement for the seventh section (and thus replacing the missing choral movement at the end of section seven).

The protagonists in the opening scene of Thymich's libretto are four shepherds, named after characters from the Old Testament: Abel, Laban, Jacob, and David. While Thymich's text is clearly influenced by the popular genre of the secular shepherds' play,[89] he does not borrow names from shepherds in pagan bucolic literature.

(Kassel: Bärenreiter, 1970), 291–93; and Susanne Alberts, *Musik in Naumburg/Saale 1650–1720: Kirchliches und höfisches Musikleben in Naumburg an der Saale zur Zeit der Sekundogenitur* (Saarbrücken: VDM Verlag, 2008), 17–19.

[88] See the description of Kuhnau's piece in Markus Rathey, "Rehearsal for the Opera–Remarks on a Lost Composition by Johann Kuhnau from 1683," *Early Music* 42 (2014): 409–20.

[89] For the tradition of the pastoral singspiel in Germany, see Mara Wade, *The German Baroque Pastoral "Singspiel,"* Berner Beiträge zur Barockgermanistik 7 (Bern: Peter Lang, 1990); for the merging of classical and biblical traditions, see esp. 70–71.

Some other contemporary Christmas plays occasionally introduce names from the Petrarchan tradition, such as Dafnis, Coridon, Menalkas, or Mopsus.[90] The names in Thymich's play are clearly rooted in the Judeo-Christian tradition.[91]

The text of Thymich's *Hirten-Freude* consists primarily of dialogues between the four shepherds, in which song-like arias are inserted (some of them strophic) to be sung by one, two, or four singers. Four additional movements are labeled as "Chor" (chorus), including a piece for double choir, juxtaposing a choir of angels and a choir of shepherds. The texts for the arias are in the style of song-like arias from the central German repertoire of the second half of the seventeenth century. We can therefore expect that they were set with a mostly syllabic upper voice and a simple, straightforward accompaniment. The same is true of the choir movements (although we cannot rule out a more polyphonic texture). The remainder of the text was either spoken, as was customary in contemporary school plays, or sung in the style of a recit. The use of instruments is nowhere indicated in the libretto. It is likely that the *Collegium musicum* employed both string and woodwind (including reed) instruments, as they are mentioned in the text of the libretto. All together, we can expect a group of approximately fourteen performers: the four shepherds who sang their solo parts and also performed as the "choir of shepherds" (they could have been doubled by additional singers), the choir of angels (with one angel as soloist), possibly a solo voice for the part of Mary, and a group of instrumentalists (at least two violins and woodwinds), including a *basso continuo* group. /

The Christmas play opens with the longest scene of the work, depicting the four shepherds on the meadows close to Bethlehem. While the Prologue had urged the listeners to sing and to praise God, the scene (sec. 1) turns to the opposite: David laments that the fifes were frozen, and Abel adds that nobody paid attention to "the loud crying of the sounding shawms" ("Das laute Schreyen / der schallenden Schallmeyen").[92] The mention of the fifes and shawms, flutes and reed instruments

---

[90] See, for instance, the Görlitz Christmas play described by Hans Mersmann, "Ein Weihnachtsspiel des Görlitzer Gymnasiums von 1668," *Archiv für Musikwissenschaft* 1 (1918/19), 260; see also a Christmas play performed in Goslar in 1695, which introduces the shepherds Tityrus and Coridon into the nativity scene (*Das versperrte und wieder eröffnete Paradeiß in einem Weinacht-Singe Spiel vorgestellet* [Goslar 1695]).

[91] We find a similar choice of names already in some Christmas plays from the sixteenth century, as in Johann Cuno's Christmas comedy ("Weihnachtskommödie"), featuring two good shepherds named Jacob and David, and two bad shepherds, Laban and Nanal; see Johann Cuno, *Ein schön Christlich Action von der Geburt und Offenbarung unders Herrn und Heylandts Jhesu Christi, wie er zu Bethlehem im Stall geboren, den Hirten und Weysen offenbaret* (Magdeburgk: Duncker 1595). See also the short description and analysis of Cuno's play in Alfred Lowack, *Die Mundarten im hochdeutschen Drama bis gegen das Ende des Achtzehnten Jahrhunderts: Ein Beitrag zur Geschichte des deutschen Dramas und der deutschen Dialektdichtung*, Breslauer Beiträge zur Literaturgeschichte VII (Leipzig: Hesse und Becker, 1905), 40–42.

[92] Paul Thymich, *Geistliche Hirten-Freude*, 5.

evokes the conventional association of the shepherds with woodwind instruments found in Renaissance iconography.[93] The inability to sing (or to make music in general) is an inversion of one of the characteristics of the bucolic *locus amoenus*, envisioned as a place of rest, peace, and music. The lack of music characterizes the place of the shepherds as a *locus terribilis*, which is underscored by the chilling temperatures and summarized in a lament by the shepherd Laban: "Mein Freund es singt sich nicht / Wenn Hertz und Mund umbzüngelt ist / Mit lauter Furcht und Schrecken" (My friend, one cannot sing when heart and mouth are besieged by fear and fright).

The second section ("Abtheilung") of Thymich's play describes an apparition of the angels and culminates in a paraphrase of the Gloria, which stays remarkably close to the biblical text. This is the first movement in the libretto assigns to a choir:

| *Hirten-Freude* | *Luke 2:14* |
|---|---|
| Ehre sey GOtt in dem Himmel! | Ehre sei Gott in der Höhe |
| Fried auff diesem Welt-Getümmel / | Und Friede auf Erden |
| Und den Menschen Kindern allen | Und den Menschen |
| Ein vergnügtes Wohlgefallen! | Ein Wohlgefallen |
| | |
| May Honor be to God in Heaven | May honor be to God on high, |
| And peace in the commotion on earth | and peace on earth, |
| And with his human children | and to humankind |
| A joyful pleasure. | [God's] great pleasure. |

The third section reports the departure of the shepherds and their reflections on the meaning of the angel's message. This thread is continued later in the fifth section, when the shepherds approach the manger. For a moment, though, the shepherds' scene is interrupted in section four with a scene of Mary and the angels singing lullabies to the newborn child. The scene resembles the traditional Kindelwiegen,[94] a tradition that, as we have seen, was still alive in Leipzig in the 1680s.

The fifth section returns to the shepherds and describes their arrival at the manger. In their encounter with the newborn child, our bucolic scene has finally reached

[93] We can find a similar association in Weise's shepherds' play. The preface to the play says: "Die Music bestehet mehrentheiles in Paucken und Schalmeyen / weil das gantze Spiele eine Schäfferey abbilden sol." (The music consists mainly of timpani and shawms because the play is supposed to depict a shepherds' play.). See Weise, *Biblische Dramen II*, 6. Bach also employs oboes in his *Christmas Oratorio* to signify the shepherds.

[94] For the tradition of Kindelwiegen, see Loos, *Weihnachten in der Musik*, 32–34.

its state of *locus amoenus*. The *locus terribilis* of the beginning, symbolized by the darkness and coldness of the scene, gives way to a renewal of the world through the coming of Christ. Abel sings:

ABEL

Wie die Schäfer sich erfreuen
An den Reyen/
Wenn sich Welt und Feld
    verneuen/
So erfreut sich mein Muth/

ABEL

How much the shepherds
Enjoy the dance/
When world and meadows are
    renewed/
Similarly, my mind is refreshed/

The renewal of nature again reflects the renewal of the spirit: the outer world is a symbolic reflection of the inner world. The bucolic scene is once more reinterpreted from a Christian perspective.[95] In the sixth and seventh sections, the shepherds finally return from the manger and proclaim what they have seen and heard. The scene culminates in Laban's song, admonishing his companions to praise God with fifes and strings. The mention of these two families of instruments again denotes the sonic spheres of the shepherds (fifes and flutes) and the angels (strings). The shepherds' fifes that had been frozen at the beginning of the play are now playable again and the shepherds can join the angelic orchestra (realizing the *locus amoenus* on a sonic level). The sonic unification of divine and human spheres, of angels and shepherds, finally becomes reality in the closing movement. Laban's song (with its admonition to sing) is immediately followed by a polychoral dialogue between the choirs of the angels and shepherds, based on a free paraphrase of the Gloria:

ENGEL CHOR
Ehre / Ehre/

CHOIR OF THE ANGELS
Glory, Glory

HIRTEN CHOR
Ehre / Ehre

CHOIR OF THE SHEPHERDS
Glory, Glory

ENG[EL:] Ehre sey Gott in der Höhe /
    Jetzt und auch in Ewigkeit!

ANGELS: Glory to God in the highest
    Now and in eternity

---

[95] Thymich, *Geistliche Hirten-Freude*, 18. For the use of spring and summer metaphors in Baroque poetry, see Cornelia Rémi, *Philomela mediatrix: Friedrich Spees Trutznachtigal zwischen poetischer Theologie und geistlicher Poetik*. Mikrokosmos. Beiträge zur Literaturwissenschaft und Bedeutungsforschung 73 (Frankfurt/M.: Peter Lang, 2006), 166; cf. also Hansjacob Becker, "Es ist ein Ros entsprungen," in *Geistliches Wunderhorn: Große deutsche Kirchenlieder*, ed. H. Becker in collaboration with M. Rathey (Munich 2001: Beck), 139–40.

| HIRTEN: Der uns sämmtlich hat befreyt / Seine Herrligkeit bestehe. | SHEPHERDS: Who has liberated us all His glory shall last |
|---|---|
| ZUSAMMEN Ehre sey Gott in der Höhe. | TOGETHER Glory to God in the highest |

The polychoral juxtaposition (and unification) of shepherds and angels is already familiar from previous Christmas scenes like the ones by Schelle and Sebastian Knüpfer. We will see that Bach also uses this feature in the second part of his *Christmas Oratorio*.

## Christmas in Leipzig

Commentators on Bach's *Christmas Oratorio* have frequently lamented the scarce evidence for Christmas traditions in Leipzig in the late seventeenth and early eighteenth centuries. The discussion about the Leipzig *Larvae Natilitiae* and the libretto by Thymich provides additional material that fills in some of the blank spots. Despite being written for a single occasion, Thymich's libretto reflects theological, ritual, and musical traditions that transcend the singular event of its performance in Leipzig in 1685/86. The libretto provides us with some insight into extraliturgical Christmas traditions. It also serves as an example of a madrigalistic text that rephrases the biblical text and adds its own interpretation of the Christmas narrative—something we do not find in the liturgical Christmas compositions that were used in Leipzig at that time. Of equal importance is the fact that both Johann Schelle's and Johann Magnus Knüpfer's works were composed and performed at a time when the traditions and rituals of the celebration of Christmas were highly disputed. Johann Gabriel Drechssler's treatises and the ban on the *Larvae Natilitiae* are indicative of a rejection not only of the folk traditions associated with Christmas but also of a elimination of the physical and corporeal components of this celebration, in favor of an increasingly spiritualized religiosity. Narratives that were not founded in the biblical text were banned, including the renunciation of the Knecht Ruprecht character in the *Larvae*. Even though Thymich paraphrases and expands the biblical Christmas story and embellishes the narrative with several extensive shepherds' scenes, his imagery and the names of the characters draw on biblical material (from both the Old and the New Testaments).

The following years in Leipzig saw an even further reduction of folk elements that had a physical component, including the eventual rejection even of the Kindelwiegen. We still see the culminating effects of this shift about fifty years later in Bach's *Christmas Oratorio*, which celebrates the coming of Christ with physical metaphors (love, beloved) that have become thoroughly spiritualized. While there is no evidence that Bach knew Schelle's *Actus Musicus* (as Walter Blankenburg suggested[96]), he was undoubtedly aware of accepted and rejected folk traditions. He would have encountered the play in Arnstadt in 1706; and indeed, similar plays still existed in central German cities throughout the 1720 and '30s.

Was the old Christmas play really dead in Bach's Leipzig? A curious print from 1720 suggests not. The print preserves a traditional Christmas play with an adult "Heilig Christ," who, accompanied by a host of angels, St. Peter, and other characters, comes down to earth to examine the children and to give them their Christmas gifts.[97] The play also features St. Martin and St. Nicholas as well as St. John, King David, and Christ's coachman, Hans Pfriem (from the medieval legend of an argumentative waggoner who goes to heaven).[98] The title page credits Leipzig as the place of printing, but it neither states an author nor whether the text was to be used by the children in Leipzig. We should be cautious not to jump to the conclusion that the Christmas plays were still widespread around the time when Bach began his tenure in Leipzig in 1723.[99] However, the print also suggests that the tradition was not entirely dead. Even though the city streets had been purged from carnivalesque behavior, some traditions might still have existed in private houses.

*[handwritten note: How much is Rupert a rebuy for jitch ?]*

---

[96] Blankenburg, *Das Weihnachts-Oratorium*, 26.

[97] Knecht Ruprecht is no longer present in the play; instead, Jesus asks St. Peter to give him the rod to punish the children.

[98] *Die heilige Christfart: das ist: ein holdseliges und gantz liebliches Gespräch wie sich der frommeheilige Christ mit seinen lieben Ertz-Engeln und andern Heiligen gegen itzt künfftigen heiligen Christ-Abend auf seinem himmlischen Kammer-Wagen und güldenen Schlitten herümmer zu fahren aufgemacht* . . . —Der lieben Jugend zu Nutz u. Dienst aufs neue zum Druck befördert, Leipzig 1720; the text is also accessible in a print from the early twentieth century: Ernst Kroker, "Hans Pfriem im Märchen und im Weihnachtsspiel," in *Schriften des Vereins für die Geschichte Leipzigs* 7 (1904), 177–240; here 213–40.

[99] Kroker assumes based on the language of the text that the play must originate from the first half of the seventeenth century, probably ca. 1600–1630; see Kroker, "Hans Pfriem," 206.

# 3

# Layers of Time

## *The Theology of the* Christmas Oratorio

Chapter 2 explored the shifts in the understanding of Christmas in the seventeenth and early eighteenth centuries. This chapter turns to the concepts of the feast that superseded the older traditions. These shifts were not instantaneous. The existence of a print with a Christmas play in Leipzig from 1720 (whatever its function might have been) demonstrated that some traditions were quite resilient, even forty years after their official discontinuation. While the changes in the theological under-standing of Christmas are rooted in the sixteenth century, the new understanding of the feast was firmly established around the middle of the seventeenth century; this coincides with the time when the critique of the *Larvae Natilitiae* became more intense.[1] The analysis of the seventeenth- and early eighteenth-century perception of Christmas leads us to a clearer understanding of the libretto for the *Christmas Oratorio,* and elucidates several choices made by Bach in the compositional process.

The libretto for Bach's *Christmas Oratorio* is characterized by a continuous shift in perspectives and chronological layers. These different layers frequently posed difficulties for post-eighteenth-century listeners: the familiar biblical narrative is interrupted by hymn stanzas and newly written poetry that oscillates between the topics of death, the mystical love of bride and bridegroom, and the Day of Judgment. Interpreters have occasionally explained these different perspectives of the libretto as an amalgamation of Lutheran orthodox and Pietist influences.[2]

---

[1] It is historical irony that the increasingly spiritual and internalized understanding of Christmas, which was supposed to replace the "Papist abuses," was rooted in medieval theology as well and can be traced back to Bernard of Clairvaux in the twelfth century.

[2] In his recent study on the *Christmas Oratorio,* Ignace Bossuyt suggests that the use of the biblical text was influenced by Lutheran orthodoxy while the (emotional) arias showed influences of the Pietist movement. Even though Bossuyt admits that Bach probably was not a dedicated Pietist himself, this "did not, however, prevent the occasional appearance of Pietistic concepts in some of the texts, as, for instance, in the symbolism of the bride and the bridegroom (representing the soul and Christ), with their fervent longing to be united, and the intimate, loving and emotionally-charged relationship with

However, the ideas of mystical love and the foreshadowing of death were part of a common understanding of Christmas among Lutheran orthodox theologians in the seventeenth and eighteenth centuries. The individual piety that is sometimes identified as "Pietist" can be found in numerous Lutheran orthodox writings from Bach's time.[3] Furthermore, the imagery of bride and bridegroom is rooted in a strand of religiosity in German Protestantism that emerged toward the end of the sixteenth century and which had originated in a revival of medieval mystical texts, particularly those by Bernard of Clairvaux (1090–1153). This type of devotional imagery was not at all limited to the Pietist movement; it influenced orthodox Lutherans as well.[4] In fact, the *Christmas Oratorio* libretto, which might have been written by Picander, never leaves the realm of early eighteenth-century Lutheran theology.

The theological landscape of the eighteenth century is foreign to most listeners today. It would be erroneous to infer present understandings of piety (and of Christmas) to an interpretation of Bach's oratorio and equally incorrect to reduce Bach's (and his librettist's) theology to a reiteration of Luther's understanding.[5] Instead we have to leave these assumptions behind and, not unlike an ethnographer, need to map the understanding of divine incarnation and the Christmas feast in the seventeenth and early eighteenth centuries in order to grasp the religious profile of Bach's oratorio. This chapter also sheds light on some peculiarities of the libretto and of Bach's composition, namely the highly emotional metaphors and the frequent references to death and dying in a piece that celebrates the coming of Christ. This leads to a reassessment of the temporal structure of the oratorio as a whole. The theological basis for this analysis of the understanding of Christmas in Bach's time

Jesus found particularly in the chorales of Paul Gerhard, the so-called 'Ich-Lieder,' texts written in the first person . . . and other free texts." Bossuyt, *Johann Sebastian Bach: Christmas Oratorio (BWV 248)*, trans. Stratton Bull (Leuven: Leuven University Press 2004), 31.

[3] The common misidentification of texts in Bach's church music that express Lutheran dogma as "orthodox" and those that are more emotional as "Pietist" has already been criticized by Wolfgang Herbst in his dissertation on Bach and Lutheran mysticism; however, the misconception is so deeply ingrained in Bach scholarship that it is constantly perpetuated; see Herbst, *Johann Sebastian Bach und die Lutherische Mystik*, PhD diss., Friedrich-Alexander-Universität Erlangen, 1958, 2.

[4] Regarding the reception of Bernard's texts in the seventeenth century, see Ferdinand van Ingen, "Die Wiederaufnahme der Devotio Moderna bei Johann Arndt und Philipp von Zesen," in *Religion und Religiosität im Zeitalter des Barock*, ed. Dieter Breuer, Wolfenbütteler Arbeiten zur Barockforschung 25 (Wiesbaden: Harrassowitz, 1995), 467–75; and Martin Brecht, "Das Aufkommen der neuen Frömmigkeitsbewegung in Deutschland," in: *Geschichte des Pietismus I: Der Pietismus vom siebzehnten bis zum frühen achtzehnten Jahrhundert*, ed. M. Brecht (Göttingen: Vandenhoeck & Ruprecht, 1993), 127–30.

[5] The latter approach was recently criticized by Rebecca Joanne Lloyd, *Bach Among the Conservatives: The Quest for Theological Truth*, PhD diss., King's College London, 2006; see also the summary of the main thesis in Lloyd, "Luther's Musical Prophet?" *Current Musicology* 83 (2007): 5–32.

*That's it?*

is the concept of the *threefold coming of Christ*, which represents the common view of the birth of Jesus at that time and connects the historical event to a chronological continuum with the present and with the end of times.

## The threefold meaning of Christmas

The Christmas festival was an integral part of salvation history: the physical birth of Jesus was the natural precondition for his death on the cross and his resurrection. At the same time, incarnation was also the theological precondition for divine solidarity with men. Christ had to become human (and therefore be born like every other mortal), or else, his death at the cross would not have been a real sacrifice but merely a staged and thus illusory death of an immortal God.[6]

Christmas was commonly interpreted as having a threefold meaning that transcended the historical narrative transmitted in the New Testament. Lutheran theology in the seventeenth and eighteenth centuries differentiated between three modes of Christ's coming, which were theologically interconnected and dependent on each other. Theologians spoke of the "threefold coming" (dreifache Ankunft) of Christ: in the flesh, in the spirit, and in glory, representing his coming in the past, in the present, and in the future. These three categories form the theological background for Bach's *Christmas Oratorio*. As a jumping-off point, instead of using a scholarly theological treatise, I refer to a simple didactic book intended for school children. The author of the book, Johann Joachim Neudorf (169?–1752), was a Lutheran theologian from Hamburg. In 1727 he published a didactical treatise for schoolboys explaining the meaning of Advent, Christmas, and New Year's Day.[7] Neudorf employs a catechistic sequence of questions and answers, supplementing his own text with a collection of poems and hymns. Thanks to the clear and systematic presentation of this material, the book serves as a comprehensive overview of the common theological understanding of Christmas at the time. In Neudorf's book we are presented with knowledge that was expected to be familiar to every educated Christian, instead of the more academic knowledge of university theologians. It helps circumvent the question of whether Bach knew all this—he surely did. This was fundamental knowledge, vital to the Lutheran culture in which Bach lived, worked, and worshipped.

---

[6] In other words, any kind of Docetism was rejected.

[7] Johann Joachim Neudorf, *Christlicher Unterricht, für die Jugend, wie die H. Advents-Zeit, das H. Christ-Fest und das Neue Jahr GOttgefällig zu feyren sey*. Nebst einer Vorrede von Erdmann Neumeistern (Hamburg: Kißner, [1727]). Since the title page does not mention the author but only his much more famous colleague Erdmann Neumeister, who provided the preface, the print is often erroneously attributed to Neumeister (e.g., see Jaroslav Pelikan, *Bach Among the Theologians* [Philadelphia: Fortress, 1986], 4).

While Bach probably did not own or even know Neudorf's book, he was familiar with most of the material printed in it and with the theological understanding of Christmas propagated by Neudorf. The supplementary material that follows Neudorf's questions and answers are borrowed from cantata librettos by Benjamin Schmolck (1672–1737) and Erdmann Neumeister (1671–1756) who also wrote the preface for the book, and they also contain prayers, some of them taken from the *Leipziger Kirchenstaat*, a prayer book for the liturgy in Leipzig published in 1710.[8] In his elaborations on the meaning of Advent as the coming of Christ, Neudorf differentiates between the three modes of Christ's coming ("Zukunft Christi"[9]):

1. Ins Fleisch, (oder zu unserer Erlösung,) die ist vergangen.
2. In unsere Hertzen, (zu unserer Heiligung,) die ist gegenwärtig, (oder geschicht täglich.)
3. Zum Gericht, die ist zukünftig.[10]

1. Into the flesh (or for our salvation); this one has passed.
2. Into our hearts (for our sanctification); this one is the present [mode] (or happens daily)
3. For the [Final] Judgment; this one lies in the future.[11]

Neudorf's understanding of the three modes of Christ's coming have their roots in the theology of Luther and—even earlier—in the sermons by Bernard of Clairvaux, who was widely read by theologians in the seventeenth century.[12] Martin Luther refers to the threefold advent of Christ in his first lecture on the Psalms (1514), differentiating between incarnation, *adventus spiritualis* (coming in the spirit), and the return at the end of times, summarized in the formula: "Triplex est adventus eius"

---

[8] *Leipziger Kirchen-Staat: das ist deutlicher Unterricht vom Gottes-Dienst in Leipzig . . .; nebst darauff eingerichteten Andächtigen Gebeten und denen dazu verordneten Teutsch- und Lateinischen Gesängen; welchem zuletzt noch mit beygefüget Geistreiche Morgen- und Abend-Segen auf jeden Tag in der Woche* (Leipzig: Groschuff, 1710).

[9] "Zukunft" has a slightly different meaning than it has today. Instead of denoting "future," here it means "coming."

[10] Neudorf, *Christlicher Unterricht*, 5.

[11] All translations, if not indicated otherwise, are my own.

[12] Cf. Ferdinand van Ingen, "Die Wiederaufnahme der Devotio Moderna bei Johann Arndt und Philipp von Zesen," in *Religion und Religiosität im Zeitalter des Barock*, ed. Dieter Breuer, Wolfenbütteler Arbeiten zur Barockforschung Band 25 (Wiesbaden 1995), 467–75. Text in the tradition of Bernardinian piety were popular devotional texts during the seventeenth century; several of them were also used by composers in motets and concertos. Mary Frandsen has traced the influence of these texts and their musical reception in Saxony in *Crossing Confessional Boundaries: The Patronage of Italian Sacred Music in Seventeenth-Century Dresden* (Oxford: Oxford University Press, 2006), 101–58.

(His advent is threefold).[13] According to Bernard, Christ came on Christmas for the first time (first advent) to gather and save the lost (cf. Lk 19:10); at his second advent he comes not in an incarnate form but spiritually into the hearts of men. As Bernard put it, those who love God, obey his word, and prepare their hearts will be rewarded with Christ's coming into their hearts.[14] The third advent of Christ is the return of Christ at the end of times for the Day of Judgment. As Ulrich Knöpf has shown, the threefold advent provided Bernard with the framework for his understanding of salvation history, which positions the encounter with Christ at the center of his theology of salvation.[15]

The most influential exposition on the threefold advent in Lutheran Orthodoxy can be found in Johann Gerhard's *Postille* (1617), a widely read collection of sermons by one of the leading Lutheran theologians in the first half of the seventeenth century. In his sermon for the First Sunday of Advent, Gerhard describes the threefold coming of Christ ("dreierlei Zukunft des HErrn Christi"):

Erstlich ist die Zukunft Christi **ins Fleisch**, wie Er nämlich in die Fülle der Zeit wahre menschliche Natur angenommen . . .
Die andere Zukunft ist die **geistliche Zukunft**, da nemlich der HErr Christus durchs Wort uns seine Gnade anbeut und in unsern Herzen sein Gnadenreich anfangen will. . . .
Die dritte Zukunft ist nun **zum Gericht,** da Er nemlich einmal am Ende der Welt kommen wird mit großer Kraft und Herrlichkeit in den Wolken des Himmels zu richten die Lebendigen und die Todten. . . .

The first is the coming of Christ **in the flesh,** as he took on human nature when the time was fulfilled . . . The other coming is the **spiritual coming**, as the Lord Christ offers us through the word grace and wants to begin in our hearts his kingdom of grace. . . . The third coming is now the coming **for judgment,** as He will come at the end of the world with great power and glory in the clouds of heaven, to judge the living and the dead. . . . These are the three kinds of the coming of Christ; the first has

---

[13] Martin Luther, *Dictata super Psalterium*: 1513–16, WA 4, 344. Cf. Renate Steiger, *Gnadengegenwart: Johann Sebastian Bach im Kontext lutherischer Orthodoxie und Frömmigkeit*. Doctrina et Pietas II/2 (Stuttgart-Bad Cannstatt: Frommann-Holzboog, 2002), xvii; see also Ulrich Asendorf, *Heiliger Geist und Rechtfertigung* (Göttingen: Vandenhoeck & Ruprecht, 2004), 201.

[14] See Jean Leclercq, *St. Bernard et l'esprit cistercien*, Maîtres spirituels 36, 3rd ed. (Paris: Éditions du Seuil, 1975), 30. Cf. Michael Stickelbrock, *Mysterium Venerandum: Der trinitarische Gedanke im Werk des Bernhard von Claixvaux* (Münster: Aschendorf, 1994), 246.

[15] Ulrich Knöpf, *Religiöse Erfahrung in der Theologie Bernhards von Clairvaux*. Beiträge zur Historischen Theologie 61 (Tübingen: J. C. B. Mohr/Paul Siebeck, 1980), 228; Knöpf refers to Bernard of Clairvaux's important Advent sermon "In Adventu Domini," in *Patrologia Latina* (Paris: Migne, 1966), 183. 35–56.

Dieß sind die dreierlei Arten der Zukunft Christi, der erste ist vergangen, die ander geschieht noch täglich, die dritte ist noch zu gewarten. Die erste siehet auf die andere, denn darum ist Christus Mensch geworden und hat in seiner angenommenen Menschheit das Werk der Erlösung verrichtet, auf daß Er solche Wohlthaten durchs Wort austheile und ihm eine Kirche sammle. Die andere siehet auf die dritte, denn darum glauben wir an Christum und dienen ihm in seinem Gnadenreich, auf daß wir einmal in der letzten Zukunft Christi zum Gericht vor ihm bestehen mögen und ins Reich der Herrlichkeit aufgenommen werden.[16]

already passed, the other one still happens daily, the third still has yet to come to pass. The first one leads to the second, as Christ has become man and has in his assumed manhood done the work of salvation so that he may distribute such blessings through the word and that he may assemble a church. The second one leads to the third since we do believe in Christ and serve him in his kingdom of grace so that we can stand the judgment at his last coming and be accepted into his kingdom of glory.

Gerhard not only lays out the three modes of Christ's coming but also demonstrates their theological interdependence, with the second advent being the present realization of the first and the precondition of the third: the second advent is seen as the existential center. We will see later that this is the very understanding of Christmas on which the libretto of Bach's oratorio focuses most. It is essential for Gerhard's understanding of the Second Coming that it is mediated through the "word" and not understood as an independent divine revelation. As the biblical scriptures serve as the norm for Lutheran orthodox theology, Gerhard can only think of this Second Coming as mediated through scripture. Thus, the second advent, according to Gerhard's theology, is realized in Christ's spiritual arrival in the liturgy through the sermon, the sacraments, and the coming of Christ into the hearts of the believers. Gerhardt—and other contemporary theologians—called this dwelling in the heart either *inhabitatio* (indwelling) or used the German term "Gnadengegenwart"—a concept that has its roots in the theology of Bernard of Clairvaux as well.[17]

---

[16] Johann Gerhard, *Postille das ist die Auslegung und Erklärung der sonntäglichen und vornehmsten Fest-Evangelien über das ganze Jahr . . . Nach den Original-Ausgaben von 1613 und 1616: Vermehrt durch die Zusätze der Ausgabe von 1663.* 1st ed. (Berlin: Schlawitz, 1870), 11–12.

[17] The concept of Christ's indwelling can be traced through numerous treatises and across religious camps from the end of the seventeenth to the middle of the eighteenth century. For a small sample of theological writings on this topic, see Georg Serpilius, *Gloria, Pax Et Alleluja. Das ist: Gott geheiligte Sing-Und Früh-Stunden: Welche auß dem Geistreichen Psalm/Lob-Gesang und Lieblichen Advents-Liede: Gott sey danck durch alle Welt. . . . Nach der Dreyfachen Zukunfft Christi angestellet* (Regensburg: Seidel/

Advent hymns from the seventeenth century can serve as an indicator of the wider reception of Bernard's and Gerhard's ideas. The dogma of the incarnation, which had been emphasized in hymns from the sixteenth century, fades noticeably into the background during this time, while the Second Coming in the believer gains prominence.[18] Helene Werthemann pointed out that the idea of the second advent, even though already present in Luther's theology, was individualized and motivically connected with the image of the heart during the seventeenth century.[19] A popular example of this shift in seventeenth-century hymnody is the Christmas hymn "Wie soll ich dich empfangen" by Paul Gerhard. As Elke Axmacher has demonstrated, the structure of the text closely follows the theological concept of the threefold advent by addressing the first advent of Christ as a historical event in stanzas 3–5 ("Als Leib und Seele saßen/in ihrem größten Leid . . . da bist du, mein Heil kommen," stanza 3), the second advent in stanzas 6–8 ("Das schreib dir in dein Herze," stanza 6), and the return of Christ at the end of times in stanzas 9–10 ("Er kömmt zum Weltgerichte," stanza 10).[20] The shift in emphasis in seventeenth-century hymnody explains the selection of hymns for Bach's *Christmas Oratorio*. With a few exceptions, most of the hymns in the oratorio are from the seventeenth century, while Reformation-era hymns are underrepresented, as most hymns from that time did not provide the librettist with the view of Christmas Bach wanted to present in the oratorio; only seventeenth century hymns reflected on the coming of Christ in the three-partite temporal pattern that is at the core of the libretto.

The concept of the threefold coming of Christ serves as hermeneutic key for the understanding of Christmas in Neudorf's book. Like Gerhard, Neudorf emphasizes that the second advent was mediated though scripture and baptism, or, more generally, through word and sacraments:[21]

---

Hanckwitz, 1697). Serpilius's book is a collection of hymn sermons, based on the Advent hymn "Gott sei Dank durch alle Welt," which is interpreted according to the doctrine of the threefold coming of Christ. The Pietist theologian Georg Johann Hencke from Halle published the following collection of Advent sermons in 1720: *Die Dreyfache Zukunft Unsers Herrn und Heylands Jesu Christi: Aus einigen auserlesenen Oertern Alten und Neuen Testaments Jn der Heil. Advents-Zeit betrachtet* . . . (Halle: Hendel, 1720). Finally, the year before Bach's *Christmas Oratorio*, the radical Pietist (and lawyer) Tobias Eisler published a short, catechistic booklet on the threefold coming of Christ: *Christlicher Unterricht von der dreifachen Zukunft Jesu Christi, insonderheit von der innern geistlichen Zukunft oder Geburt Christi in uns* . . . (n.p.), 1733.

[18] Cf. Helene Werthemann, *Studien zu den Adventsliedern des 16. und 17. Jahrhunderts*, Basler Studien zur Historischen und Systematischen Theologie 4 (Zürich: EVZ, 1963), 81.

[19] Cf. Werthemann, *Studien zu den Adventsliedern*, 84–85; Karl Hauschildt, *Die Christusverkündigung im Weihnachtslied unserer Kirche. Eine theologische Studie zur Liedverkündigung*, Veröffentlichungen der Evangelischen Gesellschaft für Liturgieforschung 8 (Göttingen: Vandenhoeck & Ruprecht 1952), 80–81.

[20] S. Axmacher, "Die dreifache Zukunft des Herrn," 93.

[21] Neudorf, *Christlicher Unterricht*, 6, hereafter noted in text.

| | |
|---|---|
| Welches ist die Beschaffenheit der andern Zukunft? Das Christum zu den Gläubigen kommt, durchs Wort und die heiligen Sacramenten, und sich mit ihnen vereiniget. (Neudorf, 20) | Of what nature is the other coming? That Christ comes to the believers though the word and the holy sacraments and unifies himself with them. |

In Neudorf's treatise, the Second Coming occupies the central position as it vouch-safes the existential relevance of the first and third advents:

| | |
|---|---|
| Ohne die andere Zukunft würde uns weder die erste, noch die dritte, heilsam seyn. Dahero man eben bey dieser Advents-Zeit das neue Kirchen-Jahr mit danckbarer Erkenntlichkeit solcher hohen Wohlthat billig anfangen soll, daß GOtt noch durchs Wort, und die heiligen Sacramente, zu uns kommt. (Neudorf, 7) | Without the second advent neither the first nor the third [advent] would save anyone. Therefore, one has to thankfully begin this new ecclesiastical year during this advent and remember that God comes to us through the word and the holy sacraments. |

Even though Gerhard and Neudorf describe the relationship between the three modes of Christ's coming in slightly different terms (Gerhard as a linear sequence of events and Neudorf almost concentrically, with the two other modes revolving around the middle), both theologians affirm the importance of Christ's coming into the heart and the logical interdependence of the three modes. The three "advents" of Christ in the past, present, and future are inseparable. Neudorf repeats this later in his chapter about the meaning of Christmas:

| | |
|---|---|
| . . . wer den herrlichen Nutzen aus der Geburth JEsu Christi haben will, der muß solchen in wahrem Glauben annehmen. Zu welcher gläubigen Annehmung nicht nur eine **rechtschaffene Erkäntniß JEsu,** und seiner erworbenen Güter, auch **eine zuversichtliche Zueignung und Ergreifung,** da man alles, was JEsus gethan und gelitten hat, so ansiehet, daß man Theil daran habe, und es sich zueignet: da man JEsum in sein Hertz fasset. (Neudorf, 88) | . . . whoever wants to have the wonderful benefit of the birth of Jesus Christ, has to accept such true beliefs. He [the believer] has not only faithfully to accept the **truthful knowledge of Jesus** and the gifts he [Jesus] has earned but he has to **faithfully embrace that one is part** of everything Jesus has done and suffered and that it is done for oneself: that one lets Jesus in one's heart. |

Neudorf also highlights that the coming of Christ gives consolation in the tribulations of present life:

| | |
|---|---|
| Wie können wir uns dieser Einwohnung im Leiden getrösten? Wo GOtt wohnet, da tröstet er den Geist der Leidenden. . . . Diese Einwohnung wird auch durch den zeitlichen Tod nicht getrennet, sondern bleibet ewig, und in der Ewigkeit soll erst die Herrlichkeit dieser Vereinigung offenbahr werden.(23–24) | How can we draw consolation from this indwelling when we suffer? Where God dwells, there he consoles the spirit of those who suffer. . . . This indwelling will not end with death but is eternal and only in eternity the glory of this unification [between Christ and man] will be revealed. |

The second advent guides the believer from fear to happiness and joy:

| | |
|---|---|
| Welches ist der Nutz dieser Zukunft? Die seelige Einwohnung Christi, und, um dessen willen, auch des Vaters und Heiligen Geistes, in uns: Als in welcher Vereinigung des Dreyeinigen GOttes mit den gläubigen Menschen dieser ihre höchste Glückseeligkeit besteht. (Neudorf, 21) | What is the benefit of this coming? The blessed indwelling of Christ, and, through this, also of the Father and the Holy Spirit in us: As the highest happiness is in such a unification of the Trinitarian God with the faithful man. |

Christmas can therefore become a consolation in times of death and thus be part of an *ars moriendi*, a preparation for the time of death:

| | |
|---|---|
| Durch die Geburth Christi wird ihr Sterbe-Tag ein Gebuhrts-Tag zum ewigen Leben. Denn da gelangen sie, als Kinder GOttes, zu ihrer seeligen Erbschaft.(Neudorf, 89) | Their [the Christians'] day of dying becomes a birthday in eternal life through the birth of Christ, because on this day they become as God's children, his blessed heirs. |

We can trace the idea of the threefold coming of Christ as a theological concept to Bach's immediate religious environment, and chronologically to the time of the composition of the *Christmas Oratorio* (1734/35). The *Schemelli Gesangbuch* from 1736, a hymnal to which Bach contributed several settings (and probably some melodies as well), provides the following sequence of chapters for the beginning of the liturgical year. These four categories (the first two form a unity) reflect the three modes of Christ's advent ("Zukunft") in the flesh, the heart, and the Day of Judgment:[22]

| | |
|---|---|
| 6. Von Christi Zukunft ins Fleisch | 6. About the coming of Christ into the flesh |
| 7. Von der Geburt JEsu Christi | 7. About the birth of Jesus Christ |
| 8. Von Christi Zukunft ins Herz | 8. About the coming of Christ into the heart |
| 9. Von Christi Zukunft zum Gericht | 9. About the coming of Christ for judgment |

The doctrine of the threefold advent of Christ provides a key for the understanding of the different layers of meaning in the libretto of Bach's *Christmas Oratorio*. From the beginning, the libretto blends the two temporal layers of historical narrative and present significance. The biblical narrative serves as the backbone, both structurally and theologically, while the emphasis of the interpretation shifts gradually from the second to the third coming: The opening part of the oratorio begins with reflections on the first two modes of Christ's advent. The biblical narrative reports the first coming of Christ; the invocation of the Daughter of Zion (mvts. 3 and 4) relates this to the announcement of the coming of the Messiah in the Old Testament—an aspect that is also described in Gerhard and Neudorf.[23] These two also mention the ardent love of the believer for the "bridegroom" Christ, a metaphor tightly connected to the idea of the presence of Christ in the heart. The text for the first part culminates in a representation of Christ's second advent. The hymn stanza "Ach mein herzliebes Jesulein" is an invitation to Jesus to make his bed in the believer's heart.

Mvt. 3

| | |
|---|---|
| Nun wird mein liebster Bräutigam, | Now will my most beloved |
| Nun wird der Held aus Davids Stamm | bridegroom, |
| Einmal geboren werden. | Now will the champion from the tribe |
| Auf, Zion, und verlasse nun das | of David at last be born. |
| Weinen | Arise, Zion, and forsake weeping now; |

Mvt. 4

| | |
|---|---|
| Bereite dich Zion, mit zärtlichen | Make yourself ready, Zion, with |
| Trieben, | tender desires, |
| Den Schönsten, den Liebsten, bald | To see the Most Handsome, the Most |
| bei dir zu sehn! | Beloved soon at your side! |

---

[22] *Musicalisches Gesang-Buch herausgegeben von George Christian Schemelli* . . . (Leipzig: Breitkopf, 1736, repr., Hildesheim/New York 1975), Erstes Register [no pagination; following p. 654].

[23] Neudorf, for instance, refers to texts from Zechariah 2:10 and 9:9 in his theological interpretation of the first coming.

| Mvt. 9 | Oh my beloved little Jesus, |
| Ach mein herzliebes Jesulein | Make for yourself a perfectly soft |
| Mach dir ein rein sanft Bettelein, | little bed, |
| Zu ruhn in meines Herzens Schrein | To rest in the shrine of my heart |

The early movements of the oratorio emphasize the current meaning of the events by making extensive use of words like "heute" (today), and "nun" (now), as is mvt. 1: "glorify what the Most High has done *today*"; mvt. 3: "*Now* will my most beloved bridegroom, *now* will the champion from the tribe of David"; and mvt. 4: "*Today* your cheeks must sparkle much lovelier." The focus on the present meaning of Jesus's coming even motivates Bach and his librettist to make a significant change to the biblical text. The first four parts of the oratorio set the familiar Christmas story from Luke 2: 1–21. The biblical text is complete except for the second verse: "This was the first registration and was taken when Cyrinius was governor of Syria." The omission is noteworthy; it is the only omission of a biblical verse in the entire oratorio. The function of the verse within the narrative by Luke is to locate the event of the census in a historical framework, thus giving it an additional degree of credibility.[24] Within the temporal structures of the libretto of the *Christmas Oratorio*, the verse reminds us of the chronological distance between the historical event and the contemporary listener.[25] Eliminating the one verse blurred this chronological distance.

The third advent of Christ is explicitly mentioned for the first time in the second part, in the hymn "Brich an, o schönes Morgenlicht": "Dazu den Satan zwingen / und letzlich Frieden bringen." ([Shall] vanquish Satan, too, and finally bring peace!). A similar apocalyptical outlook is also present in the hymn stanza "Ich will dich mit Fleiß bewahren" in the third part of the oratorio:

| Dir will ich abfahren, | To you will I retreat; |
| Mit dir will ich endlich schweben | With you will I at last hover, |
| Voller Freud | Full of joy, |
| Ohne Zeit | Time no longer, |
| Dort im andern Leben. | There in the afterlife. |

---

[24] See François Bovon, *Luke 1: A Commentary on the Gospel of Luke 1:1–9:50*, trans. Christine M. Thomas, ed. Helmut Koester (Minneapolis: Fortress Press, 2002), 83; Joseph A. Fitzmyer, *The Gospel According to Luke (I–IX)*, Anchor Bible (New York: Doubleday, 1981), 171–92.

[25] Biblical interpretations of Bach's time used the opening verses of Luke 2 to date the events of Jesus's birth, as can be seen in the Calov Bible, a copy of which Bach owned at least since 1733; see Abraham Calov, *Das Neue Testament / verdeutschet durch D. Martin Luthern / Nach der eigentlichen Intention und Meinung des Heil. Geistes . . . fürgestellet* (Wittenberg: Schröder, 1682), 431.

This is continued in the second to last movement of the oratorio, a recit for the four soloists (no. 63):

| | |
|---|---|
| Was will der Höllen Schrecken nun, | What will the horrors of hell intend now, |
| Was will uns Welt und Sünde tun, | What will World and Sin intend to do to us, |
| Da wir in Jesu Händen ruhn? | Since we rest in Jesus's hands! |

And it is confirmed in the last movement, a chorale setting (no. 64):

| | |
|---|---|
| Nun seid ihr wohl gerochen | Now you all are well avenged |
| An eurer Feinde Schar, | Of your band of enemies, |
| Denn Christus hat zerbrochen, | For Christ has broken apart |
| Was euch zuwider war. | What was against you. |
| Tod, Teufel, Sünd und Hölle | Death, devil, sin, and hell |
| Sind ganz und gar geschwächt; | Are completely diminished; |
| Bei Gott hat seine Stelle | The human family |
| Das menschliche Geschlecht. | Has its place by God. |

The libretto for the *Christmas Oratorio* essentially follows the aforementioned threefold pattern. Even though the focus constantly shifts throughout, it is clear that the text has three gravitational centers: the historical event of the birth of Jesus, the existential meaning of this coming expressed in the image of Christ's dwelling in the believer's heart, and the return of Christ at the end of time.

The temporal layering and the trajectory from the past to the future has an impact on the musical structure of the oratorio and on Bach's use of aria forms in particular. Karol Berger in his book *Bach's Cycle, Mozart's Arrow* demonstrated that a shift in the perception of time, which took place during the Enlightenment, is reflected in compositions by two major eighteenth-century composers—Johann Sebastian Bach and Wolfgang Amadeus Mozart. Bach, Berger posits, represents a pre-Enlightenment concept, while Mozart's music shows signs of a new understanding of time. While Bach's music is cyclical, Mozart's music is driving forward, pointing toward the future like an arrow.[26] A key element of Bach's "cycle," as shown by Berger, is his use of *da capo* forms, especially in his arias. Simply put, the *da capo* aria with its ABA structure epitomizes the concept of the cyclical form: we end where we have started. There is no place for real development, since we repeat

---

[26] Karol Berger, *Bach's Cycle, Mozart's Arrow: An Essay on the Origins of Musical Modernity* (Berkeley: University of California Press, 2007).

the first section without alterations. The countermodel would be Mozart's sonata allegro form, which also features the repetition of the opening section but with significant changes that are influenced and shaped by what had happened in the development.

Berger's study serves as a jumping-off point for John Butt's book *Bach's Dialogue with Modernity* (2012), in which he draws a more nuanced picture of time-concepts in Bach's music. While he does not disagree with Berger's observation that a shift in the perception of time did indeed take place in the eighteenth century, and that Bach—more than Mozart—is a proponent of that older concept, Butt shows that already within Bach's own works, we can see a certain shift. Butt argues that the *St. John Passion* represents a " 'classical' sense of time as something rooted in eternity, emphasizing the eternal consistency of Christ's divinity, and the sense of all the events as foreordained."[27] The *St. Matthew Passion*, on the other hand, "suggests a more linear concept of time by alluding to what will happen in the end times; there is a sense that much must happen and develop before the expected fulfillment occurs" (Butt, 99). Butt sees this "modern" temporality of the *St. Matthew Passion* manifested in the arias, especially in the use of strict and modified *da capo* forms. In the first half of the *St. Matthew*, Bach almost exclusively uses strict *da capo* arias; the turning point is the moment of Jesus's arrest with the aria "So ist mein Jesu nun gefangen," in Butt's words, "the moment at which events begin to seem irreversible" (Butt, 106). Almost all the arias after this are either modified *da capo* arias (ABA′) or through-composed arias. Butt summarizes: "Thus, in the progression of arias at least, Bach first establishes a cyclic sense of temporality for the most of Part I, which is mainly concerned with Jesus's prophecies and teaching up to the point of his arrest, [he then] moves toward more linear, progressive models for the trial and crucifixion" (Butt, 106–7). In other words, the use of different aria forms has a specific function within the temporal-dramatic framework of the work itself.

The understanding of Christmas in Bach's time was shaped by a temporal framework. An overview of the twelve arias in the oratorio shows a progression that resembles John Butt's observations in the *St. Matthew Passion*:

| | | | |
|---|---|---|---|
| 4 | Bereite dich, Zion | ABA | *da capo* |
| 8 | Großer Herr | ABA | *da capo* |
| 15 | Frohe Hirten | AB | bipartite |
| 19 | Schlafe, mein Liebster | ABA | *da capo* |

[27] John Butt, *Bach's Dialogue with Modernity: Perspectives on the Passions* (Cambridge: Cambridge University Press, 2012), 99. For a critical assessment of Berger's and Butt's studies, see Jeremy Begbie, *Music, Modernity, and God: Essays in Listening* (Oxford: Oxford University Press 2013), 41–72.

| 29 | Herr, dein Mitleid | ABA | *da capo* |
| 31 | Schließe, mein Herze | ABA' | modified *da capo* |
| 39 | Flößt, mein Heiland | AB | bipartite |
| 41 | Ich will nur dir | ABA | *da capo* |
| 47 | Erleucht auch meine | ABA' | modified *da capo* |
| 51 | Ach, wenn wird die Zeit | ABA' | modified *da capo* |
| 57 | Nur ein Wink | AB | bipartite |
| 62 | Nun mögt ihr stolzen Feinde | ABA' | modified *da capo* |

The *Christmas Oratorio* features five strict *da capo* arias, three bipartite arias, and four modified *da capo* arias. The three bipartite arias—which do not repeat the opening section at the end—all have a text that expresses either temporal or kinetic directionality: no. 15 urges the shepherds to go to the manger, no. 39 follows the way from the divine "no" to the divine "yes" in the famous echo-aria (and a return to the "no" would have been theologically out of the question); and no. 57 describes the destruction of the enemies at the end of times. The four modified *da capo* arias show also, for the most part, a strong directionality; the urging for the coming of Christ in no. 31 and the terzet no. 51, the giving of the divine light in no. 47, and again the destruction of the enemies at the end of times in no. 62.

Bach's calculated use of specific aria forms is confirmed by function of the strict *da capo* arias in the oratorio. Maybe with the exception of no. 4, which expects the coming of Christ, all of them have an essentially meditative character; contemplating the greatness of God (no. 8), singing the baby Jesus to sleep (no. 19), meditating on God's compassion (no. 29), and promising to honor God in eternity (no. 41). Even more striking than the correspondence between musical structure and text is the distribution of the arias within the oratorio. Similar to the structure John Butt had discovered in the *St. Matthew Passion*, the strict *da capo* arias are concentrated in the first half of the piece (interrupted only by the strongly directional bipartite aria that urges the shepherds to run to the manger), while the arias in the second half are almost exclusively modified *da capo* arias and bipartite arias; again with one exception: the *da capo* aria "Ich will nur dir zu Ehren leben," the promise to honor God in eternity. The cyclical nature of the divine praise is reflected in the strictly cyclical structure of the aria form. Bettina Varwig has characterized the concepts of temporality in Bach's time as being "suspended between apocalyptic linearity and everyday circularity."[28] The doctrine of the threefold coming of Christ represents both the circular aspect of Christ's presence in the heart and the return in the third coming at the end of times. The arias become increasingly directional; moving from

[28] Bettina Varwig, "Metaphors of Time and Modernity in Bach," *Journal of Musicology* 29 (2012): 159.

a cyclical concept of time in the first half of the *Christmas Oratorio* to a directional one as Bach uses the arias purposefully within the temporal-dramatic framework of his two oratorios. The turning point in the *St. Matthew Passion* is, as Butt has identified, the moment of Jesus's arrest; the "point of no return." The turning point here in the *Christmas Oratorio* is no. 31, "Schließe mein Herze" (My heart, embrace this blessed marvel). The point may be less obvious but does mark a crucial moment within the narrative and temporal framework of the oratorio as well as within the theological understanding of Christmas in Bach's time. This moment was crucial for Bach as well: he had originally sketched a different beginning for the aria, which was then rejected before he composed the piece we have now. Why did he invest a considerable amount of work in this specific piece?

The aria is part of a sequence of movements that reaches from the gospel narrative no. 30 to the chorale setting no. 33. These movements represent the threefold coming of Christ in a nutshell and take the listener from the first advent to the third, while dwelling extensively on his presence in the second advent. The sequence of movements begins with the report that the shepherds arrive at the manger, find Mary, Joseph, and the child, and are surprised by all they had heard and seen. Mary, however, keeps all these words in her heart. The narrative is followed by an alto aria with obbligato solo violin. The text elaborates on the words in Mary's heart and on the miracles seen and heard: both the miracle and the words are a source of strength and consolation. The libretto takes the listener from the historical event of the First Coming to the spiritual presence of Christ in the heart of the believer. Just as Neudorf had explained, the presence of Christ, or *inhabitatio*, is, to be sure, a source of that strength and consolation. The aria is followed by an accompagnato recit, sung again by the alto and is a short confirmation of the presence of the divine word in the heart. The final movement of this sequence broadens this view. The believer promises to keep Christ in his present life, in the hour of his death, and finally in the timelessness of the "other life," the end of times, at the Third Coming of Christ.

Bach's composition reflects this threefold event in some remarkable ways. The first movement is a secco recit, as is the custom for most of the biblical texts in the oratorio. The basso continuo line is mostly static; the text is pronounced in simple declamation over extended notes in the accompaniment. The text itself consists of four sentences, and Bach separates every single one with an increasingly longer rest. Only during these rests does the basso continuo develop more independence: in mm. 4 and 8 a sixteenth-note motif bridges the gap between the first three sentences, and the motif returns later during the last sentence in m. 13. The transition between sentences 3 and 4 is bridged by a simpler cadential phrase in quarter notes. The repeated sixteenth-note motif guarantees a certain coherence within the recit and adds some interest to the otherwise rather simple movement. But the motif has a rhetorical function as well. While in the first two occurrences the motif appears to have a primarily ornamental function, toward the end it corresponds to the words sung by the tenor: Mary moved and pondered the words in her heart (Lk 2:19). The sixteenth-note motif, combined with the following chromatic descent depicts the movement as well as the heightened emotional state of the presence of the word in the heart (ex. 3.1).

Example 3.1 J. S. Bach, BWV 248/30, mm. 1–15

The connection between the sixteenth-note motif and the "word" sheds some light on its use earlier in the recit. Already the previous sentences of the recit mentioned the "word," the "talk" about the child in the manger, which is then finally "moved" (around) or contemplated in Mary's heart. The sixteenth-note motifs serve thus not only as a depiction of the movement itself, but also relate the "word of the manger" to the movement in the heart, even before the text explicitly mentions it. We have evidence that Bach did indeed conceive the sixteenth-note motif motivated by the final line of the text. The autograph score of the *Christmas Oratorio*, P 32, allows a reconstruction of the compositional process (fig. 3.1). The first two instances of the motif were added later: m. 4 in the continuo originally had a half note (discernible by its thicker head), which was then changed into the first note of our motif. In m. 8 Bach originally wrote two quarter notes that were then transformed into the sixteenth-note motif. The only instance where the motif represents the primary version is m. 13, where it was directly motivated by the text. In other words, the motif in mm. 4 and 8 was added in retrospect, as a sort-of afterthought, probably as a reaction to its use in the final line of the recit. This confirms our reading that the motif indeed stands in correspondence with the movement of the word in the heart; or to put it into seventeenth-century theological lingo, with the *inhabitatio Christi* in the heart of the faithful.

Considering the importance of the Second Coming of Christ in the seventeenth and eighteenth centuries, it is understandable that Bach put particular effort into this section. This is evident in the following aria. While all the other arias in the *Christmas Oratorio* are parodies, based on secular cantatas Bach had composed in

*Figure 3.1* J. S. Bach, BWV 248/30, tenor recit (D-B Mus. ms. Bach P 32, fol. 31ʳ) (bpk, Berlin/Mendelssohn-Archiv, Staatsbibliothek zu Berlin, Stiftung Preussischer Kulturbesitz, Berlin, Germany/Art Resource, NY)

1733/34, the aria "Schließe, mein Herze" is an original composition. In the score, Bach sketched the beginning of an aria for alto, flutes (later changed to one flute), strings, and basso continuo. He drafted the beginning of the instrumental ritornello but after about twenty measures discarded the draft and crossed it out. He then composed an aria for alto, basso continuo, and two violins, which he ultimately changed into "violini [*sic*!] solo."[29] The final result is an aria in modified *da capo* form; it is the "turning point" in the progression of arias I outlined earlier, marking the moment when the heart embraces the presence of Christ. Later movements will be able to state this presence as a *fait accompli*; in mvt. 45 the alto sings "Seek him in my breast" and in the terzet no. 51 the same voice confirms "he really is already here."

The aria keeps an intricate balance between circularity and directionality. By avoiding a strict *da capo* form, Bach creates a form that is forward looking. Even though the text of the A-section is repeated in A', and some of the musical material returns, we do not go back to where we started. This is mainly due to the fact that Bach designs the A-section in a way that directly leads to the B-section but makes a literal repetition impossible: the A-section modulates from the home key of B minor to F♯ minor, the key both of the interlude and of the B-section. Only a short modulation, separating the B- and A'-sections, brings us back to B minor. The harmonic progression of the aria is forward striving, not static. The text urges the heart to embrace the miracle, to establish a unity between the Word of God (Christ) and the believer. Only when this urgency has found its completion can the heart can rest, and the aria return to the music (and the key) of the beginning. The music is never cyclical, revolving around itself and around the presence of Christ, but instead drives forward to embrace him in the believer's heart. We will return to this aria and its complex compositional process in the discussion of part III of the oratorio (see chap. 8, this book).

The following recit continues the thought of keeping the word in the heart and introduces the new parameter of *time*: "at this pleasing time, for its [eternal] blessedness." The pleasing time is the time of the narrative, but it is also the time of the believer (the alto) who reflects on the meaning of this; in other words, it is the time of the second advent. And it is the time of the "*eternal* blessedness"—the third advent of Christ. This is then further elaborated in the hymn "Ich will dich mit Fleiß bewahren" (I will safeguard you with diligence). The four-part setting is simple, but numerous chromatic progressions in the bass line give the movement special tension and evoke at the same time the chromatic lines we saw earlier in the gospel recit when the text said that Mary contemplated the words in her heart. In Bach's *St. Matthew Passion* it had been the arrest of Jesus that motivated the shift from cyclical to directional aria forms; in the *Christmas Oratorio*, it is the moment of the *inhabitatio Christi*, which inevitably leads from the divine presence to his return at the end of times. It is the theological point of no return.

---

[29] Bach obviously neglected to change the plural form to singular.

## Second advent and *unio mystica*

The second advent of Christ—as it is the focal point of both Neudorf's and Bach's understanding of Christmas—warrants closer examination. The indwelling of Christ in the believer's heart (*inhabitatio*) was tightly connected with the idea of a mystic unity (*unio mystica*) between the believer and Christ.[30] The concept was widely (and sometimes controversially) discussed in German Lutheranism during the seventeenth century. The essential idea of God's dwelling in the heart of the believer and the spiritual connection with Christ were not contested in the major theological camps. They were concepts supported by such biblical texts as Paul's letter to the Ephesians: Eph 3:17: *Inhabitatio Christi In cordibus nostris* (dwelling of Christ in our hearts); Eph 5:32: *Mysticum Christi et Ecclesiae conjugium* (mystical marriage of Christ and the church).[31] Lutheran orthodox theologians in the seventeenth and eighteenth centuries referred frequently to these verses to describe the close relationship between God and the individual.[32] What was contested was the degree of intimacy to which God and men were joined in this unity. For example, sixteenth-century spiritualists, such as Valentin Weigel (1533–88), advocated a complete and essential unity of God and man.[33] Lutheran orthodox theologians in the late sixteenth and early seventeenth centuries, such as Friedrich Balduin (1575–1627) and Martin Chemnitz (1522–86), rejected the Weigelian view and advocated for a unity in which Christ was present in his essence in the heart of the believer. While Christ's power impacted the individual, the human did not become god-like by acquiring part of the divine essence. The coming of God into human flesh, the incarnation (first advent), was a unique historical act and represented the only time that divine and human nature were united in one person. *Inhabitatio* (the second advent) was therefore theologically distinct from the unique *incarnatio* (the first advent).[34]

[30] The term, while appropriate and also used by seventeenth- and eighteenth-century theologians, has to be used with some caution as it denotes here a Lutheran version of the mystic unity that should not be confused with concepts found in medieval mysticism, as Herbst has already pointed out; see Herbst, *Bach und die Lutherische Mystik*, 19–20.

[31] For Luther's view of *unio* and *inhabitatio* and for the ethical implications of these concepts in his theology, see the excellent study by Jennifer A. Herdt, *Putting on Virtue. The Legacy of the Splendid Vices* (Chicago: University of Chicago Press, 2008), 178–79.

[32] Cf. Karsten Lehmkühler, *Inhabitatio: Die Einwohnung Gottes im Menschen,* Forschungen zur systematischen und ökumenischen Theologie 104 (Göttingen: Vandenhoeck & Ruprecht, 2004), 154.

[33] Cf. Theodor Mahlmann, "Die Stellung der unio cum Christo in der lutherischen Theologie des 17. Jahrhunderts," in:*Unio: Gott und Mensch in der nachreformatorischen Theologie,* ed. Matti Repo and Rainer Vinke, Schriften der Luther-Agrikola-Gesellschaft 35, (Helsinki: Luther-Agrikola-Gesellschaft, 1996), 81.

[34] See the overview in Mahlmann, "Die Stellung," 81–84. It was essential for seventeenth Lutheran orthodox theologians that *inhabitatio* did not describe a blending of the human and divine essences: that is, the human did not become divine when God dwelled in him. This insistence on

Johann Arndt (1555–1621), one of the most influential religious authors from the first half of the seventeenth century, whose *Books on True Christianity* integrally shaped Protestant piety during the German baroque, describes the unity between Christ and the believer in his 1620 treatise *De unione credentium cum Christo capite ecclesiae*. The German translation (published later that same year) was subsequently incorporated in an extended version of Arndt's popular book, published as the *Six Books on True Christianity*; in that way, the primarily apologetical treatise became part of a widely read book of religious edification.[35] Arndt had been accused of Weigelianism before, and not entirely without foundation. The *De unione credentium* was an attempt to clarify his view of *inhabitatio* in opposition to Weigel and demonstrate accordance with Lutheran orthodox theology. For Arndt the goal of human life was unification with God;[36] communion between God and the believer is established through God's word (as God is present in his word) and through the sacraments:

| | |
|---|---|
| Im Wort aber und H. Sacramenten ist das rechte Gedächtniß des Namens GOttes gestiftet. Darum wird er auch durch das Wort und Sacrament mit uns vereiniget. Welches unser Heyland mit dem schönen und lieblichen Spruch bekräftiget: Wer mich liebet, der wird mein Wort halten, und mein Vatter wird ihn lieben, und wir werden zu ihm kommen und Wohnung bey ihm machen[,] Joh. 14,13.[37] | In the words and in the holy sacraments is laid down the true memory of the name of God. That is why he is unified with us through the word and the sacrament; which was confirmed by the Savior through the beautiful and lovely saying: He who loves me will keep my word and my father will love him and we will come to him and dwell with him (Jn 14:13). |

In other words, *inhabitatio* is not to be understood as a new revelation but is, instead, mediated by word and sacraments. Furthermore, *inhabitatio* does not grant the

---

separation of the essences became even more crucial during the seventeenth century as the concept of "mixture" received a more and more intense (and increasingly positive) attention from both the sciences and philosophy; see Wolfram Schmidgen, *Exquisite Mixture: The Virtues of Impurity in Early Modern England* (Philadelphia: University of Pennsylvania Press, 2013), 20–29. While commingling of cultures, languages, and races could be seen as an improvement over the unmixed entities, a mixture of human and divine elements led necessarily to a weakening of the divine.

   [35] Mahlmann, "Die Stellung," 89; Johann Sebastian Bach also owned a copy of this book, see Robin A. Leaver, *Bach's Theological Library: A Critical Bibliography*, Beiträge zur theologischen Bachforschung 1 (Neuhausen-Stuttgart: Hänssler, 1983), 184–87.

   [36] Cf. Mahlmann, "Die Stellung," 89, 97.

   [37] Johann Arndt, *Sechs Bücher vom Wahren Christenthum … Nebst dessen [Arndt's] Paradieß-Gärtlein* (Altdorff: Zobel, 1735), 634 (bk. 5, chap. 3, § 3).

believer any knowledge about the divine that goes beyond (or against) the revelation already codified in the scriptures and sacraments administered by the church. The dwelling of God in the heart of the believer is for Arndt the closest and most intimate connection between God and the believer; he compares this mystic unity (in accordance with Eph. 5:32) with a marriage:

Durch die geistliche Ehe und Vermählung geschiehet die Vereinigung des HErrn Christi mit der gläubigen Seele.

Wenn der Bräutigam kommt, so freuet sich die H. Seele, und giebt genaue und fleißige Achtung auf seine Gegenwart; denn durch seine fröhliche, Herz-erquickende und H. ankunft vertreibet er die Finsterniß und die Nacht. Das Herz hat süsse Freude, es fliessen die Wasser der Andacht, die Seele schmelzet vor Liebe, der Geist freuet sich, die Affecten und Begierden werden inbrünstig, die Liebe wird entzündet, das Gemüth jauchzet, der Mund lobet und preiset, und thut Gelübde, und alle Kräfte der Seelen freuen sich in und wegen des Bräutigams. Sie freuet sich, sage ich, daß sie den gefunden hat, welcher sie liebt, und daß der sie zur Braut auf- und angenommen, welchen sie ehret. O welche Liebe! O welch ein feuriges Verlangen! O welche liebreiche Gespräche! O wie ein keuscher Kuß, wann der H. Geist herab kommt, wann der Tröster überschattet, wann der Höchste erleuchtet, wann das Wort des Vatters da ist, die Weißheit redet, und die Liebe freundlich sie umfänget.[38]

The unification of the Lord Christ with the faithful soul is caused by the spiritual marriage and wedding.

When the bridegroom arrives, the holy soul [*Seele*] is happy and pays exact and diligent attention to his presence; as his joyful, heart-refreshing and holy arrival drives away darkness and night. The heart has sweet joy, the waters of devotion flow, the soul melts for love, the spirit is full of joy, the affects and desires turn fervent, the love is ignited, the soul [*Gemüt*] rejoices, the mouth praises and extols and utters vows, and all the powers of the soul [*Seele*] rejoice in and because of the bridegroom. She [the soul] is full of joy, so I say, because she has found the one who loves her and because he has taken her as a bride. She honors him. O what love! O what burning desire! O what conversations full of love! O what a chaste kiss, when the Holy Spirit descends, when the Consoler overshadows, when the Most High illuminates, when the word of the Father is there, when [it] talks wisdom and when love embraces her warmly.

---

[38] Arndt, *Sechs Bücher vom Wahren Christenthum*, 641–42 (= bk. 5, chap. 7, § 1).

The spiritual marriage serves as a metaphor for the mystic unity established through the indwelling of Christ in the believer's heart.[39] It is important to notice that the spiritual marriage (an image that can again be traced back to Bernard of Clairvaux and which derives its imagery predominantly from the Song of Songs)[40] is not an independent act but rather illustrates what theologians described as the "second advent" of Christ. Therefore, the mystic unity in seventeenth-century Lutheran orthodoxy was, as Arndt points out toward the end of the passage quoted earlier, mediated through biblical scripture and was not just a mystical experience.

By about 1640, as Theodor Mahlmann pointed out in his seminal study on the idea of *unio* in orthodox Lutheran theology, the *unio mystica* was established as a central part of Lutheran school dogmatics.[41] Johann Andreas Quenstedt (1617–88) describes the mystical unity and *inhabitatio Christi* in his influential *Theologia didactico-polemica* from 1685 in the following quotation, representing the widely accepted view in Lutheran orthodoxy in the second half of the seventeenth century:

| | |
|---|---|
| Unitio fidelium cum DEO mystica est actus gratiae Spiritus S. applicatricis, quo substantia hominum justificatorum atque fidelium anima & corpore substantiae SS. Trinitatis, & carnis Christi, mediante fide, verbo imprimis Evangelii & Sacramentorum usu accensa, vere, realiter & arctissime, impermixtibiliter tamen, illocaliter & incircumscriptive conjungitur, ut facta spirituali communicatione, DEus familiariter & constanter praesens sancta operetur; | The mystic unification of the faithful with God is an act of active grace by the Holy Spirit, through which the substance of the justified and believing man (both his soul and body) is unified with the substance of the most Holy Trinity and the body [flesh] of Christ, mediated through faith, which was ignited by the word (in particular the gospel) and the use of the holy sacraments; [this unification] is true, real, and most close, but also un-mixed, un-local, and |

---

[39] The metaphor created unity between Christ and the believer, but it also facilitated the unity among the believers as the common emotional response to the divine, which was initiated by marriage-like unity and established what Barbara Rosenwein has called an "emotional community." She describes these communities as "groups in which people adhere to the same norms of emotional expression and value—or devalue—the same or related emotions." Rosenwein, *Emotional Communities in the Early Middle Ages* (Ithaca, NY: Cornell University Press, 2006), 2.

[40] Cf. E. Ann Matter, *The Voice of My Beloved: The Song of Songs in Western Medieval Christianity* (Philadelphia: University of Pennsylvania Press, 1990); see also the excellent collection of primary sources in Denys Turner, *Eros and Allegory: Medieval Exegesis of the Song of Songs,* Cistercian Studies Series 156 (Kalamazoo: Cistercian Publications, 1995).

[41] See Mahlmann, "Die Stellung," 118–19.

Fideles autem DEO & Redemptori suo ad gloriam Majestatis divinae conjuncti, per mutuam immanentiam vivificae facultatis & omnium Christi beneficiorum participes facti, de praesentissima gratia, amoreque paterno & subsecutura gloria certiores redditi in statu filiorum DEI atque unitate fidei & charitatis, cum reliquis corporis mystici membris perseverent, aeternumque salventur.[42]

without spatial extension. For the very purpose that God, after consummation of this spiritual community, may be known and continuously present and that he may cause holy actions; the believers, however, who are joined with God and their savior for the glory of the divine majesty, can be sure of the life-giving power and all blessings of Christ, the most present grace, and the fatherly love, that are granted through this community; and they can remain in the state of God's children and the unity of faith and love, together with the other parts of the mystical body and be blessed forever.

In Johann Joachim Neudorf's book for school children this rather complex theological concept is simplified into a set of easily comprehendible texts and a sequence of questions and answers. It is clear that Neudorf understands the second advent concept and *unio mystica* in similar terms as Quenstedt and other theologians of his time. The goal of this unity is the sharing of all of Christ's blessings, as Quenstedt pointed out. Neudorf writes:

Was haben wir insonderheit für eine Glaubens-Lehre hierbey zu fassen? Aus dieser Zukunft und Vereinigung entsteht eine solche Gnaden-volle Gemeinschaft, daß ein Gläubiger JEsum und sein gantzes Verdienst, nebst dem Vater und dem Heiligen Geiste, zu eigen bekömmt.[43]

What teaching of faith do we have to grasp here? From such coming and unification results such a merciful community that a believer receives as his own Jesus and all that he has done, besides the Father and the Holy Spirit.

---

[42] Johannes Andreas Quenstedt, *Theologia didactico-polemica, sive systema theologicum, in duas seciones, didacticam et polemicam, divisum* (Wittenberg, 1685), III, 622b; cf. Lehmkühler, *Inhabitatio*, 153–54.

[43] Neudorf, *Christlicher Unterricht*, 22.

The idea of *inhabitatio* and the divine presence in the human heart was omnipresent in devotional iconography in the seventeenth and early eighteenth centuries.[44] Johann Rittmeyer's *Himmlisches Freuden-Mahl*, a hymn- and prayer book—first published in Helmstedt in 1655 but then over the next 120 years in at least twenty editions—prints several engravings that show Jesus's actions in the human heart: Jesus searching the heart (symbolized by Jesus carrying a lamp), Jesus purging the heart (Jesus driving out snakes with a broom), and others (figs. 3.2 and 3.3).[45] Other devotional books had similar images, for instance the *Leipziger Kirchen-Andachten* (1694), which showed Jesus singing in the heart. I have demonstrated in chapter 1 that Bach himself used the image of the heart repeatedly in part IV of the *Christmas Oratorio*.

The unity between the divine and the human thus established is described as a spiritual marriage or *unio mystica* (mystical unity).[46] As the libretto of Bach's *Christmas Oratorio* reflects the doctrine of the threefold advent of Christ, so it also draws a connection between the indwelling of Christ and the *unio mystica* by employing aural and textural metaphors of spousal affection. The third and fourth movements of the oratorio, the accompagnato recit "Nun wird mein liebster Bräutigam" (Now will my most beloved bridegroom) and the following aria "Bereite dich Zion" (Make yourself ready, Zion), both sung by the alto, address Christ as bridegroom and most beloved, admonishing "Zion" (here understood as the church) to ardently love the most handsome bridegroom. The librettist employs the language of mystical love, which is deeply rooted in the doctrine of the second advent and the coming of the divine into the heart of the believer.[47] The chorale stanza that follows the aria is the first verse from Paul Gerhard's Advent hymn "Wie soll ich dich empfangen."[48] It synthesizes these two perspectives and

---

[44] For the significance of the heart in Protestant devotion, see Barbara Kiefer Lewalski, *Protestant Poetics and the Seventeenth-Century Religious Lyric* (Princeton: Princeton University Press, 1979), 179–212. The image of the heart was not limited to Protestant devotion, but it became increasingly popular in Catholic piety as well during the second half of the seventeenth century; cf. Scott Manning Stevens, "Sacred Heart and Secular Brain," in *The Body in Parts: Fantasies of Corporeality in Early Modern Europe*, ed. David Hillmann and Carla Mazzio (New York: Routledge, 1997), 263–82.

[45] I am grateful to Robin Leaver for bringing these images to my attention.

[46] It is significant that Lutheran theology adopted the image of a spiritual marriage at a time when physical expressions of religiosity, like processions and other rituals, were increasingly frowned upon. Physical religiosity was replaced with spiritual religiosity; at the same time, though, the metaphorical language of faith was charged with erotic metaphors, transferring physicality to a metaphorical level; cf. chap. 2 of this book.

[47] Cf. Isabella van Elferen, *Mystical Love in the German Baroque: Theology, Poetry, Music*, Contextual Bach Studies 2 (Lanham: Scarecrow Press, 2009), 225–49.

[48] Axmacher, "Die dreifache Zukunft des Herrn," 92–95.

*Figure 3.2* Johann Rittmeyer, *Himmlisches Freuden-Mahl*, Berlin 1731, next to p. 57 (bpk, Berlin/Mendelssohn-Archiv, Staatsbibliothek zu Berlin, Stiftung Preussischer Kulturbesitz, Berlin, Germany/Art Resource, NY)

*Figure* 3.3  Johann Rittmeyer, *Himmlisches Freuden-Mahl*, Berlin 1731, next to p. 121 (bpk, Berlin/Mendelssohn-Archiv, Staatsbibliothek zu Berlin, Stiftung Preussischer Kulturbesitz, Berlin, Germany/Art Resource, NY)

gives the *unio mystica* a theological foundation by associating it with the Word of God, the very instance that mediates the second advent:

*5. Chorale*

| | |
|---|---|
| Wie soll ich dich empfangen | How shall I receive you, |
| Und wie begegn' ich dir, | And how shall I meet you, |
| O aller Welt Verlangen, | O desire of all the world |
| O meiner Seelen Zier? | O decoration of my soul? |
| O Jesu, Jesu setze | O Jesus; Jesus, set |
| Mir selbst die Fackel bei, | The torch next to me yourself, |
| Damit, was dich ergötze, | So that whatever brings you enjoyment |
| Mir kund und wissend sei. | May be manifest and known to me. |

The "Fackel" (torch) in line 6 refers, as Michael Marissen and others have shown, to Psalm 119:105: "Your word is a lamp for my feet, and a light on my path."[49] This interpretation is further confirmed by the following lines referring to the manifestation and knowledge of God's will, which result from the giving of the torch/word.

As mentioned in chapter 1, *inhabitatio* and emotional unity are also quite prominent in the fourth cantata of the *Christmas Oratorio*, celebrating New Year's Day as the festival of Christ's circumcision and naming. In mvts. 38 and 40 Bach combines a recit text in the bass voice with a hymn text in the soprano.[50] In the center of mvt. 38 Bach layers the following two sections of the texts (the hymn text is printed in bold):

| | |
|---|---|
| **Jesu, du mein liebstes Leben,** | **Jesus, you, my most beloved life,** |
| **Meiner Seelen Bräutigam,** | **My soul's bridegroom,** |
| Komm! Ich will dich mit Lust umfassen, | Come! With delight I will embrace you, |
| Mein Herze soll dich nimmer lassen. | My heart shall never leave you. |

By featuring a bass and soprano, Bach already evokes the image of male and female counterparts and thus sonically represents the metaphor of bride and bridegroom. Even though the text of the duet does not assign clear roles to the two singers (it is

---

[49] Marissen, *Bach's Oratorios*, chap. 5, fn. 8.

[50] See a more extensive discussion of these movements in Markus Rathey, "Drama and Discourse: The Form and Function of Chorale Tropes und Bach's Oratorios," *Bach Perspectives* 8 (2010): 59–62.

not a dialogue between the soul and Christ, as we find in other pieces by Bach), the texture of the movement still aurally represents the harmony between a female and a male character (bride and groom) that the words of the libretto evoke (ex. 3.2). The short example combines the two important images of the second advent, the emotional intimacy denoted by the word "bridegroom" and the "heart" as the place of the unification between Christ and the believer. Here, Bach highlights the emotionality of the mystic unification and the longing for each other by leading the two singers in harmonious thirds and sixths—a feature also familiar from operatic love duets of the time.[51] The invitation to Christ to live in the believer's heart is later repeated in the second chorale-recit (no. 40), which begins with the words:

*Example 3.2* J. S. Bach, BWV 248/38, mm. 10–13

---

[51] The music of religious longing and desire has recently been explored by Susan McClary in her study, *Desire and Pleasure in Seventeenth-Century Music* (Berkeley: University of California Press, 2012); especially relevant to Bach's own musical heritage is her analysis of Heinrich Schütz's "Anima mea liquefacta est," 148–58.

| Wohlan, dein Name soll allein | Well then, your name alone shall |
|---|---|
| In meinem Herzen sein. . . . | Be in my heart! . . . |
| So will ich dich entzücket nennen, | These are what I, in a trance, will call you, |
| Wenn Brust und Herz zu dir vor Liebe brennen. | When [my] breast and heart burn with love for you. |

The "name" evoked here in the recit on the feast of the Naming of Jesus, represented for seventeenth- and eighteenth-century theologians the essence of Christ's being and could therefore stand for the entire person and his salvific meaning. The literal meaning of the Latin name "Jesus" (*Yesous* in New Testament Greek, *Yeshua* in Aramaic) is "God is salvation" or "God rescues." Neudorf continues:

| Was für ein Glaubens Trost fliesset aus diesem Nahmen? 1) Daß Jesus dasjenige, was sein Nahme heisset, wahrhaftig geleistet, und uns alle erlöset habe. 2) Daher ist dieser Nahme eine lebendige Quelle alles Trostes, und ein Begriff aller Göttlichen Wohlthaten.[52] | What a faithful consolation does flow from this name? 1) That Jesus has truly done what his name says and that he has redeemed all of us. 2) Therefore, this name is a living source of all consolation and a symbol for all divine blessings. |
|---|---|

In other words, if the "Name of Jesus" is present in the believer's heart, the essence of his being is also present, according to the doctrine of the *inhabitatio*. Movement 40 of the oratorio therefore captures the central meaning of Christmas for the eighteenth-century Lutheran: the essence of Christ dwells in the human heart and is engaged in a mystical unity with the believer.

Within this theological framework of the *Christmas Oratorio*, the alto voice plays a crucial role. The alto sings most of the texts associated with the *inhabitatio Christi* and the *unio mystica* between Christ and the believer: the recit/aria pair at the beginning of the oratorio, invoking the coming of the bridegroom; the intimate aria "Schlafe, mein Liebster" (no. 19); the aria "Schließe, mein Herze" (no. 31); in addition, the alto is the one voice that proclaims Jesus's presence in the terzet "Ach, wenn wird die Zeit erscheinen" (no. 51). The singer also appears in several accompagnato recits that touch on the same topic. The central status of the alto voice has been highlighted by several scholars, which has led to a variety of interpretations. Walter Blankenburg sees the alto as the voice of Jesus's mother Mary. In Blankenburg's interpretation of the oratorio she sings the lullaby for the child (no. 19), and the aria "Schließe, mein

[52] Neudorf, *Christlicher Unterricht*, 70.

Herze" (no. 31) is the expansion of the gospel text reporting that Mary had included the words of the shepherds in her heart. Mary then becomes the example of humility and a model of faith for all believers and for the church in general. Ernst Koch has shown that Blankenburg's interpretation, while it might work in the first half of the oratorio, becomes incoherent in the second half because Mary as a character is no longer present in the narrative. Furthermore, Blankenburg's theory falls apart in the last part, where even he must concede that the mvts. 61 and 62 should have been sung by the alto and not the tenor.[53] Koch shows that Blankenburg's interpretation is problematic because it tries to see dramatic action in the oratorio where there is none. Bach's oratorio concept in the 1730s is that of a nondramatic, contemplative oratorio and not that of a "sacred opera" with identifiable characters (see chap. 4, this book).

Koch suggests that the voice of the alto should be interpreted as the voice of the Holy Spirit.[54] He refers to several sermons and emblems from the seventeenth century that develop a typology of meanings for the four voices of the vocal ensemble. In this, the alto consistently represents the voice of the divine spirit.[55] This identification does not imply that *every* alto part in Bach's music (or that of his contemporaries) has to signify the Holy Spirit. It would be easy to find numerous counterexamples. But it suggests that for a text about the presence of the Holy Spirit the alto would have been the first and most natural choice. The connection between the alto signifying the divine spirit and the *inhabitatio Christi* is indeed close. Several of the theological sources quoted earlier have already mentioned the Spirit as a means though which Christ is present in the human heart. Heinrich Müller, in his *Göttliche Liebes-Flamme* (1659/77), a book owned by Bach, draws this connection explicitly:

| | |
|---|---|
| GOtt hat seinen tempel in deinem hertzen/darinnen lehret er durch seinen Geist. Er lehret nicht allein äusserlich/wann er sein wort predigen lässt/sondern auch inwendig/wann er das hertz auffthut.[56] | God has his temple in your heart, in which he teaches [you] through his spirit. He not only teaches externally when he lets his word be preached, but also internally, when he opens your heart. |

The concepts of Jesus's presence in the heart or the presence of the Holy Spirit are (in the context of the Trinitarian understanding in seventeenth-century theology) interchangeable. In other words, the alto is the voice of the divine presence in

[53] Blankenburg, "Die Bedeutung der solistischen Alt-Partien," 233–34, 236.

[54] Koch, "Die Stimme des Heiligen Geistes," 72. For a critique of Blankenburg's views, see also Konrad Klek, "Die Mär mit der Maria: Zur Symbolik der Altstimme im Weihnachtsoratorium Johann Sebastian Bachs," *Concerto* 29 (2012): 14–15.

[55] Koch, "Die Stimme des Heiligen Geistes," 62.

[56] Heinrich Müller, *Göttliche Liebes-Flamme* (Frankfurt/M., 1677), 221.

the human heart, a symbol for the *inhabitatio Christi*. The voice of the alto in the *Christmas Oratorio* is the voice of the heart that first strives toward and then accomplishes the unification with God in Christ and the Holy Spirit.

Bach is not unique in his emphasis of the *inhabitatio Christi* in a Christmas composition. An example for the broader tradition is Carl Heinrich Graun's *Oratorium in Festum Nativitatis Christi,* which combines excerpts from the biblical narrative with lengthy meditations on the meaning of the coming of Christ and of his birth in the manger.[57] The coming into the believer's heart plays an important role in the libretto for Graun's composition. The oratorio is interspersed with numerous hymn stanzas; however, while most of them appear in simple homophonic settings (similar to the style in Graun's more famous *Tod Jesu*), the setting of the hymn stanza "Ach mein herzliebes Jesulein" is sung by a solo soprano and embedded into a multi-sectional movement. The hymn text is the thirteenth stanza of Luther's Christmas hymn "Vom Himmel hoch, da komm ich her." It expresses an invitation to Jesus to make the heart his manger and his dwelling place. Graun maintains the original melody, unlike Johann Schelle's 1683 treatment in his *Actus musicus,* but turns the hymn into an intimate arioso. A repetitive sixteenth-note motif in the accompaniment, which also separates the lines of the hymn with short interludes, gives the hymn setting the character of a lullaby (ex. 3.3).

*Example 3.3*  Carl Heinrich Graun, *Oratorium in Festum Nativitatis Christi*, no. 5, mm. 68–71

[57]  Carl Heinrich Graun, *Oratorium in festum nativitatis Christi für Soli (SATB), Chor (SATB), zwei Querflöten, zwei Oboen, zwei Fagotte (ad lib.), zwei Hörner, drei Trompeten, Pauken, zwei Violinen, Viola, Viola pomposa und Basso continuo,* ed. Ekkehard Krüger and Tobias Schwinger (Beeskow: Ortus, 1998).

The structure of Graun's movement and the compilation of various textual genres (biblical texts, poetry, hymn) draw a connection between the first advent of Christ (announced in the framing movements from Isa 9:6) and the second advent in the central hymn setting. The hymn and biblical texts are connected through reflective accompagnato recits, also sung by the soprano:

| | |
|---|---|
| Uns ist ein Kind geboren . . . (Isa 9:6) | coro+soli |
| [Unto us a child is born][58] | |
|     Du durch mein dringendes Gebet erbetnes Wort . . . | rec. accomp., |
|     [You promised child, word of answer to my urgent prayers] | soprano |
|         **Ach mein herzliebes Jesulein** . . . | **Soprano** |
|         **[Oh my beloved little Jesus]** | |
|     Doch welcher banger Zweifel fesselt mich . . . | rec. accomp., |
|     [But what is the anxious doubt that binds me] | soprano |
| Welches Herrschaft ist auf seiner Schulter . . . (Isa 9:6) | coro |
| [To bear the symbol of domination on his shoulder] | |

The movement from Graun's oratorio is paradigmatic as an example for the multi-faceted meaning of the "Advent of Christ," with its deep emotionality, mystic unity, and the theologically central position of the *inhabitatio*. Graun depicts intimacy by assigning the melody to a solo voice and by accompanying it with a soothing lullaby. An important keyword within the framework of eighteenth-century piety is the mention of the "Word" (Wort) in the first accompagnato recit, which is, as we have seen, the mediator for the indwelling solicited in the following hymn stanza.

The librettist for Bach's *Christmas Oratorio* likewise places a setting of the stanza "Ach mein herzliebes Jesulein" in a prominent position at the end of the first part of the six-part cycle. The stanza summarizes the understanding of Christmas as a historical, existential, and emotional event, as it is interpreted in the preceding movements. It also refers back to the idea of a *mystic unity* as explored in the third and fourth movements. However, while the inclusion of the thirteenth stanza of "Vom Himmel hoch" was more than logical for the librettist from a theological perspective, and represented an appropriate endpoint for the first part of the oratorio, Bach's setting is significantly different from Graun's version. The emotionally charged lines of the hymn are interrupted by festive and joyful fanfares, played by the trumpets, which stand in stark contrast to the character of the hymn setting. The movement seems anything but mystical. It is possible that the librettist of the *Christmas*

---

[58] The English version of the text follows, with a few changes, trans. Astrid Reisener and Kim Moore, in Graun's *Oratorium in festum nativitatis*.

*Oratorio* intended the stanza simply to be a summary of the ideas of the second advent, but Bach composes a chorale movement that fulfills several functions at once. The *gestalt* of the movement reflects a multifaceted amalgam of structural and theological aspects. The chorale setting itself, stripped of its regal interludes, may be seen as a reflection of the intimate character of the text: a smooth and uninterrupted eighth-note-motion that threads through the accompanying voices and surfaces occasionally in little embellishments of the melody. Similarly, the chromaticisms in the harmonic texture are features often found in settings of devotional poetry in the seventeenth and early eighteenth century. Here, both underscore the intimacy of the *unio mystica*. The chorale setting also continues a train of thought from the immediately preceding movements, which deal with the dichotomies of Christ's incarnation: the seventh movement, a combination of chorale and recit, revolves around the dichotomy between Jesus's nature as Son of God and his humble birth in a manger. Toward the end of the recit the dichotomy is resolved (or rather revealed as not representing a logical problem) and the following aria ("Großer Herr, o starker König") celebrates Jesus as the "lord" and "mighty king" who sleeps in "harsh mangers."[59] The aria features a solo trumpet, which signifies the regal character of the newborn child. The final chorale setting, with its juxtaposition of regal trumpets and a simple hymn setting, sonically represents this dichotomy between weakness and strength. Finally, the chorale movement has a structural function within the first cantata as well, as the instrumentation of the final chorale sonically balances the first movement of the cantata, which features the same instrumentation.[60]

So far we have left out one source that attests to Bach's familiarity with the doctrine of Christ's *inhabitatio*. A German term frequently used in the seventeenth and eighteenth centuries to describe the indwelling of Christ in the heart of the believer is "Gnadengegenwart," (presence of grace) which resonates with terms from theological discourse, like Quenstedt's "unio spacialis gratiosa"[61] or Conrad Dietrich's term for the second advent of Christ, "adventus mentis sive gratiae."[62] Johann Sebastian Bach himself used the term "Gnaden Gegenwart"[63] in an annotation in his *Calov Bible*. The remark appears next to the text of 2 Chronicles 5:13 and reads, "With a devotional music God is always in his presence of grace."[64] This short remark, written

---

[59] For a discussion of that movement, see Rathey, "Drama and Discourse," 57–59.

[60] In most of the cantatas of the *Christmas Oratorio,* Bach creates a sonic balance between the first and the last movements of a cantata.

[61] Quenstedt, *Theologia didactico-polemica*, III, 615a.

[62] Dieterich, *Analysis evangeliorum dominicalium*, 7.

[63] Bach's handwriting is not entirely clear; the spelling could either be "Gnaden Gegenwart" (as Martin Petzoldt suggests) or "Gnadengegenwart," proposed by Renate Steiger; see Steiger, *Gnadengegenwart*, 243. The different spellings, however, do not affect the meaning of the annotation; see also Walter Wallmann's extensive review of Steiger's study in *Pietismus und Neuzeit* 29 (2003), 327–32.

[64] Hans T. David and Arthur Mendel, eds., *The New Bach Reader: A Life of Johann Sebastian Bach in Letters and Documents*, rev. exp. ed. by Christoph Wolff (New York: Norton, 1998), 161 (no. 165d).

on the margins of the voluminous Bible, is not dated; however, Bach dated the book himself in 1733, which marks the year in which the Bible was acquired and therefore the *terminus post quem* of the annotation. It is possible that the remark was written in close chronological proximity to the composition of the *Christmas Oratorio* (1734/35). In any case, the entry in the Bible makes it unequivocally clear that Bach was well aware of the doctrine of *inhabitatio Christi* when working on his oratorio.

Gnadengegenwart, as Bach and his contemporaries would have understood the term, means more than simply "presence of grace" or "merciful presence," as some interpretations have suggested, but is rather a clearly defined theological term and a central doctrine of Lutheran orthodoxy.[65] Renate Steiger was able to show that Bach's remark was probably influenced by a section in Johann Gerhard's *Schola Pietatis* (1622/23),[66] one of the many theological tomes Bach owned:

*Gratiosa DEI inhabitatio.* Gottes gnädige Einwohnung/2. Paral. 5. v. 13[.] Als die Stimme vom Lobe deß HErrn gehöret wurde / daß Er gütig ist / und seine Barmhertzigkeit ewiglich währet / da ward das Haus des HErrn erfuellet mit einem Nebel / welcher Nebel ein Symbolum und Anzeigung war der sonderbaren gnädigen Gegenwart GOttes / darum stehet Ps. 22. v. 4[:] GOtt wohne unter dem Lob Israel / das ist / im heiligen Tempel / da man zusammen kömmt / Ihn zu loben und zu preisen. Wie nun GOtt der HERR im Tempel zu Jerusalem mit seiner Gnadengegenwart gewohnet / also will Er auch noch heutiges Tages wohnen in den Hertzen derer / so ihn loben und preisen.[67]

The gracious dwelling of God. 2. Chr 5.13. As the voice praising God was heard–that he was good and that his mercy lasted forever—the house of the Lord was filled with a fog; this fog was a symbol and a sign of the special and gracious presence of God. Therefore, it is written in Ps. 22:4, God dwelled in the praises of Israel, that is: in the holy temple where one gathers to worship and praise him. Just as God the Lord has dwelled in the temple in Jerusalem with his gracious presence, in the same way he will still today live in the hearts of those who worship and praise him.[68]

[65] S. Lucia Haselböck, *Bach-Textlexikon: Ein Wörterbuch der religiösen Sprachbilder im Vokalwerk von Johann Sebastian Bach* (Kassel: Bärenreiter, 2004), 90–91. Bossuyt misunderstands the term "Gnadengegenwart" as well when he suggests a connection to Luther's "sola gratia"; cf. Bossuyt, *Christmasoratorio*, 30, fn. 30 and 31.

[66] Steiger, *Gnadengegenwart*, 244.

[67] Johann Gerhard, *Schola pietatis, das ist: Christliche und Heilsame Unterrichtung, was für Ursachen einen jeden wahren Christen zur Gottseligkeit bewegen sollen, auch welcher Gestalt er sich an derselben üben soll*: Nunmehr zum siebendemal aufgelegt, (Nürnberg: Endter, 1691), III, 24.4 (= p. 621).

[68] My translation borrows some ideas from Sven Rune Havsteen's rendition but translates some phrases differently; see Havsteen, "Aspects of Musical Thought in the Seventeenth-Century Lutheran Tradition," in *The Arts and the Cultural Heritage of Martin Luther*, ed. Eyolf Østrem et al., 166 (Copenhagen: Museum Tusculum Press, 2003).

Even though it is impossible to reconstruct when exactly Bach annotated his Bible or when he acquired Gerhard's *Schola pietatis*, we can, in light of the general importance of the doctrine of the *inhabitatio* assume that he was familiar with it long before the 1730s.[69] More important is the meaning of the annotation and its impact on our understanding of Bach's *Christmas Oratorio*. If Gnadengegenwart is understood as the substantial and real presence of Christ in the heart of the believer, mediated by word and sacrament, music—at least "devotional music" as Bach puts it—becomes a mediator itself.[70] The divine grace is not "in" the music itself but it serves as a mediator. Though not a direct divine revelation, music mediates revelation and God's presence. As God is understood as being present in the word, music, pious music, mediates that "Word," the Word of God. We will return to this revelatory and theological function of music in the discussion of part II of the oratorio in chapter 7.

*[handwritten annotation:] what does that mean?*

*[handwritten annotation:] a means of the means*

[69] Nicolaus Stenger, a theologian who had several ties to the Bach family, uses the term frequently. August Pfeiffer, another seventeenth-century theologian whose books Bach owned (cf. Leaver, *Bach's Theological Library*, 147) talks about God's *Gnaden-Gegenwart* in his *Antimelanchcholicus oder Melancholey-Vertreiber* (Leipzig, 1684), 406, as the presence of the Holy Spirit in the believer; we also find it mentioned in sermons by Johann Adolph Frohne, Bach's superior during his time in Mühlhausen in 1707/8. In his sermon for the introduction of the new town council in 1697, Frohne talks about "Gnaden-Gegenwart" that God grants the good ruler: "GOTT nahet sich zu einem Christlichen Regenten mit dem Licht seiner Gnaden-Gegenwart," Frohne, *Der Erleuchtete und in seiner Amts-Last Erleichterte Regent bey Auffuehrung Eines . . . Neuen Rahts der . . . Stadt Mühlhausen im Jahr Christi 1697 . . .* (Mühlhausen: Pauli, 1697), 266.

[70] The relationship between mystic unity, God's dwelling in the heart, and the power of music was already reflected in seventeenth-century writings. Christoph Frick states in his *Music-Büchlein* (1631): "Denn das Hertz des Menschen sol GOttes Wohnung seyn. nicht weit vom Hertzen / hat Gott die Lunge/die *arteriam*, die Lufftröhre / den Mund vnd die Zunge gesetzt / welche die Stimm vnd den Gesang machen. auff daß der Mensch wenn er sich selber anschawet / sich erinnete er solte seiner Gliedmaß vmb das Hertz also gebrauchen / daß Gott/der in dem Tempel vnsers Hertzens wohnen wil / gelobet vnd aus warer Danckbarkeit angesungen werde." (For the heart of man should be the abode for God. God has placed the lung, the artery, the windpipe, the mouth and tongue, which produce the voice and the singing, near the heart, so that man when he observes himself will remember to use these body parts around the heart in such a way that God—who wants to dwell in the temple of our heart—will be praised with singing in an attitude of true gratitude.), Frick, *Music-Büchlein oder Nützlicher Bericht von dem Uhrsprunge, Gebrauche und Erhaltung christlicher Music* (Lüneburg: Sternen, 1631, repr., Leipzig: Zentralantiquariat d. DDR, 1976), 58; English trans. in Havsteen, "Aspects of Musical Thought," 163.

# 4

# Bach's Oratorio Concept

The composition of oratorios was not part of Johann Sebastian Bach's contractual obligations in Leipzig. In fact, when he assumed his position as cantor at St. Thomas's in 1723, he had to pledge to "arrange the music that it should not last too long, and shall be of such a nature as not to make an operatic impression, but rather incite the listener to devotion."[1] Oratorios, though not staged, were considered the sacred sister of the opera. Bach's cousin Johann Gottfried Walther had defined in his dictionary of music from 1732, "Oratorio . . . eine geistliche Opera" ("a sacred opera").[2] It was not until the early 1730s that Bach began using the term "oratorio."[3] Within approximately four years he composed and performed three pieces, all of which bear the label "oratorio" in his autograph scores. The first composition in this genre was the *Christmas Oratorio* from 1734/35, followed by an oratorio for Ascension Day, BWV 11, in 1735.[4] Around 1738 he performed his *Easter Oratorio*, BWV 249. These three pieces were not only conceived in chronological proximity to each other (with BWV 249 having an earlier predecessor), but they also share several essential features, which allows us to see the pieces as a group

---

[1] Mendel, David, Wolff, *New Bach Reader*, 105.

[2] Johann Gottfried Walther, *Musikalisches Lexikon oder musikalische Bibliothek* (Leipzig: Deer, 1732), 451.

[3] A print of the libretto for the 1725 version of the *St. John Passion*, published in Nuremberg in 1728 bears the title "Das schmählich- und schmerzliche Leiden Unsers HErrn und Heylandes JEsu Christi/in einem *ACTU ORATORIO* besungen (capitalization original); see the reproduction of the title page in Christine Blanken, "A Cantata-Text Cycle of 1728 from Nuremberg: a Preliminary Report on a Discovery relating to J. S. Bach's so-called 'Third Annual Cantata Cycle,'" *Understanding Bach* 10 (2015), 17. If this was the original title, Bach would have already used the term "oratorio" in 1725; however, it is absent from the manuscript sources from 1725 and it is therefore likely that the title was added later by the editor of the Nuremberg print.

[4] The date for this oratorio is not entirely sure but it is the accepted consensus among Bach scholars; see *BWV Kleine Ausgabe*, 282, Tobias Janz, "Oratorien: Entstehungsgeschichtlicher Kontext," in *Das Bach-Handbuch 3: Bachs Passionen, Oratorien und Motetten*, ed. by Reinmar Emans and Sven Hiemke (Laaber: Laaber Verlag 2009), 225.

and at the same time differentiating them from the related genre, the Passion. The oratorios were composed for the "jubilant ecclesiastical feasts" of the year and all feature a celebratory instrumentation of trumpets and timpani in addition to the strings and woodwinds.[5] The Passions, on the other hand, due to their liturgical place and subject matter, do not use brass instruments and lack the overtly cele-bratory character of the oratorios.[6] The Passions and oratorios also differ in their liturgical functions. While the settings of the suffering and death of Christ were per-formed during the annual vespers service on Good Friday afternoon, the oratorios were conceived as "Hauptmusik" (main music) in the morning services on Sundays and festival days, where they were performed in place of the regular church cantata before the sermon.[7] The vespers service on Good Friday provided Bach with ample time to perform a large-scale, multihour piece, while in the morning service he had to remain within a much narrower time frame, roughly between twenty and thirty minutes. The *Easter Oratorio* already stretches these limits as it is slightly longer than forty-five minutes. The *Christmas Oratorio*, however, would not have fit into the time frame of a regular service. Bach and his librettist thus conceived the piece in six parts that each roughly corresponded to the length of a regular church can-tata. In spite of these differences, Bach's oratorios and Passions also share numerous features, such as their narrative-dramatic character and the combination of biblical narrative and reflective poetry. Both Passions and oratorios use a biblical story as the backbone, which differentiates them from other contemporary oratorios, which frequently presented the biblical narrative only in poetic paraphrase, and also from Bach's regular church cantatas, which do not feature a coherent narrative. As Bach's Passions and oratorios share these stylistic features, there might have been some cross-fertilization in the compositional process as well. Christoph Wolff has rightly noted that "Bach's work in the oratorios may also have prompted the major revi-sions to which he subjected the Passions in 1736 and later."[8] It is remarkable that

---

[5] Christoph Wolff, "Under the Spell of Opera?," 1.

[6] This, however, did not prohibit Bach from alluding to the connotations associated with brass instruments. In his *St. John Passion*, the aria "Es ist vollbracht" features a vivid middle section with the text "Der Held aus Juda siegt mit Macht" which uses fanfare-like motifs in both the vocal part and the instrumental accompaniment. Under other circumstances Bach would have set this section with brass instruments. Robert Schumann, in an instrumentation of the passion, sensed this and added trumpets for this movement (see Meinrad Walter, *Johann Sebastian Bach: Johannespassion: Eine musikalisch-the-ologische Einführung* [Stuttgart: Carus Verlag and Reclam, 2011], 182–84); while the addition of the brass instruments is both anachronistic and contradicts liturgical conventions, it nevertheless shows a clear understanding for Bach's musical ideas. An excellent recording of Schumann's version of the *St. John Passion* was recorded by the Rheinische Kantorei and Das Kleine Konzert, directed by Herman Max (cpo 777 091-2), released in 2007; I am grateful to Michael Marissen for this recommendation.

[7] The pieces were normally repeated during the vespers service in the other main church as well as during the "old service' in the University Church, see Wolff, "Under the Spell of Opera?" 2. But the primary performance was always in the morning service at one of the two main churches.

[8] Wolff, "Under the Spell of Opera?" 3.

Bach began to rework his Passions (composed between 1724 and 1731) during the years from 1736 to 1744, immediately following the composition of the oratorios.

Why did Bach begin composing oratorios at this point in his career? He was already approaching fifty and was an accomplished composer who had covered a wide range of genres and forms. Why did he not compose oratorios earlier?[9] And why did he begin composing them in 1734? While Bach does not answer these questions, it is possible to name several models that might have served as an inspiration and thus triggered Bach's decision to turn his attention to this genre.

## *Model:* Joseph

The lack of oratorio compositions before 1734 is understandable, as the musical environment in Leipzig did not provide an easy venue for oratorio performances. A public concert hall did not exist. Bach's situation in Leipzig was different from places like Hamburg, where Georg Philipp Telemann had spaces available to perform larger scale works in a public concert. An unusual exception is the musical drama *Joseph*, which Bach might have encountered during his earlier years in Leipzig. Unfortunately, the piece poses more questions than it provides answers. Performed by Georg Balthasar Schott's Collegium musicum, *Joseph* could be a unique piece, but it could also be the only representative for an otherwise lost group of works.[10] Only the libretto for this *dramma per musica* survives. The length of the text is shorter than in other oratorios of the time, and it represents the type of a larger, dramatic cantata, not unlike the secular *drammi per musica* Bach composed during his tenure. With its use of a biblical story in an extraliturgical piece it also continues the tradition we have observed earlier with Thymich's and Knüpfer's Christmas piece from 1685. The libretto tells the story of the second journey of Jacob's sons to Egypt (Gen 43–45) and consists of eleven arias (four for chorus), two soliloquies, and longer sections labeled recitative. Michael Maul argues convincingly that the piece was probably performed in Leipzig between 1725 and 1729.[11] The performance took place not in a church but during the usual performances of the ensemble in the coffee houses and coffee gardens in Leipzig,[12] which was also the usual performance venue for the secular cantatas by Bach.

The surviving libretto print for *Joseph* mentions that this was the "anderer Theil" (second part), suggesting that a first part must have existed. Therefore, the complete

---

[9] Alfred Dürr stated in his 1967 study on the *Christmas Oratorio* that the reasons for Bach's interest in the genre in the early 1730s were unknown; see Dürr, *Johann Sebastian Bach. Weihnachts-Oratorium BWV 248* (Munich: Fink, 1967), 3.

[10] For a facsimile of the libretto see Michael Maul, "Neues zu Georg Balthasar Schott, seinem Collegium musicum und Bachs Zerbster Geburtstagskantate," *Bach-Jahrbuch* 93 (2007): 98–103.

[11] Maul, "Neues zu Georg Balthasar Schott," 91.

[12] Maul, "Neues zu Georg Balthasar Schott," 77.

piece might have been about double the length, which brings it closer to the dimensions of a conventional oratorio. The remark also suggests that the piece was performed in at least two parts; the printing of a libretto in two parts makes sense only if the performance was divided in two parts as well. We can assume that the complete piece was too long for a performance during one of the usual performance sessions in a coffee house and thus was broken up into two halves and played on two different days. Listeners who had heard the first part probably were enticed to come back to the coffee house for the continuation. It is not farfetched to see the breaking-up of a larger composition into multiple sections, and the performance on different days, in relation to the performance of Bach's *Christmas Oratorio*, which was performed in cantata-sized parts over six days. While we will see later that a similar practice existed for sacred compositions in other cities as well, the *Joseph*-drama provides a local model for Bach, performed in Leipzig within a decade before the *Christmas Oratorio*. *Joseph* is not explicitly called an oratorio and there is no indication that it was seen as such. But as a setting of a biblical subject featuring different characters in a quasi-dramatic setting, without any indication of being staged, it qualifies as an oratorio even though the libretto does not use this label.

## Literary models

In 1725, Picander, Bach's librettist and possibly the author of the text for the *Christmas Oratorio*, published the libretto for a Passion oratorio, *Erbauliche Gedanken ... über den Leidenen Jesum, in einem Oratorio entworfen*.[13] The text follows the model of the Passion oratorios by Brockes and Hunold. The biblical text does not employ Luther's translation but is rendered in free poetic paraphrase. Picander's text was never set to music; however, some of the movements appear in revised form in Picander's libretto for Bach's *St. Matthew Passion* a few years later. The performance of a composition based on Picander's libretto from 1725 at the two main churches, St. Thomas and St. Nicholas, would have been out of the question for about another decade.[14] A performance in a nonliturgical context, as with the Christmas piece by Thymich or the *Joseph*-drama, would have been problematic

---

[13] Picander, *Erbauliche Gedancken auf den Grünen Donnerstag und Charfreitag Über den Leidenden JEsus, In einem Oratorio Entworffen* (1725); the libretto was printed in Picander's collection *Sammlung Erbaulicher Gedancken über und auf die gewöhnlichen Sonn- und Fest-Tage in gebundner Schreib-Art entworffen* (Leipzig: Boetius, [1725]), 193–206; see also the description in Irmgard Scheitler, *Deutschsprachige Oratorienlibretti. Von den Anfängen bis 1730*, Beiträge zur Kirchenmusik 12 (Paderborn: Schönigh, 2005), 345–46.

[14] The situation was different at the Neukirche in Leipzig, where in 1729 a setting of Brockes' "Der für die Sünde der Welt gemarterte und sterbende Jesus" was performed. The composition was probably by Christian Gottlieb Fröber; s. Andreas Glöckner, *Die Musikpflege an der Leipziger Neukirche zur Zeit Johann Sebastian Bachs* (Leipzig: Nationale Forschungs und Gedenkstätten J. S. Bach, 1990), 88 and 97.

given the subject of the work. Nonetheless, Bach was surely aware of this oratorio-libretto by a poet with whom he began a fruitful collaboration in that same year.[15]

Bach was familiar with both the term "oratorio" as well as the genre before he embarked on his collaboration with Picander. In Italy, the genre had emerged around 1600, the term having been in use since 1640.[16] In Protestant Germany, the development of the oratorio took a slightly different turn than in the Catholic regions south of the Alps, where the genre had originated in the meetings of a religious community in the context of the Catholic reformation. While the performance of an oratorio in the Italian tradition would have been out of the question in most Lutheran worship services, a related form, the *historia*, flourished in Protestant churches.[17] The *historia* grew out of the chanting of the scripture in the liturgy. Characterized by the presence of the original text in Luther's translation, the biblical sections were interrupted by hymns or free poetic interpolations. Schelle's *Actus musicus* follows this form, and Bach's Passions adhere to the same model. A more modern form of the oratorio in Protestant Germany, which uses the biblical text in poetic paraphrase, developed primarily in the north around 1700 in close proximity to the opera house in Hamburg. There, librettists like Barthold Heinrich Brockes, Christian Friedrich Hunold, and Erdmann Neumeister wrote and published librettos that were set to music by composers who were likewise associated with the opera, like Johann Mattheson, Georg Philipp Telemann, or Reinhard Keiser. The genre soon became popular in central Germany as well, as the example of Gottfried Heinrich Stölzel shows and who became an important influence for Bach.

The term "oratorio" was not clearly defined. As quoted earlier, Johann Gottfried Walther compared it liberally to the opera, and in his *Versuch einer Critischen Dichtkunst* from 1751, the Leipzig poet Johann Christoph Gottsched describes it in general terms:

> Church pieces generally called oratorios—that is, prayer pieces [*Betstücke*]—resemble cantatas in that they, too, contain arias and recitatives. They also generally introduce various speaking personae so that there might be variety amongst the singing voices. Here now the poet must introduce biblical persons, from the gospels or other texts, even Jesus and

---

[15] Wolff goes so far as to suggest that the libretto might have "encouraged [Bach's] collaboration with Picander" (Wolff, "Under the Spell of Opera?," 5); while this is probably not the case, it definitely attests to an interest on the poet's part in writing an oratorio and a familiarity with the genre on the side of Bach.

[16] For the early history of the genre, see Howard E. Smither, *A History of the Oratorio 1: The Oratorio in the Baroque Era: Italy, Vienna, Paris* (Chapel Hill: University of North Carolina Press, 1977), 77–206; see also Christian Speck, *Das Italienische Oratorium 1625–1665: Musik und Dichtung* (Turnhout: Brepos, 2003).

[17] Cf. Bernd Baselt, "Actus Musicus und Historie um 1700 in Mitteldeutschland," *Hallesche Beiträge zur Musikwissenschaft* Ser. G 1 (1978/69), 77–103.

God himself, or allegorical figures representing religious functions such as Faith, Love, Hope, the Christian Church, Sacred Bride, Shulamite, Daughter Zion, or Faithful Soul, and the like in a speaking manner so that the outcome corresponds to purpose and place.[18]

Consequently, not only large-scale pieces could be called oratorio but also cantata-sized compositions like the pieces in one of Telemann's cantata cycles, known as the *Oratorischer Jahrgang* (oratorio cycle) from 1730/31.[19] A definition of the oratorio that is close to Bach's understanding is given in Christian Friedrich Hunold's handbook *Die allerneueste Art, zur reinen und galanten Poesie zu gelangen* from 1707. The book is largely based on the lectures on literature by the Hamburg poet and theologian Erdmann Neumeister. Hunold's definition of the oratorio reflects a more conservative form that resembles the model of the seventeenth-century *historia* in its combination of biblical text, reflective arias, and hymns:

| | |
|---|---|
| Eine Oratoria ist eine vortrefflich schöne Art, und vornehmlich wird sie uns in geistlichen Sachen und Kirchen-Stücken contentiren. Sie ist aber kürzlich also beschaffen, dass ein Biblischer Text und Arien unter einander gewechselt werden. Bisweilen tut man auch ein oder ein Paar Gesetze [stanzas] aus einem Choral Gesang dazu.[20] | An oratorio is an exceptionally beautiful genre; it is primarily used for sacred subjects and for pieces composed for the church. In short, it is structured thus: a biblical text alternates with arias. Sometimes are added one or a couple stanzas from a chorale. |

The quote from Hunold describes very well the structure of both Bach's *Christmas Oratorio* and of his Passions. The libretto, according to Hunold, does not necessarily require a dramatic-operatic plot. Essential is the combination of biblical narrative and contemplative interpolations in arias and hymn-settings. Christoph Wolff

---

[18] Quoted after Wolff, "Under the Spell of Opera?" 5; the German original is printed in: Johann Christoph Gottsched, *Versuch einer Critischen Dichtkunst* (Leipzig, 1751), 728.

[19] Ute Poetzsch, "Ordentliche Kirchenmusiken, genannt Oratorium—Telemanns 'oratorische' Jahrgänge," in *Musikkonzepte—Konzepte der Musikwissenschaft, Bericht über den Internationalen Kongreß der Gesellschaft für Musikforschung Halle (Saale) 1998, Bd. 2: Freie Referate,* ed. Kathrin Eberl and Wolfgang Ruf (Kassel: Bärenreiter, 2001), 317–24; and Ralph-Jürgen Reipsch, "Der Telemann Bestand des Notenarchivs der Sing-Akademie zu Berlin—ein Überblick," in *Telemann, der musikalische Maler/ Telemann Kompositionen im Notenarchiv der Sing-Akademie zu Berlin* (Telemann-Konferenzberichte XV), ed. Carsten Lange and Brit Reipsch (Hildesheim: Olms, 2010), 275–363.

[20] Friedrich Christian Hunold (Menantes), *Die Allerneueste Art, zur reinen und galanten Poesie zu gelangen* (Hamburg, 1707), 275; see also Meinrad Walter, *Johann Sebastian Bach: Weihnachtsoratorium* (Kassel: Bärenreiter, 2006), 21.

has suggested that J.G. Walther's description of the oratorio as a sacred opera in his *Musikalisches Lexicon* from 1732 might have inspired the composer to embark on his oratorio project.[21] Although it is impossible to rule this out entirely, two other sources of inspiration seem to be of greater importance. Two compositions, both performed on Good Friday 1734, might have been the trigger for Bach's increasing interest in oratorios.

## Model: Hasse

The first piece was performed in Dresden, the Saxon capital. On Good Friday 1734 the court capellmeister and celebrated opera composer, Johann Adolph Hasse (1699–1783), performed his first oratorio in that city. *Il cantico de' tre fanciulli*, based on a libretto by Stefano Benedetto Pallavicino (1672–1742), tells the story of the three young men in the fiery furnace from Daniel 3. The text stays close to the biblical text but, as is typical for the modern Italian oratorio, is a poetic paraphrase of the narrative.[22] Dresden had seen oratorio performances before. In 1730 the court chapel had performed Caldara's *Morte e Sepoltura di Cristo*.[23] Still, the performance of Hasse's piece was a significant event and begun a tradition of oratorio performances that continued for the next several decades. In years when Hasse was not present, as in 1735, the duty of composing a new oratorio for Lent was taken over by Jan Dismas Zelenka (1679–1745).

Hasse's oratorio *Il cantico de' tre fanciulli* is firmly grounded in the tradition of the Italian oratorio. Its twenty-two movements include nine recitatives, nine arias, a terzet, and two choral movements.[24] As is common for a dramatic oratorio at this time, the libretto does not feature a narrator (*testo*); all the action is carried by the dialogue (or monologue) of the protagonists. The number of choral movements is reduced to two, and the oratorio mainly consists of a sequence of solo movements.

Hasse's oratorio was performed for the first time on April 23, 1734, in Dresden.[25] As can be expected, there are no direct musical connections between Hasse's oratorio and Bach's first oratorio, the *Christmas Oratorio*, which was performed about eight months later. Bach's and Hasse's styles were too different for a direct

---

[21] Wolff, "Under the Spell of Opera?" 12.

[22] Cf. Michael Koch, *Die Oratorien Johann Adolf Hasses: Überlieferung und Struktur. Erster Teilband: Wirkungsgeschichte, Überlieferung und Gestalt der Oratorien* (Pfaffenweiler: Centaurus), 1989, 135.

[23] See Ursula Kirkendale, *Antonio Caldara. Life and Venetian-Roman Oratorios*, rev. and trans. Warren Kirkendale (Firenze: Olschki, 2007), 167–69.

[24] For later performances in 1740 and 1743 the text and the music were slightly changed and expanded; see Koch, *Die Oratorien Johann Adolf Hasses*, 99.

[25] Koch, *Die Oratorien Johann Adolf Hasses*, 55–56.

borrowing. What is more important for Bach's oratorio project is the date: Hasse composed an oratorio for the court in Dresden in 1734. Bach was then at a point in his career where he was dissatisfied with his position in Leipzig and was looking for opportunities outside the city, particularly at a court like Dresden. In a famous letter to his friend Georg Erdmann in Danzig,[26] he inquired about employment opportunities and in 1733, after the death of Elector Friedrich August II (the strong), he sent his two Mass movements (Kyrie and Gloria of what would later be known as the *B-Minor Mass*) to the court in Dresden, hoping to be awarded the title of court composer. In his accompanying letter Bach writes:

> To Your Royal Highness I submit in deepest devotion the present small work of that science which I have achieved in *musique*, with the most wholly submissive prayer that Your Highness will look upon it with Most Gracious Eyes, according to Your Highness's World-Famous Clemency and not according to the poor *composition*; and thus deign to take me under Your Most Mighty Protection. For some years and up to the present moment, I have had the *Directorium* of the Music in the two principal churches in Leipzig, but innocently had to suffer one injury or another, and on occasion also a diminution of the fees accruing to me in this office; but these injuries would disappear altogether if Your Royal Highness would grant me the favor of conferring upon me a title of Your Highness's Court Capelle, and would let Your High Command for the issuing of such a document go forth to the proper place. Such a most gracious fulfillment of my most humble prayer will bind me to unending devotion, and I offer myself in most indebted obedience to show at all times, upon Your Royal Highness's Most Gracious Desire, my untiring zeal in the composition of music for the church as well as for the orchestra, and to devote my entire forces to the service of Your Highness, remaining in unceasing fidelity Your Royal Highness's most humble and most obedient servant.
>
> Dressden, July 27, 1733
> JOHANN SEBASTIAN BACH[27]

It took until 1736 for Bach to finally receive the title of court composer. But it is clear from this letter and from the dedication of the two parts of the Mass that Bach was looking to Dresden not just for protection but also that he hoped to work for the court, if not in a permanent and local position then at least from his current place in Leipzig as "Capellmeister von Haus aus." Bach sent the two parts of the

---

[26] Mendel, David, Wolff, *New Bach Reader*, 151–52.
[27] Mendel, David, Wolff, *New Bach Reader*, 158.

Mass to Dresden as a sample of his accomplishments, but he obviously designed the Mass movements in a style that was close to the musical styles of sacred music in Dresden.[28] Janice Stockigt suggests that Bach might even have written the Mass movements "with the capabilities of the instrumentalists and singers—the castrati especially—of the Dresden *Hofkapelle* [in mind]. . . . Already in 1731 he had heard these musicians when he and Wilhelm Friedemann traveled to Dresden to hear a performance of Hasse's *Cleofide*."[29] In spite of several differences between Bach's Mass movements and the Mass style favored at the court in Dresden, Stockigt concludes that "in matters of large-scale structuring, consideration of the abilities of the solo singers . . . and most of the instrumental organization and writing, the *Missa* conformed with models of this era."[30]

Bach was well informed about the musical life in the Saxon capital. And there was, of course, a constant exchange of news between the capital Dresden and the economical center of Saxony, Leipzig. The news of the upcoming performance of an oratorio by Hasse might easily have traveled from Dresden to Leipzig within a few days. Bach was also familiar with Hasse's music. In September 1731 he had visited Dresden to play concerts on the Silbermann organ of the Sophien-church. One such concert was on September 14, 1731. The evening before was the first performance of Hasse's opera *Cleofide* in Dresden. Bach scholars have argued convincingly that Bach might have attended this significant performance.[31] Bach's contact with Dresden continued. On June 23, 1733, Bach's oldest son, Wilhelm Friedemann, had been elected organist at the Sophien-church in Dresden, where he would stay until 1746.[32] Friedemann kept in close contact with numerous musicians at the

---

[28] See Janice B. Stockigt, "Consideration of Bach's *Kyrie e Gloria* BWV 232I within the Context of Dresden Catholic Mass Settings, 1729–1733," *International Symposium: Understanding Bach's B-minor Mass: Discussion Book,* vol. I, ed. by Yo Tomita, et al. (Belfast: School of Music & Sonic Arts, 2007), 59–60; George B. Stauffer, *The Mass in B Minor. The Great Catholic Mass* (New Haven: Yale University Press, 2003), 16–23.

[29] S. Christoph Wolff, "Anmerkungen zu Bach und 'Cleofide' (Dresden 1731)," in *Johann Sebastian Bachs Spätwerk und dessen Umfeld. Bericht über das wissenschaftliche Symposium anläßlich des 61. Bachfestes der Neuen Bachgesellschaft, Duisburg 1986,* ed. Christoph Wolff (Kassel: Bärenreiter, 1988), 167–69, as well as Reinhard Strohm's article in the same volume, "Johann Adolph Hasse's Opera 'Cleofide' und ihre Vorgeschichte," 170–176.

[30] Stockigt, "Consideration of Bach's *Kyrie e Gloria*," 63.

[31] *Bach-Dokumente* (Leipzig and Kassel, 1963–72), 294 (II), 653–64 (III).

[32] David Schulenberg suggests that Friedemann was personally acquainted with Hasse; he also proposes that Hasse's *Cleofide* might have had a direct impact on Friedemann's music, see David Schulenberg, *The Music of Wilhelm Friedemann Bach* (Rochester, NY: University of Rochester Press, 2010), 6 and 173–75. For Wilhelm Friedemann Bach's contact to the music at the court in Dresden, see also Gerhard Poppe, "Ein Sohn des Thomaskantors in der kursächsischen Residenzstadt—Annotationen zum Thema 'Dresden und Wilhelm Friedemann Bach,'" in *Wilhelm Friedemann Bach und die protestantische Kirchenkantate nach 1750,* ed. Peter Wollny and Wolfgang Hirschmann (Beeskow: Ortus, 2012), 69–78.

Dresden court and would have been aware of the performance of Hasse's oratorio as well. Johann Sebastian Bach was also familiar with the styles and genres favored in Dresden and was eager to emulate the style, be it for a composition for the Electoral court, or within his own position in Leipzig. Since taking over the *Collegium musicum* in 1729, he had an opportunity to perform both instrumental music and secular cantatas, and during the early 1730s he became increasingly interested in music dramatic genres, as attest the *Hercules Cantata*, BWV 213, from 1733 and the *Coffee Cantata*, BWV 211, from 1734. Given Johann Sebastian Bach's interest in the musical life at the court and his numerous connections, he must have heard about the performance of Hasse's oratorio on April 23, 1734. And given his interest in bringing some of the "flavor" of Dresden's music to Leipzig, turning to the very genre Hasse had just begun to introduce in Dresden was a logical step.

This is not to say that Bach necessarily depended on Hasse as a direct model. Oratorio composition lay in the air, so to speak, in the early 1730s. While Hasse began his oratorio production in 1734, George Frideric Handel was performing his oratorios in London in 1732, with *Esther* and *Acis and Galatea*, closely followed by *Deborah* and *Athalia* in 1733.[33] But England was far away, and Handel, while a native German, was not a direct competitor for Bach. Dresden, however, was much more intriguing. Bach's oratorios of the 1730s—the *Christmas Oratorio* from 1734/35 and the *Ascension Oratorio* from 1735, in particular—are examples of Bach's attempt to adopt musical developments from the Dresden court. Yet, the two pieces were not part of his attempt to gain a position at the court. Not only were they stylistically too different but a German oratorio would not have been of any interest to the court. By composing oratorios, though, Bach was able to transplant some of the Dresden forms into his own musical world in Leipzig.[34]

## Model: Stölzel

The first step in this direction was not the composition of an oratorio but rather the performance of a piece that had been composed more than a decade prior by Gottfried Heinrich Stölzel in Gotha. On the same day as the performance of Hasse's new oratorio in Dresden, Good Friday 1734, Bach performed Stölzel's piece that was highly innovative by Leipzig standards. Modern Bach scholarship

---

[33] See the overview in Matthew Gardner, "Öffentlichkeit als Veranstaltungsform. Werkgestalt, Primärrezeption und Umstände der Aufführungen von Händels englischen Oratorien," in *Händels Oratorien, Oden und Serenaten*, ed. Michael Zywietz, *Das Händel-Handbuch* 3 (Laaber: Laaber Verlag 2010), 59–74.

[34] Hasse's oratorio would later be performed in Leipzig as well, but it would take until the 1750s for Bach's successor Doles to mount a performance; see Koch, *Die Oratorien Johann Adolf Hasses*, 43.

had assumed until recently that the liturgical conventions in Leipzig did not allow the performance of a Passion oratorio in one of the main churches, St. Thomas or St. Nicholas. However, the discovery of a printed libretto for Good Friday 1734 shows that Bach did indeed perform a piece that presented the Passion narrative in free poetic paraphrase and not, as Bach's own Passions, in its original form. The piece Bach performed on March 23, 1734, was the Passion *Ein Lämmlein geht, und trägt die Schuld* by Gottfried Heinrich Stölzel. The discovery of the libretto is quite significant as it confirms that Bach was interested in performing an oratorio at this time. The libretto further demonstrates that the religious authorities in Leipzig permitted the performance of a piece that left behind the models of the seventeenth-century *historia,* with its combination of biblical narrative and interpolated interpretations.

Stölzel was one of the forerunners in the creation of the new poetic oratorio in central Germany in the early eighteenth century. When he assumed his position as capellmeister in Gotha in 1720, he had already gained experience with opera in Hamburg and had traveled extensively in Italy where he was able to study both Italian opera and oratorio. He met Vivaldi in Venice and Domenico Scarlatti in Rome; before coming to Gotha, he had lived for three years in Prague, where he had composed secular and sacred works, and at least three oratorios. Right from the start in Gotha, Stölzel showed great interest in the genre. In 1720 he composed his first Passion oratorio, for which, as the libretto states, he also provided the text.[35]

Stölzel's first Passion oratorio for Gotha was a contemplative oratorio.[36] While he also composed works of a more dramatic character (for instance in 1723) it was this first piece from 1720 that Bach chose to perform in Leipzig. Stölzel's Passion consists of a sequence of short meditations (*Betrachtungen*). While a libretto from Gotha divides the work into twenty of these *Betrachtungen,* the Leipzig libretto subdivides the piece into twenty-two sections.[37] Besides these structural differences and some minor textual changes, the versions are identical.[38] The different distribution of the *Betrachtungen* in the Leipzig and Gotha librettos does not affect the musical

[35] The preface mentions the "well set poetry and composition of the current Capellmeister" ("wohlgesetzte Poesis und Composition Dero nunmehrigen Herrn Capell-Meisters," *Der Leidende und am Creutz sterbende Liebe Jesu/in der Hoch-Fürstl. Sächß. Hof-Capelle zum Friedenstein Musicalisch Aufgeführet* (Gotha 1720, fol.)(7)).

[36] Of the two manuscripts of the music that survive, the manuscript in the Schloßmuseum Sondershausen is closer to the Gotha and Leipzig librettos and represents the original form of the piece, while a copy in the Staatsbibliothek Berlin exhibits some deeper changes and revisions. See Tatjana Schabalina, "'Texte zur Music' in Sankt Petersburg. Neue Quellen zur Leipziger Musikgeschichte sowie zur Kompositions- und Aufführungstätigkeit Johann Sebastian Bachs," *Bach-Jahrbuch* 94 (2008): 79.

[37] The division into twenty-two meditations was not unique for Leipzig; the same division was made for librettos that were printed for performances in Nuremberg and Rudolstadt in 1736; see Scheitler, *Deutschsprachige Oratorienlibretti,* 343.

[38] See Schabalina, "'Texte zur Music' in Sankt Petersburg," 79–80, and Scheitler, *Deutschsprachige Oratorienlibretti,* 343.

substance. In fact, the manuscript sources from Sondershausen (a short score and a set of parts) do not mention the division into *Betrachtungen* at all but divide the oratorio into four parts of approximately equal length.[39] It is not clear whether the four parts reflect a particular performance practice, but a note at the beginning of the score suggests that the piece was performed in two parts on two subsequent days: one part on Maundy Thursday and the other parts on Good Friday. The same division shows up in the next Passion by Stölzel, his dramatic Passion oratorio from 1723.[40]

The two oratorios are only a small portion of oratorios composed by Stölzel. According to his obituary, printed in Mizler's *Neu eröffneter Musicalischer Bibliothek*, the composer wrote approximately fourteen Passion and Christmas oratorios ("ohngefehr vierzehn Paßions und Weyhnachts Oratorien").[41] While seven of the Passion oratorios are known, the identity of the Christmas oratorios is unclear. No pieces with this name are extant or known through other sources, although it is possible that some of the cantata cycles for Christmas could be combined into oratorio-like works. It is also possible that some cantatas, which are listed individually, were seen by the composer as sections of an oratorio. This could be the case for a cycle of three Christmas cantatas Stölzel performed in 1719. The printed libretto suggests that the cantatas together formed an entity: *Liebes-Andachten, nach dem Jahrgang aus denen EVANGELIIS eingerichtet, Und in Hoch-Fürstl. Fieden-steinis. Schloß-Capellen am Weyhnacht-Fest 1719. musiciret.* The three cantatas do not recount the Christmas narrative but are meditations on Christ's love, revealed through his birth.[42] The *Liebes-Andachten* (devotions) are similar to the meditative Passion oratorio for the following year. It is probable that other Christmas cantatas by Stölzel can be grouped in a similar way. It is also possible that Stölzel did indeed compose several Christmas oratorios that have not come down to us; the oratorios might be lost—as are most of Stölzel's other compositions. Therefore, we cannot rule out that Bach's decision to compose a Christmas oratorio was partly inspired by a piece by Stölzel, and one with the same title.

The only influence by Stölzel that can be quantified at this point is the Passion that Bach performed in 1734. It is necessary to summarize the stylistic characteristics of that piece briefly before we move on to Bach. Most of the *Betrachtungen* follow the same simple structure: an evangelist, a role alternatively assigned to the tenor or the bass, sings a free paraphrase of the gospel text in a secco recitative. This is followed by an accompagnato recitative and an aria by the "faithful soul"

---

[39] Part I: Betrachtung 1–6; Part II: Betrachtung 7–12; Part III: Betrachtung 13–18; Part VI: rest (=Betrachtung 19–20 or 19–22).

[40] Scheitler, *Deutschsprachige Oratorienlibretti*, 343.

[41] Johann Lorenz Mizler von Koloff, *Neu eröffnete Musicalische Bibliothek*, vol IV (Leipzig, 1754), 152.

[42] Cf. Scheitler, *Deutschsprachige Oratorienlibretti*, 339.

(Gläubige Seele), which is sung in alternation by one of the four soloists. Each of the *Betrachtungen* ends with a homophonic hymn-setting in four-part harmony, identified in the libretto as the voice of the "Christian church" (Christliche Kirche). Stölzel deviates from this basic structure only in the framing movements. The opening *Betrachtung* features a longer sequence of recitatives, while nos. 20–22, reporting the death of Jesus, omit the meditative arias and contain longer choral movements.

The instrumentation in the movements is standardized. Strings and bc are the norm; in several arias the first violin is doubled by an oboe. Three of the arias feature the oboe as a solo instrument, and two arias use a flute or a viola da gamba respectively as obbligato instruments. The structure of the arias is similarly standardized, usually following a regular *da capo* form. Noteworthy exceptions are no. 14, a strophic aria for bass, and no. 7, a duet for cantus and alto. The voice-leading in the arias is simple and mostly syllabic. Longer melismas only appear on central keywords and are normally not very extensive; this occasionally gives the arias a song-like character. The obbligato parts in most of the arias have a similar cantabile quality. Finally, the recitatives follow a clear pattern as well: the gospel paraphrases are secco recitatives, with the exception of the depiction of the earthquake in *Betrachtung* 20. The accompagnato recitatives are, for the most part, accompanied by long, extended chords played by the strings; sometimes replaced by short chords, setting rhythmic accents. The most remarkable exception is a recitative in *Betrachtung* 5, "Ach! daß ihr Augen Quellen wärt" (Ah! If your eyes were wells), where the flowing of the tears is depicted by groups of sixteenth notes played by the strings. The clear functional differentiation between the recitatives in gospel texts (secco) and free meditations (accompagnato) reminds us of the pattern Bach employs in the *Christmas Oratorio*.

With its focus on contemplation over drama, Stölzel's Passion does indeed foreshadow Bach's *Christmas Oratorio*. Bach was obviously intrigued by Stölzel's works, since he not only performed the Passion on Good Friday 1734 but also performed a larger number of Stölzel's cantatas in 1735, shortly after completing the *Christmas Oratorio*. He even used one of the arias from the Passion as a model for one of his own compositions. Peter Wollny has shown that Bach's aria "Bekennen will ich seinen Namen," BWV 200, was directly modeled on Stölzel's aria "Dein Creutz, o Bräutigam" from *Betrachtung* 13.[43] In spite of the differences that a modern listener might hear between the styles of Bach and Stölzel, Bach saw in Stölzel's work material that was worthwhile performing in the liturgy in Leipzig, and he also viewed it as inspiration for his own compositions.

[43] Peter Wollny, "'Bekennen will ich seinen Namen'–Authenzität, Bestimmung und Kontext der Arie BWV 200. Anmerkungen zu Johann Sebastian Bachs Rezeption von Werken Gottfried Heinrich Stölzels," *Bach-Jahrbuch* 94 (2008): 123–58.

*Table 4.1* **Bach chorale tropes**

| Movement (Year) | Poetic text | Chorale | Scoring |
|---|---|---|---|
| BWV 23/2 (1723) | Ach! gehe nicht vorüber | Christe, du Lamm Gottes | T, str, ob I +II, bc |
| BWV 70/9 (1723) | Ach, soll nicht dieser große Tag | Es ist gewißlich an der Zeit | B, tr, str, bc |
| BWV 5/4 (1724) | Mein treuer Heiland tröstet mich | Wo soll ich fliehen hin | A, ob I, bc |
| BWV 38/4 (1724) | Ach! daß mein Glaube noch so schwach | Aus tiefer Not schrei ich zu dir | A, bc |
| BWV 122/3 (1724) | Die Engel, welche sich zuvor | Das neugeborne Kindelein | S, rec I–III, bc |

One of the most interesting movements from Stölzel's Passion has left its mark on the *Christmas Oratorio*. The final *Betrachtung* features an accompagnato recitative for soprano and tenor. While the tenor sings a poetic text meditating the burial of Jesus, the cantus intones two stanzas of the Passion chorale "O Traurigkeit, O Herzeleid" (ex. 4.1). The two singers are accompanied by the strings. The second violin and viola provide a harmonic backdrop in long note values, the first violin doubles the cantus melody. The movement is a chorale trope, combining a free poetic text and a hymn; it is a genre that was used by Bach quite frequently as well.[44] What is unusual in comparison to Bach's chorale tropes is the simultaneous combination of recitative and vocal chorale. Bach combined a chorale melody with a recitative in five cantatas (see table 4.1), but in all cases the melody had been played by an instrument and had not been sung by a voice.

Bach avoided this type of chorale trope because the simultaneous combination impeded the understandability of the recitative text. Concurrent chorale tropes are more frequent in Bach arias, where text repetitions were the norm, so that the listener could perceive both layers of the text. If Bach used chorale tropes in recitatives, he usually presented the two layers (chorale and poetic text) in alternation. The only exception from this norm are two recitatives in the *Christmas Oratorio*, mvts. 38 and 40, in the fourth part of the oratorio. These two movements belong together, as they share the same chorale stanza from a hymn by Johann Rist ("Jesu, du mein liebstes Leben"); the first half of the stanza is quoted in no. 38 and the second half in no. 40. Both are sung by the soprano and combined with a recitative layer assigned to the bass. A closer comparison between Bach's setting in no. 40 and Stölzel's trope shows that Bach modeled his setting on the piece by Stölzel (exx. 4.1 and 4.2).

---

[44] For a definition of this genre, see Markus Rathey, "Drama and Discourse: The Form and Function of Chorale Tropes in Bach's Oratorios," *Bach Perspectives* 8 (2011): 42–68.

*Example 4.1* Gottfried Heinrich Stölzel, *Ein Lämmlein geht*, no. 22/2, mm. 1–8

*Example 4.2* J. S. Bach, BWV 248/40, mm. 1–51

Both settings use the same instrumentation. They begin with a string accompaniment against which the recitative voice sings the beginning of its statement before the chorale voice enters a little bit later, doubled by the first violin. The similarities extend into the voice-leading of the chorale as both voices begin with a descending gesture, which, in Stölzel's case, is part of the original chorale melody and in Bach's case, the composer's own invention. Bach clearly took the inspiration from Stölzel's piece, which he had just performed a few months prior, and then composed a type of chorale trope he had not used before. But the two pieces also exhibit a number of significant differences. In contrast to Stölzel, Bach uses the words of the chorale but not the melody traditionally associated with it. This is unusual for Bach and unique among his chorale tropes. The melody Bach composes resembles a song rather than a chorale and is not unlike his melodies for the

*Schemelli Gesangbuch,* published in 1736.[45] Bach's reason for composing his own melody was the highly emotional character of the text, which was insufficiently captured in the original tune by Johann Schop (ca. 1590–1667).[46] The newly composed melody also gives Bach the opportunity to disregard the bar-form (AAB) of the original tune and to create a through-composed melody instead, one that can more closely follow the affect and meaning of the individual words of the text. Still, Bach loosely follows the "grammar" of a traditional hymn melody, by ending what was the end of the A section in no. 38 in the dominant C major (m. 17) and modulating back to the tonic F major for the B-section in no. 40 (m. 16).

Bach's piece is significantly more complex than Stölzel's movement. The voice-leading in Stölzel's recitative layer is formulaic and constantly repeats a short motif on different pitch levels. Differences can also be seen in the accompaniment. Stölzel supports the chorale melody in the lower strings with a simple harmonic backdrop, while the accompaniment in mvt. 40 of the *Christmas Oratorio* is rhythmically and melodically independent. Bach uses Stölzel as a model but, at the same time, transcends this model. These stylistic differences notwithstanding, Stölzel's Passion was an important inspiration for Bach at a time when he showed an increased interest in the composition of oratorios. Other movements from the Stölzel Passion did not leave direct traces in BWV 248, which is not surprising, considering that most of the arias in the oratorio were parodies from earlier works. Finally, the structure of Stölzel's oratorios, consisting of sections that resembled cantatas, could have been one motivation for Bach to compose an oratorio that consisted of individual cantatas to be performed on consecutive days.

[45] Cf. Renate Steiger, *Gnadengegenwart: Johann Sebastian Bach im Kontext lutherischer Orthodoxie und Frömmigkeit,* vol. 2, bk. 2, Doctrina et Pietas. Zwischen Reformation und Aufklärung. Texte und Untersuchungen, II 2 (Stuttgart-Bad Canstatt: Frommann-Holzboog, 2002), 177–85; Martin Geck refers to the melody as an example for the Pietist aria, see *"Denn alles findet bei Bach statt": Erforschtes und Erfahrenes* (Stuttgart: Metzler, 2000), 104–5. The association with Pietism made by Geck is problematic because this style, even though favored by some Pietist composers and theorists, was not limited to this religious camp. In fact, the *Schemelli Gesangbuch* was intended to serve as a more orthodox counterpart to the popular Pietistic songbooks of the time.

[46] The concept of abandoning a preexisting chorale melody in order to better capture the emotional qualities of a hymn text has its models in the seventeenth century. Bach's predecessor as cantor at St. Thomas's in Leipzig, Johann Schelle (1648–1701) composed a setting of "Ach mein herzliebes Jesulein," the thirteenth stanza of Luther's hymn "Vom Himmel hoch," in which he replaces the familiar chorale melody with his own setting (see. chaps. 2 and 3, this book) that emphasizes the emotive qualities of the text; cf. Markus Rathey, "Rezeption als Innovation: Zur Aktualisierung traditioneller geistlicher Texte durch die Musik im 17. und frühen 18. Jahrhundert," in *Aedificatio. Erbauung im interkulturellen Kontext der Frühen Neuzeit,* ed. Andreas Solbach (Tübingen: Niemeyer, 2005), 234–36.

Passion performances on several days are documented in Protestant central and southern Germany during the seventeenth and early eighteenth centuries.[47] A Passion in Rudolstadt in 1705 (probably a piece that dates back to 1688) was performed on the six days of Holy Week, from Palm Sunday to Good Friday.[48] The music, which was presumably composed by Philipp Heinrich Erlebach (1657–1714), is lost, but the libretto clearly lays out a division into six *actus* and a performance over six days. Similar multiday performances of Passions are known from Nuremberg (1699)[49] and Eisenach (1711).[50] While the sections of the Passions in Nuremberg were performed on the four Sundays of Lent and on Maundy Thursday and Good Friday, the Erfurt-Passion was divided into ten parts, which were sung on Thursdays and Sundays during Lent, beginning on *Invocavit* Sunday, the first Sunday in Lent. The details of the performances differ, yet it is clear that it was not unusual to divide the Passion narrative into shorter sections and to perform it over several days, ranging from two days in Stölzel's Gotha to ten days in Eisenach. Given this evidence, it is likely that Bach's decision to perform the six parts of the *Christmas Oratorio* spread out over six days has its model in the practice of Passion performances in central Germany.[51]

[47] See Daniel R. Melamed, "Multi-Day Passions and J. S. Bach's *Christmas Oratorio*," *Eighteenth Century Music* 11 (2014): 215–34.

[48] See Scheitler, *Deutschsprachige Oratorienlibretti*, 111–16.

[49] Scheitler, "Ein Oratorium in der Nürnberger Frauenkirche 1699 und seine Nachfolger," *Morgen-Glantz* 14 (2004): 179–211.

[50] Die höchst-tröstliche Fasten-Zeit Wurde nebst andern gottseligen Betrachtungen über das bittere Leiden und Sterben unsers HErrn und Heylandes JEsu Christi / auch mit Harmonischer Devotion, nach Anleitung der Vier Evangelisten zugebracht / Also/daß wöchentlich zweymal / nemlich Sonntags und Donnerstangs / von Invocavit an bis auf Palmarum des 1711ten Jahres / bey öffentlichem Gottesdienste / einen Theil davon musicalisch aufführete Ihr. Hochfl. Durchl / zu Sachsen-Eisenach Capelle, Gotha: Reyher [1711].

[51] Kerala Snyder has suggested that Bach's model for the multipartite structure of the *Christmas Oratorio* might have been Dieterich Buxtehude's *Abendmusiken* in Lübeck. The Lübeck *Abendmusiken* were a concert series performed on five Sundays between St. Martin's Day (Nov. 11) and Christmas. Frequently, Buxtehude mounted an oratorio that was spilt up into shorter sections, which were to be performed in consecutive concerts. Bach had visited Buxtehude in 1705/6, and he might have learned about this practice. In 1705, however, Buxtehude did not produce a multipartite oratorio but performed two "Extraordinaire Abendmusiken," so although Bach might have heard about the practice, he would not have witnessed the performance of a multipartite oratorio; see Kerala J. Snyder, "Oratorio on Five Afternoons. From the Lübeck Abendmusiken to Bach's *Christmas Oratorio*," *Bach Perspectives* 8 (2011): 71. Snyder might be a bit too enthusiastic about Buxtehude's influence, though. The Lübeck-experience was already almost three decades in the past when Bach began his work in the *Christmas Oratorio*. The performances of pieces like the *Joseph* drama in the 1720s (probably over two days) and the division of Passions over several days, as it is known from Gotha and other places, had a more immediate influence.

# Shaping a model

With the literary and musical traditions in Leipzig, and the oratorios by Hasse and Stölzel as models, how did Bach himself understand the genre "oratorio"? Bach's own concept of the genre in the 1730s, between traditional *historia* and modern, dramatic oratorio, comes into sharpest relief not in the *Christmas Oratorio* but in the *Easter Oratorio*, BWV 249, the last part of Bach's "Oratorio Trilogy."[52] Like the other oratorios, the *Easter Oratorio* parodies an earlier composition by Bach, but in this case, even the sacred parodies have a longer history before the composer attached the label "oratorio." The piece is based on the "Shepherd's" cantata, *Entfliehet, verschwindet, entweichet ihr Sorgen*, BWV 249a, composed for the birthday of Herzog Christian of Sachsen-Weissenfels on February 23, 1725. The libretto for the secular cantata was written by Picander and "enacts" dialogues between the shepherds Menalcas and Damoetus and the shepherdesses Doris and Sylvia. The secular cantata resembles a little operatic scene, a feature that would have been easily recognized by the audience, as the court in Weissenfels had a long-standing tradition of opera performances.[53] At the same time, the piece transcends the realm of purely dramatic music. Particularly remarkable is the extensive duo-aria at the beginning,[54] featuring in the A and B sections of the *da capo* form the two shepherds and, in the repetition of the A section, the two shepherdesses. Bach transplants the form of a conventional opening movement of a cantata with its *da capo* structure into the realm of dramatic music. The result, however, is not dramatic but instead, the mere juxtaposition of the two groups of speakers lacks dramatic and dialogical qualities.

Bach reused the work several times. In 1726 he reworked the music into a birthday cantata for Graf Joachim Friedrich von Flemming (*Verjaget, zerstreuet, zerrüttet, ihr Sterne*, BWV 249b); this revision was preceded by a sacred parody in the Easter cantata *Kommt, gehet und eilet*, BWV 249, performed on April 1, 1725. Bach parodied the arias and ensemble movements from the secular model while the recitatives were, as per usual in parodies, newly composed.[55] Like the secular cantata, the piece is a little dramatic scene, featuring a conversation between two male protagonists

---

[52] For a short overview of Bach's oratorios for Easter and Ascension, see Markus Rathey, *Bach's Major Vocal Works: Music, Drama, Liturgy* (New Haven: Yale University Press, 2016), 138–65.

[53] Cf. Eleonore Sent, ed., *Die Oper am Weißenfelser Hof*, Weißenfelser Kulturtraditionen 1 (Rudolstadt: Hain Verlag, 1996); see also the older overviews by Erdmann Werner Böhme, *Die frühdeutsche Oper in Thüringen*, PhD diss., Greifswald, 1931, 203–16; Arno Werner, *Städtische und fürstliche Musikpflege in Weißenfels* (Leipzig: Breitkopf und Härtel, 1911); and Renate Brockpähler, *Handbuch zur Geschichte der Barockoper in Deutschland* (Emsdetten: Lechte, 1964), 369–79.

[54] The two instrumental movements at the beginning of the piece could have been part of the original shepherd's cantata, but it is also possible that they were added when the piece was revised for its sacred parody, see Dürr, *Cantatas*, 802–5.

[55] Christoph Wolff suggests that Bach might have decided to parody the secular piece because of the "tight schedule" between the performance of the last work of the chorale cantata cycle, BWV 1

(Petrus and Johannes) and two female characters (Maria Magdalena and Maria Jacobi). The sacred cantata follows its secular model in that the four characters are identified by name, bringing the piece close to a dramatic oratorio.

It is unusual that Bach does not use any hymns in his Easter cantata. This is in part due to the model for the cantata, but it would have been possible for Bach to insert hymn stanzas (either during the piece or at the end) and thus make it similar to his standard cantata-form. The lack of a hymn is even more remarkable as the cantata was written immediately after he had prematurely ended the chorale cantata cycle, a group of forty cantatas that were entirely based on hymns. The motivation for Bach was probably a dramatic one: the final chorus is an ensemble piece for the four protagonists praising God. Had Bach ended the cantata with a chorale (a genre that had traditionally been identified with the voice of the church or congregation, as it is done in Stölzel's Passion), the protagonists would have spoken out of character and abandoned their roles as historical figures.

The 1725 version of the Easter cantata needs to be viewed in connection with the *Joseph* drama performed by the *Collegium musicum* (1725–29) and Picander's Passion oratorio libretto (1725): all three paraphrase the biblical text and transform it into a dramatic scene. In spite of these features, Bach does not call this version of the cantata an oratorio. This label appears only in connection with another revision in the 1730s, probably around 1738.[56] But now Bach also changes the nature of the composition: in the later version the names of the characters are eliminated. Instead of a dialogue between four biblical characters, the words can now be heard as a meditation *about* the biblical text. The text would have been familiar to the audience as the cantata was performed in the liturgy immediately after the reading of the Gospel for Easter Sunday. Bach's revised version of his Easter cantata from 1725 is decidedly less naturalistic and now much closer to the type of contemplative oratorio represented by Stölzel's Passion.

In summary, Bach's revisions eliminate the operatic, dramatic character of the piece and change it, as Christoph Wolff describes, from "theatrical to devotional."[57] In other words, as soon as Bach calls BWV 249 an "oratorio," he eliminates some of its operatic features. In its emphasis on the contemplative devotion, the revised *Easter*

---

(*Wie schön leuchtet der Morgenstern*), and the performance of the second version of the *St. John Passion*; Wolff, "Under the Spell of Opera?" 7. However, it is more likely that Bach had originally planned to continue the chorale cantata cycle on Easter Sunday but had to change his plans after the librettist for the chorale cantatas was no longer available. The parody of the secular cantata would then be a similar reaction to this circumstance, as is the fragmentary revision of the *St. John Passion*. See Rathey, "Johann Sebastian Bach's *St. John Passion* from 1725: A Liturgical Interpretation," *Colloquium: Music, Worship, Arts* 4 (2007): 123–39, and Daniel Melamed, *Hearing Bach's Passions* (Oxford: Oxford University Press 2005), 66–77.

[56] Janz, "Oratorien: Entstehungsgeschichtlicher Kontext," 225.
[57] Wolff, "Under the Spell of Opera?" 9.

*Oratorio* resembles Stölzel's work that Bach had performed in 1734. The same concept of an oratorio is already present in the two earlier oratorios by Bach, composed for Christmas and Ascension. The *Ascension Oratorio*, BWV 11, written in 1735, is a parody based on two secular cantatas from 1725 and 1732 respectively. Only the recitatives and the two hymn-settings were newly composed.[58] The framing movements are an expression of praise; the affect is underscored by the use of festive trumpets and timpani. In the other movements Bach alternates between biblical texts and madrigalistic poetry. For the biblical texts, Bach's librettist borrowed a compilation from Johannes Bugenhagen's *Evangelienharmonie* (Gospel harmony, 1524).[59]

The biblical narrative of the ascension is, as usual, sung by a tenor. The only section with direct speech appears when two men in white clothes address the disciples: "Ihr Männer von Galiläa" (Ye men from Galilee). The section is set for tenor and bass. But even though Bach introduces a dramatic element by representing the two men with two singers, he limits this moment of verisimilitude by having the tenor sing both the evangelist and one of the two men.[60] Interpolated into the biblical narrative are reflective accompagnato recitatives, arias, and a hymn-setting. As in the *Christmas Oratorio*, Bach musically differentiates between gospel sections and the structure of the oratorio becomes clear: a short biblical text, sung by the tenor in secco recitatives, motivates reflective responses by other singers in either accompagnato recitatives or arias. After this, the biblical text continues and motivates further reflections.

The *Ascension Oratorio* lacks both dramatic character and operatic dialogue. Instead, Bach focuses on the narrative and a reflective interpretation of the biblical texts in the poetic interpolations. Instead of creating a "sacred opera," as Johann Gottfried Walther's definition spelled out, he chose to emphasize the narrative/ reflective element over the dramatic. He even revised his earlier Easter cantata in a way to fit this concept. Thus, he amalgamated elements from the traditional *historia* with the reflective oratorio model in Stölzel's Passion.

## The Christmas Oratorio and Bach's oratorio concept

This oratorio concept shapes all aspects of the *Christmas Oratorio*. The biblical text from Luke and Matthew serve as backbone for the libretto; they are interrupted by

[58] See Dürr, *Cantatas*, 336–40.

[59] See Martin Petzoldt, "Auswahl und Gebrauch geistlicher Texte durch Bach, dargestellt am Himmelfahrtsoratorium (BWV 11)," in *Kirche als Kulturfaktor*, ed. Ulrich Kühn, Festschrift Johannes Haupt (Hannover: Lutherisches Verlagshaus 1994), 88–115, here 98; see also Petzoldt, *Kantaten Kommentar* II, 922.

[60] It is clear from the original parts that both the narrative and the direct speech were sung by the same performer; cf. PL Kj Mus.ms. Bach, St. 356, tenor part.

*Table 4.2* **Leipzig cantata form and the *Christmas Oratorio***

| Normal Cantata | Part I | Part II | Part III | Part IV | Part V | Part VI |
|---|---|---|---|---|---|---|
| Chorus | Coro | Sinfonia | Coro | Coro | Coro | Coro |
|  | Evangelista | Evangelista | Evangelista | Evangelista | Evangelista | Evangelista |
| Recitative | Recitative | Chorale | Chorus | Recit./ Chorale | Coro/Rec. | Recitative |
| Aria | Aria | Evangelista | Recitative | Aria | Chorale | Aria |
|  | Chorale | Recitative | Chorale | Recit./ Chorale | Evangelista | Evangelista |
|  | Evangelista | Aria | Aria duetto | Aria | Aria | Chorale |
| Recitative | Chorale/ Recit. | Evangelista | Evangelista | Chorale | Evangelista | Evangelista |
| Aria | Aria | Chorale | Aria |  | Coro/Rec. | Recitative |
| Chorale | Chorale | Recitative | Recitative |  | Evangelista | Aria |
|  |  | Aria | Chorale |  | Aria terzetto | Recit. à 4 |
|  |  | Evangelista | Evangelista |  | Recitative | Chorale |
|  |  | Chorus | Chorale |  | Chorale |  |
|  |  | Recitative | Coro |  |  |  |
|  |  | Chorale |  |  |  |  |

reflections in recitatives, arias, and choral settings. The previous chapter has made clear how Bach's librettist uses this feature to interpret the biblical text from the perspective of the threefold coming of Christ. The six-partite structure of the oratorio, on the other hand, is determined by its performance context on six separate days. It consists of six self-contained parts, each of which resembles structurally a conventional church cantata, albeit in an expanded form. Table 4.2 shows how the blueprint of the six parts conforms to Bach's standard Leipzig cantata form. The resemblance is most clear in part I of the oratorio. The major difference is the inclusion of gospel recitatives, which are interpolated between the arias and recitatives.[61]

The seemingly small difference between the normal church cantata and the parts of the *Christmas Oratorio* points to an important structural difference. Bach's regular cantatas follow a hermeneutic pattern that can be described as *dictum–explicatio–applicatio–confirmation* (biblical text–explanation–application–confirmation).[62] The first movement presents a biblical verse (often referring back to the biblical

---

[61] See also the overview in Wolff, "Under the Spell of Opera?" 11.

[62] Cf. Wolff, *Bach, Learned Musician*, 255.

readings that preceded the cantata in the liturgy), followed by a recitative and an aria, which explore the meaning of this text, and a recitative/aria-pair, which interprets the moral and practical meaning therein. The final chorale is often a confirmation, sung in the name of the congregation. This outline of the cantatas follows a standard sermon format, as they were preached in Bach's time.[63] The *Christmas Oratorio* maps this pattern albeit on a smaller scale. The opening movements are not biblical dicta but general expressions of praise or, as in the case of part II, an instrumental movement that sets the stage for the following pastoral scene. The first biblical text appears in the second movement of each part. The text is then interpreted in the ensuing movements, followed by the next section of biblical text, which, in turn, triggers a new sequence of interpretations. Although the parts of the oratorio might look like cantatas (and they fulfill the same function within the worship service), their hermeneutical principle is slightly different.

Within this framework, the six parts are realized with a large degree of diversity. Part II begins with an instrumental sinfonia instead of a choral movement; in part III Bach repeats the opening chorus at the end, and the final chorale settings in each of the six parts can either be a simple four-part setting or an elaborate setting with obbligato instruments and instrumental interludes. The number of movements that follow a section from the biblical text is variable as well. The part I presents a rather regular pattern. Both sections of the gospel text are followed by recitative, aria, and chorale. But the sequence of movements in part II is already less regular: the first gospel text is followed by a chorale, the second by a recitative and an aria, and the third by the succession of chorale, recitative, and aria. Although the number of movements following a section of the gospel text is flexible, they are always an immediate reaction to the biblical texts.

The meditations on the biblical texts can sometimes be misconstrued as utterances of characters from the biblical narrative. Chapter 3 has shown that the naturalistic identification of the alto voice in the oratorio with the Virgin Mary obscures the symbolic meaning of the alto as the divine voice in the human heart. Another example is the movement "Schlafe mein Liebster" (no. 19) from the second part of the *Christmas Oratorio*. After the angel's announcement that the shepherds will

---

[63] For the relationship between Bach's cantatas and contemporary sermons, and for the structure of a typical sermon in Bach's time in particular, see Jochen Arnold, *Von Gott poetisch-musikalisch reden: Gottes verborgenes und offenbares Handeln in Bachs Kantaten* (Göttingen: Vandenhoeck & Ruprecht, 2009), 60–69. The Leipzig superintendent Salomon Deyling employed a similar structure in a cycle of sermons preached in Leipzig in the year before the performance of the *Christmas Oratorio*. In the published outline of the sermons from 1734, every sermon comprises three steps: 1. "Eine herrliche Glaubens-Lehre" (a marvelous doctrine of faith); 2. "Eine nöthige Lebens-Pflicht" (a necessary duty in life); 3. "Ein süsser Glaubens-Trost" (a sweet consolation of faith); Deyling, *Herrliche Dinge wurden in der Stadt Gottes geprediget, und in einem Jahrgange 1734 der Gemeine zu St. Nicholai in Leipzig auf jeden Sonn- und Festtag . . . vorgetragen* (Leipzig, [1734]).

find the child in a manger, swaddled in cloth (no. 16), follows a chorale setting, an accompagnato recitative, and the aforementioned aria. The recitative encourages the shepherds to sing this lullaby for the child: "Sleep, my Most Beloved, enjoy your rest." Albert Schweitzer and others have argued that this movement as a lullaby was out of place, since the shepherds had not even embarked on their journey to the manger and thus could not possibly sing a song for the newborn child.[64] If we read the oratorio as a coherent narrative, the lullaby indeed seems out of place. But if we view the text instead as a reaction of the individual believer to the gospel narrative, the lullaby makes sense: both the accompagnato recitative and the following aria meditate on the announcement of the angel by speaking to the shepherds, but from a place *outside* of the narrative, removed by time and space. The words are spoken (or sung) by the faithful believer who immerses herself into the action; not by one of the acting characters.

Our exploration of Bach's view of oratorios shows that his concept is not that of a sacred opera. Bach's changes to the earlier version of BWV 249, which turned the Easter "cantata" into an Easter "oratorio," have eliminated some of the natural-istic, dramatic features of the piece. A similar reduction of dramatic features can be seen in Bach's parody of two older movements in the *Christmas Oratorio*. The *aria à 2*, "Herr, dein Mitleid, dein Erbarmen" (no. 29) was originally a duet for alto and tenor in the *Hercules Cantata*, BWV 213, in which Hercules and Virtue engaged in an agitated love dialogue. The version in the oratorio lacks this dramatic quality: the two voices sing the same text, and Bach is more interested in projecting the idea of love and harmony as a principle than in staging an amorous dialogue. The same is true for the terzet "Ach, wenn wird die Zeit erscheinen" (no. 51) in part V of the ora-torio. The original version of the movement probably belonged to a secular cantata wherein three characters engaged in a conversation. In the oratorio, Bach juxtaposes two texts, one sung by the two outer voices, the other sung by the alto. But even here, the three singers cannot be identified as characters from the narrative. Rather, we hear the juxtaposition of doubt (in soprano and tenor) and confidence (alto) about the presence of Jesus in the human heart.

The libretto did not leave much opportunity for dramatic action. Most of the oratorio is narrative; only on two occasions do characters appear in direct speech: the angel in part II (no. 13) and King Herod in part VI (no. 55). Additionally, Bach composes three choral movements based on biblical texts that were spoken by groups of people (turba choruses): the choir of angels in part II (no. 21), the choir of shepherds in part III (no. 26), and the chorus of the wise men in part V (no. 45) of the oratorio. Bach lets pass two other opportunities for direct speech in order to not interrupt the flow of the piece. Movement 16 continues the announcement of the angel from mvt. 13, but instead of giving the sentence to the soprano who had

---

[64]  Schweitzer, *Bach*, vol. 2, 308–9; see also Blankenburg, *Weihnachts-Oratorium*, 65.

sung the part of the angel before, the words are simply reported by the evangelist. A second passage of the libretto that would have lent itself for direct speech is no. 50 in part V. The evangelist reports in a secco recitative that King Herod had gathered the high priests and inquired about the birthplace of Christ (Mt 2:5–6). The answer from the high priests is direct speech; but Bach decides to emphasize the quotation from the Old Testament instead (Mt 2:8), which is embedded into the answer. The beginning of the answer of the high priests (mm. 6–8) is still rendered as a simple secco recitative. The voice-leading only changes with the quotation; the tenor sings an arioso (indicated by the tempo marking "andante"), accompanied by a continuous stream of eighth notes in the bc. The autograph score shows that this passage was of some importance for Bach. We will return to this movement chapter 5 when we reconstruct the compositional process.

There was no reason why Bach and his librettist should not have introduced more direct speech and individual characters. Even if there were regulations (explicit or implicit) that prohibited the use of paraphrased biblical texts in the Good Friday vespers (a tradition that Bach had broken in 1734 with the performance of Stölzel's Passion), the *Hauptmusik* for Sundays and festival days did not have any regulations of this kind. In contrast to the Passions, Bach was not required to quote any biblical text at all. Nonetheless, the transformation of the Easter cantata into an oratorio and the form of the *Ascension Oratorio* have shown that Bach intentionally conceived the pieces the way he did. Bach and his librettist realized the *Christmas Oratorio* as a contemplative oratorio that combined the biblical narrative with the metanarrative of the Second Coming (and eventual Third Coming) of Christ into the human heart.

# 5

# Planning the Oratorio

## The sources

Inspired by his encounter with Stölzel's Passion oratorio and the news about oratorio performances in Dresden, Bach, supported by his librettist, began preparing an oratorio to be performed during the Christmas season of 1734. The sources allow us to trace the development of the project, the planning, and even the shaping of single musical ideas in the final composition. The reconstruction of Bach's compositional process is possible because Bach's score, the performance parts, and the original print of the libretto are extant.[1] The main source comes from Johann Sebastian Bach's autograph score (Mus. ms. Bach P 32), housed today in the Deutsche Staatsbibliothek Berlin-Preußischer Kulturbesitz. The piece originally consisted of six independent scores, one for each of the six parts of the oratorio.[2] Each part of the score has its own title line, indicating the liturgical function, and each ends with the remark "Fine SDGl [Soli Deo Gloria] 1734."[3] The way the score is listed in Carl Philipp Emanuel Bach's estate catalogue[4] suggests that the whole piece was not yet bound in the late eighteenth century but that each part was kept with its respective performance parts wrapped in cover paper.[5] The score was not bound until the

---

[1] Every study of Bach's compositional process, like this book, is deeply indebted to Robert L. Marshall's landmark study *The Compositional Process of J. S. Bach. A Study of the Autograph Scores of Vocal Works*, 2 vols. (Princeton: Princeton University Press 1972).

[2] The score is accessible in an excellent facsimile edition by Alfred Dürr: Johann Sebastian Bach, *Weihnachts-Oratorium*, BWV 248, (Leipzig: Deutscher Verlag für Musik, 1984); and online at http://www.bachdigital.de

[3] The fourth part ends with the remark "Fine" (end), but this difference is probably just an accident and not in any way significant.

[4] See NBA II/6 KB, 7. It is likely that Carl Philipp Emanuel Bach did not inherit the score from his father directly. Peter Wollny has shown that the score for BWV 248 first went to Johann Christoph Friedrich Bach; only toward the middle of the 1770s did the score end up in the possession of Carl Philipp Emanuel; see Wollny, "Johann Christoph Friedrich Bach und die Teilung des väterlichen Erbes," *Bach-Jahrbuch* 87 (2001): 63–66.

[5] Cf. NBA II/6 KB, 11.

nineteenth century, a procedure that was reversed in the second half of the twentieth century.

The music in the score is in Bach's own hand, with a few additions by later hands, which clarify passages that were hard to read (especially in corrections), indicate musical forces if they were missing in the score, and add to the texts; the latter two based on the performance parts.[6] The most extensive additions and clarifications were made by Carl Philipp Emanuel Bach's main copyist, Johann Heinrich Michel, who was commissioned by Carl Philipp Emanuel to copy the score in the 1780s.[7] Johann Sebastian Bach's autograph score for the *Christmas Oratorio* is an indispensable source and one that shows the genesis of the work. Movements that are parodies from earlier works appear in clear handwriting and show only occasional corrections and changes, but the newly composed movements have a multitude of corrections and revisions. In most instances, the score immediately reveals whether a movement is an original composition or a parody.

The second main source for the oratorio is that of the original performance parts, which were copied by Bach and his students at the St. Thomas School.[8] Bach himself revised the parts; he corrected mistakes, added performance instructions such as slurs, trills, staccato marks, dynamics, and the like.[9] Finally, he composed additional flute parts for some of the movements in part II of the oratorio, which had not been present in the score. Bach did not always pay much attention to the performance material of his cantatas; consequently, his attention to detail in the parts for the *Christmas Oratorio* shows a special interest in that piece. The parts are exclusively based on the autograph score; this is the case even for parody movements. The doublet parts for the last part of the oratorio are the exception. The part books for the two violins, the bc, and a transposed organ part belong to an earlier cantata (BWV 248a), which is now lost. The parts reflect earlier versions of the movements,

---

[6] NBA II/6 KB, 75. Further additions, like page numbers and marks by later copyists can be neglected here in this context.

[7] The copy is now in the Bibliothèque Nationale in Paris, F-Pn D. 551 (1–6). A scan of this manuscript is available online at http://gallica.bnf.fr/ark:/12148/btv1b84511589. While there is no evidence that C. P. E. Bach ever performed the entire piece in Hamburg, he used the opening movement in his Easter Cantata *Jauchzet, frohlocket*, H 804, from 1778; see Stephen Lewis Clark, *The Occasional Choral Works of C. P. E. Bach* (PhD diss., Princeton University, 1984), 154–74; see also Clemens Harasim, *Die Quartalsmusiken von Carl Philipp Emanuel Bach: ihre Quellen, ihre Stilistik und die Bedeutung des Parodieverfahrens* (Marburg: Tectum, 2010), 177–83. Carl Philipp Emanuel Bach also planned to borrow the chorale setting "Ich steh an deiner Krippen hier" (248/59) for his Passion for 1769 (with the text "O Jesu hilf zur selben Zeit"); however, he deleted the chorale again before the performance; see introduction to *Carl Philipp Emanuel Bach. The Complete Works, Vol IV/4.1: Passion according to St. Matthew 1769*, ed. Ulrich Leisinger (Los Altos: PHI, 2008), xiv.

[8] See the overview in NBA II/6 KB, 121–27 as well as the updated overview at http://www.bach-digital.de

[9] Cf. Dürr, *Weihnachts-Oratorium*, 15.

but Bach made several changes so that they could be used for the performance of the oratorio. We will return to this earlier piece in our discussion of part VI of the oratorio in chapter 11 of this book.

The third group of musical sources are the scores and parts for the cantatas that were parodied in the *Christmas Oratorio*. The autograph scores for all three cantatas, BWV 213, 214, and 215, are preserved and show the origins of these earlier movements before they became part of the oratorio.[10] Finally, the print of the libretto that was sold to the members of the congregation in Leipzig in 1734 has been preserved in several copies.[11] The text occasionally shows slight variations in comparison to the score, which suggests that Bach either made some minor changes to the libretto or that the handwritten manuscript he had received from the librettist was changed before it went into print. We will return to some discrepancies between the libretto print and Bach's score in our analysis.

## First plans

The *Christmas Oratorio* was planned in close collaboration between Bach and his librettist. This collaboration involved the selection of the movements from earlier works that were to be parodied and probably also decisions regarding their placement within the oratorio. The name of the librettist is not mentioned on the print of the libretto from 1734 and Bach's score also does not identify the author. Nonetheless, Bach scholarship agrees that Christian Friedrich Henrici (1700–1764), known by the pen-name Picander, is a likely candidate for the authorship of the libretto.[12] Picander held the title of "Ober-Post-Commissarius" in Leipzig and was known as quite a prolific author of occasional poetry. Bach's collaboration with the poet began in 1725. Picander wrote the texts for the *St. Matthew Passion*, BWV 244, from 1727, and he had also provided the libretto for one of the parody models Bach had borrowed for the oratorio, the *Hercules Cantata, Laßt uns sorgen,*

---

[10] All three scores are housed in Staatsbibliothek zu Berlin—Preußischer Kulturbesitz: BWV 213 (D-B Mus. ms. Bach P 125); BWV 214 (D-B Mus. ms. Bach P 41, Faszikel 2); BWV 215 (D-B Mus. ms. Bach P 139).

[11] Two extant copies are known; one is owned by the Bach Archiv Leipzig; the second one is transmitted in a convolute of prints collected by Merseburg teacher Balthasar Hoffmann (Universitäts und Landesbibliothek Sachsen-Anhalt in Halle, 76 L 1034 (1734–35); see the description in Marc-Roderich Pfau, "Ein unbekanntes Leipziger Kantatenheft aus dem Jahr 1735: Neues zum Thema Bach und Stölzel," *Bach-Jahrbuch* 94 (2008): 101 and 117. For a facsimile edition of the copy at the Bach Archiv, see: *Weihnachts-Oratorium BWV 248: Faksimile des originalen Textdruckes von 1734*, Faksimile-Reihe Bachscher Werke und Schriftstücke, Neue Folge 6, with an introduction by Christoph Wolff (Leipzig: Bach-Archiv, 2012).

[12] Cf. Dürr, *Weihnachts-Oratorium*, 4; Blankenburg, *Weihnachts-Oratorium*, 21; Walter, *Weihnachtsoratorium*, 14.

BWV 213. What sheds some doubts on Picander's authorship is that the text for the oratorio does not appear in Picander's collections of poetry, which were published between 1727 and 1751 and contain the texts for other works composed by Bach.[13] Picander might have had some reason to exclude the text, but it is also possible that the libretto for the oratorio was written by some other poet in Leipzig. Bach collaborated with a number of authors during this time, such as the unknown author of the text for the other parody model, BWV 214 (*Tönet, ihr Pauken! Erschallet Trompeten!*), or the author of the text for BWV 215 (*Preise dein Glücke, gesegnetes Sachsen*), Johann Christoph Clauder. The question of authorship must remain open, but what we can say, however, is that neither poetic style nor theological reasons speak against Picander. The theological profile of the oratorio, as outlined in chapter 3, echoes Christmas libretti by Picander that are published in his printed collections. What also speaks in Picander's favor is that he is the only poet who provided Bach with texts both for smaller cantatas and with larger libretti for works like the *St. Matthew Passion*, BWV 244 and *St. Mark Passion*, BWV 247. Picander therefore remains the most likely author for the libretto of the *Christmas Oratorio*.

Inextricably linked to the matter of the librettist is the question of when Bach decided to parody some of his secular cantatas into an oratorio. It has been suggested that Bach had already composed the cantatas *Laßt uns sorgen, laßt uns wachen*, BWV 213, by September 1733 and *Tönet, ihr Pauken! Erschallet, Trompeten*, BWV 214, by December 1733, with the objective of using them in the *Christmas Oratorio*.[14] This, however, cannot substantiated by the sources. While it is very likely that Bach intended to reuse the secular cantatas with a sacred text, as he did with numerous secular cantatas in Leipzig,[15] there is no evidence that plans for the composition of a *Christmas Oratorio* had begun to emerge in the fall or winter of 1733. The assumption that the secular cantatas were conceived with specific sacred versions in mind from the outset perpetuates the frequent misconception that the sacred works were of higher value and importance, and that Bach's religious compositions represented his "ultimate goal" ("Endzweck") while the secular cantatas were only a necessary byproduct.

---

[13] Picander, *Ernst-Schertzhaffte und Satyrische Gedichte*, 5 parts (Leipzig 1727, 1729, 1732, 1737, and 1751).

[14] This was suggested by Wilhelm Rust in the preface for vol. 5.2 of the old *Bach Ausgabe* (Leipzig, 1856), viii–ix; it was later repeated by Friedrich Smend, *Kirchen-Kantaten V* (Berlin: Christlicher Zeitschriftenverlag, 1966), 33. Most recently Christoph Wolff has alluded to this possibility, see Wolff, "Bachs weltliche Kantaten: Repertoire und Kontext," in *Die Welt der Bach Kantaten II: Johann Sebastian Bachs weltliche Kantaten*, ed. Christoph Wolff (Stuttgart/Kassel: Metzler/Bärenreiter 1997), 14–15. Richard D. P. Jones in his recent study of Bach's creative development still considers this a possibility, see Jones, *The Creative Development of Johann Sebastian Bach, Volume II: Music to Delight the Spirit* (Oxford: Oxford University Press 2013), 309.

[15] This possibility has been suggested by Hans-Joachim Schulze, *Die Bach-Kantaten*, 634.

If the *Christmas Oratorio* had been projected as early as fall 1733, this would suggest that other secular pieces from that time would have been conceived as models for the oratorio as well. A viable model for a parody would have been *Schleichet, spielende Wellen,* BWV 206, originally planned for the celebration of the birthday of Elector August III on October 7, 1734. The unknown librettist had already written the text for the piece and Bach had embarked on composing it when he learned that the Elector would visit Leipzig during the Michaelmas fair from October 2 through 6. Instead of a birthday cantata, Bach now needed a piece that celebrated the first anniversary of August's election as king of Poland. The composer abandoned the fragment of BWV 206, and within just a few days wrote the *dramma per musica Preise dein Glücke, gesegnetes Sachsen,* BWV 215.[16] It would take several years (probably until 1736) before Bach completed the score for BWV 206.[17] If Bach had had long-term plans for the *Christmas Oratorio,* BWV 206 would have been a possible source for parody movements as the libretto for the birthday cantata contains two choral movements and four arias. If the oratorio had been planned in advance, several of these movements could have been borrowed for the sacred work, but this is not the case. The texts for the cantata show no resemblance in rhyme, meter, or number of lines to any of the movements of the *Christmas Oratorio.* Therefore, we can rule out that the text for the secular cantata was written with a later parody in the oratorio in mind. Instead, Bach parodied in his oratorio an aria from the cantata he composed in place of BWV 206, "Durch die vom Eifer entflammeten Waffen" from BWV 215, a piece that was not composed before the beginning of October 1734.

A second cantata, composed about the same time as BWV 215, is the model for the last part of the *Christmas Oratorio.* Andreas Glöckner has suggested that the parts for the lost cantata (BWV 248a) were probably written in September/October 1734, and he has proposed that it might have been a cantata for Michaelmas on September 29, 1734.[18] Again, the text for the last part of the oratorio could only have been written *after* the completion of the music for that cantata. The libretto for the *Christmas Oratorio* was thus conceived after early October 1734, and Bach most likely embarked on composing the oratorio during the fall of that year. As Bach's interest in the genre "oratorio" was sparked by those of Hasse and Stölzel, concrete plans for the parody movements from BWV 213 and 214 most likely emerged in the second half of 1734, rather than in the final months of 1733. This does not rule out that Bach kept the secular cantatas close to his desk for a possible sacred parody, but these vague plans did not necessarily include the possibility of a large-scale oratorio.

[16] See for the genesis of the piece, see Stephen A. Crist, "The Question of Parody in Bach's Cantata 'Preise dein Glücke, gesegnetes Sachsen,' BWV 215," *Bach Perspectives* 1 (1995): 135–61.

[17] Cf. Dürr, *Cantatas,* 847, and Wolff, *Bach, Learned Musician,* 360–64.

[18] Andreas Glöckner, "Eine Michaeliskantate als Parodievorlage für den sechsten Teil des Bachschen Weihnachts-Oratoriums?" *Bach-Jahrbuch* 86 (2000): 317–26.

Most of the work on the oratorio was done in the two-and-a-half months between the electoral visit in early October and Christmas 1734.[19]

It is not entirely clear what other pieces Bach composed or performed while completing the oratorio, as his calendar for his cantata performances and compositions in late 1734 is incomplete. Although he must have performed cantatas on the Sundays in October and November 1734, only one piece can be dated with some certainty: the cantata *Herr Christ, der einige Gotts Sohn*, BWV 96, was probably performed on October 24. The piece had been composed in 1724 as a part of Bach's chorale cantata cycle and was now repeated about ten years later.[20] No new compositions of regular Sunday cantatas from this time are known, and so it is likely that his students sang exclusively older works in late 1734. The only new composition after the electoral visit in early October was a cantata for the introduction of the new rector of the St. Thomas School, Johann August Ernesti, BWV Anh. I, 19 (*Thomana saß annoch betrübt*), the music of which is lost.[21] The performance took place on November 21, 1734. The libretto by Johann August Landvoigt (1715–66) a pupil of the school, contains a charming little echo movement (no. 4), which is noteworthy because Bach was just then transforming the echo aria "Treues Echo dieser Orten" from BWV 213 into a movement for part IV of the *Christmas Oratorio*. While the movement does not stand in a parody relationship to the other two pieces, it does demonstrate Bach's interest in echo-techniques at this time outside of the oratorio. Besides performances of earlier pieces of his own, Bach might also have performed cantatas by other composers. The performance of Georg Philipp Telemann's cantata *Machet die Tore weit* (TVWV 1:1074) on the first Sunday of Advent 1734 is documented. It was the last cantata Bach had to perform until Christmas, as the liturgical traditions in Leipzig prohibited the use of concerted music during the "quiet" time of Advent.[22] The use of older pieces of his own or of works by other composers gave Bach ample time in fall 1734 to put together the *Christmas Oratorio*. He and his librettist had several months to develop a concept, plan the outline, write the libretto, and finally compose the piece. Considering that Bach had composed the cantatas of his first Leipzig cycles within a week, and that it took him only a few days to write BWV 215, there is no reason to assume that the concrete plans for BWV 248 materialized any time sooner that October 1734.

---

[19] While the simultaneous conception of original and parody is the case in the *Trauerode* and the *St. Matthew Passion* (two pieces that were written at about the same time), there is no evidence that Bach proceeded in a similar way with the piece for Christmas 1734.

[20] See Markus Rathey, "Der zweite Leipziger Jahrgang—Choralkantaten," in *Bachs Kantaten. Das Handbuch*, ed. Reinmar Emans and Sven Hiemke, Das Bach-Handbuch 1/1 (Laaber: Laaber-Verlag, 2012), 388–90.

[21] See *BachDok* II, 358 and 357. It is possible that the Ernesti-cantata featured parodies as well, see NBA I/39 KB, 16.

[22] Günther Stiller, *Johann Sebastian Bach and Liturgical Life in Leipzig*, ed. Robin A. Leaver, trans. H. J. A. Bouman et al. (St. Louis: Concordia, 1984), 58–60.

The genesis of the *Christmas Oratorio* can be divided into three stages: (1) a planning stage, (2) a composition stage, and (3) a revision stage. The *planning stage* includes the conceptualization of the overall structure of the piece, the selection of the parody movements, their placement within this structure, and also the writing of the libretto. The *composition stage* encompasses the parody of the earlier movements as well as the new composition of the remaining movements. During the composition stage, Bach made some changes to the original plans that have an impact on the overall concept of the oratorio (like the balance between individual movements and the "dramatic flow") as well. During the *revision stage*, Bach made minor adjustments to the musical substance of the movements by adding musical details or by clarifying the performance instructions. It is significant that these final revisions affect both the newly composed movements as well as the parodies. Differentiating between these three stages will help view the oratorio as a unity consisting of parts that were not only unified by an overarching concept but that are connected by an artistic vision that transcends the sum of its parts.

## The "parody problem"

At some point in the second half of 1734, Bach and his librettist decided to embark on the creation of an oratorio for the upcoming Christmas season. A plan had to be worked out, the parody movements needed to be selected. This selection process included, as the previous chapters have shown, situating the movements within a formal pattern that outlined a specific theological-narrative concept. The general outline of each of the six parts had to be drafted, and finally the text had to be written accordingly. Thus, the librettist had to work under certain formal constraints, a factum to which an eighteenth-century poet was accustomed. Early on in the planning process, Bach and his librettist had to decide on which older movements should (and could) be parodied. When Bach decided to make extensive use of older works that had been composed for a different text, he followed a convention that was familiar in the eighteenth century and was employed by composers such as Handel, Hasse, and Gluck. While the transformation of a secular into a sacred piece was a familiar practice, it was not entirely uncontested. The Hamburg critic Johann Mattheson—one of the writers on music from the first half of the eighteenth century who had contributed significantly to the terminological and esthetic differentiation between sacred and secular music—criticized, in *Der musicalische Patriot* (1728), the reuse of opera-melodies in religious compositions: "Now no one will readily approve that a melody . . . which has just been heard by thousands of people at the opera, should be sung, by way of a parody, to sacred words."[23] As sharp

---

[23] Johann Mattheson, *Der musicalische Patriot* (Hamburg: [s.n.], 1728), 109; in "Parody and Contrafactum: A Terminological Clarification," trans. Robert Falck, *Musical Quarterly* 65 (1979): 5–6.

as Mattheson's criticism was, it had only tangential relevance for Bach. The critic's main concern are the implications of an intertextual *contamination* of the sacred composition with the text of the secular original. This problem was much more crucial in the case of opera, Mattheson's main focus, because the pieces were performed repeatedly and certain melodies were well known to the audience. Bach's secular compositions, on the other hand, were performed only on a single occasion, and hearing the melodies more than a year after their original performance would not likely have triggered a recollection of the original text. While it cannot be ruled out that movements might have sounded familiar to some listeners, it was less probable than in the case of a popular operatic melody.

The "parody problem" was not a dilemma for Bach and his contemporaries. The esthetic predicament that the music had not originally been composed for the words with which it was now combined would be a concern of a later time and not of the eighteenth century.[24] Gottfried Ephraim Scheibel pointed out in 1722 that a parody was not an esthetic problem as long as the model and the resulting piece shared the same affect: "I don't know what one could object to. I take a secular composition from a cantata, and make a parody upon it of a spiritual nature, and express thereby the same affect as the original composition."[25] Most composers (including Bach himself) took a somewhat practical approach to the issue, as did Bach's cousin Johann Gottfried Walther in a letter from 1729 about the parody of a wedding cantata: "The enclosed parody on the wedding cantata which I recently sent will clear up the first point as to its origin. . . . The cantata "Lobsinget ihr Christen" is likewise of this kind. It originally had another text, but was subsequently supplied with this one for the sake of utility."[26] Instead of being a problem, parody was part of the compositional process. It allowed Bach to return to older compositions, to adapt them, and to make small changes that were not always due to the new text but could also represent an improvement of the older piece.[27]

[24] Cf. Ludwig Finscher, "Zum Parodieproblem bei Bach," in *Bach-Interpretationen*, ed. Martin Geck, FS Walter Blankenburg zum 65. Geburtstag (Göttingen: Vandenhoeck & Ruprecht 1969), 94: a parody is "zumindest ästhetisch auf den ersten Blick befremdlich." For the evaluation of parodies in the nineteenth century, and Bach's parodies in particular, see: Nicole Schwindt-Gross, "Parodie um 1800: Zu den Quellen im deutschsprachigen Raum und ihrer Problematik im Zeitalter des künstlerischen Autonomie-Gedankens," *Die Musikforschung* 41 (1988): 16–45; and Wolfgang Sandberger, *Das Bachbild Philipp Spittas: Ein Beitrag zur Geschichte der Bachrezeption im 19. Jahrhundert*, Beihefte zum Archiv für Musikwissenschaft 39, (Stuttgart: Steiner, 1996), 277–286.

[25] Gottfried Ephraim Scheibel, *Zufällige Gedanken von der Kirchenmusik* (Frankfurt and Leipzig, 1722); English trans. after Falck, "Parody and Contrafactum," 5.

[26] See Wilhelm Jerger, "Ein unbekannter Brief Johann Gottfried Walthers an Heinrich Bokemeyer," *Die Musikforschung* 7 (1954): 207; English transl. after Falck, "Parody and Contrafactum," 6.

[27] This has been pointed out by Hans-Joachim Schulze, "Bachs Parodieverfahren," in Wolff, *Die Welt der Bach Kantaten II*, 183.

Werner Neumann has differentiated between two types of parody in Bach's works; the *poetic parody* ("dichterische Parodie") and the *compositional parody* ("kompositorische Parodie").[28] The first category describes pieces for which a librettist wrote a new text for an already existing composition. Bach only had to make small adjustments in the composition in order to improve the relationship between music and text. For parodies of the second category, Bach adapted an older composition to an already existing text, often a biblical verse or a liturgical text from the ordinary of the Mass. The small Kyrie-Gloria masses (BWV 233–236) as well as most of the movements from the *B-Minor Mass*, BWV 232, belong to the second category. In contrast, Bach's parodies of secular cantatas from his time in Cöthen that were adapted for the liturgy in Leipzig belong to the group of poetic parodies. The "dichterische Parodie" is also often characterized by *en bloc parodies*, in which entire cantatas (or larger parts thereof) are provided with a new text, conventionally excluding only the recits. In his compositional parodies, on the other hand, Bach often selected individual movements from several models and combined them with new material.[29] The parodies in the *Christmas Oratorio* are poetic parodies; for parts I–III, Bach's librettist wrote new texts for movements that were for the most part borrowed from the secular cantatas *Laßt uns sorgen*, BWV 213, and *Tönet, ihr Pauken*, BWV 214 (see table 5.1). One additional movement was borrowed from the cantata *Preise dein Glücke, gesegnetes Sachsen*, BWV 215, while the terzet "Ach, wenn wird die Zeit erscheinen" (no. 51) is taken from an unknown model. Part VI of the oratorio is almost entirely based on a sacred cantata of unknown origin. The parody practice in the first four parts resembles the en bloc technique that Neumann has associated with the poetic parody. Yet, Bach does not maintain the original order in which they appear in the model. Instead, the movements are rearranged to fit both the dramatic and musical trajectory of the oratorio, and this provided Bach and his librettist with a greater degree of freedom than in a conventional en bloc parody.

The expanded form of the standard church cantata required two framing movements and two arias for each part of the oratorio. Since the final movement was a chorale, Bach could borrow parodies only for the opening movements while the final hymn-settings had to be newly composed. The two secular cantatas contained four choral movements. As Bach had decided to begin part II of the oratorio with an instrumental pastoral instead of a vocal piece, he already had the opening movements for five of his six parts. The opening movement for part VI was borrowed from the now lost church cantata BWV 248a.

[28] Werner Neumann, "Über Ausmaß und Wesen des Bachschen Parodieverfahrens," *Bach-Jahrbuch* 51 (1965): 72–73.

[29] Neumann, "Über Ausmaß und Wesen des Bachschen Parodieverfahrens," 72–73; see also Finscher, "Parodieproblem," 97.

*Table 5.1* **Parodies in the *Christmas Oratorio***

| I | 1. Coro "Jauchzet, frohlocket" | 214/1 "Tönet, ihr Pauken" |
|---|---|---|
| | 4. Aria "Bereite dich, Zion" | 213/9 "Ich will dich nicht hören" |
| | 8. Aria "Großer Herr, o starker König" | 214/7 "Kron und Preis gekrönter Damen" |
| II | 15. Aria "Frohe Hirten" | 214/5 "Fromme Musen" |
| | 19. Aria "Schlafe, mein Liebster" | 213/3 "Schlafe, mein Liebster" |
| III | 24. Coro "Herrscher des Himmels" | 214/9 "Blühet, ihr Linden" |
| | 29. Aria Duetto "Herr, dein Mitleid" | 213/11 "Ich bin deine" |
| IV | 36. Chorus "Fallt mit Danken" | 213/1 "Laßt uns sorgen" |
| | 39. Aria "Flößt, mein Heiland" | 213/5 "Treues Echo" |
| | 41. Aria "Ich will nur dir zu Ehren" | 213/7 "Auf meinen Flügeln" |
| V | 47. Aria "Erleucht auch" | 215/7 "Durch die vom Eifer" |
| | 51. Aria Terzetto "Ach, wenn wird die Zeit" | [model unknown] |
| VI | 54, 56, 57, 60–64 | based on a now lost earlier sacred cantata (BWV 248a) |

Bach had limited options, both musically and theologically, when placing the movements. The cantata for first day of Christmas demanded a highly festive opening movement, so that the opening chorus from BWV 214, featuring trumpets and drums, was the most appropriate choice. The second day of Christmas was traditionally celebrated as St. Stephen's Day, remembering the first martyr of the Christian Church; even if Bach did not refer to the martyr in part II of the oratorio, the Epistle reading and the sermon was probably on St. Stephen, so that Bach would need to maintain the more subdued character of the day. The final movement of BWV 214 was used as opening movement for part III, which again features trumpets and drums.

For the remaining parts of the oratorio, Bach had the framing movements of BWV 213 at his disposal. He selected BWV 213/1 to open the cantata for New Year's Day (part IV), and he originally intended to use the final movement of BWV 213 for part V, performed on the Sunday after the New Year. For the selection of the arias from the secular cantatas, Bach arranged the existing pieces into a sequence that featured primarily arias in a regular *da capo* form for the first half of the oratorio; beginning with mvt. 31, though, he favored modified *da capo* forms and through-composed arias (see chap. 3 for the dramatic function of this order). A second pattern that influenced the placement of the arias is tonality, in that one of the arias is normally in major and the other one in minor. The only exception is in the part V where both arias are in a minor key, which suggests that the pattern was probably of only secondary importance to Bach:[30]

|          | 1st aria | 2nd aria |          | 1st aria | 2nd aria |
|----------|----------|----------|----------|----------|----------|
| Part I   | A minor  | D major  | Part IV  | C major  | d minor  |
| Part II  | E minor  | G major  | Part V   | F♯ minor | B minor  |
| Part III | A major  | B minor  | Part VI  | A major  | B minor  |

With most of the movements from BWV 213 and 214 having been used in parts I–IV, Bach needed to look for new models for the final two parts of the oratorio. When he decided to use one aria from BWV 215, he chose the only one that had been newly composed for this cantata. The two other arias in BWV 215 were parodies themselves (at least in part), and the martial affect of the movements would have been out of place in part V of the oratorio.[31] The terzet in part V is puzzling, though: no parody model exists for it, although the meticulous and clear handwriting in the autograph score suggests that it *is* a parody and not a new composition. We suggest a possible model for this movement in chapter 10.

## Liturgy as a performative context

With the sequence of parody movements in place, and with the understanding that the oratorio would consist of six parts, the librettist could embark on writing the text for the oratorio. Each of the six parts of the *Christmas Oratorio* is performed at the place in the liturgy normally occupied by a cantata. This posed a particular challenge for the structure of the oratorio. The cantata, the Hauptmusik, (principal music) was performed between the reading of the Gospel and the sermon, which was usually based on a specific biblical text. The cantata was followed by the congregational singing of the German version of the creed ("Wir glauben all' an einen Gott") before the preacher began with his sermon. The cantata was thus closely embedded into the liturgical framework, as it constituted a bridge between Gospel

---

[30]  Ulrich Siegele has suggested that this pattern was of major importance for Bach; however, Bach breaks with the pattern in part V, and in part VI this pattern was already predetermined by the model of BWV 248a; see Ulrich Siegele, "Das Parodieverfahren des Weihnachtsoratoriums von J.S. Bach als dispositionelles Problem," in *Studien zur Musikgeschichte: Eine Festschrift für Ludwig Finscher*, ed. Annegrit Laubenthal (Kassel: Bärenreiter, 1995), 258–59.

[31]  See Crist, "The Compositional History," 152–57.

and sermon. The text of the Hauptmusik frequently referred directly to the readings of the day, often to the Gospel but in numerous occasions to the Epistle reading as well.[32]

The cantata was repeated in the afternoon vespers service. The sermon in those services was based on the Epistle for the day.[33] The cantata was less closely embedded into the sequence of readings and stood at the beginning of the vespers service, following an organ prelude and a Latin motet. The sermon came much later in the liturgy. Thus the cantata in the afternoon service was less a direct reflection of the reading and more of a general reminder of the liturgical character of the specific day. Considering that the cantata was part of the liturgy in the morning service, it is noteworthy that the Gospel texts that serve as the basis for the *Christmas Oratorio* align only in part with the Gospel readings for those days. As table 5.2 shows, the librettist had to rearrange some of the texts from the Gospels in order to distribute the narrative to the feast days. The table also lists the texts on which the preachers based their sermons during the Christmas season 1734/35.

The prescribed Gospel texts for the six feast days would not have constituted a coherent narrative. For example, the Gospel for the first day of Christmas was Luke 2:1–14, and the sermon would have been based on that text. On the second day of Christmas, the reading was the continuation of the Lukan Christmas story, but the sermon would have been based on the story of the first Christian martyr, Stephen (Mt 23:34–39); the day would have been celebrated both as a day of remembrance of the first blood-witness of Christ and as a celebration of Christ's birth. Earlier cantatas by Bach bear witness of this dual character of the day: *Darzu ist erschienen*, BWV 40, composed during Bach's first year in Leipzig, focuses on Christ's coming into the world and his fight against the devil. The text alludes briefly to the story of St. Stephen,[34] but it neither references the martyr directly nor does it evoke the bucolic sphere of the second part of the *Christmas Oratorio*. A clearer connection is made in the dialogue cantata *Selig ist der Mann* (BWV 57) from 1725, which does not reference Christmas at all but is instead a celebration of martyrdom, as the opening movement demonstrates: "Blessed is the man who endures temptation; for after he is tested, he will receive the Crown of Life" (Jas 1:12).[35] The cantata from the chorale cantata cycle, *Christum wir sollen loben schon*, BWV 121, on the other

---

[32] See Dürr's discussions of the texts in *Cantatas*, 22–24.

[33] With the exception of Advent and Lent: During Advent the sermon was based on a section from the catechism while during the weeks before Easter, the sermon interpreted sections from the Passion harmony by Bugenhagen; cf. Ulrich Meyer, "Liturgie und Kirchenjahr," in *Bachs Kantaten: Das Handbuch*, ed. Reinmar Emans and Sven Hiemke, Das Bach-Handbuch 1/1 (Laaber: Laaber-Verlag, 2012), 198.

[34] The phrase "nimmt sich seiner Küchlein an" in mvt. 7 of BWV 40 uses an image also encountered in the Stephanus-narrative (Mt 23:37).

[35] BWV 57, quoted after Dürr, *Cantatas*, 114.

*Table 5.2* **Liturgical texts for the Christmas season and Bach's *Christmas Oratorio***

|  | First Day of Christmas | Second Day of Christmas | Third Day of Christmas | New Year | Sunday after New Year | Epiphany |
|---|---|---|---|---|---|---|
| Gospel | Lk 2:1–14 | Lk 2:15–20 | Jn 1:1–14 | Lk 2:21 | Mt 2:13–23 | Mt 2:1–12 |
| Sermon morning (Gospel) | Lk 2:1–14 | Mt 23:34–39 (St. Stephen's Day) | Jn 21:15–24 (second Gospel) | Lk 2:21 | Mt 2:13–15 | Mt 2:1–12 |
| Sermon vespers (Epistle) | Isa 9:2–7 | Acts 6:8–15; 7:55–60 | – | Gal 3:23–29 | – | Isa 60:1–6 |
| Oratorio | Lk 2:1; 3–7 | Lk 2:8–14 | Lk 2:15–20 | Lk 2–21 | Mt 2:1–6 | Mt 2:7–12 |
| performance morning | St. Nicholas | St. Thomas | St. Nicholas | St. Thomas | St. Nicholas | St. Thomas |
| performance vespers | St. Thomas | St. Nicholas | – | St. Nicholas | – | St. Nicholas |

hand, refers concisely to the second day of Christmas by mentioning the manger and the choir of angels: "Yet how does it see You in Your crib? My heart sighs: with shaking and almost closed lips it presents its grateful offering . . . then let me, with the angel choirs, hear a jubilant song of praise and thanks." (recit, no. 5).[36]

The traditional Gospel reading for the third day of Christmas was the Prologue to the Gospel of John (Jn 1:1–14: "In the beginning was the Word"), providing a different view of the coming of Christ from the one given in the Synoptic Gospels. Alternatively, the Gospel reading could be John 21:20–24, the very end of that Gospel, also known as the "Farewell Discourse." The text reports the final dialogue between Jesus and his disciples John and Peter, and revolves around the love between the two disciples and Jesus, adding the command to Peter to "shepherd his flock." The sermon in the morning service of December 27, 1734, would have been based on this text. While it lacks a direct connection to Christmas, the motif of the shepherd (here Peter) links it to the bucolic sphere of the shepherds' scenes in the Christmas narrative. Additionally, the topic of love, which is of theological significance for the *Christmas Oratorio*, appears here as well. It would have been easy for a preacher (or even a listener) to draw a connection between the text of the oratorio and the text for the sermon.[37]

---

[36] BWV 121, quoted after Dürr, *Cantatas*, 111.

[37] In Bach's cantata *Sehet, welche Liebe*, BWV 64, from 1723, the aspect of love receives more attention while the bucolic motifs that are present in the Gospel text do not appear: "[1] Sehet, welche eine Liebe hat uns der Vater erzeiget, daß wir Gottes Kinder heissen. [5] Aber was mir Jesus gibt und was

For the composition of the *Christmas Oratorio* libretto, it was necessary to rearrange the texts from Luke 2:1–20 to cover the three days of Christmas and thus create a coherent narrative over the three feast days. The librettist decided to use only the first half of the Gospel reading for the first day of Christmas (Lk 2:1.3–7) and shift the second half (Lk 2:8–14) to the second day of Christmas. The text for that day was then used in the musical setting for the third day of Christmas (Lk 2:15–20). The division of the text in Luke 2 was not arbitrarily chosen by the librettist but rather reflects a long-standing tradition. In his *Hauspostille*, a widely read collection of sermons, the Lutheran theologian Johann Gerhard provided several sermons for the days of Christmas. In the first three sermons he elaborates on the Gospel for Christmas Day, dividing the text into three sections, with Luke 2:1–7 being the first, Luke 2:8–12 the second, and Luke 2:13–14 the last (the verses 15–20 were not used on Christmas Day).[38] A similar division of the Gospel can be found about one hundred years later in August Hermann Franke's sermon *Erfreuung des Menschlichen Herzens durch die Geburt Christi*, which deals with Luke's text in three sections: vv. 1–7, 8–14 (without the Gloria), and the so-called angelic hymn (Lk 2:14).[39]

The Gospel text for New Year's Day consisted of one verse only, the naming of Jesus and his circumcision (Lk 2:21). Bach's librettist used this verse without changes: this is the only instance in which the designated Gospel reading and the oratorio have the same text. Bach and his librettist then had to make another important decision: just as the second day of Christmas had a dual character as celebration of Christ's birth and as St. Stephen Martyr day, New Year's day could be celebrated as feast of Christ's circumcision and naming but also (with a more secular undertone) as the beginning of the secular new year. Most cantatas outside of the *Christmas Oratorio* cover both aspects; for instance the New Year's cantata, *Singet dem Herrn ein neues Lied* (BWV 190) from 1723. The text asks for the blessing of the New Year and requests Jesus's blessings for church, school, and authorities (mvt. 6), but it also contains a lengthy litany about the name of Jesus (mvt. 5), celebrating the name of the savior.[40]

---

meine Seele liebt, bleibet fest und ewig stehen." (1) See what love the Father has shown to us, in that we are called God's children. (5) But what Jesus gives me and what my soul loves remains firm for ever), quoted after Dürr, *Cantatas*, 121–22.

[38] Johann Gerhard, *Postille, das ist Auslegung und Erklärung der sonntäglichen und vornehmsten Fest-Evangelien über das ganze Jahr* ... Teil 1: *Von Advent bis Pfingsten*, nach der Original-Ausgabe von 1613 und 1616, vermehrt durch die Zusätze der Ausgabe von 1663 (Berlin: Schlawitz, 1870).

[39] August Hermann Franke, *Erfreuung des Menschlichen Hertzens durch die Geburt Christi am 1. Christ-Tage A. 1717 in einer über den ordentlichen Evangelischen Text Luc. II, 1–14. in der Stadt-Kirchen zu Blaubeuren im Hertzogthum Würtemberg* ... (Halle: Waisenhaus, 1740), 12.

[40] See for BWV 190: Markus Rathey, "'Singet dem Herrn ein neues Lied' (BWV 190). Johann Sebastian Bachs Auseinandersetzung mit dem Te Deum laudamus," in *Bachs 1. Leipziger Kantatenjahrgang*, ed. Martin Geck, Dortmunder Bach Forschungen 3 (Dortmund: Klangfarben Musikverlag, 2002), 287–301.

In the two final parts of the oratorio, Bach's librettist had to rearrange the texts again. The prescribed Gospel text for the Sunday after New Year's (Mt 2:13–23), tells of the flight of Jesus and his parents to Egypt. This is followed on Epiphany (January 6) by the story of the three wise men (Mt 2:1–12). While the inverted chronology (first the flight and then the arrival of the three men and their encounter with King Herod) was not a major problem within the liturgical calendar, it must have seemed problematic within the narrative structure of an oratorio. The feast of Epiphany was traditionally connected with the story of the three wise men, and therefore it was not possible to invert the two texts from Matthew 2 and present them in chronological order. Instead, Bach's librettist decided to shift the first half of the text from Epiphany to the Sunday after New Year, and to present the rest of the text (Mt 2:7–12) on its allotted day. This led to some tension between the Gospel reading and sermon text for the Sunday after New Year, which focused on the flight to Egypt, and the text set in the oratorio. The texts are still thematically connected, as the narrative in the oratorio reports the fear of King Herod, and the sermon would have focused on his reaction, the killing of the young boys, and the subsequent flight of Jesus and his family.

Bach and his librettist favored narrative coherence over liturgical order. Some listeners might have noticed that biblical texts were rearranged and moved to different feast days. This, however, was less problematic than it might seem to a modern observer. First, not all cantatas by Bach are very closely related to the Gospel text. Some of them relate in a more general way to the theological topics of the day without quoting ideas or verses from the biblical readings. Second, since we do not know the sermons for the six days during which Bach's *Christmas Oratorio* was performed in Leipzig's main churches, it is impossible to determine whether the preacher drew a connection between his sermon and the text for the oratorio of some sort. Sermons in the Baroque era were rarely monothematic; instead, they frequently began with an introduction, the *exordium*, which could have a different focus from the rest of the sermon. In hymn sermons, for instance, the interpretation of the hymn took place in the *exordium* (which could be very extensive) while the main body of the sermon was an exegesis of the Gospel text. For example, Bach probably would have been familiar with the collection of hymn sermons by the Leipzig preacher Johann Benedict Carpzov.[41] Preachers could also use the *exordium* to interpret the Gospel text and then turn to a different text in the main body of the sermon to focus on a specific theological question. Romanus Teller's *Grosser Unterscheid* from 1720, a collection of sermons preached at St. Nicholai in Leipzig is one example of this kind of structure. In his sermon for the first day of Christmas, Teller first interprets the Gospel for the day (Lk 2:1–14), for approximately three pages, before introducing a

---

[41] Markus Rathey, "The Chorale Cantata in Leipzig: The Collaboration between Schelle and Carpzov in 1689–1690 and Bach's Chorale Cantata Cycle," *Bach* 43 (2012): 46–92.

new text (Gen 3:15) to preach about the antagonism between Christ and the devil, and the implications for the just and the godless.[42] The second part of the sermon is seventeen pages long. The same model is used in the other sermons of the collection. The two examples show that discrepancies between the texts used in the oratorio and the other liturgical texts for the day did not necessarily mean that parts II and V of the oratorio were without connection within the framework of the liturgy. In fact, the nonlinear approach was a widely accepted practice. The polyphony of voices and topics in a Baroque-era sermon makes it seem less problematic to have a piece between the Gospel reading and the sermon that veered in a different direction than the framing liturgical elements. Without knowing the content of the contemporary sermons, it is impossible to determine the specific connection between the oratorio and the liturgical context.

It is also important to consider the other circumstances of the performance. In Leipzig, performances of cantatas alternated traditionally between the two main churches, St. Thomas's and St. Nicholas's. According to a rule instituted in 1658, the choir at the St. Thomas School had to perform on the first and third days of the major feasts in St. Nicholas's Church and only on the second feast day at St. Thomas's.[43] Thus, part I of the *Christmas Oratorio* was performed on Christmas Day in St. Nicholas's, part II the next day in St. Thomas's, and so forth. If a vespers service was celebrated, the piece from the morning service was repeated in the early afternoon in the other church. However, since no vespers were held on the afternoons of the third day of Christmas and the Sunday after Christmas, two days when the main music was performed in St. Nicholas, the congregation at St. Thomas's would not have had an opportunity to hear the compositions for these specific days. Additionally, Bach had to perform four times a year on high feast days in St. Paul's Church during the so called "old service," and so the part I (and only that one) would have been performed in St. Paul's.[44] While the oratorio was conceived as a unity, the congregations would have perceived only those parts within their liturgical context as single "cantatas" without the larger narrative thrust. The congregations in the afternoon services would also not have been able to see the unity between readings, music, and sermon, because the sermons in these services were based on the Epistles for the day and not on the Gospel. All this shows that the liturgical contexts, while important, are not the only determining factor for the shape of the oratorio. While it was composed for liturgical purposes, it emancipates itself from a purely liturgical function due to its own narrative and musical principles.

---

[42] Romanus Teller, *Der grosse Unterscheid zwischen den Gerechten und Gottlosen, zum theil aus denen ordentlichen Sonn- und Fest-Tags-Evangeliis, grösten theils aber aus hierzu auserlesenen . . . Sprüchen* (Leipzig: Braun, 1720).

[43] See Martin Petzoldt, *Texthefte zur Kirchenmusik aus Bachs Leipziger Zeit: Die 7 erhaltenen Drucke der Jahre 1724–1749 in faksimilierter Wiedergabe* (Stuttgart: Carus, 2000), 6.

[44] See the overview of Bach's duties in Wolff, *Bach*, 252.

# Hymns

Next to the Gospel texts, the second source for preexisting material were the hymns, most of them had familiar texts and melodies. Bach had probably trusted his librettist with the selection of the hymns as well. The only hymn melody that was—more or less—determined was that for the final hymn, which was already part of the earlier BWV 248a. Bach's librettist could have easily included the hymn into the oratorio as the melody was connected to several Christmas texts as well, such as "Wie soll ich dich empfangen," which is quoted in part I of the oratorio. The hymns (see table 5.3) were selected based on textual considerations; this led to the, for Bach, uncharacteristic prevalence of seventeenth century hymns over those from the time of the Reformation, since the concept of the *inhabitatio Christi* was more prominent in texts from the time after 1650.[45]

In the completed version of the oratorio, most of the final hymns of each part are extended chorale-settings with instrumental interludes, while the internal hymn-settings as simpler movements without obbligato instrumental parts. However, the final chorales for parts III and V, which both end with simpler chorale harmonizations, stand as an exception.

# Plans abandoned

Between the first concepts, the writing of the libretto, and the preparation of the score Bach seems to have changed some of his initial plans. Two of the newly composed movements were substitutes for what were originally planned to have been parody movements: the choral movement "Ehre sei dir Gott" (no. 43) and the aria "Schließe, mein Herze" (no. 31). In the course of their preparations for the oratorio, Bach and his librettist originally decided to place the final movement of BWV 213 at the beginning of part V (no. 43). The librettist wrote a text that conformed to the model in the number of syllables per line (8 7 7 7 3 8 10) and in meter. The only (minor) discrepancy between the two texts is a difference in the rhyme scheme, a feature that did not necessarily affect the composition:

BWV 213, 13: *abcccab*

BWV 248, 43: *abccbab*

Although the new text would have fit the model, Bach changed his plans before he embarked on composing the chorus. The secular movement from BWV 213 is

---

[45] After Dürr, *Christmas Oratorio*, 45; some dates and attributions have been updated.

*Table 5.3* **Hymns in the *Christmas Oratorio***

| No. | Text | Poetry | Melody |
|---|---|---|---|
| 5 | Wie soll ich dich empfangen | Paul Gerhard, 1653, 1st stanza | Hans Leo Hassler, 1601 (Herzlich tut mich verlangen) |
| 7 | Er ist auf Erden kommen arm | Martin Luther, 1524, 6th stanza of "Gelobet seist du, Jesu Christ" | Martin Luther, 1524 (original melody) |
| 9 | Ach mein herzliebes Jesulein | Martin Luther, 1535, 13th stanza of "Vom Himmel hoch" | Martin Luther, 1539 (original melody) |
| 12 | Brich an, du schönes Morgenlicht | Johann Rist, 1641, 9th stanza of "Ermuntre dich, mein schwacher Geist" | Johann Schop, 1641/ Darmstadt, 1687 (original melody) |
| 17 | Schaut hin, dort liegt im finstern Stall | Paul Gerhard, 1667, 8th stanza of "Schaut, schaut, was ist für Wunder dar" | Martin Luther, 1524 (original melody) |
| 23 | Wir singen dir in deinem Herr | Paul Gerhard, 1656, 2nd stanza of "Wir singen dir, Immanuel" | Martin Luther, 1524 (original melody) |
| 28 | Dies hat er alles uns getan | Martin Luther, 1524, 7th stanza of "Gelobet seist du, Jesu Christ" | Martin Luther, 1524 (original melody) |
| 33 | Ich will dich mit Fleiß bewahren | Paul Gerhard, 1653, 15th stanza of "Fröhlich soll mein Herze springen" | after Johann Georg Ebeling, 1666 (Warum sollt ich mich denn grämen) |
| 35 | Seid froh, dieweil | Christoph Runge, 1653, 4th stanza of "Laßt Furcht und Pein" | Dresden, 1593 (Wir Christenleut) |
| 38, 40 | Jesu, du mein liebstes Leben | Johann Rist, 1642, 1st stanza | Bach's own composition |
| 42 | Jesus richte mein Beginnen | Johann Rist, 1642, 15th stanza of "Hilf, Herr Jesu, laß gelingen" | Bach's own composition |
| 46 | Dein Glanz all Finsternis verzehrt | Georg Weissel, 1642, 5th stanza of "Nun, liebe Seel, nun ist es Zeit" | Nuremberg, 1581 (In dich hab ich gehoffet) |
| 53 | Zwar ist solche Herzensstube | Johann Franck, 1655, 5th stanza of "Ihr Gestirn, ihr hohlen Lüfte" | Heinrich Albert, 1642 (Gott des Himmels und der Erden) |
| 59 | Ich steh an deiner Krippen hier | Paul Gerhard, 1656, 1st stanza | Wittenberg, 1535 (Nun freut euch, lieben Christen g'mein, 2nd melody) |
| 64 | Nun seid ihr wohl gerochen | Georg Werner, 1648, 4th stanza of "Ihr Christen auserkohren" | Hans Leo Hassler, 1601 (Herzlich tut mich verlangen) |

a lighthearted, homophonic piece, rhythmically resembling a gavotte.[46] The piece itself has a rather complex history. Bach composed the earliest version for a secular cantata (BWV 184a), the text of which is unknown, at the court in Cöthen sometime between 1717 and 1723[47]. That version of the movement was revised for the sacred cantata *Erwünschtes Freudenlicht*, BWV 184, performed in Leipzig on May 5, 1724. The sacred cantata was repeated at least once in Leipzig, in 1731.[48] Bach then reworked the earlier movement again and incorporated it into his *Hercules Cantata*, BWV 213. Bach's audiences in Leipzig had thus heard it once as a secular piece and probably several times in its sacred version. This alone might have motivated Bach to abandon the plan of using that particular chorus in his oratorio. Another reason may have been the musical form of the movement. The chorus has a simple ritornello form. The first two lines of the text in BWV 213, the praise of the young Saxon prince Friedrich, served as a refrain and are sung, according to the libretto, by the Chorus of the Muses. The Muses are interrupted by the god Mercury (a metaphor for the city of Leipzig) with two short solo statements, each with the same text. The movement reflects Bach's interest in instrumental genres during his time in Cöthen, here combining a solo concerto form with a joyful dance rhythm.[49]

Had Bach adhered to the original plan of using the movement in the *Christmas Oratorio*, the two lines "Ehre sei dir, Gott, gesungen / Dir sei Lob und Dank bereit" would have been used for the ritornello while the remaining lines would have been assigned to a solo voice. While the juxtaposition of solo and tutti in BWV 213 had a dramatic purpose and reflected a dialogue between the muses and a god, in the parody this would have been a purely musical feature without dramatic or semantic function. Furthermore, the tone of the movement is rather light, and Bach might have found it too much so for a poetic paraphrase of the angelic Gloria. Instead of borrowing a preexisting chorus, Bach eventually decided to compose a new setting, which features a *da capo* structure instead of a ritornello form. The autograph manuscript shows extensive revisions that reflect the effort the composer put into the movement. Using the earlier setting would have been easier and less time-consuming, but it is obvious that Bach was not satisfied with that option. The final version is festive and joyful but eschews the dance-like lightness of the secular chorus. Chapter 10 will demonstrate that the final version is a movement, which is on par with the other opening movements of the *Christmas Oratorio*, like "Jauchzet, frohlocket" at the beginning of part I or the opening sinfonia of part II.

---

[46] Cf. Dürr, *Cantatas*, 826.

[47] Cf. Dürr, *Cantatas*, 826; and NBA I/35 KB, 138–42.

[48] NBA I/14 KB, 173–74.

[49] For the influence of instrumental form and genres on Bach's cantatas in Cöthen, see: Markus Rathey, "Instrumentaler Satz und Orchesterbehandlung in den Köthener Glückwunschkantaten," *Cöthener Bach Hefte* 11 (2003): 116–35.

A second movement that has to be discussed in this context is the aria "Durch die von Eifer entflammeten Waffen" (BWV 215/7). The secular model was composed in early October 1734 as part of the cantata in honor of the Elector of Saxony, who had unexpectedly decided to visit Leipzig. The piece earned some negative repute for the strenuous circumstances of its open-air performance on October 5, which led to the untimely death of the famous trumpet player Gottfried Reiche (1667–1734). Stephen Crist has shown that the movement in BWV 215 was specifically composed for this occasion and that it is the most recently composed parody movement in the *Christmas Oratorio*.[50] It has been suggested that the piece was originally intended as a parody model for "Schließe, mein Herze."[51] Bach then decided to compose a new movement and to use the secular setting as a model for "Erleucht auch meine finstre Sinnen" in part V of the *Christmas Oratorio*.[52] Some similarities between the texts of "Schließe, mein Herze" and "Durch die von Eifer" seem to suggest that the sacred text was conceived to fit the preexisting music. The major difference is that the second line is missing in the sacred text, which, as Alfred Dürr has suggested, might have been omitted:[53]

| *BWV 215/7* | *BWV 248/31* |
|---|---|
| Durch die von Eifer | Schließe, mein Herze, dies |
|     entflammeten Waffen |     selige Wunder |
| Feinde bestrafen | |
| Bringt zwar manchem Ehr und Ruhm; | Fest in deinem Glauben ein! |
| Aber die Bosheit mit Wohltat | Lasse dies Wunder, die |
|     vergelten, |     göttlichen Werke |
| Ist nur der Helden, | Immer zur Stärke |
| Ist Augustens Eigentum. | Deines schwachen Glaubens sein! |

Dürr's suggestion, which has been adopted by other interpreters, has its problems. While the number of syllables in each line and the rhyme scheme are the same, there is no indication that a second line from the sacred text was omitted. While in BWV 215/7 the first two lines are tied by an enjambment (the first line is grammatically incomplete), the first two lines of BWV 248/31 form a unity as the second line

---

[50] Crist, "The Question of Parody," 139.
[51] Dürr, *Weihnachts-Oratorium*, 5–6.
[52] NBA II/6 KB, KB, 215.
[53] Dürr, *Weihnachts-Oratorium*, 5.

grammatically completes the first one. There is no poetic reason to assume the dele-tion of a line. It is difficult to fathom why Bach should have omitted a line and then later composed an entirely new movement, which could have accommodated any number of lines he wanted. Musical reasons speak against an association between BWV 215/7 and BWV 248/31 as well. Bach interprets the beginning of the secular text not as a dactyl, which would have required a downbeat on the first syllable, but as an iambus, setting it with an upbeat (ex. 5.1). While this rhythmic shift works well with the secular text, it would be impossible for the beginning of the text in the *Christmas Oratorio* (ex. 5.2).

*Example 5.1* J. S. Bach, BWV 215/7, mm 1–4

Durch die    von___    Ei – fer ent – flam – me-ten    Waf – fen,

*Example 5.2* J. S. Bach, music from BWV 215 with text from BWV 248/31

Schlie - ße,    mein___    Her – ze dies se – li – ge    Wun – der

Dürr recognizes this problem but draws a different conclusion. He suggests that, since the visit of the Elector was announced at the last minute and Bach had to complete his composition within only a few days, the plan for the text of the ora-torio must have been made *before* the composition of the music for BWV 215/7; otherwise, parody would have been impossible.[54] This does imply that the librettist, while writing the text for the oratorio, knew the text for the secular aria but not the music. This, however, is unlikely as we have to assume that the text for BWV 215 was written by J. C. Clauder at the last minute as well.[55] Text and music were created within a few days and it seems a great coincidence that the librettist for BWV 248 would have written his mismatched text during the days between the completion of the text and Bach's composition. It is more plausible that this particular aria was not intended as a model for BWV 248/31. The two texts share some formal features but nothing more. Musically and poetically the two texts are too different to assume a parody relationship.

A second factor that sheds some doubt on Dürr's assumption is the fact that the librettist wrote an aria for part V of the oratorio (no. 47) which goes much better with the music from the secular cantata. Therefore, it is more likely that this text had

---

[54]  Dürr, *Weihnachts Oratorium*, 6.

[55]  See NBA I/37 KB, 65–69.

already been written with the music from BWV 215 in mind. If Dürr's assumption were correct, the librettist would have written his text only after Bach had already rejected the secular model for "Schließe, mein Herze." But this does not mean that BWV 248/31 was not intended to have been a parody. Chapter 8 will demonstrate that Bach worked particularly hard on composing that aria, rejecting several compositional ideas before arriving at the final form; he might have rejected earlier plans for a parody as well. In that case, though, it would have been an unknown model from one of the cantatas from the early 1730s and not BWV 215/7.

These two examples demonstrate that the plans for the oratorio, even after the completion of the libretto, were still in flux and that Bach made changes as necessary. These changes also meant additional work for the composer and created time constraints toward the eventual completion of the oratorio. Some details in part VI suggest that he did indeed need to save time and thus did not make the changes that were necessary to bring the final part in line with the remainder of the piece. We will return to this problem in chapter 11.

## Concepts for the recitatives

From the outset, Bach developed a variety of patterns for the musical realization of the libretto. These patterns include the use of certain textures for specific text genres, the systematic use of instruments, and structural considerations for each of the six parts. These plans can be seen in his settings of the recitatives. The biblical narrative was set as secco recits, while reflective recits were composed as accompagnati, which is in line not only with his own practices in large scale works like the *St. Matthew Passion* but also with Stölzel's Passion Bach had performed in 1734. This common compositional decision had two primary purposes: it created a sonic differentiation between the biblical narrative and its reflective interpretation, and it allowed the composer to react musically to the often more emotional texts of the accompagnati. In addition, the accompagnato recits often asked for the same musical forces as the arias that follow them, so that recit and aria were connected as musical pairs. An example for such a pair is the first alto aria ("Bereite dich, Zion, mit zärtlichen Trieben"). The preceding alto recit is accompanied by two oboi d'amore while the aria features an oboe d'amore as obbligato instrument.

The use of an accompagnato instrument was sometimes motivated by semantic reasons; in other cases the choice is purely musical. The oboe d'amore in part I of the oratorio, for instance, is featured in two accompagnato recits (nos. 3 and 7) both of which thematize the love between Christ and the believer. The "love-oboe" here is used to underscore the idea of spiritual love. In the accompagnato recits of part II (nos. 14 and 18) Bach employs the choir of oboes (d'amore and da caccia) to denote the bucolic sphere of the shepherds, whereas the angel in recit, no. 13 is sonically represented by the strings. In part III, both accompagnato recits are accompanied by two flutes; this time the instruments are used without a symbolic function but to established a sonic contrast. The accompagnati in part IV feature the chorus of strings. The same is the case for the accompagnati in part V (nos. 45 and 49), with the exception of a short alto recit that precedes the final choral movement and features the two oboi d'amore instead of the strings. The reason is again a symbolic one, as the text returns to the topic of mystical love.

Part VI of the oratorio represents a special case. The surviving sources suggest that the two recits (nos. 56 and 61) were originally secco in the model for the parody. In order to bring them in line with the remainder of the oratorio and to differentiate them from the newly composed Gospel recits, Bach added instrumental accompaniment. In contrast to the other parts of the oratorio, the two recits in part VI do not use the same instrumentation, although the first one features strings while the second one brings back the oboi d'amore. Ulrich Siegele has suggested that Bach might simply have followed the instrumentation of the aria to which the recit is linked; the first aria is accompanied by the string ensemble (with oboe 1 mostly doubling the first violin), while the second recit prepares the transition to the aria for tenor and two oboi d'amore, "Nun mögt ihr stolzen Feinde."[56] While Siegele's observation is correct, the instrumentation also follows patterns for the semantic use of instruments in the previous parts: in the text for recit no. 61, the beloved (Christ) promises to remain with the believer, which Bach underscores by bringing back the "love-oboes." The first recit, no. 56, on the other hand, expresses the rejection of the "deceitful one" and the use of oboi d'amore would simply have been out of place here.

The overview of Bach's patterns of instrumentation in the accompagnato recits demonstrates that the use of instruments was planned in advance of the composition of the oratorio and that it follows both systematic and semantic paradigms: Bach typically uses the same instruments in all accompagnati of each part, and the choice of the instruments is based on the text. The text however, can also necessitate a deviation from this basic pattern. The choice of instruments often have a semantic function (as the bucolic reed-chorus in part II or the "love-oboes" in part I), but the instruments are also used to create sonic diversity without a symbolic meaning. Structural and semantic aspects strike a balance in Bach's planning of the instrumentation of the *Christmas Oratorio*.

Bach determined the patterns of instrumentation during the planning stage. During the composition stage, though, Bach decided to make some changes to the original plans. A change of this kind appears toward the end of part II. The autograph score shows that it was Bach's original plan to have the newly composed choral movement "Ehre sei Gott" followed by an accompagnato recit for bass. The recitative was supposed to be accompanied by the oboe-choir (da caccia and d'amore) and the strings (vl 1 + 2 and vla). Bach wrote down the clefs and key signatures for

---

[56]  See Siegele, "Das Parodieverfahren des Weihnachtsoratoriums," 260.

all nine parts not only on the first page of the recitative but on the second page as well; he also added the text for the piece.[57] In other words, the score suggests that Bach planned a richly scored movement that was supposed to follow the setting of the angelic praise. In this original plan, the recitative would have been followed by a simple four-part chorale setting. The autograph score shows that Bach had already written the clefs and time signatures for five parts (SATB and bc) for the closing chorale. Thus, the formal outline of the end of the second part of the oratorio was significantly different from what it is now. Modern listeners are familiar with the balanced structure of part II, with the opening and closing movements corresponding musically. The musical ideas of the sinfonia, the siciliano and pastoral motifs, and the juxtaposition of string and reed chorus return at the end in the final chorale setting. In its initial form, though, part II was much closer to usual church cantata with a large-scale opening movement and a simple, four-part chorale at the end. The climax of this "cantata" would have been the praise of the angels in "Ehre sei Gott." The following recit and especially the final chorale would have appeared as an anti-climactic afterthought. While composing the final chorale setting, Bach changed his mind. The score suggests the following thought process: After the composition of the choral movement "Ehre sei Gott," he marked the necessary lines for the following accompagnato recit and then wrote its text. This indicated how much space he would need for the movement and thus could return later to compose the music for the recit. He then moved on to the final chorale and marked the five lines for a simple chorale setting. At some point, however, he decided to compose an elaborate choral movement. But this movement would still have been different from the one we know today. Bach entered the melody first in the violin part in regular quarter notes and in common time (C): a crossed-out measure after m. 5 still preserves this earlier version. Only then he decided to conceive the chorale-setting as a counterbalance to the opening movement; he changed the time signature to 12/8 and dotted the notes of the chorale melody. The crammed bc line with the siciliano motif still shows that the spacing for the movement was not designed to accommodate such an elaborate bass line.

The change of plans shifted the balance within part II. Now the opening and closing movements served as two balanced side-wings to the edifice of the composition. The originally projected accompagnato recit before the hymn-setting appeared out of place. Bach would have had three richly scored movements: the praise of the angels, the recit, and the final chorale. What he needed, however, was a moment of repose between the festive "Ehre sei Gott" and the closing hymn. Therefore, he decided to modify his plans for the recit and composed the text as a simple secco recit instead. This contradicted the general pattern that set reflective recits as accompagnati, but it fit better into the context of the work. This example demonstrates that

---

[57] He even wrote down one note (*g*) in the accompaniment in the first oboe d'amore.

Bach handled his initial plans quite liberally and that some of the ideas that seem to be constitutive for the *Christmas Oratorio* emerged only during the compositional process.

Movement 45 from part V shows a change of plans on a smaller scale. Bach combines sections from the Gospel of Matthew with short reflective interpolations. In the final version, the text is sung by the chorus while the two recit interpolations are presented by the alto, accompanied by the strings. In the score, however, Bach initially notated only the first recit section for alto but the second one for bass. After finishing the movement he added "NB. Dieß Recit muß im Alt transponiert werden" (NB. This recit has to be transposed for the alto).[58] While it is possible that Bach simply made a mistake, it is more likely that the earlier version was deliberate. Movement 47 is an aria for bass. And the text of the recit is thematically related to the aria, as both pay tribute to the shining of the light of God:

no. 45 (recitative)

Wohl euch, die ihr dies Licht gesehen,
Es ist zu eurem Heil geschehen!
Mein Heiland, du, du bist das Licht,
Das auch den Heiden scheinen sollen,
Und sie, sie kennen dich noch nicht,
Als sie dich schon verehren wollen.
Wie hell, wie klar muss nicht dein Schein,
Geliebter Jesu, sein!

no. 47 (aria)

Erleucht auch meine finstre Sinnen,
Erleuchte mein Herze
Durch der Strahlen klaren Schein!
Dein Wort soll mir die hellste Kerze
In allen meinen Werken sein;
Dies lässet die Seele nichts Böses
    beginnen.

Well for you, you who have seen this light;
It has taken place for your salvation!
You, my Savior, you are the light
That shall shine also to the gentiles,
And they, they do not know you yet,
[Even now] as they already want to revere
    you.
How bright , how clear must not your
    luminosity be,
Beloved Jesus!

Light up, too, my dark inclinations,
Light up my heart
With the clear luminosity of your
    streams of light!
Your word shall be the brightest
    candle to me
In all my works;
This will let the soul embark on
    nothing evil.

Bach might have understood this section of the recit as a preparation for the aria, from which it is separated only by the chorale-setting, no. 46. His decision to change the soloist was then motivated by the attempt to create more coherence

---

[58] Cf. NBA II/6 KB, 66.

within the movement. With both recit statements sung by the alto, the setting now alternates between chorus and alto voice. The change also draws the two statements theologically closer together: The "King of the Jews" from the first part of the recit, who can be found in the "breast" of the believer, is the savior, who is the light and who is finally identified as the beloved Jesus. Considering that the "light" is a metaphor for the word of God (as it is later spelled out in mvt. 47), the dwelling in the believer's heart and the presence through the Word are theologically interrelated, and represent a key aspect of the Lutheran orthodox understanding of *inhabitatio*. It is impossible to tell whether Bach was motivated here by deeper theological reasoning or whether he just aimed to create a movement that was more coherent. The result, however, is a theologically enhanced version of the original plan.[59]

## The hymns as structural problem

The genesis of the final chorale setting for part II of the *Christmas Oratorio* already reminds us that some of the structural features were not worked out during the planning stage. It also appears that the selection of the closing hymns was not made by the composer but by the librettist, which posed some challenges for Bach and which necessitated some interesting solutions. For example, part III ends with a setting of the chorale stanza "Seid froh dieweil," mvt. 35. The melody associated with the text is in F♯ minor. If Bach wanted to close the individual parts of the oratorio in the same key in which they had opened, he had to find a way to return to the key of the opening movement (D major). Another problem was the balance between the opening chorus and the final movement. In the two previous parts of the oratorio, Bach had composed expanded chorale-settings that borrowed musical ideas from the opening choruses. This would have been difficult with the melody of "Seid froh dieweil," for both structural and harmonic reasons. If he wanted to accomplish the impression of symmetry in part III, Bach either had to choose a different hymn, or he had to add another movement that mirrored the character and the instrumentation of the opening movement and facilitated a return to the home key D major. Bach's solution is simple but ingenious: he sets the chorale as a simple four-part setting, followed by a repetition of the opening chorus (the

---

[59]  There is an instance in which Bach changed the forces for a recitative is probably only the correction of mistake. In the short recitative no. 32 in part III, "Ja, ja, mein Herz soll es bewahren," Bach initially wrote a bass clef for the solo voice but then changed it to alto. Considering Bach's typical compositional procedures, he would have written the clefs, time signatures, and the text for the complete recitative and then at a later point (or immediately thereafter) composed the movement. Since the second line for the solo voice is notated in alto clef, we can assume that the use of the bass clef at the very beginning was only a mistake that was corrected before he wrote the second line of the alto part.

shortest one of its kind in the oratorio). The encore performance of the first movement was apparently Bach's decision; the printed version of the libretto does not
mention a repetition of the opening chorus.

The final chorale for part IV posed a similar problem. The librettist again suggested a text that was associated with a melody in the minor mode. In order to have
an ending that corresponded to the opening movement in major and that underscored the festive character of New Year's Day, Bach composed a new melody, this
one in F major. The setting of this "chorale melody" is an expanded chorale-setting
with instrumental interludes, which resembles the final movements in parts I and
II and which invokes the musical character of the opening movement of part IV.[60]
Bach's decision to compose a new melody for the chorale text is unusual but not
entirely out of context. In the early 1730s Bach had collaborated on the *Schemelli
Gesangbuch* (1736) to which he had contributed several new melodies for existing hymn texts.[61] The project might have encouraged Bach to do the same in the
*Christmas Oratorio*. A second case, even closer than the *Schemelli Gesangbuch*, are
mvts. 38 and 40 in part IV of the oratorio. Bach uses a preexisting hymn text but
again composes his own melody, which is then combined with a bass recit in a
chorale trope.

Part V is the only part of the *Christmas Oratorio* that does not refer back to the
opening movement in its final chorale. This probably has practical liturgical reasons,
as the cantata was performed on a regular Sunday (the first Sunday after the New
Year), and the simple chorale-setting conforms to the pattern for a standard church
cantata. Part VI did not require changes as the opening and closing movements
already came from the parody model, which had a closing hymn in an expanded
chorale-setting. Overall, the planning stage for the *Christmas Oratorio* determined
some general patterns, but Bach showed flexibility and was willing to modify these
plans during the compositional process. This included structural aspects, the choice
of voices for certain movements, and even the replacement of parodies for newly
composed movements, as in the case of the opening chorus for part V.

## Composition stage

As mentioned earlier, the movements of the *Christmas Oratorio* were not composed
in their final order. It is not possible to determine in what order the six parts of the

---

[60]  A repetition of the opening movement was probably out of the question since the first chorus of
part IV is about five-and-a-half minutes long, whereas the first movement of part III was, with less than
two minutes, rather short.

[61]  The exact number of these melodies is unknown and the identification of the melodies that were
actually written by Bach is impossible; however, the preface states that Bach was involved in the composition of (some) of the chorale melodies; Mendel, et al., *New Bach Reader*, 170.

oratorio were composed because the scores for every part are independent and start with new pagination in Bach's own handwriting.[62] Every part begins with a new gathering of score paper so that the final pages of a part sometimes stay empty; parts II and V have one empty page, and part III has two-and-a-half pages. The separation into six independent scores reflects the practical circumstances of their original performance on six different days since one large score for the entire piece would have been impractical. The independence of the six scores implies that Bach could have worked on several parts of the oratorio simultaneously—even though there is no conclusive evidence for this. Nonetheless, the order of composition within each of the six parts is clearer. Bach first wrote the opening movements; these were either parodies of earlier works and could be copied from the existing sources (parts I, III, IV, VI); or they were new compositions (parts II and V), which were then composed directly into the score. The opening movements were the most extensive movements, both in terms of length and vocal-instrumental forces.

The size of the opening movements determined the spacial placement for the remaining movements. In several cases Bach had more staff lines available on a page than he needed for the opening movements, and this allowed him to enter some of the following movements at the bottom of the pages. In part I, for instance, the long opening chorus extended from pages 1 through 20. Since each page has twenty-two staff lines but the chorus required only sixteen, Bach repurposed the remaining lines for other movements. That way, he was able to enter mvts. 2–7 at the bottom of the pages. Beginning with no. 8, the aria "Großer Herr," Bach began to use the entire page. The opening movements for the other parts of the oratorio were entered in a similar way; with the exception of the instrumental sinfonia of part II. The smaller musical forces allowed the composer to enter several systems on each page, which did not leave space for additional movements. The movements that follow the opening chorus in each part of the oratorio could be entered only after the opening movements had been written down. The second movement entered in all six parts was the first Gospel recit. Bach notated the clefs, key-, and time signatures, and then wrote the complete text for the recit. By entering the text Bach could determine how much space was needed for the movement. This allowed him to enter the following movements without composing the music for the recit first.[63]

Movements that had to be entered completely (copied or newly composed) were the arias and some of the accompagnato recits as well as the turba-choruses; in short, all the movements where the length was not determined by their text or a

[62] For details see NBA II/6 KB, 10–11.

[63] Robert Marshall has already demonstrated this in his study on Bach's compositional process, see Marshall, *Compositional Process of J. S. Bach*, vol. 1 , 90–91.

given melody alone. We will see, however, that some of the seemingly predictable movements turned out to be less predictable than Bach had anticipated.

## Composing the recitatives

Recitatives typically follow the declamation of the text, without repetitions or longer instrumental interpolations. It was common among Baroque composers to enter the text first and to write the music afterwards.[64] Bach followed this convention, as can be seen in the first recit (no. 2). The text is written in a fluent hand and without any larger spaces between the syllables of the words, while the spacing of the notes is aligned with the text and the bar lines (after m. 4) are interrupted in order not to interfere with the text. Even in the following accompagnato recit (no. 3, "Nun wird mein"), the spacing of the notes follows the text, suggesting that the words were written before the music. These general paradigms suggest that Bach composed the movements of part I in the following order:

| | |
|---|---|
| 1. | Coro "Jauchzet, frohlocket" [parody] |
| 4. | Aria "Bereite dich, Zion" [parody] |
| 7. | Chorale/Recit "Er ist auf Erden" [new] |
| 8. | Aria "Großer Herr, o starker König" [parody] |
| 9. | Chorale "Ach mein herzliebes Jesulein" [new] |
| 2. | Recit "Es begab sich aber" [new] |
| 3. | Recit "Nun wir mein liebster Bräutigam" [new] |
| 5. | Chorale "Wie soll ich dich empfangen" [new] |
| 6. | Recit "Und sie gebar ihren ersten Sohn" [new] |

The assumption that Bach postponed the composition of the recitatives is confirmed by the beginning of part V. As usual, Bach wrote down the first movement (in this case, a new composition). The instrumental forces for the opening movement (no. 43) occupy just ten staff lines, and Bach could fit two systems on one page and still had two staff lines left for the first Gospel recit. After writing the text

---

[64] Bach's two contemporaries, George Frideric Handel and Johann Adolph Hasse, are prime examples for this conventional procedure. For Handel, see David R. Hurley, *Handel's Muse: Patterns of Creation in his Oratorios and Musical Dramas, 1743–1751* (Oxford: Oxford University Press, 2001), 20; and for Hasse, Frederick L. Millner: *The Operas of Johann Adolf Hasse*, Studies in Musicology 2 (Ann Arbor, MI: UMI Research Press, 1979: 65, 77, 85. This was more recently confirmed by Roland Dieter Schmidt-Hensel, *La musica è del Signor Hasse detto il Sassone. . . . Johann Adolf Hasses "Opere serie" der Jahre 1730 bis 1745. Quellen, Fassungen, Aufführungen*, Teil I: Darstellung, Abhandlungen zur Musikgeschichte 19.1. (Göttingen: Vandenhoeck & Ruprecht, 2009), 128–30.

for the complete recitative on the first two pages Bach realized that the following movement, a turba-chorus with the words "Wo ist der neugeborene König der Juden" ("Where is the newborn King of the Jews?" no. 45) could not possibly fit underneath the opening chorus. As the turba-chorus was part of the Gospel narrative, it had to follow *attacca* after the recit. Bach therefore decided to abandon the sketched recit and enter the text again after the opening chorus. He could now compose a direct transition between the text of the evangelist and the turba-chorus of the wise men.

Bach's custom to enter the music for recits later is further confirmed by some additional details. In recit no. 18 of part II, the bc line overlaps with the title for the following aria. A similar case appears in part V, recit no. 50. Bach composed the music *after* the parody of terzet, no. 51, had been entered. He wrote the text for the recit, not yet anticipating that he would compose a short postlude of two measures in the bc. In the final version, the final bar line for the recit now overlaps with the title for the terzet, which had already been written at this point.

Recitative 50 is interesting for the compositional process for another reason. The recit contains a quotation from the Old Testament, a combination of Micah 5:1 and 2 Samuel 5:2: "And you Bethlehem in the Jewish region are by no means the smallest among the princes of Judah; for out of you shall come to me the leader who would be a ruler over my people Israel." Bach's setting of the Gospel text reflects the change from the New Testament narrative (Mt 2:5–6) to the quotation from the Old Testament by changing from a simple secco recit with extended bc notes and declamatory voice leading in the tenor into arioso style, which is additionally highlighted by the word "Andante." The change in the character of the voice is supported by the instrumental bass line, which changes into a continuous chain of eighth notes. From a performers' perspective, these changes implied the switch from a free declamatory style to a metered style (*alla battuta*). A glance at the score, though, shows an oddity, that has not been mentioned in the critical commentary for the NBA or in other interpretations of the piece: Bach's handwriting changes slightly at the transition from the Gospel text to the prophetic quote. The letters in the prophetic text are rounder than in the preceding text; this is especially the case for the letter "e" (fig. 5.1). The handwriting in the prophetic text resembles Bach's Latin script instead of his usual German script. As usual, Bach wrote the text first and only later returned to compose the music. The change from German to Latin script indicated that these words had to be set differently from the previous text. The differentiation in script also indicates an alteration in the musical texture. In other words, the change of Bach's handwriting incorporates distinct fonts that almost serve the function of a musical sketch.[65] And if we assume that the gap between the

---

[65] Bach does occasionally change the script when quoting prophetic texts from the Old Testament in his works. A similar case can be found at several places in the fair copy of the *St. Matthew Passion* (D-B

*Figure 5.1* J. S. Bach, BWV 248/50, changes in Bach's handwriting. See the letter "e" in the word "Bethlehem" in lines 1 and 2 (D-B Mus. ms. Bach P 32, fol.55ᵛ) (bpk, Berlin/ Mendelssohn-Archiv, Staatsbibliothek zu Berlin, Stiftung Preussischer Kulturbesitz, Berlin, Germany/Art Resource, NY)

writing of the text and the composition may have been longer (as is known in the case of Handel's compositions), this would have been even more helpful for Bach when he returned to the recit after copying the terzet. We will return to this movement later in the discussion of part V of the oratorio in chapter 10.

While it is not possible in all cases to confirm that Bach composed the recits last, all the cases in which a succession is visible suggest that he did. In no case is there an indication that Bach must have composed a secco recit (or a simpler accompagnato recit) *before* he composed the surrounding movements. The only exception from this rule are those recits that are embedded into a larger context, like the chorale trope in mvt. 7, the combination of turba-chorus and recit in mvt. 45, and especially the chorale trope in mvts. 38 and 40, where Bach simultaneously combined a recit with a chorale. Consequently, Bach's handwriting in these movements, the size of the letters, and the spaces between the words look more uneven than in the other recits, all of which suggests that the text was not written beforehand but rather during the compositional process (and after entering the notes).

## Arranging the hymns

As for the composition of the chorale movements (with the exception of the expanded chorales at the end of parts I, II, and IV), it is clear that Bach entered the melodies first and then composed the remaining voices. The prioritization of the melody can be seen in the final movement of part II, where Bach changed the time signature; but it is also apparent in several of the simpler chorale-settings, especially where the lower voices have more movement than does the melody. Bach

mus.ms. Bach P 25). Since P 25 is a fair copy, the change of script indicates the different character of the text, but it does not serve as a reminder that the text had to be set differently.

occasionally ran out of space and had to squeeze in the notes or even disregard the margins of the bar lines. A typical example is the chorale no. 28 in part III.[66]

## Connections and coherence

The order of composition, as it can be reconstructed from the autograph score, allowed Bach to create a framework primarily based on the large-scale choral movements and arias because they are mostly parodies. The recits then serve as links, a connecting tissue, leading harmonically from one key to the next, but also motivically, as Bach could pick up motivic details from parody movements and then connect the disparate parts into a new coherent unity. We will return to the details of the compositional process in relationship to the texts later; first, here is a brief overview of the third stage, the revision stage.

## Revision stage

While it is methodologically useful and necessary to differentiate between the planning, composition, and revision of the *Christmas Oratorio*, the division is often not as clear-cut as the terminology suggests. We have already seen that Bach changed some of the original plans in the course of the composition, or he realized musical ideas that emerged during the compositional process. The same can be said of the *revision stage*. Bach composed his movements and often made changes—adding details, inserting motifs, or evening out musical transitions. It is often not clear when these changes were made, except that most of them have happened between the composition and the copying of the parts because the performance parts already have most of these revisions. In several cases it is unclear whether the changes were made while he was still working on a specific movement or whether he returned to it after working on a different movement. In spite of this uncertainty, the revisions are still an important source for our understanding of the way Bach manipulated his material and how musical ideas, those that seem to be so natural when we hear them today, emerged. Revisions can be found both in the newly composed movements as well as in the parodies. In both layers of the composition Bach revised the material and added little musical details. At this point in the creation of the oratorio, the parodies and the newly composed movements are treated equally.

An instructive example for a revision in a newly composed movement can be found in part II, mvt. 18, the recit "So geht denn hin." The sextuplet motion in the

---

[66] D-B Mus. ms. Bach P 32, part III, 7. It was a usual procedure for Bach to enter the melody first and then compose the rest of a chorale setting "around" it. This can be seen in numerous examples in the *Orgelbüchlein*; see Russell Stinson, *The Orgelbüchlein* (Oxford: Oxford University Press, 1999), 36–37.

second half of the movement was not original. Initially, Bach composed a sixteenth-note motif that was later changed to sextuplets by inserting two additional notes to each group of notes (ex. 5.3). The new version underscores the lullaby character of the text, mirroring the rocking motion of a cradle. It is not clear when Bach made this change but it was clearly made *after* the completion of the movement. Small revisions of a different kind are also encountered in the opening movement of the oratorio, which was a parody of a chorus from BWV 214. In the secular piece, the flutes played a short motif in m. 2. In the parody at the beginning of BWV 248, Bach first copied the motif but then gave it a sharper profile by adding a rest and turning the initial sixteenth notes into thirty-second notes. The score shows that Bach inserted the original version first and then applied the revision.

*Example 5.3* J. S. Bach, BWV 248/18, earlier and final versions of the bc

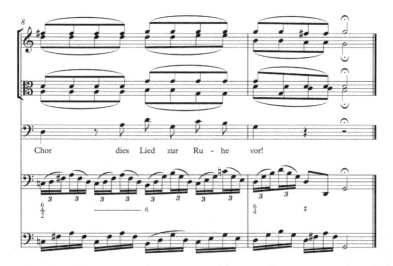

The revision stage was the point in the compositional process at which Bach could add details that either helped to emphasize or interpret the text, or which added interest and rhythmic profile to a movement, as in the case of the first movement. A final step in the revision stage was the recasting of the instrumental and vocal parts Bach's copyists had made based on his score. This was an opportunity for Bach to make corrections and to add performance instructions such as slurs, staccato marks, and tempo markings. In one case, the copying of the parts even involved a return to the composition stage. The instruments in the second part of the oratorio had originally been oboe d'amore I + II, oboe da caccia I + II, violin I + II, viola, and bc. After completing the score Bach decided to give the obbligato part in aria no. 15, "Frohe Hirten" to the first flute and to add flauti traversi to the instrumentation of the rest of the second part as well. The situation was easy in the first half of the part, as the flutes either simply double the violins (nos. 10 and 12) or play the obbligato solo part (no. 15); Bach could instruct his copyist Johann Gottlob Haupt to copy the lines from those instruments into the flute parts. In the second half of part II, however, the designation of the flute parts was more complicated. In the angelic Gloria, "Ehre sei Gott," the lines of the flutes are derived from other instrumental parts; they sometimes double the strings and at other occasions the oboi d'amore. Bach, therefore, took over from his copyist and copied (or rather created) the flute parts for the mvts. 17–23. After finishing the parts for the first flute, he also copied the entire part book for the second flute.[67]

The following chapters analyze some of the revisions made by Bach as far as they either represent a significant step within the compositional process or highlight a particular aspect in Bach's understanding of the text of an aria, recit, or movement for chorus. It is not the goal to replace (or to narrate) the critical commentary, and many smaller changes will have to be left unmentioned.

[67] I am grateful to David G. Rugger for sharing with me an unpublished article about the traverse flute in part II of the *Christmas Oratorio*.

# 6

# Dichotomies (Part I)

Chapter 3 demonstrated how the libretto for the *Christmas Oratorio* oscillates between three layers of time. The "threefold coming" of Christ—in the past, in the human heart, and at the end of times—serves as a hermeneutical key for the interpretation of the Christmas narrative. While the libretto moves back and forth between these three layers, the text also describes a gradual shift from the first and second comings in the earlier parts, to the third coming at the very end of the oratorio. Part I of the *Christmas Oratorio* is characterized by two binary oppositions: on the one hand, the dichotomy between the then and now, the first and second coming of Christ; on the other hand, the dichotomy between the royal office of Christ and his humble birth in a manger. While this second dichotomy is already present as a problem in the Gospel text, it is expanded and elaborated in Bach's own theological tradition where sermons and theological treatises focus extensively on what theologians understood as the "paradox" of Jesus's birth. Based on these two dichotomies, the first part of the *Christmas Oratorio* can be divided into two halves. The first five movements establish the juxtaposition of historical past and existential presence. In the second half of part I (mvts. 6–8), the focus shifts to the paradox of Christ's status between royalty and humility. The existential interpretation of this paradox also problematizes the conflict between human reason and divine will—one that was of particular interest during the early enlightenment.[1] The final movement of part I, the chorale setting "Ach mein herzliebes Jesulein," represents a synthesis of the two main topics of part I, as it amalgamates the idea of the *inhabitatio Christi* and the royal office of Christ. The opening chorus, "Jauchzet, frohlocket," while belonging to the first sequence of movements, also sets the stage for the second topic, as it evokes with its trumpets and timpani a royal soundscape, to which Bach then returns in the second half of part I. The strong presence of binary opposites allowed

---

[1] Cf. Elke Axmacher, "Aus Liebe will mein Heiland leben: Zum Text des Weihnachts-Oratoriums BWV 248 von Johann Sebastian Bach," in *Im Klang der Wirklichkeit: Musik und Theologie. Martin Petzoldt zum 65. Geburtstag*, ed. Norbert Bolin and Markus Franz (Leipzig: Evangelische Verlagsanstalt, 2011), 112–14.

Bach to employ musical juxtapositions as well, especially in the second half of part I where the composer makes extensive use of these musical contrasts.

## Temporal dichotomies (mvts. 1–5)

The libretto for part I interprets the historical narrative of Jesus's birth not only as an event of existential relevance but as taking place simultaneously in the past and in the present. The opening movement encourages the praise of the "highest" for what he has done "today": "Rühmet, was *heute* der Höchste getan!"[2] The Gospel recit (no. 2) is then followed by an accompagnato recit for alto, which highlights the present significance even more by opening three of its lines with "now":

| | |
|---|---|
| *Nun* wird mein liebster Bräutigam, | *Now* will my most beloved bridegroom, |
| *Nun* wird der Held aus Davids Stamm . . . | *Now* will the champion from the tribe of David . . . |
| *Nun* wird der Stern aus Jacob scheinen. | *Now* will the star out of Jacob shine. |

The following alto aria anticipates the immediate arrival of the "most beloved" as an event that takes place "today": "Deine Wangen müssen *heut* viel schöner prangen" (*This day* your cheeks must sparkle much lovelier). The use of present tense underscores the immediacy of the narrative. Seen within the context of the "second coming" of Christ, the two alto movements in particular transpose the historical narrative into the present. The opening movement already sets the stage by referring to *today*, and the chorale-setting no. 5, "Wie soll ich dich empfangen" (How shall I receive you), while not determining the reception of Christ temporally, summarizes the present significance by asking its question in the voice of the Christian congregation. Later movements of the *Christmas Oratorio* will return to the notion of Christ's birth as a current event, albeit less frequently than in part I:

| Part II, 22 | Daß es uns *heut* so schön gelinget | that for us *this day* has prospered so beautifully |
|---|---|---|
| Part II, 23 | *nun*mehr eingestellet hast | have *now* presented yourself |
| Part III, 24 | Wenn wir dir *itzo* die Ehrfurcht erweisen | when we *now* show you reverence |
| Part IV, 39 | Sollt ich *nun* das Sterben scheuen | Shall I *now* shy away from having to die |

[2] The emphases here and in the following quotes from the libretto are mine.

| Part V, 43 | Weil *anheut* unser aller Wunsch gelungen | because *today* the wish of all of us has come true |
| Part V, 51 | er *ist* schon *wirklich* hier | he really *is already* here |

The understanding of Christ's coming as a present-tense occurrence reflects the doctrine of the threefold coming of Christ. The opening movements thus provide the hermeneutical key for the understanding of the entire biblical narrative in the oratorio. This concept also ties in with Bach's oratorio concept in the early 1730s, as we read in chapter 4. Bach's oratorios are not sacred operas but rather meditations on the biblical narrative: they provide a metanarrative that transposes the historical event into the present. In addition to the juxtaposition of past and present, part I of the oratorio is subdivided into a section on the expectation of the coming of Jesus (Advent) and his birth. The first five movements of the oratorio express this expectation and longing and could be aptly called the "advent-portion" of the *Christmas Oratorio*. Since performances of concerted music after the first Sunday in Advent were not permitted in Leipzig until Christmas, these opening movements give Bach and his librettist the opportunity to touch on some of the topics that were frequently treated in Advent cantatas. Tobias Heinrich Schubart, in his collection of cantata texts from 1733, prints the following opening movement for the fourth Sunday in Advent:[3]

CHOR DER FRÖLICHEN
Lieblicher Saiten ergetzendes Schallen,
Lockender Flöten besänftigtes Lallen,
Schärffet die Töne doch! Greiffet auch an!
Lasset das Klingen umd Singen itzt
    streiten!
Lasst es die Stimme Johannis begleiten[4]

CHORUS OF THE CHEERFUL
Delightful sound of the lovely strings,
calming babble of the enticing flutes,
Sharpen the sounds! Start the attack!
Let the sound [of the instruments]
    and the singing begin their contest!
Let them accompany the sound of
    John [the Baptist]

Schubart's text displays some similarities with mvt.1 of BWV 248. Similarly, its enumeration of different instruments also resembles the parody model for this movement from BWV 214.[5] Even closer to the libretto for the *Christmas Oratorio* is the text of a

---

[3] The text was composed by G. Ph. Telemann, TVWV 1:1048.

[4] Tobias Heinrich Schubart, *Ruhe nach geschehener Arbeit: in unterschiedlichen Gedichten und Uebersetzungen, der Ehre Gottes und dem Dienste des Nächsten gewidmet* (Hamburg: Kißner, 1733), 177–78.

[5] BWV 214/1: "Tönet, ihr Pauken! Erschallet, Trompeten! Klingende Saiten, erfüllet die Luft!" (Sound, you drums! Ring out, you trumpets! Resonant strings, fill the air!).

cantata for the first Sunday of Advent by Gottfried Ephraim Scheibel from 1725.[6] The libretto begins with a movement of striking resemblance to the one used by Bach. Both texts paraphrase freely the beginning of Psalm 100, "Jauchzet dem Herrn alle Welt! Dienet dem Herrn mit Freuden, kommt vor sein Angesicht mit Frohlocken," (Make a joyful noise to the Lord, all the earth. Worship the Lord with gladness, come into his presence with rejoicing). In the following movements Scheibel introduces the metaphor of bride and bridegroom and implores Jesus to come to the believer; later he also praises Christ as the king. The opening movement reads:[7]

| | |
|---|---|
| Jauchzet, frolocket, ihr Völcker der Erden! | Shout, exult you people of the Earth! |
| Jerusalem stimme der Säyten Thon an! | Jerusalem, let the sound of the strings ring! |
| Erschallt ihr hellen Lüffte! | Resonate, you bright gales! |
| Erthönet Zions Klüffte! | Resound, clefts of Zion! |
| Laßt euch vermelden: | Let it be known to you: |
| Wir haben den König, wir grüssen den Helden, | We have the king, we greet the hero, |
| Bestreut ihm zu Ehren mit Palmen die Bahn.[8] | Honor him by spreading palm branches on his path. |

In spite of the similarities between Bach's oratorio and Scheibel's text, it is not necessary to assume that the libretto of BWV 248 was in any way modeled on Scheibel. Rather, it demonstrates the conventionality of motifs, topics, and images employed by the libretto for the *Christmas Oratorio*.[9] But it does show that the first movements of Bach's oratorio touch on topics that were traditionally associated with the season of Advent. This is confirmed by a cantata libretto by Gottfried Scherzer, written for Gera and published in 1722. The text for the first Sunday in Advent begins with a biblical dictum from Zechariah 2:10 (which was probably set as a chorus) and is

[6] I am grateful to Robin A. Leaver who drew my attention to this text.

[7] The text was set by Johann Balthasar Christian Freißlich (1687–1764) in a cantata for the first Sunday in Advent; Freislich's cantata only uses strings and flutes and no brass or reed instruments. The score is preserved in Stadt- und Kreisbibliothek Sondershausen (D-SHs/Mus.A7:6).

[8] Gottfried Ephraim Scheibel, *Poetische Andachten Uber alle gewöhnliche Sonn- und Fest-Tage, durch das ganze Jahr: Allen Herren Componisten und Liebhabern der Kirchen-Music zum Ergötzen* (Leipzig/ Breßlau: Rohrlach, 1725), 1.

[9] We find a similar text in Georg Philipp Telemann's *Harmonischem Gottesdienst* (1725/26), "Jauchzet, frohlocket, der Himmel ist offen" (TVWV 1:953), Cantata 70 for the second day of Christmas, in *G.Ph. Telemann, Musikalische Werke V*, new ed. (Kassel and Basel: Bärenreiter).

followed by a recit that draws a connection between the daughter of Zion, the image of the bride from the Song of Songs, and the *inhabitatio Christi*:

[I.] [CHORUS?]:

| | |
|---|---|
| Freue dich und sey frölich, du Tochter Zion; denn siehe ich komme und will bey dir wohnen, spricht der HErr. | Be cheerful and rejoice, Daughter Zion; for I will come and dwell among you, says the Lord. |

[II.] Recit:

| | |
|---|---|
| Auf auf! betrübter Geist | Up, up! distressed spirit |
| Die Stimme deines Freundes läst sich hören, | The voice of your friend is being heard, |
| Der dein Verlobter heist, | Who is called your betrothed. |
| Will nun dein Ach! in Freuden=Lieder kehren. | [He] will turn your sigh [Ach!] into songs of joy. |
| Er wehlet sich dein Hertzens Hauß | He has chosen your heart as his house |
| An statt des Himmels Kostbarkeit | Instead of the wealth of heaven |
| Zur frohen Wohnung aus; | And he will dwell there joyfully; |
| Ach so bemühe dich es würdig zu bereiten.[10] | Be diligent in preparing it [the heart] properly. |

## The opening movement

Bach's librettist combines these customary Advent motifs with the portion of the Christmas narrative from Luke 2 that immediately precedes the birth of Jesus. The sequence of five movements begins with the opening chorus "Jauchzet, frohlocket, auf, preiset die Tage, rühmet, was heute der Höchste getan" (Shout, exult, arise, praise the days, glorify what the Most High this day has done"). The music of the movement is a parody of the first chorus from the secular cantata *Tönet, ihr Pauken! Erschallet, Trompeten*, BWV 214 (1733). The use of instruments closely follows their mention in the secular text; first, it introduces the timpani, followed by the trumpets, then the strings, and finally the poets:

| | |
|---|---|
| Tönet, ihr Pauken! Erschallet, Trompeten! | Sound, you drums! Ring out, you trumpets! |
| Klingende Saiten, erfüllet die Luft! | Resonant strings, fill the air! |
| Singet itzt Lieder, ihr muntren Poeten | Sing songs now, you lively poets! |

[10] Gottfried Heinrich Scherzer, *Texte zur Kirchen-Music, So Mit Gott Aufs 1722. Jahr in Gera soll aufgeführet werden* (Leipzig: Tietze, [1721]), 3.

The order of the text is reflected in an effective sonic depiction by the timpani solo at the beginning (m. 1), a trumpet fanfare (m. 5), the entrance of the strings (m. 5), and the chorus (m. 33). The correspondence between text and music in BWV 214 follows a long established model in Baroque musical poetry. Dieterich Buxtehude sets an analogous enumeration of musical instruments in a similar way (*Schlagt, Künstler, Ihr Pauken und Saiten* BuxWV 122);[11] as does Telemann in the first bass aria of his Christmas oratorio *Hirten bei der Krippe zu Bethlehem*, TVWV 1:797 (1759).[12] But Bach's movement is not simply a literal translation of the text into music. While the entrance of the instruments roughly follows their mention in the text, Bach introduces additional instruments, such as flutes (m. 2) and oboes (m. 4). The opening measures thus already go beyond the groups of instruments listed in the libretto. Although the details were clearly motivated by the text, Bach's instrumental color-pallet is much larger. He composes the universal praise of the Saxon Electress and Polish queen that draws its universality from the succession of the different instrumental sounds in his orchestra. The autograph score of BWV 214 (Mus ms P 41 adn. 1) shows that this extraordinary beginning of the movement was not Bach's initial concept but the result of a revision (ex. 6.1). The drum motifs were originally enveloped by a descending motif in the strings (similar but not identical to the ones we now find from m. 5 on). The movement still has a buildup of sound at the beginning, but the individual instruments (and especially the timpani) are less exposed than in the final version. The original plan for the opening movement of BWV 214 had been to create a much fuller sound. Bach then reduced the instrumentation to juxtapose the different instrumental groups in an intricate dialogue. Robert Marshall has suggested that Bach's decision to revise the beginning of the movement came somewhat hesitantly as such blatant effects contradicted his esthetic ideals. It was, according to Marshall, a concession to (or even a fascination with) newer operatic ideals because they were popular at the courts of Dresden and other German operatic centers.[13] Considering that Bach's oratorio was an attempt to transfer a "new" genre from Dresden to Leipzig (see chap. 4), the opening with an effective timpani motif was a fitting way to begin the piece.

When Bach parodied the movement in the *Christmas Oratorio* he took this as an opportunity for additional, albeit smaller, revisions in the opening measures. One of these changes appears at the very beginning. Bach originally copied the

---

[11] See Kerala J. Snyder, *Dieterich Buxtehude: Organist in Lübeck*, rev. ed. (Rochester, NY: University of Rochester Press, 2007), 413.

[12] In Telemann's aria the text lists the instruments played by the shepherds, and the mention of each instrument by the bass singer is followed by a short phrase played by the specific instrument.

[13] Robert L. Marshall, "Bach at Mid-Life: The Christmas Oratorio and the Search for New Paths," *Bach* 43 (2012): 10.

*Example 6.1* J. S. Bach, BWV 214/1, rejected draft, mm. 1–8

version from the secular model and then subsequently inserted rhythmic changes that sharpened the rhythmic profile of the flute and oboe parts. Some interpreters have viewed the opening movement of the oratorio as esthetically inferior to its secular model because it lacks the close correspondence between text and music. However, I suggest viewing the parody as a further step in the compositional process, which in this case leads from the rejected beginning in BWV 214 to the executed version and finally to the rhythmically more intricate version in BWV 248 (ex. 6.2).

*Example 6.2*  Flute parts in BWV 248/1 and BWV 214/1

The opening chorus follows a regular *da capo* form. An extensive ritornello of thirty-three measures establishes the main musical material for the entire movement, and the first eight measures are a grand elaboration of the D-major triad. While harmonically static, the measures highlight the differences in instrumental color by juxtaposing the individual instrumental groups. The first eight measures serve as *vordersatz* (initial statement) in the ritornello, followed by a sequential *nachsatz* (secondary statement) in mm. 9–16. Alfred Dürr has shown that the opening sixteen measures now become a large vordersatz by themselves, followed by a nachsatz of sixteen measures that ends the ritornello.[14] This final section creates a climax by featuring sequential material for eight measures, first in the strings and woodwind instruments, before the motifs are handed over to the first trumpet (mm. 25–33). Although Bach employs a large ensemble, the ritornello is characterized by a constant change of instrumental groups and instrumental colors within the orchestra. Tutti passages are reserved for structurally important moments: the cadence at the end of the first sixteen-measure section and the final cadence of the ritornello in mm.

---

[14]  Dürr, *Weihnachts-Oratorium*, 36.

31/32.[15] The opening ritornello is also a continuous expansion of sonic space; from the dry timpani calls in the opening measures to the instrumental crescendo in mm. 5–9, and finally to the regal trumpet solo in mm. 25–33. This sonic climax is supported by a constant play with the harmonic tension. Only at the very end does Bach return to the tonic chord, which had been featured so prominently in the first eight measures but then had been avoided. Bach's original plans for the opening movement of BWV 214 had lacked this gradual expansion. Thus, the revision of the beginning has larger esthetic ramifications as it affects the overall rhetoric of the ritornello, which is that of a gradual expansion, culminating in the trumpet solo.

The first vocal part (mm. 33–137) is divided into five smaller sections, which differ in text and their use of ritornello material. Sections $A_1$ and $A_3$ not only share the same text but also make extensive use of the ritornello material by either quoting it literally or by building the chorus into quotations of the first sixteen measures of the ritornello. The sections are, as Dürr has pointed out, dominated by the instruments, while the voices are limited to declamatory phrases and a homophonic texture[16]:

| 33–50 | $A_1$ | D->V of D[17] | Jauchzet, frohlocket! auf, preiset die Tage, Rühmet, was heute der Höchste getan! | Shout, exult, arise, praise the days, glorify what the Most High this day has done! |
|---|---|---|---|---|
| 50–81 | $A_2$ | V of D->A | Lasset das Zagen, verbannet die Klage, Stimmet voll Jauchzen und Fröhlichkeit an! | Leave off faintheartedness, ban lamenting; break forth into song, full of shouting and rejoicing! |
| 81–89 | Rit | A->D | | |
| 89–106 | $A_3$ | D->V of D | Jauchzet, frohlocket! auf, preiset die Tage, Rühmet, was heute der Höchste getan! | Shout, exult, arise, praise the days, glorify what the Most High this day has done! |
| 106–37 | $A_4$ | V of D->D | Lasset das Zagen, verbannet die Klage, Stimmet voll Jauchzen und Fröhlichkeit an! | Leave off faintheartedness, ban lamenting; break forth into song, full of shouting and rejoicing! |

[15] Measures 25–33 involve the entire ensemble as well, but a listener perceives the measures as a trumpet solo with accompaniment.

[16] Dürr, *Weihnachts-Oratorium*, 36.

[17] While the music moves toward A (the $V^{th}$ degree of D) the dominant is not confirmed by a clear modulation.

This balance shifts in sections A$_2$ and A$_4$ where the voices dominate in a polyphonic texture, while the instruments assume an accompanying role. The fourteen measures of polyphonic imitation are based on an ascending trill-figure, which is briefly foreshadowed by a short motif played by the oboes and flutes (mm. 2 and 4) at the beginning of the ritornello.[18] Toward the end of subsection A$_2$, Bach returns to the homophonic vocal texture, which is now built into the final sixteen measures of the opening ritornello. A short instrumental interlude of seven measures, loosely based on the ritornello (mm. 9–12), leads to the second half of the A section (A$_3$ and A$_4$), which is a slightly varied version of the first half. The most significant differences are changes in the entrance of voices (the order of instrumental groups in mm. 90–94 and the order of vocalists in the polyphonic section, m. 106), and the harmonic trajectory, as Bach now modulates back to the tonic D major at m. 89. The separation of the extensive A section into two contrasting parts allowed Bach to react to the text of the secular model more directly. In the secular model, the two opening lines express the praise of the Electress through the sound of musical instruments (A$_1$), while line 3 urges the poets to sing songs, which consequently leads to an emphasis of the vocal layer (A$_2$). Line 4 of the A section then returns to a praise of the Electress, which Bach sets in homophonic declamation with a vivid instrumental accompaniment. In the parody in the *Christmas Oratorio*, the contrast between A$_1$ and A$_2$ (and accordingly between A$_3$ and A$_4$) has a different purpose. The first and second lines of the text praise what "the highest" has done "today," while line 3 articulates the absence of despair and mourning before the final line of the A section returns to the topic of praise.

The B section consists of two contrasting parts: B$_1$ (mm. 138–70) stands in darker B minor and features a dense polyphonic texture in the voices, accompanied only by short staccato-motifs in the strings. The first exposition (mm. 138–54) of the polyphonic material is followed by a second one (mm. 154–70) in which the instrumental participation is increased by doubling the voices in the strings while the staccato-motifs are taken over by the woodwinds. The listener perceives it as a logical continuation of this instrumental crescendo when the following short interlude (mm. 170–85) adds the first trumpet and then features a short dialogue between the strings and woodwind group. The motivic material of this interlude is derived from the ritornello, mm. 9–12, which had already been used for the short instrumental section between A$_1$/A$_2$ and A$_3$/A$_4$. After the interlude, Bach returns to the last sixteen measures of the opening ritornello for the final line of the text. After this, the whole A section is repeated in a complete *da capo*.

The entire movement is constructed from the material established in the ritornello; a technique that Bach commonly used as a structural paradigm in his vocal

[18] Dürr characterized the polyphonic sections of the opening movement as independent from the ritornello ("ritornellfrei"), Dürr, *Weihnachts-Oratorium*, 36. While he is correct that these sections do not quote entire measures from the ritornello, the musical material used in the imitation is still present in the instrumental introduction as well.

and instrumental works. Laurence Dreyfuss compared Bach's ritornello technique to the construction of an "ideal machine."[19] The structure of the movement is motivated by the text, but it also allows Bach to explore the wide array of musical possibilities inherent in the material of the instrumental introduction. Dürr has perceptively pointed out that this form of motivic unification is encountered again in the aria "Bereite dich, Zion," the very first aria of the oratorio.[20] The extensive use of the ritornello material also establishes a second layer of structure in the movement, which is embedded in the simple *da capo* form (ABA): after presenting the entire ritornello, Bach separates the two halves of the instrumental introduction and interpolates a short polyphonic section. Following a short interlude (derived from a musical motif in the ritornello), the section is repeated with some variations. For the B section, Bach introduces a new musical idea (again a short polyphonic section), followed by a short interlude that harkens back to the first interlude, before the B section ends with a version of the second half of the ritornello:

| | | | |
|---|---|---|---|
| Rit a | 1–16 | Rit | Rit |
| Rit b | 17–33 | | |
| Vocal section a | 33–50 | $A_1$ | |
| Vocal section c | 50–64 | | |
| Vocal section b | 65–81 | $A_2$ | |
| Rit [a] | 81–89 | | A |
| Vocal section a | 89–106 | $A_3$ | |
| Vocal section c | 106–20 | $A_4$ | |
| Vocal section b | 121–37 | | |
| Vocal section d | 138–70 | $B_1$ | |
| Rit [a] | 170–85 | | B |
| Vocal section b | 186–201 | $B_2$ | |

Viewed from a structural perspective, the B section is a modification of the A section: The opening part of the ritornello is eliminated and the order of events (free section (d) and interlude) is inverted. This resemblance and rearrangement of

[19] See the excellent analysis of Bach's ritornello technique in Laurence Dreyfus, *Bach and the Patterns of Invention* (Cambridge, MA: Harvard University Press, 1996), 59–102.

[20] Dürr, *Weihnachts-Oratorium*, 36.

familiar material creates a tension that must be resolved with a complete state-ment of the opening section, which then takes place in the repetition of the entire A section.

Since the text for the parody was modeled on the secular text, major changes to the music were not necessary when Bach adapted the movement from BWV 214 for the *Christmas Oratorio*. The changes are mostly subtle and fall into three categories. The first category includes additions of performance instructions, like trill signs, staccato marks, or slurs. An early example is encountered in mm. 13–15, where Bach adds staccato points in the strings and a trill sign in the first trumpet and the strings. The staccato points are only added in the performance parts while the trill already appears in Bach's score. These additions (more of which occur through-out the rest of the piece) do not constitute substantial changes, and it is possible (even likely in many cases) that they merely codify performance practices that were already applied in the performance of the secular model in 1733.

The changes of the second category are more substantial and include manipula-tions of smaller musical details. An example is the sharpening of the rhythm in the flute and oboe motif in mm. 2 and 4. Bach makes the same changes later throughout the movement (for instance mm. 34, 36, 38). These revisions were not necessary for correct voice-leading or text but show instead Bach's wish for continuous improve-ment on his compositions. The small modification of the voice-leading in the bass in m. 47 falls into a similar category. The original line in BWV 214/1 had three *f*♯s, which are now changed into *f*♯–*d'*–*f*♯. The change breaks up three repeated notes in the three lower voices, adding more variety to the voice-leading.[21] This striving for perfection also included the correction of some compositional mistakes. In m. 27 the secular model has the forbidden parallel fifth followed immediately by a parallel octave between viola and bc. After copying the problematic measures into the score, Bach must have noticed the errors and corrected them by erasing the original note and overwriting it with a version that avoided the parallel progressions.[22]

Most of the significant changes fall in a third category and are motivated (or necessitated) by the new text. Even though the model and the parody shared the same general affect, the new words sometimes required small adjustments to accen-tuate the right keywords or to imbue particular phrases with the proper affective properties. A change of this kind was especially necessary in the setting of the third line of the A section. The secular model admonishes the poets to sing songs, while the sacred text mentions "fearheartedness" and "lamenting." Measures 58–66 illus-trate how Bach makes the necessary adjustments while still maintaining most of the musical texture (ex. 6.3): A vivid descending melisma in the tenor on "Poeten" in m. 59 is reduced to a simpler descending eighth-note motion on "Zagen," now

---

[21] This change was already made while Bach was copying the piece from BWV 214, as the auto-graph score shows no corrections.

[22] A similar case can be found in mm. 75 and 77, see NBA II/6, KB, 27.

progressing in parallel thirds with the vocal bass. In m. 60 Bach keeps a melisma on the same word, which now motivically prepares the entrance of the same motif on "verbannet" in the bass. The motif in the alto adds emphasis to the word "Klage" and underscores its lamenting affect. A heightened state of emotionality also characterizes mm. 65/66, where Bach accentuates the word "verbannet" with an expressive melismatic embellishment in soprano and bass. While the voice-leading departs from the secular model, the notes were simply borrowed from the first violin for the soprano and the bc for the bass respectively. By merely redistributing lines from the model, Bach was able to change the vocal parts without having to compose any new music.[23]

*Example 6.3* J. S. Bach, BWV 214/1 and BWV 248/1, mm. 58–66

---

[23] The changes in mm. 115-20, based on the same text, are slightly different but have the same effect.

While the words "lebe" in BWV 214 and "Jauchzen" in BWV 248 have a match-ing, joyful affect, the new text necessitates a change in mm. 78/79. In BWV 214 the composer sets the word "lebe" (living) with long notes in the framing voices while the tenor expresses the liveliness of the text through a vivid melismatic line. This worked perfectly for the secular text, but the word "Jauchzen" in BWV 248 elicited a more brilliant setting. Bach thus borrows a motif from the oboes and gives it to the soprano, while modifying the other voices accordingly. Only the melismatic line in the tenor stays the same.

A significant change, more covert than the previous one but symptomatic of Bach's parody technique, is encountered in mm. 190–92. The secular model has the text "Königin lebe und blühe" (May the Queen live and blossom), which had origi-nally motivated Bach to set the words in the bass with a vivid flourish of sixteenth notes against the simple, syllabic eighth-note declamation in the upper voices. In spite of the obvious textual motivation, the two measures do not sound very elegant. This is especially the case in m. 191, where the vocal bass does not move in unison with the instrumental bass. Bach changed the measures in the oratorio and reduced the bass to simpler declamation (ex. 6.4). This last example falls somewhere between categories two and three. While the original bass line was motivated by the text, Bach could have kept the two measures of music with the new words; he does so at places where they sounded less awkward, as in mm. 199–200 in the alto. The change was probably more motivated by Bach's wish to improve the musical texture than by the new text of the sacred parody.

*Example 6.4* J. S. Bach, BWV 214/1 and BWV 248/1, mm. 190–92

Outside of our three categories of subtle musical changes falls a curious correction in the opening movement, one that also reflects a characteristic feature of the parody process. In mm. 33–47 and 89–100 Bach entered a phrase from the text of the secular cantata in all four voices. The wrong text even included a mistake he had already made in the secular model, writing "gestimmete" (tuned) instead of "klingende" (sounding) at the end of the soprano part (mm. 46/47).[24] Alfred Dürr has suggested that Bach must have copied the score from BWV 214 to BWV 248 rather mechanically and thus replicated the earlier mistake.[25] While this error might

[24] See the critical commentary for BWV 214: NBA I/36, KB, 110.
[25] NBA I/36, KB, 110.

shed some light on the attention Bach spent on copying the earlier movement for the *Christmas Oratorio*, it does not sufficiently explain the quotation of the earlier, secular text in the sacred composition. Two explanations are likely:

(1.) Bach simply made a mistake while copying; in fact, copying mistakes in the score of BWV 248 are not unusual. The problem of this assumption is that it does not explain sufficiently why Bach made the same mistake twice; first in mm. 33–47 and then again later in mm. 89–100.

(2.) The half-sentence "Tönet ihr Pauken, erschallet Trompeten" was originally meant to be the first line for the *Christmas Oratorio*. This explanation was considered as an option by Meinrad Walter[26], and Alfred Dürr mentioned this possibility as well.[27]

One option we can exclude is the possibility that an earlier version of the text began with "Tönet ihr Pauken" and then continued with a version similar to the current text. A closer analysis of the written text, especially the shades of the ink, shows that Bach did not write a conflation of the two texts. This is clearly visible in mm. 45/46 in the vocal bass: while "Tage" (the last word of the correction) and "rühmet" (the first word of the continuation after the correction) have exactly the same light shade of ink, "Trompeten" (from the secular libretto) in mm. 44/45 is written in darker ink. The same applies to the soprano line in mm. 46/47. The different shades of ink cannot be differentiated in all instances, but where the text before and after the correction is in a different shade of ink, the correction and the continuation always have the same color. In other words, the entry of the "wrong" text and the entry of the complete "correct" text represent two distinct stages in Bach's work on the first movement. There is no evidence that Bach wrote a version of the text that combines the words from BWV 248 and 214. Since there is no apparent reason for Bach (or the librettist) to change the words at the last minute, we can assume that Bach simply made a mistake while he was copying the music from BWV 214. It is still peculiar though, that Bach makes the mistake in all for voices and not just in one. To understand this we should consider how Bach copied the piece, that is, we have to assume that he copied the music for the entire movement first, before he set out to insert the new text and before he applied some of the minor musical changes to the music. While copying the music he must have inserted some of the text from the original as well. Our analysis of the movement has already shown that its complex structure with different sections derived from the same material but with different texts. Bach's reason for entering

---

[26] Walter, *Weihnachtsoratorium*, 44.

[27] KB NBA II/6, 201, fn. 5.

the text at the beginning of sections $A_1$ and $A_3$ was to indicate when the first text had to be repeated. In other words, it is a textual marker for the structure of the piece—which in this case, unfortunately, used the wrong text. We will encounter another wrong text-marker (with the correct text albeit at the wrong place) in the opening chorus, mvt. 43, part V, of the *Christmas Oratorio*: in m. 64 of this chorus Bach originally inserted the word "Dir" (you) in all four voices; yet, in the final version of the piece the voices enter one measure later (and not at the same time as in the first sketch but staggered), so that he has to cross out the words again. Even though the circumstances are slightly different, this example shows that Bach uses the text-fragments as markers to clarify the structure of a composition. While these markers might be correct in most cases (so that we do not recognize them as such), the cases in which they are wrong they may cause some confusion.

The opening movement of part I of the oratorio has been criticized for relying too much on the underlying secular text and thus establishing a less compelling connection with the new words in the *Christmas Oratorio*. We have seen that the movement is more than a simple musical translation of the secular text as Bach already transcends the text in the opening measures. He then creates a complex musical structure that expands the long ritornello and highlights the different facets of praise. It is noteworthy that Bach utilizes the material from the second half of the ritornello much more than from the first half, thus featuring the pictorial opening less frequently. If we look beyond the obvious text-painting at the beginning, the movement is about expansion: The ensemble is systematically expanded from a simple and dry timpani motif to the full tutti; from a single instrumental color to the entire pallet of Bach's orchestra. While the whole movement as a *da capo* form is cyclical, the opening measures are highly directional. A second characteristic of the ritornello is its regal sonority, produced by the trumpets and timpani. The regal instruments are first introduced in the first half of the ritornello in a fanfare-like fashion; and in the second half of the ritornello Bach builds up tension that culminates with the special entrance of the first trumpet at m. 129. As explained earlier, the oratorio commences with a sequence of movements that evokes poetic and biblical images frequently associated with Advent. The second half of part I explores the meaning of the royal office of Christ, and so this opening movement thus bridges the two topics of part I: the instrumental crescendo with its directional temporality can be heard as a metaphor for the expected advent of Christ, which, once it has taken place, leads to his continuing presence in cyclical time. The pronounced use of the trumpet (and the first trumpet in particular), on the other hand, highlights Jesus as the newborn king, as it is expressed in the aria that brings back the trumpet in the second half of part I, "Großer Herr, o starker König." This way of listening to the opening chorus might be ahistorical in so far as it neglects its prehistory in BWV 214. But it *is* historical as an attempt to hear the chorus within the context of the beginning of the oratorio and especially within the context of the religiosity of Bach's listeners in 1734.

# First recitatives and an aria—setting the stage
## (mvts. 2–5)

With nineteen measures, the first recit of the *Christmas Oratorio* is one of the lon-gest Gospel recits in the entire oratorio. It covers the narrative from the decree by Emperor Augustus for a general census until shortly before the birth of Jesus (Lk 2:1, 3–6). As explained earlier, the libretto leaves out the second verse: "And this census was the very first: and it took place at the time that Cyrinius was gover-nor in Syria,"[28] to de-emphasize the chronological distance between the historical event and the contemporary listener.

Like most of the Gospel recits in Bach's oratorios and Passions, the setting of the text follows a recurring melodic formula, which is employed liberally and can be modified.[29] Each phrase of the text is treated independently, separated from the next one by a rest in the voice. The phrases typically begin with a fourth (ascending or descending), and the movement ends with a falling fourth. Within this framework, which has its origin in the operatic recit as much as in liturgical models for cantil-lation, Bach uses a wide array of variation, based on the specific text. The rhythm of the voice follows the natural speech-rhythm and central words usually coincide with high notes (like "Joseph" in m. 8), or are highlighted by demonstrative har-monic settings, as the name "David" in m. 11, which is emphasized by a harsh dis-sonant chord that lifts it out of the otherwise harmonious context.

The autograph score for the movement shows that, at some points, Bach was unsure about the exact rhythmic realization.[30] A change that demonstrates Bach's attempt to maintain a rhythmic flow and, at the same time, use cadences to highlight the syntactic structure of the text can be seen in mm. 15–16: the second to last note in the tenor in m. 15 was $c\sharp'$ and the first note in the following measure was $a$. Bach changed this to $b$–$g\sharp$–$e\sharp$–$e\sharp$, prolonging harmonic tension with the 6/5 chord on $e\sharp$ in the bc on "Weibe" (wife), which is then resolved in the final half-sentence with the phrase "die war schwanger" (who was pregnant). With his change, the harmonic tension is resolved the very moment when Mary's pregnancy (the motivation for the entire oratorio) is finally revealed.

The story told in the Gospel recit ends immediately before the birth of Jesus, and the two following movements for alto—an accompagnato recit and an aria—transfer

---

[28] The translation follows the translation of the libretto of Bach's oratorios by Michael Marissen, *Bach's Oratorios*, 4, fn. 1.

[29] Cf. the analysis of these recit formulas by Bossuyt for the *Christmas Oratorio* (Bossuyt, *Christmas Oratorio*, 65) and by Konrad Küster for the *St. Matthew Passion* (Küster, "Die Vokalmusik," in *Bach Handbuch*, ed. K. Küster (Kassel/Stuttgart: Bärenreiter/Metzler, 1999), 462–64).

[30] In m. 9 the second note was originally followed by a sixteenth rest and two sixteenth-notes; and in m. 12 the last four notes in the tenor were probably eighth-notes, which were then shortened to lead to a climax on the words "[Ge-] schlechte Davids war" (now in eighth notes).

the anticipation of his birth to the expectation of his Second Coming. The text borrows images from the Song of Songs (bridegroom, beloved, etc.), which are traditionally connected to the idea of mystic unity. The accompagnato (mvt. 3) also refers back to the previous Gospel recit by addressing the bridegroom as the "champion from the tribe of David." The bridegroom is expected to be the "salvation of the earth" and a source of consolation. The rhyme "Bräutigam" and "[Davids] Stamm" in lines 1 and 2 of the recit appears frequently in seventeenth- and eighteenth-century poetry based on the Song of Songs. The best-known example is the first stanza of the chorale "Wie schön leuchtet der Morgenstern," which draws the line from Jacob to David and then to Christ: "Du Sohn Davids aus Jacobs Stamm, mein König und mein Bräutigam" (You, Son of David, from the tribe of Jacob, my king and my bridegroom). But the connection is also limned in a later hymn, published as a Christmas song in the *Schemelli Gesangbuch* from 1736, "O Fürstenkind aus Jacobs Stamm, O meiner Seelen Bräutigam" (O child of princes from the tribe of Jacob, bridegroom of my soul).[31]

The second half of the alto recit introduces visual imagery (likewise rooted in the Old Testament), such as the "star out of Jacob" that breaks forth as a stream of light. The libretto later connects the light metaphor to the *inhabitatio Christi* as well, by comparing the Word of God with a torch (no. 5). The connection to the Second Coming is deepened in the following aria, admonishing Zion (here used as a term denoting the church)[32] to prepare herself as a bride with tender desires, to welcome the "Most Handsome" and "Most Beloved." Bach created the two movements as a pair: both feature the same soloist (alto), and they are sonically connected through the use of the oboi d'amore. In addition, the movements are motivically joined through a shared melodic phrase at the beginning of the recit and the aria. Bach probably copied the aria first, before he composed the recit.[33]

---

[31] Schemelli, no. 202, p. 135; the hymn is sung to the same tune as "Wie schön leuchtet der Morgenstern," which adds another intertextual connection to the Song of Songs; the hymn by Philipp Nicolai makes extensive use of images from the biblical love poem.

[32] A brief survey of publications with the term "Zion" in their title shows that it was frequently used for hymnals and also as an emphatic term for the Protestant church. See, for instance, the Zeitz hymnal from 1736: *Das Gott-lobende Zion, oder, Zeitzisches Kirch- Schul und Haus- Gesang-Buch*; a survey of the churches in Nuremberg from 1733: Johann Jacob Carbach, *Nürnbergisches Zion: worinnen. . . Kirchen-Pflegere, Prediger, Capläne, Rectores und Collegae, sowohl vor als nach der Reformation . . . zu finden sind*; or a book published in celebration of the 200th anniversary of the Augsburg Confession in Jena in 1730: Lorenz Etzdorff, *Des Evangelisch-Lutherischen Zions erfreuliche Vorbereitung zum Andern Jubel-Fest der Augspurgischen Confession*. The examples reflect a broad variety of usages but they also demonstrate that listeners of the opening movements of the *Christmas Oratorio* did not hear the term "Zion" solely as a historical term but that they saw themselves included when the alto aria demanded: Make yourself ready, Zion. The biblical basis for this interpretation of "Zion" is found in Hebrews 12:22–23.

[33] For the order of composition in the oratorio see chapter 5.

The text for the alto recit consists of three sentences, and Bach creates a climactic arch within the settings of each of them. The first phrase of the first sentence ascends to *c♯″* and the second one reaches even higher to *e″* (on the name "David"); this is followed by a sharp descent leading down to *d♯′* on the word "Erden" (accompanied by a harmonically unstable and dissonant seventh-chord with an augmented fourth). The melodic descent reflects the divine descent that takes place with the birth of Jesus.[34] We will see later in the second cantata that Bach makes extensive use of high-low contrasts to depict the difference between the divine and human sphere. The setting of the first sentence ends in the middle of the ambitus of the recit (in neutral territory) with the statement that the child was about to be born. For the first time since the beginning of this movement, Bach reaches a moment of slow harmonic rhythm with an extended E-major chord in root position. A small melismatic embellishment on the word "geboren" (m. 4) not only highlights a central keyword but also links the accompagnato recit back to the preceding Gospel recit, which ended with a similar melodic gesture on "gebären" (give birth, m. 18). The second sentence features visual images and the shining of the "Star of Jacob." Bach again creates a climax by ascending to *c♯″* in the first half, and then superseding this with a leap of a minor seventh from *f♯′* up to *e″* in the second half, coinciding with the word "Strahl." The climax highlights the shining of the "ray," and Bach's score shows an interesting revision of the original alto line: The final note in m. 6 had originally been *c♯″*, so that the leap on "Strahl" would only have been a third. Bach changed this to a minor seventh—obviously to increase the effect of the high note. The final sentence admonishes Zion to cease its crying because its welfare was ascending. The climax of this final section of the recit is reached on the last phrase, coinciding with the words "welfare" and "up."

Even though it had been Bach's plan from the outset to differentiate the Gospel recit and the reflective recits by setting the former as seccos and the latter as

*Figure 6.1* J. S. Bach, BWV 248/3, score with revisions (D-B Mus. ms. Bach P 32, fol. 2ʳ) (bpk, Berlin/Mendelssohn-Archiv, Staatsbibliothek zu Berlin, Stiftung Preussischer Kulturbesitz, Berlin, Germany/Art Resource, NY)

---

[34] We can see a similar use of ascent-descent in the mvt. 7 of part I; in m. 42 Bach sets the text "Des höchsten Sohn kömmt in die Welt" with a descending octave from *d′* to *d*.

accompagnati, the score shows that Bach intended a much simpler accompaniment for this movement, featuring plain extended notes in the two oboi d'amore (not unlike most of the reflective recits in Stölzel's Passion that Bach had performed on Good Friday 1734). After writing down the accompaniment he decided to insert small eighth-note motifs between the phrases of the text. It is clearly visible that the first notes of each group of eighth notes are thicker and that they were changed from a half note. Only in the final cadence is the group of eighth notes original (fig. 6.1 and ex. 6.5).

*Example 6.5*  J. S. Bach, BWV 248/3, reconstruction of original version and final version

The aria "Bereite dich, Zion" (no. 4) follows organically from the preceding recit, as the opening motif picks up the beginning of that piece. The close connection between recit and aria nearly makes us forget that the music was written for a very different text. The choice of an aria that was originally composed to express the distain of the young hero Hercules for the seductive vice Pleasure appears quite odd at first sight. A juxtaposition of the texts for BWV 213/9 and BWV 248/4 brings the contrary affects into sharper relief:

BWV 213/9                                    BWV 248/4

Ich will/mag dich nicht hören, ich will/    Bereite dich, Zion, mit zärtlichen
   mag dich nicht wissen,                      Trieben,
Verworfene Wollust, ich kenne               Den Schönsten, den Liebsten bald bei
   dich nicht.                                 dir zu sehn!
Denn die Schlangen,                         Deine Wangen
So mich wollten wiegend fangen,             Müssen heut viel schöner prangen,
Hab ich schon lange zermalmet,              Eile, den Bräutigam sehnlichst zu
   zerrissen.                                  lieben!

I do not want/like to listen to you,        Make yourself ready, Zion, with tender
   I do not want/like to                       desires,
   acknowledge you,                         to see the Most Handsome, the Most
depraved Pleasure, I know you not.             Beloved, soon at your side!
For the serpents                            This day your cheeks must sparkle
that would seize me in my cradle               much lovelier;
I have long since crushed and torn.         hurry on, to love the Bridegroom most
                                               ardently.

In the process of planning the oratorio, neither Bach nor his librettist seem to have seen a problem in transferring Hercules's aria of rejection into an aria welcoming Jesus. This is because the music had to fulfill two requirements: as part of the first half of the oratorio it needed a regular *da capo* form, and it should also be highly emotional. Both requirements were met by the alto aria from BWV 213. It was also sung by the same voice-type (alto) and did not need to be transposed. Bach only changed the obbligato instruments from violins in the secular model to first violins and oboe d'amore in the oratorio. He also toned down the aggressive undertone of the model, which asked the violins to play staccato, by omitting this performance instruction and by adding slurs (some of them only in the performance parts) to give the accompaniment a smoother and more pleasing character. Additionally, Bach made some changes in the B section of the aria in order to adapt the music to the new text.[35]

---

[35] For the principles of parody in this aria, see Ludwig Finscher, "Zum Parodieproblem bei Bach," in *Bach-Interpretationen*, ed. Martin Geck (Göttingen: Vandenhoeck & Ruprecht, 1969), 100–104, and

The movement is a regular *da capo* aria, which derives much of its material from the opening ritornello.[36] The vordersatz consists of two segments of four measures each; some of the material is echoed in both the upper voice and the basso continuo voice as well. This is followed by a *fortspinnung* (spinning out), sequentially played with broken triads (2+2 mm.) and then leading to a moment of stagnation with a neighbor-note-motif (1+1 mm), before the ritornello ends with a cadential formula.[37] Dürr has explained that vordersatz and fortspinnung are characterized by contrasts: strong rhythmic declamation vs. flowing motion, and tight vocal ambitus vs. wider, instrumental ambitus.[38] The ritornello sets the stage for the decisiveness expressed in both texts through the forceful, declamatory character of the beginning, paired with the ascending fourth that demands attention. The A section of the *da capo* structure is almost exclusively constructed from the material of the ritornello. The first vocal part begins with a statement of the vordersatz, sung by the alto and doubled by the instruments (mm. 17–23). In the beginning of the fortspinnung, Bach interpolates short interjections by the vocalist. The text in the secular original is "ich will nicht" (I do not want to) and "ich mag nicht" (I do not like to), expressing in an almost obstinate way Hercules's rejection of Pleasure. In the parody, Bach uses these short interjections to repeat the two keywords "den Schönsten" (most handsome) and "den Liebsten" (best loved); what had been an obstinate rejection now turns into an emotional affirmation of the beloved bridegroom. The rest of the A section is similarly derived from the ritornello material.[39] The A section closes with a literal repetition of the ritornello, with only a slightly modified cadence.

While Bach needed only small adjustments in the A section to accommodate the new text, the B section demanded more extensive changes. What remains unchanged, however, is a long melismatic line in the bc voice in mm. 90–99, which had originally been motivated by the "snakes" that attempted to capture the young hero Hercules. Bach keeps this line, which now loses its pictorial function and merely serves as a reminder of the fortspinnung-motif from the ritornello. A moment where the new text does not mesh smoothly with the old music is mm. 103–5, where the original text "lange" (long) was set with a long *b'-natural* in the alto. The sacred text now has the word "eile," and the hastening expressed in the text is hard to reconcile with the resting of the singer on one note. The second time the long note appears (mm. 107–9), Bach combines it with the word "sehnlichst" and the listener can hear the long note as an expression of the ardent longing for the bridegroom.

Hans-Jürgen Möller, "Das Wort-Ton-Verhältnis im Weihnachtsoratorium Johann Sebastian Bachs," *Neue Zeitschrift für Musik* 113/12 (1972): 688–89.

[36] The movement has the following structure:
mm. 1–16   Ritornello | mm. 17–72   Vocal section A | mm. 73–88   Ritornello |
mm. 89–138   Vocal section B | *da capo* (mm. 1–88)

[37] See also the description in Dürr, *Weihnachts-Oratorium*, 29.

[38] Dürr, *Weihnachts-Oratorium*, 29, cf. Walter, *Weihnachtsoratorium*, 57.

[39] Cf. Dürr, *Weihnachts-Oratorium*, 29–30, for a more detailed harmonic and thematic analysis of the movement.

*Example 6.6*  J. S. Bach, BWV 213/9 and BWV 248/4, mm. 103–14

But back to mm. 103–5: here, Bach must have felt the discrepancy, and in the *Christmas Oratorio* he changed the dotted quarter note in m. 103 into an eighth rest followed by two eighth notes on *b'*, combined with a repetition of the text "eile" (hurry on) (ex. 6.6). This resolved, at least in part, the discrepancy between the music and the text without requiring major changes to the model composition. Measures 110–12 of the secular cantata, however, required more significant changes in the *Christmas Oratorio*. Bach had set the words "zermalmet, zerrissen" with wide leaps and separated them by rests, sonically staging the shredding of the snakes by Hercules. It is hard to imagine a way to reconcile the former setting with the new text, which talks about the ardent love for the bridegroom. Bach decided to add two new measures in the oratorio and to set the text with a flowing motion of groups of sixteenth-note pairs (ex. 6.6). But even here, Bach resorts to material from the ritornello, as m. 111 alludes to the bass line from the beginning of the ritornello (m. 6 to the first note of m. 7). We see once more how Bach constructs his music as a skillful elaboration of the musical ideas developed in the opening measures of a piece. The quotation of the ritornello in mm. 110–12 is then followed by a modified version of the vordersatz in the instruments. This leads to the second half of the B section, which is now completely built into an extended version of the fortspinnung. Within this harmonic framework, Bach re-composes the final sixteen measures of the B section. The first eight measures maintain the instrumental accompaniment from the secular model but include a variant melodic line, while the last eight measures are entirely newly composed. The reason for the change was again the text, which indulges in the beauty of the bridegroom's cheeks and their lovely sparkle. A long melisma on "prangen" (sparkle) is the most striking addition in these final measures. The new additions in these measures are immediately visible in the score, as Bach made several corrections in the voice-leading of the alto in mm. 129 and 131 as well as in the bc line in mm. 132–33. Yet, the additional work Bach invested in the final measures of the B section is not exclusively due to the new text. He could have easily used the existing instrumental accompaniment from the secular cantata and modified the alto part in a way to better conform to the new words. Instead, the composer decided to emphasize the sensuality of the relationship between the believer and Jesus, the radiant beauty of the bridegroom. This change, as well as the changing of measures 110–11 in the secular cantata to a new passage of measures 110–13 in the oratorio, can only be understood in light of the sensual language and imagery of the *unio mystica*, which provides the linguistic and metaphorical framework for the understanding of the coming of Christ in the *Christmas Oratorio*.

The opening movements of part I foreshadow the final movements of the oratorio. The alto recit, no. 3, is echoed in the alto recit, no. 61, which similarly evokes the images of bride and bridegroom and is also set for alto and two oboi d'amore. The text is interrupted by short instrumental interpolations, similar to the antecedent accompagnato recit. The first and last recits of the oratorio have a bookending effect, suggesting the first welcoming of Jesus in the believer's heart and the final confirmation of his enduring presence:

| BWV 248/3 | BWV 248/61 |
|---|---|
| Nun wird mein liebster Bräutigam, | So geht! Genug, mein Schatz geht nicht von hier, |
| Nun wird der Held aus Davids Stamm | Er bleibet da bei mir, |
| Zum Trost, zum Heil der Erden | Ich will ihn auch nicht von mir lassen. |
| Einmal geboren werden. | Sein Arm wird mich aus Lieb |
| Nun wird der Stern aus Jakob scheinen, | Mit sanftmutsvollem Trieb |
| Sein Strahl bricht schon hervor. | Und größter Zärtlichkeit umfassen; |
| Auf, Zion, und verlasse nun das Weinen, | Er soll mein Bräutigam verbleiben, |
| Dein Wohl steigt hoch empor! | Ich will ihm Brust und Herz verschreiben. |
| | Ich weiß gewiss, er liebet mich, |
| | Mein Herz liebt ihn auch inniglich |
| | Und wird ihn ewig ehren. |
| | Was könnte mich nun für ein Feind |
| | Bei solchem Glück versehren! |
| | Du, Jesu, bist und bleibst mein Freund; |
| | Und werd ich ängstlich zu dir flehn: |
| | Herr, hilf!, so lass mich Hülfe sehn! |
| Now will my most beloved bridegroom, | So go! [It is] enough that my Treasure will not go from here; |
| now will the champion from the tribe of David— | he stays with me; |
| for the consolation, for the salvation of the earth— | I will also not let him [free] from me. |
| at last be born. | His arm will embrace me out of love |
| Now will the star out of Jacob shine; | with gentle desire |
| its stream of light is already breaking forth. | and greatest tenderness; |
| Arise, Zion, and forsake weeping now; | he shall remain my bridegroom; |
| your well-being lifts on high! | I will entrust breast and heart to him. |
| | I know for certain that he loves me; |
| | my heart also loves him deeply |
| | and will honor him eternally. |
| | Now, at such good fortune, |
| | how could any enemy harm me! |
| | You, Jesus, are and remain my friend; |
| | and if I anxiously beseech you: |
| | "Lord, save [me]!," then let me see salvation! |

The similarities between the beginning and the end of the oratorio are to a lesser degree continued in the following arias (nos. 4 and 62), both of which emphasize the presence of the beloved. Due to the context, the aria in the final part has a more forceful martial character. But here, Bach draws a connection between the two movements by again using the oboi d' amore (now as a pair and without the strings); the singer in the later aria is a tenor.[40] A closer relationship between the first and last parts of the oratorio is created by the use of the same chorale melody in mvt. 5 ("Wie soll ich dich empfangen") and mvt. 64 ("Nun seid ihr wohl gerochen"). Since the final movement had already been composed when Bach wrote the first chorale setting, the design of the opening sequence of movements is based on the later part (and not the other way around). Bach and his librettist thus create the frame that connects the first and last parts of the oratorio. Part I expresses the wish for Jesus's coming (understood as his second coming "today") while Part VI confirms his enduring presence and widens the perspective to his return in the third coming. The foundation for this frame was laid, of course, by the author of the text, but Bach made sure that the movements were connected through musical means as well.

The Advent portion of part I ends with a simple chorale-setting, which, as usual in Bach's cantatas and oratorios, represents the voice of the congregation. The text by Paul Gerhard from 1653 conflates the individual response ("Wie soll ich dich empfangen") with the congregational perspective. The hymn as a whole is an extensive elaboration on the threefold doctrine.[41] The text expresses the uncertainty regarding how to welcome Jesus, but at the same time it confirms that the answer lies in the "torch of Jesus," which is a familiar metaphor for the biblical Word. The melody that Bach uses has given some reason for speculation. It is the same as that of the Passion chorale ("O Haupt voll Blut und Wunden") and has led to the assumption that it might have been Bach's goal to allude to a deeper theological connection between Christmastide and Passiontide. Carl von Winterfeld had already highlighted Bach's use of the same chorale in the *St. Matthew Passion* and in the *Christmas Oratorio*,[42] and the editor of the oratorio for the *Bach Gesellschaft Ausgabe*, Wilhelm Rust, drew a direct theological connection to Bach's Passions.[43] The same

[40] An interesting, albeit accidental detail, is that arias no. 3 and no. 61 both begin with the same melodic phrase: an ascending fourth, followed by a third, and then a descending half-tone step. This similarity is purely accidental, as the two arias were composed for different purposes at different times, but it still creates unity between these two movements.

[41] See chap. 3, and Axmacher, "Die dreifache Zukunft des Herrn," 91–102.

[42] Carl von Winterfeld, *Der evangelische Kirchengesang und sein Verhaltnis zur Kunst des Tonsatzes*, vol. 3 (Leipzig, 1847; repr., Hildesheim: Olms, 1966), 345. The complex nineteenth-century history of this idea has been analyzed by Carolyn Carrier-McClimon, "Hearing the 'Töne eines Passionsliedes' in "J. S. Bach's Christmas Oratorio: The Nineteenth-century Critical Reception of BWV 248," *Bach* 45 (2014): 34–67.

[43] Wilhelm Rust, preface to *Johann Sebastian Bachs Werke* V² (Leipzig: Breitkopf und Härtel, 1856), vi.

view was subsequently adopted by Philipp Spitta in his Bach biography,[44] and by other biographers like Bitter and Pirro.[45] The theory was later rejected by Friedrich Spitta, Philipp's brother, who had already shown in 1907 that Bach's choice of melody was simply a reflection of customs in Leipzig.[46] Still, the association between the two texts within Bach's own oeuvre, that is, between the *Christmas Oratorio* and the *St. Matthew Passion*, proved to be too strong and too intriguing for interpreters of Bach's music.[47]

Nonetheless, Bach's use of the Passion-chorale melody in the *Christmas Oratorio* is not the result of theological reasoning: it was simply the tune that was commonly associated with this text in the Bach's Leipzig hymnal, the *Ordentliches und Vermehrtes Dreßdnisches Gesang-Buch* (Dresden: Leipzig, 1725).[48] The melody that Bach uses in the oratorio originated in a secular song by Hans Leo Hassler (1564–1612), but it was soon combined with a sacred text. It was thence commonly known as "Herzlich thut mich verlangen." The text expresses the wish for an imminent death and the longing for community with Jesus.[49] It was subsequently combined with a broad variety of texts: from "O Haupt voll Blut und Wunden" to "Befiehl du deine Wege" to "Wie soll ich dich empfangen." The thematic diversity of texts associated with the melody suggests that it did not have a specific connotation (except for the more somber affect due to its Phrygian modality). Unfortunately, scant sources exist for the perception of certain melodies in the seventeenth and eighteenth centuries.

[44] Philipp Spitta, *Johann Sebastian Bach: His Work and Influence on the Music of Germany, 1685–1750*, trans. Clara Bell and J. A. Fuller-Maitland, vol. 2 (London: Novello, 1889, repr., New York: Dover, 1979), 579.

[45] Karl Hermann Bitter, *Johann Sebastian Bach*, vol. 2, 2nd ed. (Berlin, 1881, 178); André Pirro, *J. S. Bach* (Paris: Librairie Félix Alcan, 1906); hereafter the German ed: *Bach sein Leben und seine Werke*, autorisierte deutsche Ausgabe von Bernhard Engelke (Berlin/Leipzig: Schuster & Loeffler, 1910), 3. bis 6. Aufl. 1920, 145.

[46] Friedrich Spitta, "Die Melodie 'Herzlich tut mich verlangen' in J. S. Bachs Weihnachtsoratorium," *Monatsschrift für Gottesdienst und kirchliche Kunst* 13/1 (Jan 1908): 25–27.

[47] More recently, the theory has been favored by Robin A. Leaver, "The Mature Vocal Works and Their Theological and Liturgical Context," in *Cambridge Compendium Bach* (Cambridge: Cambridge University Press, 1997), 86–122 (there 98–99); Günther Jena, *Brich an, o schönes Morgenlicht: Das Weihnachtsoratorium von Johann Sebastian Bach* (Freiburg, Herder, 1999), 53; Anne Leahy, J. S. Bach's "Leipzig" Chorale Preludes: Music, Text, Theology (Lanham: Scarecrow Press, 2011), 144–45; and Günther Massenkeil, *Oratorium und Passion* I, Handbuch der musikalischen Gattungen 10/1 (Laaber: Laaber Verlag, 1998), 220. However, that theory has been rejected by Walter Blankenburg, *Weihnachts-Oratorium*, 46–47 as well as by Meinrad Walter, *Weihnachtsoratorium*, 58.

[48] The current well-known melody that appeared in the *Schemelli Gesangbuch* and which is attributed to Bach (BWV 469) did not appear before 1736; it would have been unusual to set a hymn text with a newly composed melody. Although part IV of the *Christmas Oratorio* shows in two cases that Bach was not opposed to this option.

[49] Interestingly, the final line of the first stanza reads as "O Jesus, komm nur bald," thus alluding to the third coming of Christ. Within the context of the *Christmas Oratorio*, it is this connection that would make more sense.

Hymn sermons primarily talk about the text but not about the affect of the melody. A rare exception, albeit dating to more than half a century later, is a book by Gottlob F. W. Bekuhrs (+1795). His characterization of the melody that he lists both under "Herzlich lieb hab ich dich" and "Wie soll ich dich empfangen" confirms that the tune was associated with a somber affect but not specifically with the Passion:

"Herzlich tut mich verlangen" ("Wie soll ich dich empfangen"), . . . Sofern die Gelassenheit und eine nachdenkliche Stille des Geistes erweckt werden soll, ist die Musik geschickt dazu. Sollte aber sich der Geist zu einer größern Freudigkeit und Munterkeit erheben, so wäre die von "Valet ich will dir geben passender."⁵⁰

"Herzlich tut mich verlangen" ("Wie soll ich dich empfangen"), . . . if the goal is to express composure and thoughtful silence, this music is appropriate. If the spirit should be elevated to greater joy and liveliness, the melody of "Valet ich will dir geben" is more fitting.

Based on Bekuhrs's characterization and on the variety of ways that particular melody was used in Leipzig in Bach's time, we have to infer that a connection to the Passion (and more specifically to the *St. Matthew Passion*) was not intended. This does not mean that a modern listener cannot hear the chorale melody that way. In fact, such a perception would be in line both with Lutheran theology in general and the theology of the *Christmas Oratorio* in particular. The problem here is not that hearing the chorale melody as an allusion to Christ's Passion was historically incorrect, as the term "historically correct" hearing is impossible. Listeners will always construct their own meanings based on the music and their own musical (and extramusical) experiences. And sometimes a modern listener can hear "meanings" that are true and valuable even though they were not intended by the composer. While the connection between the Passiontide and Christmastide would be supported by the text of the *Christmas Oratorio*, the modern association overshadows the actual function of the two chorales in the oratorio that have the same melody (nos. 5 and 64). The connection apparently drawn by Bach (and his librettist) is not between Christmas and Good Friday but rather between the beginning and the end of the oratorio, aurally bridging the second and third comings of Christ: Christ's real presence in the life of the believer and his return at the end of times. If we hear these chorales just with the *St. Matthew Passion* and other works in mind, we miss

⁵⁰ Gottlob Friedrich Wilhelm Bekuhrs, *Ueber die Kirchen Melodien* (Halle: Johann Christian Hendel, 1796), 47; the tune "Valet ich will dir geben" was used repeatedly by Bach; most prominently in the organ chorales BWV 735 and 736; see also Peter Williams, *The Organ Music of J. S. Bach*, 2nd ed. (Cambridge: Cambridge University Press, 2003), 479.

their significance within the theological and musical framework of the *Christmas Oratorio*.

## Dichotomies of status (mvts. 6–8)

In the second half of part I of the *Christmas Oratorio*, the focus of the libretto shifts from the "temporal dichotomies" to the "dichotomy of status" between Jesus's regal office and his lowly birth. As we read at the beginning of this chapter, Christian theologians understood this as a paradox that challenged human reasoning. The conflict between reason and divine providence is a recurring theme in the eighteenth century, where Enlightenment philosophy and established theological doctrines struggled to coexist, often within the work of a single scholar. Numerous cantatas by Bach allude to the conflict, and as can be expected, side with divine providence.[51] It was incomprehensible to reason that God would become man and be born in a manger since the Messiah had been expected, according to the promises in scripture, to come as a king to liberate his people.

For example, Johann Christoph Wentzel, a teacher at the school in Zittau and occasional poet, summarizes this paradox in a school play, performed by the schoolboys in 1718.[52] In the second scene, reason (ratio) approaches the manger. He uses a technical device, a telescope, as a symbol for his modern, scientific approach, but he refuses to accept that the unassuming child could be the son of God:

| | |
|---|---|
| . . . tritt Ratio auf und siehet mit einem Fern-Glaß nach der Krippe und Kinde JEsu/gestehet aber/daß sie sich nimmermehr überreden werde/das unansehliche Kind vor Gottes Sohn zu erkennen.[53] | . . . enter Ratio searching with a telescope for the manger and the child Jesus; however, he confesses that he will never be persuaded to accept the shabby child as the Son of God. |

---

[51] See the chapter on reason and divine providence in Eric Chafe's study *Tonal Allegory in the Vocal Music of J. S. Bach* (Berkeley: University of California Press), 1991, 225–53, esp. the summary on 247–48.

[52] Wentzel's school plays stand in the tradition of Christian Weise's plays, using the theater as a place for moral and religious education. We encountered Wentzel earlier in chap. 2 as one of the librettists who had written Passion librettos modeled after Thymich's Christmas play. Wentzel had been in Jena when Knüpfer performed his play in 1693. The present play, however, departs from Thymich's model and uses the Christmas narrative as a basis for a morality play.

[53] Johann Christoph Wentzel, *Der unerkandte Jesus zu Christlicher Vorbereitung auf das Heilige Weyhnacht-Fest von der studierenden Jugend in Zittau den 21. Decembr. 1718 in einem kurtzen Dramate vorgestellet* (Budißin: David Richter, 1719), 11; for the complete text recited by *ratio*, see Wentzel, 47–48.

Wentzel's text echoes a more general discourse about the meaning of the manger in Protestant theology at that time. We know from Bach's estate catalogue that he, Bach, owned Martin Geier's sermon collection *Zeit und Ewigkeit*. He might have read the following section on the reasons for Jesus's lowly birth in Geier's sermon for the first day of Christmas. Here, Geyer interprets the manger as a soteriological necessity:

| | |
|---|---|
| Sehen wir hier ein armes schwaches kind in der krippe / das sich muß elendich behelffen / so fragt sichs: warum ist doch dieses kind so arm worden? Antwort: darum / daß du und ich und wir alle mit einander / die wir blut-arm waren / durch seine armuth reich würden / 2. Corinth. 8,9. und also das ewige erbe durch ihn erlangen möchten.[54] | We see here a poor and weak child in the manger, who lives under miserable circumstances. We ask ourselves: why has this child become so poor? Answer: so that you and I and we all together, who have been anemic [literally: poor of blood], would become rich through his poverty, 2 Cor 8:9, and that we therefore gain the eternal inheritance. |

Martin Luther, in his sermon from the *Hauspostille*, another book Bach owned, explores this idea more deeply. The birth in the manger and the disparity between Jesus's divine and royal heritage and his birth highlights the dimensions of salvation. The appropriate response is, according to Luther, thankfulness:

| | |
|---|---|
| Warum malt doch der Evangelist diese Geburt so arm und elend? Darum, daß du daran gedenken und nimmermehr vergessen sollst, und dirs auch lassest zu Herzen gehen, und sonderlich, weil du hier hörst, es sei dir zu gut geschehen, daß du darüber fröhlich und Gott auch dankbar seiest.[55] | Why does the Evangelist paint this birth so poorly and miserably? [He does it,] so that you may remember it and never forget it; and so that you keep it in your heart; especially since you hear that it happened for your benefit, so that you may rejoice and thankful to God for it. |

---

[54] Martin Geier, *Zeit und Ewigkeit nach Gelegenheit der ordentlichen Sonntags-Evangelien in des HErrn Furcht heibevor der Christlichen Gemeine in Leipzig Anno 1664 fürgestellet* (Leipzig: Friedrich Lanckischens Erben, 1715), 129. Geyer's sermons, although dating from the second half of the seventeenth century, were still widely read in Leipzig during Bach's time. The Leipzig superintendent Salomon Deyling edited the collection again in 1738 with a new preface; see the list of editions of the sermons between 1670 and 1738 in Leaver, *Bach's Theological Library*, 119.

[55] *Dr. Martin Luther's Sämmtliche Schriften 13: Die Hauspostille nach Veit Dietrich*, ed. Johann Georg Walch (St. Louis: Concordia, 1904), *col. 47.*

The seventeenth-century theologian Johann Gerhard joins the soteriological aspect of Jesus's lowly birth with the image of an engagement, a marriage contract, tying it to the familiar metaphor of bride and bridegroom. The phrase "Pfand des H. Geistes" (pledge of the Holy Spirit) in the following quote further relates Gerhard's understanding of the manger to the *inhabitatio Christi*. He subsequently continues to underscore the humility of the birth by pointing to Mary's role[56]:

| | |
|---|---|
| Wir sollen hierbei erinnert sein, daß, wenn wir den Nutzen dieser Geburt geniessen wollen, wir uns durch wahren Glauben mit GOtt verloben müßen, wie Hos. 2, 19 stehen, und von ihm das Pfand des H. Geistes bekomme, welcher gegeben wird allen gläubigen Herzen, welche durch göttliche Erkenntnis und durch wahren Glauben mit GOtt verlobet sind. . . . Darum als ihn die Mutter gebähren sollte, wurde sie aus den Oertern, welche sonst menschlicher Wohnung bequem, in einen Stall, für das unvernünftige Vieh erbauet, gewiesen. . . . Und wenn wir diese Historie hin und her wenden, findet sich nichts darinnen, als Dürftigkeit und Armuth.[57] | If we want to benefit from this birth, we should be reminded that we have to be betrothed to God through our faith, as Hosea 2:15 writes; and that we receive from his the pledge of the Holy Spirit, which is given to all believing hearts, which are betrothed to God through divine understanding and genuine faith. . . . As his mother was about to give birth to him [Jesus], she was led from the common dwelling places of humans to the stable that had been erected for the animals that lack reason and understanding. . . . However we spin this story, we do not find anything but meagerness and poverty. |

Gerhard concludes that Jesus could have come into the world differently, but that he chose to be born as a child in a manger, since his own humiliation was the precondition for man's elevation and salvation.[58] But the birth in the manger was not only seen as a necessity in the context of a forensic soteriology, it was also viewed as an expression of the divine love. Gerhard's mention of the engagement already pointed

---

[56] For Mary as a model of humility and simplicity in Lutheran theology, see Beth Kreitzer, *Reforming Mary: Changing Images of the Virgin Mary in Lutheran Sermons of the Sixteenth Century* (Oxford: Oxford University Press 2004), 112–14.

[57] Johann Gerhard, *Postille, das ist Auslegung und Erklärung der sonntäglichen und vornehmsten Fest-Evangelien über das ganze Jahr, auch etlicher schöner Sprüche heiliger Schrift* . . . Nach den Original-Ausgaben von 1613 und 1616 vermehrt durch die Zusätze der Ausgabe von 1663 (Berlin: Schawitz, 1870), 56–57.

[58] Gerhard, *Postille*, 57.

in this direction. Heinrich Müller, in his *Evangelische Schlußkette* (likewise owned by Bach), contrasts human love (and the reasons for this love) with the motivations for divine love. While human love can have a variety of motivations, divine love, as it is expressed in the image of the manger, challenges human reason ("Ursach zur Verwunderung") and therefore transcends human understanding:

| | |
|---|---|
| Würde sich ein grosser Monarch in ein armes Bettel-Mädchen verlieben / möchte dasselbe zwar vielen eine Ursach zur Verwunderung / doch nicht ohn Ursach seyn. Vielleicht reizt ihn ihre Schöne / vielleicht ihre Tugend / vielleicht raset er für Brunst. Daß aber Gott die Menschen lieber / gibt darumb desto grössere Ursach zur Verwunderung / weil diese Liebe keine ander Ursach hat als seine unverdiente Barmhertzigkeit.[59] | If a great monarch fell in love with a beggar girl, this would be reason for astonishment for many but it would not be without a certain cause. Maybe he is attracted by her beauty, maybe by her virtue, maybe he is maddened by desire. However, much more surprising is the fact that God loves man since this love has no other cause that his mercy, which we did not earn by ourselves. |

Müller views it as an expression of divine love that God descends from heaven to become man: "Die Liebe stellt sich dem Geliebten gleich" (Love descends to the same level as the beloved) (Müller, Festteil 1). And he adds that it was an expression of love as well as of divine mercy:

| | |
|---|---|
| Im Stall wird der HErr der Herrlichkeit geboren. Ist das nicht Liebe? Gnade ists / wann ein grosser Herr bey seinem armen Unterthan in sein Strohhüttlein einkehrt. Gnade über Gnade / daß der HErr aller Herren/da er kommt das Himmelreich zu bringen/mit dem Stall vorlieb nimmt (Festteil, 7). | The Lord of glory is born in a stable. Is that not love? It is an expression of mercy if a high lord enters the little straw-hut of one of his poor subjects. Mercy over mercy, that the Lord of all Lords, who comes to bring the Kingdom of God, makes do with a stable. |

Müller quotes a verse from a poem that epitomizes his view of Jesus lowly birth: "Komm / zuckersüsses Jesulein / Laß unser Hertz dein Kripplein seyn / Und führ

---

[59] Heinrich Müller, *Evangelische Schluß-Kette / und Krafft-Kern / oder Gründliche Außlegung der Sonn- und Fest-Tags-Evangelien* . . . (Frankfurt a.M.: Balthasar Christoph Wust, 1698), Festteil, 1 (hereafter cited in text).

uns in den Himmel ein! Amen" (Come, sugar-sweet little Jesus; let our heart be your manger and lead us to heaven! Amen) (Müller, Festteil, 2). The coming of the "sweet" Jesus has bidirectional ramifications; it is a coming into the human heart, which serves as his manger, and at the same time it leads the believer into heaven. In other words, the manger is a symbol for the *inhabitatio Christi* as well as a symbol for salvation. All of this is, as Wentzel and others point out, incomprehensible to the human mind. A congregational hymn that brings this paradox into focus is Luther's "Gelobet seist du Jesu Christ" (Praise be to you, Jesus Christ), first published in 1525 and since then an integral part of the Christmas section of Lutheran hymnals. The eighteenth-century theologian Johann Martin Schamelius, in his *Lieder-Commentarius* (1724), aptly introduces the hymn with the following headline: "Wohlthaten der Geburt Christi durch lauter *Paradoxa* besungen" (The benefits of the birth of Christ sung in several paradoxes).[60] Bach's librettist chose a stanza ("Er ist auf Erden kommen arm") from this hymn as the centerpiece for the second half of part I (no. 7). In an intricate play of hymn text and free poetic interpolations in a bass recit, mvt. 7 discusses the incomprehensibility of Jesus's birth in a manger. The recit is preceded by a short Gospel recit (no. 6), which briefly reports the birth of Mary's son, her swaddling him and laying him in a manger. Bach's short recit highlights the dichotomy between the divine sphere and God's descent by setting the first phrase of the text with an ascending line that comes to a halt on the word "Sohn" (son). From there on, the three following phrases are all descending until the tenor reaches the low *d* on the final word "[Her-]berge" (m. 5).[61] Harmonically the most startling moment is the setting of the word "Krippe" ("manger," the scandalon or stumbling block for eighteenth-century theologians). The recit as a whole gradually modulates from e minor to G major, staying within the range of sharp keys. Unexpectedly, Bach sets the two syllables of "Krippe" with two f-naturals, cadencing on a D-minor chord. This harmonic twist highlights the keyword that will be at the center of the following movement.[62]

In mvt. 7, Bach's librettist combines the four lines of the sixth stanza of Luther's hymn in the soprano with interpolations by the bass that question the meaning of the paradox. The two voices engage in a dialectic discourse, leading from the question "Wer will die Liebe recht erhöhn?" (Who will properly extol the love?) to

[60] Johann Martin Schamelius, *Evangelischer Lieder-Comentarius, worinnen das glossirete Naumburgiche Gesang-Buch weiter ausgeführet und verbessert wird*, vol. 1 (Leipzig: Friedrich Lankischens Erben, 1724), 105.

[61] Bach repeats a pattern he had already used in the two preceding recits. In the Gospel recit, no. 2, the sharp descent to a low *d♯* occurs on the word "Nazareth" (mm. 9–10) and in the accompagnato recit, no. 3, Bach reaches the *d♯* on "Erden" (Earth) (m. 4). In both cases Bach employs the descent to a low note to express lowliness and God's descent.

[62] There is nothing unusual about the way Bach reaches D minor as he proceeds in a regular circle of fifths: B-E-A-d.

the affirmative statement "So will er selbst als Mensch geboren werden" (That he himself wants to be born as man). Meanwhile, the chorale proclaims Christ's incarnation in poverty. The hymn comments on the paradoxical dichotomy of rich and poor in the Gospel while the bass questions this view and, only toward the end, agrees with the words sung in the chorale. The text-combination provided by the librettist is a chorale trope and left Bach with a number of options. He could have set the entire recit for one voice, as he had done with a similar case in BWV 93/5;[63] or he could have juxtaposed a solo voice for the recit sections and a four-part chorale setting for the lines from the hymn, as in the *St. Matthew Passion* (BWV 244, mvt. 19, "O Schmerz"). Even a simultaneous combination of the two textual layers would have been possible, as seen later in mvts. 38 and 40 of the *Christmas Oratorio*. Instead, Bach chooses to set the text as a dialogue between two solo voices, soprano and bass. In his setting of the chorale trope, Bach alternates between the lines of the hymn (soprano) and sections from the recit (bass). The alternation of the musical material goes along with a change in meter (the hymn is in $\frac{3}{4}$ while the recit sections are in common time). The sonic contrast between the two layers is further emphasized by a change in the accompaniment. The chorale sections are accompanied by a trio of two oboi d'amore and continuo while the recit sections are set as secco recit, interspersed with occasional ragged motifs in the oboes. The short oboe motifs have a syntactical function within the movement as they connect the otherwise disjoint spheres of the chorale and the recit. Bach's choice of instruments also has a symbolic function. The two oboi d'amore are commonly associated with the topic of love, and Bach had already used them in the two alto movements, which had expressed the ardent waiting for the beloved bridegroom. The two instruments, especially in their progression in parallel thirds, draw a sonic connection to the topic of love. The bass represents the voice of reason, a believer voicing doubts about the humble birth of Christ. The soprano represents the voice of the church (or the congregation), which has already grasped the soteriological meaning of Christ's poverty and holds this view against the doubts of the individual.

The entire movement is framed by a twelve-measure ritornello that provides the motivic material for both the short interludes between the sections and for the accompaniment of the chorale. When the ritornello returns again at the end of the movement in slightly modified form, the last phrase of the chorale ("Kyrieleis") is built into the beginning of the instrumental trio, leading to a synthesis of chorale and ritornello. In the course of the movement, the motivic material never appears in its original version but is transposed several times during the chorale sections and interludes, beginning in G major, then in E minor, D minor, A minor, then finally back into C and G major. Ignace Bossuyt has suggested (based on Blankenburg's interpretation) that the "series of modulations moves constantly "downwards," as

---

[63]  See for this movement, Rathey, "Der zweite Leipziger Jahrgang—Choralkantaten," 361–65.

if to indicate that God had to lower himself to the level of humanity."[64] It should be added, however, that toward the end, the modulations ascend again back to G major. Bach uses descent and ascent to symbolize the incarnation as a process in which Christ descends while the human heart ascends to God, the very idea that is expressed in the text of the hymn. The dichotomy of decent and ascent also shapes the melodic line of the bass voice. Bach employs a melodic descent in his setting of the words of the bass "Des Höchsten Sohn kömmt in die Welt" (The Son of the Most High comes into the world), which is set with a descending line from $d'$ down to $d$ (mm. 42–43); this is followed by a leap of an octave up from $e$ to $e'$ on "Mensch" (man) in m. 53. The movement thus continues to use the juxtaposition of ascent and descent that had been employed in the preceding Gospel recit. The dialogue between reason and faith is resolved when the bass confesses that God came into the world as a humble child because it was his will and for man's salvation. The libretto confirms this change of attitude in the following bass aria. The singer now accepts that the "Lord" and "King" has rejected the splendor of the world and that the divine son has to sleep in a crude manger. The paradox is still there, but it has been resolved as an act of divine will not to be questioned by (human) reason.

For the bass aria, Bach reuses an aria from BWV 214, which had already featured the regal trumpet as a solo instrument. The aria thus ties back to mvt. 1, in which the trumpet had had a similar symbolic function. In its original secular context, the aria had served as praise of the Saxon Electress as the trumpet not only alludes to her being member of the royal family but was also the common attribute of the goddess "Fama"[65] who sings the aria in honor of the Electress in the secular cantata:

| | |
|---|---|
| Kron und Preis gekrönter Damen, | Crown and prize of crowned ladies, |
| Königin! mit deinem Namen | O Queen, with your name |
| Füll ich diesen Kreis der Welt. | I fill the circle of the world. |
| Was der Tugend stets gefällt | What is ever pleasing to virtue |
| Und was nur Heldinnen haben, | And what only heroines have, |
| Sein dir angeborne Gaben. | May they be to you innate gifts. |

Bach adopted the aria from the secular model without transposition and he also kept the bass as the soloist. Even though the score of BWV 248 has the same instrumentation as the model, Bach added a flute to double the first violin in the performance parts for the *Christmas Oratorio*. The ethical "perfection and flawlessness" of the Electress, which the text of the secular cantata praises, is mirrored in a flawlessly balanced and symmetrically structured *da capo* aria. The A section is eighty measures

---

[64] Bossuyt, *Christmas Oratorio*, 80; cf. Blankenburg, *Weihnachts-Oratorium*, 47.

[65] A famous example for the symbolic connection of Fama and her trumpet is Baldassare Galuppi's aria "Alla tromba della fama" (from an unknown opera).

long, consisting of two ritornelli of fourteen measures each, which frame a vocal part of fifty-two measures. The following B section—with forty measures, exactly half the length of A—is constructed from two vocal parts (sixteen measures each), which are separated by an instrumental interlude of eight measures. The result is a movement that is not only symmetrical on a macro scale (ABA) but in which each of the sections is symmetrical as well (14 + 52 + 14 // 16 + 8 + 16 // 14 + 52 + 14). Thus, the main musical material for the A section is presented in the opening ritornello; a vordersatz of eight measures (divided into two similar sections of four measures each) is followed by a fortspinnung of four measures and a (tonally open) cadential epilogue of two measures. The motif is characterized by an embellishment of a D-major triad. The vocal line of the B section establishes a contrast by favoring more stepwise motion and a syncopated rhythm. This contrast is prompted by the text of the secular model, as the A section emphasizes the general praise of the female ruler,[66] while the B section has a more restrained quality in highlighting her virtuous character.

The aria appears almost as a textbook case for a *da capo* aria, with one significant exception. The obbligato trumpet employs the material from the ritornello during the vocal sections (as it would be usual for an aria in the first half of the eighteenth century), but then it introduces a new motif that is played four times during the A section. The writing for the trumpet is idiomatic, featuring a typical fanfare motif. Bach's use of the trumpet in the movement was motivated by the regal connotations that were associated with the sound of the trumpet in eighteenth-century music. Fanfares were a symbol for the highest layers of the stratified society and could—in a metaphorical use—symbolize God as the divine ruler as well. Klaus Hofmann has convincingly suggested an additional layer of meaning.[67] He has identified several pieces by Bach in which a similar motif occurs, all of which use a variation of the same pattern (ex. 6.7).[68] In Hofmann's examples, the first three notes are always played as a upbeat, while the octave (note 4) falls on a downbeat. Hoffmann shows that the motif was not invented by Bach but can be traced to the horn- and trumpet-literature of the eighteenth century.[69] It appears, among others, as a signal for

---

[66] The gender typologies in the secular aria and its parody in the oratorio have been explored by Christine Siegert, "Genderaspekte in und um Johann Sebastian Bachs 'Weihnachtsoratorium,'" in *Frauen hör- und sichtbar machen: 20 Jahre "Frau und Musik" an der Universität für Musik und darstellende Kunst Wien*, ed. Sarah Chaker and Ann-Kathrin Erdélyi (Wien: Institut für Musiksoziologie, 2010), 47–69.

[67] Cf. Klaus Hofmann, "'Großer Herr, o starker König': Ein Fanfarenthema bei Johann Sebastian Bach," *Bach-Jahrbuch* 81 (1995): 36–37, 38.

[68] The examples listed by Hofmann are BWV 1046a and 1046/1; BWV 1066, Gavotte II; BWV 143/5; BWV 70a/1 and 70/1; BWV 119/7; BWV 127/4; BWV 52/1; BWV 214/7, and BWV 248/8, in "'Großer Herr, o starker König,'" 32; in a later article he adds BWV 132/3, see Hofmann, "Nochmals: Bachs Fanfarenthema," *Bach-Jahrbuch* 83 (1997): 178.

[69] Hofmann lists as references Horace Fitzpatrick, *The Horn and Horn-Playing in the Austro-Bohemian Tradition from 1680 to 1830* (London: Oxford University Press, 1970), 20 and 60–62; Bertil

greeting the ruler in the table ceremonies at the Dresden court,[70] and Hofmann suggests that the motif could have been used as an entrance fanfare and as a greeting for members of the electoral family as well. The use of the trumpet motif in BWV 214/ 7 would thus signify not only the royal attributes of the dedicatee of the composition but also serve as a greeting to a royal person.[71] In the case of the secular model, the welcoming of the Electress at this point of the cantata would be appropriate as it is the first movement that addresses the her directly (Hofmann, 38). In the context of the *Christmas Oratorio*, the movement appears after the birth of Jesus and is thus the first direct address of the newborn child (Hofmann, 39). If we assume that Bach's listeners would have been familiar with the trumpet signal, they might have heard the insertion of the call in the aria "Großer Herr" both as an allusion to Jesus's regal heritage and as a welcome to the newborn child.

*Example 6.7* Outline of Bach's trumpet fanfare

The aria is sung at a crucial moment in the development of part I of the oratorio, following the movement that had discussed the dichotomy between the lowly birth and the regal office of Christ. The text for the aria still maintains some of this dichotomy by juxtaposing Christ's lordship and his disregard for the splendor of the world in the A section, while the B section shifts the focus to his role as creator of the world and sleeping in a manger. What still appears as a dichotomy in the text is resolved in Bach's music as it highlights these regal characteristics. Meinrad Walter has suggested that Bach, if he had composed the aria from scratch, would have used the phrases "Großer Herr, o starker König" and "Liebster Heiland, o wie wenig" to establish a stronger contrast.[72] While it is true that Bach's possibilities

van Boer, "Observations on Bach's Use of the Horn, Part I," *Bach* 11 (1980): 21–28; and Edward H. Tarr, "Monteverdi, Bach und die Trompetenmusik ihrer Zeit," in *Bericht über den musikwissenschaftlichen Kongreß Bonn 1970* (Kassel: Bärenreiter, 1971), 592–96.

[70] An example of the model used for this purpose in Dresden is printed in Hofmann, " 'Großer Herr, o starker König,' " 35; see also Detlef Altenburg, *Untersuchungen zur Geschichte der Trompete im Zeitalter der Clarinblaskunst*, Kölner Beiträge zur Musikforschung 75 (Regensburg: Bosse, 1973), 105–6.

[71] Hofmann, " 'Großer Herr, o starker König,' " 37–38 (hereafter cited in text). Malcolm Boyd adds in his reaction to Hofmann's article that Telemann uses a similar motif to greet the new day, thus confirming Hofmann's identification of the trumpet call as a musical symbol for greeting; but he also adds that Telemann uses the motif as a military symbol as well; Malcolm Boyd, "Bach, Telemann und das Fanfarenthema," *Bach-Jahrbuch* 82 (1996): 148–49.

[72] Walter, *Weihnachtsoratorium*, 66; the lack of contrast due to the parody was also criticized by Jones, *Creative Development II*, 309.

were limited by the secular model, the present combination of text and music stresses the fact that the paradox is already resolved: Jesus reveals himself as king in the poverty of the manger.

*Example 6.8*  J. S. Bach, BWV 214/7 and BWV 248/9, mm. 61–66 and 81–86

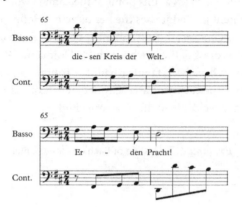

However, Bach does make some subtle changes to the parody model. In m. 65 (bass) he embellishes a cadential phrase by inserting a short melismatic motif on "Erden," a change that both smoothens the melodic line and highlights the word. In the bass voice in m. 84 he lowers the long note from g to e and adds the two descending sixteenth notes on the first beat (ex. 6.8). Additionally, he ties the note to the eighth note e in the following measure, thus adding to the syncopations in the B section.[73] The change also increases the musical coherence between the musical phrases in the B section. In the secular model, the first four measures of section B (mm. 81–84) represent a closed phrase, concluding with an authentic cadence in E minor (B major–E minor); the movement comes to a halt for a moment, with eighth notes in the accompaniment on the first beat of m. 84 and the half note in the vocal part. The sixteenth notes in the first violin merely appear as a transition to the next phrase. In the revised version of BWV 248/8, the motion in the vocal part continues and comes to a halt only when the flute and

<hr />

[73] Bach originally copied the version from the secular model but then changed it into the current version.

violin take over with a sixteenth-note gesture in m. 88. Bach made another change in mm. 109–10. Again, the revision of the model ties together two phrases of four measures into a longer, eight-measure phrase. It is possible that Bach decided to link the notes in mm. 109–10 and to add a small melismatic descent in m. 110 to express the duration of God's maintaining involvement in the world by lengthening the duration of the word "erhält" (maintain). But it is noteworthy that the change is not only due to the text but also has ramifications for the syntactic structure of the aria movement as well.

Somewhat related to these musical changes is a discrepancy between the text of the printed libretto, which has the text "die ganze Welt *gemacht*" and Bach's "die ganze Welt *erhält*." The verb "gemacht" seems to be a better fit from a textual perspective as it rhymes with "Pracht" in line three. On the other hand, the verb "erhält" is closer to the verb "gefällt" in the secular model, and it is possible that Bach wanted to keep the same "ä"-sound as in the model composition. The fact that the text did not rhyme in this case was less problematic, as the third line appears in the A section and the fourth line opens the B section. A listener would not have heard that the two lines were not rhyming, and from a theological standpoint, the change is only a shift of nuance. In Lutheran understanding, God was not only the creator but also the maintainer of his creation. Bach (and his contemporaries) would have memorized this when they learned Luther's *Small Catechism* by heart: "I believe that God has created me and all that exists; that he has given me and still sustains."[74] However, the shift is in line with the general focus of the *Christmas Oratorio*, as it again directs attention from an event in the past ("gemacht") to the present time ("erhält"). The change thus fulfills a similar function as the omission of the second verse of the Gospel text in mvt. 2, as it blends out the historical past and highlights the present significance. The aria serves as a greeting to the newborn child, but it can also be seen within the context of the second coming of Christ: his presence in the time of the listener. An interesting musical detail alludes to this: Bach had already employed the same fanfare in an earlier cantata, which focuses on this second coming of Christ. In cantata BWV 172, composed in Weimar in 1714, Bach uses the trumpet motif in the third movement, which is also an aria for trumpet and bass.[75] The text for that aria shows some remarkable resemblance to ideas in the *Christmas Oratorio*, which is rooted in a similar theological understanding of the presence of Christ:

[74] Martin Luther, "The Small Catechism (1529)," in *Martin Luther's Basic Theological Writings*, ed. Timothy F. Lull (Minneapolis: Fortress Press, 1989), 479.

[75] Boyd had already pointed out that the motif used in BWV 172 is derived from the one presented by Hofmann (see Boyd, "Bach, Telemann und das Fanfarenthema," 147), and Hofmann had agreed that the motif was indeed present, albeit more veiled than in his original list (Hofmann, "Nochmals: Bachs Fanfarenthema," 178).

| Heiligste Dreieinigkeit, großer Gott der Ehren, | Most Holy Trinity, great God of honor, |
|---|---|
| Komm doch, in der Gnadenzeit bei uns einzukehren, | Come in this time of grace and stay with us; |
| Komm doch in die Herzenshütten, | Come into the tabernacles of our |
| Sind sie gleich gering und klein, | hearts, |
| Komm und laß dich doch erbitten, | Though they be slight and small; |
| Komm und kehre bei uns ein! | Come and let us beg You, |
| | Come and stay with us! |

Hofmann poses the question whether Bach might have remembered his cantata from 1714 when he composing his oratorio in 1734.[76] This is possible since Bach did not even have to think back to 1714 he had performed the cantata several times in Leipzig. A performance is documented for 1731 and another performance had taken place sometime after 1731, perhaps also in 1734.[77] Yet it is not necessary to assume that Bach remembered BWV 172 when he wrote the aria for the *Christmas Oratorio.* The similarity between the arias from BWV 172 and BWV 248, mvt. 8, shows that the musical realization in the Christmas piece was not only due to the secular model, as in BWV 248, the aria from the Pentecost cantata of 1714 musically passes over the poverty of the heart as the dwelling place of Jesus in favor of highlighting the regal office of the divine.

## *"Ach mein herzliebes Jesulein" (mvt. 9)*

A keyword connection, as was common for eighteenth-century homiletics, leads from the text of the bass aria to the final hymn setting. The "most beloved Savior" ("liebster Heiland") from line 2 of the aria now becomes the "beloved little Jesus" ("liebes Jesulein"). The common keyword highlights love as one of the central topics of part I of the oratorio and harkens back to the first half of part I. The final chorale, mvt. 9, serves as a conclusion that draws together several strains (both textually and musically) of the piece. Even though the stanza was part of Martin Luther's popular sixteenth-century Christmas hymn "Vom Himmel hoch, da komm ich her"[78]

[76] Hofmann, "Nochmals: Bachs Fanfarenthema," 178.

[77] A performance of a cantata with the same text in the Saxon city of Delitzsch is documented for 1735; only the text is preserved and it is not clear whether it was Bach's cantata or a piece based on the same text; see Schulze, *Die Bach Kantaten,* 253.

[78] Regarding the theology and history of this hymn, see Gerhard Hahn, *Evangelium als literarische Anweisung: Zu Luthers Stellung in der Geschichte des deutschen kirchlichen Liedes,* Münchener Texte und Untersuchungen zur deutschen Literatur des Mittelalters 73 (München: Artemis, 1981), 133–43.

it acquired a broader meaning during the seventeenth century and led an almost independent life during the seventeenth and eighteenth centuries in theological treatises, hymn interpretations, and musical settings. Already in the 1630s, sermons appeared that only used this one stanza, no. 13, of the Christmas song, some of them not related to Christmas at all.[79] In 1642 the Erfurt theologian Nicolaus Stenger (who would later preside over the marriage of Bach's parents and whose writings would find their way into Bach's own library[80]) published three sermons on the indwelling of God in the heart of the believer (*Der Hochtröstliche Artickel Von der Einwohnung Gottes in den Gläubigen*), originally preached during the three days of Pentecost 1642.[81] Stenger's understanding of *inhabitatio* conforms to the Lutheran orthodox views outlined earlier in chapter 3: God is substantially present in the heart of the believer through word and sacrament without any mixing of the divine and human substances.[82] A brief paraphrase of the stanza from "Vom Himmel hoch" serves as a summary of the ideas; Stenger combines the paraphrase with the familiar bride/bridegroom metaphors known from the *unio mystica*:

Der hat vns / als seine Braut / durch einen blutigen Krieg vnd gewaltigen Sieg von den Hellischen Philistern erstritten / vnd wil gerne in vnsers Hertzens Schrein / als auff einem sanfften Bette ruhen / vnd bey vns wohnung machen.[83]

He has saved us, as his bride, in battles from the hellish Philistines through a bloody war and overpowering victory, and he wants to rest in the shrine of our hearts, like on a comfortable bed, and dwell among us.

Even without an explicit mention of the Christmas hymn as a source, it must have been apparent to his listeners (and readers) that the preacher was referring to this text. The popularity of the stanza (and the theological concept it expressed) can also be seen in its reception in contemporary hymnody. Several seventeenth-century poets used Luther's stanza as a model for extensive sacred songs about the indwelling of Christ.

[79] Cf. Martin Rössler, *Bibliographie der deutschen Liedpredigt*, Bibliotheca Humanistica & Reformatorica 19 (Niewkoop: de Graaf, 1976), 273.

[80] Cf. Robin A. Leaver, *Bach's Theological Library: A Critical Bibliography* (Neuhausen-Stuttgart: Hänssler, 1983), 117–18.

[81] Nicolaus Stenger, *Der Hochtröstliche Artickel Von der Einwohnung Gottes in den Gläubigen oder: Von der Gäubigen Vereinigung mit GOTT* (Erfurt: Birckner, [1642]); see also the study by Ulman Weiss, "Nicolaus Stenger und Ezechiel Meth im Jahre 1640. Des Pfarrers Versehgang bei einem Verirrten," in *Nicolaus Stenger (1609–1680): Beiträge zu Leben, Werk und Wirken*, ed. Michael Ludscheidt (Erfurt: Ulenspiegel-Verlag, 2011), 65–77.

[82] Stenger, *Der Hochtröstliche Artickel*, Cʳ; C IIʳ.

[83] Stenger, *Der Hochtröstliche Artickel*, E IVʳ.

Those new hymn texts generally adopted the first line literally and then continued freely, as the song "Ach mein hertzliebes Jesulein, Gotts und Mariens Söhnelein" (O my beloved little Jesus, little son of God and Mary), written by Tobias Kiel (1584–1626), which appeared for the first time in Michael Altenburg's *Kirchen- und Haus-Gesänge* (Erfurt 1620); it was later incorporated into the Gotha hymnal *Cantionale Sacrum* (1646), making it available for congregational singing. Every stanza begins with that one phrase and then sets different theological accents in the ensuing lines.[84] Seventeenth-century piety found in Luther's stanza a fitting summary of some of its core ideas and used its first (and easily recognizable) line in hymns about all kinds of topics, including the art of dying. A functional change of the stanza can also be seen in a remark by the theologian and hymnologist Johann Martin Schamelius (1668–1742).[85] In his *Lieder Commentarius* (1724) the stanza is accentuated with bold print (the only one in this hymn) and Schamelius adds, "Mit diesem Sprüchelgen solte billig ein jedweder auffstehen und zu Bette gehen" (With this little verse everybody should duly get up and go to bed), turning the stanza into a prayer for the daily morning and evening routine. With the *inhabitatio* being a central doctrine of Lutheran piety at that time, it seemed appropriate to begin and end the day with a prayer for Christ's presence in one's heart and to connect this metaphorically with the believer's own bed, thus turning an everyday experience into a theologically charged image. A later example for the independent life of Luther's stanza can be found in a short exegesis of the verse in Gottfried Christian Goetze's *Kirchen-Buch Gläubiger Beter* (1728). His brief meditation on "Ach mein herzliebes Jesulein" highlights the comforting nature of God's presence in the heart:

Wie sich die Christliche Kirche in diesem Seuffzer öffers hören lässet / und in denselben um die Gnadenreiche Beywohnung des Hertzens ihr JEsulein beweglichst anfleht: Also zweiffelt sie auch nicht / ihre Bitte werde nicht unerhöret bleiben / sondern vergnügliche Gewehrung erhalten.[86]

Just as the Christian church frequently lets itself be heard by repeating this sigh, and as it earnestly asks the little Jesus for his graceful presence in the heart, she also does not doubt that her request is heard and that it is happily granted.

---

[84] For the complete text, see Albert Fischer/Wilhelm Tümpel, *Das deutsche evangelische Kirchenlied des 17. Jahrhunderts* I (Gütersloh: Brockhaus, 1904, repr. Hildesheim: Olms, 1964), 28–29.

[85] Cf. Andreas Lindner, *Leben im Spannungsfeld von Orthodoxie, Pietismus und Frühaufklärung: Johann Martin Schamelius, Oberpfarrer in Naumburg*. Kirchengeschichtliche Monographien 3 (Giessen/Basel: Brunnen, 1998).

[86] Gottfried Christian Goetze, *Kirchen-Buch Gläubiger Beter oder Zufällige Gedancken über einige Lieder-Seuffzer, welche in Denen Evangelisch-Lutherischen Kirchen öffentlich gebraucht werden* (Lübeck: Willers, 1728), E 2ʳ.

Toward the end of this meditation, Goetze (1702–36), while explaining the meaning of the stanza for the understanding of Christmas, also keeps his focus on the general idea of God's *inhabitatio*. He ends the study with by quoting the tenth stanza of Johann Rist's Christmas hymn "Ermuntre dich," which again combines the image of God's dwelling in the heart with the love metaphors of the *unio mystica* ("Schönster"/most beautiful; "lieber hab"/love most dearly):

| | |
|---|---|
| . . . rechtschaffene Christen / und Christliche Hertzen haben nichts liebers in ihren Munde / als ihren JEsum / und wissen von keiner süsseren HErtzens Freude / als welche dieses liebe Kind ihnen schaffet und zu wege bringet. . . . O liebes Kind / o süsser Knab / holdselig von Geberden / mein Bruder den ich lieber hab / als alle Schätz auf Erden: Komm Schönster in mein Hertz hinein / komm laß es deine Krippe seyn / komm / komm/ich will bey Zeiten / ein Lager dir bereiten.[87] | . . . upright Christians and Christian hearts do not have anything dearer on their tongues than their Jesus and they do not know a sweeter joy in their hearts than that which is given and accomplished by this dear child. . . . Oh dear child, oh sweet boy with beloved features, my brother whom I love more dearly than all treasures on earth; come, most fair, into my heart; come, let it be your manger; come, come, I will, in time, prepare a bed for you. |

Given the popularity of the stanza, it is not surprising that Bach's librettist chose to place the chorale "Ach mein herzliebes Jesulein" at the end of part I of the oratorio. It is still a Christmas hymn—but it is more than that as it resonated on more than just one level with Bach's listeners. Even more remarkable, given this background, is Bach's setting, which combines the intimate text with instrumental interludes, played by the trumpets and timpani and which recall the musical language of the opening movement. The instrumental interludes were part of certain traditions of congregational singing,[88] and Bach had used similar techniques in numerous hymn settings in his cantatas. What is noteworthy is the sonic contrast between the rather quiet, calm lines of the hymn (which correspond to the quiet, calm character of the text) and the festive, celebratory brass interludes.

The vocal lines are in a world by themselves. The melody is sung by the soprano, while the lower voices accompany in delicate harmony. As the melody is mostly unadorned at the beginning, the lower voices increasingly pick up movement,

[87]  Goetze, *Kirchen-Buch Gläubiger Beter*, E 2ᵛ.

[88]  See the discussion of the chorale interludes in Bach's organ works in Matthias Schneider, "Bachs 'Arnstädter Choräle"—komponiert in Weimar?" in *Bachs Musik für Tasteninstrumente*, ed. Martin Geck, Berich über das 4. Dortmunder Bach-Symposium 2002 (Dortmund: Klangfarben Musikverlag, 2003), 287–308.

which then gradually transforms the chorale melody. The increasing degree of movement reaches its apogee in the final line: in the first line only one voice, then two voices briefly move in eighth notes against the melody in quarter notes. In the second line, the eighth-note gestures become longer and now involve three voices; in line 3 (esp. m. 8), all four voices move in flowing eighth notes, including the melody; and finally, in line 4, the lower voices are engaged in an eighth-note motion, and the soprano joins in during the final cadence. The smooth, flowing motion resembles many of the seventeenth- and eighteenth-century settings of the melody and even shares some characteristics with Graun's solo setting (see chap. 3, this book). It expresses the text as a highly emotional poem that awaits the presence of Christ. The instrumental interludes that separate the individual lines, on the other hand, invoke the regal sphere of the opening movement and the bass aria. The interludes represent the "other side" of part I of the oratorio, the celebratory, regal side. By combining them in one movement, Bach leads the dichotomy to a synthesis. Christ is both the one who dwells in the poverty of the stable (and in the poverty of the sinful human heart) and the king of the world, for which the preceding aria had celebrated him.

Some of the details of this movement were again the result of intensive compositional work. The autograph score shows that Bach had originally notated the first line of the melody in C major instead of D major. Since it is unlikely that Bach had planned a final chorale in C, we have to assume that he made a mistake because the transposing brass instruments were notated without accidentals. Bach corrected the mistake before he wrote down the other lines of the chorale.[89] More significant are changes to the voice-leading in the chorale setting. In mm. 11–12 Bach changes the first note on the bass voice from *a* to *b*, creating a sharp dissonance with the bc voice, and in m. 12 the fourth note in the tenor voice is changed from *d* to *e*, creating dissonant tension with the alto. Both changes aim to harmonically sharpen the sound of the movement and thus increase the expressivity of the chorale setting. Bach also made several changes to the interludes, which shows that some of the characteristic features of the interpolations only developed during the compositional process. At the end of m. 2, Bach changes the bass line from *d–f♯–g* to *d–f♯–d* (something similar happens at beat 2 of m. 3). The change, which most likely occurred immediately after he had notated the initial reading, is significant, as it introduces a recurring idea in the bass that will return in all of the interludes. In m. 7 a revision adds rhythmic interest to the line of tromba III by replacing a simple eighth-note line with a vivid sixteenth-note motif.[90] A similar case is the final cadence in tromba III, where Bach again changes simple eighth notes into a rhythmically charged brass motif (ex. 6.9).

---

[89]  This assumption is also confirmed by Dürr in NBA II/6, KB, 31.

[90]  See the reconstruction in NBA II/6, KB, 33.

*Example 6.9* J. S. Bach, BWV 248/9, tromba III, m. 15.

It is indicative of the character of the two contrasting musical layers in the cho-rale setting that Bach makes primarily harmonic changes to the chorale setting, effectively increasing the expressive harmonic tension. In contrast, the changes in the interludes lead to the creation of characteristic motifs and to a higher complex-ity of rhythm. This little detail in the compositional process highlights again the play with dichotomies that fundamentally shapes the first part of the *Christmas Oratorio*.

# 7

# Mundane and Celestial Harmonies (Part II)

The regulations of Leipzig's St. Thomas School from 1733 described the musical duties of the students at the school by comparing them to a choir of angels:

Wenn sie singen, so sollen sie an die Natur und die Verrichtungen der heiligen Engel fleissig gedencken, und daraus urtheilen, was der Gesang der geistlichen Lieder vor eine herrliche Verrichtung sey, und wie ehrerbietig man sich bey demselben aufführen müsse. Es hat ein alter Kirchen-Lehrer die heiligen Engel mit Rechte ζῷα λογικὰ ὑμνολογικὰ d.i. vernünftige Geschöpfe genennet, welche beständig in dem Singen des Lobes Gottes ihre gröste Lust finden. Diese Beschreibung schicket sich sehr wohl auf einen rechtschaffenen Thomas-Schüler.[1]

When they are singing, they shall diligently remember the nature and the duties of the holy angels; this shall teach them that the singing of sacred songs is a glorious duty and how they should behave honorably while singing these songs. An ancient teacher of the church has aptly called the holy angels [zoa logika hymnologika], that is reasonable creatures, which steadfastly find their greatest joy in singing the praise of God. This description is also appropriate for any upright student at St. Thomas's.

The text employs stereotypical images of heavenly and angelic music as a model for musical activities on earth. But this is more than an exercise in traditional rhetoric and conventional metaphors. The cosmological concept of sacred music, which is rooted in the medieval *musica speculativa*, is encountered frequently in theological

---

[1] *Gesetze der Schule zu S. Thomae* (Leipzig: Breitkopf, 1733), 5–6.

treatises of the early eighteenth century.[2] In his book *Veritophili* (1717), a theological defense of music, Christoph Raupach writes about the music in heaven:

Obgleich nun keine gründliche Nachricht vorhanden / wie die Englische Music eigentlich eingerichtet sey / oder was für unzehliche *Modos* dieselbe von Anfang her mit sich geführet und ferner in alle Ewigkeit mit sich führen werde; So ist doch aus der Heil. Schrift bekandt / und unserm Christlichen Glauben gemäß / daß hauptsächlich der Freude des ewigen Lebens die allergrösseste / vollkommenste und wichtigste ist / indem sie beydes in dem höchsterfreulichen Anschauen Gottes / und im laut-singend- und klingenden Loben besteht / wir davon beim Esaia / C. 6. v. 3. Paulo / 2. Cor. 12/4. den Bethlehemitischen Hirten im Evangelio S. Lucae 2. Cap. wie auch in den Offenbahrungen S. Johannis / Cap. 5/ 8. Cap. 14. v.2. Cap. 15. v. 2. C. 22. v. 8. und anderswo daselbst mehr nachlesen können.[3]

Although we do not have comprehensive knowledge about the music of the angels, or what different kinds there have been since the beginning and that will be there in eternity, we do know from the Holy Scripture (and it is according to our Christian belief) that the joy about eternal life is the greatest, most perfect, and most important [joy], since it consists of the beholding of God and of the praise [of him] in the act of singing and of playing [instruments]; this we can read in Isaiah 6:3, Paul's second letter to the Corinthians 12:4, the shepherds of Bethlehem in Luke 2, as well as in the Revelation of St. John 5:8, 14:2, 15:2, 22:8 and at numerous other places [in the Bible].

Raupach makes a point that music on earth is but a foretaste of heavenly harmonies:

So man demnach / mit dem Beystand GOttes des H. Geistes / sich bestrebet / daß die Kirchen-*Musiqu*en heilig /

Thus, if one endeavors (with the assistance of God, the Holy Spirit) to create church music (that is holy,

[2] For a summary of these concepts, see Melanie Wald, "Kanon, Kombinatorik, Echokompositionen: Die musikalische Vermittlung zwischen Himmel und Erde in der Frühen Neuzeit," *Musiktheorie* 23 (2008): 51–70; the fundamental study of this allegorical view of music is Rolf Dammann, *Der Musikbegriff im deutschen Barock,* 3rd ed. (Laaber: Laaber-Verlag, 1995).

[3] Christoph Raupach, *Veritophili: Deutliche Beweis-Gründe / worauf der rechte Gebrauch der MUSIC, beydes in den Kirchen / als ausser denselben / beruhet* (Hamburg: Benjamin Schillers Erben, 1717), 41–42. On Raupach and his concept of heavenly music see also the study by Joyce L. Irvin, *Foretastes of Heaven in Lutheran Church Music Tradition: Johann Mattheson and Christoph Raupach on Music in Time and Eternity,* trans. and ed. Joyce L. Irvin (Lanham: Rowman & Littlefield, 2015).

verständig / lieblich / und zu rechter Zeit / bald demüthig und ernsthafftig / bald auch frolockend und jauchzend / nach der besten Kunst eingerichtet und wol zu Gehöre gebracht werden; kan man darauf beym Anhören derselben sich den Vorschmack der Himmlischen ewigen Freuden-Music desto besser und nachdrücklicher einbilden. Denn / durch die von Hertzen fliessende ungezwungene Musicalische Vorstellungen heiliger *Affect*en kommt man der Englischen- und Himmlischen Music nahe / indem schon hier auf Erden dadurch ein brünstiges Verlangen nach dem seligen Anschauen GOttes / nach der Fülle und Brunnquell der Freuden und nach dem ewigen lieblichen Wesen / so zur Rechten GOttes ist/angezündet wird. Darum denn auch alle auf die erbauliche Andacht zielende / woleingerichtete / Gottselige Music-Verrichtuneng / mit gutem Fug / Vorpiele des ewigen Freuden-Lebens zu nennen sind.[4]

understandable, pleasant, and at the proper times either devout and serious or rejoicing and gleeful) which is both fashioned according to the proper rules of the art and that is [also] well performed, then one can—when listening to that music— better imagine it being a foretaste of the heavenly, eternal music of joy. For, one comes closer to the angelic and heavenly music with the aid of the musical representation of holy feelings that freely flow from the heart. [This is the case because music] already here on earth sparks an ardent desire for the blessed beholding of God; [a desire] for the fullness and the fountain of joy and for the eternal [and] beloved being that sits at the right hand of God [the father]. Therefore, any devout [and] well-ordered musical practice that is geared toward edifying contemplation can with complete justification be called a prelude to the eternal life of joy.

Visual representations of this correspondence between celestial/angelic and mundane/human music appeared in numerous prints from the seventeenth and early eighteenth centuries. On title page of Michael Praetorius's *Musae Sioniae* (fig. 7.1) God—symbolized by the tetragram, his name in Hebrew letters—is surrounded by a host of angels who sing and play in his honor. In the middle and lower part of the image we see three human choirs, singing the praise of God as well. Several quotations from biblical texts appear with or without musical symbols. One biblical verse is divided between the heavenly and earthly spheres, prominently linking the upper and lower margins of the image: *"Pleni sunt coeli . . . et terra . . . Gloria tua"* (Heaven and earth are full of the glory of God). What appears in Praetorius's print as a model

---

[4] Raupach, *Veritophili*, 49; for a discussion of Raupach, Mattheson, and their theological views of music in relation to Bach's works, see Eric Chafe, *Tears into Wine: J. S. Bach's Cantata 21 in its Musical and Theological Contexts* (New York: Oxford University Press, 2015), 279–311.

*Figure 7.1  Musae Sioniae V* (1607). (public domain)

(and justification) for polychoral music, returns a few decades later in Heinrich Müller's *Göttliche Liebes-Flamme* (1676) with a spiritual purpose (fig. 7.2).[5]

---

[5]  Heinrich Müller, *Göttliche Liebes-Flamme Oder Auffmunterung zur Liebe Gottes: Durch Vorstellung dessen undendlichen Liebe gegen uns: Mit vielen schönen Sinnebildern gezieret* (Frankfurt a.M.: Wust, 1676), 1018.

*Figure 7.2* Heinrich Müller, *Göttliche Liebes-Flamme* (1676) (private copy, Eric Chafe, Boston)

Here, the music of the heart is a direct echo and reflection of the music in heaven, as seen at the top of the image. The subscriptio reads, "With all my heart do I praise you since you gladden my mind with your mercy, O wonderfully great God. Heaven praises you; I have heaven here on earth when I praise you: thus, one must become angelic."[6] Heavenly music in the eighteenth century was indeed both a exemplar and a justification for liturgical music. Johann Mattheson, who had already provided a preface for Raupach's *Veritophili* in 1717, published a defense of sacred music (both vocal and instrumental) in 1747. In his *Behauptung der himmlischen Musik*, Mattheson asserts that only humans and angels were able to make music with intelligent reflection (contrary to the music of birds).[7] He rejects assumptions that heavenly music was only metaphorical and maintains that the angels did indeed use instruments—even if details of this music might be difficult to comprehend:

Ueberhaupt haben alle diejenigen, welche insonderheit das Klingen oder Spielen der Engel uns Seligen noch etwas mehr, als das eigentliche Singen derselben, leugnen wollen, keinen andern Vorwand, als die vermeynte Unbegreiflichkeit der himmlischen Instrumenten, samt der Art und Weise, solche zu handhaben: denn es gehet alles über ihren Verstands-Kreis.[8]

Those who want to deny us blessed ones the sounding and playing of the angels (even more than their singing) have no other argument than the alleged incomprehensibility of the heavenly instruments, including the way in which they [the instruments] might have to be handled: because that simply goes beyond what they [the ones who deny this music] are able to comprehend.

Consequently, Mattheson can appreciate human music as a reflection or echo of the music of angels. He quotes the seventeenth-century theologian Johann Conrad Dannhauer to support his assertion: "The entire church, both the Church Militant and the Church Triumphant, is divided into two choirs, in an upper choir and a lower choir. The one takes form in heaven and the other one down here on earth. Our earthly music is, so to speak, nothing but an Echo or a resounding of heavenly [music]."[9]

---

[6] "Von Hertzen lob ich dich, weil du mit deiner Güte / O wundergrosser Gott erfreuest mein Gemüthe. / Der Himmel lobet dich, den Himmel hier auf Erden, / Hab ich wenn ich dich lob: so muß man Englisch werden."

[7] Johann Mattheson, *Behauptung der himmlischen Musik aus den Gründen der Vernunft, KirchenLehre und heiligen Schrift* (Hamburg: Herold, 1747), 1–2. Mattheson's reflections on sacred music in this very late treatise were analyzed by Erik Dremel, "Matthesons 'Behauptung der himmlischen Musik,'" in *Johann Mattheson als Vermittler und Initiator: Wissenstransfer und die Etablierung neuer Diskurse in der ersten Hälfte des 18. Jahrhunderts*, ed. Wolfgang Hirschmann and Bernhard Jahn (Hildesheim: Olms, 2010), 443–61.

[8] Mattheson, *Behauptung der himmlischen Musik*, 4.

[9] "Die ganze christliche, so wohl streitende, als triumphierende, Kirche theilet sich in zween Chöre, nämlich, in den obern und untern. Jener figurieret im Himmel; dieser hernieden auf Erden. Unsere irdische Musik ist, gewissermaßen, nichts anders, als nur ein Echo oder Wiederhall der himmlischen." Mattheson, *Behauptung der himmlischen Musik*, 65; Mattheson quotes Johann Conrad

The correspondence of angelic and human music along with the function of music as a human response to the divine word are fulcrum points for part II of the *Christmas Oratorio*. The regulations of the St. Thomas School from 1733 encouraged the pupils (who would sing the *Christmas Oratorio* in the following year) to envision themselves as being in a polychoral dialogue with the choir of angels, echoing the celestial sounds from above. The gospel text for the second part of the *Christmas Oratorio* (Lk 2:8–14), does not explicitly mention music. However, it had been the traditional understanding that the angels did indeed sing their praise, "Ehre sei Gott in der Höhe." Some theologians had challenged this tradition, but for Mattheson and others there is no question that the angels not only sang their Gloria, but that they also used instruments: "die Engel sungen und spieleten stark" (the angels sang and played [their instruments] with gusto),[10] and the interpretation in the *Calov Bible* calls the angelic chorus "a beautiful Angelic sermon, a magnificent festival music."[11] The librettist for the *Christmas Oratorio* draws on these understandings of music in his depiction of the angels' praise. Aptly, part II of the oratorio begins with a *sinfonia*, a purely instrumental movement, which sonically stages the dialogue between heaven and earth.

## Sinfonia (mvt. 10)

Newly composed for the *Christmas Oratorio*, the instrumental movement consists of three sections of approximately equal length. The structure is symmetrical. Section 1 (mm. 1–18) begins in the key of G major and modulates via the dominant D major to the relative minor E minor. The middle section (mm. 18–44), a transposed

Dannhauer, *Hodomoria Spiritus Calviniani*, (Straßburg: von der Heyden, 1654), 1244. The idea of a musical correspondence between the Church Militant and the Church Triumphant goes back to earlier models. It is one of the twenty effects of music that the late fifteenth-century music theorist Johannes Tinctoris listed in his famous *Complexus effectuum musices*: "Ecclesiam militantem triumphanti assimilare" (to make the Church Militant like the Church Triumphant). Tinctoris, *On the Dignity & the Effects of Music: Two Fifteenth-Century Treatises*, trans. J. Donald Cullington, ed. J. Donald Cullington and Reinhard Strohm (London: Institute of Advanced Musical Studies, King's College, 1996), 51.

[10] Mattheson, *Behauptung der himmlischen Musik*, 108. See also a similar discussion of the sound of the angels in Erdmann Neumeister's sermon collection *Priesterliche Lippen* (1714). While Neumeister admits that nothing is known about the performance of the words, he posits that the sound must have been sweeter and more pleasant than the most perfect harmony on earth (Neumeister, *Priesterliche Lippen in Bewahrung der Lehre. Das Ist: Son[n]- und Festtags-Predigten durchs gantze Jahr* [Leipzig/Görlitz: Laurentius, 1714], 108). Other theologians, like Christian Münden, held similar positions; see Münden, *Bey der Geburt Christi Gott lobende Stimme Der Himmlischen Heerschaaren* (Helmstädt: Schnorr, 1729), 7.

[11] Abraham Calov, *Das Neue Testament / verdeutschet durch D. Martin Luthern*, 435: "diese schöne Englische Predigt / eine herrliche Fest-Music."

variant of the first section, continues in E minor but then modulates over D major to B minor. A short transitional section (mm. 41–43) modulates back to the home key. The final section (mm. 44–63) is another variation of section 1. The harmonic progression within the movement, while not particularly unusual, resembles that in the second newly composed movement of part II of the *Christmas Oratorio*, the angelic chorus "Ehre sei Gott in der Höhe" (except for its modulation to D minor at m. 31) This chorus can thus be divided into two major parts, each of which is subdivided (based on the text) into three shorter sections:

| | | |
|---|---|---|
| A | Ehre sei Gott in der Höhe | G–>D–>e–>b |
| B | und Friede auf Erden | b–>d |
| C | und den Menschen in Wohlgefallen | [G]–>C |
| A' | Ehre sei Gott in der Höhe | C–>G |
| B' | und Friede auf Erden | G–>G |
| C' | und den Menschen in Wohlgefallen | G–>G |

We will return to details of that movement later, but here I suggest that the opening sinfonia already anticipates some characteristics of the later Gloria movement. The harmonic progression in both movements moves from the home key of G major to E minor and then the minor dominant (B minor) before returning again to the home key. Both movements also share an extensive use of pedal points, which alternate with the more vivid motion of the bass voice. Since the dialogue between the heavenly sphere and the human sphere (i.e., between the angels and the shepherds), is central to this part of the oratorio, it is significant that both large-scale movements begin with the heavenly sphere and then descend to the human sphere. Both ultimately return (though transformed) to the heavenly realm, creating a synthesis of mundane and celestial musical signifiers.

The musical dialogue between heaven and earth in the opening sinfonia manifests itself within each of the three sections. Since each section is based on the same principle, we examine the first one more closely. The sinfonia begins as a regular siciliano: the upper instruments play a lilting dotted eighth-note figure, while the continuo line proceeds in a pulsating alternation of quarter notes and eighth notes. In the second half of m. 4, the upper voices and the bc exchange their roles, but the basic rhythmic pulse stays intact. The autograph score shows that the final version took shape in steps. Bach's original idea for this movement was only the siciliano motif in the strings. The bass line began with quarter notes and rests (as it is still the case in the viola); after a few measures, however, Bach decided to change it to the current version, which gives the beginning of the movement a stronger rhythmic profile (fig. 7.3).

As we read in chapter 4, the two flauti traversi do not appear in the autograph score, but their parts were added shortly before the first performance in 1734. The sound Bach originally intended here in the opening movements was therefore the sound of the string instruments playing a siciliano.[12] It is a musical topos that was frequently associated with the angelic sphere, as in Bach's cantata for Michaelmas 1726, *Es erhub sich ein Streit,* BWV 19, in which the aria "Bleibt, ihr Engel, bleibt bei mir" (no. 5) features a similar motif (ex. 7.1).[13]

*Example 7.1*  J. S. Bach, *Es erhub sich ein Streit* BWV 19, aria "Bleibt, ihr Engel, bleibt bei mir" (no. 5)

---

[12] The siciliano as a musical topos has been analyzed by Reinhard Wiesend, "Siciliana: Literarische und musikalische Traditionen" (PhD diss., University of Würzburg, 1986); for Bach's use of the siciliano, see in particular Reinhard Wiesend, "'Erbarme dich', alla Siciliana," in *Bach und die italienische Musik / Bach e la musica italiana,* ed. Wolfgang Osthoff and Reinhard Wiesend (Venice: Centro Tedesco di Studi Veneziani, 1987), 19–41.

[13] Günter Jena has also pointed to this similarity, see Jena, *Brich an, o schönes Morgenlicht,* 78.

*Figure 7.3* J. S. Bach, BWV 248/10, corrections in score (D-B Mus. ms. Bach P 32, fol. 13ʳ), mm. 1-5 (bpk, Berlin/Mendelssohn-Archiv, Staatsbibliothek zu Berlin, Stiftung Preussischer Kulturbesitz, Berlin, Germany/Art Resource, NY)

The sound color of the sinfonia in the *Christmas Oratorio* as well as the rhythmic profile of the movement changes in the second half of m. 9: Bach introduces a choir of reed instruments (oboi d'amore and da caccia), which play a descending, pulsating motif derived from the opening motif in the bc. The section for the reed chorus sounds much more grounded as Bach sets the reed section over a pedal point, played by the second oboe da caccia, which gives the whole section more the character of a pastoral (or a musette) than a siciliano.[14] The section for reed instruments is mostly homorhythmic, featuring first-inversion chords in parallel motion over a pedal point. This contrasts sharply with the more differentiated rhythmic layering in the string section at the beginning of the sinfonia. Later we will see that Bach uses similar pedal points in "Ehre sei Gott" (no. 21) to set the text of "und Friede auf Erden" (and peace on Earth), which supports my earlier suggestion that that the introductory movement depicts the juxtaposition of heavenly and earthly music thus foreshadowing the later angelic praise.

The first section of the sinfonia ends in a tightly knit polychoral dialogue between the two groups of instruments, with the strings featuring the siciliano motif while the reed instruments repeat the pastoral motif. Bach's choice of both the instrumentation and the rhythmic character has a symbolic function. The instrumental movement at the beginning of part II of the *Christmas Oratorio* evokes a bucolic scene:

---

[14] Cf. for Bach's use of pastoral dance idioms, Doris Finke-Hecklinger, *Tanzcharaktere in Johann Sebastian Bachs Vokalmusik*, Tübinger Bach-Studien 6 (Trossingen: Hohner, 1970), 79–83.

the image of shepherds on the fields outside of Bethlehem, immediately before they encounter the angel. Philipp Spitta heard the opening sinfonia as an almost romantic painting of a bucolic idyll:

> Thus, to be perfectly in sympathy with the instrumental symphony which opens the second part, we shall do well to imbue our minds with the sentiment on which the scene of the shepherds by night was based in the Christmas plays. A combination of opposite factors—which presented no difficulties to the naïve minds of the people—of the grace of the Eastern [oriental] idyll with the severity of the starlit boreal winter's night, gave the fundamental feeling of this symphony. This wonderful composition, woven as it were of silver rays, and enchanting us by harmony of hoes, is full of calm rejoicing, and yet unutterably solemn, child-like, and overflowing with yearning. The romantic feeling for nature, which so unmistakably breathes from it, also pervades the magnificent chorus of angels, "Glory to God in the highest!" where the sparkling accompaniment makes us feel as if we are gazing into the vault of the stars.[15]

Spitta's suggestion to hear Bach's sinfonia as depicting of a starry night in front of Bethlehem stands in the tradition of the romantic tone poem. While he misunderstands the musical vocabulary of Bach's setting, he is right in his observation that the opening sinfonia and the "Glory to God" are closely linked. Albert Schweitzer's interpretation of the sinfonia, while still influenced by romantic program music, focuses more on the dramatic function of the movement:

> Bach is once more writing music that depicts a situation. The shepherds in the fields awake and blow their pipes; over them there hovers already the band of angels that is about to appear to them. Their music blends with that of the angels. Bach thus intends the movement to be an introduction to the recitative "And there were shepherds in the same country, abiding in the field . . . and lo, an angel of the Lord stood by them."[16]

Schweitzer's view evokes more the idea of a Baroque painting than a nature scene, with putti hovering over a bucolic scene in which the shepherds play their instruments. He recognizes the dramatic function of the movement but falls short of seeing it within the context of the rest of the second part of the oratorio. The movement has a more complex function than either Spitta and Schweitzer suggest. Here, Bach draws on established musical symbolism in his use of instruments. The strings in

---

[15] Philipp Spitta, *Johann Sebastian Bach*, 2:580–81.

[16] Albert Schweitzer, *J. S. Bach*, English translation by Ernest Newman (New York: Dover, 1966), 2:307.

Renaissance and Baroque iconography have often been associated with the heavenly sphere.[17] The most famous example is probably the "Concert of Angels" in the Isenheim Altarpiece (1512–15), where the nativity scene is accompanied by an angelic string orchestra, playing under a Gothic baldachin. Reed instruments, on the other hand, were conventionally employed for the sonic representation of the shepherds.[18] Numerous images, especially from the Renaissance and the early Baroque depict shepherds with reed instruments, as Robert Campin's *Nativity* (ca. 1425) or the shepherds in the nativity scene of Albrecht Dürer's *Marienleben* (ca. 1501–11) show. Countless pre-Bach composers combined this sonic stereotype with the pastoral genre that was both stereotypically and nominally associated with the shepherds. A similar example of Bach's use of the reed instruments to depict the shepherds' sphere is the *Sonata pastorella* from Johann Schelle's *Actus musicus* from 1683, an instrumental piece for reed instruments, which evokes a bucolic scene before the arrival of the angels. A related use of reed instruments can also be found in Johann Rudolph Ahle's little Christmas concerto "Fürchtet euch nicht," in which the shepherds are accompanied by a chorus of bassoons.[19] Johann Sebastian Bach was familiar with all of these conventions and stereotypes. George Stauffer has recently pointed out that around 1734 Bach performed Pietro Locatelli's (1695–1764) *Concerto grosso in F minor*, op. 1, no. 8 (from 1721).[20] The concerto ends with a "Pastorale," which exhibits similarities to Bach's sinfonia.[21] Both movements are in major keys (Locatelli's in F and Bach's in G), and both composers juxtapose different sections of the ensemble; in Locatelli's case it is the concertant juxtaposition of soli and tutti, while Bach pits the strings against the reed instruments. What is missing in Locatelli's piece, however, is a motivic differentiation between the two groups, which fulfills

---

[17] Meredith J. Gill has analyzed the "Music of Angels" in her art-historical study, *Angels and the Order of Heaven in Medieval and Renaissance Italy* (Cambridge: Cambridge University Press, 2014), 112–34.

[18] The association of shepherds with reed instruments has left its mark not only on numerous compositions from the seventeenth and eighteenth centuries but can also be traced to common knowledge from books of this time that were not written for musical professionals. Adam Friedrich Kirsch writes in his *Neu-verfertigtes und in zwey Theil eingerichtetes Kunst-, Hauß-, Arzney- und Wunder=Buch* (Nuremberg, 1720), in the chapter "Von der Viehezucht," that sheep had a special proclivity for the sound of the schalmey and that thus shepherds used this instrument (131); and the dictionary *Curieuses Natur-Kunst-Gewerk und Handlungs-Lexicon* (Leipzig, 1722), adds that sheep developed better if the shepherds played a schalmei (shawm) or another kind of pipe for them (1242). In spite of lacking scientific basis for this assumption (and for some others the *Lexicon* presents on the impact of music on a wide variety of animals), the two books demonstrate the close connection between shepherds and the sound of reed instruments, outside of the musical discourse proper.

[19] See Markus Rathey, *Johann Rudolph Ahle, 1625–1673: Lebensweg und Schaffen,* (Eisenach: Wagner, 1999), 391.

[20] George B. Stauffer, "Music for 'Cavaliers et Dames': Bach and the Repertoire of His Collegium Musicum," in *About Bach*, ed. Gregory G. Butler et al. (Urbana-Champaign: University of Illinois Press, 2008), 139–40 and 151.

[21] This has recently been emphasized again by Robert Marshall, "Bach in Mid-Life," 11.

an important semantic function within Bach's composition. While it is possible that Bach's decision to compose a pastoral at the beginning of part II of the *Christmas Oratorio* was "inspired" by Locatelli's pastoral, as Robert Marshall has suggested,[22] the piece was no more than a general inspiration and did not serve as a direct model. Closer to Bach's sinfonia is the *Pastorale per la Notte della Nativitate Christi* by the Dresden composer Johann David Heinichen (1683–1729). The composition uses a typical siciliano rhythm and thus resembles more closely the opening of Bach's sinfonia. While maintaining the concerto principle by pitting soli against tutti, Heinichen also juxtaposes the sound of the reed instruments and the rest of the orchestra; a technique that closely resembles Bach's sinfonia (ex. 7.2).[23]

*Example 7.2* Johann David Heinichen, *Pastorale per la Notte della Nativitate Christi*

[22] Marshall, "Bach in Mid-Life," 11.

[23] Heinichen's piece has been brought into dialogue with Bach's sinfonia by Hermann Jung (*Die Pastorale: Studien zur Geschichte eines musikalischen Topos*. Neue Heidelberger Studien zur Musikwissenschaft 9 (Bern: Francke, 1980), 188–89), but the connection has not been followed so far.

In contrast to Locatelli's piece, which Bach had performed around the time he composed the *Christmas Oratorio*, there is no evidence that Bach knew Heinichen's *Pastorale*. Yet, given Bach's increasing interest in the musical life in Dresden during the early 1730s, it is possible that he drew upon a piece by a Dresden composer as inspiration for his own sinfonia.[24] But maybe these speculations lead in the wrong direction altogether. Both the pastoral and the siciliano were established musical styles, and Bach was aware of them long before he encountered the pieces by Locatelli and Heinichen. In fact, he can use these stereotypes in the opening movement of the second part of the *Christmas Oratorio* exactly because they *were* conventional and familiar to his listeners.[25] Bach and the other Baroque composers who made use of the pastorale, both sonically and rhythmically, often employed both strings and reeds in their various pastorales. The sound of the bucolic pastoral was, of course, a sonic fantasy of the courts and city-dwellers in the seventeenth and eighteenth centuries. It is the sound of the Arcadian shepherd in the tradition of Ovid and the baroque and medieval shepherd's plays. The real shepherds, who tended their sheep outside of the walls of Leipzig, were excluded from this imaginary soundscape[26]—as were their instruments, which were seen as "dishonest" instruments. In the seventeenth century, sons of shepherds were still not allowed to become "honorable" artisans, and the *Statutes of the Saxon Collegium of Town Musicians* listed, in 1653, the bucolic bagpipe as a questionable instrument that must not be played by an honorable musician.[27] When the Dresden court in 1697 hired Polish-style bagpipers, the musicians fed the desire for Otherness and for an exotic sound.[28] Their hiring confirmed this marginalization and did nothing to alleviate it.

The symbolic use of string and reed instruments in Bach's sinfonia sets the stage for the following movements of part II of the oratorio. The announcement of the angel in mvt. 13 is accompanied by the strings playing a halo-like accompaniment. On the other hand, the two reflective accompagnato recits (nos. 14 and 18), which explore the meaning of the announcement of Jesus's birth to the shepherds, are

---

[24] It is also possible that Bach and Heinichen knew each other personally.

[25] Another "shepherds symphony" from the eighteenth century is the famous *Pifa* from Handel's oratorio *The Messiah*, which employs a pastoral idiom similar to Bach's.

[26] See for the perception of shepherds in the early modern period: Werner Danckert, *Unehrliche Leute: Die verfemten Berufe* (Bern/München: Francke, 1963), 174–80; see also the more recent analysis by Kathy Stuart who locates the shepherds "on the periphery of dishonor," *Defiled Trades and Social Outcasts: Honor and Ritual Pollution in Early Modern Germany* (Cambridge: Cambridge University Press, 1999), 94–97

[27] Stephen Rose, *The Musician in Literature in the Age of Bach* (Cambridge: Cambridge University Press 2011), 79, 94; for the articles from 1653, see also Martin Wolschke, *Von der Stadtpfeiferei zu Lehrlingskapelle und Sinfonieorchester: Wandlungen im 19. Jahrhundert*, Studien zur Musikgeschichte des 19. Jahrhunderts 59 (Regensburg: Bosse, 1981), 33–36, and Adolf Koczirz, "Das Kollegium der sächsischen Stadt- und Kirchenmusikanten von 1653," *Archiv für Musikwissenschaft* 1 (1920/21): 280–88.

[28] Rose, *Musician in Literature*, 97.

accompanied by reed instruments. Bach also assigns both of the recits to the bass, the masculine voice that not only denoted the masculine sphere of the shepherds but also contrasted with the soprano voice of the angel in mvt. 13.

Yet, the sinfonia is more than the sonic painting of a bucolic scene. The movement begins with the light texture of the string ensemble, which can be heard as a depiction of the heavenly or angelic realm; this is followed by a depiction of the shepherds, with their reed instruments and pastoral pedal points. These two choruses subsequently engage in a dialogue (mm. 9–16). In mm. 16–18 the oboes suddenly introduce a falling fifth in a descending sequence, followed by an ascending gesture in the strings. Here Bach again uses descent and ascent to contrast the two spheres before finally, in mm. 18–23, combining the two sonic layers. The strings play their siciliano motif while the reed instruments continue their pulsating pastoral motif until they finally (m. 22) join the "angels" in their song. Bach's autograph score shows several corrections in mm. 19–22, which demonstrates that the combination of the two layers, which previously has existed independently, presented a compositional challenge.[29] In the second section, at mm. 23–41, Bach features the same juxtaposition of the two instrumental choirs but now in a minor key: the strings begin with their siciliano, followed by a dialogue between the strings and the reed instruments. The descending leaps are now played by both the strings and reeds (mm. 33–34). Meanwhile, the reeds also present the siciliano motif for a short moment before Bach simultaneously layers the two sonic spheres, each one with its original musical material (mm. 36–41); but as a twist, the violin picks up briefly the motif from the reed ensemble as well (m. 38). A short modulatory passage (mm. 41–44) leads from B minor back to the home key of G major, and the last section begins as a reprise of the beginning. In the final section of the movement (mm. 44–63), the statements of the two instrumental groups are abbreviated. The first statement of the sicilano, which had been eight measures long, is condensed to its first four measures. Bach is more interested in playing with the dialogue of the two instrumental groups, and in the final measures, the reed instruments take over the siciliano motifs from the string chorus for a second time.[30] Even more, in m. 62 the reed instruments have a short solo statement of the siciliano motif, echoing the previous phrase of the strings, before all the instruments play the final chord together.

The sinfonia is a rare piece of program music in Bach's works.[31] Bach evokes the sonic sphere of the shepherds as so many composers had done before him in their Christmas compositions. Bach establishes two sonic spheres, differentiated by their

---

[29] See NBA II/6, KB, 32 for the corrections.

[30] Some massive corrections in the second violin suggest that Bach again worked intensively on the layering of the two sonic spheres; unfortunately, the previous version is not legible; see NBA II/6, KB, 33–34.

[31] Interestingly, another piece of program music might have been part of the third version of the *St. John Passion* from ca. 1732. The gospel text about the earthquake and the resurrection of the dead

rhythmic profile, texture (siciliano versus pastoral), and sound (strings versus reeds). If this piece is about the juxtaposition of the two spheres, it is also about the synthesis of these spheres. All three sections culminate in the simultaneous combination of the two instrumental choruses and in the take-over of the "angelic" material by the shepherds. The function of the movement is multilayered: on a purely sonic level, it establishes the sonic spheres of angels and shepherds, which Bach continues to juxtapose in the following movements of part II. But the combination of the two spheres also has a theological meaning, one that might reflect an interpretation of the Christmas narrative in Martin Luther's *Hauspostille*. The reformer writes:

| | |
|---|---|
| Aber er ist nicht allein unser HErr, sondern auch der Engel HErr; die sind nun mit uns und wir mit ihnen dieses HErrn Hausgesinde, zählen sich unter diesen HErrn zugleich mit uns, daß wir Menschen, die wir zuvor des Teufels Knechte waren, durch dies Kindlein zu solchen Ehren kommen, daß wir nun in der Bürgerschaft der lieben Engel angenommen sind. Die sind jetzt unsere besten Freunde.[32] | But he is not only our Lord but he is also the Lord of the angels; and together with the angels we are members of the Lord's domestic community. While we had been servants of the devil before, now the child has honored us by elevating us to the citizenry of the angels. They are now our best friends. |

The humans, in the oratorio represented by the shepherds, participate in the angelic sphrere by joining in their music. Or, to come back to the discussion of heavenly music from the beginning of this chapter, the shepherds use the angelic music as a model for their own music. Human and divine music engage in a polychoral dialogue and finally become one as the reed instruments take over the musical motif from the strings. A theological treatise from 1746 formulates this synthesis thus: "In Christo und durch Christum stimmen himmel und erde, Gott, Engel und menschen wieder zusammen" (In Christ and through Christ heaven and earth, God, angel, and men sound together).[33] A third function of the sinfonia within the larger context of the oratorio is its anticipation of the praise of the angels later in part II. We

---

after Christ's death was followed by a movement called "Sinfonia," (see Daniel R. Melamed, *Hearing Bach's Passions* [Oxford: Oxford University Press, 2005], 75 and 146) The movement is lost and we only know about it because it is mentioned in the contemporary performance parts; however, it is more than likely that the "Sinfonia" was a musical depiction of the earthquake that followed the death of Christ. Musical depictions of earthquakes, storms, and thunderstorms had been a staple of contemporary opera for a while and considering Bach's increased interest in operatic forms in the early 1730s is it likely that he made careful attempts to introduce programmatic instrumental movements in his sacred works as well.

[32] Luther, *Hauspostille*, col. 62–63.

[33] Christoph Starke, *Synopsis Bibliothecae Exegeticae in Novum Testamentum: Kurzgefaster Auszug Der gründlichsten und nutzbarsten Auslegungen über alle Bücher Neues Testaments, In Tabellen,*

have already pointed out the similarities between the sinfonia and the chorus "Ehre sei Gott" (no. 21). Both the sinfonia and the choral "Ehre" movement were newly composed for the *Christmas Oratorio*, and Bach designed these two movements as corresponding pillars within the second- part framework of the oratorio.

## The angelic Gloria (mvt. 21)

Part II of the *Christmas Oratorio* is the only one that does not open with a large-scale choral movement. The listener has to wait until the second half of part II to hear the setting of the angelic chorus, "Ehre sei dir Gott," and this delay increases the impact of the chorus when it enters later. With the exception of the chorale settings, the listeners had not yet heard the entire ensemble in a tutti movement in part II. The setting of "Ehre sei dir Gott" formally resembles a motet: the instruments are never dominant and either play short motifs or simply go colla parte with the vocal parts. Consequently, most of the corrections in the autograph score reflecting the compositional process appear in the vocal lines while the instruments show a rather clear handwriting. The text of the movement consists of three short phrases, which, as usual in a motet, are set with different musical material: (A) "Ehre sei Gott in der Höhe," (B) "und Friede auf Erden," and (C) "und den Menschen ein Wohlgefallen." The structure of the movement is well balanced. The first section (A)—the invocation of God in the highest—is twenty-five measures long. The other two sections (B and C) focus on the human side, the earthly sphere. These sections are six and nineteen measures long, adding up to twenty-five measures as well. In the last part of the composition Bach goes through the entire text again, shortening the setting of the heavenly praise to eight measures, while the settings of sections B and C are condensed to five and five measures respectively. As mentioned earlier, the large-scale structure of the choral movement juxtaposes the divine and human spheres. The harmonic progression in the movement resembles the one in the opening sinfonia of part II. The repetition of the material in shortened fashion at the end of the movement allows Bach to treat the text differently. In the first, more extensive setting (mm. 1–49), he establishes a transition from the home key G major to the subdominant

---

*Erklärungen, Anmerkungen und Nutzanwendungen . . .*, vol. I (Biel: Heilmann, 1746), col. 1039. We find a similar view of human and angelic music in Telemann's *Hirten bei der Krippe* (1759), based on a text by Karl Wilhelm Ramler. The two-part oratorio celebrates the music of the shepherds in the first half: "Hirten aus den gold'nen Zeiten, blast die Flöten, rührt die Saiten, euer Tagewerk sei Freude, euer Leben sei Gesang." Telemann's setting transfers these musical actions directly into music: "Flöten" follows a little interjection by the two flutes (mm. 17–18); after "Saiten" comes a similar passage by the strings (mm. 19–20); and the word "Gesang" is set with a long melisma, featuring eighth-note triples and duplets as well as sixteenth-notes. The first part ends with a dialogue between two soli (S and B) and the choir, which celebrates the unification of earthly and heavenly music: "Erd' und Himmel sei, wie vor, in den Allerhöchsten Ohr ein Gesang ein Chor" (mm. 33–112). See Telemann, *Musikalische Werke 30*, ed. Wolf Hobohm (Kassel: Bärenreiter, 1997).

C major and the minor dominant B minor. The second time the complete text is set (mm. 49–65), Bach establishes a return to the home key G major. The first nine measures (A') lead back from C major to G major, while the final two sections (B' and C') are firmly rooted in the tonic G major. In addition to the structural necessity of returning to the key of the beginning, the transposed recapitulation of the material in the last seventeen measures of the movement also allows Bach to elevate the human texts from sections B and C to the "heavenly realm" by transposing them to G major. The unification of the divine and human realm that had already shaped the structure of the opening sinfonia is here realized on a harmonic level. We will see more similarities when we explore the movement in more detail.

The first section of mvt. 21 consists of three polyphonic expositions of the text. Each one of the expositions are of equal length (nine measures with each exposition eliding at the ninth measure). The first exposition (mm. 1–9) presents the text in a tight polyphonic web, with the four voices (SATB) entering at a distance of only half a measure from each other. The head of the subject emphasizes the word "Ehre" through a syncopated leap. At its second entrance, the word "Ehre" is then expanded by a long melisma, both underscoring the glory of God and the praise of the angels. The regular polyphonic entrance of the voices at the beginning of the movement is somewhat obscured by an accompanying countersubject in the lower voices, which is sung until these voices take over the main subject as well. The effect is that Bach on the one hand composes a highly polyphonic, motet-like movement that at the same time opens with nearly the full available forces, thus reflecting the splendor of the angelic praise. The dense polyphonic opening of the movement required special attention by the composer. In mm. 3 and 4, Bach has to deal with the increasingly complex polyphonic texture after the movement had begun, using a canon of soprano and alto and a simple accompaniment in the two lower voices. The numerous corrections cover some of the original notes, but an earlier version of these two measures had the parts of alto and tenor exchanged from note 5 of m. 3 to note 4 of the following measure; the leap in the first two notes of the soprano of m. 3 was a third ($a'-c\sharp''$) instead of a sixth ($a'-f\sharp''$), and the second note in the bass was a different pitch (probably $g$ or $a$). The revised version emphasizes the leaps in soprano, alto, and bass, which had been thirds or fourths, by turning them into more pronounced ascending sixths. Overall, the change underscores the upward trajectory of the beginning.

A second characteristic feature of section A is an ostinato-like bc line, which is repeated three times with each one of the expositions of the polyphonic material. Alfred Dürr has called this first section a "Passacaglia," a term, which, if loosely applied, is indeed fitting.[34] The constant motion of the bc line also gives the section a high degree of kinetic energy. The texture of the vocal and instrumental parts

---

[34] John Butt has criticized Bossuyt's use of the term "passacaglia" for this movement, "Review of I. Bossuyt, 'Johann Sebastian Bach: Christmas Oratorio,'" *Music and Letters* 87 (2006): 656. Bossuyt is only partly to blame because he borrows the term from Dürr. The term is problematic if used strictly; however, loosely applied, it is quite useful as it highlights the repetitiveness of the bass line.

is in constant motion and the chain of eighth notes is rarely interrupted. One of the voices is regularly maintaining this motion. This continuous chain of energy is essential for the A section, as can be seen in a correction Bach made to the tenor in mm. 10/11. In version 1, the energy would have been interrupted on beat 3 of m. 10 with a quarter note in alto and tenor and a half note in the bass. By changing the text underlay and the rhythm (version 2), Bach keeps the motion going and creates an ideal backdrop for the entrance of the subject in the soprano in m. 11 (ex. 7.3).

*Example 7.3* J. S. Bach, BWV 248/21, revisions in tenor voice, mm. 9–12

When he turns to "peace on earth" in section B, Bach dramatizes the shift from the heavenly to the earthly sphere by way of sharp contrasts. Instead of *forte*, as the first section, the score now indicates *piano*; the harmonic progression arrives in B minor (with Picardy third), and the walking-bass line has abruptly come to a halt in extended pedal points. The reed chorus in section B plays a simplified colla parte accompaniment. The simplicity and the pedal points hark back to the reed sections of the opening sinfonia. In spite of the contrast between sections A and B, Bach still establishes a sense of continuity. The subject he uses for the point of imitation in soprano and alto is a rhythmically varied version of the subject from the section A: an ascending leap of a fourth followed by a descent in stepwise motion. The tempo appears to be slowed down as the third note is lengthened to a half note. This, together with the slowing down of the harmonic rhythm underscores the strong contrast to the preceding section. The strings, instead of short chords, play legato motifs on weak time, resembling the sigh motifs Bach had used in the *St. Matthew Passion* in the chorale-trope "O Schmerz, hier zittert das gequälte Herz" (no. 19). He employs a musical texture that expresses the somber conditions of men in contrast to the glory of heavens. Martin Luther emphasizes the lowness of the shepherds in his *Hauspostille*; he also operates within the spacial juxtaposition of the low shepherds and the high angels (and the high and mighty rulers in Jerusalem):

| | |
|---|---|
| Das ist auch etwas Neues, daß GOtt die großen Herren zu Jerusalem läßt sitzen, und schickt so seine herrliche Botschaft vom Himmel herunter zu den armen Bettlern, den Hirten, auf dem Feld. . . . Ob nun wohl die Hirten geringe, einfältige Leute sind, gleichwohl halten die Engel sich selbst nicht so für heilig und hoch, daß sie nicht sollten von Herzen willig und fröhlich sein, solche Botschaft ihnen anzusagen.[35] | It is something new that God stands up the mighty men in Jerusalem and instead sends such a wonderful message down from heaven to the poor beggars, the shepherds, on the fields. . . . Although the shepherds are only humble, simple people, the angels nevertheless do not deem themselves too holy and high; with a willing heart and with joy they deliver such a message to them [the shepherds]. |

The short B section is followed by a longer setting of text-phrase C, "und den Menschen ein Wohlgefallen." The section is again highly polyphonic, the beginning even shaped as a canon. The subject has once more a downward trajectory, gradually descending by a fourth from $d''$ to $a'$. The entries of the four voices (SATB) are also descending. Section C thus continues the idea of descent that is

---

[35] Luther, *Hauspostille*, col. 64–66.

present in several of the parameters of the composition. At the same time, section C creates a climax by increasing the motion within the polyphonic texture. While section A featured mostly melismatic lines in eighth notes and section B slowed down this motion, the third section has long sixteenth-note melismas on the word "Wohlgefallen" (satisfaction, goodwill), emphasizing the final goal of the coming of Christ, the pleasure of men over the advent of God's son. This "Wohlgefallen" is the very joy that was announced by the angel immediately before the other angels enter with their hymn of praise, "See, I announce great joy for all mankind." Johann Gerhard writes in a similar vein in his *Postille*. He points out that, while the joy is expressed by the angels, it is the humans who have to be joyful about Christ's coming:

| | |
|---|---|
| Weil nun die Engel sich so herzlich über der Geburt Christi freuen und lobsingen, so doch Christus nicht um ihretwillen Mensch worden, wie vielmehr will uns gebühren, mit fröhlichem Herzen und Munde GOtt zu preisen, sintemal um unsertwillen GOttes Sohn Mensch geboren ist und alle Wohlthaten dieser Geburt dem menschlichen Geschlecht, nicht den Engeln, zu gute kommen.[36] | While the angels are joyful and sing wholeheartedly about the birth of Christ, Christ did not become man for them; how much more do we have to praise God with a cheerful heart and mouth, since the son of God has become man for us; and it is we who benefit from this birth and not the angels. |

Section C presents an interesting combination of previous musical ideas, establishing a synthesis of sections A and B. The strings and flutes go colla parte with the vocalists, while the reed instruments play a harmonic backdrop that resembles their function in section B. The bc line returns to the walking-bass line from section A, albeit now not in a strict, passacaglia-like manner but rather as a continuous accompaniment to the polyphonic texture in the upper voices. Section C also returns dynamically to the opening section by prescribing *forte* instead of *piano*. Bach thus creates a correspondence between sections A and C, while he also maintains a continuity between B and C. The Danzig theologian Aegidius Strauch suggests, in a sermon for the first day of Christmas, published in Leipzig in 1702, a spatial understanding of the three lines of the praise of the angels:

| | |
|---|---|
| [Wir haben] auff die Englische Posituren oder Stellungen zu sehen. Denn anfänglich wenden sich die | [We have] to pay attention to the positions or directions of the angels. At the beginning, they turn |

---

[36] Gerhard, *Postille*, 69.

| | |
|---|---|
| Engel über sich zu GOtt / und lassen sich hören mit einer unvergleichlichen Lob-Stimme: Ehre sey GOtt in der Höhe. Bald darauff wenden sie sich herunter zu den Menschen mit einer fröhlichen Wuntsch-Stimme: Friede auff Erden. Endlich sehen sie gleich aus / und lassen erklingen eine Evangelische Lehr-Stimme: Und den Menschen ein Wohlgefallen.[37] | themselves upwards toward God and they let themselves hear with the incomparable voice of praise: "May honor be to God on high." Soon they turn their gaze down toward men [and sing] with a joyful [and] wishful voice: "and peace on earth." Finally, they look straight and let sound the voice of teaching of the gospel: "and to humankind great pleasure." |

It is unknown whether Bach or his librettist knew Strauch's sermons. However, Strauch's use of spatial images: upward for the first line of the text, downward for the second line, and a leveled trajectory for the rest, can help explain the juxtaposition of high and low in the first two sections of Bach's setting and the jubilant character of the third section. What is not present in Strauch's account, however, is the gradual descent that characterizes Bach's piece, and the synthesis of the human and angelic spheres at the end of the piece. With the recapitulation of the three previous sections from m. 49 on, Bach composed abbreviated versions of each of the sections: section A' presents the text once, based on the ostinato bass line from the beginning (now transposed to C major); section B' brings back the pedal point (now in the home key G major); and section C' shortens the canonic entrance of the voices by opening with the alto voice but then introducing soprano and tenor in parallel sixths, and by assigning the bass a modified version of the subject that facilitates the transition into the final cadence in mm. 64/65.

This movement is not a parody but was newly composed for the *Christmas Oratorio*. Bach's score exhibits numerous corrections so we can clearly identify it as a composition score. However, even though Bach did not parody an older movement, the praise of the angels uses existing pieces as structural models. One general model is the opening sinfonia, in which Bach had juxtaposed the heavenly and earthly spheres, employed pedal points and reeds to signify the earthly realm of the shepherds, and led the two realms to a final synthesis. The other model is the Gloria from the *B-Minor Mass*, completed just over a year before the composition of the *Christmas Oratorio*. In the Mass, Bach sets the praise of the angels ("Gloria in excelsis Deo") in a jubilant, concerto movement in D major. On the text "Et in terra pax," Bach transitions quickly to the subdominant G major, the texture becomes homophonic and rests on an extended pedal point (with the remark *"tasto solo"* as

---

[37] Aegidius Strauch, *Starcke und Milch-Speise / hiebevor der Christlichen Gemeine daselbst in hundert sechs und siebentzig Sonn- und Fest-Tags-Predigten vorgetragen*, 2nd rev. ed. (Leipzig 1702), 66.

in the *Christmas Oratorio*); additionally, the strings play a sigh-like accompaniment that expresses a similar somber mood as the setting of the same text in the oratorio. Analogous to the movement in the *Christmas Oratorio*, the pedal-point section is followed by a vivid, polyphonic setting. And finally, as in the oratorio, the phrase "*[bonae] voluntatis*" (good will) is highlighted by a long, jubilant sixteenth-note melisma. Bach used similar ideas to set the German version of the Gloria text as he had in his Latin Mass setting. What is missing in the Latin version is a synthesis of the "Gloria" and "et in terra" sections (or, metaphorically speaking, of the divine and human spheres) toward the end of the movement. This was prohibited because Bach was using preexisting music in his Mass. The two sections of the Latin Gloria were probably taken from different model compositions.[38] But a synthesis was also less necessary than in the *Christmas Oratorio*, where the unification of divine and human spheres in music was an essential part of the narrative and a central topic in the second part of the oratorio.[39]

## United choirs (mvts. 22 and 23)

Bach's settings of both the sinfonia and the "Ehre sei Gott" chorus already led to a synthesis of the heavenly-angelic and human-bucolic spheres. The final recit of part II (no. 22) confirms this and admonishes the listeners to join the chorus of the angels as well: "So recht, ihr Engel, jauchzt und singet . . . wir stimmen mit euch ein" (Quite right, you angels: shout and sing . . . we will join with you in song). As explained in chapter 5, Bach abstains from setting the text as an accompagnato recit, as he had originally intended, in order to create a moment of repose between the joyful setting of the biblical text and the final chorale. In addition to revising the plans for the instrumentation, Bach also made several changes in the voice-leading of the movement. The recit originally began in C major (the key of the human sphere in the previous movement) and highlighted different aspects of the text. In the first version, the exposed high notes (ex. 7.4) appear on "En-[gel]" (angel) and "heut" (present time).

---

[38] While it is clear that Bach parodies two earlier models in the Gloria of his Mass, the sources of these movements are not known, cf. Alfred Dürr, "Zur Parodiefrage in Bachs h-Moll-Messe: Eine Bestandsaufnahme," *Die Musikforschung* 45 (1992): 117–38; and George B. Stauffer, *Bach: The Mass in B Minor, The Great Catholic Mass* (New Haven: Yale University Press, 2003), 65–71.

[39] For a comparison of Bach's setting of the Gloria with Handel's rendition of the chorus in his *Messiah*, see Jin-Ah Kim, "Händel und Bach als Akteure ihrer musikalischen Produktion," *Archiv für Musikwissenschaft* 65 (2008): 289–308. Kim contrasts Handel's "dramatic" approach to the text with Bach's "hermeneutical" approach and locates the differences within the sociological contexts of both pieces.

*Example 7.4* J. S. Bach, BWV 248/22, transformation of the recitative, mm. 1–3

The version emphasized the angels as the bringers of the good news and it also accentuates the present meaning of this praise (the "heut" alludes to the time of Christ's Second Coming). While the present meaning of Christ's coming is of central importance for the entire *Christmas Oratorio*, the emphasis in part II is on other aspects. Bach thus revised the first version: he transposed the movement to G major, and he also modified the first notes of the bass voice (ex. 7.4). Now the jubilation of the angels is highlighted. This reading of the recit text is more in line with the emphasis on music (heavenly and earthly) in the rest of this part of the oratorio. What is still less convincing in this version is the threefold repetition of the note *d'* in m. 2. Bach subsequently abandoned the sketch and crossed it out in order to begin fresh on the following page. The final version now begins with an exclamatory "So recht," emphasized by an ascending leap of a fourth, a high note (*d'*) on the word "jauchzt," and a second high *d'* on the word "schön." Bach here highlights the esthetic beauty of the angelic praise—or in extension, the esthetic beauty of the music made in honor and as praise of God. The following descending fifth on "Auf denn!" mirrors the "So recht" from the beginning and demands attention for the admonition to sing a hymn of praise together with the angels. Here the libretto finally embraces the synthesis of the two spheres that had been present in Bach's music since the very beginning of part II. The final movement of the second part, a setting of the Paul Gerhard hymn "Wir singen dir in deinem Heer," answers the command to join the choir of angels. This first line "We sing to you [Jesus] amid your host [of angels]" is a logical sequitur to the penultimate line of the preceding recit: "wir stimmen mit euch ein" (We will join with you [angels]). The first line of Gerhard's stanza, the mention of the divine host ("deinem Heer") connects the hymn to the praise of the angels. The text also mentions the advent of the guest (Christ) whose coming had been so long desired. This coming of the "guest" has again a dual temporal meaning. Within the temporal framework of the narrative it is the first coming of Christ. But it is also the desired coming of Christ in the heart of the believer, the second advent of Christ.

The end of part II bears some resemblance to the Christmas play by Paul Thymich and Johann Magnus Knüpfer from 1685. The seventh "Abtheilung" (or scene) of their *Hirten-Freude* closes with the statement of the shepherd Laban, encouraging his companions to sing a song of praise and join with the chorus of the angels, "Wir müssen ein fröhliches Dancklied bereiten/die himmlischen Sänger die stimmen mit an" (We have to prepare a joyful song of praise; the heavenly singers join in [with us]). The final movement in Thymich's libretto is a polychoral dialogue between the chorus of angels and the chorus of shepherds. The text is a free poetic paraphrase of the Gloria, which culminates in the two choruses singing together "Ehre sey Gott in der Höhe." As conceded earlier, there is no evidence that Bach or his librettist knew Thymich's text or Knüpfer's composition. Nonetheless, this similarity displays a commonality of certain patterns of understanding. As explained in chapter 5, the present version of the final chorale was not part of the original plan. Bach intended to compose a simple four-part chorale setting in common time. He then changed his plans and projected an extended chorale setting, still in common time but with instrumental accompaniment. Finally, he decided to compose an extended chorale setting in 12/8 time (the same time signature he had used in the opening movement of part II), and to quote the siciliano motif from the sinfonia in the accompanying bc line. The individual lines of the chorale, which are accompanied by the string ensemble, are interrupted by short interjections of the wind instruments. The oboe interludes resemble the pastoral motifs from the opening sinfonia, including the pedal points that are characteristic of the pastoral genre. The final chorale is again a dialogue between the divine chorus (musically denoted by the siciliano motif in the bc) and the chorus of the shepherds, playing its bucolic reedy pastoral. But now the angelic instruments (strings) are joined by the chorale, which traditionally represents the voice of the congregation. The human and the angelic spheres are finally united.

## The sign of the manger (mvts. 16 and 17)

The three large-scale movements—nos. 10, 21, and 23—form the framework for the interpretation of the announcement to the shepherds in part II of the *Christmas Oratorio*. They represent the ideal of both heavenly and human music. The final chorale also demonstrates that the appropriate response to the announcement of the coming of Jesus is praise, and in particular, praise through music. As the regulations for the St. Thomas School had stressed, the boys should be "reasonable beings, who find their greatest joy in singing the praise of God." A pair of movements that emphasizes the uses of music as a human response to the divine revelation is the recit "So geht denn hin" (no. 18) and the following aria "Schlafe, mein Liebster." They are part of a sequence of movements that react to the second half of the announcement of the angel: "Und das habt zum Zeichen: Ihr werdet finden das Kind in Windeln gewickelt und in einer Krippe liegen." (And take this for a sign: you will find the child wrapped in bands of cloth and lying in a manger).

The biblical verse by itself does not necessarily lead to a musical response, and Bach's setting of the text does not evoke musical images. Instead, he presents a setting of the text that focuses on the skandalon (stumbling block) of the birth of God's son, swaddled in diapers and lying in a manger. The recit begins rather unspectacular with D-major chord in first inversion, with a pedal point on $f\sharp$ in the bc, and the outline of the D-major triad in the tenor voice. The second phrase consists of repeated notes on $a$ and then slowly ascends to $e'$ on the word "Windeln." Only on the verb "[ge-]wickelt" does Bach introduce an unexpected half-diminished seventh chord, based on $f\natural$, as part of a chromatic progression in the bass line ($f\sharp-f$). The bc drops farther down by a tritone to $b\natural$. The tenor voice follows with a drop of a diminished fifth ($d'-g\sharp$) on "und in" (and in) and an ascending leap of a diminished 7th ($g\sharp-f$) on "in einer" (in a). Chromaticism and dissonant leaps underscore that the lowly birth of Jesus in a manger is, as in part I, musically depicted as a skandalon and a paradox.[40] The following chorale confirms this understanding of Jesus's birth in the manger. It juxtaposes the "dark stable," which had merely been the place of nourishment for cattle, with the all-encompassing lordship of the child of the virgin.[41] This movement, in C major, marks the middle of part II; it is the subdominant of the home key G major of part II and constitutes the deepest descent within the harmonic progression at this part of the entire *Christmas Oratorio*. Eric Chafe has argued convincingly that Bach frequently employs a descending harmonic progression in a symbolic way to depict aspects like divine descent, human sinfulness, or despair.[42] We have seen a similar descent in Bach's juxtaposition of the divine and the human spheres in mvt. 21 ("Ehre sei Gott") and the choice of key here follows a similar rationale. The subdominant highlights the divine descent from his rulership to the manger of Bethlehem; from heaven to the "dark stable."[43]

[40]  Bach made a small change in his autograph score. The second note of m. 3 in the bc was originally a half-note $b$, which was then changed into a quarter-note $b$ and a quarter-note $c$, resolving the harshness of the tritone from the first half of the measure at the end of m. 3 instead of at the start of m. 4.

[41]  The chorale stanza is the eighth stanza of Paul Gerhard's Christmas hymn "Schaut, schaut, was ist für Wunder dar" from 1667.

[42]  Eric Chafe, *Analyzing Bach Cantatas* (Oxford: Oxford University Press, 2000), 104–5 and 148–49.

[43]  The same has already been suggested by Blankenburg, *Weihnachts-Oratorium*, 64.

In spite of its simplicity, the chorale setting of "Schaut hin, dort liegt im finstern Stall" (no. 17) features some noteworthy details. Bach inserts several ascending and descending lines into the bass voice. In mm. 2–3 the bass line ascends in a scalar motion over the interval of a ninth from *A* to *b♭* and later in mm. 4–5 it descends again by a ninth from *a* to *G*. A partial scalar descent follows in mm. 7–8 from *e* down to *F*. The scales overreaching the octave—the all-encompassing interval, or in Greek *diapason* (overall)—is a musical depiction of the word "überall," which qualifies the all-encompassing lordship of Christ. This ascending line appears for the first time in combination with the text "des Herrschaft gehet [überall]" (he whose lordship ranges over all).[44] A second compositional detail is a syncopation in the bass line in the penultimate measure. It paints the word "ruhet" (rests, sleeps) and leads to a small moment of hesitation in the chorale setting. The syncopation highlights the very word that will be of importance in the following two movements, the accompagnato, no. 18, and especially the aria, no. 19, "Schlafe, mein Liebster" (Sleep, my most beloved). But before we come to these movements, we need to return again to the beginning of part II.

## Shepherds and angels (mvts. 11–15)

The unification of the human and divine spheres in music in the mvts. 10 and 21 of the second part of the *Christmas Oratorio* is procedural. They are not joined at the beginning but rather they stand in opposition, both in their placement within the range of the musical scale (high versus low) as well as in the musical material employed to represent them. This procedural aspect reflects the development within the narrative. The opening sinfonia of part II is a real piece of program music, but it is also proleptic as it creates a unity that will be accomplished only later in the story. At their first encounter with the angel, the shepherds are frightened. Bach's rendition of this encounter in recit no. 11 follows immediately after the opening sinfonia. The shepherds are tending to their sheep in the fields near Bethlehem. It is night, dark, and Bach's setting of the description leads the voice of the Evangelist down to the deepest note of the recit (*d♯*) by way of a diminished triad (*a–f♯–d♯*), which is then followed by a surprising and attention-grapping leap up to *c'*. The darkness of the shepherds is contrasted with the light of the angels: the voice of the tenor raises on "und siehe" (and look) and reaches a peak when the text announces that an angel of "the Lord" ("des Herren") had appeared (m. 6). The radiance of the Lord

---

[44] Blankenburg also argues that the descending scale in mm. 4–5 symbolized Christ's humiliation in his birth in a manger. While this would make sense within the theological framework of the oratorio, it might overstretch the symbolism in this piece. The fact that Bach uses the interval of a ninth to make his point seems to be more important.

surrounds the shepherds and the encounter with the divine does not cause joy but instills fear. Bach sets this fear with a threefold descending triad, each one outlining a diminished fifth (mm. 7–9): $g'$–$e'$–$c\sharp'$–$e'$–$c\sharp'$–$a\natural$–$b$–$g\sharp$–$e\natural$. And the "divine radiance" ("leuchtet um sie") is not set any differently from the way the "night" had been set a few measures earlier: $e'$–$c\sharp'$–$a\natural$. This fear-causing encounter with the divine light is also echoed in the bc. In mm. 8 and 9 the instrumental bass plays a little arch-like figure that can be heard both as a depiction of the "radiance" of the angel's apparition ("Klarheit des Herrn"), but it also depicts the fear (as in the use of the diminished chords), as the first figure descends by a diminished octave and the second one by a diminished seventh. Bach inserted this figure after drafting a different version: m. 8 originally had a much simpler progression of a half note and two quarter notes. But after writing down the notes, he decided otherwise and turned the first note into a quarter note and the two other notes into a chain of sixteenths. He then repeated a similar figure in the following measure, now without corrections.

The recit continues the juxtaposition of the human and divine spheres but without a synthesis. The reactions to the divine light are shock and fear. The ensuing chorale setting picks up on this and addresses the shepherds directly: "Du Hirtenvolk, erschrecke nicht" (You shepherd folk, do not be alarmed). The chorale, the ninth verse of Johann Rist's hymn "Ermuntre dich, mein schwacher Geist" (1641), is one of the rare occasions in the oratorio that a chorale becomes part of the narrative by addressing one of the protagonists directly.[45] However, similar to other chorales, the hymn text interprets one or more of the keywords from the previous narrative, in this case the light-metaphor ("schönes Morgenlicht," lovely morning light) and the fear of the shepherds ("erschrecke nicht," do not be alarmed). The chorale anticipates the following angelic announcement and explains the salvific meaning of the little child in the manger. The simple chorale setting employs an unusual version of the melody in common time instead of its original version in triple meter, a version which Bach uses in his other compositions.[46] Walter Blankenburg has suggested that Bach might have independently changed the meter for the version in the oratorio;[47] but it is likewise possible that he found that version in a local tradition,[48] so we should not

---

[45] This was already pointed out by Meinrad Walter, *Weihnachtsoratorium*, 78.

[46] BWV 11/6 (*Ascension Oratorio*), and BWV 43/11 (*Gott fähret auf mit Jauchzen*).

[47] Blankenburg, *Weihnachts-Oratorium*, 58.

[48] Different traditions seem also to be responsible for a mistake at the end of the first line of the melody (mm. 3/4). He originally wrote $c''$–$b'$–$a'$–$g'$–$g'$–$f\sharp'$–$g$, a version that is closer to Schop's original version (Zahn, 5741a) than the one that was used in Leipzig during Bach's time. It is possible that he had known this different version and accidentally used the phrase when he copied down the chorale melody. The correction, however, was made before he entered the alto line, because it has the same last notes as the different melody version: $g'$–$f\sharp'$–$g'$.

put too much stock in this difference. More important is what Bach does with this chorale melody. Little details in the setting underscore the hymn text. A chromatic ascent in m. 11 on the words "unser Trost und" (our comfort and) leads to a climax that is reached on the word "Freude" (joy, m. 12), the same word the angel will use in the next recit to qualify the birth of the child. The two lower voices sing an eighth-note motif in parallel tenths on the words "[Satan] zwingen" (vanquish Satan, m. 14), a detail that gives the setting a martial character by suddenly increasing the motion in the accompaniment, as Walter perceptively suggests.[49]

After a short introduction by the evangelist (no. 13), the angel, sung by the soprano and accompanied by a halo of strings, sings his "Fürchtet euch nicht!" (Fear not!). It had been a long-standing tradition to assign this section to a soprano; we find similar cases in the seventeenth-century Christmas scenes by Sebastian Knüpfer, Johann Schelle, Johann Rudolph Ahle, and Heinrich Schütz. Also the instrumental halo had been a tradition of sorts, as it is used in Knüpfer's *Christmas Concerto*; and Schelle employs an additional obbligato trombone to accompany the announcement of the angel. Bach himself has frequently set a divine voice (often the voice of Christ, as in the *St. Matthew Passion*) with a halo-like accompaniment.[50] The use of strings in this movement of the *Christmas Oratorio* is also in line with the practice of assigning strings to the angelic orchestra (in contrast to the reed instruments of the shepherds), and it perpetuates the symbolic use of the instruments he had established in the opening movement of part II. Bach had originally planned a slightly different beginning for the recit. The autograph score shows that the movement was supposed to begin in G major (probably with a chord in first inversion in the bc); this beginning would have maintained the key of the previous chorale. It is not possible to determine when Bach changed the beginning into a more "surprising" version, but now the recit begins with an A-major chord in first inversion. He also changed some rhythmic details in the string accompaniment in the final two measures of the recit, turning a simple progression of mostly half notes into a rhythmically more intricate cadence.[51]

---

[49] Walter, *Weihnachtsoratorium*, 81; the score shows that Bach worked on this measure. The first note in the alto was originally an *f♯′* and the second beat in the bass was a quarter-note *a*; Bach changes this, giving the two lower male voices a parallel movement of four notes instead of two, which increases the "martial" affect.

[50] Cf. Martin Geck, "Die *vox-Christi*-Sätze in Bachs Kantaten," in *Bach und die Stile*, ed. Martin Geck. Bericht über das 2. Dortmunder Bach-Symposion 1998 (Dortmund: Klangfarben Musikverlag, 1999), 79–101. In his Christmas cantata *Das neugeborne Kindelein*, BWV 122, from 1724, Bach uses a halo of three recorders over the bc to accompany a poetic paraphrase of the announcement of the angel (soprano recit, no. 3); in BWV 122 the instruments do not play sustained harmonies but a (very quiet) harmonization of the chorale melody "Das neugeborne Kindelein."

[51] See NBA II/6, KB, 34.

The announcement of the angel, answering directly to the fears of the shepherds, sets the stage for the first pair of accompagnato recit (no. 14) and aria
(no. 15) in part II. The two movements are assigned to different singers. The
accompagnato recit is sung by the bass (again representing the sphere of the
shepherds) and the aria by the tenor. Instead of meditating on the joy that had
been announced by the angel, the accompagnato recit "Was Gott dem Abraham
verheissen" focuses on the significance of the announcement to the shepherds.
The text draws a typological connection between the shepherd Abraham,[52] who
had been promised the coming of a Messiah (Gen 12:2; 17:6–8; 18:18; 22:17),
and the shepherds before Bethlehem. Some interpreters have called this recit
"strange,"[53] and Philipp Spitta remarks that the text for the recit "seems to contain an obscure reference. The insipid antithesis of Abraham as a shepherd, and
the shepherds of Bethlehem, can hardly have been the whole motif of the poem;
the author must rather have had in mind an idea of praising the shepherd's calling
generally."[54]

The purpose of the allusion comes in sharper relief if we consider the understanding of the shepherds in seventeenth- and eighteenth-century religious discourses. The text follows the theological model of promise and fulfillment. The
new covenant (with Christ) is understood as the fulfillment of the old covenant
(beginning with Abraham). The Old Testament is read as a prophetic pointer
toward the coming of Christ as the redeemer. And in their encounter with the
promised Messiah, the shepherds finally become preachers of Christ, as Luther
remarks in his *Hauspostille*: "The other benefit is that the shepherds become
preachers themselves, and tell everybody what they have heard about this
child."[55] Earlier, Thymich's *Hirten-Freude* from 1685 draws a close connection
between the shepherds of the Old Testament (represented by names taken from
the Hebrew Bible) and the shepherds of Bethlehem.[56] But in addition to this
typological connection between Abraham and the shepherds in the Christmas
narrative, the text of the accompagnato recit also refers back to Luke 1:54–55,
the mention of Abraham in the Magnificat: "He has helped his servant Israel in
remembrance of his mercy, according to the promise he made to our ancestors,
to Abraham and to his descendants forever." The proximity between the seemingly "strange" recit in the oratorio (accompagnato bass recit) and the Magnificat
comes into even sharper focus in a paraphrase (here, a tenor recit) of the Song

---

[52]  For the typological connection Abraham–Christ, see Petzoldt, *Bach-Kommentar*, 2:187.

[53]  Schulze, *Die Bach-Kantaten*, 637.

[54]  Spitta, *Bach*, 2:580.

[55]  Luther, *Hauspostille*, col. 78: "Die andere Frucht ist, daß die Hirten auch zu Predigern warden,
sagen jedermann, was sie von diesem Kindlein gehört haben."

[56]  See Rathey, "Die Geistliche Hirten-Freude," 583–86.

of Mary from Bach's chorale cantata *Meine Seele erhebt den Herrn*, BWV 10,[57] composed in 1724:

| BWV 10/6 (beginning) | BWV 248/14 |
|---|---|
| **Was Gott den Vätern** alter Zeiten Geredet und *verheißen* hat, *Erfüllt* er auch im Werk und in der Tat. **Was Gott dem Abraham**, Als er zu ihm in seine Hütten kam, Versprochen und geschworen, Ist, da die Zeit *erfüllet* war, geschehen. | **Was Gott dem Abraham** *verheißen*, Das lässt er nun dem Hirtenchor*Erfüllt* erweisen. Ein Hirt hat alles das zuvorVon Gott erfahren müssen. Und nun muss auch ein Hirt die Tat, Was er damals versprochen hat, Zuerst *erfüllet* wissen. |
| **What to the fathers** in the days of old God spoke and *pledged*, he also *fulfills* in work and deed. **What to Abraham**, when he came to him in his tents, God promised and swore did happen when the *fullness* of time came. | **What God had** *pledged* to Abraham, he now lets be shown to the chorus of shepherds as *fulfilled*. About all of this a shepherd had to hear from God beforehand; and now also a shepherd has to be the first to come to know the deed— what he [God] at that time had promised— as *fulfilled*. |

What is added here in the *Christmas Oratorio* is the "chorus of shepherds," and this is due to the emphasis on music in this part of the oratorio. The text refers back to the sonic representation (reeds) of the "Hirtenchor" in the opening sinfonia.[58] The representation is reflected in the setting of the text. Bach uses long pedal points at the beginning (more than half of the recit rests on the pedal point G),[59] and he accompanies the solo bass with the chorus of reed instruments.

While the accompagnato recit had inserted a theological interpretation for the revelation to the shepherds, the following aria returns to the topic of joy that had been mentioned in the announcement of the angel. As we read earlier, the movement is the only aria in the first half of the *Christmas Oratorio* that is not in *da capo*

---

[57] For Bach's cantata 10 and its relationship to the Magnificat, see the article by Mark Peters, "J. S. Bach's *Meine Seel' erhebt den Herren* (BWV 10) as Chorale Cantata and Magnificat Paraphrase," *Bach* 43 (2012): 29–64.

[58] If not intentionally by the librettist, definitely in Bach's setting.

[59] The long pedal point on G was not the original version of this recitative. In m. 3, Bach originally wrote a half-note F♯, which was subsequently changed into G.

form. The binary structure (AB) reflects the forward-moving urgency of the text that admonishes the "joyful shepherds" to "hasten" to the child in the manger. The binary structure was, of course, part of the secular model for the parody, but here, in the context of the *Christmas Oratorio*, it acquires an additional significance. The sacred text in the *Christmas Oratorio* and the model in the secular cantata share almost no common words, except for the word "Freude" (joy) in line 4 and the general affect of joy. Even the line structure in the secular text (2 + 2 + 2) and in the sacred libretto (3 + 3) is different:

|  BWV 214/5  |  BWV 248/15  |
| --- | --- |
| Fromme Musen! meine Glieder! | Frohe Hirten, eilt, ach eilet, |
| Singt nicht längst bekannte Lieder! | Eh ihr euch zu lang verweilet, |
|  | Eilt, das holde Kind zu sehn! |
| Dieser Tag sei eure Lust! |  |
| Füllt mit Freuden eure Brust! | Geht, die Freude heißt zu schön, |
|  | Sucht die Anmut zu gewinnen, |
| Werft so Kiel als Schriften nieder | Geht und labet Herz und Sinnen! |
| Und erfreut euch dreimal wieder! |  |
|  |  |
| Devout Muses! My members! | Joyful shepherds, hurry, oh, hurry, |
| Do not sing long-familiar songs! | before you tarry too long; |
|  | hurry, to see the pleasing child! |
| May this day be your delight! |  |
| Fill your breast with joy! | Go, the joy is all too lovely; |
|  | seek to gain the refinement; |
| Throw down both quill and script | go and refresh your hearts and minds! |
| And rejoice three times over! |  |

While in BWV 214/5 the first two lines are set in the A section of the binary aria and the last lines form in the B section, the version in the *Christmas Oratorio* distributes the lines evenly to both sections, a decision that conforms to the structure of the libretto.[60] The movement was originally an alto aria, accompanied by an oboe d'amore and was sung in honor of the birthday of the electress of Saxony and queen of Poland, Maria Josepha. Cantata 214 celebrates the electress as protector of the Muses. In this aria, the goddess of the arts and sciences, Pallas Athene, admonishes her Muses to enjoy the day instead of singing well-known songs. In his parody in the oratorio Bach transposes the aria from B minor to E minor and assigns the vocal part to the tenor. Bach's decision to change the singer was motivated by the function of the alto in the *Christmas Oratorio*, which mostly serves as the voice of the divine in the human heart, often associated with the topic of *inhabitatio Christi*. While the

---

[60] Walter Blankenburg points to this example when he emphasizes how carefully Bach designed his parodies, see Blankenburg, *Weihnachts-Oratorium*, 61.

sacred text does mention the heart, Christ's dwelling in the human heart is not the main idea, so that Bach chose not to use the alto in this case. A second, more practical reason might have been that the tenor had not had an aria so far in the oratorio, so Bach wanted to give this singer a larger solo movement.

Bach also reassigned the obbligato instrument from oboe d'amore to solo flute. The reason for the change of the instrument is less clear than the change of the vocal soloist. While the oboe d'amore is often connected with the alto in movements that present the *inhabitatio Christi*, as in "Bereite dich, Zion" (no. 4), it also, per usual, denotes the bucolic sphere of the shepherds, especially here in the second part of the oratorio. The use of the oboe for a movement that urges the shepherds to hasten to the manger would have been appropriate within the logic of instrumentation in the *Christmas Oratorio*. It appears that Bach was perhaps undecided about which instrument to use in this particular aria: the original score lacks the designation of an instrument. The designation that appears in the score today (*"Fl. 1ᵐᵒ solo"*) was added later by C. P. E. Bach's Hamburg copyist Johann Heinrich Michel.[61] The possibility that Bach might have intended a different instrument (maybe the original oboe d'amore[62]) is supported by the fact that the score for the second part of the oratorio lacks flutes altogether. The flutes were added only when the parts for the piece were written out after the oratorio had already been completed. Soon after the completion of the score Bach must have decided to add the flutes.[63] The flutes have no independent tasks in the entire second part with the exception of aria no. 15. Since Bach initially left the instrumentation for the aria open he might have considered giving the obbligato to an oboe or to a violin. However, this part, while technically possible, lays rather low and is quite awkward for an oboe. Maybe this was ultimately the reason for giving the solo to a flutist instead. In any case, the result is a virtuosic aria for tenor and flute, a combination Bach has used frequently in earlier cantatas, for instance in his chorale cantatas cycle.[64]

The A and B sections of the aria in the secular cantata (BWV 214/5) represent a juxtaposition of the "old songs" the Muses are discouraged to sing and the state of enthusiasm they are called to feel and express instead. The Muses are now urged to sing in extroverted exaltation, leaving behind outdated and established modes of praise. Bach's composition of the text expresses this dichotomy through a highly contrastive musical setting. The A section opens with a ritornello of sixteen measures, following a regular and square structure. The ritornello is constructed from two halves of eight measures each (indicated by a rest in the solo oboe d'amore in m. 8), and each half in itself consists of two-measure segments. At the beginning

---

[61] Michel based his designation of the flute on the instrumental parts for the oratorio. In his own copy of the score for the oratorio (Paris, F-Pn D. 551 [2], 13) Michel added the instrumentation.

[62] This was also suggested by Dürr, *Weihnachts-Oratorium*, 15.

[63] See chap. 5 for details about the added flute parts.

[64] See Reinmar Emans, "Zu den Arien mit einem obligaten Flöteninstrument," in *Vom Klang der Zeit: Besetzung, Bearbeitung und Aufführungspraxis bei Johann Sebastian Bach*, ed. Ulrich Bartels and Uwe Wolf, Klaus Hofmann zum 65. Geburtstag (Wiesbaden: Breitkopf&Härtel, 2004), 73–85.

we hear twice a descending motif, beginning with an eighth note and followed by a chain of sixteenth notes (this will be the first motif used in the vocal part). The four opening measures are followed by a *fortspinnung*, coming to a halt at the rest in m. 8. The second half of the ritornello introduces a new motif, again two measures long, which is presented twice and continues in a *fortspinnung*. This second motif, which returns primarily in the vocal section as instrumental accompaniment, is derived from the first motif. The initial eighth note is omitted, and the sequence of leaps in the second measure leads upward instead of down, but the listener still hears the second motif as an organic development of the first one.

The rhythmic design of the ritornello (as well as of the entire aria) has the joyful, lighthearted affect of a minuet.[65] The vocal A section of the binary movement (mm. 17–56) presents the first two lines of the text. The setting maintains the extremely regular structure established by the ritornello. While the minuet rhythm underscores the joyful character of the text, the repetitiveness with which the voice and the solo instrument hand the simple opening motif back and forth (esp. mm. 36–43) highlights the technique of the "old songs," which the text says should no longer be repeated.

The final four lines of the text ask for an emotional response by the Muses, a response not guided by these old songs. While not abandoning the regularity of the A section (Bach still operates with regular segments of four measures), he introduces exuberant runs and melismatic lines in the solo instrument as well as in the vocal part. The B section establishes a clear contrast to the first half of the aria: The thirty-second-note motif on the downbeat (used repeatedly) challenges the regular rhythmic flow that was set up at the beginning. It is a negation of the square, established order of the old songs; the same is the case for the syncopation on the word "werft" in m. 77, depicting the gesture of throwing away or, even more acutely, of throwing off the regular order of the old song. The extensive thirty-second-note melismas in the B section appear in combination with the words "Freuden" and "erfreut" as well as "füllt [mit Freuden]," thus painting the emotion of joy. But Bach could have accomplished this simple text-painting easily with the sixteenth-note melismas he had employed in the A section. Here, it was essential to establish a kind of joy that was categorically different from the "scripted emotionality" of the old song in the A section. Bach goes through the text of the B section twice (mm. 69–96 and 100–124). In both cases the climax is reached on the final "erfreut." Bach builds up this climax, this eruption of unrestrained emotion, by presenting the verb "erfreut" with static tone repetitions, accompanied by the oboe d'amore,

---

[65] Meredith Little and Natalie Jenne label it "minuet like" in *Dance and the Music of J. S. Bach* (Bloomington: Indiana University Press, 2009), 231–32 and 301, while Doris Finke-Hecklinger identifies it as "Passepied-Menuett" ("Tanzcharaktere in Johann Sebastian Bachs Vokalmusik," *Tübinger Bach-Studien 6*. [Trossingen: Hohner, 1970], 106).

then two instances of the word "dreimal" (thrice) leading finally to a long, eruptive melisma on "erfreut." The aria concludes with an abbreviated version of the opening ritornello, which serves as a formal closure but not as a restitution of the old song from the beginning. Bach's setting of the secular libretto follows the affect of the text but, again, it is more than mere text-painting; it is the expression of exuberant joy through music; it is the "new song," a heart-felt enthusiasm that leads to a spilling over of melismatic lines.

The parody in the *Christmas Oratorio* required more than a few changes to the model. The first change was the division of the text. While the secular libretto expressed a juxtaposition between the first two and the final four lines of the text, in the oratorio the first three and the final three lines form a unity. The sacred text also lacks the stark contrast between the texts for the A and B sections, which had motivated Bach to establish the musical contrast discussed earlier. The entire poem in the oratorio urges the "joyful shepherds" to hasten to the manger, and Bach makes some subtle changes to the beginning of the aria that reflect this difference. The regularity of the rhythmic flow represents the old order of the scripted (and thus restrained) enthusiasm. Bach promptly disturbs this order in m. 2, and then again in m. 4 by inserting thirty-second notes and appoggiaturas in the first motif, anticipating and foreshadowing some of the rhythmic diversity of the B section of the aria. The autograph score shows that Bach had originally copied the secular piece as he found it in the model but then decided to change the obbligato part. Since these changes still occur as corrections in the interlude between the A and B sections (mm. 56–68), Bach must have made up his mind rather late in the game, probably while he was writing the B section of the aria. The changes lead to a stronger unification of the two sections—without completely covering their musical dichotomy. The increase in motion and tempo in the second half of the aria can now be perceived as an increase in urgency, with which the shepherds are admonished to hasten to the manger.

In addition to these large-scale revisions, Bach had to make smaller adjustments to fit the music to the new text. In mm. 49/50 he adds a longer melisma to depict the word "eilt" (hurry); the original words had been "Tag sei eure Lust" (may this day be your delight), which had received only a mostly syllabic setting. The new version (which was already written down while Bach was copying the composition), fills out the notes present in the secular version with passing notes. Bach thus maintained both the accompaniment in the obbligato instrument as well as the bc.[66] The changes in m. 109 fall into a similar category, where the setting of the word "Kiel" ("quill," here a term with negative connotations) is changed into a smooth melisma on "Anmut"

---

[66] The change in m. 52 is clearly a revision, where Bach changes a descending line on "eure" (here with a neutral affect and leading to the more important word "Lust" in m. 53) into an ascending line on "eilt."

(grace). The awkward placement of the beams shows that Bach had again originally copied the original version and then changed in to better conform to the new text.

The changes Bach makes to the secular model conform to the parody techniques we can observe in other movements of the *Christmas Oratorio*. The reduction or insertion of melismatic lines are a way to change a preexisting piece to fit a new text. The modifications that are not directly motivated by word-music correspondences hold greater significance, like the rhythmic changes at the very beginning of the aria. This shows that the parody process implied more than just a mechanical adaptation of older music to a new text. In its new version, the aria highlights the urgency with which the shepherds are sent on their way by the angels, and it expresses the affect of joy that had been invoked by the angel in the gospel recit, no. 13 ("verkündige euch große Freude"). While the words of the aria change from the secular model to the sacred movement in the *Christmas Oratorio*, the music maintains its general affect of joy and—even more—the exuberant enthusiasm that is expressed by the music. Bach originally composed the B section of the aria as an expression of an enthusiastic outburst of the Muses, the goddesses of music and the arts, leaving behind the "old songs" and extolling a heartfelt excitement. Even without the original words, the aria maintains this exuberance. With this emphasis on the power of music, the aria fits well into the second part of the *Christmas Oratorio*, which is an essay on the power of music as a link to the heavenly spheres.[67]

The aria "Frohe Hirten" has posed problems for some interpreters. Konrad Küster (echoing remarks by Philipp Spitta) questions the dramatic function of the movement in the context of part II as the shepherds are asked to hasten to the manger while they still had to wait for the rest of the angelic announcement and the praise of the angels in "Ehre sei Gott." The aria would make sense only later in the narrative. Küster suggests two explanations. One is that the libretto added the extended shepherds' scene (of which the aria is a part) as "added action" ("hinzuerfundene Handlung"), complementing the primary action of the gospel text. A second explanation is that composer and librettist decided to anticipate in the aria a section of the narrative that would be at the center of part III of the oratorio (the embarking of the shepherds to the manger), since this part had been performed only in St. Nicholas's Church and not in St. Thomas's. According to Küster, the aria would have been the attempt to give the congregation in St. Thomas's a glimpse of this

---

[67] A contemporary of Bach's, the preacher at the Ritteracademie in Copenhagen, Franz Julius Lütgens, expressed this thus: "Behold, I bring you great joy. . . . One should sing of this kind, this savior of the world, and rejoyce in him like a bride rejoices in her bridegroom; because rejoicing are singing are an effect of joy."(Siehe, ich verkündige euch grosse Freude. . . . Man soll singen von diesem Könige, dem Heiland der Welt, und sich über ihne freuen, wie eine Braut über ihren Bräutigam. Denn das Jauchtzen und Singen ist eine Wirckung der Freude). Lütgens, *Geistreiche und erbauliche Evangelium-Predigten* (Leipzig: Campen, 1727), 117.

further development, which they would not have heard the next day.[68] Both explanations are problematic since completeness was not the goal of Bach and his
librettist—otherwise they would not have divided the oratorio the way they did.
Additionally, the congregation at St. Thomas's would still have heard the complete
gospel narrative in the liturgical readings, even if they had not heard the setting
within the oratorio. It is true that the aria seems to be out of place within the narrative flow of the oratorio. The shepherds are encouraged to leave for the manger at a
point when they still have to wait for further instructions by the angels. But Küster's
(and Spitta's) readings suggest a dramatic coherence that is not constitutive for the
*Christmas Oratorio.* Instead, the song to the "joyful shepherds" has to be understood
as an immediate interpretative reaction to the angel's announcement that the baby
in the manger was a reason for joy. As theological interpreters of the biblical narrative repeatedly stress, the proper reactions to the announcement—regardless of
the further narrative—is the feeling of joy and the inner urge to see the child that
has been announced by the angel. The term "frohe Hirten" (joyful shepherds) is
a stereotype in Christmas poetry and theology in the early modern tradition. An
example is Thymich's *Hirten-Freude* from 1685. Similarly, joy as human reaction is
the tenor of Martin Luther's sermon on the gospel of the first day of Christmas. He
writes in his *Hauspostille*:

| | |
|---|---|
| Jetzt sagen wir allein von der Ehre, daß GOtt uns so nahe geworden ist, daß er unser Fleisch und Blut, und ein persönlicher Mensch ist, wie ich und du sind, allein das ausgenommen, daß er ohne Sünde ist. Mit dieser unaussprechlichen Ehre hat er das menschliche Geschlecht gezieret. Das wollte der Engel den Leuten gern einbilden und spricht: "Ich verkündige euch große Freude, die allem Volk widerfahren wird.". . . Er ist fröhlich und guter Dinge darüber, brennt und springt vor lauter Freude, schämt sich der armen Hirten gar nichts, daß er ihnen predigen soll, sondern ist guter Dinge drüber, und wollte gern, daß jedermann solches zu Herzen ginge, wie ihm, und alle | For now we just say about the "Glory" that God has come so near to us that he has [taken on] our flesh and blood, that he is a real person, like you and me, with the only exception that he is without sin. He has adorned the human race with this unspeakable honor. This is what the angel wanted to impress upon the people when he said, "I announce to you great joy, which will come to all people." . . . He [the angel] is full of joy and in good spirits, he burns and jumps, out of pure joy. [The angel] is not ashamed that he has to preach this to the poor shepherds but instead, he is in a good mood about this. He wants this [message] went into the hearts of everybody, like it filled his own heart. |

---

[68] Küster, "Die Vokalmusik," 479.

Menschen solche große Ehre lerneten
erkennen, daß die menschliche Natur
zu der Herrlichkeit gekommen ist,
daß der Sohn GOttes, durch welches
alles erschaffen ist, die hohe Majestät,
unser Fleisch und Blut geworden ist.[69]

[The angel wishes] that all mankind
learned about this great honor that
human nature had been elevated to
great glory, because the son of God,
though whom everything was created,
the high majesty, has been incarnated
in our flesh and blood.

Luther states that the joy over the coming of Christ is one of exuberance. It is a
degree of joy that makes the bringer of the news leap and "burn." In other words,
it is the kind of joy that is expressed in the music of the aria "Frohe Hirten," the joy
that transcends the time of the narrative but includes both the shepherds and the
present listener. While dramatically problematic, it is theologically justified, even
necessary.

## Images of music beyond part II

Part II of the *Christmas Oratorio* explores the functions and the meaning of music:
music is the unification of the divine and human choruses; the human praise is
an emulation of the angelic praise; and music is the expression of the exuberant
joy that follows from the announcement of the angel. Humans (and the pupils at
the St. Thomas School in particular) were encouraged to become *zoa logika hym-
nologika*, emulating the chorus of the angels. As mode of God's real presence, his
*Gnadengegenwart*, music was a way for Christ to enter the human heart. In short,
music is a mode of encounter between the human and the divine. It is a means
through which humans can and do respond to the divine presence. While part II of
the oratorio is centered on the exploration of music, it is not the only place in this
work where music is mentioned as a mode of divine praise. The first chorus of part
I begins with a praise of God through the means of music:

Jauchzet, frohlocket, auf, preiset die Tage,
Rühmet, was heute der Höchste
    getan! . . .
Stimmet voll Jauchzen und
    Fröhlichkeit an!
Dienet dem Höchsten mit herrlichen
    Chören . . .

Shout, exult, arise, praise the days,
Glorify what the Most High this
    day has done . . .
Break into song, full of shouting
    and rejoicing!
Serve the Most High with glorious
    choirs . . .

---

[69] Luther, *Hauspostille*, sp. 56.

If we see the opening chorus of the *Christmas Oratorio* through the lens of the second part, the function of music as an expression of joy comes into even sharper relief. The "glorious choirs," mentioned here in the last line, can be interpreted as the choirs of both angels and men, praising together the name of God. Seen within this context, the array of musical instruments at the beginning of the opening chorus—timpani, flutes, reed, strings, and brass—seems an intriguing choice even if it lacks a direct connection with the parody text. The opening chorus is a celebration of music as a means for the expression of the joy that will be announced by the angel later in the oratorio. A similar case can be made for the opening chorus of part III:

| | |
|---|---|
| Herrscher des Himmels, erhöre das Lallen, | Ruler of heaven, give heed to our babble, |
| Laß dir die matten Gesänge gefallen, | Let our feeble songs please you, |
| Wenn dich dein Zion mit Psalmen erhöht! | When your Zion extols you with psalms! |
| Höre der Herzen frohlockendes Preisen . . . | Hear the exultant praises of our hearts . . . |

Again, music, now the songs and psalms sung in the honor of God, is used to celebrate the birth of Christ. The last line combines the image of the "heart" (to be understood as the dwelling place of Christ) and the exultant praises sung to the gory of God. Even the opening chorus for part IV, while not mentioning music directly, invokes the thanksgiving and praise that are often associated with music: "Fallt mit Danken, fallt mit Loben" (Bow with thanksgiving, bow with praise). Consequently, the opening chorus for part V mentions music as well, even in a direct paraphrase of the angelic Gloria. Thus, we are referred back to the model for human praise of God presented in part II: "Ehre sei dir, Gott, gesungen, Dir sei Lob und Dank bereit" (May honor, God, be sung to you, may praise and thanks be extended to you.). Only the opening movement for part VI lacks a direct reference to music; it focuses instead, on the juxtaposition of the proud enemies and the steadfast faith of the believers.

## Shepherd's lullaby (mvts. 18 and 19)

Singing lullabies to the newborn Jesus had been a long-standing tradition, as both a ritual and a poetic metaphor. The practice of "Kindelwiegen," the rocking of the child Jesus was established in medieval times but continued long after the Lutheran Reformation. Heinrich Schütz suggests in his *Historia der Geburt Jesu Christi* that the cradle-rocking could be done during the *intermedia*.[70] The tradition belonged to the

---

[70] Heinrich Schütz, *Historia der Freuden- und Gnadenreichen Geburth Gottes und Marien Sohnes, Jesu Christi (Weihnachtshistorie)*, SWV 435/435a, ed. Friedrich Schöneich (Kassel: Bärenreiter, 1976).

physical and corporal rituals around Christmas that were abolished around the turn of the seventeenth century. Still, it continued in some areas and survived as a sonic metaphor in the singing of lullabies for the baby Jesus, which often became a poetic substitute for the practical act. The tactile intimacy with the child Jesus is thus replaced with poetic (and sonic) intimacy. Movements 18 and 19 of the oratorio celebrate this intimacy and also refer to the function of music within this act of human and divine approximation. It is fitting, then, that the first time in the oratorio humans plan to approach the manger, they do so to sing the newborn Jesus a "song of rest," as the text of recit, no. 18, puts it.

Those two movements form a sonic pair, with the words of the recit directly preparing the text for the following aria. The librettist might have expected Bach to give the two movements to the same singer. Within Bach's dramatic concept of the *Christmas Oratorio*, however, the two mvts. 18 and 19 belong to two different realms. The recit addresses the shepherds and admonishes them to go to the manger and sing a lullaby at the cradle of the newborn Jesus. The noun "Wiegen" is the cradle or bed in which the child lays; the verb "wiegen" refers to the rocking motion of the traditional Kindelwiegen. This association will be important for Bach's setting of the text. As the recit is addressed to the shepherds, Bach uses the bass voice and adds the bucolic chorus of reeds (oboi d'amore and da caccia) as an accompaniment. The following aria, "Schlafe, mein Liebster," employs images that are closely related to the concept of *inhabitatio*—images of the "breast," sensation of "delight," and joy of the heart—primarily assigned to and sung by the alto voice in the *Christmas Oratorio*, the same voice that now sings this aria.

The text for the accompagnato recit consists of eight lines. The first four lines are an expanded paraphrase of angel's announcement. The second half turns to music, an aspect not present in the biblical text.[71] Bach sets the first four lines of the recit in a simple declamatory style with short chords in the reed chorus that resemble the accompagmental figures from the previous accompagnato recit. Instead of the long pedal point from no. 14, however, Bach introduces a sixteenth-note motif in the bc, which outlines broken triads. The vivid bass motifs can be heard as an expression of the urgency with which the shepherds are admonished to hurry to the manger. This correlates with the text, which uses the word "geht" twice. In the terminology of classical rhetoric this is an *epanadiplosis*, a rhetorical emphasis: "So *geht* denn hin, ihr Hirten, *geht*." Other details of the music emphasize and interpret the words of the text as well: a melodic ascent on the words "des Höchsten Sohn" in mm. 3/4; a dissonant D-minor chord with diminished seventh in second inversion (m. 2), depicting the miracle ("Wunder") of the child in the manger; and a harsh seventh chord on the word "harten" in m. 4. The character of the recit changes in the second half. The reed instruments pick up momentum and play a pulsating motif of

---

[71] Martin Petzoldt has suggested that the second half of the recit could be a reference to Sirach (or Ecclsiasticus). 47:8–11, one of the foundational texts for religious music in the Old Testament; see Petzoldt, *Bach Kommentar* II, 191.

repeated eighth notes while the bc group accompanies the singer with a flowing chain of wave-like triplets. The soothing triplet motion is an allusion to the rocking of the cradle and prepares motivically for the following lullaby. The decision to compose a rocking motion was not necessarily triggered by the text, which only refers to the sweet sound and to the song of rest and quietness. Bach's decision here was rather motivated by stereotypes traditionally associated with the lullaby, the rocking of the child. The rocking motion in the bass line, however, was not Bach's original idea: it grew out of the compositional process. The autograph score shows that the composer originally wrote an accompaniment in regular sixteenth notes. In order to insert the sextuplets he had to squeeze in additional sixteenth notes in each measure (see ex. 5.3 and fig. 5.2, chap. 5).

Instead of using a sextuplet motive, the following aria establishes the image of the rocking cradle through octave leaps in the bc. Originally composed for BWV 213, the aria was a song by the vice Pleasure in her attempt to seduce the young hero Hercules by lulling him to sleep:

| BWV 213/3 | BWV 248/19 |
|---|---|
| Schlafe, mein Liebster, und pflege<br>    der Ruh, | Schlafe, mein Liebster, genieße<br>    der Ruh, |
| Folge der Lockung entbrannter<br>    Gedanken. | Wache nach diesem vor aller<br>    Gedeihen! |
| Schmecke die Lust | Labe die Brust, |
| Der lüsternen Brust | Empfinde die Lust, |
| Und erkenne keine Schranken. | Wo wir unser Herz erfreuen! |
| | |
| Sleep, my Most Beloved, and take<br>    your rest, | Sleep, my Most Beloved, enjoy<br>    your rest, |
| follow the enticement of inflamed<br>    thoughts. | awake after this for the flourishing<br>    of all! |
| Taste the pleasure | Refresh your breast, |
| of the wanton breast | feel the delight, |
| and know no bounds. | where we gladden our hearts! |

As the librettist modeled the new text closely after the secular text, most of the changes Bach made to the music are slight. While several changes were necessary in the B section of the *da capo* aria, the handwriting in the A section in Bach's score is clear and has only a few smaller corrections and revisions.[72] The original

---

[72] Several corrections of mistakes apply to errors made during the transposition of the original; the original piece was a third higher; cf. NBA II/6, KB, 36–37. These corrections occur especially in the early measures of the piece.

composition was an aria for soprano, accompanied by two violins, viola, and bc in B♭ major. Bach transposed the piece to G major and gave the solo part to the alto; the original instrumentation is kept, but the strings are now doubled by the chorus of oboes, denoting the sphere of the shepherds. Additionally, the solo voice is doubled at the octave by the flute,[73] probably to balance the alto against the other accompanying instruments. The aria is a textbook case for the polysemy of musical signs. In the sinfonia and "Ehre sei Gott" we identified a texture characterized by a pedal point, a simple, homophonic texture, and the use of reed instruments as a sign indicating the shepherds. This aria begins with a very similar texture: oboe da caccia II and viola play a long pedal point while the upper voices feature calm lines in simple, parallel motion; additionally, the bc resolves the pedal point into a "rocking" motion with pulsating eighth notes. In BWV 213, the texture is used to instill calmness in the young hero, but within the context of the *Christmas Oratorio*, the beginning of the aria acquires an additional set of connotations. By adding the reed instruments to the accompaniment, Bach immediately locates the aria within the bucolic sphere of part II of the oratorio. The simple texture and the pedal point do the same. Both refer back to the reed passages of the introductory sinfonia and anticipate the "und Friede auf Erden" sections in the later chorus, which is separated from the aria only by a short, four-measure passage of gospel recit. The listener without knowledge of the parody model will just hear the aria as a motivic continuation of the sinfonia.[74] Another aspect that ties the aria into the concept of this part of the *Christmas Oratorio* brings us directly to the music. The aria begins with a long instrumental ritornello. With twenty-eight measures it is one of the longest ritornellos in the oratorio. The extensive instrumental presence harkens back to the beginning of part II, where Bach had, with purely musical terms, depicted the merging of the heavenly and earthly choruses. The ritornello with its soothing rhythm and parallel motion in the instruments highlights music's ability to induce sleep through soothing melodies and a gently rocking rhythm. And as this part is about the capabilities of music,

---

[73] As in other movements of part II, the flute does not appear in the score but only in the performance parts.

[74] Walter Blankenburg has entertained the possibility that the aria in BWV 213 might have already been planned and composed by Bach with its later use in the *Christmas Oratorio* in mind: "Bei dieser Arie kann man vermuten, daß Bach sie bei der Arbeit an dem Dramma per Musica BWV 213, Satz 3, gleichzeitig mitkonzipiert hat; wird sie doch dem Text des Weihnachts-Oratoriums letzten Endes besser gerecht, als dies in der Vorlage geschieht" (Blankenburg, *Weihnachts-Oratorium*, 66). Blankenburg's assumption is problematic and, for all we know, wrong. We argued earlier that Bach began planning his oratorio only in the second half of 1734, more than half a year after the composition of BWV 213. Secondly, Blankenburg's thesis is based on a judgment of taste and on the assumption that there is only one original text that fits a composition. Since he feels that the sacred version fits better, this must be the original one. And last, if Blankenburg were correct, one would have to ask why Bach had to rework the B section of the aria to fit the sacred text. If the text in the oratorio had been the intended one, he could have composed the piece in a way that would have made it easier to underlay the sacred text.

the opening measures of the ritornello demonstrate the soothing affect of music in an exemplary way. The aria is already a sleep-inducing lullaby before the alto sings her long "Schlafe" in mm. 28–32.

Bach constructs the beginning of the ritornello with two distinct motifs, encountered in different permutations (ex. 7.5). Motif (a) appears in m. 1 and consists of an arch-like melodic line, beginning on the third of the home key G major and ascending stepwise to D and then descending in stepwise motion down to G. Motif (b) follows in m. 2 and creates a rocking motion through a series of two downward leaps. Motif (a) is then repeated and leads to an harmonically unstable second-inversion C major on the pedal point G. Both motifs are repeated (enveloped in a dissonant accompaniment), leading to a modified version of (a), but now with a simple figure instead of the dotted eighth note. Permutations of motif (b) follow (mm. 9–11) and lead to another moment of stagnation on a seventh chord. The first part of the ritornello ends with a variation of (b), (a), and a cadential formula that culminates in m. 16 not into the expected G-major chord but in a deceptive cadence to E minor, or more precisely, an E-minor seventh chord. The structure of the ritornello is quite straightforward yet provides an unexpected twist: it consists of segments of single measures that form groups of two measures; these two-measure groups then form groups of four measures, and these four-measure groups are combined into groups of eight measures, before eliding at m. 16 into a syncopated group. The listener is deceived into expecting a continuation of the established pattern, but instead the syncopations drive the energy for thirteen measures. While the four-measure groups in the first half of the ritornello have each ended with a moment of stagnation of motion, the second half builds up energy. As calming as the motifs, the pedal point, and the regular structure at the beginning are, the piece does not come to rest. Rather, the harmonic instability drives the movement forward. Only once, in m. 8, does Bach end a phrase in the home key G major. In all other instances, the movement in the upper voices comes to a halt in dissonance and longs for resolution. The unrest that is present under the surface of the first half of the ritornello becomes more prevalent in the second half. In the original composition, the restlessness foreshadows the first word of the second line, "folge" (follow), which in the oratorio is replaced with the keyword "wache" (wake). In both cases, the libretto indicates action that is contrary to sleep. The music in the second half of the ritornello is characterized by syncopations, larger leaps both in the upper voices and the bc, and a faster harmonic rhythm (contrasting especially to the pedal-point passages at the beginning of the ritornello). The second half begins, rather jarringly, with the deceptive cadence that ended the first half of the ritornello. Bach now introduces two new motifs (ex. 7.5): a syncopated motif (c) in m. 16 and a motif in eighth notes in the following measure (d). He again combines the two motifs in changing permutations, and the idea of syncopation finally becomes prevalent (mm. 20–25) before the ritornello ends with a smoother cadential formula that finally leads back to G major.

*Example 7.5* J. S. Bach, BWV 248/19, motifs a, b, c, and d (mm. 1/2 and 16/17)

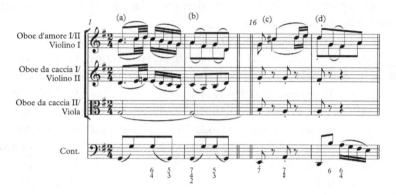

The ritornello already portrays the dichotomy between sleep and awakening that will be at the center of the A section of the aria. The beginning of the first vocal part is constructed from sections of the ritornello. For the most part, Bach takes groups of four measures and interpolates them with newly composed groups of the same length. In the first vocal section (mm. 28–96), Bach uses the technique of *Vokaleinbau* and "builds" the line of the vocalist into the ritornello material. While the alto sings the word "Schlafe" over an extended note that evokes the sleeping child in the manger, the instruments play the beginning of the ritornello. The second phrase (now with a lengthened note on "Liebster") uses the same material in transposition. The third phrase, with the text "genieße . . . " (mm. 37–44) is an almost literal repetition of m. 5–12 from the ritornello. Bach now inserts another new group of four measures (mm. 45–48), before he repeats almost verbatim the opening measures of the ritornello, leading to a cadence on the dominant D major (mm. 49–56). The result is a "calming" regular structure. Since the text of the model composition and the aria in the *Christmas Oratorio* follow the same pattern, Bach can take the musical material without major changes. The most obvious change is the final note of this section. In the *Christmas Oratorio* version, Bach reaches the word "Ruh" at mm. 51–52 with a smooth descending motion and an appoggiatura on the final note. In the secular cantata, the voice abruptly rises by a leap of a sixth from *g'* to *e"*, establishing dissonant tensions with the B♭ pedal point in the bc. Meinrad Walter has suggested that leap to the higher note in the *Hercules Cantata* shows that the peace or rest that is being promised is not really restful, that the vice Pleasure is deceiving the young Hercules.[75]

A short statement of the second phrase of the text "wache nach diesem vor aller Gedeihen" (awake after this for the flourishing of all) leads to a repetition of the second section of the ritornello (mm. 56–68), which represents the musical realization

[75] Walter, *Weihnachtsoratorium*, 89.

of the state of waking. The dichotomy between sleeping and waking (or in the secular model between sleeping and following), expressed by the juxtaposition of the first and second sections of the ritornello, is synthesized after the instrumental interlude when Bach repeats the entire text again. Bach layers the two states (rest and action) at the same time. The lullaby motif (a and b) is now simultaneously combined with the syncopated motif (c). This section again demonstrates the polysemy of musical motifs. In mm. 77–80 Bach composed a small point of imitation with the two violins mimicking and "following" the solo voice. What had been a rhetorical depiction of the text, "folge," is now in the new context ("wache") merely a neutral polyphonic imitation without extramusical meaning. We encounter a similar case a few measures later in mm. 92–95. The long melismatic line with syncopations, leading to an ascending *tirata*, was originally combined with the text "[ent-]brannten" and served as an expression of the agitated state—and maybe even of the spiking flames the text metaphorically evokes. In the version in the *Christmas Oratorio*, Bach keeps the melisma but now it is employed to set the word "aller" (all); the image of flames now moves to the background, and the accumulation of notes in the melisma can be heard as a depiction of the word "aller" instead.

While only a few modifications were necessary to adapt the A section of the secular aria to the new text,[76] deeper changes were required in the B section (mm. 113–52). The B section is primarily based on a simple melismatic motif, a descent from $b'$ to the lower sixth $d\sharp$, which is derived from the first two motifs of the aria, creating motivic unity between the two sections. The texts for both the secular model and the sacred parody did not require a contrasting stetting (the contrast is already inherent in the A section); thus Bach was free to connect the A and B sections through a similar musical idea. Contrast is established by the instrumentation. The first oboe d'amore, at m. 121, plays an obbligato line (in the secular model played by the first violin), echoing the line of the alto, while the strings interject with short sixteenth-note motifs. Even here Bach makes some subtle changes by rearranging these string interjections when he transforms the model composition into the sacred parody. The aria in BWV 213 alternates between the short string interjections and a motif based on descending triads in the second violin. In the sacred parody, Bach eliminates this second motif and inserts additional instances at which the string interjections are played. This again contributes to a musical and motivic unification of the movement. In mm. 132–33 Bach revises the composition to make the use of the motifs more coherent: In m. 132 the motif appeared in the second violin; Bach then crossed it out and assigned it to the viola. He also added the same motif, a third higher, in m. 133 in the second violin, overwriting a whole-measure rest he had already written. Finally, in m. 135, he entered the motif without first having entered the measure's BWV 213 reading (fig. 7.4).

[76] Cf. NBA II/6, KB, 37.

*Figure 7.4* J. S. Bach, BWV 248/19, corrections in score (D-B Mus. ms. Bach P 32, fol. 19ᵛ-20ʳ), mm. 123–39 (bpk, Berlin/Mendelssohn-Archiv, Staatsbibliothek zu Berlin, Stiftung Preussischer Kulturbesitz, Berlin, Germany/Art Resource, NY)

These changes are an instructive case for how Bach, while copying, made changes to the music, in the first instance by revising what he had copied, and in the second instance by directly recomposing certain material while he was otherwise simply copying. Other changes in the sacred parody represent Bach's recomposition of some of the melismatic lines to accommodate the new text of the B section. In mm. 117–20, the original text was "[er-]kenne keine Schranken," and Bach sets this text syllabically. In the sacred parody, on the other hand, the text expresses the joy of the heart, and the word "erfreuen" (gladden) motivates a more exuberant setting, which leads Bach to the composition of a longer melisma.[77] It appears that he had originally copied some of the original material and then revised it to fit the new text.[78] A similar case occurs in mm. 129–30, which differs significantly from the model composition. Bach made numerous changes that render the passage virtually illegible. The composer then clarified the voice-leading with the help of tabulature

[77] The short melisma on "labe" in m. 125 is also new, within a compositional revision of mm. 123–38.

[78] Measure 118 shows numerous corrections and while not everything is clearly legible, the original version seems to have been the one from BWV 213, which Bach then revised in a second step.

symbols. The corrected version that now appears at the bottom of the page of the score was written by Johann Heinrich Michel, based on the performance parts.[79] This melismatic outburst is even expanded in mm. 137–38 with rapid thirty-second notes in the vocal line and the flute. The movement ends with an extended allusion to the second half of the ritornello with its syncopated material, in which Bach builds the complete text of the B section, culminating in a long and exuberant melismatic outbreak on "[er-]freuen," mm. 144–52, a section that is literally borrowed from the secular model.[80]

Bach's librettist for the *Christmas Oratorio* designed the text to fit the preexisting music from the secular cantata. The music demanded a text that created a juxtaposition between two emotional states in the two opening lines of the A section and an intimate mood (though no strong contrast) in the B section. The librettist accomplished this by establishing a contrast between sleeping and waking in the A section and images of intimate love and joy in the B section. While the A sections in the model and the parody exhibit a similar degree of contrast, this contrast is of a different nature. In BWV 213, the lullaby sung by the vice Pleasure has the purpose of seducing the young hero Hercules. By falling asleep and resting, he would follow the enticing thoughts that lead him to join Pleasure. In the *Christmas Oratorio*, though, the two states follow each other chronologically. The young child is asked to rest for a while, because he will soon have to wake "for the flourishing of all"; in other words, to fulfill his soteriological mission. The music of the aria reflects this transitory nature of the rest, not only through the restlessness of some of the material (especially the syncopations in the second half of the ritornello) but also through the restless harmonic progression in the "lullaby" sections. Furthermore, the simultaneous combination of the material toward the end of the A section highlights the transitory nature of this rest.

The placement of the aria at this point in the oratorio has been criticized by several scholars. Albert Schweitzer had even suggested moving the aria to the place where the shepherds have arrived at the manger and are thus physically able to sing the song of the child.[81] Schweitzer's criticism, even though it might sound

---

[79] Cf. NBA II/6, KB, 37.

[80] The main difference is, besides the transposition and the different instrumentation, the fact that Bach deleted the "adagio" indication from m. 150.

[81] Schweitzer, *Bach*, 309. Walter Blankenburg suggests a different interpretation: "Sicherlich ist der Gedanke eigentümlich, den Hirten das Wiegenlied, das sie spielen sollen, zunächst vorzumusizieren. Aber darum geht es tatsächlich. Würde man die Arie an dieser Stelle wegnehmen, verlöre das vorangehende Accompagnato- Rezitativ seinen Sinn, und obendrein käme das gesamte Gefüge der Gliederung ins Wanken. Daß diese Arie dem Alt zugeteilt ist, dem Sinnbild der Mutter Maria, erscheint nach unseren bisherigen Beobachtungen zwangsläufig" (Blankenburg, *Weihnachts-Oratorium*, 65). While I do not agree with Blankenburg's Marian interpretation of the alto, his insistence that the aria has its correct place here is convincing.

convincing at first sight, is again based on the incorrect premise that the *Christmas Oratorio* is a piece with a dramatic plot that is enacted both in the gospel recit as well as in the arias.[82] Bach's own concept of an oratorio, however, was different in the early 1730s, as we learned in chapter 4. The arias are not sung by protagonists of the biblical narrative but they are meditations, removed from the drama in time and space. If we see part II of the *Christmas Oratorio* as an essay on music, understood as an art that facilitates the encounter between the human and the divine, the recit and the aria as the "song of rest" have their place firmly within the context of this part of the oratorio.

If part II is about music and the power of music in particular, then the genesis of the lullaby "Schlafe, mein Liebster" raises implicitly the question of the ambivalent power of music. In BWV 213 the lullaby seduces Hercules; in BWV 248, part II, the same notes serve as a cradle song for the newborn Jesus. It raises the question of whether music was to be seen as a vice or a virtue. This question was the basis for an ongoing dispute about the use of music in the liturgy, an argument that stretched from the Reformation to the eighteenth century, and one that was often divided along the lines of orthodox Lutherans (who supported the use of music) and Pietists (who challenged it).[83] For a theologian in the Lutheran tradition, the answer was rather straightforward: the ethical character of music was not inherent to the music itself but to its use, as Luther had emphasized his preface to Georg Rhau's *Symphoniae iucundae* (1538), one of the founding documents of a Lutheran theology of music. Here, music was seen as part of the divine creation and thus was good; it could, however, be used in a way that contradicted the divine plan, in which case it needed to be rejected. If used properly, the art was to be commended.[84] In other words, a lullaby like the "Schlafe, mein Liebster, genieße der Ruh" aria could be employed by vice and virtue alike. The context (and the text associated with it) determined its ethical impact, so that the seductive lullaby could become a song of rest for the newborn Son of God.

The "song of rest" is separated by only a short recit from the "song of praise" in the chorus of the angels (no. 21). Part II of the oratorio, then, continues with an accompagnato recit (no. 20) that not only encourages the angels to sing but also invites the listeners to join the heavenly choir. This is finally realized in the closing chorale setting, "Wir singen dir in deinem Heer," in which Bach returns to the siciliano motif from the opening sinfonia and thus brings the second part to a close.

[82] For a criticism of Schweitzer see also J. Merrill Knapp, "The Luke 2 Portions of Bach's Christmas Oratorio and Handel's Messiah," in *A Bach Tribute: Essays in Honor of William H. Scheide*, ed. Paul Brainard and Ray Robinson (Kassel: Bärenreiter, 1993), 159.

[83] See Joyce L. Irwin, "German Pietists and Church Music in the Baroque Age," *Church History* 54 (1985): 29–40.

[84] Martin Luther, "Preface to Georg Rhau's *Symphoniae iucundae*," in *Liturgy and Hymns*, vol. 53, ed. Ulrich S. Leupold (Philadelphia: Fortress Press, 1965), 323.

# 8

# Inward Mobility (Part III)

The third part of the *Christmas Oratorio*, performed on December 27, 1734, was the last of the three cantatas for the Christmas feast proper and concluded the story of the shepherds at the manger. Bach recognized the narrative arch within these three parts of the oratorio by returning to the key (D major) and to the sonic characteristics (trumpets and timpani) of part I. The gospel text for part III reports several departures: that of the angels after the announcement of the birth of Jesus; that of the shepherds for the manger; and later, after they have found the child, their return from the manger. The libretto, however, does not dwell much on this spatial movement. The movement of the angels and shepherds does not serve as a model for physical motion. Instead, the libretto turns this dynamic movement inward. This interpretation of the biblical narrative reflects the shift in the celebration of Christmas outlined in chapter 2: the transformation of the feast of folk rituals (which often involved movement, on the streets, from house to house, or the physical "rocking" of the child) into a celebration of interiority and personal devotion. Chapter 3 has already shown that part III of the oratorio contains the turning point in the temporal structure of the piece. The gospel recit no. 30 states that Mary "kept all these words [which she had heard from the shepherds] and pondered them [or rather in German "bewegte," moved] in her heart" (Lk 2:19). The focus of part III of the *Christmas Oratorio* is the internalized motion within the human heart. This is spelled out in the aria, the accompagnato recit, and the hymn, all of which immediately follow the gospel recit. We will return later to mvts. 30–34 and their musical realization of the *inhabitatio Christi*. Let us first look at the opening movements of part III, which develop their own theological focus with the idea of salvation as an expression of divine love. This topic was quite common in sermons and cantata texts for the third day of Christmas. Bach's cantata for this day from 1723, BWV 64 (*Sehet, welch eine Liebe hat uns der Vater erzeiget*), centers on the same theological idea.[1]

---

[1] *Sehet, welch eine Liebe hat uns der Vater erzeiget*, BWV 64 (See what love the Father has shown to us). While the libretto for this cantata does not reference the readings for the feast day directly, it does explore the topic of love that is the main theme of one of the gospel texts (Jn 21:20–24) for this day; see a short description of the cantata in Dürr, *Cantatas*, 121–24.

The first sequence of movements in part III of the oratorio after the opening chorus (see the discussion at the end of this chapter) ranges from the gospel recit no. 25 to the duet "Herr, dein Mitleid" (no. 29). The movements follow a similar theological trajectory as the opening movements of part I: Jesus is introduced as the savior of Israel and then typologically interpreted as the savior of mankind, of the faithful individual in particular. In this summary of salvation history, the coming of Jesus is viewed as an expression of God's mercy and of his divine love. What had been expected and promised at the beginning of the oratorio has now come to pass; the shepherds are the first witnesses and represent typologically the Christian congregation. The librettist in parts I and III not only employs a similar theological concept but also uses two stanzas from the same Lutheran hymn, "Gelobet seist du, Jesu Christ" to express this idea. Both parts join a stanza from the hymn with a text about God's love and compassion; in part I, the chorale is interspersed with free poetry in a chorale trope while in part III the meditation on God's compassion appears in the following aria. The comparison demonstrates that parts I and III are not only musically linked by their home key and instrumentation but that they also share an analogous theological focus:

| Part I | Part III |
|---|---|
| 3. Nun wird mein liebster Bräutigam . . . <br> Zum *Trost*, zum Heil der Erden . . . <br> Auf, *Zion*, und *verlasse nun das Weinen* | 27. Er hat sein Volk *getröst'* . . . <br> Die Hülf aus *Zion* hergesendet <br> Und *unser Leid geendet*. |
| [Now will my most beloved bridegroom . . . <br> for the consolation, for the salvation of the <br> earth . . . <br> Arise, Zion, and forsake weeping now] | [He has comforted his people . . . <br> sent salvation out of Zion, <br> and ended our suffering] |
| **7. Er ist auf Erden kommen arm,** <br> **Daß er unser sich erbarm . . .** | **28. Dies hat er alles uns getan,** <br> **Sein groß Lieb zu zeigen an . . .** |
| [He has come on earth poor, <br> that he might have mercy on us . . . ] | [All this he has done for us <br> to show his great love . . . ] |
| *interpolations in 7:* | 29. Herr, dein *Mitleid*, dein <br> Erbarmen |
| Wer will die *Liebe* recht erhöhn . . . <br> Wie ihn der Menschen *Leid* bewegt . . . | Tröstet uns und macht uns frei. <br> Deine holde Gunst und *Liebe* . . . |
| [Who will properly extol the love . . . <br> how human suffering moves him. | [Lord, your compassion, your mercy <br> comforts us and makes us free. <br> Your pleasing favor and love . . . ] |

As usual, the sequence of movements begins with a portion of the Christmas narrative. The first verse of the gospel text (Lk 2:15) is divided into a short narrative passage sung by the tenor (no. 25) and a turba chorus by the shepherds, "Lasset uns nun gehen gen Bethlehem" (no. 26). The short gospel recit directs the gaze from the heaven, the angelic sphere, down to earth, the realm of the shepherds. The melodic line of the tenor voice descends from *e'* at the beginning down to *e* for the final note. What stands out in this katabatic line is the upward leap of a seventh on the word "Himmel" (heaven) in m. 2. Bach's composition score shows a number of revisions to this simple recit. While the original version also had a descent and featured a leap on "heaven," the revised version now outlines a descending triad in E major, followed by the expressive leap of a seventh up to *d'* on "heaven" (ex. 8.1).

*Example 8.1* J. S. Bach, BWV 248/25, corrections in the recit

Bach also changed the voice-leading in the bc in m. 2. Instead of keeping the half note in the second half of the measure, he changed the *a* to a quarter note followed by *c♯*. While the harmony stays the same (the *c♯* serves as the basis for a first-inversion A-major chord), the bass line picks up momentum that is continued in a walking-bass line in the following turba chorus. The second half of the gospel verse ("Lasset uns nun gehen") is set as a polyphonic chorus. The texture of the movement stands in the tradition of earlier Christmas *historiae*. Already seventeenth-century composers—like Johann Rudolph Ahle and Johann Schelle—had composed contrapuntal settings depicting the shepherds walking from their fields near Bethlehem to the manger. Even the shape of Bach's fugue subject is conventional. Schelle's fugue begins with an ascending fifth; Bach simply fills this interval in stepwise motion. Ahle even features the same stepwise ascent as Bach does. It is not necessary to assume that Bach intentionally referred either one of the compositions or that he used them as a model (although they were composed by his predecessors in Mühlhausen and Leipzig respectively). The similarities instead demonstrate that he employed a stereotypical model to depict the march of the shepherds. More important is what he adds in comparison to his predecessors: these seventeenth-century composers write straightforward points of imitation. Bach, on the other hand, fabricates a more complex texture by leading two of the four voices in contrary motion. Tenor and soprano ascend while the alto and bass descend. It would be wrong to try decoding the combination of the fugal subject and its inversion as a theological message.[2] Rather it is Bach's typical attempt to add contrapuntal complexity to an established compositional model. Bach also adds an independent instrumental line to this model. In an almost uninterrupted continuous sixteenth-note motion, the two flauti traversi and the first violins accompany the polyphonic vocal texture, while the vocalists are doubled by the remaining strings and oboes. This combination of a vocal setting with a single independent instrumental line is not unusual for Bach's turba choruses; he used a similar technique in the movements "Jesum von Nazareth" (no. 2b) and "Wir dürfen niemand töten" (no. 16d) of his St. John Passion. Here in the Christmas Oratorio, the two elements also have a symbolic function. The scalar motion of the fugal subject evokes the walking of the shepherds, while the rushing instrumental line alludes to their hurrying.[3]

The score of the movement in P 32 exhibits numerous corrections and it is easily identifiable as a composition score.[4] The uneven spacing of the notes on the page also reveals the compositional process: Bach first composed the vocal lines; the music moves mostly in eighth notes and the individual note signs are evenly spaced. He then added the instrumental line in sixteenth notes above the voices. On numerous occasions Bach did not leave enough space, and the smaller note values made it necessary to squeeze the instrumental line into the margins of the already

---

[2] Cf. Friedrich Smend, *Joh. Seb. Bach: Kirchen Kantaten, Heft 5 (vom 1. Sonntag im Advent bis zum Epiphanias-Fest)*, 3rd ed. (Berlin: Christlicher Zeitschriftenverlag, 1966), 36–37), for instance, tries to see an expression of repentance and turning in the juxtaposition of the ascending and descending lines. The problem of this interpretation is that the motif of spiritual/moral inversion is neither present in the libretto nor does it figure prominently in eighteenth-century sermons on this passage.

[3] A similar interpretation of the movement was already suggested by Walter, *Weihnachtsoratorium*, 108.

[4] Ortwin von Holst has suggested that the movement might be a parody; however, Bach's handwriting in the score and the number of corrections clearly disproves this assumption; see von Holst, "Turba Chöre des Weihnachts-Oratoriums und der Markuspassion," *Musik und Kirche* 38 (1968): 229–33, esp. 231–33.

written bar lines. While being unevenly spaced and sometimes spilling over the bar lines, the instrumental line does not exhibit a lot of corrections or revisions, which attests to its formal and harmonic simplicity: the harmonic progression had already been determined by the vocal layer; the instruments simply move within this framework, using scalar motion, circular figures, and oscillations between neighboring notes. The vocal layer, on the other hand, exhibits numerous corrections. Some of the changes are corrections of the harmonic progression, others are intended to maintain the rhythmic flow of the movement. In m. 4 (on beat 1) Bach changes the final note of the subject in the tenor part from a half note to a quarter note followed by a quarter-rest. The change was probably made after writing down the vocal bass line, which has a half note on the same beat as well. The purpose of the change is to avoid rhythmic stagnation in the two voices and it also delineated the end of the tenor phrase. Later, in m. 6 Bach corrects the third note in the bass from *d* to *e*. While *d* would have been the corresponding pitch in this statement of the fugue subject, it would have sounded awkward with the *c♯* in the alto and the *e* in the tenor, both of which already had been written down.

Keeping the rhythmic flow was also the reason for Bach's revision to the alto line in m. 7. The first note was a half note,[5] which was then shortened to a quarter note. The reason for the change is clear, as the bass already has a half note as part of the head of fugal subject and the tenor sings two quarter notes on the same pitch (also part of the fugal subject). Having a half note in the alto would have brought the motion in the measure to a premature halt and would have taken some of the kinetic energy out of the march of the shepherds. In the revised version, the alto shortens the last note of the subject to a quarter note and immediately begins with another statement of the subject. Together with the fragments of the subject in the soprano and in the following measure in the tenor, Bach creates a stretto-like effect, thus increasing the energy of the movement instead of bringing it to a halt. The stretto opens an episode of freer play with still smaller fragments of the subject,[6] culminating with a cadence (mm. 14–15) even though the subject *does* appear at mm. 12–15 in the vocal bass line. After this, Bach introduces the second half of the sentence of the text "und die Geschichte sehen" (and see what the story is) and a new musical idea, which is also treated polyphonically. In this second half of the movement, Bach struggles more with the distribution of the text than with details of the polyphonic texture. Bach accidentally inserts in mm. 17–19 (soprano) and 19–21 (alto) the end of the text "die uns der Herr kund gethan hat" (which the Lord has made known to us) instead of the correct words, "die da geschehen ist" (that's taking place there).

After the shepherds have embarked for the manger the drama comes to a halt. The following three movements—an accompagnato, a hymn, and a duet—explore

---

[5] Cf. NBA II/6, KB, 47.

[6] Further corrections appear in the tenor, mm. 9–10; cf. NBA II/6, KB, 47.

the theological meaning (or rather, *one* theological meaning) of the biblical narrative. Instead of elaborating on the movement of the shepherds, the libretto looks
back to what the text calls the "story" that God has revealed through his angel. In this
case, the "story" refers to the announcement by the angel in part II of the oratorio.
The libretto for part III harkens back to ideas from part II, such as the understanding of the shepherds as representing Israel (recit no. 14). But the "story" is the story
of salvation, not only of the shepherds and of Israel but also of the entire Christian
congregation: "Und *unser* Leid geendet" (and ended *our* suffering), as the recit
no. 27 claims. This typological interpretation of the narrative is continued in the
following hymn setting, "Dies hat er alles *uns* getan" (All this he has done for *us*).[7]
The text of the hymn ("Gelobet seist du, Jesu Christ") by Martin Luther resonates
with several aspects of the earlier parts of the oratorio. The "story" has happened
for "us," it is an expression of God's "love," and it is, as the angel had announced in
recit no. 13, a reason for "great joy." The spatial aspect of the shepherds' journey to
the manger is completely ignored in the following movements. Instead, the libretto
directs the gaze inward, culminating in the duet no. 29, which interprets the divine
compassion expressed in the incarnation as an indication of divine love. The metaphors of love and desire in the text of the duet harken back to the images of bride
and bridegroom in part I of the oratorio. Although the libretto makes a clear shift
away from what the biblical narrative reports, the movements are clearly theologically connected; mvts. 25–29 are also linked through common keywords: the word
"kundgetan" (had announced) from mvt. 26 returns in modified form in mvt. 27
as "getan" (He has done this) and in no. 28 as "uns getan" (He has done for us).
The final "Kyrieleis" (God have mercy) from the chorale (no. 28) is transformed
in no. 29 into "Herr, dein Mitleid, dein Erbarmen" (Lord, your compassion, your
mercy). The close connection of the texts of the movements has motivated Bach
to create an unusually close link between the turba chorus no. 26 and the following
accompagnato recit by extending the final chord in the bc from the chorus and using
it to harmonically support the beginning of the recit. Later in part V Bach will create
a similar, even closer connection of gospel chorus and interpretative accompagnato,
mvt. 45.[8] Similar to the accompagnato recits referring to the shepherds in part II,
the recit no. 27 in part III is again sung by a bass. However, instead of the bucolic
reed instruments of the previous part, Bach now introduces two flauti traversi to
accompany the singer. The reason for this is not entirely clear. In terms of the semantic meaning of the instruments, it would have made sense to use the oboi d'amore
again, especially since the soprano-bass-duet (no. 29) employs these instruments
as well. However, the use of the flutes creates a greater continuity with the flute

---

[7] My emphasis.

[8] Interestingly, this later movement also transforms spatial movement within the narrative into an
internalized motion toward the human heart.

figurations in the turba chorus. Here, sonic coherence[9] seems to be more important to Bach than sonic symbolism.[10]

While the accompagnato recit (no. 27) and the duet (no. 29) are not connected by a similar instrumentation, Bach does join them motivically. The music for the duet already existed in a secular cantata, which allowed Bach to anticipate musical material in the recit that would return in the later movement. We have seen an earlier example for this type of connection in mvts. 3 and 4 from part I. Here in part III the connecting musical idea is a dotted eighth note followed by two thirty-second notes, which figures prominently in the duet. Bach inserts the motif twice in the flute part of the recit (mm. 5 and 7) as short interpolations between textual phrases. This musical detail was the result of a revision. In m. 5 (and possibly in m. 7) the flutes originally had a simple quarter note, which was then turned into the motif borrowed from the duet. The score P 32 clearly shows the stages of composition. The motivic link suggests that the two movements have to be seen as a unity, comparable to conventional recit-aria pairs in contemporary opera. The motivic connection bridges the two movements and are separated by the interpolation of the hymn, representing the voice of the congregation.

The chorale "Dies hat er alles uns getan" appears in an elaborate harmonization. Bach had set the same melody eleven years earlier, in 1723, for BWV 64/2, his first Leipzig cantata for the third day of Christmas. This setting from Bach's first year in Leipzig begins very simply and mostly homophonic, perhaps the simplest setting imaginable for the melody. Eleven years later, Bach composes a highly complex movement with rhythmically intricate textures in the accompanying voices and an extended final cadence. Even within the context of the four-part hymn settings of the *Christmas Oratorio*, the independence of the accompanying voices is remarkable. In BWV 64/2 Bach begins with a homophonic texture. In the second half, the motion in the lower voices is slightly increased, highlighting central words such as "alle," "dank ihm," and "Ewigkeit." The final "Kyrieleis" staggers the entrances of the final phrase by an eighth note. In short, the hymn setting from 1723 creates a climax that culminates in the final line. The setting from 1734 begins like an embellished version of the earlier movement. The bass line of BWV 248/28 expands the bass from BWV 64/2 into a descending chain of eighth notes. But already in the first cadence, the later version opts for a modern authentic cadence (A–D), while the earlier setting had maintained a more archaic character by cadencing in A minor (BWV 64/2 is a whole step lower). Even more striking is the independence of the middle voices. Not only does the eighth-note motion from the bass line spill over

[9] In Bach's original plan the text of the aria "Schließe, mein Herze," no. 31, was supposed to be given an entirely different musical setting, one that featured the two flutes as obbligato instruments. Bach revised that plan after he had already assigned the first accompagnato to the two flutes.

[10] A symbolic interpretation of the flutes has been suggested by Walter Blankenburg, see Blankenburg, *Weihnachts-Oratorium*, 80–81.

into the other voices, Bach also lengthens the word "alles" in the bass by inserting a dotted quarter note (m. 1), adds a syncopation on "uns" in the tenor (m. 2; another one on "zeigen" in m. 4), and embellishes the word "Ewigkeit" with a long melisma (m. 8, bass). All of these embellishments can be explained as simple emphasis of central words of the text, but they also point ahead to later movements: the emphasis on the eternity of God's love foreshadows the second half of part III, where Bach goes through the three temporal states of Christ's presence, culminating in his third coming at the end of times. Similarly, the drawn-out "Kyrieleis" will be taken up again in the following duet with the praise of God's mercy. Judging from Bach's score, the idea for the chorale setting grew during the compositional process. While the melody in the soprano was entered first and is evenly spaced, Bach has a hard time inserting the florid lower voices. Had the composer planned a complex setting like this from the start, he would probably have left more room.

## Transforming a love duet (mvt. 29)

The first half of part III ends with the duet for soprano and bass, "Herr, dein Mitleid" (Lord, your compassion). We have to remind ourselves that the libretto is still technically an interpretation of the journey of the shepherds in Luke 2:15. The journey to manger is now turned into a journey inside, to the manger of the human heart. The duet is a typical love duet, celebrating the *inhabitatio Christi* as an expression of divine love, implicitly alluding to the image of bride and bridegroom from part I.

The duet "Herr, dein Mitleid" (no. 29) is a parody movement with a complex history. The immediate model for the movement in the *Christmas Oratorio* was a duet for alto and tenor in the *Hercules Cantata* BWV 213 ("Ich bin deine," no. 11) from 1733. However, that movement might have been a parody from an earlier work as well.[11] To make things even more complicated, Bach's score for the duet BWV 213/11 has the beginning of a duet—now crossed out at the top of the page[12]—that would later become part of the *B-Minor Mass* as a setting of the text "Et in unum dominum." While Bach only inserted the first four measures of the first instrumental part, he also bracketed the first six staves of the page, creating the space for the three instruments, two singers, and bc.[13] The four measures Bach inserted differ from the later version in the Mass only in the key, which is C major instead of G major. The C-major version would have allowed Bach to write a duet for alto and tenor (as required in the context of BWV 213) with the alto singing

[11]  Cf. Schulze, *Die Bach-Kantaten*, 640.

[12]  D-B Mus.ms. Bach P 125, fol. 15ʳ.

[13]  The version in the *B-Minor Mass* is set for two violins, viola, soprano, alto, and bc., and two oboes that move colla parte with the violins.

what is sung in the Mass by soprano I and the tenor what is sung by the alto. The discarded fragment in the score of BWV 213 suggests that Bach was not composing a new piece but that the movement was planned as a parody of an earlier duet of unknown provenance.[14] Bach's reasons for giving up his original plans are not known. The movement could have been quite fitting; the two voices move in close proximity, sometimes in parallel thirds, sometimes even interlocking, underscoring the text that talks about ardent love, betrothal, and tender kisses. After writing down the opening measures Bach must have changed his mind and decided to choose another movement from his repertoire to sonically enact the engagement of Hercules and Virtue. A possible reason for Bach's change might have been the motivic similarity between the first aria of the cantata, "Schlafe, mein Liebster" and the duet that he eventually chose to use in the cantata. The opening motifs of the two movements both feature a characteristic dotted figure, parallel motion in the instrumental lines, and stepwise ascending lines in mm. 9–11 (no. 3) and 5/7 (no. 11). The two movements look like a pair, and it is possible that both of them were parodies from the same earlier model.

Through the motivic correspondences between the two movements, this choice underscores the formal and dramatic structure of the *Hercules Cantata*. Two similar pieces now appear as the first and last arias in the *dramma per musica*, featuring the three protagonists: Pleasure (soprano) in no. 3, and Hercules (alto) and Virtue (tenor) in no. 11. The two movements are part of a symmetrical ground plan:

| no. | voice | genre | voice | no. |
|---|---|---|---|---|
| 1 | | Chorus | | 13 |
| 2 | A | Recit | B | 12 |
| 3 | S | Aria/Duet | AT | 11 |
| 4 | ST | Recit | AT | 10 |
| 5 | A | Aria | A | 9 |
| 6 | T | Recit | T | 8 |
| 7 | T | Aria ("Auf deinen Flügeln") | | |

---

[14] Klaus Häfner has tried to reconstruct the history of this movement. He suggests that the duet was originally composed for a wedding cantata in 1725. Häfner's thesis rests on the assumption that Bach made major changes in the B section of the duet when he borrowed it for the Mass setting. This attempted reconstruction is not entirely convincing, as only in the A section does the music and the preserved text from 1725 go well together; see Häfner, *Aspekte des Parodieverfahrens bei Johann Sebastian Bach. Beträge zur Wiederentdeckung verschollener Vokalwerke*, Neue Heidelberger Studien zur Musikwissenschaft 12 (Laaber: Laaber Verlag, 1987), 305–27.

The movements of the cantata are symmetrically arranged around three movements sung by Virtue: the aria "Auf deinen Flügeln" and its two framing recits. This is the turning point in the dramatic development. The movement before this trias feature Pleasure's attempt to seduce Hercules (no. 3 and 4) and the young hero's search for the right path to follow (no. 2 and 5). In the second half of the cantata, Hercules rejects Pleasure and engages in a love relationship with Virtue, leading to their engagement and eventual marriage. The symmetrical juxtaposition and motivic similarity of arias 3 and 11 highlight the dramatic tension between them: both texts represent a form of love. Pleasure addresses her "most beloved" and attempts to lull him into sleep with the goal of seducing him, "Schmecke die Lust der lüsternen Brust" (Taste the pleasure of the wanton breast). The vice promises fulfillment of carnal desire, yet the desire remains unfulfilled. Only the instruments enact what the text promises as they move in close harmony. The music is seductive while Pleasure stays and sings alone. The desire is promised by the sound of the instruments but not physically realized by the joining of soprano (Pleasure) and alto (Hercules). Only in the final duet between Hercules and Virtue is the desire fulfilled. The instruments again play in close harmony, but now the two singers perform together, depicting the intimate embrace of Hercules and Virtue. The physicality of this intimate embrace is morally justified by the libretto as the hero and Virtue become engaged to get married. Instead of following their carnal desire, as promised by Pleasure in no. 3, the two singers now, in no. 11, realize their physical connection in the chastity of marriage.[15] Bach uses the proximity of alto and tenor voices (a more unusual pair in Bach's cantatas) to musically enact this physical entanglement. Not only do the two voices imitate one another and move in parallel thirds, the voices also cross occasionally (mm. 79, 83, 97–98, 120, and 126), and twice the two singers finish their phrase in unison (mm. 42 and 75). Both unison moments occur on the word "(küsse) dich/mich" (kiss you/me); Bach transposes the physical touching of the two bodies into music. In their juxtaposition at the beginning and the end of the *Hercules Cantata*, the two similar movements stand for unfulfilled promise versus fulfillment. We will return to the function of these two movements later.

When Bach parodied the duet in his oratorio he made several fundamental changes. He transposed the duet from F major to A major, replaced the violas of the model with two oboi d'amore, and changed the singers from alto/tenor to soprano/bass. The inclusion of the oboes has a symbolic function as Bach employs the "love-oboes" in the oratorio frequently to signify the spiritual love between

---

[15] During the Protestant Reformation in the sixteenth century the ethical ideal of the chaste woman (symbolized in the middle ages by the nun) was replaced with a married woman who limited her sexual activity to her husband; cf. Joel F. Harrington, *Reordering Marriage and Society in Reformation Germany* (Cambridge: Cambridge University Press, 1995), 59–84; and Lyndal Roper, *The Holy Household: Women and Morals in Reformation Augsburg* (Oxford: Oxford University Press, 1989), 232f.

Christ and the believer. The sound of the reed instruments also connects the duet with the sonic domain of the shepherds, which Bach had established in part II. The transposition by a third was necessary to fit the duet into the harmonic context of the oratorio. More importantly, though, the transposition allowed Bach to give the part of the alto to the soprano and assign the tenor part (one octave lower) to the bass. The result is a soprano-bass duet, a combination Bach uses frequently to depict the mystical love between the bridegroom (Christ) and the bride (the human soul). This can be heard most prominently in the two love-duets from BWV 140, *Wachet auf, ruft uns die Stimme,* composed only three years before the *Christmas Oratorio.*[16] The change of voices also brings the movement in line with the three other movements for two vocalists, all of which feature soprano and bass: the chorale setting no. 7 ("Er ist auf Erden kommen arm") in part I and the two "pseudo" chorale tropes no. 38 and 40 in part IV. All four movements share the general topic of love. With the chorale setting no. 7, the duet no. 29 is additionally connected through the use of oboi d'amore as obbligato instruments as well as a sigh-like motif in the instrumental part, which evokes the sense of longing and desire. The four soprano-bass duets in the oratorio are further united by the fact that none of them feature dramatic dialogue, as is the case in BWV 140 and other Christ/soul dialogues by Bach. While Bach uses the same texture in the oratorio, it is not possible to identify acting persons. We hear a symbolic representation of love but not a dramatic one.[17] Bach uses the sound of a love duet to highlight a central subject of the text without "staging" this love as some of his cantatas do.[18]

[16] An overview of the dialogue composition is given in Mary Jewett Greer, "The Sacred Duets and Terzets of Johann Sebastian Bach: A Study of Genre and Musical Text Interpretation." PhD diss., Harvard University, 1996, 238–41, 256–58, and 282–301; for a critical evaluation of the gender identities in BWV 140, see Susan McClary, "The Blasphemy of Talking Politics during Bach Year," in *Music and Society: The Politics of Composition, Performance and Reception,* ed. Richard Leppert and Susan McClary (Cambridge: Cambridge University Press, 1987), 13–62

[17] Walter Blankenburg has suggested an identification of the two voices in the duet as the shepherds hastening to the manger: "Man kann sich dieses nur als Äußerung der in froher Erwartung zum Stall nach Bethlehem eilenden Hirten vorstellen. Die beiden Oboen d'amore bestätigen dies," Blankenburg, *Weihnachts-Oratorium,* 81. (One can only imagine that these words were unttered by the shepherds who are hastening to the stable in Bethlehem in joyful anticipation. This is confirmed by (the use) of the two oboi d'amore.). The problem with Blankenburg's suggestion is that he tries to insert a dramatic quality into the aria that had been eliminated by Bach himself when he changed the duet into an aria for two. Furthermore, the combination of soprano and bass is so typical for love duets in Bach's works that it is hard to imagine that this could be a dialogue between two shepherds.

[18] Meinrad Walter suggests a different reading which maintains a dialogical understanding of the duet but takes into account Bach's changes: "Denn doch ist die Botschaft immer auf eine Zweigliedrigkeit angelegt, die musikalisch nutzbar gemacht ist. Im Wortlaut dialogisieren nun undramatisch 'Mitleid' und 'Erbarmen' sowie 'Gunst' und 'Liebe,'" Walter, *Weihnachtsoratorium,* 110 (However, the message still relies on the juxtaposition of two elements, of which the music makes use. In the text "compassion" and "mercy" as well as "favor" and "love" now engage in a dialogue.). While Walter's suggestion

By transposing the movement, the two kissing characters are now separated in sonic space, leaving no opportunity for voice crossing. Only once, for the brief moment of an eighth note (m. 75), do the two singers sing together.[19] What remains in mvt. 29 is the mere allusion to a love duet through the emotive qualities of the music, like the parallel motion of the two voices and the use of a pair of voices, which the listeners of Bach's sacred music were accustomed to decoding as bride and bridegroom. Overall, the sensual love of the secular duet is transformed into a symbolic representation of love.[20] This act of de-dramatization was intentional, as the text for the movement shows. Bach's librettist must have been aware that he was writing the text for a movement that had been designed as a duet between two voices. However, the text does not differentiate between two characters, both voices sing the same words, and the text does not utilize the dramatic potential of the existing music. A similar case appears in part V, when Bach transforms a movement that had been a conversation between three characters into a terzet in which two of the voices engage in a conversation with the third voice (no. 51). One of the surprising peculiarities of the *Christmas Oratorio* is that its only duet has the text of a regular aria and its only terzet the text of a duet. Again, the drama is internalized. External action like the kissing of lovers, is turned inward as an act of inward mobility. This is not to deny or diminish the dramatic potential and the emotional import of the duet in the context of the oratorio, but it is not the external drama of the opera or the secular *dramma per musica*.

In retrospect, we can suggest a slightly modified reading of aria no. 19 in part II ("Schlafe, mein Liebster"). In the secular model, BWV 213, the aria describes the desire and promise of carnal unity with the vice Pleasure, which remains unfulfilled. Only at the end of the cantata, in the duet no. 11, is Hercules allowed to exchange kisses, but now with Virtue. In the *Christmas Oratorio* the two movements are "neighboring" arias. No. 19 is the last aria of part II, and no. 29 is the first movement in aria form in part III. Of course, they are separated by nine other

has its merits, it is not warranted by the text since these abstract principles never engage in a dialogue. Instead of searching for dialogical elements, an interpretation of the movement should rather ask for the semantic function of the dialogical texture within the context of the oratorio.

[19] And this moment is lost in most performances because the eighth-note is the last beat of a long, extended note in the bass which is often shortened to afford the singer an opportunity to breath before the beginning of the next musical phrase.

[20] We find a similar symbolic representation of love in the three Christological duets of the *B-Minor Mass*, "Christe eleison," "Deum de Deo," and "Et in unum Dominum." Two of the movements were completed about seventeen months before the *Christmas Oratorio* for the Kyrie-Gloria Missa that Bach dedicated to the court in Dresden; and the model for the third one is quoted coincidentally in the score for BWV 213 where it was eventually replaced with the duet that provided the model for mvt. 29 of the oratorio.

movements. Thus, the modern listener has to wait about eight-and-a-half minutes between the two arias (not to mention the original performance where they were separated by about twenty-four hours). Nonetheless, Bach connects the two movements by putting them close to each other in the oratorio and by associating them both with the narrative of the shepherds who are on their way to the manger. The texts for both movements turn this motion toward the manger into an inward motion that recasts the journey to the stable in Bethlehem as a journey toward Jesus in the believer's heart. Analogous to the function of the aria and the duet in BWV 213, representing promise and eventual fulfillment, the two movements have a similar function in the oratorio. "Schlafe, mein Liebster," the sacred parody of Pleasure's seductive aria, is sung before the shepherds have reached the manger. It is a response to the message of the angel, expressing an ardent desire to be united with Jesus. This desire has to stay unfulfilled for those eight-and a-half more minutes (or twenty-four hours); the choir of angels has to sing their hymn of praise first, and the shepherds have to embark on their journey to the manger. Only when close to reaching the manger—the arrival is narrated immediately after the duet—do we hear the duet that celebrates the mystical unity symbolically, combining soprano and bass in a musical dialogue. The sonic fulfillment of the desire is here connected to the local proximity of the shepherds to the stable and the Christ child.

Bach designed the structure of the duet in BWV 213 to underscore the emotional (and physical) proximity of hero and Virtue. The duet has an extensive *da capo* form. The opening ritornello (mm. 1–16) presents the main material in two-measure segments (the following bar-number and keys refer to the version in the *Christmas Oratorio*): a characteristic opening gesture by the first oboe (mm. 1–2), which is immediately repeated in parallel motion with the second oboe (mm. 3–4), and the ascending, stepwise motif mentioned earlier (mm. 5–6), repeated sequentially (mm. 7–8). This is followed by a short play with fragments of the second half of the opening motif (mm. 9–10), loosely imitated by the second oboe (m. 11). Before the final cadence, Bach introduces a short "knocking" motif (mm. 13–14). These three musical ideas provide the main building blocks for the duet. The opening measures of the first vocal section (mm. 17–20) are an almost literal repetition of the beginning of the ritornello (mm. 1–4). But Bach superimposes the characteristic knocking motif, thus telescoping the different ideas from the ritornello. The first vocal section ends in m. 42, giving way to a repetition of the opening ritornello, transposed to E major (mm. 42–58). The listener might expect the B section of the *da capo* aria, but instead Bach inserts another statement of the text of the A section (A$_2$, mm. 58–98), followed by a complete statement of the opening ritornello (mm. 98–114) including some minor changes throughout. These changes are mostly due to the need to stay in

A major instead of modulating to the dominant E major, as the opening ritornello had done. Bach's decision to extend (in fact, double) the A section was motivated by the text and the dramatic function of the movement in the secular cantata. In BWV 213 the duet is the manifestation of the conjunction of Virtue and Hercules. The dual setting of the dialogic text allows Bach to begin the duet as a dialogue. Hercules sings "Ich bin deine" (I am yours) and Virtue answers "Du bist meine" (you are mine). When the text returns in section $A_2$, the voices now enter simultaneously. The unity is already a *fait accompli*, and the music mirrors this by introducing the two voices together. While the duet loses its dialogical character in the *Christmas Oratorio*, the extensive elaboration of "love" does indeed emphasize the central foundation of the human-divine relationship as it is seen by the text of the oratorio: the foundation of his liberating compassion and mercy is God's love. The double treatment of the text is now not dramatic but emphatic.[21]

The B section of the duet (mm. 115–66) is in comparison much more compact. The musical material is derived from the second half of the opening ritornello, juxtaposing the Lombard thirty-second-note motif from m. 9 and the "knocking" motif from m. 13. Bach almost literally recalls the second half of the opening ritornello in an instrumental interlude (mm. 134–42) that separates the first and second halves of the B section.[22] The text for the sacred parody follows the affective trajectory of the secular model. Keywords of the oratorio text line up well with melodic features of the existing music: like the dotted eighth notes accentuating "Herr" and "dein" (mm. 17–19), long notes on the word "frei" (mm. 26–28), or the highly emotional, descending melismas on "tröstet" (mm. 34–36).[23] Most of the changes due to the text occur in the B section, from mm. 118–34. The sacred text ends with a central keyword that has two syllables, "Lie-be" (love) while the secular text mentions the noun "Verlobte" (betrothed) earlier and ends with the three-syllable verb "ver-binden" (join). For the secular version, the fall of an octave at mm. 121 on the final verb works well; but the noun "Liebe" in the oratorio required a stronger, more melodic treatment (ex. 8.2).

---

[21] Richard D. P. Jones misses this point when he criticizes that in "the Christmas version [of the duet] the subject is no longer love but divine mercy and compassion; hence the justification for the operatic love-duet style is no longer clearly apparent," Jones, *Creative Development II*, 310–11. Divine love and divine mercy are intrinsically intertwined in early eighteenth-century theology in general and in the theology of Bach's *Christmas Oratorio* in particular. Bach's use of the "love-duet idiom" in the movement "Et misericordia" from the *Magnificat* BWV 243/243a shows that "love" and "mercy" were conceived by the composer as related concepts, which elicited a similar musical treatment.

[22] On Bach's use of the Lombard rhythm, see Gerhard Herz, "Lombard Rhythm in Bach's Vocal Music," in Herz, *Essays on J. S. Bach*, Studies in Musicology 73 (Ann Arbor, MI, 1985), 233–68.

[23] The melismas had originally been associated with the word "küsse."

*Example 8.2* J. S. Bach, BWV 213/11 and BWV 248/29, mm. 118–24

As in earlier examples, Bach integrates his changes into the harmonic and motivic framework of the essentially unaltered instrumental layer. Most of the changes were already made while Bach was copying the music from the score for BWV 213. The handwriting in the autograph P 32 is clear and without significant corrections. However, major changes in the melismatic lines in mm. 125–28 are visible as corrections in the autograph score. The same is true for the soprano line in mm. 130–33, where Bach revises the music in several stages to adapt it to the new text.[24] In addition to changes motivated by the text, Bach also continues to clarify performance details, like the addition of staccato marks in the knocking motif, which are missing in the performance material for BWV 213 (although it might reflect how the secular aria was performed as well). The simplification of the voice parts in mm. 142–44 is quite unusual for Bach's parody method, which usually lends a higher degree of complexity and musical detail. Bach smoothens the sequence of appoggiaturas and trill motifs into a calm and simple descending line, which culminates in the three-note gesture on "Liebe." The erotic excitement of the connection of the two lovers in the secular cantata gives way to a calm sonic representation of God's "pleasing favor and love." The duet ends the first half of part III of the *Christmas Oratorio*. While the shepherds in their journey approach the manger, the inward journey celebrates the unity with Christ. Kinesis gives way to contemplation.

## The threefold coming (mvts. 30–35)

The discussion of the threefold coming of Christ in chapter 3 as the hermeneutic key for the understanding of Christmas in Bach's time has shown that the second half of part III encapsulates this overarching theme of the oratorio. We have already identified the aria "Schließe, mein Herze" as the turning point in the temporal framework of the entire *Christmas Oratorio*. The analysis of the first half of part III has also made clear that the journey of the shepherds is interpreted as an internalized motion toward Christ who dwells in the heart of the believer. In the gospel recit that opens the second half of part III, the shepherds reach their destination and the "Word"—mediator of the presence of Christ in Lutheran orthodox theology—reaches its "destination" in Mary's heart where Christ's mother (who is to be understood as

---

[24] The changes mostly affect requirements of the new text-declamation in the parody movement; for the changes see NBA II/6, KB, 48–49; another change is the voice exchange between the singers in mm. 158–63.

the model for the faithful believer)[25] contemplates and "moves" (bewegt) it. We have already analyzed Bach's setting of this gospel recit (no. 30) in chapter three. The aria "Schließe" then admonishes the heard to "embrace" the miracle. Given the theological and structural centrality of this aria within the *Christmas Oratorio*, we can appreciate the effort Bach put into the composition of this very movement. It might have been planned as a parody at the beginning,[26] but Bach soon decided to compose an entirely new aria. The first sketch for the movement—an alto aria for strings, flutes, and continuo—suggests a large-scale, dance-like piece, and the rhythm resembles a lighthearted siciliano. While the sketch was soon discarded with emphatic crisscross strokes of the pen, the fragment affords valuable insights into the compositional process. Bach begins with the main theme in the upper voice of the instrumental ensemble (flute 1). The composition of the ritornello already exhibits numerous revisions. While the siciliano opening motif (mm. 1–4) is quite clear from the start, the fortspinnung had to be developed, and the corrections show Bach's thought process. Measures 7–8 in the flute originally had a different shape, and the thirty-second-note cascade in m. 16 was at first a third lower. Bach also changed the bc in mm. 5–6 from a simpler cadential arrival to a broken triad (fig. 8.1 and ex. 8.3).

*Example 8.3* Transcription of rejected sketch for BWV 248/31

---

[25] It was quite common in Lutheran theology to view Mary's "pondering of the words" as a model for the believer; see Kreitzer, *Reforming Mary*, 114.

[26] See the discussion of this issue in chap. 5.

The thirty-second-note cascade in m. 16 and the return to the opening motif in the following measure suggests that the ritornello was projected to be sixteen measures long and that the voice would have entered in m. 17, together with the instruments. During his work on the ritornello, Bach decided to reduce the instrumentation. After entering the first three measures of the part for flute 2 (playing in unison with flute 1), he wrote "Trav. 2 tacet." in the score and changed the header from "due Trav" to "una Trav." The second staff (originally intended for the second flute) is now no longer needed and Bach is free to use it to sketch alternative versions of the first flute part, as in m. 9 (ex. 8.3). After drafting the opening measures of the flute

*Figure 8.1* Rejected sketch for BWV 248/31 (D-B Mus. ms. Bach P 32, fol. 31ᵛ) (bpk, Berlin/Mendelssohn-Archiv, Staatsbibliothek zu Berlin, Stiftung Preussischer Kulturbesitz, Berlin, Germany/Art Resource, NY)

part, and indicating that the first violin had to go colla parte with the flute, Bach begins to add the bc line but breaks it off after m. 12. The next step in the compositional process would have been to add a second violin, which would probably have moved a third below the upper voice. Then he would have added a viola part to fill out the harmony. But all these steps were not actually taken. Having broken off the bc after m. 12, Bach abandons the sketch altogether. The elimination of the second flute earlier in the work on the movement already indicates that Bach had doubts about the size of the instrumentation as it was now too massive to do justice to the intimate character of the text.[27] Bach decided instead to highlight the intimacy

[27] The second half of the ritornello was very vivid and might have been motivated by the idea of "movement" in the preceding gospel recit.

of the *inhabitatio Christi,* crossing out the entire sketch to begin over from scratch. Walter Blankenburg suggests that Bach might have deemed the lively 3/8 meter "inappropriate" for the text.[28] But this is not the case. We find a very similar movement, with almost the same text, a few years prior in another of Bach's Christmas cantatas, *Ehre sei Gott in der Höhe,* BWV 197a.[29] That aria is in 6/8 meter, stands in D major, and combines a siciliano opening with a fortspinnung with broken triads in sixteenth notes for the ritornello (ex. 8.4). When Bach embarked on composing the movement for the *Christmas Oratorio,* he clearly had something like the aria from BWV 197a in mind.[30] Thus, the sketch in the oratorio was not as inappropriate as Blankenburg suggests. Rather, Bach thought in 1734 that there was a better solution in this particular context.

*Example 8.4* J. S. Bach, *Ehre sei Gott in der Höhe* BWV 197a, mvt. 3: "Ich lasse dich nicht," mm 1–10

---

[28]  Blankenburg, *Weihnachts-Oratorium,* 86.

[29]  The piece was composed in 1728 or in one of the following years.

[30]  Another movement that shows a close resemblance to the rejected aria fragment from the *Christmas Oratorio* is the alto aria "Erbarme dich" from the *St. Matthew Passion* BWV 244. Both pieces feature a characteristic siciliano rhythm, stand in B minor, use repeated notes in the bc line, and introduce more vivid figurations in the second half of the ritornello. The longing affect of "Erbarme dich" is rather close to the mood of the text of "Schließe, mein Herze." It is clear that the siciliano rhythm itself did not motivate the rejection of the draft.

Even in the newly composed aria, Bach continues to reduce the instrumentation. In the abandoned sketch he had already eliminated the second flute. The new piece does not use the flute at all; instead, Bach employs unison violins, finally reducing the instrumentation to just one violin by changing the header from "Violini unisoni" to "Violini [*sic!*] solo." The large ensemble from the first sketch is finally condensed to a solo instrument. Bach also opted for a piece with a different character. Instead of a siciliano with outbreaks into extensive instrumental figuration, the composer develops a simpler, syncopated theme. Bach uses the terzet (no. 51) from part V of the *Christmas Oratorio* for a model. The terzet is, again, a parody from a secular cantata, and the terzet music already existed when Bach began to write the music for the "Schließe" aria. The texts of "Schließe" and the terzet, "Ach wenn wird," are related as both thematize the presence of Christ in the human heart. Bach borrows the syncopated opening motif from the terzet, as well as the broken triads in the second half of the ritornello, the accompaniment in short eighth notes, and even the key (B minor). This analysis will further show that the terzet influenced the aria, even in smaller details. What connects the two movements even more is the symbolic use of the alto as the voice that Bach employs to speak about Christ's presence in the heart. By designing the newly composed aria as a sister movement to the later terzet, Bach creates an aria pair that expresses a similar theological idea with analagous musical material, albeit with a different set of musical forces. Thus, it resembles the aria-pair "Schlafe" (no. 19) and "Herr, dein Mitleid" (no. 29) discussed earlier in this chapter. In both cases, Bach establishes a musical connection transcending the individual parts of the oratorio.[31]

The final version of the aria Bach composed for the *Christmas Oratorio* is a movement for alto, violin, and bc in modified *da capo* form. The A section is considerably longer than the compact B section. This emphasizes the opening two lines of the text and the "embracing of the miracle," while the three lines of the B section (presenting the benefits of this miracle) receive a less extensive treatment:

|   |       | ritornello    | b–> b   |
|---|-------|---------------|---------|
|   | 1–24  | ritornello    | b–> b   |
| A | 25–61 | vocal part I  | b–> f♯  |
|   | 61–72 | ritornello    | f♯–> f♯ |
| B | 73–98 | vocal part II | f♯–> f♯ |

---

[31] While Bach evidently creates unity by borrowing musical features from another movement in the oratorio, the musical features taken by themselves are, of course, not unique. A similar aria for alto, accompanied by a single instrumental line with a syncopated motif and accompanied by a bc line in short eighth-notes is the Agnus Dei from the *B-Minor Mass*, which in turn is a parody of the aria "Entfernt euch" from the lost wedding cantata *Auf, süß entzückende Gewalt*, BWV Anh. I 196, from 1725. That aria also served as a model for the alto aria "Ach bleibe doch" from the *Ascension Oratorio*, BWV 11, performed about six months after the *Christmas Oratorio*. What connects all these pieces is that they are all for alto and have an intimate, contemplative text.

|     | 99–102 | ritornello | b–> b |
| A'  | 103–34 | vocal part III | b–> b |
|     | 134–46 | ritornello | b–> b |

The vocal declamation is mostly syllabic or employs short, two-note motifs. By eschewing virtuosity, the vocalist underscores the intimacy of the text and thus continues the process of simplification visible in the compositional process. Within this context, the few melismatic lines are highlighted and even more powerful. They appear in the A section on the central term "Glauben" (faith) (mm. 31/32, 35, etc.) and in the B section on the contrasting terms "Stärke" (strengthening) (m. 78) and "schwachen" (weak) (mm. 89/90). Constitutive for the character of the aria is Bach's use of syncopations, which have already been introduced in the opening measures of the movement. The first motif begins with an eighth note on the first beat, gliding into a quarter note. This is developed in m. 3 and followed by another syncopation in mm. 4/5. The syncopations give the music a certain degree of viscosity and density, making the clear rhythmic flow seem always a bit stagnant. The text associated with the syncopations are "schließe," "selige," and "fest." Especially the words "fest" and "schließe" correlate with the impression of viscosity, as both of them express the closeness with which the human heart embraces the divine word (and thus the divine presence). The music embodies the tightness with which the heart holds Christ. If we take the metaphorical correlation between *inhabitatio* and Bach's setting one step further, we can see the viscosity of the music as a sonic representation of the metaphor of Jesus being "glued" to the heart, as it was described by some seventeenth-century theologians. While the syncopations represent the closeness and proximity of Christ and the human heart, the second coming of Christ, understood as *unio mystica*, is additionally represented by Bach's extensive use of unison between the voice and the solo instrument.[32] Four times throughout the aria (mm. 34–36, 54–58, 112–14, and 125–26) the two lines are briefly led in unison. The text of these unison moments is always "in deinem Glauben ein [schließe]" (hold fast in your faith). Considering the rarity of unison passages like this in Bach's arias and how easily they could have been avoided in this movement, it is clear that Bach used them intentionally to sonically denote the idea of unity. We have seen a similar technique in the duet from BWV 213, where Bach used voice-crossings between the two singers and the meeting of the two protagonists on one note as a signifier for their unification (and kissing).

"Schließe" is the only aria in the *Christmas Oratorio* that was written for this work in particular and is not a parody. The Bach's autograph score shows numerous traces

---

[32] This reading of the unison measures has already been suggested by Walter, *Weihnachtsoratorium*, 112–13.

of the compositional process and reflects details of his reasoning in composing this movement. It is worthwhile to trace some of his compositional steps to clearer understand the character of the aria. Robert Marshall has shown in his study of Bach's compositional process that Bach not only derives much of his musical material for his arias and choral movements from the opening ritornellos, but that the ritornelli also exhibit some of the heaviest compositional revisions.[33] This holds true for the opening measures of "Schließe" as well. The autograph score shows some work on the material of the ritornello and demonstrates that Bach worked on several instances to emphasize the syncopations that are characteristic for the movement. We also find several traces of influences of the terzet from part V. The first correction is encountered in the bc in m. 2. The first note was originally a *d*, which was then changed into B. While we can rule out that Bach was planning to have a D-major chord, it is likely that his original plan was a B-minor chord in first inversion, the same chord he had used in the terzet. However, he decided otherwise and corrected the note to B. A second correction in mm. 4/5 is more substantial (see ex. 8.5 for the original violin part).

*Example 8.5* J. S. Bach, BWV 248/31, versions of the violin part in mm. 1–7

The ritornello would have continued the eighth-note motion of the opening and then would have become static in m. 5. The revised version now turns the descending triad into a smooth sixteenth-note descent and adds the syncopation from m. 4 to m. 5, which in turn creates a rhythmic tension that drives the movement forward. The syncopation developed here will be an important feature in the following measures: mm. 5/6 (bc), 7/8 (bc), and 8/9 (violin). Bach thus prolongs the rhythmic tension and employs it as a central feature throughout the first half of the ritornello. The following measures consist mostly of sequential treatment of the material. The lack of major revisions or corrections clearly reveals that this task was quite straightforward for Bach. Further corrections appear in mm. 12/13 at the transition from the first to the second half of the ritornello. In its original version, the first half of the ritornello ended in the violin on an eighth note *d'*, followed by a quarter note *f♯"* and two descending sixteenth notes (see ex. 8.6). Bach then squeezed another measure

---

[33] Marshall, *Compositional Process of J.S. Bach*, 119–30.

of music into the violin line right after m. 11, by entering a half note on *d* (this he then changed into a quarter note followed by a quarter rest) and inserted a bar line separating this new final note of the first half of the ritornello from the ascent to *f♯''*. The upswing to *f♯''* thus now appears in the next measure, at the beginning of the second half of the ritornello. The two versions, the new m. 12 and the former m. 12 (*cum* 13), look very much alike (ex. 8.6). Now, however, the revision changes the character of the motif. In the original version, the opening *d'* is also the final note of the previous phrase and thus an endpoint for the first half of the ritornello. The *f♯''*, spatially and sonically disjunct from the previous note, might then be perceived as the first note of a new motif. By ending the previous phrase on *d'* in m. 12 and by beginning the following measure with the ascending gesture *d'–a'–f♯''*, Bach creates a motif that continues the syncopic energy of the first half of the ritornello; at the same time, it is a motif that expresses a feeling of longing (here for the coming of Christ). On a syntactic level, the change also guarantees a clearer separation of the two halves of the ritornello. Why did Bach originally plan a different version? He might have been influenced by the instrumental ritornello of the terzet. In mm. 12/13 of the terzet a sequential chain of broken triads ends on the first beat of m. 13 on a G-major chord, prepared by a seventh-chord in the bc. The *g'* in the violin is embellished but the listener has a clear sense of arrival on G. The ritornello then continues with a quarter note on the off beat, followed by a chain of sixteenth notes, quite like the second half of the ritornello in "Schließe, mein Herze."

*Example 8.6* J. S. Bach, BWV 248/31, versions of the violin part in what became mm. 13–15

A close connection with the terzet is also exemplified by a number of changes in m. 16. In the first half of the violin part, Bach originally wrote ♫♩ but then changed this during the composition into ♫♩. While the sharpening of a rhythmic phrase is a familiar feature in Bach's revisions during the compositional process, it again picks up a musical idea from the later movement. The version with two thirty-second notes would have resembled a similar motif in the terzet (mm. 13, 15, etc.). However, Bach does not repeat his use of the thirty-second-note motif again in the aria. He therefore reverted this change again in the part book for the violin (the change seems to be in Bach's own hand).[34] In other words, an idea from the terzet

---

[34]  See NBA II/6, KB, 279.

appears briefly but is then discarded. Bach's revisions in the ritornello for the aria show two things. First, several of the details in the musical material were not entirely worked out from the start; they took shape in the course of the compositional process. And second, the terzet from part V of the oratorio served as a model for the aria; not only in regard to some of the musical material but also in some compositional decisions, some of which were eventually rejected.

With the composition of the ritornello, Bach had developed the majority of the musical ideas that would carry the entire aria. Composing the beginning of the vocal part (m. 25) was therefore a straightforward task. The beginning of the A section is built into the opening measures of the instrumental introduction (*vokaleinbau*). Measures 25–28 in the alto are derived from mm. 1–4 from the ritornello, while mm. 5–14b from the ritornello are quoted in the violin at mm. 29–37b. The character of the compositional process is confirmed in the autograph score, as Bach does not have to make major corrections until m. 44.[35] The violin part in mm. 44–46 is almost illegible. Here, Bach made several revisions, erased notes, wiped out others, crossed out ideas, and clarified his intentions (at least in m. 46) by adding tabulature symbols. The moment at which these revisions occur is more important than a detailed reconstruction of the changes (which is impossible). Thus, we can see that the revisions in mm. 44–46 mark a crucial point in the development of the aria. Bach had left the technique of literal *vokaleinbau* a few measures earlier; he is now combining the material in a new way. Measure 44 serves as a transition to the final complete statement of the text of the A section, which now appears in F♯ minor. Additionally, Bach combines at m. 44 a version of the first ritornello motif with a variant of the second ritornello motif (the wide leap, m. 13). In other words, Bach increases the harmonic and motivic complexity in this last statement of the A-section text, which, even for a composer like Bach, made it necessary to work out the compositional problems. In spite of the overall illegibility of the measures in the violin, it is apparent that the second note in the violin in m. 45 was at one point a quarter note, just like the alto. In the final version, the part of the violin is changed into a fluent sixteenth-note motion, thus rendering the texture rhythmically more complex. The wish for a more complex texture was also the motivation for several revisions in mm. 48–50. In m. 48 Bach changed a descending triad of eighth notes in the violin into a scalar descending line of sixteenth notes, thus avoiding a rather static progression of eighth notes in all three voices. In the following measure he changed the progression in the bc line. The original notes are illegible, but it is clear that the composer erased an earlier version of the measure to change it into the version we have today. This is followed by changes in m. 50. The violin part in the second half of the measure originally had a simple line of sixteenth notes, descending

---

[35] The few changes are minimal and represent either corrections of mistakes (m. 31) or smaller details (m. 33 in alto, or 36 in violin).

from $f\sharp''$ to $c\sharp''$, which would have been a sequential repetition of the line in the first half of the measure. Instead, Bach changed it into a syncopated motif, which begins an entire chain of syncopations, increasing the rhythmic tension toward the end of the A section: mm. 50/51 (vl); 51/52 (A), and culminating in a unison passage for instrument and voice (mm. 54/55–58). The change in m. 50 harkens back to an earlier moment in the aria where a similar syncopation appears in mm. 28/29; the mm. 51–53 are indeed a transposed (and slightly modified) version of mm. 29–31.

The corrections and revisions in the autograph score reflect Bach's compositional process. The musical ideas are developed in the ritornello. When this material is reused without major changes, the handwriting is clean; if the harmonic development makes changes necessary, this can necessitate corrections. The same is true for those measures in which Bach wants to increase the motivic or rhythmic complexity of the music. Consequently, the instrumental interlude that separates the A and B sections of the aria shows several revisions. The compositional problem Bach had to solve (or rather, challenged himself to solve) was how to manipulate the motivic material from the opening ritornello to create a shortened version of the ritornello that could serve as a transition from section A to section B. The interlude begins as a transposed variant of the opening ritornello (now in F♯ minor); mm. 1–8 are almost identical with mm. 61–68. It looks as if Bach had experimented with his material in the violin in m. 64. The measure is mostly illegible due to smudges and crossed-out notes. Whatever Bach's plan was (eighth-note descent on C♯ triad?), the version that appears in the part book for the violin is simply a transposed version of the line Bach had already used in the opening ritornello.

Bach abandons the thematic content of the opening ritornello in the second half of m. 68 to compose a transition to the B section. It is at this point where we again find major corrections. In m. 69 he wrote an idea for the violin part (without the bc), then crossed out the entire measure and started afresh in the empty space of what would have been the following measure. He now also added a bc line, which was again corrected by erasing the original version (probably $b\sharp$ and $g\sharp$, changed into $f\sharp$ and $b$). Measure 70 shows massive corrections as well and would be almost completely illegible if it were not for some tabulature symbols Bach added to identify the notes.[36] The following measure begins with a smaller correction in the violin ($f\sharp'–a'$, changed into $a'–c\sharp''$) before the interlude ends with a descending scale (identical to the end of the opening ritornello). In spite of some motivic similarities with the A section, the B section of the aria posed a new compositional problem: the new text required the invention of fresh musical material. Numerous corrections and revisions document how Bach worked on his material. The alto in m. 74 originally had two sixteenth notes, followed by an eighth note; this version was erased and replaced with two sixteenth notes and a quarter note. This

---

[36] The bc voice was corrected by erasing an earlier version.

new motif not only resembles the syncopation at the beginning of the aria but it also accentuates the central word "Wunder" (marvel). Bach's changes in m. 78 are more extensive. The word "Stärke" was originally set with a simple, diatonic idea (Stär-ke: ♩ ♩);[37] but Bach then decided to compose a longer, melismatic line with larger leaps and syncopations, a type of voice-leading that resembles the material from the A section. The revision was made while he was working on the vocal part and before he wrote the violin part for this measure. This order of events is clearly visible in the score. The corrected notes called for ledger lines above the staff, and Bach did not have enough space to insert the notes for the violin at their proper place and thus had to shift them slightly to the left.[38]

Even though he had to make some corrections, Bach had a vision for how to compose the text for the B section. Ideas were flowing when he reached the end of the page . . . and he had to wait until the ink was dry. Lest he would forget how to continue, he wrote the continuation of the vocal line in an empty stave at the bottom of the page. The sketch (described by Marshall as "continuation sketch"[39]) is eight measures long (mm. 91–98) and contains both the music and the text. In the penultimate measure he originally wrote $a'$–$g'$–$f\sharp'$ but then changed to $f\sharp'$–$g'$–$f\sharp'$, the version that also appears on the final version of the movement. When Bach was able to turn the page, he copied the eight measures from the sketch and added the instrumental accompaniment. After writing down this version, he made a final revision by changing the rhythm of the alto part in m. 95. In his sketch as well as in the first version of the measure, the word "deines" is set with a syncopated motif: ♪ ♩ ♪, a rhythmic motif Bach had used twice before in the B section, with the word "Wunder" (m. 74) and with the word "Stärke" (m. 94). Bach smoothened the rhythmic flow and changed the syncopation into an even chain of eighth notes. Thus he avoided the repetition of the rhythmic motif from the measure immediately before and opted instead for a calmer version, which now leads into the final cadence of the B section. The opening measures (99–103) of the A′ section has no corrections as they are entirely based upon the opening ritornello. Also the A′ section overall has a lesser amount of revisions and corrections, and none of them affects the character of the musical material. Large parts of the A′ section are derived from the A section by voice-exchange between alto and violin. Only where Bach deviates from his model, as in mm. 115–20, the number of smaller corrections slightly increases (here especially in the bc); however, the revisions affect only small details and do not touch the spirit of motivic substance or the character of the voices.[40]

---

[37]  Cf. NBA II/6, KB, 53.

[38]  Another example where the violin part has to be squeezed in after the writing the vocal line is m. 82.

[39]  Marshall, *Compositional Process of J. S. Bach*, 141–47.

[40]  For m. 116–120 in the bc, see NBA II/6, KB, 54.

We have discussed this movement more extensively because it provides valuable insights into Bach compositional process: the way in which he shapes his ideas
in the ritornello, how he reuses and manipulates the material in the course of the
movement, and how sections of earlier material alternate with measures where the
musical development forces the composer to work out new musical solutions. That
all of this happens in this particular aria is no surprise, as the text encapsulates the
center of the meaning of Christmas, the *inhabitatio Christi*. The intimate character of
the movement, which was by itself the result of a complex process, went along with
an increasing reduction of the instrumental forces. The result is an aria that reflects
the intimacy of the *unio mystica*. Bach captures this mystic unity in the unison measures, encountered twice in the A section and twice in the A′ sections. The aria text
expresses the wish for Christ's presence in the human heart: it does not talk about
his actual presence. (The fulfillment is postponed until the terzet in part V of the
oratorio, when the soprano and tenor ask when "He" would finally appear, to which
the alto replies, "he really is already here!")

The aria is followed by a short alto recit, "Ja, ja, mein Herz soll es bewahren,"
no. 32, confirming that the heart will indeed safeguard what it has learned and seen.
In this accompagnato recit the alto is supported by simple, extended chords in the
traverse flutes, the same instruments Bach had used for the first accompagnato recit
in this part of the oratorio (no. 27). At no. 32 Bach accidentally wrote a bass clef
for the vocalist and then changed it to an alto clef (the first accompagnato recit did
indeed feature the bass). Did Bach plan to set this recit for bass as well and then
changed his mind? Keeping with his usual compositional practice, he would have
entered the clefs for the singer and the instruments first, and then added the text.
Only after these preparatory steps (possibly at a later point) would he have composed the music. While it is possible that Bach intended to assign the recit again to
the bass voice, it is more likely that he simply made a mistake, as the text for the recit
is of the kind that is typically given to the alto voice. And in addition, it is theologically very different from the first recit in part III.[41]

The simple four-part setting of "Ich will dich mit Fleiß bewahren,"[42] ends this
sequence of movements that had begun with the arrival of the shepherds at the

---

[41] Hans-Joachim Schulze (*Die Bach-Kantaten*, 639) has suggested that Bach might have changed
the order of the movements in this part of the oratorio. Viewing the aria and the recit as a unity, he
assumes that the original order had been the usual sequence of recit and aria, which was inverted by
Bach to bring the aria closer to the biblical text to which it refers, and the recit closer to the following
chorale, with which it has some theological connections. While Schulze's assumption is justified by
the convention of having an aria preceded by a recit (a convention that Bach maintains frequently in
his works), there is no evidence that he did change the order of the two movements in this case. The
printed libretto presents the two movements in the same order as the score, and the textual connections between biblical narrative and aria text on the one hand, and the recit and the chorale on the
other are much easier explained if they were intended by the librettist.

[42] Stanza 15 of Paul Gerhard's hymn "Fröhlich soll mein Herze springen."

manger and Mary's keeping in her heart all the things she had seen and heard. The chorale now represents the response of the Christian congregation; a commitment to diligently keep Christ in their hearts as well, not only now in this life but in the hour of death and "in the other life." In other words, to safeguard Christ in their hearts at his Second Coming and to be with him ("hover" with him,[43] as the text says) at his third coming. As shown in chapter 3, the hymn stanza brings to a close the sequence of movements that ran the gamut from the First Coming (in the biblical narrative) to the Third Coming at the end of times. Bach's setting of the chorale stanza is simple yet not without some harmonic intricacies, like the chromatic descent in m. 2 on "Fleiß bewahren" (*a–ab–g*) in the bass line, immediately followed by a chromatic ascent in mm. 3/4 on "ich will dir" (*g–g♯–a*), which is later (m. 9) repeated (though under a different harmony) on "schweben" (hover). These chromatic lines indeed give the movement a "hovering" quality.

Part III of the oratorio continues with a short gospel recit (no. 34), reporting that the shepherds returned and praised God for everything they had heard and seen. The text shifts the focus again, now back to the historical narrative and to praise as the human answer to the divine revelation. The tenor reaches its highest note on the word "preiseten" (praised) with an upward leap of an octave, and it is this idea of praise that is the focus in the following two movements: the setting of the chorale stanza "Sei froh dieweil" and the final chorus "Herrscher des Himmels," which is the repetition of the opening chorus. The chorale text is the fourth stanza of Christoph Runge's hymn "Laßt Furcht und Pein," a hymn that did not appear in contemporary Leipzig hymnals, as Walter Blankenburg had pointed out.[44] Bach's librettist chose the text because it expresses joy and praise starting in its opening line, "Be joyful meanwhile." It then moves on to summarize the reason for this joy, the salvation through the God who had become man in the city of David. While the text was ideal for this purpose, the hymn posed a difficulty for Bach, as shown earlier. The F♯-minor melody did not lend itself to the type of expanded chorale setting Bach had composed to end the first two parts of the oratorio, and it certainly did not provide a proper basis for a celebratory setting that could have balanced the opening movement of part III. Thus Bach decided to repeat the opening movement instead, which gave this third part a balanced frame and made it possible to close it in the celebratory key of D major. The limitations of the chorale melody notwithstanding, Bach's setting does still project the joyful character of the text. An ascending melisma on "froh" in the first full measure in the bass voice already captures the affect of the text. And the eighth-note motion in the bass, which increasingly

---

[43] Michael Marissen has pointed out that this chorale line refers to a verse from Isaiah 58:14: "Then you will have delight in the Lord, and I will have you hover over the heights of the earth . . . for the mouth of the Lord has spoken it." Marissen, *Bach's Oratorios*, 14, fn. 40.

[44] Blankenburg, *Weihnachts-Oratorium*, 90.

permeates the other voices, underscores this joyful affect. The setting culminates in the final line ("unsre Wohlfahrt befestiget steht"/our welfare has been confirmed). The simple melodic line is accompanied with a *gradatio* in the bass voice,[45] a gradually ascending line that chromatically inches up from *f♯* to *c♯*, thus endowing the final line of the hymn with additional harmonic tension.

## A celebratory frame (mvt. 24)

Part III of the *Christmas Oratorio* is framed by the choral movement only loosely connected to the major theological themes of this part. The word "Wohlfahrt" (welfare) corresponds to the topic of salvation in the first half of part III, while the word "Herzen" (heart) resonates with the *inhabitatio Christi* in both halves. Overall, though, the text and the character of the music reflect the general affect of praise. The more introspective, centripetal trajectory of the core movements of part III is balanced by the extroverted framing movement(s). Within the narrative framework of the oratorio, the opening movement utters the praise that is expressed in the final gospel recit: "Die Hirten . . . preiseten und lobten Gott" (The shepherds . . . praising and lauding God).[46] The text of the framing movement admonishes the listener to praise God with psalms, and interestingly, the text itself is, as Martin Petzoldt has shown, primarily constructed from psalm verses.[47] Bach probably did not recognize this. In spite of the psalm-based text, he repeatedly wrote the text incorrectly and penned "Palmen" (palm branches) instead of "Psalmen" (psalms). The wrong text here would not have been entirely out of place as the praise of Jesus with palm branches features prominently in the story of Jesus arrival in Jerusalem on Palm Sunday. The story was not only part of the Passion narrative but was also one of the readings for the first Sunday in Advent.[48] Bach's erroneous version would have emphasized the "coming" of Christ, whereas the correct text highlights the praise of Jesus through songs from the Old Testament. However, the praise is inadequate, as the text expresses; it is "Lallen." The verb denotes the inarticulate speaking and often refers to babbling, the attempts to speak by young children.[49] It then is a reversal of roles when the Christian community greets the newborn Jesus by highlighting

[45] This was already remarked on by Blankenburg, *Weihnachts-Oratorium*, 92, and Walter, *Weihnachtsoratorium*, 115.

[46] Martin Petzoldt, *Bach-Kommentar*, 2:237, has already pointed out this connection. Petzoldt rejects Walter Blankenburg's notion that the final gospel recit was only an unimportant detail, see Blankenburg, *Weihnachts-Oratorium*, 76.

[47] Petzoldt, *Bach-Kommentar*, 2:235.

[48] Gottfried Ephraim Scheibel's cantata for the first Sunday in Advent (1725), for instance, features an opening movement that ends with the line, "Bestreut ihm zu Ehren mit Palmen die Bahn"; see Scheibel, *Poetische Andachten*, 1.

[49] Cf. Petzoldt, *Bach-Kommentar*, 2:239.

their own linguistic infancy. The use of the verb was not unique to the libretto of the oratorio. It is encountered occasionally in texts related to the Christmas feast. In Paul Thymich's libretto *Hirten-Freude* from 1685 the shepherds have the following dialogue while they are on their way to the manger:

| | |
|---|---|
| AB[EL] Geht doch ein wenig leise | ABEL Walk a bit quietly |
| L[ABAN] Hier ist die Davids Stadt / | LABAN Here is David's city / |
| AB[EL] Und hier der Stall / | ABEL And here is the stable / |
| JAC[OB] Der Himmel auff der Erden / . . . | JACOB Heaven on earth / . . . |
| DAV[ID] Ach! Liebes Jesulein hör unser | DAVID Ah! Dear little Jesus, hear |
| Lallen[50] | our babbling |

The cantata for the feast of Epiphany in Gottfried Scherzer's *Texte zur Kirchen Music* in Gera from 1722 (Leipzig) features an aria that uses a similar image: "Jesus nimmt mein hertzlich Lallen / Und ein gläubig Niederfallen/von betrübten Sündern an." (Jesus, takes my heartfelt babble, and a faithful prostrating, from the distressed sinner).[51] Johann Sebastian Bach's setting, however, is anything but inarticulate. It is a vivid and festive choral movement in ritornello form, rhythmically resembling dances in fast triple meter like gigue or passepied.[52] Like a dance movement, the texture of the chorus is simple and the harmonies mostly alternate between tonic and dominant. The chorus is the parody of the final movement of the secular cantata BWV 214.[53] The structure of the movement resembles a concerto, juxtaposing homophonic ritornello sections and episodes with lighter textures:

| | | | |
|---|---|---|---|
| | 1–16 | Ritornello I | D–> A |
| A | 17–32 | vocal "solo" part I | D–> D |
| | 33–48 | vocal ritornello I | D–> A |
| | 49–64 | Ritornello II | A–> D |
| B | 65–80 | vocal "solo" part II | D–> A |
| | 81–96 | vocal ritornello II | A–> D |

Bach does not differentiate between soli and tutti in this movement. But even without such a differentiation, the "solo" sections are distinguished by their lighter,

---

[50] Thymich, *Hirten-Freude*, 16.

[51] Scherzer, *Texte zur Kirchen-Music*, 26.

[52] Cf. Walter, *Weihnachtsoratorium*, 106; Finke-Hecklinger, *Tanzcharaktere*, 96; and Little/Jenne, *Dance and the Music of J. S. Bach*, 289 and 306.

[53] The original text begins as "Blühet, ihr Linden in Sachsen, wie Zedern" (Blossom, you lindens, in Saxony, like cedars).

polyphonic texture and a reduced instrumentation. The (virtual) differentiation in soli and tutti section and the bipartite AB structure describe the movement only in part. The entire movement is derived from a motivic idea presented in the first four measures. The first two solo sections juxtapose variants of the motif in a polyphonic dialogue between the three upper voices. The first vocal ritornello (mm. 33–48) is derived through *vokaleinbau* from the instrumental ritornello. The second instrumental ritornello presents a modified version of the opening motif; it now appears in descending direction, a version of the opening motif that had already been used by the tenor in the first solo episode. The second vocal ritornello is then consequently created through *vokaleinbau* from the second instrumental ritornello. Thus, the movement could also be called monothematic or it could be identified as a modified *da capo* form without the contrasting middle part.

Bach was able to use the model composition from the secular cantata without significant revisions. Two changes, which were necessitated by the new text, affect the musical texture and appear at the end of the vocal ritornelli.[54] While the meter and rhyme scheme in the model and the sacred parody were the same, the syntactic structure was slightly different. The original text ends in line 3 with a phrase is four syllables long ("lebe auch lang") whereas the final phrase in the sacred text is one syllable longer ("mit Psalmen erhöht"). This difference not only makes necessary a modification of the vocal texture but also gives Bach the opportunity to change the voice-leading. The lively melisma on "lebe" (mm. 46/47) in the soprano is turned into a simple long note on "Psalmen." Although the "lively" melisma had been motivated by the text, it was not necessary to make the change since the word "Psalmen" would have worked perfectly with either version. Textual necessity and esthetic improvement go again hand in hand. Bach made a similar change at the end of the second vocal ritornello (mm. 93–96), where he had to transform a phrase of four syllables ("lebe noch lang") into one that could accommodate five syllables ("befestiget steht"). In both cases Bach reuses as much material as possible, lifting lines from one voice to another, as in mm. 45/46 where the tenor takes over parts of the soprano voice while he composes a new line for the soprano.

The final movement of part III ended the first half of the *Christmas Oratorio* and also concluded the parts that were written for the three days of Christmas. The praise expressed in the final movement grows directly out of the message of the last gospel recit (no. 34), which had reported that the shepherds left the manger and praised God. On a larger scale, the movement also serves as a counterpart for the opening chorus of part I of the oratorio, as it returns to the key, meter, and celebratory brass of the first movement.

---

[54] The changes in the continuo in mm. 37/38 are only corrections of writing mistakes and are not compositional revisions.

# | 9 |

# "What's in a Name?" (Part IV)

## Understandings of January 1

Liturgical traditions in early-modern Lutheran Germany saw a plethora of ways to celebrate the first day of January. The day could be observed as the beginning of the New Year, as a commemoration of the circumcision of the newborn Jesus,[1] or as a celebration of the naming of Jesus. The theologian Martin Moller in his *Praxis Evangeliorum* from 1601 differentiates between these three modes:

| | |
|---|---|
| Zum ersten/Wie wir recht Christlich das Neue Jahr anheben sollen. | Firstly, how we properly and Christianly should begin the New Year. |
| Zum andern / von der Beschneidung des HErrn Christi. | Secondly, about the circumcision of the Lord Christ. |
| Zum dritten / von dem hochtröstlichen Namen JEsus.[2] | Thirdly, about the highly consoling name of Jesus. |

The beginning of the secular year on January 1 was generally celebrated as a day of "thanksgiving and prayer." Johann Joachim Neudorf wrote that it was a day of thanksgiving for the blessings of the bygone year, an occasion for repentance for the sins committed during the year, and a day of prayer for the year to come. He described it as a day to give thanks for the spiritual and material blessings received

---

[1] The circumcision traditionally took place eight days after the birth of a child; with December 25 designated as the birthday of Jesus, January 1 was the logical date for his circumcision.

[2] Martin Moller, *Praxis Evangeliorum, Das ist: Einfältige Erklärung und nützliche Betrachtung der Evangelien . . . Erster Theil. Vom Advent biß auff Laetare* (Lüneburg: Johann Stern, 1651), 94; see also Steiger, *Gnadengegenwart*, 179.

by God, including both the sacred authorities as well as the secular authorities (city, school, government, dukes, princes, and the emperor), which are understood as being instituted by God to provide the framework for the well-being of all.[3] The tenor of the day was praise, as the preacher at Leipzig's St. Nicholas's Church, Romanus Teller, explained in a sermon published in 1720.[4] After touching briefly on the gospel for New Year's Day, Teller based his sermon on verses from Psalm 34. The exegesis highlights the celebratory character of the day:

Der gantze 34. Psalm schickt sich sehr wohl zum anfange des neues Jahres. Denn es ist solches 1. ein überaus schöner Lob- und Danck-Psalm. Also fängt er sich an: **Ich will den HErren loben allezeit / Sein Lob soll immerdar in meinem Munde seyn. Meine Seele soll sich rühmen des HErrn / daß die Elenden hören und sich freuen. Preiset mit mir den HErrn / un[d] laßt uns miteinander seinen Nahmen erhöhen.** Wan könte doch uns und allen rechschaffenen Christen besser anstehen, da wir nun wieder durch GOttes Gnade ein altes Jahr glücklich überlebet, und unter GOttes Schutz und Seegen das Neue angefangen haben, als daß wir GOtt für allen Dingen recht hertzlich loben für die grosse Wohlthat, die Er uns bisher erwiesen, da daß wir einander recht auffordern und ermuntern zu solchem Lobe und Preise GOttes.[5]

The entire psalm 34 is very appropriate for the beginning of the new year, because (1) it is an extremely beautiful psalm of praise and thanksgiving. It begins thus: '**I will praise the Lord always. His praise shall be in my mouth at all times. My soul shall boast of the Lord, so that the distressed shall hear it and be happy. Praise with me the Lord, and let us elevate his name together.**' What would be more fitting for us and for all honest Christians, now that we have survived another year and begin a new one under God's protection and blessing, than to praise God (more than anything else) with all our heart for the great blessings he has afforded us? Therefore, we ask and encourage each other to praise and to glorify God.

[3] Neudorf, *Christlicher Unterricht*, 140, 141, 144.

[4] Teller served as Bach's confessor after 1736; for Teller and his relationship to Bach, see Martin Petzoldt, "Johann Sebastian Bach in theologischer Interaktion: Persönlichkeiten in seinem beruflichen Umfeld," in *Über Leben, Kunst, und Kunstwerke: Aspekte musikalischer Biographie. Johann Sebastian Bach im Zentrum*, ed. Christoph Wolff (Leipzig: Evangelische Verlagsanstalt, 1999), 154–55.

[5] Romanus Teller, *Der grosse Unterscheid zwischen den Gerechten und Gottlosen, zum theil aus denen ordentlichen Sonn- und Fest-Tags-Evangeliis, grösten theils aber aus hierzu auserlesenen . . . Sprüchen/ Vorgetragen* (Leipzig: Braun, 1720), 173.

The celebration of the New Year as a reason for praise is a constant element in sermons and cantata libretti for that day. A second focus of the celebrations was the commemoration of the circumcision of Jesus. The circumcision, mentioned in the gospel for the day, was commonly reinterpreted from a Christian perspective.[6] The sermons for the day frequently elaborated on the relationship between circumcision and baptism, both rites of passage for the introduction of a child into the religious community. Aegidus Strauch, a pastor in Danzig, wrote that baptism replaced circumcision in the Christian tradition.[7] Similarly, the Leipzig pastor Martin Geier preached in the 1660s about circumcision as a sign for the old covenant that was superseded by baptism, a symbol for the new covenant.[8] In a sermon from 1662, Johann Michael Dillherr, preacher and professor of theology in Nuremberg, drew the following connection between circumcision, baptism, and naming:

Gleichwie die Kindlein / in dem Alten Testament / bei der Beschneidung / ihren Nahmen bekamen / und sich dabei deß Bundes / den GOTT / in der Beschneidung / mit ihnen / gemacht hatte / erinnern mussten: also bekommen auch wir / In dem Neuen Testament / in der H. Tauff / die/an statt der Beschneidung / ist eingesetzet worden / unsere Nahmen; und sollen uns dabei auch deß Bundes / den GOTT / in der H. Tauff / mit uns / gemacht hat / erinnern.[9]

Like the children who, in the Old Testament, received their name during the circumcision and who are reminded in that circumcision of the covenant God had made with them, in the same way, we receive our name in holy baptism, which was instituted in the New Testament instead of the circumcision; and we should be reminded of the covenant God has made with us in the holy baptism.

A second aspect in sermons from this era that emphasize the circumcision of Jesus is the detail that the ritual is the first time that Jesus sheds blood, albeit only a few

---

[6] As Luther points out in his *Hauspostille*, for a Christian the circumcision only could have a symbolic and metaphorical meaning; see Luther, *Hauspostille*, col. 104.

[7] Aegidius Strauch, *Starcke und Milch-Speise, Hiebevor der Christlichen Gemeine daselbst in hundert sechs und siebentzig Sonn- und Fest-Tags-Predigten vorgetragen*, 2nd. enl. ed. (Leipzig: Gleditsch, 1702), 116. In a sermon published in 1727, the preacher at the Ritterakademie Copenhagen, Franz Julius Lütgens, similarly stressed that Christian baptism replaced the Jewish circumcision as a rite of passage. Lütkens, *Geistreiche und erbauliche Evangelium-Predigten* (Leipzig: Campen, 1727) 193.

[8] Geier, *Zeit und Ewigkeit*, 183.

[9] Johann Michael Dillherr, *Heilsame Beschneidung / und Tröstliche Benahmsung unsers liebsten Christkindleins: In der ordentlichen Neu-Jahrs-Predigt / Aus dem Evangelisten Luca 2. Cap. v. 21. Gezeiget*, (Nürnberg: Endter, 1662), 15.

drops, which some preachers interpreted as a symbolic foreshadowing of the shedding of Jesus's blood at the cross. Heinrich Müller calls the drops of blood a deposit ("Angeld") for the salvation in the crucifixion.[10] A similar interpretation is suggested by Erdmann Neumeister in a sermon for the Feast of Circumcision from 1714.[11] Most preachers, while drawing the connection between the bloodshed during the circumcision and the crucifixion then move on to elaborate on the salvific meaning of Christ's blood and his sacrifice, thus integrating Jesus's rite of passing into salvation history.[12] This view of the circumcision can be found in Salomon Deyling's outline of a sermon for New Year's Day preached at Leipzig's St. Nicholas's Church in January 1, 1734, one year before the performance of part IV of the *Christmas Oratorio*:

1. **Die Glaubens-Lehre:** Die Quelle alles Heyls kanst du in JEsu finden, ergreiff sein theures Blut, das macht dich rein von Sünden.

2. **Die Lebens-Pflicht:** Soll diese neue Zeit dir seyn ein Jahr der Freuden, so mach dein Hertze neu, und laß dich heut beschneiden.

3. **Der Glauben-Trost:** Wenn du wirst Christi Blut in wahren Glauben fassen, solst du gesegnet seyn, der HErr will dich nicht lassen.[13]

1. **The doctrine of faith:** You can find the source of all salvation in Jesus; embrace his precious blood, which cleanses you from sin.

2. **The duty in life:** If this new time shall be a joyful year for you, then renew your heart and let it be circumcised today.

3. **The consolation of faith:** If you do grasp the blood of Christ in true faith, you shall be blessed, the Lord will not abandon you.

Although the complete sermon is not extant, it is clear that the blood of Christ was the focus, and Deyling would certainly have drawn a connection between the blood

---

[10]   Müller, *Schlußkette*, Festteil, 70. A similar connection is drawn in the Calov Bible that Bach had owned since 1733, see Abraham Calov, *Das Neue Testament / verdeutschet durch D. Martin Luthern*, 437.

[11]   Erdmann Neumeister, *Priesterliche Lippen in Bewahrung der Lehre; Das Ist: Sonn- und Festtags-Predigten durchs gantze Jahr* (Leipzig/Görlitz: Laurentius, 1714), 192. The sermon for New Year's Day by Johann Gottfried Olearius from 1669 takes a similar position: "Ferner schencket uns der HErr JEsus auch seine Heilige erste Blutströpflein / welche Er bey seiner Schmertzlichen Beschneidung zum Angeld unser Erlösung / fliessen lassen" (Further does the Lord Jesus grant us his holy, first drops of blood, which were shed during his painful circumcision as a deposit on our salvation). Olearius, *Geistliches Seelen-Paradies und Lust-Garten, des allerheiligsten Lebens Jesu Christi unseres hochgelobten Herrn und Heylandes: Darinnen Die Geheimnüsse solches Lebens, in 24. Capiteln kürtzlich und erbaulich betrachtet, Wie auch vermittelst so viel schöner meistentheils Biblischer Gewächse und Blumen anmuthig fürgestellet und in schöne Kupfer abgebildet, Und zu Erweckung schuldiger Dancksagung mit Gebeten und Gesängen andächtig angewendet werden* (Nürnberg: Hoffmann, 1669), 80.

[12]   See, for instance, Moller, *Praxis Evangeliorum*, 148–50.

[13]   Salomon Deyling, *Herrliche Dinge in der Stadt Gottes gepredigt* (Leipzig, 1734), 6.

during the circumcision and the blood at the cross. The second section also referred to the image of the circumcision of the heart, another image frequently employed by preachers at that time.[14] A cantata libretto by Bach's Weimar librettist, Salomo Franck, employed extensive use of the blood metaphor. The text was published in Franck's *Evangelische Sonn- und Fest-Tages-Andachten* (1717), a collection that includes texts set by Bach while he was in Weimar. The text for New Year's (which was, as far as we know, not set by Bach), includes the following aria:

| | |
|---|---|
| Komm, komm mein Hertz, und eile mit Verlangen, | Come, come my heart, and hurry with desire |
| Die kostbarsten Bluts-Tropffen aufzufangen, | To capture the most precious drops of blood |
| Die itzt dein JEsulein so milde läßt von seinem Leibgen fliessen. [15] | Which now flow most generously[16] From the little body of your Jesus. |

The third focus of the New Year's Day festivities is the naming of Jesus. Interpreters view the name of Jesus as the essence of his being. Martin Luther had already emphasized the importance of the name in his *Hauspostille*: "von dem Namen JEsu, von welchem der Evangelist das sonderlich meldet, wie er vom Engel ernennet sei, ehe denn das Kind im Mutterleib empfangen ist. Darum muß an solchem Namen sehr viel gelegen sein" (about the name of Jesus, about whom the evangelist announces, how he was named by the angel, even before he was conceived in the womb. Therefore, the name must be of particular significance).[17] And he continues in a second sermon:

| | |
|---|---|
| Nun heißt aber der Name JEsus auf Deutsch, wie wir eigentlich reden und sagen, als viel als ein Heiland. . . . Diesen Namen laßt uns mit Fleiß lernen und merken, daß dies Kindlein | The name Jesus means in German, the language we speak, "Savior." . . . Let us diligently learn this name and remember that this little child is called Jesus and that he is a savior |

---

[14] For instance in Strauch, *Starcke und Milch-Speise*, 116–19; or Müller, *Schlußkette*, Festteil, 69.

[15] Salomo Franck, *Evangelische Sonn- und Fest-Tages-Andachten . . . / in Geistlichen Arien erwecket* (Weimar/Jena: Bielcke, 1717), 13.

[16] The literal translation of the German word "milde" would be "tenderly, but the eighteenth-century meaning of the term is closer to the English word "generously." See the discussion of the meanings in Michael Marissen, "Historically Informed Rendering of the Librettos from Bach's Church Cantatas," in *Music and Theology: Essays in Honor of Robin Leaver on his Sixty-fifth Birthday*, ed. Daniel Zager (Lanham: MD: Scarecrow Press, 2007), 103–20, esp. 113–15. I'm grateful to Michael Marissen for pointing me to this article.

[17] Luther, *Hauspostille*, col. 103–4.

JEsus heiße und sei ein Heiland,
der von dem höchsten und größten
Jammer, nämlich, von Sünden helfe,
und nicht von der Noth und losen
Anfechtung, die dies Leben mitbringt.
(Luther, col. 114–15)

who liberates us from the highest and
greatest pain, from sin; [he does not
liberate us] from need and temptation,
which are just part of life.

His name identified "Jesus" as the savior. Johann Jacob Rambach writes in a similar vein, emphasizing that both the human and divine nature of Jesus are unified in the person and the name of Christ:

Fliesset aus dieser Bedeutung, daß der
Sohn GOTTES unaufhörlich willig
sey, uns zu helfen. Hat er sich mit
der menschlichen Natur persönlich
vereiniget, und sich mit dieser
armen und geringen Braut so innig
verbunden, daß er auch so gar ihre
Schwachheiten mit angenommen.[18]

We can deduce from this meaning
[of the name] that the son of God is
incessantly eager to help us. He has
unified his person with human nature
and has joined himself with the poor
and humble bride so tightly that he has
also assimilated her weaknesses [into
his person].

It is essential for Rambach's understanding that the name not only symbolizes his essence but also underscores his human nature. Furthermore, Rambach introduces the image of the bride, which connects his theology of the name of Jesus with the idea of mystic unity. The knowledge of the name and the calling of the name establishes a close, intimate relationship between the caller and the called. A second title (or name) for Jesus is "Immanuel," "God with us," (Isa 7 and 8), and the two names are typically used synonymously. Rambach explains the proper use and understanding of the names by differentiating between four points: (1) The name highlights and reminds us of the separation between God and the sinful mankind; (2) The name consoles and is a defense against the devil.

Der dritte Gebrauch, daß die Seele
ihrem im Glauben ergriffenen
Immanuel das Hertz zur Wohnung
einräumet, daß aus demselben eine

The third way of using [the name of
Jesus] is that the soul may faithfully
give her heart to Immanuel as a
dwelling place. . . .

---

[18] Johann Jacob Rambach, *Betrachtungen über das Evangelium Esaiä: von der Geburt Jesu Christi, Cap. IX, 6 wie auch über dessen trost-vollen Namen Immanuel* 3rd. ed. (Halle: Waisenhaus, 1729), 130. Rambach's first edition appeared in 1724.

Hütte GOttes werden möge. . . . Den vierten Gebrauch, daß sie den Namen ihres Immanuels zu einer Losung gebrauchet gegen ihre Feinde. . . . Hier ist Immanuel, der mir ist grösser als der in der Welt ist. Rüstet sich gegen sie der Satan, und will ihr GOtt als einen Feind vorstellen, so spricht sie: Hier ist Immanuel, der mich mit GOtt versöhnet hat. Zeiget sich der Tod in seiner fürchterlichen gestalt, so erschrickt sie nicht, denn ihr Immanuel hat dem Tode die Macht genommen. (Rambach, 138–40)

The fourth way of using [the name] is to employ the name as a defense [literally: watchword] against their enemies. . . . Here is Immanuel who is greater than the one who is in the world [the devil]. If Satan prepares for onslaught [on the faithful] and attempts to present God as their enemy, she [the soul] replies: "Here is Immanuel who has reconciled me with God." If death presents himself in his most threatening form, she [the soul] is not startled because her Immanuel has taken the power away from death.

Rambach establishes a close connection between the name "Immanuel" and the idea of *inhabitatio*. He also introduces the idea of the name being a defense against enemies and in the hour of death.[19] We will see later in our discussion of the text for part IV of the *Christmas Oratorio* that these concepts play an essential role for Bach's libretto as well. Even more essential than the fearfulness of the name of Jesus (or Immanuel) is its pleasantness for those who are willing to follow him. This idea of the "sweetness" of the name of Jesus had already been developed in the sermons by Bernard of Clairvaux, as so many aspects of the understanding of Christmas in Bach's time were. Heinrich Müller quotes a passage from Bernard's fifteenth sermon on the Song of Songs, praising Jesus as "mel in ore, melos in aure, in corde jubilus" (honey in the mouth, melody in the ear, a jubilee in the heart).[20]

Finally, the knowledge of the name provides the believer with power over the divine son. In an exegesis of the gospel for the fourteenth Sunday after Trinity (Lk 17:11–19), Müller gives the following account of the authority of the name of Jesus. While he is referring to a different gospel text, the connection to the gospel for the first day of the year is evident:

Kurtz / aber doch kräfftig. JESU. Dieser sein Tauffname zeichnet sein

Short but powerful. Jesus. This name, given in his baptism, signifies his

---

[19]  For a similar idea, see also Müller, *Schlußkette*, Festteil, 77.

[20]  Müller, *Schlußkette*, Festteil, 77; Rambach quotes from Bernard's sermon no. 15 on the Song of Songs; for a modern edition of the text, see Bernard of Clairvaux, *Sermones super Cantica canticorum* 19.7, ed. J. Leclercq, C. H. Talbot, and H. M. Rochais, in *S. Bernardi opera* 1 (Rome, 1957), 112.

Hertz. Voll Heyls der Name / das
Hertz voll Heyls. Ein Heyland heisst
/ ein Heyland ist er/und ist in keinem
andern Heyl / als in ihm. Wann ich
meinen Jesum nenne / so nenne ich
das eintzige Heyl meiner Seelen. JESU
/ du heisst ein Heyland / wollen sie
sagen / so heile; ein Helffer heisst du
/ so hilff uns auch. Sein Name muß
ihn zwingen.[21]

heart. The name is full of salvation,
the heart is full of salvation. He is
called a savior and he is a savior. There
is salvation in nobody but him. When
I call [the name of] my Jesus, then
I call upon the only salvation of my
soul. Jesus, you are named the savior,
so they say: then save [literally: heal];
you are named a helper, so do help us.
His name has to compel him [to save].

The different facets of the celebration of New Year's Day—praise, circumcision, and naming—although theologically distinct, they are not mutually exclusive. They are often combined in both sermons and texts for church music. Most of the preachers quoted earlier touch on a number of aspects of the day. Bach's cantatas for New Year's Day typically cover several of the aspects as well. We frequently find the sacred meaning of the day mentioned along with an invocation of the blessings for the government. The cantata *Singet dem Herrn ein neues Lied*, BWV 190, (1724) begins with a praise of God, quoting the German *Te Deum* ("Herr Gott, dich loben wir"), a hymn often associated with political celebrations.[22] The "secular" aspect becomes more explicit in mvt. 6 of that cantata, a recit for tenor: "May Jesus bless church and school, may he bless all faithful teachers . . . may he bless [town] council and seat of judgment."[23] And the final hymn adds blessings for the "fatherland." Side by side with this celebration of January 1 as the beginning of the new, secular year stands an invocation of the name of Jesus in a duet for tenor and bass, aria no. 5:

Jesus soll mein alles sein,
Jesus soll mein Anfang bleiben
Jesus is mein Freudenschein,
Jesus will ich mich verschreiben.
Jesus hilft mir durch sein Blut,
Jesus macht mein Ende gut.

Jesus shall be my all,
Jesus shall be my starting-point,
Jesus is my light of joy,
To Jesus will I assign myself.
Jesus aids me through his blood,
Jesus makes my end good.

---

[21] Here quoted after Steiger, *Gnadengegenwart*, 179.

[22] Rathey, "'Singet dem Herrn ein neues Lied' (BWV 190)," 287–301. For a theological interpretation of the cantata within the context of the liturgical and theological understanding of New Year's Day, see Jochen Arnold, *Von Gott poetisch-musikalisch reden. Gottes verborgenes und offenbares Handeln in Bachs Kantaten* (Göttingen: Vandenhoeck & Ruprecht, 2009), 405–22.

[23] "Es segne Jesus Kirch und Schul, er segne alle treue Lehrer . . . Er segne Rat und Richterstuhl."

The cantata covers all three aspects of New Year's Day. The most veiled allusion is to the aspect of circumcision. The word "verschreiben" (line 4) refers to the covenant (and thus to baptism and circumcision), and the reference to the "blood" in the penultimate line resonates with the idea that the blood Jesus shed during the circumcision was foreshadowing his death at the cross. The cantata for the following year, BWV 41 (1725), is part of the chorale cantata cycle, and so the text is thus closely linked to the hymn "Jesu, nun sei gepreiset." Here, the focus is on the praise of God for the blessings of the bygone year, combined with a plea for protection in the coming year.[24] In the New Year's cantata from 1729, *Gott, wie dein Name, so ist auch dein Ruhm*, BWV 171, the librettist again highlights the salvific and consolatory qualities of the name of Jesus: "You sweet Name of Jesus, in you is my repose, you are my comfort on earth" (recit, no. 3).[25] The following aria adds, " 'Jesus' shall be my first word in the New Year."[26] Later, the libretto invokes blessings for the government in the mvts. 5 and 6. Any reference to Jesus's blood is absent.

The theological landscape of the interpretation of the cantata of January 1 as well as Bach's own cantatas from previous years provide a backdrop for the understanding of the text for part IV of the oratorio, performed on New Year's Day 1735. Given the broad variety of topics, it is important that Bach's libretto for this part of the *Christmas Oratorio* focuses almost exclusively on one aspect: the name of Jesus and his presence in the believer's heart. The two other aspects are not entirely absent (contrary to Blankenburg's assessment[27]) but they appear only in fleeting allusions. Most clear is the aspect of praise and thanksgiving commonly connected to the celebration of the first day of the new secular year. It is present in the opening movement ("Fallt mit Danken, Fallt mit Loben") and the aria no. 41 ("Ich will nur dir zu Ehren leben").[28] The aspect of praise is quite general and does not necessarily allude to the secular New Year, but the secular perspective is not explicitly excluded either. The final movement, no. 42, opens with the line "Jesus richte mein Beginnen." In the liturgical context of the cantata within the New Years service on January 1, 1735, the "beginning" alludes of course to the beginning of the new year; even more so, as the text was taken from a New Year's hymn that was known to the congregation, "Hilf, Herr Jesu, laß gelingen." This is lost on a modern listener. In the context of the oratorio, though, especially when it is performed in a concert setting, it loses this

---

[24] For a detailed analysis that draws a connection between circular aspects in the cantata and the circularity of the year, see Eric Chafe, *"Anfang und Ende*: Cyclic Recurrence in Bach's Cantata *Jesu, nun sei gepreiset*, BWV 41," *Bach Perspectives* 1 (1995): 103–34.

[25] "Du süsser Jesus-Name du, In dir ist meine Ruh, Du bist mein Trost auf Erden."

[26] "Jesus soll mein erstes Wort in dem neuen Jahre heißen."

[27] Blankenburg, *Weihnachts-Oratorium*, 93.

[28] Meinrad Walter has suggested that the opening movement with its celebratory character emphasized the secular (human) aspect of the feast, similar to the two cantatas with *Te Deum* quotations, BWV 190 and 16. Walter, *Weihnachtsoratorium*, 123.

connotation and listeners will rather hear it as an invocation of Jesus's support in general.

The blessing for the sacred and secular authorities is entirely missing, which is not surprising given the focus of the *Christmas Oratorio*. The only reference to the circumcision of Jesus appears in a rather veiled allusion. This is noteworthy as the gospel would have allowed a reflection on the meaning of the circumcision and a connection to the Christian rite of passage in baptism. Only the first movement contains a reference that is almost unnoticeable: here, line 2 of the text mentions "des Höchsten Gnadenthron." "Gnadenthron" or "Gnadenstuhl" refers to the lid of the Ark of Covenant in the Temple, on which the blood of the sacrifice was spilled. Later it becomes a symbol for forgiveness as the apostle Paul refers to it as a symbol for Christ (Rom 3:25; also mentioned in Heb 4:14–16.[authorship unknown]). "Gnadenstuhl" in Lutheran orthodox theology symbolizes the forgiveness of sins that is granted through the suffering of Christ at the cross, and especially through the shedding of his blood.[29] The texts for Bach's cantatas use the term quite frequently,[30] so for a listener in 1735 the meaning of the term would have been quite obvious.[31] It is still remarkable that Bach's librettist does not insert more than a fleeting reference to the circumcision.[32] This brings into sharper relief the primary focus of part IV: the name of Jesus and his presence in the believer's heart. Again, the text (and the music) for part IV elaborates extensively on the meaning of the name of Jesus and the intimate relationship (*unio mystica*) between the believer and Jesus. The center of the fourth part (both theologically and numerically) is the famous echo-aria, no. 39, which is framed by two recits/chorale tropes. These three central movements are preceded by the only gospel text, a single line from the Christmas narrative, of which the following movements are an interpretation. We will analyze these four movements first before we come to the remaining movements of part IV.

---

[29] See for an overview of the use of Gnadenstuhl and the synonymous Gnadenthron, see Helene Werthemann, "Jesus Christus, vorgestellt zu einem Gnadenstuhl durch den Glauben in seinem Blut: Der alttestamentliche Sühnedeckel und seine Erfüllung in Christus," in *Das Blut Jesu und die Lehre von der Versöhnung im Werk Johann Sebastian Bachs*, ed. Albert A. Clement (Amsterdam: Royal Netherlands Academy of Arts and Sciences, 1995), 63–78.

[30] "Gnadenthron": BWV 55/4, BWV 76/3, and in the *St. John Passion*, mvt. 22; "Gnadenstuhl": BWV 83/3, BWV 194/2; and 125/5 as "Stuhl der Gnaden."

[31] The image of the Gnadenstuhl/Gnadenthron is also sometimes connected to the manger. In his *Labrores Sacri*, Johann Heermann writes in 1624 about Mary: "Ihr höchster Schatz, der Gnadenthron, / Dis schöne liebe Kindlein / legte sie fein säuberlich / in die Krippen neben sich, / verhüllt in grobe Windeln." (Heermann, *Labrores Sacri*, 51). Johann Olearius's Christmas hymn "Wunderbarer Gnadenstuhl," published in his *Christliche Bet-Schule* in 1665, makes a similar connection. Olearius's *Bet-Schule* might have been known by Bach as it was the book that served as a model for the order of the texts in Bach's *Actus tragicus*, BWV 106.

[32] We have to contradict Steiger who, by analyzing the meaning of the term "Gnadenthron" suggests that the circumcision was a central aspect in part IV of the oratorio (Steiger, *Gnadengegenwart*,

# Gospel and echo (mvts. 37–40)

The gospel text for part IV consists of only one verse: "And as eight days were up, when the child would be circumcised, his name was called Jesus [the name he] was called by the angel, before he was conceived in the womb" (Lk 2:21). The tenor begins his gospel recit (no. 37) in C major and gradually modulates to A minor. However, the harmonic relations are more complex. A listener will perceive F major as the tonal center, as it had been the home key of the preceding opening movement. This key of F is reached within the recit just at the moment when the tenor sings the name "Jesus," which receives additional weight by being set with the highest note ($a'$) of the movement. This setting captures within a brief moment the entire focus of part IV.

The aria "Flößt, mein Heiland" (no. 39) is a parody from the *Hercules Cantata Laßt uns sorgen*, BWV 213. In its original context it is sung by the young Hercules (alto) who is faced with the decision whether to follow the path of Virtue or to give in to the alluring promises of the vice Pleasure:

| | |
|---|---|
| Treues Echo dieser Orten, | Faithful Echo of these parts, |
| Sollt ich bei den Schmeichelworten | should I be led astray by honeyed words' |
| Süßer Leitung irrig sein? | sweet guidance? |
| Gib mir deine Antwort: Nein! | Give me your answer: No! |
| (Echo) Nein! | (Echo) No! |
| Oder sollte das Ermahnen, | Or should the warning |
| Das so mancher Arbeit nah, | that so much work is at hand |
| Mir die Wege besser bahnen? | better lead the way for me? |
| Ach! so sage lieber: Ja! (Echo) Ja! | Ah! then say rather Yes! (Echo) Yes! |

The aria was sung by two altos (Hercules and his echo) and accompanied by an obbligato oboe d'amore. In the *Christmas Oratorio*, though, Bach transposed it from A major to C major, assigned it to two sopranos, and exchanged the oboe d'amore with a regular oboe. Bach's handwriting in the score is particularly tidy and shows only a few minor corrections. The librettist furnished the new text in a way that allowed Bach to use the preexisting music without major changes.[33] In the *Hercules Cantata*, the echo aria features a dialogue between Hercules and Echo; however, it is clear from the outset of the cantata that the desire for virtue is an inborn desire,

---

181 and 185). If this were the case, Bach's librettist would have had ample opportunity to make this clearer (as did Franck in his libretto); but the libretto for BWV 248 sets a different emphasis.

[33] The echo aria in the *Hercules Cantata* itself could be a parody of an earlier cantata. A similar text appears in a cantata for the name day of Elector August the Strong on August 3, 1732, BWV Anh. 11. It is also possible that the similarities between the text from BWV Anh. 11 and the music in BWV

given by a divine instance, so that the choice of Hercules is not an actual choice but the realization of his predetermined destiny. In other words, the dialogue between Hercules and Echo is as much an external dialogue between the hero and the mythical figure as it is an internal dialogue within Hercules's mind, between his virtuous identity and his carnal desires.[34] In the *Christmas Oratorio*, the aria explores the affective response to the name of Jesus. In the first half of the aria, the singer inquires whether the name instilled fear, which is answered with "no"; the second half confirms that there was no need to fear death because of the presence of God's word. The name should instead instill joy in the believer, which is affirmatively echoed by the second singer:

| | |
|---|---|
| Flößt, mein Heiland, flößt dein Namen | Is it, my Savior, is it [true] that your name instills |
| Auch den allerkleinsten Samen | even the very tiniest seed |
| Jenes strengen Schreckens ein? | of the stark horror? |
| Nein, du sagst ja selber nein. (Echo) Nein! | No, yes you yourself say, "no" (Echo) No! |
| Sollt ich nun das Sterben scheuen? | Now shall I shy away from having to die? |
| Nein, dein süßes Wort ist da! | No, your sweet word is there! |
| Oder sollt ich mich erfreuen? | Or shall I rejoice? |
| Ja, du Heiland sprichst selbst ja. (Echo) Ja! | Yes, you yourself, Savior, declare, "yes" (Echo) Yes! |

The libretto correlates with the theological interpretation of the name of Jesus as outlined earlier. Heinrich Müller stresses in his sermon for New Year's Day that the name of Jesus was a source of fear for the devil and the enemies of the faithful: "Der Name JEsus ist ein schröcklicher Name. Schröcklich ist er den Teuffeln . . . Schröcklich den Feinden/die ihn verfolgen" (The name of Jesus is a terrible name. It terrifies the devils . . . it terrifies the enemies who pursue him).[35] But for the faithful, so Müller, the name is a source of joy and consolation. The libretto

---

213 are only a coincidence and that that the echo aria in the *Hercules Cantata* is the original and thus independent from the lost aria from 1732. It is problematic to assume that Bach would have composed only one echo aria that he then recycled during the following years. What also speaks against a parody is the number of corrections and revisions in the score for BWV 213 (D-B Mus. ms. Bach P 125), which suggests that it is a composition score and not the revision of an existing movement.

[34] The echo in mythological texts of the Baroque was never understood as a simple, mechanical and sonic reflection but as the answer of a divine instance; cf. Wald, "Kanon, Kombinatorik, Echokompositionen," 57.

[35] Müller, *Schlußkette*, Festteil, 77.

renders this view of the name in a dialogue. The opening lines of the echo aria refer back to the preceding recit, which had explicitly mentioned the fear of death. The text makes it clear that there was no reason to be afraid of death and that the name of Jesus did not instill any fear of dying. We are reminded of Rambach's sermon, which had stated, "Zeiget sich der Tod in seiner fürchterlichen gestalt, so erschrickt sie nicht, denn ihr Immanuel hat dem Tode die Macht genommen" (If death presents himself in his most threatening form, she [the soul] is not startled because her Immanuel has taken the power away from death).[36] The aria, in its second half, turns directly to the topic of death and juxtaposes the fear of death (line 5) and the presence of the "sweet word." This presence has to be seen within the context of the ever present concept of the *inhabitatio Christi* and thus alludes to the presence of Christ through his word in the heart of the believer. This "süßes Wort" is Christ himself; this becomes clear if we see the aria in connection with the preceding recit where the name of the newborn child, "Immanuel" is indeed the "sweet word." In the same way as the name of Christ was understood as the representation of his essence, the presence of the sweet word in the believer's heart signified his very presence.[37] The text for the aria finally turns to the joy the presence of Christ instills in the believer, and this is affirmed through the "yes" spoken by the *Heiland* himself ("Yes, o Savior, You Yourself say yes. (Yes!)".

The decision to use the echo aria from BWV 213 at this point in the oratorio has struck some interpreters as odd. Hans Engel, for instance, calls the movement "sinnlos" (nonsense).[38] However, Bach and his librettist consciously decided to use it in the oratorio and to use it at this point in the work. It would easily have been possible for Bach to exclude the aria as unsuitable.[39] Ernst Koch has suggested that the use of the echo has to be understood within the framework of seventeenth- and eighteenth-century theology. As Koch shows, the metaphor of the echo was frequently evoked by preachers and theologians to denote the dialogue between the divine and the human. Johann Conrad Dannhauer, for instance, calls the prayer an "echo of God's word."[40] Also church music was occasionally described as an echo because

---

[36] "daß die Seele ihrem im Glauben ergriffenen Immanuel das Hertz zur Wohnung einräumet, daß aus demselben eine Hütte GOttes werden möge" (that the soul may give Immanuel, whom she has embraced in faith, the heart as a dwelling place; and that it [the heart] may become a hut of God). Rambach, *Betrachtungen über das Evangelium Esaiä*, 140.

[37] Rambach, *Betrachtungen über das Evangelium Esaiä*, 138.

[38] *MGG* 3, s.v. "Echo," by Hans Engel, col. 1079.

[39] This, for instance, happened to the aria "Blast die wohlgegriffnen Flöten" from BWV 214, the only aria from that cantata that was not parodied in the *Christmas Oratorio*.

[40] Johann Conrad Dannhauer, *Catechismus Milch/Oder Erklärung deß Christlichen Catechismi Sibender Theil* (Straßburg: Spoor, 1659); see also Ernst Koch, "Tröstendes Echo. Zur theologischen Deutung der Echo-Aria im IV. Teil des Weihnachts-Oratoriums von Johann Sebastian Bach," *Bach-Jahrbuch* 75 (1989): 206.

it was perceived as the human response to the divine revelation.[41] But the image of the echo could also be applied in reverse direction. Johann Andreas Olearus, for instance, described God's answer to the human prayer as an echo.[42] The meaning of the image of the echo was not fixed but multivalent in the wide array of meanings and functions of the echo in Renaissance and Baroque poetry.[43] Even in the writings of one preacher, the image could be used in several ways, as Heinrich Müller in his *Evangelische Schlußkette* employed the image of the echo to describe the human response to God's word, both in prayer and in action and also to visualize the divine response to human prayer.[44] A visual representation for the echo-like dialogue between the believer and Christ is given in another sermon collection by Heinrich Müller, *Geistlicher Danck-Altar* from 1670 (fig. 9.1). The image—identified through the title as "Dulce assonat echo" (Sweetly resounds the echo)—juxtaposes the plea "Erbarm dich mein" (Have mercy on me) by the human in the lower left-hand corner, and the response "Erbarm mich dein" (I have mercy on you).

Koch suggests a book by Johann Hecht—published in Leipzig in 1684—as an earlier example. It is a collection of sacred dialogues for the Sundays and festival days of the year, titled *Dialogus Christi cum Anima* (Dialogue between Christ and the soul). The text for New Year's Day combines the idea of an echo with an allusion to the name of Jesus:

| | |
|---|---|
| JEsus süsser Nahme klinget / | The sweet name of Jesus resonates, |
| Den der Himmel selbst erdacht! | Which was invented by heaven! |
| JEsus; dieses Wort bezwinget | Jesus, this word overcomes |
| Allen Wust der Höllen-Macht. | All chaos of the powers of hell. |
| JEsus hilff / daß Mir dein Nahme fall' ein / | Jesus help, so that I remember your name, |
| Wenn mir die Trübsal zu mächtig wil seyn. | If distress seems to be too powerful. |
| Sünde / Tod / Hölle sind schreckliches Schalles; | Sin, death, and hell emit a horrible sound, |
| Dieses verschwindet / wo JEsus ist / alles! | But it disappears where Jesus is everything! |
| JEsus-Echo: JEsus ist alles![45] | Jesus-echo: Jesus is everything! |

---

[41] Koch, "Tröstendes Echo," 207; see also our discussion of Bach's concept of mundane vs. celestial music in chap. 7 of this book.

[42] Koch, "Tröstendes Echo," 207; see also Axmacher, "Aus Liebe will mein Heiland leben," 118.

[43] See Ferdinand van Ingen, *Echo im 17. Jahrhundert: Ein literarisch-musikalisches Phänomen in der Frühen Neuzeit* (Amsterdam: Koninklijke Nederlandse Akademie van Wetenschappen, 2002).

[44] See the summary of Müller's "Echo Theology" in Steiger, *Gnadengegenwart*, 179–80.

[45] Quoted after Koch, "Tröstendes Echo," 209.

*Figure 9.1* Heinrich Müller, *Geistlicher Danck-Altar*, Frankfurt/M, 1700 (Sächsische Landes- und Universitätsbibliothek Dresden/Digitale Sammlungen, Theol.ev.asc.1506) Structure of BWV 248/39

The similarities between Hecht and Bach's libretto—the invocation of the name of Jesus at the time of death and the reference to the "sweetness" of the name—reflect very common themes and images in the theology and poetry of the time. And this example suggests that the echo voice in Bach's aria is the voice of Jesus; or more specific, the voice of Jesus residing in the heart of the believer.[46] The aria is the dialogue

---

[46] Another sacred echo composition that was performed in Leipzig is documented by a libretto print from 1703 (*Texte zur Leipziger Kirchen-Music auff die Heiligen Oster-Feyer-Tage/1703*); the texts by an unknown author were presumably composed by Johann Kuhnau; the music is lost. The libretto

between the believer and Christ in the believer's heart.[47] It is an inner dialogue within the individual that is dramatically transposed into an external one. Thus, the echo aria in the *Christmas Oratorio* follows a similar logic as the model in BWV 213. There it was the hero in a dialogue with his inborn, and divinely instituted, desire for virtue, who answered his questions. Here it is the divine presence in the human heart.

The text for the aria, both in the secular and sacred versions, describes the transition from negation to affirmation, from "no" to "yes." Given the directionality of the text, Bach decided to write a through-composed aria instead of a *da capo* aria. The result is still a tripartite movement, as Bach sets the second half of the text in two separate sections (ABB'):

| 1–18 | Ritornello | C–> G |
|---|---|---|
| 19–61 | Vocal section A | C–> G |
| 61–69 | modified Ritornello | G–> G |
| 69–91 | Vocal section B | G–> a |
| 91–99 | modified Ritornello | a–> a |
| 99–127a | Vocal section B' | a–> C |
| 127b–38 | modified Ritornello | [G]–> C |

The 6/8 meter and the simple voice-leading is consistent with stereotypes of the bucolic sphere of the musical pastoral. While part IV is not a continuation of the shepherd's scene in parts II and III, we still need to imagine the action taking place in the environment of Jesus's birth.[48] The instrumental ritornello sets up both the

for the third day of Easter features a "Geistliches Echo" in which a section for solo voice is followed by a short echo of the last phrase, which is then itself repeated by a chorus. For a description of the piece and an excerpt of the text, see Werner Braun, "Bachs Echoarie," in *Die Quellen Johann Sebastian Bachs: Bachs Musik im Gottesdienst*, ed. Renate Steiger (Heidelberg: Manutius Verlag, 1998), 120–21; see also Werner Braun, "Beiträge zu G.F. Händels Jugendzeit in Halle (1685–1703)," *Wissenschaftliche Zeitschrift der Universität Halle* VIII/4–5 (1959): 853–54.

[47] Some interpreters have suggested a more naturalistic view; like Blankenburg (*Weihnachts-Oratorium*, 103), who sees the aria as a dialogue between the faithful soul and the Jesus child himself. While Blankenburg's view is not entirely wrong, we are indeed dealing with a dialogue between the human and the divine, the religious literature of Bach's time supports the assumption that it is the Jesus of the second advent and not the Jesus of the first advent who engages in a dialogue with the singer. See also "Greer, Sacred Duets and Terzets": 271–75.

[48] Cf. Jung, *Pastorale*, 213.

main musical material for the aria as well as the echo principle. It begins with a short motif of one-and-a-half measures, which is immediately followed by a *piano*-repetition, an echo, of the last three notes. Throughout the aria, the statements of the "character" Echo are all unaccompanied by the bc whenever this character is indeed imitating the principal soprano,[49] creating the impression that the echo-sections constitute a different sphere from the one of the main voice. The opening motif is varied in the subsequent measures, continuing the echo-dialogues. A short modulatory passage (mm. 9–12) leads to the dominant G major and introduces a new type of echo, now consisting of sigh-like motifs, that are handed back and forth between *forte* and *piano* before the opening ritornello cadences in G major. The first vocal section begins as *vokaleinbau*, with the soprano taking over the *forte*-parts of the oboe and the oboe playing the short echo calls. Soon, however, Bach leads the voice and the obbligato instrument simultaneously. The oboe now continues its alternation between *forte* and *piano* while the soprano sings the complete text of the A section. After having established the echo principle and after having presented the text for the A section, Bach introduces at m. 45 a second soprano voice, the character Echo, who repeats single words "No" or "Yes" as an echo (but which are not indicated to be performed *piano* or at a distance). For these vocal echoes, Bach only uses the sigh-like echo sequence he had introduced toward the end of the instrumental ritornello, while the echo-repetition of the opening motif is restricted to the oboe.

The three voices (two sopranos and oboe) create either simple alternating echo effects (mm. 20, 22, 47, 54) or a double echo, in which the motif is first repeated by the vocal echo voice and then again (*pp*) by the oboe (mm. 45–46, 47–48, 44–59). The "natural order" of the echo is disturbed in mm. 60/61: while the soprano sings the beginning of the textual phrase "du sagst ja selber," the last word is added by the echo voice: "nein!" Bach will use the same device again later in the second half of the aria (at m. 127). This break with the natural order goes back to the secular model in the BWV 213. There, Bach had even changed the text in order to let the echo-voice speak by itself. The original text by Picander reads "Gib mir *doch zur* Antwort: Nein! [Echo:] Nein!"[50] In BWV 213 Bach changes this into: "Gib mir *deine* Antwort: Nein! [Echo:] Nein!" The small textual adjustment made it possible to introduce the echo not only as a natural phenomenon that repeated mechanically what the voice had said, but it qualifies it as something,

---

[49] This with the exception of some of the instrumental echoes that appear as accompaniment of the vocal line. In those cases, as in m. 32, the instrumental bass line mostly continues.

[50] Cf. Braun, "Bachs Echoarie," 126.

if not external, still distinct from the individual. And too, in BWV 213, it was the divinely ordained desire for virtue that speaks to the young hero. Here it is Christ, dwelling in the heat of the believer, "Du sagst ja selber: [Echo:] nein!," or later, "Du Heiland sprichst ja selbst [Echo:] ja!"

A short instrumental interlude (derived from the opening ritornello) serves as a bridge to the B section of the aria. Since the texts for the A and B sections did not differ significantly in their affect (with the exception of the final words: yes and no), Bach does not establish a clear contrast but maintains the same motivic material. A new element, however, is a long melismatic line on the word "erfreuen" (mm. 75–77), which more than doubles in length in section B' (mm. 105–11). The melisma sticks out in the context of the otherwise simple, mostly syllabic voice-leading. While the melisma is a simple text-painting of the word "erfreuen" (in the model composition it painted the word "bahnen"/pave [the way]), it also endows the last two sections of the aria with a slightly different character than in the A section. Bach even creates a climax by increasing the length of the melisma in the last section. This contributes to an emphasis of the affirmative sections of the aria in comparison to the negative beginning. The different character of negation and affirmation is also reflected in the shape of the echo motif that is handed back and forth between the voices and instruments. In the "Nein" section, it is a sigh-like motif, while the word "Ja!" either appears either as a single note, or even more as a confident and joyful "ja, ja" with an ascending leap. The final word in the aria has the echo voice with the exclamation "ja," this time again independently, without echoing a text sung by the other soprano (as was true for the word "Nein" in m. 61). The aria ends with a modified ritornello, featuring the sigh-like echo sections from the opening ritornello.[51] The similarities between the model and the parody made it possible for Bach to use the movement with only minimal alterations. One example of a change is m. 23, where Bach transforms what had originally been a statement of the bc motif, which is used throughout the piece, into a line of descending sixteenth notes. The reason for this change is probably the word "flößt" that is sung by the soprano and that motivated a "flowing" line in the bc instead of the usual motif. It also corresponds to the use of a similar constellation of notes in m. 24 (on "flößt") and m. 26 (on "kleinsten"). The new bc motif can now be heard as an anticipation of these two measures (ex. 9.1).

[51] The concluding ritornello consists of the first four measures of the first interlude, followed by the last eight measures of the opening ritornello.

Example 9.1  J. S. Bach, BWV 213/5 and BWV 248/39, mm. 22–27

Two modifications of the voice-leading, due to the new text, were necessary in mm. 31 and 33, as the word "Schreckens" required additional notes compared to the monosyllabic word "sein." Both changes were already made while Bach was copying the piece; they do not appear as corrections in the score. A final change, again of smaller nature than in other parodies in the *Christmas Oratorio,* appears toward the end of the melismatic outburst on "erfreuen" (m. 109). While the melisma as such was borrowed from the secular model, where the paving of the way (for Hercules) is depicted, Bach now, for a short moment, changes the regular eighth-note motion into sixteenths, emphasizing the joyous affect of the text. The change also fits into the climatic character of the movement, as Bach gradually moves from a primarily syllabic declamation (A) to a shorter melisma (B) to a longer melisma (B').

The harmonic development within the aria adds another significant layer. The opening ritornello and the A section both move from the home key C major to the dominant G major. Section B then modulates from G major to a minor, from where the B' section picks up, ultimately returning to the home key. Bach touches C major briefly during the "erfreuet" melisma in m. 106, but the home key is only clearly and stably affirmed in m. 127, with the last "yes" followed by the return of the ritornello. Thus, the final answer and the clear confirmation of the home key coincide in m. 127.

The echo aria is framed by two extensive accompagnato recits (no. 38 and 40). If we follow the printed libretto, we have to divide the first recit (no. 38) into two—one regular recit and one recit (starting at "Komm! Ich will dich mit Lust umfassen") with a chorale (or chorale trope). Bach's setting, however, interprets these two sections as one entity. It is possible that the manuscript with the oratorio text that Bach received from his librettist did not yet clearly delineate the margins of the texts. But it is also possible that Bach intentionally combined two movements that were designed as separate by the author, since their texts are closely related.[52] The opening lines of the recit no. 38 resemble invocations of the name of Jesus as they appear in earlier cantatas by Bach for New Year's Day. Immanuel is referred to as the "sweet word" (which will later return in the echo aria), followed by an invocation of the name of Jesus as shelter, life, and joy.[53] Lines 7 and 8 identify him as "pleasure" (or even "desire") who refreshes "heart and breast"; both terms belong to the typical vocabulary of *unio mystica*.

For lines 9–15 of the text, the bass is joined by a soprano in a chorale trope. Bach's librettist juxtaposes sections from Johann Rist's hymn "Jesu, du mein liebstes Leben" and free poetic interpolations. Rist's hymn stanza is divided into two halves. The first half of the stanza is quoted in no. 38 while the second half follows in no. 40. The chorale and the interpolations in no. 38 evoke the imagery of bride and bridegroom and the idea of a mystic unity between Christ and the believer. Only

---

[52] Walter Blankenburg pointed out the close connection between the parts; he only preferred a separation because it allowed him to view the aria as the middle and center of part IV and thus suggest a symmetrical outline, which revolved around the echo aria, see Blankenburg, *Weihnachts-Oratorium*, 94.

[53] Bach accidentally wrote "Hirt" (shepherd) in m. 3 in the score; this was then copied into the bass part but then corrected to "Hort" (shelter), cf. NBA II/6, KB, 284. The mistake was probably motivated by the mention of the "Hirt" in the following chorale trope "Hirt und König, Licht und Sonne." While both versions are theologically possible, "Hort" is the one we find in the printed libretto and presumably the correct one since it rhymes with the last word of the previous line, "Wort."

after the end of the chorale text—which closes with a reference to the "bitter stem of the cross"—does the recit shift its focus to Christ's presence in the hour of death and to its consolatory nature. The echo aria then perpetuates this topic through its juxtaposition of negation and affirmation. When the recit continues after the aria, the question of death is resolved, and the dialogue between soprano and basso returns to the topic of mystic unity and the presence of Jesus's name in the believer's heart: "Wohlan, dein Name soll allein / In meinem Herzen sein" (Well then, your name alone shall be in my heart!). Both the chorale and the free interpolations in no. 40 culminate in questions, about Jesus's name and the proper way of praising him. Both texts end with a personal pronoun, *dir/dich*, addressing Jesus himself. Ending with this open question, the recit finally prepares the entrance of the following tenor aria, "Ich will nur dir zu Ehren leben" (For honor I will live only to *you*).[54]

| | | |
|---|---|---|
| *Bass* | Doch, Liebster, sage mir: | But tell me, Most Beloved: |
| | Wie rühm ich dich, wie dank ich *dir*? | How may I glorify you, how may I thank *you*? |
| *Soprano* | Hirt und König, Licht und Sonne, | Shepherd and king, light and sun, |
| | Ach! wie soll ich würdiglich, | Oh! how shall I worthily |
| | Mein Herr Jesu, preisen *dich*? | Praise *you*, my Lord Jesus? |

As pointed out earlier, Bach does not use the chorale melody but only the words, which is unusual for a chorale trope. We have discussed that the texture of the movement, the similarly unusual simultaneous combination of recit and chorale, was inspired by a movement from Stölzel's Passion, which Bach had performed a few months prior. Bach did not necessarily need to set the text of the recit as a simultaneous recit. He could have set the two layers of the text in alternating sections as he had done in mvt. 7. The possible reason for the simultaneous combination was that the two texts express essentially the same ideas, whereas in other chorale tropes in Bach's oratorios the hymn and the new texts frequently stand in a dialectical relationship.[55] The melody Bach composes resembles a song for domestic piety rather than a chorale, and it is similar to melodies in the 1736 *Schemelli Gesangbuch*.[56] Bach's new melodic

---

[54] My emphasis.

[55] See Rathey, "Drama and Discourse," 45–51.

[56] Cf. Steiger, *Gnadengegenwart*, 177–85; Martin Geck refers to the melody as an example for the Pietist aria, *"Denn alles findet bei Bach statt": Erforschtes und Erfahrenes* (Stuttgart: Metzler, 2000), 104–5. The association with Pietism made by Geck is problematic as this style, even though favored by some Pietist composers and theorists, was not limited to this particular religious camp. In fact, the *Schemelli Gesangbuch* was intended to serve as a more orthodox counterpart to the popular Pietist songbooks of the time.

composition was motivated by the elevated emotional character of the text, which was insufficiently captured in the original tune by Johann Schop (ca. 1590–1667).[57] The newly composed melody also gives Bach the opportunity to replace the bar form (AAB) of the original tune with a through-composed melody that can follow the character and meaning of the individual words of the text more closely. However, Bach still loosely follows the "syntax" of a traditional hymn melody by ending what had been the end of the A section in no. 38 on C (m. 17, here harmonized with a C-minor chord with Picardy third) and returning to F major in the B section in no. 40 (m. 16). The simple melodic contour and mostly syllabic declamation of the soprano melody in the framing chorale tropes resembles that of the soprano part in the echo aria.

The autograph score for the first recit (no. 38) shows numerous changes and revisions that not only document that the piece was newly composed for the oratorio but also highlight the sections of the recit that deserved special attention in the eyes of the composer. The opening measure originally featured half notes in the three upper strings. Bach then changed the second half note in the viola into two quarter notes ($bb'-e'$); the result is that the word "süßer" (sweet), which now sounds with the second quarter note, receives additional emphasis, highlighting the sensory quality of the relationship with Immanuel.[58] The invocation of the name Immanuel is followed by a climactic passage that invokes the divine name in increasing intensity, culminating in m. 6 with $eb'$—an overstepping of the previously highest note $d'$ in the vocal bass by a half-step—on the text "Augen [schweben]" (hover before my eyes). This again pinpoints the sensory (this time visual) proximity to Jesus. Additionally, Bach depicts the "hovering" by inserting a small eighth-note motif in the two violins (m. 6).[59] The emphasis of the sensory aspects prepares the entrance of the hymn text and the simultaneously sung text by the bass, which call Jesus the "bridegroom" who is to be embraced with "pleasure." Before the chorale enters, Bach makes some small revisions in mm. 8 and 9: He changes the second violin and the viola from originally half notes into quarter notes. The changes fulfill two purposes. On a structural level, the increased movement in the accompaniment marks the end of the first recit section before the soprano enters in m. 10; on a semantic

[57] Composers from the seventeenth and eighteenth centuries would occasionally abandon an established chorale melody to highlight the emotional qualities of a hymn text. An earlier example is Johann Schelle's setting of the thirteenth stanza of Luther's *Vom Himmel hoch*, "Ach mein herzliebes Jesulein," in which he replaces the familiar chorale melody with a highly expressive and emotional setting of his own; cf. Markus Rathey, "Rezeption als Innovation: Zur Aktualisierung traditioneller geistlicher Texte durch die Musik im 17. und frühen 18. Jahrhundert," in *Aedificatio: Erbauung im interkulturellen Kontext der Frühen Neuzeit*, ed. Andreas Solbach (Tübingen: Niemeyer, 2005), 234–36.

[58] The sweetness of Jesus and his name is, as argued earlier earlier, one of the key metaphors of Bernardian piety and was frequently quoted by preachers and religious poetry in the seventeenth and eighteenth centuries.

[59] Jena characterizes the motif aptly as "light as a feather" ("leicht wie eine Feder"), Jena, *Brich an, o schönes Morgenlicht*, 156.

level, the revised version now adds a stronger emphasis on the name "Jesus" on the last beat of m. 8, and "Herz" on the second beat of m. 9. Related to this is the small detail in m. 9: here, Bach had run out of space while writing the text of the vocal bass and had to draw a small heart instead of writing the word.

With the entrance of the soprano in m. 10, the bc turns into a continuous chain of eighth notes (a common feature in Bach's ariosi), and even the vocal bass adopts a more cantabile tone. The emphasis, then, is on the melodic line of the soprano, which is doubled by the first violin. The small two-note melismas that characterize the melody were typical for devotional songs of the time, and the entrance of the soprano on the third $a'$ supported by the $f$ in the bass immediately sets the "sweet" and emotional tone of the melody. The two voices sound together for most of the time with two significant exceptions: (1) in m. 13 the soprano sings the word "bridegroom" during a rest between two phrases of the bass recit, which is then followed by the emotional sigh "Ach" in the bass; and (2) the soprano briefly stands alone is on the phrase "Kreuzes Stamm" (stem of the cross) at the end of the chorale trope (m. 17), before the bass continues to shift the focus on the daily "crosses" of human life, such as need, danger, and dying. The final section of mvt. 38 is increasingly dissonant as Bach employs flat keys, which, as Eric Chafe has shown succinctly, can serve for Bach as a musical allegory for cross and death.[60] Throughout the compositional process, Bach even increased the dissonant nature of the movement. In m. 19 the viola originally held an $e'$ for the duration of a half note, which the composer then changed into two quarter notes $e'–c\sharp'$. The change adds emphasis to the word "[Aller-]liebste," creating harmonic tension between the $c\sharp'$ in the viola and the $b\flat$ in the vocal bass. A similar change in m. 23 (vla, notes 3–4 and bc, notes 3–4) accentuates the entrance of the final invocation of the name of Jesus.

While Bach takes measures to accentuate the name of Jesus, the score also shows his attempts to highlight the threat of death. In m. 22 the harmonic progression was originally much simpler. The bc had a half note $A$ on the first beat, and the upper strings proceed in regular half notes. In this earlier version, a static A-minor chord would have accompanied a vocal bass line that mostly consisted of notes of the A-minor triad. The text, however, talks about the terror of death. Bach thus decided to change the measure drastically: the whole note $A$ in the bass was changed into a quarter note, immediately followed by a falling diminished fourth to $E\flat$. In the second violin and the viola, the long first note is changed into a quarter note as well, so that violin II plays a $c''$ on the second beat and the viola an $f\sharp$. The result is a harsh diminished seventh chord with dramatic tension between almost every single note. Bach goes even further in m. 27 when the text refers to the fear of death, "Todes Furcht": The original half-note motion is again transformed into a dissonant series of quarter notes. The harmonic progression in this measure was so remarkable, in

---

[60] Eric Chafe, *Analyzing Bach Cantatas* (Oxford: Oxford University Press, 2000), 31–36.

fact, that Bach added bc figures, an anomaly for his score of the *Christmas Oratorio*. But this moment called for an explicit formulation of the harmonic progression. Virtually all the changes in the recit (probably done while he was still composing and not in hindsight) were made to sharpen the dissonance and to emphasize the name of Jesus and its sweetness. This approach is continued in the second half of the chorale trope after the echo aria.

The structure of mvt. no. 40 differs from the earlier recit. Bach now alternates between single measures with the recit (indicated in the score by "Recit") and sections in which the two voices are combined (indicated by "arioso"). This leads to a regular structure of single recit measures and groups of four or two measures of arioso (1 + 4 + 1 + 2 + 1 + 2 + 1 + 4 + instr. postlude). The movement again invokes the close emotional connection between Jesus and the believer in the *unio mystica*. The voice-leading of the bass resembles more of an arioso than in the first half in movement 38; it even assimilates the characteristic two-note melismas of the soprano melody. The unity that is created by the musical similarities is a sonic representation of the emotional closeness that is expressed through the text. As in the previous recit, Bach made again numerous changes during the composition. Some of these pertain to problems of voice-leading (as in m. 4 where Bach transposed a viola motif up an octave) but others again document Bach's work toward a deeper expression of the text. For one example: in m. 8, the fourth note in the bc was originally a *D*, which was then changed into *e♭*; the effect is a beautiful "sweet" parallel movement with the vocal bass on the word "Liebe," and the bass proceeds from *f♯* to *g* while the bc now has *d–e♭*. The movement ends with a short instrumental postlude of two measures, featuring a dialogue between the first violins and the lower strings using a sigh-like motif, which echoes the open question of how to glorify, thank, and praise Jesus (and his name) properly, before the following tenor aria gives the answer.

The sequence of mvts. 38–40 provides the main interpretation of the gospel text for New Year's Day. The focus is on the meaning of the name of Jesus within the general trajectory of the libretto of the *Christmas Oratorio*, the threefold coming of Christ. While the echo aria enacts the inner dialogue between the human and the divine in the heart of the believer, the framing recits explore the multitude of meanings encompassed by the name of Jesus, while simultaneously highlighting the key aspects of mystic unity. The corrections and changes in the score show that Bach put particular effort into musically highlighting these aspects.

## Songs of Praise (mvts. 41, 42, and 36)

The second aria (no. 41) in part IV, "Ich will nur dir zu Ehren leben," as well at the two framing movements express the affect of joy to different modes and degrees. The tenor aria fulfills a dual purpose in the overall construction of the oratorio. Within the dramatic structure of part IV, it presents the answer to the question posed in the previous recit; it elaborates on the consequences of the power of Jesus's name and on Christ's ongoing presence in the human heart. The proper response is a life that purposely glorifies God. This, however, can only be accomplished through the support of God:

| | |
|---|---|
| Ich will nur dir zu Ehren leben, | For honor I will live only to you, |
| Mein Heiland, gib mir Kraft und Mut, | My Savior, give me power and courage, |
| Dass es mein Herz recht eifrig tut! | That my heart will do it right zealously! |
| Stärke mich, | Strengthen me |
| Deine Gnade würdiglich | To exalt your grace worthily |
| Und mit Danken zu erheben! | And with thanksgiving! |

In the context of this part and its liturgical locus within the celebration of New Year's Day, the aria additionally articulates the general idea of praise. While the text does not mention the New Year, it expresses praise and thanksgiving, which belonged to the typical elements of sermons and cantatas for the day. The connection with New Year's Day comes into sharper relief when we put the text for the aria into a larger context. The fourth part of the oratorio ends with the fifteenth stanza from Johann Rist's New Year's hymn "Hilf, Herr Jesu, laß gelingen" (1642). Some of the stanzas in the hymn that precede the one chosen by Bach's librettist show a remarkable resemblance to the text of the tenor aria. The stanzas demand that everything done should be dedicated to the service of God, and that all human actions are to be viewed as an expression of his praise. For this, the hymn asks God for strength:

| | |
|---|---|
| 2. Alles / was ich auszurichten / Und zu reden bin bedacht / Müße mich / mein GOtt! verpflichten Deines theuren Nahmens macht / Daß auch das / was ich gedencke / Dich zu preisen stets sich lencke. | 2. Whatever I intend to do or to say I have to remember that I am obligated, my God, through the power of your precious name, to praise you. |
| 3. Meiner hände werck und thaten / Meines zungen red und wort / Müsse nur durch dich gerathen / Und gantz glücklich gehen fort; Neue krafft laß mich erfüllen Zu verrichten deinen willen. | 3. My handiwork and my actions, the speech of my tongue and my words, have to be done through you and they are blessed by you. Let me feel new strength to do your will. |

4. Was ich dichte/was ich mache/Das
   gescheh in dir allein . . .

4. What I plan and do shall
   happen in and through you
   alone . . .

5. Laß mich beugen meine knie / Nur zu
   deines Nahmens her / Hilf / daß ich
   mich stets bemühe Dich zu preisen
   mehr und mehr / Laß mein bitten und
   mein flehen Doch im himmel vor dir
   stehen.

5. Let me bend my knees only in
   honor of your name; help, that
   I always strive to praise you
   ever more; and even more, let
   my praying and my imploring
   stand in front of you in heaven.

Bach's librettist must have been aware of these lines when he wrote the words for
the aria, for he inserts the hymn-stanza immediately after the aria. The chorale and
the aria text represent a typical way of celebrating the beginning of the New Year
by praising God, dedicating all actions to him, and requesting the strength to be
able to do this. Within the context of the liturgical celebration and the intertextual
framework of hymn and aria, the tenor aria refers at least implicitly to the beginning
of the New Year as well. A listener familiar with the hymn would very likely have
noticed the connection.

The tenor aria is again a parody of a movement from BWV 213. In its original
context it was the aria of Virtue, sung for the young Hercules, in which she promised him to carry him on her wings and to let his glory shine in perfect brilliance
("Auf meinen Flügeln sollst du schweben . . . soll dein Glanz und Schimmer sich
zur Vollkommenheit erheben." (On my wings you shall hover . . . your lustre and
gleam shall rise to perfection.). In his analysis of the relationship between the echo
aria (no. 5) and this aria (no. 7) in BWV 213, Eric Chafe observes that "its function in the dramatic structure of the work celebrates the bond between Hercules
and Tugend [Virtue] that is already established by the preceding echo aria."[61] When
Bach (and his librettist) transferred the two arias from the secular model into the
*Christmas Oratorio*, the movements maintained their original relationship: the echo
aria bridges the way from negation to affirmation and describes the relationship
between the divine and mankind (culminating in the affirmative "yes"), while the
tenor aria expresses gratitude for this relationship. As in the model, the two arias are
separated only by a recit. For the parody Bach transposed the aria from E minor to
D minor and changed the instrumentation from oboe, violin, tenor, and bc to two
violins, tenor, and bc.[62]

[61] Chafe, *Tonal Allegory*, 257.

[62] In the model composition, the two higher instrumental parts are played by two sonically differentiated instruments. Bach thus demanded instrumental forces that guaranteed a high degree of
transparency. In the parody, however, Bach replaces the oboe with another violin, which created a more
homogeneous sound.

Bach's setting is remarkable. It is one of the rare occasions in his oeuvre where he combines features of a regular *da capo* aria with a four-part fugue. The main subject of the fugue, with its wide leaps and a long chain of sixteenth notes, reflects the text of the original libretto and depicts the wings of virtue that carry Hercules to eternal fame. Within the parody, the subject loses its pictorial connotations, but the melismatic lines, which Bach primarily combines with the word "leben" (live) still fulfill a music-rhetorical function. While in the model composition the "wings" were everpresent, it is now that the life in honor of God that is constantly invoked in the *Christmas Oratorio*. The continuous presence is underscored by the *da capo* form of the aria. It is the only regular *da capo* aria in the second half of the oratorio, which gives this structural feature particular weight. The aria is circular in a context of other arias that exhibit a stronger degree of directionality. In addition to the fugal subject, the texture has a semantic function as well, at least in the secular model. Chafe suggests that the fugue "with its stretti and inversions on a theme of ornate melismatic character, perfectly expresses both the discipline and exhilaration of virtue."[63] Hans-Joachim Schulze adds that the strict four-part setting represented perfection and thus stood as a symbol for ethical norms and moral qualities. In other words, the four-part fugue symbolizes the ethical perfection for which the young hero is encouraged to strive.[64] With this interpretation in mind, Schulze suggests that the setting in the *Christmas Oratorio* was a fitting expression of the honor of God to which the text refers in the first line "I will live only for your honor." Schulze's interpretation correlates with Luther's view of God's honor as being of "uncomparable perfection."[65] Just as Hercules has to strive for the perfection of Virtue, here the believer asks God for his support to live a life that conforms to the divine perfection. Nonetheless, the semantic construct is less compelling than in the secular version.

The first exposition of the fugue serves as the ritornello within the formal architecture of the *da capo* aria. The three instrumental lines enter in the regular sequence of tonic-dominant-tonic. The bc first provides a harmonic backdrop with short staccato notes before it participates in the polyphonic texture (m. 9). The second exposition begins with the entrance of the tenor (m. 13). Here, the aria exhibits a significant difference from a conventional fugue. The accompanying instruments, instead of playing a regular counterpoint, are initially limited to short staccato notes that push the tenor voice into the foreground. The opening measures of the second exposition are a classic *vokaleinbau*. Measures 13–15 are a literal repetition of mm. 1–3, now with the tenor instead of the second violin. But soon the texture becomes more complex, as Bach not only introduces the bc with the entrance of the subject that had been played in mm. 4–6 by the first violin, but now he also brings back

[63] Chafe, *Tonal Allegory*, 257.
[64] Schulze, *Die Bach Kantaten*, 180–81.
[65] Cf. Petzoldt, *Bach Kommentar II*, 88.

the first violin with an inverted variant of the fugal subject. Two more expositions follow, featuring the subject in original version, inversion, and stretto, before the A section ends with a repetition of the opening ritornello (or the first exposition of the fugue).[66] In spite of the polyphonic complexity, which, according to the text-book, should treat the four voices as equals,[67] Bach sets the vocal line apart from the instrumental voices so that it is perceived as the primary voice.

The B section introduces new vocal material accompanied by short interjections and staccato motifs in the strings. Bach gives up the fugal texture and limits the presence of the main subject to statements in the bc line[68] and to the instrumental interlude that separates the first and second halves of the B section. The interlude features a stretto version of the ritornello, transposed to G minor. The B section ends with a short adagio measure (m. 70) that dwells for a moment on the word "erheben" (exalt), before the complete A section (including the second ritornello) is repeated.

While Bach could use the parody model without major changes, he revised the music at a few places to adjust it to the new, sacred text.[69] Measure 33 is characteristic of these small changes, where he embellishes a cadential phrase that had originally carried the text "wie ein Adler" (like an eagle) to musically paint the new word "eifrig" (zealously) with a group of fast-moving notes. A case of greater structural significance is the beginning of the B section. The secular text had opened with the neutral words "Und durch mich" (and through me), which Bach had set in a simple declamatory fashion. The text for the sacred parody "stärke mich" (strengthen me) motivated the insertion of a melismatic motif that highlighted the aspect of strength. The change is significant because it alters the beginning of the B section. The new motif not only emphasizes a textual keyword but now also anticipates the use of the same motif slightly ornamented within the melisma at mm. 47 and 48 (and perhaps in modified form in m. 49). The changed version now motivically links the words "strengthen," "mercy," and "worthy," and it transfers a recurring musical motif right to the beginning of the B section. A listener, unaware of the older version, will now hear the mm. 47–49 as elaborations of this new opening motif.[70] Bach does not change the second occurrence of the syncopated motif on "Stärke" in m. 59, probably because the vocal

---

[66] The only small difference is a short voice change between the two violins in m. 45.

[67] See for instance Bach's own "textbook" on fugue composition, his *Art of Fugue: contrapunctus* 9 is based on a very similar subject; even the order of entrances is similar as the tenor enters last. But the entrance of the tenor voice in the *contrapunctus* is embedded into the polyphonic texture and does not relegate the other voices to a simple accompaniment.

[68] The bc quotes the characteristic head of the subject twice (mm. 46, 47), the entire subject twice (mm. 49, 61), and once in inversion (m. 66).

[69] Some corrections, as in the second Violin in mm. 29–30, were due to mistakes made while transposing the aria from E minor to D minor; for a list of these mistakes, see NBA II/6, KB, 59.

[70] Other small changes may be mentioned briefly: in m. 47 Bach adds a small embellishment on "deine," highlighting that it is Jesus's mercy that will strengthen the believer; Bach also embellishes the setting of the words "erheben" (exhalt) and "Danken" (here, gratitude) in mm. 50–52; both for reasons of emphasis.

line was already quite striking, coming in the way it does as a syncopated motif that arrives earlier than expected, during the cadence of the preceding ritornello.[71] No major changes were necessary for the final word of both arias, "erheben" (elevate), which is set with an ascending melismatic line. If Bach still made a little change in the first violin in m. 65 it would have been to correct a contrapuntal flaw: the score of the oratorio shows that Bach had originally transposed and copied the measure from the secular cantata. In the process he must have noticed that the tenor and violin I briefly progressed in parallel fifths: $e''$–$d''$ vs. $a$–$g$. To avoid this he added a $d''$ in the violin and changed the first two notes into sixteenth notes. The resulting parallel octaves between violin I and bc were apparently the lesser evil.

The tenor aria in part IV of the *Christmas Oratorio* is a continuous praise of the presence and power of Jesus in the life and the heart of the believer. The continuity of praise is expressed in the everpresent opening subject that even permeates the basso continuo line of the B section. The final line of the B section, "mit Danken zu erheben" (to exalt with thanksgiving), points toward an additional layer of meaning. The "elevation" of God's mercy through thanksgiving evokes the common idea that prayer is elevated and, like on wings, flies up to God.[72] Since the fugue subject already has the connotation of "wings" through its secular model, the ascending line may be heard as the ascending of the prayers of thanksgiving. This interpretation gains some credibility if we look at stanza 7 of the hymn from which the final chorale text for part IV was taken. We noted earlier that the hymn exhibits some similarities to the text of the aria. The seventh stanza reads as:

7. Mein gebet das müß' aufsteigen /
HErr! für deinen gnaden-thron /
Dan wirst du zu mir dich neigen
/ Wie zu deinem lieben sohn;
HErr! ich weiß / es wird für allen
Dies mein opfer dir gefallen.[73]

7. My prayer must raise up to you,
Lord, to your throne of mercy; then
you will lean down to me, just like
[you did] to your beloved son; Lord,
I know that my sacrifice, before all
[sacrifices], will please you.

---

[71] These changes were made during the copying process and not as a revision of the already copied and transposed musical text. It becomes clear that the copying itself was already an opportunity for changes and therefore must be viewed as a step within the compositional process.

[72] See, for instance, Christian Stock, *Homiletisches Real-Lexicon oder Reicher Vorrath zur geist- und weltlichen Beredtsamkeit: in sich haltend Der Sachen kurtzen Entwurff, die nöthigen Beweißthümer und Bewegungs-Gründe, die auserlesensten Gleichnüsse, schöne Historien, geschickte Exempel, vortreffliche Sinn-Bilder und nachdenckliche Zeugnisse So wohl Lehrer der Kirchen älterer, neuerer und neuesten Zeiten; als auch Heydnischer und anderer Profan-Skribenten, Deren sich ein Prediger und Redner bey Ausarbeitung einer erbaulichen Predigt; oder sonst geschickten Rede bedienen kan;* nebst einer Vorrede Johann Georg Walchs, 4th ed. (Jena: Hartung, 1749), 482: "Ohne Flügel kan der Vogel sich nicht in die Höhe schwingen; und ohne das Gebet kan unsere Seele sich nicht zu GOtt in Himmel schwingen" (Without wings, a bird cannot fly up high and without prayer our soul cannot soar up toward God in heaven). Heinrich Müller compares fasting to a wing that elevates the prayers to God, Müller, *Evangelische Schlußkette*, Festteil, 88.

[73] Quoted after *Kern geistlicher lieblicher Lieder* (Nuremberg 1733), 29–30.

The praise for the presence of the name of Jesus in the human heart as well as the praise of God for the New Year finds its synthesis and culmination in the closing chorale setting, which combines the litany-like invocation of the name of Jesus and the plea for the blessings of the "beginning." The chorale stanza chosen by Bach's librettist also echoes the sensuality of the experience of the divine as expressed in mvts. 38 and 40, "zäume mir die Sinnen" (tame my senses, line 3), and the emotionality of the *unio mystica*, "sei nur mein Begier" (only be what I desire). Bach made a small change to the text of the final line of the chorale. The libretto as well as the hymnals in Leipzig used the third-person form "Jesus lasse mich nie wanken" (Jesus shall never let me waver). In Bach's version Jesus is addressed directly in the second-person singular, and the negation is changed from "never" to "not": "Jesu, lasse mich nicht wanken" (May Jesus not let me waver). Since this version appears both in the score and the performance parts, we can presume that it is not a mistake but an intentional change by Bach. Later on, we will see that Bach's setting differs from the other lines, which underscores the exceptional status of this line.[74]

Again, Bach does not use one of the traditional melodies associated with this hymn text,[75] rather he composed his own tune. This allowed him to end part IV in the key of the opening movement and not in a minor key. Bach's melody is in traditional bar form (AAB) and is artfully constructed. The four lines of the melody (if we set aside the repetition) describe a climax; each subsequent line begins with a falling third one step higher: $c''$—$d''$—$e''$ until the final line emphatically ascends to the highest realms of the setting. The final line is the apogee of the entire movement (a feature Bach would not have accomplished had he used one of the melodies commonly associated with this hymn text). The climax here coincides with the line in which Bach had changed text of the hymn from an invocation of the name of Jesus into a direct address of Jesus. It is not possible to determine what came first, the change of the text or the design of the melody; but in the end, these two features complement each other and create an emphatic cry to Jesus.

The chorale movement has a ritornello structure, like the opening chorus of part IV. As in the earlier parts of the *Christmas Oratorio*, the instrumentation for the final movement is the same as in the opening chorus. The instruments accompany the four-part chorus colla parte and play a rhythmically contrasting motif between the

[74] Martin Petzoldt has noticed that the change into the second-person singular also appears in some eighteenth-century hymnals. See Petzoldt, *Bach Kommentar II*, 324. Additionally, we can also find versions of the chorale text where all the lines are changed into second-person singular; for instance in *Frommer Christen betendes Hertz und Singender Mund: Oder Altdorfisches Bet- und Gesang-Buch . . .* (Nuremberg: Endters Söhne, 1701), 56; or in Daniel Ringmacher, *Andächtiger Seelen GOtt geheiligte Sing-Ubung . . .* (Ulm: Glitzelhirn, 1737), 47. In spite of these similar cases, it was still Bach who made the change from the libretto to the version in his score, and what weighs even heavier is that Bach sets the final line musically apart from the other lines of the hymn text. The music supports the assumption that the version in Bach's score is not an error but the one the composer intended.

[75] Cf. Blankenburg, *Weihnachts-Oratorium*, 107–8.

individual lines. As in the opening movement, Bach employs the three instrumental choruses (corni da caccia, oboes, strings) as contrasting musical colors and creates the impression of a polychoral dialogue. Compared to the final movements of parts I and II of the oratorio, the instrumental involvement is expanded: Bach adds a four-measure introduction and a postlude of five measures. Each line of the chorale is finally interrupted by four measures of ritornello played by the instruments. Only the final chorale setting of the *Christmas Oratorio* (no. 64) in part VI features an even more elaborate use of instruments. The setting musically connects several of the features of the preceding composition: the concerto structure and instrumentation of the opening movement and the descending gesture of the beginning of the lines, followed by a brief melismatic embellishment of the end of the line, also resemble the melody Bach had composed for his chorale trope in mvt. 40 (ex. 9.2).

*Example 9.2* J. S. Bach, BWV 248/40, 2–3 and BWV 248/42, mm. 5–9

The chorale setting is an original composition and the score exhibits several traces of the compositional process. Revisions are especially visible in the ritornello sections. In the final version, Bach pits the three instrumental choruses against one another in a tight exchange of their characteristic musical motifs. Bach's original idea in m. 3 was to juxtapose the oboes and corni in an even more block-like dialogue. The first note in the corni was a half note, which was then changed into the present, more vivid version with eighth and sixteenth notes. Bach also added the second group of sixteenth notes in the oboes in m. 3[76] as well as the descending sixteenth notes in the corno in m. 4.[77] The goal here is the establishment of increased rhythmic diversity and a stronger rhythmic contrast to the simpler sections with the chorale lines. An example that demonstrates how Bach composed the movement is m. 16: Bach wrote the setting of the chorale melody first and copied the music into the colla parte playing instrumental lines. It is still visible that the oboes and strings had the dotted half note from the melody in m. 16; Bach then changed this into a quarter note, followed by rhythmically characteristic ritornello material, that began the transition into either the repetition of the opening ritornello or the interlude that led to the final section of the chorale setting. We see the same type of change again in m. 41, where Bach transformed the half note in the oboes and strings into a quotation of the ritornello material.

---

[76] The original version was still maintained in the oboe parts in mm. 9/10.

[77] The quarter-note rests in m. 3 in violin 2 and viola were originally eighth-note rests as in the first violin.

302 JOHANN SEBASTIAN BACH'S CHRISTMAS ORATORIO

The opening chorus for part IV, "Fallt mit Danken, fallt mit Loben," is a parody of the first movement of cantata 213, where it announced the decision of the gods to take care of the young hero Hercules. Bach's librettist modeled the new text after the words from the earlier cantata. Both texts begin with an imperative and continue with a mention the word "Erden" in line 4; the celebratory affect of both texts is the same as well. The most striking difference appears in the last lines; here the secular text mentions the miraculous career of Hercules; the sacred parody talks about the raging enemies. While the last line of the parody text would probably have motivated a more martial setting in another context, Bach does not change the music.[78]

BWV 213/1          BWV 248/4,36

| BWV 213/1 | BWV 248/4,36 |
|---|---|
| Lasst uns sorgen, lasst uns wachen | Fallt mit Danken, fallt mit Loben |
| Über unsern *Göttersohn.* | Vor des Höchsten Gnadenthron! |
| Unser Thron | *Gottes Sohn* |
| Wird auf *Erden* | Will der *Erden* |
| Herrlich und verkläret werden, | Heiland und Erlöser werden, |
| Unser Thron | Gottes Sohn |
| Wird aus ihm ein Wunder machen. | Dämpft der Feinde Wut und Toben. |
| | |
| Let us care for, let us watch | Bow with thanksgiving, bow with lauding |
| Over our Divine Son! | Before the Most High's Throne of Grace! |
| Our throne | God's Son |
| Will on earth | Is willing to become the earth's |
| Become glorious and radiant, | Savior and redeemer; |
| Our throne | God's Son |
| Will make a wonder of him. | Dampens the enemies' fury and rage |

The movement is straightforward, both texturally and structurally. It lacks the polyphonic sections we find in the other opening choral movements of the *Christmas Oratorio.* Instead, Bach composed a concerto movement that juxtaposes different groups of instruments and vocalists in a lighthearted dialogue. Rhythmically, the movement resembles a minuet,[79] and adopts its joyful and sprightly character (yet not the particular structure). The character of the movement comes into even sharper relief if we consider what Bach did *not* compose. The autograph score for BWV 213 shows for mm. 53–56 the beginning of an imitative choral section that was immediately rejected and crossed out. Instead, Bach composes long, extended notes in the upper voices that provide a harmonic backdrop for the vocal bass voice (ex. 9.3). While the polyphonic

---

[78] We find a similar case in the opening movement for the first part, "Lasset das Zagen, verbannet die Klage," where the parody model did not permit a more expressive setting of these words; in a new composition Bach would probably have set them differently.

[79] See Little/Jenne, *Dance and the Music of J. S. Bach,* 230 and 301.

section might have highlighted the labor that is involved in the caretaking of the gods, it would have given the movement a certain gravitas that does not fit the rest of the piece. Bach opts for the simplicity of a homophonic setting that now depicts the enduring care through the extended notes. Another aspect might have motivated Bach to feature the bass voice here in almost soloistic fashion. The secular cantata ends with a dialogue between the god Mercury (sung by a bass) and the choir of the Muses. Bach might have seen these measures as an anticipation of the final movement. Within the *Christmas Oratorio*, the small solo loses its semantic significance.[80]

*Example 9.3* J. S. Bach, BWV 213/1, rejected sketch from P 125, mm. [53]–[66]
J. S. Bach, BWV213/1, final version (m. 51–58)

---

[80] That is, unless we draw a connection between the bass in the opening movement and the two bass recitatives, no. 38 and 40.

The chorus is a ternary movement in modified *da capo* form. An extensive instrumental ritornello (mm. 1–24), from which mm. 9–24 are repeated literally at the end (mm. 225–40), frames two contrasting vocal sections. The vocal material in the A and A′ sections is derived from the ritornello, while the B section introduces new musical ideas. The ritornello that separates the two vocal sections in the B section is also derived from the opening ritornello:

|     |         |         |                |         |
| --- | ------- | ------- | -------------- | ------- |
|     |         | 1–24    | Ritornello     | F–> F   |
| A   | 1–96    | 25–80   | Vocal section  | F–> C   |
|     |         | 81–96   | Ritornello     | C–> C   |
|     |         | 97–120  | Vocal section  | C–> d   |
| B   | 97–160  | 121–36  | Ritornello     | d–> d   |
|     |         | 137–60  | Vocal section  | d–> a   |
| A′  | 161-240 | 161–224 | Vocal section  | F–> F   |
|     |         | 225–40  | Ritornello     | F–> F   |

The ritornello consists of twenty-four measures and follows the conventions of the "fortspinnung-type" of the Baroque ritornello. It can be subdivided into three segments of eight measures each: the *vordersatz* (mm. 1–8), a *fortspinnung* (9–16), and an epilogue (17–24). The *vordersatz* features the instruments in a compact, homophonic texture, which is followed a dialogue between the three instrumental groups, corni, oboes, and strings in the *fortspinnung*. The ritornello returns three more times, first transposed to C major (mm. 81–96) and then to D minor (mm. 121–36) before the final ritornello returns to the home key (mm. 225–40); in these later instances, however, it is reduced to *fortspinnung* and epilogue, while the characteristic *vordersatz* provides the motivic material for the vocal sections A and A' and is only heard in conjunction with the vocal ensemble.

The first vocal section presents the opening measures of the *vordersatz* literally as a motto but then (in m. 29) moves on to new material, pitting the two upper voices against the tenor, while the bass holds a pedal point. The instruments interject with short motifs, before the tutti in m. 37 repeats almost literally the mm. 1–8 from the ritornello by way of *vokaleinbau*, followed by a variant of the *fortspinnung* segment. Measures 61–80 combine again a direct quote of the motto of the ritornello with new material before the shortened ritornello (*fortspinnung* and epilogue) returns, now transposed to C major.

The B section does not literally quote from the previous material, but the gestures still resemble the motifs from section A and the listener does not perceive the B section as particularly contrasting. The sense of continuity is reinforced by the shortened ritornello (mm. 121–36), transposed to D minor, which separates the two vocal sections of the B section. The return to the modified A section is quite abrupt. Section B had ended in A minor and, without an instrumental transition, the A' section begins in the mediant key of F major. The shortened ritornello finally closes the movement.

The opening chorus for part IV of the *Christmas Oratorio* is a traditional concerto movement that exhibits a high degree of motivic economy. As so often in Bach's concerto movements, the ritornello already provides most of the musical ideas, which are then modified and varied throughout the movement. The melodic simplicity and formal constructedness of the movement goes along with a clear, mostly syllabic voice-leading. Longer melismatic lines are limited to words like "danken," "Gnaden[-thron]" in the A section, and "Heiland" and "Erlöser" in the B section. These emphasize the praise of the divine presence with all its connotations: as a historical event (as celebrated in the first three parts of the oratorio), at the beginning of the secular New Year, in the human heart (as it is celebrated especially in part IV), and for salvation (presently and at the end of times). The joyful affect prevails, and the movement thus fits right into conventional modes of celebrating the first day of January. The theological "heavy lifting," as it were, is done by the later movements.

# 10

# Paths of Enlightenment (Part V)

The schedule of feast days in the Christmas season of 1734/35 did not leave much downtime for Bach and his St. Thomas's choir. After the performance of part IV of the *Christmas Oratorio* in the morning service at St. Thomas's Church and during the Vespers service in St. Nicholas's, Bach had to mount the performance of part V on the next day, as the Sunday after New Year's Day followed right on the heels on January 2, 1735. To create a coherent narrative for the *Christmas Oratorio*, Bach and his librettist decided to skip the prescribed gospel text for the Sunday after New Year's Day, the flight to Egypt and the massacre of the young children by King Herod (Mt 2:13–16), and instead spread the gospel text for the feast of Epiphany, the story about the three wise men (Mt 2:1–12), over two days.[1] It is unlikely that the preacher in the morning service at St. Nicholas's (Diaconus Lic. Friedrich Werner [1659–1741]) would have changed the gospel reading or the text for the sermon.[2] Therefore, the listeners might have noticed a discrepancy between the text for the music and the liturgical texts but this was not perceived to be a major obstacle. We have seen similar deviations already in the second and third parts of the oratorio; and even on regular Sundays, the relationship between the liturgical readings and the cantata texts could be rather loose.

The two final parts of the oratorio are connected through their narrative. At the same time, they contrast sharply, as part V emphasizes the intimate presence of Christ and the divine light of the star of Bethlehem, whereas part VI has an exceedingly martial character and celebrates the final victory of Christ over his "enemies" at the end times. The polarity between the two parts is already inherent in the exegetical tradition of the gospel text from Matthew 2:1–12. Both aspects, intimacy and war against the enemies, is present in seventeenth- and eighteenth-century

---

[1] For the biblical context and the earliest sources for the cult of the three kings/magi see Richard C. Trexler, *The Journey of the Magi. Meanings in History of a Christian Story* (Princeton, NJ: Princeton University Press, 1997), 9–43.

[2] Petzoldt, *Bach-Kommentar* II, 353.

interpretations of the story about the three wise men. The Leipzig superintendent Salomon Deyling published an outline for his sermon on the feast of Epiphany in 1734; there he breaks the interpretation of the text into three parts:

1. **Die Glaubens-Lehre:** Die Heyden lassen sich zu Christi Krippe leiten. Wer JEsum recht erkennt, des Hertze wird voll Freuden.
2. **Die Lebens-Pflicht:** GOtt hat uns seinen Sohn zum Licht und Heyl gegeben, wer wolt in Heucheley und Finsternis noch leben?
3. **Der Glauben-Trost:** Es legt die falsche Welt den Frommen Netz und Stricke, doch GOttes Auge wacht, was schaden ihre Tücke?[3]

1. **The doctrine of faith:** The heathen [gentiles] are led to the manger of Christ. He who properly recognizes Jesus, his heart will be filled with joy.
2. **The duty in life:** God has given his son as a light and for salvation; who would want to live in hypocrisy and darkness?
3. **The consolation of faith:** The deceitful world lays out nets and traps against the pious; however, the eye of God watches, how can deceit harm [the faithful]?

The three categories listed by Deyling describe the theological scaffolding for the libretto of the two last parts of the *Christmas Oratorio*. The "heathen" or "gentiles" (i.e., the three wise men) are mentioned only briefly in recit no. 45, "das auch den Heiden scheinen soll" (that shall shine also to the gentiles). More room is given to the knowledge of Christ "in the heart" as a cause for joy. Deyling's second point is also essential to the libretto, pointing to the juxtaposition of Jesus as the divine light and the human darkness. This visual dichotomy permeates most of part V. Deyling's third point, the threat by the enemies and the divine intervention, is then the topic of the end of the *Christmas Oratorio* as we will see in part VI. The trajectory of the two final parts of the oratorio resembles the order in which Deyling had preached about the story of the three wise men one year prior.

Part V of the oratorio tells the beginning of the story of the wise men and their search for the manger, and it also continues the meta-narrative of the oratorio as a whole, the coming of Christ into the human heart. The interpretation of the gospel text in the libretto extends the process of internalization we have already observed in part III, where the journey of the shepherds to the manger was understood as an internalized journey to the human heart. In part V then, it is the search of the three wise men for the child in the manger that is interpreted as an internal event; likewise,

[3] Deyling, *Herrliche Dinge*, 7.

the star of Bethlehem is viewed as a light of internal (spiritual) illumination.[4] The
search of the wise men becomes the search for Jesus; the light of the bright star is
interpreted, referring to Psalm 119:105, as the word of God: "Your word is a lamp
to my feet and a light to my path."

## Creating energy in the opening movement (mvt. 43)

Before the story unfolds, part V begins with a festive opening movement. The
text Bach's librettist provided for the movement does not explicitly reference the
prevailing topics of this part of the oratorio. Instead, the movement is a general
expression of praise of God, similar to the opening movements of parts I, III, and
IV. The text is a free paraphrase of the Gloria in excelsis and the movement thus
also references the chorus of angels in part II. In Bach's (and his librettist's) original
plan, part V was projected to begin with a parody of the final movement of BWV
213.[5] Had Bach composed the movement as planned, it would have been a rather
lighthearted, gavotte-like chorus in *da capo* form, probably featuring a solo (as in
BWV 213) or soli (as in the actual model for that movement, BWV 184/6) in the
middle section.[6] However, Bach revised his original plan and set out to compose a
more substantial chorus in concerto form that exhibits features similar to the earlier opening movements in the oratorio. The large number and the character of the
corrections and revisions in Bach's autograph score make evident that the movement was indeed newly composed[7]: in mm. 3–6, Bach works on the main musical
material for the ritornello; between mm. 21 and 31 he eventually inserts ten additional measures on a separate sheet of paper; and a text marker at m. 64 ("Dein"/to
you), a measure that now features only the instruments, shows that Bach was still
trying to work out musical details as well as the larger musical structure while he
was composing.[8]

The festive and celebratory text for the opening of part V demanded an
equally celebratory setting. Yet, Bach had to work within the limitations and

[4] The internalization of the journey of the magi was also, at least in part, a component of the
rejection of an external cult of the magi/kings in medieval and early modern Christmas plays; see for
Luther's rejection of these practices Trexler, *Journey of the Magi*, 158–59.

[5] See chap. 5.

[6] The movement had a very complex history; see NBA I/14, KB, 164–75 and NBA I/35, KB,
138–42.

[7] Hans-Joachim Schulze has recently suggested that the movement might have had a
"Vorgeschichte" (prehistory); see Schulze, *Die Kantaten*, 647. However, the score leaves no doubt that
the movement was entirely newly composed.

[8] At the beginning of the B section (fol. 7[r] of the score for part V) Bach sketches the beginning of
the vocal line that should follow on the next page; this was usually done in new compositions and not
in parodies.

liturgical conventions of the first Sunday after New Year's Day. Normally the day provided a moment of rest for Bach's ensemble after strenuous cantata performances on the three days of Christmas and on New Year's Day. An additional reason for Bach's decision to lighten the workload for his singers on the Sunday after New Year's might have been the Leipzig tradition of New Year's Singing ("Neujahrssingen"), which was strenuous on the voices of the singers as well. The students went through the streets of Leipzig, sang sacred songs, and received money. While the best discantists and altoists were exempt from this exhausting task and received a financial compensation from the churches of St. Thomas's and St. Nicholas's,[9] Bach's ripienists might still have participated. In earlier cantatas, like BWV 153, composed for January 2, 1724, Bach only used strings and bc and gave the chorus only three simple chorale settings. In his second composition for this day, BWV 58 from 1727, Bach wrote a solo cantata for soprano and bass, leaving out the chorus entirely. The instruments in that cantata are again reduced to the minimum of strings and bc. For a performance in the first half of the 1730s, Bach slightly expanded the instrumentation with a chorus of reed instruments; still, the musical forces were smaller than in the cantatas for the preceding feast days.[10] The opening movement for part V of the *Christmas Oratorio* partially departs from these earlier conventions. With two oboi d'amore and strings, the instrumentation of part V is smaller than the other parts of the oratorio, but it is about the same size as the expanded instrumentation of BWV 58 from 1733/34. What is different, though, is that Bach does not give his chorus a break. Part V begins with a large-scale choral movement, followed by a turba chorus as well as two simpler chorale settings. The only movement that is less demanding than its equivalents in the other parts of the oratorio is the final movement. Bach did not compose an expanded chorale setting but a simple, four-part chorale harmonization.

The structure of the opening movement of part V, composed in *da capo* form, strongly favors the two opening lines of the text over the five remaining lines. So much so that the A section (97 mm.) is three times the size of the B section (29 mm.). This significant imbalance is in part due to an addition of ten measures, added after the composition had already been completed. At the end of m. 20 Bach indicates with a star-like sign and "NB" that the copyist must insert the ten additional measures that were written on a separate sheet of paper (fig. 10.1). Since the "NB" is written into the line with the abandoned text for the first recit at the bottom of the page,[11] Bach must have added the measures sometime between his decision to insert the recit *after* the opening movement and the copying of the performing

---

[9] *BachDok* II, 135–36.

[10] The performance of the revised version took place in 1733 or 1734; the additional reed instruments were oboe I and II and taille; NBA I/4, KB, 147–148.

[11] For the revision of the recitative see chap. 5.

*Figure 10.1* J. S. Bach, BWV 248/43, second page of the movement in Bach's score (D-B Mus. ms. Bach P 32, fol. 47ᵛ) (bpk, Berlin/Mendelssohn-Archiv, Staatsbibliothek zu Berlin, Stiftung Preussischer Kulturbesitz, Berlin, Germany/Art Resource, NY)

parts; in any case, this must have happened after he had already completed the movement. Even without the added ten measures, the balance between the A and B sections would be askew, but adding the measures tipped the balance even more toward the A section.[12]

For the opening movement of part V, Bach had to find a compromise between the celebratory mood of the text and the pragmatic musical limitations of the day. In a different context, the allusion to the Gloria in the opening lines might

---

[12]  One could argue that the proportions of the movement would have been more balanced without the addition. The A section consists of an opening ritornello and four vocal sections. Sections 2 and 4 are variations of sections 1 and 3 respectively. Before the addition, the ritornello and the first vocal section were each twenty-one measures long, while the two other vocal sections have a length of twenty-two measures and the B section is twenty-nine measures long. Bach added the measures because the original version did not give enough weight to the opening line of the text, which contains the praise of God ("Ehre sei dir, Gott, gesungen"). This addition allowed Bach to repeat (and thus accentuate) the text before he moved on to the second line.

have inspired Bach to use brass instruments, as in the Latin *Gloria in Excelsis Deo,* BWV 191, written for a university celebration on Christmas Day 1742 and which reuses text and music from the *Mass in B minor* of 1733[13]. While trumpets and timpani were not available for January 2, 1735, Bach could still devise musical motifs that recalled the triadic character of idiomatic trumpet fanfares and combine these with a more static harmonic foundation, as was typical for most trumpet movements. As a result, the first five measures of the opening movement stay firmly in the range of A major. Bach touches briefly the dominant E major and the subdominant D major, but the entire opening section could easily be accompanied by timpani tuned in the usual pair of tonic and dominant. From m. 5 on, triadic motifs in the oboes give way to syncopated broken triads that are rhythmically less active than the strings, while the strings continue their accompaniment with broken triads in sixteenth and eighth notes. This second motivic area of the ritornello lasts until m. 14, when the movement picks up momentum which propels the listener into the first vocal part: The pulsating eighth notes in the bc give way to an ascending sequence of *figura corta* motifs (♫), and the first violin plays sequences of a circular motif, which are an embellished variant of a gradually climbing progression in the first oboe. Bach creates the impression of a stretto-like acceleration. This section is an integral feature for the entire movement as it returns several times, contributing to the energy of the opening chorus.

The autograph score shows that Bach worked on several details in this opening ritornello. In the final version, the first four measures stage a dialogue between the vivid motif of the oboi d'amore and the broken triads in the strings. The first time the oboe presents its motif, groups of sixteenth notes frame two repeated eighth notes. The second statement of the oboes in m. 3 originally began with two falling eighth notes, similar to the notes now played by the violins. While drafting the measure, Bach changed the second eighth notes in both oboi into two sixteenth notes. The result is a repetition of the opening motif, only a sixth higher. Corrections in the score further show that the first oboe originally had two c♯″ eighth notes on the second beat. This literal repetition must have sounded too simple and too static to Bach, so he changed the second beat into a chain of sixteenth notes, circling around the pitch c♯″. This revised version, which was already devised before the second oboe was added, exhibits more driving energy than Bach's first plan (ex. 10.1).

---

[13] Markus Rathey, "Zur Entstehungsgeschichte und Datierung von Bachs Universitätsmusik *Gloria in Excelsis Deo* BWV 191," *Bach-Jahrbuch* 99 (2013): 319–28.

*Example 10.1* J. S. Bach, BWV 248/43, rhythmical changes, mm. 1–5

The creation of rhythmic energy was also the goal of a revision in m. 5. Bach changed the first note in the second oboe from a quarter note (the same value as the first oboe) into an eighth note. With this change, the second oboe is now syncopically shifted by half a beat against the $\frac{3}{4}$ meter (see ex. 10.1). Bach maintains this shift in one of the oboes throughout the second half of the ritornello, thus creating both rhythmic and (through the use of syncopations) harmownic tension between the two oboi d'amore. The rhythmic profile is further highlighted by a change in the string parts in m. 5. The last two notes in the second violin were originally *e′* and *c♯′*, outlining a broken A major triad, together with the previous note; the viola has a similar triad, *e′–c♯′–a′*, followed in m. 6 by *a′*. In his revision, Bach does not make any harmonic changes, but he replaces the broken triads with repeated notes: *a* in the second violin and an alternation between *e′* and *c♯′* in the viola. The repeated notes in the second violin in particular now emphasize the metrical accent of the measure, giving particular stress to the first beat of each measure. Bach even repeats this pattern in the following measures, suggesting that the change in m. 5 was made before the following measures were written. The compositional decision has to be seen in conjunction with the change made to the oboe part in the same measure. The lower strings now emphasize the first beat of each measure while the revised oboe part resists this very accent by means of syncopations. The result is a higher degree of rhythmic energy that propels the movement forward.

Some further revisions in the ritornello, which we can disregard here, aim to clarify the harmonic progression or to avoid awkward voice-leading.[14] A significant revision appears in the penultimate measure of the ritornello (m. 16). This is a crucial moment because Bach has to prepare the entrance of the first vocal section in the following measure. The score and original parts allow us to trace four different versions of the first three notes in the bc:

| | |
|---|---|
| Version 1: | *G♯–G♯–G♯* |
| Version 2: | *g♯–a–b* |
| Version 3: | *g♯–e–a* |
| Version 4: | *g♯–e–A* |

Bach had to arrive in m. 17 in A major. The first version, with the leading tone G♯, emphasized the dominant but it must have appeared too static, especially after the two rhythmically highly energetic measures that immediately preceded m. 16. The second version was less static but it led the bc voice up too high. Version three is the final version in the score; it marks the cadential functions with clearly articulated leaps. After copying the parts, the last note was finally transposed one octave lower.[15]

For the following vocal section Bach splices the material from the ritornello. While the first four ritornello measures provide the basis for the sections 1 and 3 of the A section, the remaining twelve measures reappear at the end of sections 2 and 4 with the voices of the chorus built into the instrumental texture. The ritornello appears that way three times throughout the A section: once in its original form, and twice in a vocal-instrumental derivate. The opening motif of the oboi d'amore is sung with the word "Ehre" (glory). As in the ritornello, the motif is assigned to pairs of voices. At the first instance (mm. 17–18) it is sung by soprano and bass, then handed to tenor and alto (mm. 22–23), and finally to tenor and bass (mm. 27–28).[16]

---

[14] Cf. NBA II/6, KB, 61.

[15] NBA II/6, KB, 61; it is not entirely clear who made this change; the transposition could be autograph but it is also possible that it was made by someone else.

[16] It appears that Bach at the outset was not clear about the assignment of these little duos. In m. 17 he first entered a version for soprano and tenor, before he replaced the tenor with the bass. It is also possible that the tenor part was simply a mistake; it is impossible to decide at this point.

The only new musical material in the A section is the fugal subject Bach introduces to set the second line of the text. A vivid, ascending line accentuates the word "Lob" (praise). The short point of imitation (mm. 31–41) culminates in a variant of the last thirteen measures of the ritornello with the vocal parts being built into the instrumental fabric. Like the opening ritornello, the end of the vocal section is infused with additional energy through the sequential ascent of the *figura corta* in the bc.

The second half of the A section (mm. 54–98) repeats the text of the first half. The musical material from the beginning is now transposed to the dominant E major. The polyphonic texture appears denser: instead of introducing the voices in simple parallel motion, Bach now adds a third voice a few beats later, which leads to the impression of increased polyphonic complexity (although all of this happens in a more or less homophonic framework). The second entrance of the voices in m. 65 exhibits several revisions that allow us to trace the compositional process. In m. 64 Bach entered the first word of the text, "Dir" (to you), in all four voices. This suggests that he, while writing the instrumental layer, had planned to compose a somewhat homophonic entrance for the four voices. The entering of the first word of the text serves as a mnemonic aid while Bach continued his work on the instrumental parts. When he finally turned to the vocal layer, he revised his original plan and delayed the entrance of the voices until the next measure (m. 65); instead of a homophonic block, the entrance of the voices is again staggered.

The opening of the second half of the A section is a variation of the beginning of the movement but with an increased degree of density. The same is true for the modified repetition of the fugal section. The first time around, Bach had introduced the voices with only the accompaniment of the bc (mm. 31–37) and brief staccato motifs in the strings. When Bach now repeats the fugal section, both the oboes and strings provide an accompaniment with continuous staccato beats, supplying a clear harmonic backdrop for the polyphonic vocal texture. Yet again, the addition of the instruments was not Bach's original plan. Measures 75–79 originally featured rests in the instrumental lines, which were then overwritten with the music.[17]

In the brief B section of the *da capo* structure, Bach introduces contrasting material. Short and mostly homophonic vocal blocks alternate with short instrumental interludes, consisting of ritornello-material. Within this simple structure, Bach establishes a climax. In the first two interludes, the opening motif of the oboi d'amore is answered by broken chords in the strings (as in the ritornello). In the third interlude, Bach inserts the string motif of mm. 2–3 again at mm. 120–21 (the bc line at m. 120 is also the same as at m. 2), but then he crosses it out and writes a variation of the oboe motif, transposed a third higher. The revision has several consequences: it breaks an established pattern and thus catches the attention of the listener. The sequential treatment of the oboe motif also creates a climax, which

---

[17] See also NBA II/6 KB, 63.

culminates in the final vocal block of the B section (mm. 121–26). The revision thus has a clear dramatic function within the structure of the movement. In summary, the compositional strategies in the opening movement of part V have the goal to generate energy and tension. The already energetic theme at the beginning is charged with even more energy at its second instance in m. 3. Bach creates rhythmic energy by adding syncopations in the ritornello (m. 5) as well as through the change of the bc pattern at the end of the ritornello. He adds momentum by revising the second entrance of the oboe motif in the ritornello as well as by changing the last instrumental interlude in the B section. He creates a sense of increased intensity by thickening the texture in the second half of the A section, both in the vocal parts and in the instrumental accompaniment of the fugal section (mm. 75–). The liturgical and practical constraints might have limited Bach's use of instruments on January 2, 1735, but he was still able to compose a highly effective, celebratory, and dramatic opening movement for part V of his *Christmas Oratorio*. It sets the stage for the arrival of the three wise men in the Christmas narrative.

## The interpretation of the three wise men

The main metaphor in part V is "Licht" (light), which is juxtaposed with "Finsternis" (darkness). While the immediate motivation for the light metaphor was the star, which had led the three wise men to Jerusalem (and subsequently to the manger in Bethlehem), the visual metaphor has a broader symbolic meaning. The light serves both as an image for Jesus as well as for the Word of God. This duality of meanings melds into one if we consider that Jesus was viewed as the Word incarnate (Jn 1) and that his presence in the human heart (his *inhabitatio*) was mediated through the word.[18] The light metaphor plays an important role in sermons and other theological interpretations of the gospel text. Johann Gottfried Olearius in his *Geistliches Seelen-Paradies* from 1669, a sacred meditation on the life of Jesus, calls Christ the light of the world[19] (in accordance with biblical verses such as Jn 8:12 and 9:5) and identifies the Word of God as the divine light, which is given for the heathen in particular:

| | |
|---|---|
| Dieses ist nun die allerfreulichste und uns allen hochtröstliche *Epiphania* oder Erscheinung / das grosse Neue Jahr / der Heyden Weihnachts-Fest / an welchem das grosse Weltlicht / | This now is the most joyful and for all of us the most consoling Epiphany or appearance, the great New Year, the Christmas feast of the heathen, on which the great light of the world, |

---

[18] See chap. 3.
[19] Olearius, *Seelen-Paradies*, 100f.

JEsus Christus auch den Armen Heyden und Japhiten zu Theil worden / 1. Buch Mos. 9. an welchen die Erstlinge der Heyden herzugebracht / und die Thür geöfnet worden uns allen / die wir von Natur auch Heiden gewesen / nunmehr aber das Licht des Göttlichen Worts / und seeligmachenden Evangelii / ja Christum selbst / in demselbigen / haben.[20]

Jesus Christ, has come to the poor heathen and to the sons of Japhet (Gen 9). On this day, the first heathen were brought [to Jesus in the manger] and the door was opened for us all, who had been heathen originally [literally: from nature] ourselves. Now we have the light of the divine word, the saving Gospel, yes, [we have] Jesus himself [in this word].

The three wise men, often identified as pagan astrologers,[21] were seen as the first "heathen" to convert to the faith in Christ[22]; their following of the star to the manger is a model for the believer's following of the Word as the divine light (and divine enlightenment). The believers are admonished to

in dem Himmlischen Lichte wandeln / den Stern deß Göttlichen Worts zu dem geistlichen Bethlehem uns regieren lassen / daselbst auch / aus dem guten Schatz unsers Hertzens unserm Ehren-Könige / das Gold des wahren ungefärbten Glaubens / den Weyrauch des Gebeths und Dancksagung / und Myrrhen der geduldigen Aufnehmung des Creutzes und Verleugnung unser selbst / williglich aufopfern / den Weg welchen Er uns führet / gehorsamlich folgen / daß Licht seiner Gnade auch mitten in Noth- und Todes Finsternüs erblicken / und in das Himmlische Vaterland eingehen sollen.[23]

walk in the heavenly light, to let the star of the divine word be the guide to the spiritual Bethlehem. There, we shall give to the king of honor from the treasure of our heart the gold of the unblemished faith, the frankincense of prayer and thanksgiving, and the myrrh of the patient acceptance of the cross and of self-denial. [We shall give these gifts] voluntarily and obediently walk the path he [God] is leading us, so that we shall see the light of his mercy in the midst of the darkness of distress and death, and that we shall enter the heavenly fatherland.

---

[20]  Olearius, *Seelen-Paradies*, 100–101.

[21]  However some interpreters also saw in the three men descendants of those who had been converted to Judaism during the Persian exile; see Neumeister, *Priesterliche Lippen*, 239.

[22]  See, for instance, Aegidius Strauch (*Starcke und Milch-Speise*, 1702, 130) who writes with reference to St. Chrysostom, "In diesen Weisen und derer Zukunfft wird die Gnaden-Thür den Heyden weit auffgethan" (In these wise men and their coming, the door of grace is opened wide for the heathen).

[23]  Olearius, *Seelen-Paradies*, 101f.

The combination of the revelation to the heathen and the interpretation of the star as a symbol for the Word already appears in seventeenth-century sermons, for instance in the *Postille* by Johann Gerhard.[24] He writes about the star: "Here, we shall remember that if we shall come to Christ, God the Lord has to lead us with his miraculous light. Our minds are so clouded with darkness that we cannot recognize Christ lest God the Lord ignites a light for us."[25] Not only does Gerhard decode the star as the light of divine revelation but he also juxtaposes the divine light and the darkness of the human mind. He continues with an exploration of the meaning of this divine light without which man is not able to even perceive the divine revelation.[26] Gerhard's reading of the gospel text resembles the interpretation we find in the libretto for part V, a hymn setting (mvt. 46) which states, "Dein Glanz all Finsternis verzehrt, die trübe Nacht in Licht verkehrt. Leit uns auf deinen Wegen" (Your luster consumes all darkness, turns the murky night into light. Lead us along your pathways); the following aria, no. 47, juxtaposes the dark human mind and the divine light, "Erleucht auch meine finstre Sinnen, erleuchte mein Herze durch der Strahlen klaren Schein!" (Light up, too, my dark inclinations, light up my heart with the clear luminosity of your streams of light!). The final chorale setting of part V adds, "Zwar ist solche Herzensstube wohl kein schöner Fürstensaal, sonden eine finstre Grube; doch, sobald dein Gnadenstrahl in derselben nur wird blinken, wird es voller Sonnen dünken" (True, such a heart-cellar is certainly no choice hall of princes, but rather a dark pit; yet, as soon as your grace-filled stream of light flashes in this same [pit], it will seem full of sunlight). The similarities between Gerhard and the libretto for the *Christmas Oratorio* point to an exegetical tradition that was quite common in the seventeenth and early eighteenth centuries.[27] This metaphorical understanding of the light of the star of Bethlehem has its model in Martin Luther's theology. Luther's sermon on the gospel text in his *Hauspostille* contrasts human reasoning, which leads into darkness, and trust in the divine word, which will lead to the light: "This we have to remember well. For, if we want to come to this

---

[24] For the revelation to the heathen see Gerhard, *Postille*, 150f.

[25] "Wir sollen allhie bedenken, wenn wir zu Christo kommen sollen, so muß auch GOtt der HErr durch ein wunderbares Licht uns herzuführen. Wir sind an unsern Verstande also verfinstert, daß wir Christum nicht erkennen mögen, wenn uns nicht GOtt der HErr ein Licht anzündet." Gerhard, *Postille*, 152f.

[26] Gerhard, *Postille*, 153.

[27] Leipzig preacher Romanus Teller, for instance, provides a similar interpretation in his sermon collection *Der große Unterscheid*, published in Leipzig in 1720: "Oh, how lucky were the wise men, when the first glimpse of mercy, which God had given into their souls, was had not been futile. They did follow it [the sign God had planted into their souls. Then God let shine his light for them evermore. . . . Not only did they search for their Savior but they did indeed find him and recognized him as the one who reveals himself more and more to their souls, as he has promised." ("O wie wohl hatten es die Weisen, als sie den ersten Gnaden-Blick, der GOtt in ihre Seelen that, nicht vergebens seyn liessen. sondern demselben nachgiengen! Darauf hat GOtt ihnen sein Licht immer mehr und mehr aufgehen lassen. . . . Sie suchen nicht nur ihren Heyland, sondern finden Ihn auch und erblicken Ihn als denjenigen, der immer mehr und mehr sich ihrer Seelen offenbaret, wie er versprochen."); Teller, *Der grosse Unterscheid*, 227.

little child and if we want to find it, we must not follow our own thoughts or reasoning but stick to the word alone and not turn away from it [the word]."[28]

A sermon that draws a similar connection is the sermon for the feast of Epiphany by Heinrich Müller, published in his *Evangelische Schlußkette* (1672).[29] Bach owned the book himself,[30] and we know that Müller's theology had a strong impact on the genesis of some of Bach's works. Elke Axmacher has succinctly shown that Müller's Passion theology served as an inspiration for Picander's text for the *St. Matthew Passion*.[31] Given Müller's impact on the genesis of the *St. Matthew Passion*, it is possible that Bach and his librettist (who might have been Picander as well) were influenced by Müller's sermon. Indeed, that sermon is theologically quite close to the libretto of part V of the *Christmas Oratorio*. The three men are a symbol for the "heathen" searching for Christ.[32] Müller also equates the wise men searching for Jesus with the searching for Jesus in one's own breast:

| | |
|---|---|
| Jerusalem deß HErrn Stadt. Wo sucht man den HErrn? In seinem Hause. Das Hertz sein Haus / Weist du nun / wo du Jesum suchen solt? In deinem Hertzen. (Festteil, 89) | Jerusalem, the city of the Lord. Where does one search for the Lord? In his house. The heart is his house, do you now know where to look for him? in your heart. |

The quote resonates with the combination of gospel text and interpretative recit in mvt. 45, which directly combines the physical search of the wise men for Jesus and the spiritual search for Christ in the heart:

CHORUS

| | |
|---|---|
| Wo ist der neugeborne König der Jüden? | Where is the newborn King of the Jews? |

RECIT

| | |
|---|---|
| Sucht ihn in meiner Brust, hier wohnt er, mir und ihm zur Lust! | Seek him in my beast, here he dwells, to my and his delight! |

---

[28] "Das laßt uns wohl merken. Denn so wir zu diesem Kindlein kommen und es finden wollen, müssen wir nicht unsern Gedanken oder Vernunft folgen, sondern bei dem Wort allein bleiben, und uns vom selben nicht lassen abwenden." Luther, *Hauspostille*, col. 124.

[29] Here quoted after the edition from 1689.

[30] See the description in Leaver, *Bach's Theological Library*, 112f.

[31] Elke Axmacher, "Ein Quellenfund zum Text der Matthäus-Passion," *Bach-Jahrbuch* 64 (1978): 181–91; see also the larger study by Axmacher, *"Aus Liebe will mein Heyland sterben": Untersuchungen zum Wandel des Passionsverständnisses im frühen 18. Jahrhundert*, Beiträge zur theologischen Bachforschung 2 (Neuhausen-Stuttgart: Hänssler, 1984; rev. ed. Stuttgart: Carus, 2005).

[32] Müller, *Schlußkette*, Festteil, 84 (hereafter in text).

Müller later adds how Christ makes his dwelling in the human heart: "[D]urch den Glauben wohnt Christus in unserm Hertzen / und wo er wohnt / da ist auch sein Reich / Gerechtigkeit / Fried / und Freud in Heiligen Geist" (It is through faith that Christ lives in our hearts; and where he lives, there is his kingdom, justice, peace, and joy in the Holy Spirit (Festteil, 91). Christ is present through faith; and faith, according to Lutheran Orthodox theology, is instilled through the Word of God. This leads Müller to a meditation on the star of Bethlehem as a symbol for the divine light that shines through the word:

Den Weisen hatte GOtt ein zweyfaches Licht angezündet / dabey sie die Weisheit suchen solten / das eine in der Lufft / das ander im Hertzen. Wer Christum finden wil / der muß beydes haben / den Stern des Worts / und das Licht des Geistes. Mancher rühmet sich des Sterns und fehlt des Geistes. Er hört eine Predigt über die ander / und wird doch / weil er keine mit Andacht höret / durch keine erleuchtet. So muß das Wort gehöret / daß die es hören / dadurch erleuchtet werden. Es kan erleuchten / es wil auch erleuchten / wann nur die / so es hören / sich wollen erleuchten lassen. Daß die wenigsten Zuhörer erleuchtet werden / kommt daher / weil sie die Finsternis lieber haben dann das Licht / zumalen ihre Wercke böse seyn. Andere rühmen sich des Geistes und verachten doch dass Wort / geben grosse Erleuchtung / heimliche Offenbarungen vor ausser dem Wort / da doch denen / die das Wort haben und hören können / kein ander Mittel zur Erleuchtung / dann das Wort Gottes versprochen ist. (Festteil, 93)

God has lit a dual light for the wise men in their quest for truth; one in the sky and the other one in the heart. In order to find Christ, one has to have both: the star of the word and the light of the spirit. Some [people] praise themselves for having the star but they lack the spirit. [They] hear one sermon after the other but they are not enlightened because they do not hear them with contemplation. The word has to be heard in a way that those who hear it are enlightened [by the word]. It only can enlighten, and it only wants to enlighten, if those who hear it want to be enlightened. The reason for the fact that only a few listeners [of the word] are enlightened is that [most listeners] prefer darkness over light, especially as their deeds are evil. Others praise themselves for having the spirit but [then] they scorn the word. They pretend having great enlightenment and secret revelations without the word. [However, they are wrong, as] those who have the word and who hear it have no other means of enlightenment than the word that God has promised.

The duality of the light in Müller's sermon is referenced in the continuation of mvt. 45 in the *Christmas Oratorio*: "Wohl euch, die ihr dies Licht gesehen . . . Mein

Heiland, du, du bist das Licht" (Well, for you who have seen this light . . . You, my Savior, you are the light). While the external light is important for Müller, it is the inner light, identified in the sermon as the "word," that is the focal point. Later in his sermon, Müller alludes to the image of the divine word as a light on the way (Ps 119:105), which also appears in the libretto for aria 47, "Dein Wort soll mir die hellste Kerze in allen meinen Werken sein" (Your word shall be the brightest candle to me in all my works).[33] Similar to the final chorale in part V, Müller emphasizes that the presence of Christ (the Word) leads to enlightenment while his absence has darkness as its final consequence:

| | |
|---|---|
| Für uns geht das Wort GOttes hin und rufft uns zu? [correct: ':'] Folge mir nach. Leben wir als das Wort lehrt / so bleiben wir auff dem Wege / sonst gerathen wir in die Irre. Im Wort im Licht / ohn Wort im Finstern. Dieser Stern führt zu Christo alle die/ so in dem Licht dieses Sterns einher gehen. Ein Leben ohn Wort ist ein Leben ohn Christo / ein Leben im Teuffel. (Festteil, 102) | The word of God walks in front of us and calls us: follow me. If we live as the word teaches us, then we will remain on the path, otherwise we will get lost. With the word [we are] in the light; without the word [we are] in darkness. To Christ this star leads everybody who walks in the light of the star. A life without the word is a life without Christ, [it is] a life with the devil. |

While the identification of the star with the Word of God remains fairly abstract,[34] Müller explains that the quote from the prophet Micah in the gospel reading, which consequently is a quote from the "word of the LORD" in the Old Testament, fulfills this paradigmatic function of being a guiding light for those who search for Jesus:

| | |
|---|---|
| Die Schrift muß Richter seyn in Glaubens-Sachen und Richtschnur in allen *Conciliis*. Denn sie ist Gottes Stimme. Wer sie annimmt / der nimmt Gott an/wer sie verwirfft/ | Scripture must be the judge in questions of faith and a guideline in all councils, since it is the voice of God. Whoever accepts it, accepts God; whoever scorns it, scorns |

---

[33] The oratorio had earlier referred to the Word of God as a light; the second half of the chorale "Wie soll ich dich empfangen" (no. 5) reads: "setze mir selbst die Fackel bei, damit was dich ergötze, mir kund und wissend sei" (set the torch next to me yourself, so that whatever brings you enjoyment may be manifest and known to me).

[34] Preachers could find the identification of the star as the word of God in exegetical handbooks; see, for instance, Starke, *Synopsis Bibliothecae exigeticae*, 50, "Der stern Christi, so viel uns betrifft, ist sein wort" (The star of Christ, as far as we are concerned, is his word).

| verwirft [!] Gott. . . . Aus der Schrifft A. Testaments ziehen die Hohenpriester and Schrifftgelehrten den Propheten Micham an. Denn ob zwar alle Propheten von Christo gezeuget / so hat doch keiner unter allen seine Geburt-Stadt / darnach Herodes fragte / so gewiß und eigentlich benennet als Michas. (Festteil, 97) | God. . . . The high priests and the scripture experts quote from the Old Testament the prophet Micah. Even though all prophets have predicted Christ, no other [prophet] among them has predicted the city of his birth so surely and clearly, about which Herod had inquired, and which had been surely and specifically been named by Micah. |

In other words, the quote from the prophetic text serves not only as a means to identify the place where Jesus can be found within the narrative but as an example for how the word of God can guide those who are searching for him. In Müller's interpretation, the quote from the prophet Micah is charged with symbolic (and theological) meaning that transcends its narrative function; it exemplifies the efficacy of scripture as a guiding light. We will see later how this particular verse received special treatment in Bach's setting.[35]

In order to find the child, the wise men have to follow the revelation through the prophet Micah, "if they want to find him [Jesus], they have to have and hear the prophet Micah."[36] It would be easy to add more examples to the list of similarities of the libretto with theological interpretations of the gospel text.[37] What our selected sample demonstrates is that the libretto participates in a discourse about the *inhabitatio Christi* that is quite common among theologians from the seventeenth and early eighteenth centuries. But it also brings into sharper relief the theological coherence of the libretto: the focal point is still the presence of Christ in the human heart

[35] Müller's interpretation shows some resemblance to Luther's sermon in the *Hauspostille*. The three wise men have trusted their own reasoning and falsely arrived in Jerusalem to find the child. But in order to find him, they have to follow the word, which tells them that the child will be found in Bethlehem, "Sollen sie es aber finden, so müssen sie dem Wort folgen. Das ist der rechte Stern und die schöne Sonne, die auf Christum weiset." (If they [the wise men] want to find it, they have to follow the word. That is the true star and the beautiful sun, which points towards Christ). Luther, *Hauspostille*, col. 125.

[36] "Sollten die ihn aber finden, mußten sie den Propheten Micham haben und hören." Luther, *Hauspostille*, col. 126.

[37] An example is the sermon in Martin Geier's *Zeit und Ewigkeit*, Bach owned the book as well (Leaver, *Bach's Theological Library*, 25). A new edition with the preface of Leipzig Superintendent Deyling, which appeared in 1738, shows that the sermon collection was still read during Bach's time. Like Luther and the other theologians quoted above, Geier interprets the star as a metaphor for the word of God, which guides the way for the one who wants to find Jesus is his own life; see Geier, *Zeit und Ewigkeit*, 209–12.

mediated through the word. The libretto for the oratorio reflects common patterns of understanding, which the two collaborators of the piece would have encountered in sermons, treatises, and even in other poetic texts, such as cantata librettos. A final example here is the libretto for the feast of Epiphany by the Weimar poet Salomo Franck. The text was published in a 1717 collection; the collection also includes several texts that were set by Bach during his tenure in Weimar[38]:

END OF ARIA 3

| | |
|---|---|
| Nimm mein Hertze zum Geschencke, | Take my heart as a gift, |
| Daß ich, JEsu, mich zu dir | So that I guide myself to you, Jesus, |
| Für und für | Over and over, |
| Nach des Wortes Leit-Stern lencke. | With the guiding star of the word. |

ARIA 4

| | |
|---|---|
| Dein Wort sey meines Hertzens Freude | Your word shall be the joy of my heart, |
| Und meiner Füsse klares Licht, | And a clear light for my feet, |
| Daß keine Nacht von dir mich scheide, | So that no night may separate me from you |
| Biß ich dein reines Angesicht | Until I can see your pure face, my Jesus, |
| In Himmels-Glantz, mein JEsu, sehe, | In the splendor of heaven, |
| Und gantz verklähret für dir stehe.[39] | And until I stand in front of you transfigured. |

## Toward the inner light (mvts. 44–47)

The first sequence of movements after the opening chorus stretches from the gospel recit (no. 44) to the aria "Erleucht" (no. 47). The text accomplishes the exegetical transfer of the narrative on the journey of the wise men to the spiritual journey to the human heart as the dwelling place of Christ. In refashioning the external movement as an internal movement within the human heart, the scene parallels the journey of the shepherds to the manger in part III of the oratorio. The two scenes also have some structural similarities; in both Bach uses turba choruses (in ex. 10.2.2) and ties them closely to the subsequent interpretation in an accompagnato recit. In part III, the turba chorus "Lasset uns nun gehen" (no. 26) transitioned seamlessly

---

[38] For Bach's collaboration with Franck, see Rainer Bayreuther, "Bachs Weimarer Wortgeber: Salomo Franck," in *Johann Sebastian Bach in Weimar (1708–1717)*, ed. Helen Geyer (Göttingen: Hainholz, 2008), 41–61.

[39] Salomo Franck, *Sonn- und Fest-Tages-Andachten*, 17.

into the bass recit "Er hat sein Volk;" the whole note c♯ in the bc was the final tone for the chorus and continues for the first measure of the recit. Bach also used two of the instruments (Fl. trav I/II) from the previous chorus as accompagnement. In part V, the turba chorus "Wo ist der neugeborne" (no. 45a) now is linked to the alto recit "Sucht ihn in meiner Brust" (no. 45b) by continuing the bc note D♯. The second half of the turba chorus, "Wir haben seinen Stern gesehen" (no. 45c) is also tied to the following alto recit "Wohl euch" by means of a similar overlap. Considering that normally the movements in the oratorio stand as independent entities and that Bach especially separates biblical narrative and its interpretation, these two moments acquire particular significance.

Movement 45 is further connected with the preceding gospel recit (no. 44). As explained earlier in chapter 5, Bach had originally written the text for the first gospel recit of part V at the bottom of page 1 of the score. He would eventually abandon this "sketch" and enter the text and the music after the end of the opening chorus. This rearrangement of movements reflects Bach's wish to keep the gospel settings in nos. 44 and 45 together. This is underscored by the attacca transition between the gospel recit and its continuation in the following turba chorus (no. 45a). A third link between the two movements is the similar contour of the melodic material. Both movements feature a broken triad, followed by repetitions of the last note, a stepwise ascent and then a leap downward. The intervals differ slightly, but the contour in the tenor voice of no. 44 and the oboe d'amore I part in no. 45a is identical (ex. 10.2.1 and 2).

*Example 10.2* J. S. Bach, BWV 248/44, mm. 1–2 and BWV 248/45a, mm. 1–2

Bach's setting of the gospel text in mvt. 44 is based on a stepwise ascending line in the bc, climbing slowly from f♯ to b; the melodic contour of the tenor line emphasizes the name of "Jesus" (leap of a 4th), and later inserts an exclamation on "siehe" by pitting a high g♯ against an a♯ in the bc. The autograph score shows a small correction in m. 6: the first note in the bc was originally a B♯. Bach then extended the A♯ from the previous measures for a half note and postponed the B♯ until the third beat of m. 6. This change maintains the harmonic tension for two more beats before the harmonic goal is reached at precisely the moment when the text mentions the destination of the journey of the three wise men, Jerusalem.

It has occasionally been suggested that the following turba chorus (no. 45) could have been a parody from the now lost *St. Mark Passion*.[40] This, however, can be ruled out since Bach's handwriting in the score unmistakably represents a composition score and not the copy of an older movement.[41] The text for the movement turns the external experience of the light of the star into the internal "enlightenment" of the faithful. The question for the whereabouts of the newborn king of the Jews is sung by the chorus in a homophonic setting, accompanied mostly colla parte by the two oboi d'amore and the strings. The first choral section ends with an open question, "wo" (where), which Bach sets effectively with a 6/5 chord, followed by a rest in the vocal parts (m. 5). The question is answered by the alto recit: "Sucht ihn in meiner Brust" (Seek him in my breast). Walter Blankenburg has suggested that we are hearing the symbolic voice of Mary.[42] However, that interpretation does not take into account the exegetical trajectory we have explained earlier. The movement is not in fact a dialogue between the wise men and Mary. Rather, the question asked by the wise men within the narrative is answered from the perspective of the believer, who had already asked for the presence of Christ in the aria "Schließe" of part III. After the alto recit, the movement continues with the second half of the choral text of the wise men: "We have seen his star in the Orient and have come to worship him." The walking of the wise men is reflected in a staggered, imitative entrance of the four voices. The subject of this short point of imitation is based on an ascending fifth; Bach uses a similar compositional idea that he employed when he set the journey of the shepherds in part III (no. 26).

The turba section leads again directly into a second alto recit ("Wohl euch, die ihr dies Licht resehen"), exploring the existential significance of the "light" for the "heathen." Bach had originally drafted this second accompagnato recit into the part for the bass voice but then added, "NB. Dieß Recit muß im Alt transponirt werden" (NB. This recit has to be transposed for the alto). Was this an accident or did Bach originally intend to give the recit to the bass? (We have already discussed this question in chapter 5, this book.) Whatever the case, the result after the correction fits into the theological concept of the *Christmas Oratorio* as a whole. The text mentions the "beloved Jesus" ("Geliebter Jesu") and corresponds to the other alto parts in the oratorio. Bach's setting of the text highlights on the one hand the emotional intimacy and, on the other hand, draws attention

[40] Gerhard Freiesleben, "Ein neuer Beitrag zur Entstehungsgeschichte von J. S. Bachs Weihnachtsoratorium," *Neue Zeitschrift für Musik* 83, nos. 29/30 (1916), 237–38 and Beilage 1–2; and Ortwin von Holst, "Turba Chöre des Weihnachts-Oratoriums und der Markuspassion," *Musik und Kirche* 38 (1968): 229–33.

[41] For a political and ideological interpretation of Freiensleben's suggestion, see Daniel R. Melamed, "Bach's *Christmas Oratorio*, BWV 248, and the Jews," *Yale Journal of Music and Religion* 1/1 (2015): 81–102.

[42] Blankenburg, *Weihnachts-Oratorium*, 113.

to the juxtaposition of light and darkness. The light is associated with high, bright sounds. In m. 19 the *e''* on "Licht" is reached by an upward leap of a minor seventh (*f♯'–e''*); the same motif is repeated a third lower in m. 22 (*d'–c''*). The light finally radiates in mm. 26/27, when Bach modulates to F♯ major. Darkness, on the other hand, is, as the overview of the exegetical context has shown, understood as the absence of Christ. Consequently, Bach reaches the lowest notes on the word "heathen" (m. 23) with a fall from *f♯'* down to *b*.

In the parousia theology of the Second Coming of Christ, the presence of the "light" is also understood as an intimate relationship between the believer and the divine. This intimacy is expressed in the phrase "mein Heiland du" (you, my Savior, mm. 21–22) which Bach sets with a sigh-like gesture that descends from *d''* to *a*, supported by a calm and static D-major chord in root position (the only case in the movement where a single consonant chord is held for an entire measure). This sigh-like gesture brings to mind similar ones in the emotional soprano-bass dialogue in part IV (no. 38), where Bach sets the phrase "Jesu, du" (Jesus, you) with a comparable motif. The recit in part V culminates in an invocation of the "beloved Jesus." The alto now features a small melismatic embellishment of the name of Jesus; again a small emotional outburst in what is otherwise a simple and syllabic recit. The melismatic embellishment could remind a modern listener of the invocation of Jesus in Bach's *Actus tragicus*, BWV 106 (at the closing measures of mvt. 2e), albeit on a much smaller scale; but here in part V of the *Oratorio*, the forty-nine-year-old Bach shows much more restraint than his twenty-three-year-old, younger ego. The burst of emotion here does not represent Bach's first plan. Originally, he had only written a single eighth note (*b'*), which he then changed into the figure as it stands now. This change went along with some rhythmic changes in the accompanying instruments. Bach transformed a simple progression in half notes into the rhythmically (and harmonically) more intricate version we have now in mm. 27 and 28[43]; all of this helped him to establish a climax on the final invocation of the name of Jesus.

The sequence of movements leads from the gospel text to the reflection in the accompagnato recits, and then to a hymn setting. The chorale "Dein Glanz all Finsternis verzehrt" continues the juxtaposition of darkness and light. It also alludes briefly to Psalm 109:105 by mentioning God's support on the "pathways" of life (line 3), thus drawing a connection to the journey of the wise men. The hymn gives a glimpse of the third advent of Christ when the final lines express the wish that "we may see your face and glorious light eternally!" The text for this hymn is the final stanza of Georg Weissel's hymn "Nun liebe Seel, nun ist es Zeit," a chorale that was assigned in Leipzig hymnals for the feast of Epiphany.[44] Quite unexpectedly, the

---

[43] For the changes, see NBA II/6, KB, 66.

[44] Cf. Blankenburg, *Weihnachts-Oratorium*, 113. Bach does not use the original melody by Johann Eccard but the melody of *In dich hab ich gehoffet*, as did the Leipzig hymnals as well; see Blankenburg, *Weihnachts-Oratorium*, 116; cf. NBA II/6, KB, 199.

chorale setting does not begin in A major but with an upbeat in F♯ minor. Beginning on that minor chord allows Bach to postpone the bright A-major sound until the second chord (m. 1), setting the word "Glanz" (luster). The bright sound on this word goes along with an ascending melisma in the alto, which extends the word "Glanz" long beyond its appearance in the other three voices.

As usual, Bach composed the chorale setting directly into score. While the melody is evenly spaced, the accompanying voices are sometimes crammed in and show numerous instances of revisions. The result is a setting with a texture of remarkably independent lower voices, full of syncopations and melismatic expansions. The ascending melisma on "Glanz" is followed by a lengthened statement of "Finsternis" (darkness) in the other three voices (mm. 1–2). The darkness contrasts sharply with the "luster": while m. 1 had begun with a bright A-major chord, m. 2 now begins with a seventh chord with an augmented fourth, featuring both a harsh second between $a$ and $b$ and a tritone between $a$ and $d$♯. When the text turns to the "murky night" in the following line, Bach muddies the waters even more. A syncopated bass line renders the rhythmic foundation unstable and the sequence of dissonant harmonies (m. 4) only brightens when in m. 5 the darkness is turned into light. The alto again adds a special feature by embellishing the word "Licht" with an ascending melisma that recalls the one from m. 1. The same melisma will appear later (m. 7) on the word "Wegen" (pathways), thus tying together the two terms that are central to Psalm 119:105: light and path. The whole movement culminates in a melismatically expanded setting of the final phrase "ewig schauen mögen" (may see . . . eternally). Some of these details are the result of Bach's compositional process. The fluid bass line in m. 2 was originally a chain of simple quarter notes before Bach changed it into a smoother eighth-note motion. The chord on the last beat of m. 3 was originally planned as an A-major chord with an added fourth (alto: $e$; tenor: $d$; bass: $a$); the change to a brighter D-major chord in the final version now renders the following gloomy chord on the first beat of m. 4 even more effective. Several major changes appear in m. 5, the very moment when the darkness is turned into light. The tenor in the first version began with three eighth notes; Bach then changed it into the syncopation we have now by tying the second and third notes together, creating a quarter note. Also the alto looked slightly different. The word "Licht" had only the first three notes of the melisma while notes $a'$ and $f$♯' appeared with the syllable "ver-." Bach changed this after finishing the composition in the autograph performing part for the alto.[45] The result is an ascending melisma that emphasizes the word "Licht." The same is the case with the second occurrence of the same melisma in m. 7; again the version in the score groups the notes into 3 + 2 while Bach's alto part puts all five notes under one slur. Finally, Bach made some changes to the rhythmic flow of the tenor in mm. 10 and 11, thus creating a

[45]  Cf. NBA II/6, KB, 301.

more rhythmically diverse texture on the line of the text that expressed the eternal view of the divine face.[46] Bach's revisions in this hymn setting call attention to the juxtaposition of light and darkness. The same dichotomy is implicit in the theme of the following bass aria, no. 47, "Erleucht auch meine finstre Sinnen" (Light up, too, my dark inclinations). The aria makes explicit the exegetical transfer from the light to the word of God, which had been implicit already in the chorale setting no. 46. In accordance with the theological understanding of the "star" as the "word of God," the bass now sings in the B section of the *da capo* aria, "Your word shall be the brightest candle to me."

The aria is probably a parody of the most recent piece that found its way into the *Christmas Oratorio*. The model is the soprano aria "Durch die von Eifer ent- flammeten Waffen" from the secular cantata *Preise dein Glücke, gesegnetes Sachsen,* BWV 215, composed in honor of the Polish king and performed during an open-air celebration on October 5, 1734.[47] The original composition was an unusual setting for soprano (doubled by oboe d'amore) and obbligato flauto traverso I/II with "bas- setto" accompaniment. It lacks a deep bc voice; instead, the lowest voice is played by the violins and the viola. Hans-Joachim Schulze explains that Bach usually employed the bassetto-technique for movements that depicted an inverted world order or something that was utterly remarkable (as was the sound of this type of setting). It usually appears with texts that speak about the lack of a strong founda- tion (or the lack of need for such a foundation), texts that state the extraordinary or incomprehensible, or it expresses light, clarity, or innocence.[48] The latter connec- tion might have inspired Bach (and his librettist) to use the aria at this point in the oratorio. However, the changes Bach makes to the piece eliminate its characteristic light sound and turn it into a more conventional aria with a regular bc line. The model was transposed from B minor to F♯ minor and the solo part was given to a vocal bass, while the instrumental obbligato is played by the oboe d'amore. The bas- setto line now becomes a regular bc line, played by the organ. Bach probably wanted to maintain some of the "airiness" of the original and did not double the bc with another bass instrument. Yet, the doubling of the line was originally intended. The instrumental parts for part V of the *Christmas Oratorio* contains two parts labeled "continuo" (B 13 and B 14) and an organ part (B 15). The aria originally appears

---

[46] For details see NBA II/6, KB, 67. Dürr suggests that the second half of m. 11 in the tenor con- sisted of two eighth notes followed by a quarter note: $f\sharp'-d'-b$. But it is also possible that the beats three and four of this measure were originally quarter notes $(f\sharp'-b)$ and that the second eighth note was added during the revision.

[47] For the history of the piece see Crist, "The Question of Parody," 135–61.

[48] Hans-Joachim Schulze, "Bachs Parodieverfahren," in *Die Welt der Bach Kantaten II: Johann Sebastian Bachs weltliche Kantaten,* ed. Christoph Wolff (Stuttgart/Kassel: Metzler/Bärenreiter, 1997), 178; see also Schulze, "Zum Themenbereich der neueren Bach-Forschung," in *Johann Sebastian Bach und Johann Joseph Fux: Bericht über das Symposium anläßlich des 58. Bachfestes der Neuen Bachgesellschaft 24.–29. Mai 1983 in Graz,* ed. Johann Trummer and Rudolf Flotzinger (Kassel: Bärenreiter, 1985), 33f.

in parts B 15 and B 13. It was then bracketed in B 13 and Bach added the remark "tacet" for the aria. The other continuo part (B 14) has an original "Aria tacet" in Bach's hand. It was probably written after the use of the continuo had already been rejected.[49] We can only speculate why Bach did not keep the original bassetto setting with soprano. The new key is harmonically a better fit in the sequence of the piece, where it follows a chorale in A major. Bach might also have wanted to give an aria to the bass as the other three voices are occupied in the terzet "Ach, wenn wird die Zeit erscheinen" (no. 51). Since the vocal forces for the terzet could not be changed (Bach needed the alto surrounded by the two other voices), the bass was the logical choice for the aria no. 47.[50]

The aria is, as most of the arias in the second half of the oratorio, in modified *da capo* form. The movement is framed by an extensive ritornello of twenty-four measures, which not only provides the musical material for the vocal parts but also partially returns as interlude between vocal parts A and B. Thus, the structure of the movement is well balanced. Between the two statements of the ritornello there are ninety-six measures, which are evenly divided between vocal section A (incl. ritornello) and vocal sections B and A'; each of the sections has forty-eight measures, the same number of measures as the two statements of the ritornello combined:

| | | |
|---|---|---|
| 1–24 | Ritornello | f♯–>f♯ |
| 25–60 | Vocal section A | f♯–>c♯ |
| 61–72 | Ritornello (2nd half) | c♯–>c♯ |
| 73–84 | Vocal section B | c♯–>b |
| 85–88 | Short interlude | b–>b |
| 89–120 | Vocal section A'[51] | V of b–>f♯ |
| 121–44 | Ritornello | f♯–>f♯ |

Next to the change of instrumentation, the most significant difference between the parody model and the aria in the *Christmas Oratorio* is the division of the text. In BWV 215 the vocal sections B and A' use the same text. The movement appears as

---

[49]  Cf. the discussion in NBA II/6, KB, 301.

[50]  Blankenburg, *Weihnachts-Oratorium*, 116, and Bossuyt, *Christmas-Oratorio*, 147, have suggested that the bass voice might be the personification of one of the three wise men. While this suggestion is intriguing in the context of the dramatic concept the two authors see in the oratorio (with the alto as Mary, etc.), it does not correspond to the rather nondramatic character of the piece we have been suggesting.

[51]  The chart can only partly do justice to the complex structure of the movement. Section A' is less a modified restatement of the A section; instead, Bach combines a rest of the text from the B section with a repetition of text from the A section, while musically, the whole section brings new material, so that it could almost be called a C section.

a bipartite aria (AB), which is framed and unified through the lengthy ritornello. In this version of the oratorio, Bach begins the third vocal part with the last line of the text from the B section ("Dies lässet die Seele nichts Böses beginnen") but then returns to the text from the A section ("Erleucht . . ."), thus turning the piece into a modified *da capo* structure. The change was motivated by the text. The secular libretto is dialectical: the A section describes the honor that is earned through the punishment of the enemies, which is contrasted with the heroic deeds of King August, who answered evil with blessings and so it would not have made sense for Bach to return to the opening lines of the aria. In the *Christmas Oratorio*, the text lacks this dialectical quality. The dialectic is already present within the A section; specifically, in the juxtaposition of the dark mind and the illumination of the heart through God's "luminosity." The text for the B section restates this in inversed order: it begins with the image of the word as the candle ("hellste Kerze") and then states that "this will let the soul embark on nothing evil." While Bach could have ended with a restatement of this sentence, the final lines of the A section—the "clear luminosity" of God's "streams of light"—convey the message much more plainly. Bach then returns to the opening text, necessitating several major changes in the voice-leading of the third vocal section.[52] As pointed out earlier, the sections of the aria have the same length; in the parody, however, the balance is shifted:

| BWV 215 | Ritornello | Vocal section I (A) | Vocal sections II+III (B) | | Ritornello |
|---------|-----------|---------------------|---------------------------|---|-----------|
| | 24 mm. | 48 mm. | 48 mm. | | 24 mm. |
| BWV 248 | Ritornello | Vocal section I (A) | Vocal sections II+IIIa (B) | Vocal section IIIb (A′) | Ritornello |
| | 24 mm. | 48 mm. | 20 mm. | 28 mm. | 24 mm. |

Bach was more interested in the delivery of the text than in maintaining the balance within the aria. Both of these arias establish a contrast. In BWV 215 this contrast is established between the texts for sections A and B, whereas BWV 248 contrasts light and darkness in both the A and B sections. This idea of contrast is

[52] These major changes speak against Blankenburg's assumption that Bach already had a parody in mind when he composed this aria (Blankenburg, *Weihnachts-Oratorium*, 116–17); the music was clearly designed for the secular cantata and not with an eye on its reuse in the oratorio. While Bossuyt concurs with Blankenburg's assumption and suggests that the music of the sacred aria fit the text better than the secular model (Bossuyt, *Christmas-Oratorio*, 147), the assumption was already rejected by Martin Petzoldt, *Bach-Kommentar* II, 358–59, with a similar argument as stated earlier.

already present in the two contrasting themes of the opening ritornello. The first twelve measures begin with an ascending leap of a fourth, followed by a circling motion around $f\sharp'$ (mm. 1–2). This opening gesture is repeated (in highly modified form and a fourth higher) in mm. 3–4 before Bach continues, leading to a cadential phrase in mm. 11/12. The second half of the ritornello begins with a bold descending gesture, which leads to a stubbornly repeated note $e'$ (mm. 13/14) and a gradual ascent with small motifs in Lombard rhythm (mm. 15–16). The second half of the ritornello is not only contrasting but is also, in a general sense, an inversion of the material in the first half: descent instead of ascent; the Lombard motif is an inversion of the dotted motif in m. 1.

Bach uses the ritornello from the secular cantata without major changes (if we disregard the transposition for a moment). Two small changes are indicative of the little adjustments Bach typically makes when parodying a movement. In m. 12, at the transition from the first to the second half of the ritornello, he adds two sixteenth notes in the bc, creating a smooth transition between the two halves. This addition was not necessary, but it adds to the "perfection" of the movement.[53] A slightly different case is a small change in the oboe d'amore part in m. 20. The model composition has two sixteenth notes and an eighth note on the first beat ($g''–f\sharp''–e''$); in the parody for the oratorio, the two sixteenth notes are changed into two thirty-second notes, followed by a dotted eighth note. The modified version now resembles m. 18, which begins with the same motif. The repeated ritornello—where the same change occurs (m. 140)—shows that Bach did not accidentally copy the version from two measures prior but made the change intentionally. This change is significant for the structure of the ritornello insofar as it now inserts a reminder of the main motif.

Several modifications were necessary in the vocal part. In mm. 43–45 and 47–49 the text underlay is changed to create longer melismatic lines for the words "erleuchten" and "Strahlen," which now sonically reflect the sparkling of the rays of light. A bigger challenge was the B section of the aria. The meter and the rhythm of the original text were completely different from the sacred parody. Subsequently, Bach had to recompose some parts of the mm. 73–77 to accommodate the new text. Further revisions were required after m. 92. Bach opted to structure the aria as a modified *da capo* aria instead of a bipartite aria. The return to the text of the A section in made it necessary to recompose the vocal line, either by simplifying melismas that were not needed any more or by adding new ones that were motivated by central terms like "erleuchte" and "Strahlen."[54]

---

[53] Bach first copied the version from the model composition but then changed it in the score. The same change occurs in the repetition of the ritornello at the end of the aria, in m. 132.

[54] Further changes occur between m. 111 and m. 116. All of them have the function of accommodating the new text.

The apogee of the secular aria are the invocation of the name of the Polish King, August, and the proclamation of his heroic character. Bach highlights this moment in the text by inserting four adagio measures (mm. 117–20) before the return of the final ritornello. The equivalent text in the sacred parody would have been "durch der Strahlen klaren Schein." While the sacred text is a central idea of the parody text as well, it did not warrant an adagio cadence. Bach thus eliminated the tempo change. The final section now transitions smoothly into the repetition of the ritornello. The score for BWV 215 exhibits some signs of revision that show that Bach sketched some ideas for the parody within the score of the secular model itself. In m. 117 he inserted the text "scheint durch," indicating the text for the final cadence of the aria.[55]

It might seem odd that Bach's decision to turn an aria with militaristic undertones—one that tells of the dealings of King and Elector August with his enemies—into an aria about the rays of the divine light. The leap of a fourth at the beginning of the ritornello suggests decisiveness and strength, and the instrumentation with the two flauti traversi in BWV 215 sonically invokes the military sphere. The change of instrumentation as well as the transposition of the aria (along with the use of a regular bc line) already eliminates some of the militaristic associations, but what seems to be more important for the parody is that the aria clearly establishes a dichotomy: already the opening ritornello introduces two dialectical musical ideas. These two diverging ideas are then combined simultaneously when the voice enters in m. 24; the bass (or soprano in the secular model) sings the first motif while the obbligato instrument plays the descending motif. Strictly musically speaking, the aria is about two contrasting, dialectical concepts that exist simultaneously. Only the first musical idea is sung by the vocalist, while the second, descending one is confined to the instrumental part, which already suggests a difference in import. While the secular aria juxtaposes the actions of August with those of his enemies, the aria in the *Christmas Oratorio* contrasts the "dark inclinations" of the heart and the illuminating presence of the divine light. It is easy to view the ascending trajectory of the opening motif as an image for the gradual illumination of the human heart; especially since Bach had already established ascent and descent as musical metaphors for light and darkness in the two preceding movements. In addition to using the dichotomy that was already present in the secular model, Bach adds features that highlight the new text, such as several melismatic lines that call attention to the "light" and the "rays." Finally, he changes the structure of the aria from a binary form to a modified *da capo* form, which gives him the opportunity to return to the "lightening up" of the heart, which is the central theological idea of the aria (and as metaphor for the *inhabitatio Christi* of the entire oratorio).

---

[55] See NBA I/37, KB, 69 and 86. Other changes in comparison to the secular model are changes of articulation and slurring; mostly, these changes are minimal and it is likely that some of the articulation was already implied in the secular model, which had been written in great haste.

## The fear of the enemy (mvts. 48–49)

The first sequence of movements (no. 44–47) had internalized the coming of the wise men and the guiding light of the star as an illumination of the human heart through the word of God. The second sequence, consisting only of a short gospel text and an interpreting alto accompagnato, continues this internalization, albeit with a new focus. The gospel text reports that King Herod, after hearing "this," was alarmed (or troubled, frightened), "and with him all of Jerusalem." The word "this" is (intentionally) ambiguous in this context. Within the biblical narrative it refers back to mvt. 45 and the announcement of the wise men that they had come to worship the newborn king of the Jews. But it also captures the general fear of an enemy of Christ who is alarmed by the fact that the "dark inclinations" are driven out by the "rays" of the divine light, as the previous aria had proclaimed. Part VI of the *Christmas Oratorio* will talk more extensively about the enemies of Christ. But on January 2, 1735, the congregation would have had another example on their minds. The gospel text for that day reported the killing of the newborn children and the flight of Jesus and his parents to Egypt (Mt 2:13–23). Even though the oratorio skipped this part of the narrative, the congregation would have heard this text before the performance of the cantata, and they would have heard a sermon on that very text immediately afterwards. In other words, the liturgical context would have provided a vivid example for the consequences of King Herod's fear.

The biblical narrative and the following interpretation are once more closely tied together; the harmonic goal of the short gospel recit (C♯ minor) is the opening harmony of the following accompagnato. Walter Blankenburg has called the depiction of Herod's fear one of the most dramatic moments of the entire oratorio.[56] The word "erschrak" (was alarmed) is reached via an upward leap from $c\sharp'$ to $a'$, which, even for Bach, was an extremely high note for his tenor recits. The note is supported (or rather destabilized) by a diminished chord on $b\sharp$. As so often is the case, this effective musical idea has a prehistory. Bach's original voice-leading here had been $g\sharp'-b$; the high note would have been on "-schrak" and Bach would immediately have returned to a lower tessitura. He then changed the voice-leading into $a'-g\sharp'$; and finally in the performance part for the tenor, Bach himself changed the note to $a'$.[57] The repetition of $a'$, followed by a short rest, shows the paralyzing fear of the news about the arrival of a new king.

The following alto recit (no. 49) begins with a violin motif that depicts the trembling of a frightened heart. The motif returns several times, before it gives way to a smoother motif in the second half of the movement. The four rapidly repeated notes of the first violin motif are a conventional musical topos to depict trembling. Some

---

[56] Blankenburg, *Weihnachts-Oratorium*, 117; similar Bossuyt, *Christmas Oratorio*, 149.

[57] Cf. NBA II/6, KB, 306.

listeners might be reminded of the shaking of an earthquake. Bach uses a trembling motion in the depictions of the earthquake after Jesus's death in both of his Passions, and Stölzel does the same in his Passion "Ein Lämmlein geht," which Bach had performed on Good Friday 1734. We mention the similarity to earthquakes here because one of the interpreters of the story of the three wise men, Aegidius Strauch (1702), compares the reaction to the news in Jerusalem to an earthquake: "So wird uns nun zum Sinn-Bilde vorgestellet eine Königliche Residentz / die nebenst ihren Regenten und Einwohnern / dergestalt erzittert / also würde alles durch ein Erdbeben beweget" (Before our inner eye a royal residence is depicted which trembles so much, including its ruler and his subject, as if it were shaken by an earthquake).[58] Both Bach's setting and Strauch's sermon imply a very strong physical reaction to the message of the birth of the new king of the Jews: an earth-shattering experience, but one that is purely internal. As usual for his recits, Bach inserted the text first and then added the music for the vocalist (alto) and the accompanying instruments. While the motifs do not show any changes or revisions, Bach worked on some of the details to make them stand out more. At m. 2, Bach had planned to extend the $c\sharp$ of m. 1 in the bc for one more measure; in the revised version he changed this to an $e$ as the foundation of a seventh chord, which highlights the word "erschrecken." Bach skillfully connects the word "erschrak" in the preceding gospel recit and "erschrecken" in the alto recit by reaching both by an ascending leap of a sixth and by a harsh, destabilizing accompaniment.[59] Around the middle of the recit, the text makes a shift. While the first half rejects the fear about the presence of Christ, the second half demands joy over his presence. Consequently, Bach changes the accompanying motif halfway. The trembling motif gives way to a smoother motif in m. 6, which Meinrad Walter aptly calls the "Freudenmotiv" (joy motif).[60]

This shift is accompanied by a beautifully harmonious and bright E-major chord on the word "-freuen" in m. 6. In an earlier version Bach had introduced the note $e$ in the bc already in the previous measure. However, he decided to prolong the $d\sharp$ from m. 4 and to delay the entrance of the $e$ until the text mentioned joy and until the first statement of the joy motif. The presence of Jesus in his Second Coming, which had been interpreted as a transition from darkness to light in the first sequence of movements, is here restated as the transition from fear to joy. In both cases Bach (and his librettist) introduce strong contrasts, and Bach's composition not only reflects these contrasts but, like the majority of his compositional revisions, have the goal of emphasizing this contrast. For Bach's theologically educated listeners it would have been evident that the transition from darkness to light and from fear to joy was a result of the Christ's presence in the Word.

---

[58] Strauch, *Starcke und Milch-Speise,* 136.

[59] In m. 2 of the alto recitative Bach also changes the vl 1 part from e" to f♯", increasing the dissonant sound of the fear motif (also, avoiding now doubling the e in the bc).

[60] Walter, *Weihnachtsoratorium,* 158.

## The written word (mvt 50)

The libretto returns to the "word" in quite unusual fashion in the following move-ment (no. 50). It is again connected by an extended bc note with the previous accompagnato recit. While the movement is thus structurally connected to its con-text, thematically it seems to stand quite separate. In contrast to other gospel recits, it is not immediately followed by a theological interpretation. Instead, mvt. 51 is a terzet that juxtaposes the questions for Christ's coming against the affirmation that he was already present. The terzet looks back to topics of mvt. 45 rather than elabo-rating on the theme of mvt. 50.

Some other features of mvt. 50 are similarly remarkable. The beginning of the gos-pel recit reports that King Herod had called his high priests and scholars of scripture ("Hohepriester und Schriftgelehrten") to inquire about the place of Christ's birth. The answer of the experts, even though it is spoken by a group, is not set as a turba chorus; instead, Bach continues with the recit. Heinrich Schütz—in his setting of the *Christmas Historia*—had opted for a more naturalistic depiction by giving the passage from the gospel to four bass voices (accompanied by a pair of trombones and bc). Bach lets this opportunity to create some musical drama pass and instead opts to prepare a "dramatic" entrance of the prophecy about the birthplace for Christ.

Commentators have noted the character of Bach's setting of the quotation from the prophet Micah (5:1–2) that begins in m. 9.[61] Walter Blankenburg describes it as "ancient venerable sublimity" (altehrwürdige Erhabenheit),[62] and Meinrad Walter compares the texture of the setting to *vox Christi* settings in other works by Bach, particularly in the *St. Matthew Passion* and in some of his cantatas.[63] Walter is correct insofar as the text—even though it is not the voice of Christ because it comes from the Old Testament—is indeed the word of God and thus deserves the "venerable sublimity" as Blankenburg notes. But the case is more complex. Bach highlights the prophetic text by changing into an arioso style. He marks "andante" in the score and the walking bc line is likewise typical for Bach's ariosi. From a performer's perspec-tive these changes implied the switch from a free declamatory style to a metered style (*alla battuta*). Bach's compositional approach to the biblical text conforms to eighteenth-century conventions: Johann Matteson has reflected a similar dif-ferentiation in volume 5 of his journal *Critica Musica*. In an essay titled "Des fra-genden Componisten," Mattheson criticizes a setting of Christian Postel's *Das Lied des Lammes*. He advocates a simple, declamatory recit style—the *stylus narrativus*, which is devoid of affections—for the narrative passages and allows a deviation only

---

[61] The quotation is not literal; it also includes a reference to 2 Sam 5:2 which is not part of the original Micah text and also references Mt 2:6.

[62] Blankenburg, *Weihnachts-Oratorium*, 118.

[63] Walter, *Weihnachtsoratorium*, 159; about the setting of the *vox Christi* in general see Geck, "Die *vox-Christi*-Sätze in Bachs Kantaten," 79–101.

to highlight certain passages. In his own setting of Postel's text, Matteson changes from the free declamation in the recit settings to a strict meter and the use of clear tempo indications. These changes highlight not only the inscription above the cross but also citations from the Old Testament. In other words, Bach follows a convention in eighteenth-century music to set central verses from a biblical text differently (see chap 5, this book, for a discussion on this movement). Bach used a change in his script to indicate the shift in texture when he drafted the movement.

Why did Bach decide to highlight this particular verse? The exegetical history of the gospel text might again be helpful here. Martin Luther had already pointed out that the revelation by the prophet Micah was essential for the wise men to find the newborn child. In other words, it fulfilled paradigmatically the function of the word of God as being a "light on the path":

| | |
|---|---|
| Sollen sie ihn aber finden, mußten sie den Propheten Micham haben und hören. Da sie nun das Wort haben, und ihre Gedanken fallen lassen, ziehen sie willig aus der heiligen Hauptstadt Jerusalem gen Bethlehem, in das geringe Städtlein, und ärgern sich nichts daran.[64] | If they [the wise men] shall find him, they have to have and hear the prophet Micah. Now, having the Word and letting their [own] thoughts go, they dutifully depart from the holy capitol city Jerusalem and travel to the humble little town of Bethlehem, and they are not offended at this. |

Heinrich Müller argues, in a similar vein, that the wise men had two lights: the star and the word of God. Both Luther and Müller, two theologians with considerable importance for Bach and with all likelihood for his librettist as well, view the prophetic word from Micah 5 as the paradigmatic word that guides the way for the wise men. Considering that the guiding light of scripture is the central issue of this part of the oratorio, it is clear why Bach decided to feature this "Wort" more prominently. It is not so much the text itself that is emphasized here but its function as a guide within the narrative.

Still, some details of the text deserved special attention by the composer. The invocation of the small city of Bethlehem in the setting of the prophetic text reaches its climax in the final lines, which Bach sets with a small melodic sequence: The short melodic idea on "denn aus dir" (out of you) at m. 14 is repeated with the text "soll mir kom-" (shall come) one step higher in mm. 14/15, and finally another step higher in m. 15 "-men der Herzog" (the leader to me), now with the short sixteenth-note melisma lengthened to eighth notes. In m. 16, when the opening interval (an ascending 4th) of the small motif returns again, Bach now continues the voice's

[64] Luther, *Hauspostille*, col. 126.

upward ascent instead of descent, as in the previous three instances. Such distinction serves to emphasize to the words "mein Volk Israel" (my people Israel). The brief instrumental postlude by the basso continuo in mm. 18/19 finally closes the sequence of interconnected recits that reached from mvt. 48 to mvt. 50.

The movements of part V of the *Christmas Oratorio* so far have stated that the word of God illuminates the darkness, turns fear into joy, and serves as guidance. Earlier parts of the oratorio had already acknowledged (in accordance with established Lutheran orthodox theology) that Christ himself was present in God's word. Mary had kept these words in her heart, and the alto had later promised to "safeguard" the word (part III, no. 32). Now again in part V, the libretto in the terzet (no. 51) confirms the presence of Christ against the questions of soprano and tenor. We have already mentioned earlier that the terzet, which is a parody from an unknown secular cantata, served as a model for the aria in part III, "Schließe mein Herze," thus connecting the two pieces that most explicitly talk about the presence of Christ in the human heart.

## Aria Terzetto—a duet for three (mvt. 51)

From a simple numerical perspective, the terzet (no. 51) fits well into the overall context of the oratorio. In parts I and II, Bach had used solo arias, in part III, he introduced two voices in a duet (no. 29), and later in part VI he will combine all four soloists in a *Recitativo à 4* in the penultimate movement of the oratorio. While such an expansion of forces might seem simplistic to us, it was a common structural principle in seventeenth-century concertos by Heinrich Schütz and his contemporaries.[65] The number "3" also conforms to the number of wise men in the Christian tradition. Schütz, for instance, in his *Christmas Historia,* had set the choruses of the wise men for three tenors.[66] While Bach composes the turba choruses of the wise men for the complete ensemble, the use of the three voices may allude to the number of magi/wise men. But even if such consideration have might have played a role for Bach, it would be misleading to view the three singers as a dramatic representation of the three men. The libretto for this movement does not introduce a conversation among three men, but the text for the terzet features a meditation, which is separated in space and time from the biblical narrative. The structure of the terzet also speaks against a direct identification, as one voice (alto) is pitted against the two other voices (soprano and tenor). The narrative about the three wise men gives no indication that one of them had been more knowledgeable than the other two.[67]

---

[65]  See, for an earlier example of such an expansion of forces, Rathey, *Ahle,* 399–40.

[66]  See Heinrich Schütz, *Historia,* Intermedium 4: Die Weisen aus Morgenlande.

[67]  Walter Blankenburg has suggested a different, quasi-dramatic understanding of the terzet. In his view, the movement expresses the questions of the wise men (soprano and tenor) before they arrived

The terzet is not so much a reaction to the previous gospel recit, but rather a continuation of the meta-narrative about the coming (and eventual presence) of Christ. The text alludes to the anticipated coming of Christ and to his actual presence. The alto (representing the soul of the believer) is already attuned to Christ's presence, while the other two voices still anticipate his coming in the future. The alto continues the "role" it had in earlier parts of the oratorio:

| | |
|---|---|
| I/4 | Make yourself ready, Zion . . . to see the most handsome |
| II/19 | Sleep, my Most Beloved |
| III/31 | My heart, include this blessed marvel |
| V/51 | He really is already here! |

The history of the terzet "Ach, wenn wird die Zeit erscheinen" (Ah, when will the time [of his coming] appear?) is somewhat of an enigma. It is the only one of its specific type in the oratorio, and it is also the only parodied movement for which we do not have a parody model. This is remarkable as the neat handwriting in Bach's autograph score clearly identifies it as a parody. Several scholars in the past have doubted that it was a parody and, given the seemingly "perfect" correspondence of music and text, have suggested that the movement must have been an original composition, even though the sources suggest otherwise. Walter Blankenburg, for example, states that "one could not image anything else but an original composition, since the terzet is, both in the logical order of the *Christmas Oratorio* and in regard to its musical treatment, one of the most unique and also one of the most profound movements of the work."[68] Blankenburg's suggestion is based on the assumption that a parody could not lead to a profound, original movement, an assumption that is challenged by most of the parodies in the *Christmas Oratorio*. Günter Jena also has a hard time believing that the movement should be a parody,[69] and Konrad Küster carefully suggests that the movement was either a new composition or "an extremely well done" parody.[70] In spite of the doubts expressed by these commentators, Bach's score forces us to

---

at the manger, which were answered by Mary (alto), Blankenburg, *Weihnachts-Oratorium*, 119. This interpretation is problematic, as it is not clear why Bach would have used two voices instead of three to represent the wise men.

[68] "Dennoch kann man sich hier kaum etwas anderes als eine Originalkomposition vorstellen; denn das Terzett gehört sowohl in der Gedankenfolge des Weihnachts-Oratoriums als auch in seiner musikalischen Bearbeitung zu den eigentümlichsten und zugleich tiefsinnigsten Sätzen des Werkes." Blankenburg, *Weihnachts-Oratorium*, 118.

[69] Jena, *Brich an, o schönes Morgenlicht*, 198.

[70] Küster, "Die Vokalmusik," in *Bach Handbuch*, ed. Küster (Kassel/Stuttgart: Bärenreiter/Metzler, 1999), 482: "eine außerordentlich gelungene Neutextierung."

conclude that the terzet is indeed a parody of an earlier composition. As the score for the terzet is remarkably devoid of corrections and revisions, the structure and the text of the model must have been very similar to the one in the oratorio. The small number of corrections in the piece are mostly limited to the three voices; some of them appear in the bc, but only two minor corrections were made to the part of the solo violin, a sure sign that Bach was dealing with a preexisting piece that had a different text.[71] Most of the changes are corrections of single notes, which were off either by a single pitch or by an octave. This suggests that the original composition might have been in a different key and was transposed to B minor for the oratorio. Bach also corrected the text underlay in mm. 101–2 and 124–25 from "kom[m] zu mir" to "ach so kom[m]" (soprano) and from "Je-su" to "ach so;" another sign of the re-texting of an earlier piece. Even some internal musical evidence speaks to the assumption that this movement is a parody. In mm. 55–59 the soprano and tenor feature long melismatic lines on the words "erscheinen" (appear) and "Seinen" (his). While it is possible to explain these melismas as an emphasis of central keywords, it is more likely that they were originally more directly motivated by another text.

It is has not been possible to find a model composition for this unusual movement. None of the printed texts by Bach's Leipzig librettists (in particular Picander) fit the structure of the terzet. Even Klaus Häfner, who has been quite creative in relating compositions by Bach to printed texts by Picander and others, has not been able to find a model for the piece.[72] But even without a model composition, it is at least possible to locate the movement in the context of Bach's own work and within forms of terzet composition in Bach's time. Terzets, vocal compositions for three voices and bc, sometimes accompanied by one or more obbligato instruments, are quite rare among Bach's compositions.[73] Six terzets are extant from Bach's sacred works.[74] Additionally, Bach used movements for three voices in two of his secular compositions (see table 10.1), and two movements seem to have been part of the now lost cantata BWV Anh I 7 (table 10.1).

While the movements listed in table 10.1 represent different types and characters, all are always placed in the second half of a cantata. The voices build up in a climax in preparation for the terzet. This is not the case with Bach's duets, which are

---

[71] For a list of the corrections, see NBA II/6, KB, 68–69.

[72] See Klaus Häfner, *Aspekte des Parodieverfahrens bei Johann Sebastian Bach: Beiträge zur Wiederentdeckung verschollener Vokalwerke*, Neue Heidelberger Studien zur Musikwissenschaft 12 (Laaber: Laaber Verlag 1987), 537.

[73] Not that they were very frequent in eighteenth-century music in general!

[74] Movements for three voices are also encountered in Bach's motet *Jesu, meine Freude* BWV 227; mvt. 4, "Denn das Gesetz," is composed for S1/S2/A and mvt. 7, "So aber," for ATB. The polyphonic texture of the movements resembles some of the terzets from 1724; see, for these two terzets, Klaus Hofmann, *Johann Sebastian Bach: Die Motetten* (Kassel: Bärenreiter 2003), 136.

*Table 10.1* **Terzet movements by J.S. Bach**

| Sacred works | | |
|---|---|---|
| [1707/8] | BWV 150/5 | ATB |
| 12/25/1723[75] | BWV 243a/10 | SSA |
| 10/29/1724 | BWV 38/5 | SAB |
| 11/26/1724 | BWV 116/4 | STB |
| 12/31/1724 | BWV 122/4 | SAT |
| 1/2/1735 | BWV 248$^v$/51 | SAT |
| **Secular works** | | |
| Summer 1734 | BWV 211/10 | STB |
| 10/5/1734 | BWV 215/8 | STB |
| [12/10/1720?] | BWV Anh. I 7/6 | ? |
| | BWV Anh. I 7/10 | ? |

even encountered as first or second movements in his cantatas.[76] Thus, the place-ment of the terzet in part V of the oratorio conforms to the convention in Bach's works. We can even assume that the model composition was also located in the second half of the secular cantata from which Bach had borrowed it.

Half of the terzets in Bach's sacred cantatas were composed as part of the chorale cantata cycle (1724/25). This might suggest that the terzet from the *Christmas Oratorio* originated in the mid-1720s as well. Upon closer examination, however, the terzets from the 1720s are quite different from the movement in the *Christmas Oratorio*. Most of the earlier pieces (BWV 38, 116, 150, and 243a) are polyphonic settings with the same text in all three voices.[77] Only the terzet from the chorale cantata BWV 122 comes close to the texture of the movement in the oratorio. Soprano and tenor sing a free poetic text while the alto intones a chorale melody. What is different, however, is the lack of a dialogical relationship between the voices. The terzet in BWV 122 rather resembles a chorale-trope motet with added cantus firmus. The terzets in Bach's secular cantatas are quite different from the one in the *Christmas Oratorio* as well. The terzet at the end of the *Coffee Cantata*, BWV 211 resembles a choral movement for three voices; the three

---

[75] Andreas Glöckner has suggested that the *Magnificat* BWV 243a might have been composed about half a year earlier than Christmas 1723 (Glöckner, "Bachs Es-Dur-Magnificat BWV 243a—eine genu-ine Weihnachtsmusik?" *Bach Jahrbuch* 89 (2003): 37–45). But this question is irrelevant in our context.

[76] For instance in BWV 131/2; 71/2; 185/1; 155/2; 161/1; and 59/1. In general, however, the duet also appears preferably toward the end of a cantata. According to the statistical overview by Mary Greer, this is the case in 85 percent of Bach's duets. Greer, "Sacred Duets and Terzets": 25 and 138.

[77] The movement from the *Magnificat*, BWV 243, has a chorale melody on top of the three-part vocal texture.

singers that are featured in the cantata are united for a final movement and sing the same text together. The same was probably the case in the final movement of BWV Anh. I 7; the libretto suggests that all three singers sang the same words. Only two terzets from Bach's secular cantatas have a slightly different structure. In BWV 215, the penultimate movement is a recit for three voices, which then transitions into a polyphonic setting. During the recit section, the voices interact in a conversation before they are brought together, singing the same text. But again, mvt. 10 from the lost cantata BWV Anh. I 7 might have been the closest to the movement in the oratorio. The libretto print indicates that the three singers occasionally have to sing two different words. It is not clear how the text was distributed among the singers:

> Auf! Lobet / Dancket dem gütigsten / herrlichsten GOTT, etc.
> Up, praise / thank the most merciful / glorious God, etc.

Even if this *Aria à 3* gets closest to the movement in the *Christmas Oratorio*, it still lacks the dramatic quality of the dialogue between the two outer voices and the alto.[78] The musical texture of Bach's earlier terzets is different as well. Most of the movements are polyphonic, written in three-part counterpoint with extensive points of imitation. The only modern element is the independent bc line. This texture is quite coherent in Bach's terzets and can be found as early as BWV 150, *Nach dir, Herr, verlanget mich* (1708/9?) and as late is in the chorale cantata *Aus tiefer Not* (1724), BWV 38. In other words, Bach's terzet movements are generally motet-like movements for three vocal voices and an independent bc. The terzet in part V of the *Christmas Oratorio* departs significantly from this model. The movement is not a motet but features two voices (ST) which sing the same text, asking for the time of Christ's coming, while the alto answers independently that "he" was already there. Although the two outer voices engage in musical imitation, we don't find the motet-like polyphony of earlier terzets. Rather, the interaction between the voices resembles duets Bach had composed around 1730: the duet "Ich bin deine" from BWV 213; "Domine Deus" from the Gloria of the *B-minor Mass*, BWV 232; the duet "Seid wachsam" from BWV 149; and "Ich lebe, mein Herze" from BWV 145. The extensive parallel movement of soprano and tenor especially reminds us of duets like the one in BWV 213 (which then found its way into the *Christmas Oratorio* as "Herr, dein Mitleid"). And so the terzet, no. 51, "Ach, wenn wird die Zeit erscheinen" departs from Bach's earlier terzet models and uses textures the composer had employed more frequently in duets during the years shortly before the composition of the *Christmas Oratorio*. This suggests that Bach used a model that was composed at about the same time as the other secular cantatas that provided the basis for the oratorio. Could models by other composers have played a role in the particular design of the terzet? We suggested in chapter 4 that the composition

---

[78] See the facsimile in NBA I/35, KB, 173.

of the *Christmas Oratorio* was (in part) motivated by the first performance of an oratorio by Hasse in Dresden. Although we cannot prove that Bach knew the piece, it is noteworthy that Hasse's *Il Cantico de' tre Fanciulli* does feature a terzet as one of the final movements of the oratorio. The movement begins with a close dialogue between two of the voices. The two singers trade musical motifs and finally move in close parallel motion when the third singer enters. Throughout the terzet, Hasse pits one singer against the other two. But here end the similarities. The three vocalists sing the same text and do not engage in a dramatic dialogue of any kind. Hasse's terzet is of interest in this context only as it represents a modern type of terzet, which is more similar to the type Bach uses, but it could not have served as a direct model.

An *Aria à 3* that is closer to Bach's setting, in fact surprisingly close, is the terzet "Sorgen machen uns im Hertzen" from Stölzel's cantata *Entweicht, ihr ungebethnen Sorgen!* (HennenbergWK A/3), composed for the birthday of Princess Elizabeth Albertine of Schwarzenburg in 1738.[79] The cantata features the personification of four different sorrows (or reasons to care) and "the sorrowless Schwarzenburg." In the terzet, the *Wohlfahrssorge* (care for welfare or well being) and the *Liebessorge* (care for love) engage in a dialogue with *Kränckungssorge* (care about insults). The libretto shows that two of the singers are set against the third:

| | | |
|---|---|---|
| Wohlfahrssorge/ Liebessorge | Sorgen machen uns im Hertzen | Sorrows cause in our hearts |
| | Statt der Wolcken Sonnenschein. | clouds instead of sunshine. |
| Kränckungssorge | Nein, das kann nicht seyn. | No, that cannot be. |
| Wohlfahrtssorge | Ja, der Hoffnung starcke Triebe, | Yes, the strong desires of hope, |
| Liebessorge | Ja, die treugesinnte Liebe | yes, the faithful love |
| à 2 | Kan, was kräncken will, zerstreun. | can destroy what wants to insult. |
| Kränckungssorge | Es gefällt Euch so zu schertzen, | You are enjoying making fun like that, |
| | Sorgen machen Pein. | Sorrows cause pain. |
| Wohlfahrssorge/ Liebessorge | Sorgen machen uns im Hertzen | Sorrows cause in our hearts |
| | Statt der Wolcken Sonnenschein. | clouds instead of sunshine. |
| Kränckungssorge | Nein, das kann nicht seyn. | No, that cannot be. |

---

[79] The performance was on April 11, 1738. The sources for the cantata are kept in the Stadt- und Kreisbibliothek "Johann Karl Wezel," Sondershausen (D-SHs/Mus.A15:11); see also Fritz Hennenberg, *Das Kantatenschaffen von Gottfried Heinrich Stölzel* (Leipzig: VEB Deutscher Verlag 1976), 73–74, and 132

The score of Stölzel's piece shows an even closer proximity to Bach than the libretto. *Wohlfahrtssorge* (soprano) and *Liebessorge* (alto) proceed in close parallel movement, whereas *Kränckungssorge* (tenor) regularly enters at the end of a phrase and has its own motivic material. Additionally, the tenor always has the last word in this conversation (ex. 10.3). Stölzel's *Aria à 3* follows the same pattern as does Bach's terzet in the *Christmas Oratorio*. Considering how important Stölzel was for Bach at the time of the oratorio composition, it seems plausible that Bach's departure from his typical terzet style was inspired by a similar piece by Stölzel. It cannot have been this particular piece, because it was composed about four years after the oratorio, but it is possible that there had been a similar terzet among the numerous Stölzel cantatas that are now lost.

*Example 10.3*  Gottfried Heinrich Stölzel, "Sorgen machen uns im Hertzen" (1738), mm. 8–21

Bach's terzet is more complex than Stölzel's piece. The two outer voices interact in an intricate polyphonic texture while Stölzel's voices simply move in parallel motion. Bach's obbligato violin develops a high degree of independent virtuosity while the orchestra in Stölzel's cantata is limited to interludes that echo the vocal lines or provide simple accompagnemental chords. But these differences in complexity do not preclude that Bach used Stölzel's works as a model. We have seen a similar case in the chorale-trope recit in part IV (no. 40); a few years later Bach would rework an aria by Stölzel for a different purpose (BWV 200 [after 1735]]).[80] Bach clearly used Stölzel's music as a model and gave it his own twist. But even if we cannot trace the influence of a particular terzet by Stölzel, the aria by the Gotha composer can tell us what the secular model for the terzet in the *Christmas Oratorio* might have looked like. It would have featured three characters (maybe vices and

---

[80]  See Wollny, " 'Bekennen will ich seinen Namen,' " 123–58.

virtues; maybe characters from Greek mythology), which engaged in a conversation. Two of these characters would have agreed, singing harmoniously to more or less the same text. The third character would have disagreed rather vehemently. It is easy to imagine a little dramatic scene in the style of Bach's *drammi per musica* in which a conversation like that develops. The existence of Stölzel's terzet supports the assumption that "Ach, wenn wird die Zeit erscheinen" is indeed a parody from a secular cantata; and if a piece by Stölzel served as an inspiration, it is safe to assume that the secular piece was composed at a time when the influence of the Gotha capellmeister was the strongest—in the first half of the 1730s.

Mary Greer has argued that the text for Bach's terzet perhaps lent itself to be set as a piece for two dialoguing voices rather than for three.[81] While this observation is correct, it turns the genesis of the piece upside down. We have to assume that the terzet already existed when Bach's librettist wrote the words for *Christmas Oratorio*. Bach does not turn a dialogue text into a terzet . . . but the text turns a terzet into a dialogue. What changed when the terzet became part of the oratorio was the elimination of its context as an element of a dramatic action. Within a secular *dramma per musica* the singers would have been introduced earlier in the piece, and the audience would have been able to identify the three singers as three protagonists of the dramatic action. In the oratorio, this dramatic context is eliminated. A listener might have identified the alto as the voice of the soul of the believer (as it is used in the remainder of the oratorio), but the two other voices lack such a clear function. The terzet is thus de-dramatized. This brings to mind the duet in part III, where Bach (and the librettist) had similarly eliminated the dramatic character of the love-duet and turned it into a more abstract representation of spiritual and emotional harmony. This de-dramatization finally corresponds to Bach's oratorio concept in general, as we have outlined it earlier in this book. Bach's oratorio concept is dramatic insofar as it stages emotion with dramatic effects, but he is not interested in putting individual and identifiable characters on an imaginary stage. What happens to both the duet from BWV 213 as well as the terzet from an unknown cantata, is the same process of de-dramatization that the *Easter Oratorio* underwent from its 1725 version to its version in the context of Bach's "Oratorio Trilogy" (see chap. 4).

The formal structure of the terzet is that of a modified *da capo* form. The movement is framed by complete statements of the ritornello for solo violin and bc (mm. 1–20 and 170–89) which begins with the exposition of the main vocal motif (mm. 1–4), a syncopated figure that will later be picked up by the two singers (S and T). The short exposition is followed by a *fortspinnung* in wide-ranging broken triads, as we have seen earlier, in the aria "Schließe, mein Herze" (no. 31). Bach introduces a new idea in m. 13, which is essentially a variation of the syncopated figure from the opening measures. The first eighth note is now resolved

[81]  Greer, "Sacred Duets and Terzets": 130.

into a Lombard gesture (♫). This energized restatement of the familiar propels the ritornello into another short *fortspinnung*, leading to a cadential phrase (mm. 19/20). As if the boost of energy is too much to halt at the arrival at the tonic cadence in m. 20, Bach adds two more measures of these Lombard gestures and syncopations before the solo violin finally comes to a rest in m. 22. The extension of the opening ritornello overlaps with the entrance of the first vocal part in m. 21. Soprano and tenor begin with a dialogue on the opening motif, accompanied by the violin with the broad garlands from the opening ritornello. The melancholic character of B minor underscores the longing in the text, the waiting for the coming of Christ. Sigh-motifs on "ach" (mm. 29, 30, etc.) add to this sad mood.

The third voice (alto) finally enters in m. 37, calling for the silence of the two other voices and asserting that he, Jesus, is already here. The two other voices do indeed drop out for a moment, before the three singers engage in a dialogue, which ends, quite expectedly, in m. 59 with a solo statement by the alto. The opening ritornello, now transposed to F♯ minor, leads to the B section of the aria, which features only soprano and tenor. The middle section of the terzet is a prime example of invertible counterpoint. The plea for the coming of Jesus is treated canonically by the tenor and soprano (mm. 80–98). Bach then inverts the roles of the singers and the soprano begins the canon, followed by the tenor. The participation of the obbligato violin is relegated to short interjections, mostly outlining simple triads. The only exceptions are a short transitional period between the two canonic statements (mm. 98–102) and the end of the B section (mm. 121–25), where the violin plays its syncopated motif from the opening of the terzet, and the two singers join in with the plea "Jesu, ach so komm [zu mir]."

In section A′ the role of the two outer voices is again inverted: the tenor begins, followed by the soprano. Otherwise, the vocal texture is more or less a transposed repetition of the A section. What is striking, though, is that Bach begins the A′-section in E minor. The arrival at the home key of B minor finally comes at m. 161. The harmonic arrival coincides with the end of a longer statement of the alto that "he is already, truly here." Soprano and tenor voice their questions a last time, but the alto counters with fanfare-like statements that the arrival had already occurred. The two outer voices now fall silent, and the alto sings a last time, "er ist schon würklich hier." Bach brilliantly uses the large-scale harmonic progression of the aria to give the listener the sense of arrival as the listener has not heard a clear statement of the home key B minor since m. 44.

Walter Blankenburg and Meinrad Walter have indicated that the final statement of the alto in mm. 168–70 bears some resemblance to the "Et incarnatus est" from the *B-minor Mass*.[82] Walter suggests that this might be more than just a coincidence. While the idea is intriguing—the coming of Christ in the terzet as the reformulation

---

[82] Blankenburg, *Weihnachts-Oratorium*, 123, and Walter, *Weihnachtsoratorium*, 160.

of the incarnation from the Creed—it is not more than a coincidence. In both cases Bach simply used a descending B-minor triad. Since the terzet was the parody of a secular model, this descending triad would already have been part of the music before Bach connected it to the incarnation. Furthermore, the "Et incarnatus est" is one of the latest additions to the Mass and was composed in the late 1740s.[83] While the ideas are theologically connected, the musical means through which these are expressed are not. Bach did not have a fixed musical vocabulary for signifying certain religious dogmas. A descending B-minor triad does not signify or mean "incarnation"; and it surely did not mean that in the secular cantata for which the terzet was originally composed. A modern listener—being familiar with the larger canon of Bach's music—might hear this phrase differently. Similar to the "Passion chorale" melody of "Wie soll ich dich empfangen" (part I/5), which one might hear as an unintended allusion to Bach's St. Matthew Passion. We may also hear the last phrase of the alto as an echo of the "Et incarnatus est" from the B-Minor Mass. Listening always creates its own meaning, and it should. This becomes a problem only if modern associations take the place of historical facts.

## A dual finale (mvts. 52–53)

After its final words in the terzet, the alto receives another opportunity to confirm the presence of Christ in the following accompagnato recit. Supported by the two oboi d'amore, the singer proclaims that Christ was the ruler and that the human heart was his throne. The image of Christ's presence in the heart—which we encountered in part I as the heart being Christ's manger—is now reimagined as the heart being the throne. Emblem books from Bach's time featured similar images. Variations on the theme "heart" were very popular. The image of the heart as being a throne is now motivated by the identification of the newborn child as the "king of the Jews" as the wise men had called him in mvt. 45. The alto had already replied in the same movement, "Seek him in my breast." The score for the recit (no. 52) shows some minor revisions in the part of the second oboe d'amore, which had a half note on the first beat of m. 2. The change into a quarter note followed by a dotted half note gives the voice some rhythmic diversity against the first oboe, which proceeds in simple half notes. Bach's revision here reminds of earlier examples we have discussed. As in the previous instances, Bach notated a simpler version of an accompagnato recit and then worked on the details.[84]

---

[83] Cf. Christoph Wolff, *Johann Sebastian Bach: Messe in h-Moll* (Kassel: Bärenreiter, 2009), 86–89; George Stauffer, *Bach: The Mass in B Minor* (New Haven, CT: Yale University Press, 2003), 116–20.

[84] The two small figures in the oboes in the final measures are a small detail that appears in the original and was not result of a revision.

Part V of the *Christmas Oratorio* ends with a plain hymn setting. The chorale harmonization is much simpler than the highly polyphonic chorale earlier in part V (no. 46), and it surely pales in comparison to the elaborate final chorales in parts I, II, and VI. The straightforward hymn setting indicates that the Sunday after New Year's Day was a regular Sunday and not a major feast day. The uncomplicated harmonization of the movement is also reflected in the lack of corrections in Bach's score.[85] The notes in the lower voices frequently flow in a smooth eighth-note motion, but the texture never develops the degree of independence we observe in earlier chorale settings. A few small details in the setting are remarkable. The alto in mm. 1/2 descends in a sigh-like chain of eighth notes, which can be heard as an expression for the longing for Christ; when the descending line sounds again at the repetition of the first measures of the chorale, it is now combined with the words "dark pit" and the alto descends into deeper regions. One measure later, the vocal bass ascends into a high tessitura, even crossing lines with the tenor, and he sings a small gesture that stands out in the context of the movement. The vocal ornament alludes to two texts that are sung with this line: the first time it depicts the beautiful (or choice) hall of princes; when the measure is repeated the text fits even better as the listener might hear it as a depiction of the "stream of light."

The text of the chorale is the ninth stanza of Johann Franck's Christmas hymn "Ihr Gestirn, ihr hohlen Lüfte," a hymn that did not appear in the Leipzig hymnals of Bach's time; it was, however, present in the 1682 edition of the Vopelius Hymnal as well as in the Wagner Hymnal from 1697.[86] The librettist used this rather unfamiliar chorale because of its text, which summarizes in a nutshell the main themes of this part of the oratorio:

| | |
|---|---|
| Zwar ist solche Herzensstube | True, such a heart-cellar is |
| Wohl kein schöner Fürstensaal, | Certainly no choice hall of princes, |
| Sondern eine finstre Grube; | But rather a dark pit; |
| Doch, sobald dein Gnadenstrahl | Yet, as soon as your grace-filled stream of light |
| In derselben nur wird blinken, | Flashes in this same [pit], |
| Wird es voller Sonnen dünken. | It will seem full of sunlight. |

The hymn stanza describes the heart as the dwelling place of Christ. Similarly, by suggesting that is was not an ornate hall of princes, it alludes to the royal office of Christ. It also looks back to the aria no. 47, in which the dark inclinations of the human heart were contrasted with the light of the divine word. The term "Gnadenstrahl"

---

[85]  See NBA II/6, KB, 69.
[86]  Cf. NBA II/6, KB, 199 and Blankenburg, *Weihnachts-Oratorium*, 125. The melody used by Bach is the familiar melody of "Gott des Himmels und der Erden" by Heinrich Albert.

resonates with images in emblem books, where the coming of Christ in the human heart was frequently depicted with a stream of light.[87]

The final chorale does not return to the musical material from the opening movement but it closes part V of the oratorio tonally. We are back in A major. Within the large-scale tonal scheme of the *Christmas Oratorio*, this is the dominant of the home-key D major, to which Bach will return for part VI.

[87] Listeners might even have associated the term "Gnadengegenwart," which describes the presence of Christ in the human heart.

# 11

# The Bridegroom and the Enemy (Part VI)

Part VI of the oratorio continues the narration and interpretation of the story of the wise men. In the outline for his sermon on this gospel text, Salomon Deyling enumerated several angles from which he intended to interpret the story: Jesus as the savior of the heathen, the heartfelt joy that is felt about the coming of Jesus, Jesus the light, and the plotting of the enemies against the faithful. Part V of the oratorio had already covered most of these topics, but the one that is still missing is the plotting of the enemies. This is the main focus of part VI. Intertwined with the struggle against the enemies is the eschatological hope that at the end of times the enemies of Christ and his followers will be overcome once and for all. This perspective reveals the last step in the threefold advent of Christ, the Third Coming at the end of times. Deyling is not the only theologian who employs the story about King Herod for an elaboration on Christ's adversaries. Heinrich Müller in a sermon for Epiphany describes Herod's deceit as an example for the enemies of Christ. After the wise men had seen the newborn child, God appears in a dream and sends them back on a different way. Müller, interprets this as God's protection against their (and Christ's) enemy Herod. He then continues:

| | |
|---|---|
| . . . **befahl ihnen im Traum / daß sie sich nicht solten wieder zu Herodes lencken.** Wir sind offt dann am sichersten / wann die Gefahr am grösten ist. Die Feinde legen unsern Füssen verborgene Stricke. Wir sehen sie nicht / und würden gleiches Fusses hinein gehen/wann uns Gott nicht wunderbarlich zurück hielte. . . . | . . . **commanded them in a dream that they should not direct themselves back to Herod.** Often we are the safest when the danger is the greatest. The enemies prepare hidden traps to catch out feet. We do not see them and would step into them if God did not miraculously hold us back. . . . God lets you sleep and keeps you safe. |

Gott lässt euch schlaffen und bewahret euch. Er streitet für euch / und ihr seyd stille. Er hilfft euch / und ihr wissets nicht einmal. Drumb lasset sich euer Hertz nicht fürchten / ob sich ein Heer wider euch aufflehnet.[1]

He fights for you and you keep quiet [about it]. He helps you but you do not even know it. Thus, do not let your heart feel fear, even if you are threatened by an army [of enemies].

Adversaries, like Herod, make secret attempts to overcome Christ and his believers. As the libretto expresses, they use "deceitful cunning" (no. 56) but "one signal from his [God's] hands" (no. 57) can overthrow these enemies. While the "insolent enemies" might horrify God, the "Treasure [and] Refuge is here" (no. 62). The patterns of understanding in the libretto and in the sermons are similar. The librettist followed established models for the interpretation of the narrative of the three wise men. Toward the end of the libretto, the interpretation even assumes an apocalyptic perspective. The recit no. 63 mentions the "horrors of Hell" and the following chorale promises the defeat of "Death, devil, sin, and hell" (no. 64). While these apocalyptic themes are implicit in the sermons by Müller and Deyling, the Leipzig theologian Romanus Teller in a sermon collection from 1720 elaborates on the end of times more explicitly:

Ach mercket doch dieses, Geliebte, in dem HErrn, daß eben diejenigen die allergröste Pein in der Hölle werden zu empfangen haben, die vor andern Christum und sein Reich sehr nahe gehabt, und doch nicht mit Ernst darnach getrachtet haben, wie sie Christi und seines Reiches möchten theilhafftig werden. Darum last es daran nicht genung seyn, daß JEsus Christus kommen ist in die Welt, daß er mitten unter uns getreten und daß das Himmelreich auch nahe herbey gekommen; sondern nahet auch ihr euch recht zu Christo und seinem Reiche. Thut Busse/und gläubet an das Evangelium. Marc. I.15.[2]

Ah, take note of this, dearly beloved in the Lord, that those will receive the greatest pain in hell, who have been close to Christ and his kingdom but who did not earnestly strive to become a part of Christ and his kingdom [like King Herod]. Therefore, do not let us be satisfied with the fact that Jesus Christ has come into the world, that he has been in our midst and that he has brought the kingdom of heaven close to us; but you shall strive to get closer to Christ and his kingdom as well. Repent and believe in the gospel (Mk 1:15).

---

[1] Müller, *Schlußkette*, Festteil, 106.
[2] Teller, *Der grosse Unterscheid*, 229.

The libretto for part VI has two thematic centers. The main theme is the enemies of Christ, as the opening movement already proclaims, "Lord, when our insolent enemies snarl" (no. 54). King Herod and his deceitful plotting against the wise men is interpreted typologically as an example for all enemies.[3] While the beginning of recit no. 56 still meditates on the individual case ("You deceitful"), the following aria addresses the "enemies" in general terms (no. 57). The focus is then shifted farther away from the concrete example to the life-threatening forces in general: "World and Sin" (no. 63) and "Death, devil [and] hell" (no. 64). The second focal point of part VI is the consoling presence of Christ in the believer's heart. The opening chorus invokes the hope for "steadfast faith" and "trust in you [God] alone" (no. 54). The tenor recit, no. 61, then continues the thought by expressing that Christ, the "treasure will not go from here." He is the friend and bridegroom who promises salvation in fear and distress. The images used in the libretto again invoke the *unio mystica*:

| | |
|---|---|
| Sein Arm wird mich aus Lieb | His arm will embrace me out of love |
| Mit sanftmutsvollem Trieb | With gentle desire |
| Und größter Zärtlichkeit umfassen; | And greatest tenderness; |
| Er soll mein Bräutigam verbleiben, | He shall remain my bridegroom; |
| Ich will ihm Brust und Herz | I will entrust breast and heart |
|    verschreiben, |    to him. |
| Ich weiß, er liebet mich, | I know for certain that he loves me; |
| Mein Herz liebt ihn auch inniglich. | My heart also loves him deeply. |

The hope for the coming bridegroom, expressed in part I, the first alto recit of the oratorio (no. 3, "Nun wird mein liebster Bräutigam"), has come full circle. He is the bridegroom, and he, Jesus, will remain the beloved bridegroom in eternity.

## Parody and models in Part VI

The prehistory of part VI of the *Christmas Oratorio* poses a particular problem. The clear and meticulous handwriting in Bach's autograph score shows that most of the movements were parodies of earlier pieces. The opening movement, for instance, is of almost calligraphic neatness. A model for the movements is not known; they do

---

[3] The cruelty of the enemy, Herod, is one of the traditional themes of the Feast of Epiphany. The vespers hymn for Epiphany (January 6) was "Hostis Herodes impie," dating from the fifth century. The hymn was later translated by Martin Luther "Was fürchtst du, Feind Herodes, sehr" and became one of the standard hymns in Lutheran hymnals.

not appear in any of the surviving secular cantatas from the years before the composition of the oratorio. There is, however, a trace of an earlier version. The set of the performing parts for the *Christmas Oratorio* contains doublets for the first and second violins (B 12 and 14), a bc part without figures (B 17), and an organ part (B 18) with figured bass and transposed, so that it could be played on an instrument in choir tone.[4] The doublets contained originally only the mvts. 54, 56, 57, and 61–64; the other movements were added later. These later additions are the two gospel recits and the hymn stanza "Ich steh an deiner Krippen hier" (no. 59). Alfred Dürr, in his comparison of the doublets—the version of part VI that is preserved in the score, and the vocal and instrumental parts for the oratorio— came to the conclusion that the doublets must have been part of a earlier cantata, which was borrowed in its entirety for the *Christmas Oratorio*.[5] That cantata is now commonly referenced as BWV 248a. Since only some of the instrumental parts are preserved, the text, function, and date of this cantata are unknown. We can assume, though, that BWV 248a had a similar instrumentation as the final part of the oratorio; it clearly featured trumpets and timpani, as they are essential to the opening movement. Some additional assumptions about the earlier cantata are possible. While Bach copied the *organum* part (B 18) himself, the scribe for three remaining doublets was Rudolph Straube (1717–ca. 1785), who had joined the St. Thomas School on January 14, 1733, as an extern student; not much later he became a regular alumnus.[6] Straube only appears as a scribe in a small number of manuscripts with Bach's music, and the sources that can be dated with confidence were written between October 1734 (BWV 215) and 1736 (2nd version of BWV 206). Straube was also one of the scribes who copied other parts for the *Christmas Oratorio*. Since Bach usually did not use external students to copy parts, Straube must have begun working for Bach sometime after he had become an alumnus. This means that the doublets for BWV 248a were written between the second half of 1733 and Christmas 1734. As Straube's hand does not appear in any sources before BWV 215 from October 5, 1734, Andreas Glöckner has concluded that the original cantata must have been composed (or at least copied) sometime in late September or early October of 1734.[7] This time frame is probably a bit too narrow as Straube could still have worked for Bach earlier in 1734 or even toward the end of 1733. The surviving sources for Bach's vocal music from this time are too scant to rule out that Straube was involved in the copying of vocal and instrumental parts

---

[4] Dürr in his critical commentary for the oratorio labels these voices B12 (vl1), B14 (vl2), B17 (cont.), and B18 (organ), NBA II/6, KB, 85–87.

[5] Dürr, *Weihnachts-Oratorium*, 7.

[6] Andreas Glöckner, "Eine Michaeliskantate als Parodievorlage für den sechsten Teil des Bachschen Weihnachts-Oratoriums?," *Bach-Jahrbuch* 86 (2000): 318. From 1740 on, Straube studied at Leipzig University.

[7] Glöckner, "Eine Michaeliskantate als Parodievorlage," 320.

before BWV 215.[8] In any case, BWV 248a must have been composed within a year or so before the *Christmas Oratorio*.

The sources allow a few more assumptions about the original cantata. The existence of an organ part and the final hymn setting imply that BWV 248a was a sacred cantata. And the fact that Bach did not use all the instrumental parts but only doublets suggests that he wanted to keep one set of parts with the original cantata, which was only necessary if Bach planned to perform the cantata again at a later date. It is therefore likely that the cantata was not composed for a special occasion (like a wedding) but for a regular Sunday or festival day during the church year. Based on this limited time frame, Glöckner has suggested that the cantata was written for Michaelmas 1734 (Sept. 29). The feast traditionally warranted a festive composition, and the martial character especially of the framing movements would have fit very well with the topic of the apocalyptic battle between the Archangel Michael and the Antichrist. Glöckner rules out that the cantata could have been written for a wedding or for the introduction of the new town council (which was celebrated on August 30, 1734).[9] Even if we assume a wider time frame (late 1733–October 1734), the possible occasions for the composition of BWV 248a are limited to those days on which Bach would use three (or four) trumpets and timpani in the liturgy in Leipzig: Easter (as in BWV 11 and 31); Michaelmas (as in BWV 19, 130, and 149); the introduction of the new town council (as in BWV 29, 69, 119, and 120); Pentecost (as in BWV 74, 34, and 172); New Year (as in BWV 41, 171, and 190); Ascension Day (as in BWV 43); the first day of Christmas (as in BWV 63 and 110); Trinity Sunday (as in BWV 129), the twelfth Sunday after Trinity (as in BWV 69a and 137); and some weddings (as in BWV 34a, 120a, 195, 197).[10] A Sunday that is still very close to BWV 215 is the twelfth Sunday after Trinity on September 12, 1734. Several of Bach's earlier cantatas for that day employed a larger ensemble, including trumpets and timpani. However, the hymns traditionally associated with that day do not use the melody of "Herzlich tut mich verlangen," which Bach uses in the final movement of BWV 248a. This does not rule out that the cantata was composed for that day, but it makes it rather unlikely. Although Glöckner's suggestion that BWV 248a was composed for Michaelmas 1734 is intriguing, it is not possible to prove without a doubt that

---

[8] A date that is probably too early is Klaus Häfner's suggestion that BWV 248a might have been composed and performed in honor of the new Elector of Saxony, August III, on April 21, 1733; see Häfner, "Zum Problem der Entstehungsgeschichte von BWV 248a," *Die Musikforschung* 30 (1977): 306. Straube was still an extern student at this time and would not have worked for Bach in his capacity as copyist; see also Glöckner, "Eine Michaeliskantate als Parodievorlage," 319, fn. 11, who rejects Häfner's suggestions as well.

[9] Glöckner, "Eine Michaeliskantate als Parodievorlage," 320.

[10] See also the overview in Ulrich Prinz, *Johann Sebastian Bachs Instrumentarium. Originalquellen-Besetzung-Verwendung*, Schriftenreihe der Internationalen Bachakademie Stuttgart 10 (Stuttgart/Kassel: Bachakademie/Bärenreiter, 2005), 62.

the unknown cantata was indeed written for September 29, 1734. It could also have been a cantata for Easter, Ascension Day, or for a wedding during the year. Glöckner's caveat that the "martial" character of the opening movement rendered it unsuitable for a wedding is not entirely compelling. We hear the movement as martial because we are familiar with the text, which talks about the battle against the enemies of Christ. If we focus only on the music, however, the trumpet plays mostly fanfare-like motifs, which are not necessarily militaristic. Handel uses almost the same motif in his soprano aria "Rejoice" from *Messiah*. In other words, Bach employs a rather conventional, celebratory motif, which could have found its place in all kinds of contexts.

Still, Bach's parody technique in the final part of the oratorio is somewhat exceptional. BWV 248a was a sacred cantata that had been performed in Leipzig within the previous year. Furthermore, he borrowed the complete cantata and added movements that were specific to its function in the *Christmas Oratorio*: the two gospel recits and a Christmas hymn. Finally, Bach not only parodied the opening chorus and the arias but also the two recits as well as the penultimate movement, the *Recitativo à 4*. He usually did not parody recits because they were so closely related to the text that it was easier to compose them anew instead of adapting a model. And because Bach was able to borrow the recits from the model composition suggests that either the text must have been very similar to the text of the oratorio, or that the librettist paid particular attention to writing a recit text that fit the preexisting music perfectly. If the text was indeed similar, the model was very likely a cantata that had the victory over the enemies as its main subject, which would again speak for either Easter or Michaelmas.

Some of the movements might even have a history that predates the sacred version from 1734. Friedrich Smend has suggested that the opening movement could have been originally composed for the cantata BWV Anh. 10, "So kämpfet nun, ihr muntern Töne."[11] While the meter and the affect do indeed fit this earlier text, the printed libretto identifies the movement as "Aria" and the cantata might have been a solo cantata, in which case the similarity would be a mere coincidence. Also the two final arias of BWV 248 and 248a betray a secular heritage. The extensive instrumental portions in "Nur ein Wink von seinen Händen" (no. 57) and its dance-like character remind us of secular models;[12] we find a similar instrumental dominance in Bach's secular cantatas for the Cöthen court.[13] While other features of the first aria—like the modern and almost gallant voice leading—do not point to Cöthen, they do point to a secular model rather than a sacred one. The same is true for the second aria. The

---

[11] Friedrich Smend, "Neue Bach-Funde," *Archiv für Musikwissenschaft* 7 (1942): 8–10. Although the music for the cantata is lost, the text by Picander was printed in the fourth volume of his *Ernst-Schertzhaffte und Satyrische Gedichte* (Leipzig: Friese, 1737), 45.

[12] Dürr points out that the ritornellos could easily be combined into an independent instrumental movement (Dürr, *Weihnachts-Oratorium*, 216); see also Petzoldt, *Bach-Kommentar* II, 393.

[13] See Markus Rathey, "Instrumentaler Satz und Orchesterbehandlung in den Köthener Glückwunschkantaten," *Cöthener Bach Hefte* 11 (2003): 116–35.

opening motif of the aria "Nun mögt ihr stolzen Feinde schrecken" (no. 62) shows a stark resemblance to an early version of the Allegro movement from Carl Philipp Emanuel Bach's Trio in D Minor (Wq 145).[14] The younger Bach dates the version in his *Nachlassverzeichnis* with 1731. If this date is correct, he would have modeled his trio on a piece by his father (probably an aria composed around that time), which would then later (1734) be used for a parody in the cantata BWV 248a.

Bach's parody technique in the last part of the oratorio differs significantly from parts I–V. Not only did he borrow a complete cantata instead of "mixing and matching" movements as in parts I–V, but he also did not change the keys for any of the movements, which means that he used the voices as they stood in the earlier model. This leads to several unusual features. In mvts. 61–63 the tenor has to sing three movements in a row: the gospel recit in no. 61, followed by an accompagnato recit and an aria. The gospel recit was added to the already existing movements, leading to the exceptional sequence of three movements for the same voice back-to-back. Did Bach originally plan to assign the last recit-aria-pair to a different singer? The text suggests that he did. Earlier commentators have already noticed that the text features some topics that are typical for alto arias in the *Christmas Oratorio*.[15] In the accompagnato (no. 61) the singer addresses Jesus as the treasure and as a friend; he is the bridegroom; heart and breast are promised to him. In the following aria the singer adds that Christ, the treasure, was with him and that he dwelled "here." All these are typical metaphors of the *unio mystica* and the Second Coming of Christ, topics that are characteristic for the alto movements. Did Bach intentionally abandon the voice pattern he had maintained during the oratorio? Did he not care as much as it seemed? Or had Bach planned to make some changes to the model composition but, as the performance drew nearer, had run out of time and thus decided to use the material as it was? The latter seems to be the most likely explanation. We have already established that he composed the *Christmas Oratorio* between early October 1734 and the end of that year. The last part is signed with "Fine SDGl 1734," so the composition was completed sometime before December 31. The composition of the oratorio as a whole, however, took longer than anticipated: While he had probably planned to use an existing piece for the aria "Schließe, mein Herze" (no. 31) in part III, he decided to write a new composition, then rejected his first draft and started again from scratch. For part V his librettist had written a text that went well with the last movement of BWV 213. But again, Bach rejected the original plan and composed an entirely new piece of rather large dimensions. He even went back and added ten measures to the finished composition before he handed over the score to his copyists. If we consider Bach's usual speed in composing complex cantata movements, the unexpected additional work must still have cost him extra time that had not been planned for. In order to finish the composition on time so that his

---

[14] See Christoph Wolff, "Carl Philipp Emanuel Bachs Trio in d-Moll (BWV 1036/Wq 145)," *Bach-Jahrbuch* 95 (2009): 184–85.

[15] Blankenburg, *Weihnachts-Oratorium*, 133; similar in Jena, *Brich an, o schönes Morgenlicht*, 223.

copyists could write out the parts, he apparently decided against major changes in part VI and used as much older material as was possible.

## The insolent enemies (mvt. 54)

It is quite unusual for an opening chorus in Bach's *Christmas Oratorio* to directly allude to topics from the following movements. The first choruses in parts I, III, IV, and V have a general celebratory character and do not touch on the central narrative. An exception to this is the sinfonia in part II, which paints the bucolic scene in which the dialogue between the shepherds and the angels unfolds. The first chorus of part VI, however, goes into *medias res* by juxtaposing the insolent, arrogant enemies—equipped with sharp claws—and the trust of the faithful in God's strength and salvation. It is this dichotomy that will play out throughout the final part of the oratorio. The "insolent enemy" was for Bach's listeners on January 6, 1735, more than just a religious metaphor. The war of Polish succession that had begun after the death of August the Strong in 1733 was still very much on the minds of the citizens of Leipzig. It had been the topic of Bach's cantata BWV 215, performed in early October 1734 and technically, the war was not over until peace negotiations in December 1735.[16] While the final part of the oratorio was not part of political war propaganda (as BWV 215 had been), it did evoke images that must have resonated deeply with Bach's audience. The enemy was a real entity—not just a metaphysical idea.

Another unusual feature of part VI is the identical verse structure of the opening movement and the tenor aria no. 62. The two movements are not only formally identical but also resemble each other thematically. It is possible that the model composition already had two corresponding movements. Here in the oratorio, the parallelism between the two movements highlights the juxtaposition of the central conflict, between the "insolent enemies" and the divine intervention:

| 248/54 | 248/62 |
|---|---|
| Herr, wenn die *stolzen Feinde* schnauben, | Nun mögt ihr *stolzen Feinde* schrecken; |
| So gib, dass wir im festen Glauben | Was könnt ihr mir für Furcht erwecken? |
| Nach deiner Macht und Hülfe sehn! | Mein Schatz, mein Hort ist hier bei mir. |
| Wir wollen dir allein vertrauen, | Ihr mögt euch noch so grimmig stellen, |
| So können wir den scharfen Klauen | Droht nur, mich ganz und gar zu fällen, |
| Des Feindes unversehrt entgehn. | Doch seht! mein Heiland wohnet hier. |

---

[16]  The peace treaty was ratified on May 1, 1737. See also chap. 10, this book, for more on BWV 215.

| Lord, when our insolent enemies snort, | Now you insolent enemies might horrify; |
| Then grant that we in steadfast faith | [Yet] how could you arouse any fear in me? |
| Will look to your strength and salvation! | My Treasure, my Refuge is here with me! |
| We want to put our trust in you alone, | You do still so like to feign being fierce; |
| So that we can escape | Just [go ahead and] threaten to bring me down completely; |
| The enemy's sharp claws unharmed. | But look! my Savior dwells here. |

Andreas Glöckner and Meinrad Walter have called the opening movement a "musi-kalisches Schlachtengemälde," a musical battle scene.[17] The ritornello is dominated by fanfare-like motifs in the first trumpet (mm. 1–8), followed by highly virtuosic trum-pet soli, supported by the instrumental ensemble. At the same time, it is a highly con-trapuntal movement, layering the virtuosity of the trumpet part on top of an intricate polyphonic texture.[18] Alfred Dürr has outlined the formal structure of the movement:

|   | measure | instruments | Chorus |
|---|---------|-------------|--------|
|    | 1–48 | Ritornello a, b, c | |
|    | 49–68 | (accompanying) | 1st fugue a ("Herr, wenn . . .") |
| **A** | 69–88 | (accompanying) | 2nd fugue a ("so gib . . .") |
|    | 89–104 | (accompanying) | imitative ("nach deiner . . .") |
|    | 105–20 | Ritornello b | *vokaleinbau* ("so gib . . .") |
| **B** | 121–44 | (accompanying) | free canon in fifth ("Wir sollen. . .") |
|    | 145–60 | Ritornello c', b' | *vokaleinbau* |
|    | 161–84 | (accompanying) | 3rd fugue a ("Herr, wenn. . . so gib. . .") |
| **A'** | 185–204 | (accompanying) | imitative ("nach deiner . . .") |
|    | 205–40 | Ritornello b', c | *vokaleinbau* ("so gib . . .") |

The opening ritornello establishes three distinct musical ideas: (a) the fanfare-like opening (mm. 1–8), (b) the virtuosic *fortspinnung* (9–24), and (c) a section Dürr

---

[17] Glöckner, "Eine Michaeliskantate als Parodievorlage," 321; Walter, *Weihnachtsoratorium*, 172.

[18] Arno Forchert had remarked on the quite unusual combination of traditional polyphony and a very modern phrase structure in this movement. See Forchert, *Johann Sebastian Bach und seine Zeit* (Laaber: Laaber Verlag, 2000), 247–48.

calls a "Coda" and which features an inversion of the opening fanfare (mm. 32–37) and an extended cadence leading to the first vocal section.[19]

The vocal sections alternate between strictly fugal episodes, passages of free imitation, and instances of *vokaleinbau* in which the voices of the singers are built into sections of the ritornello.[20] The result is, as is common in Bach's opening movements, a high degree of motivic and formal coherence. Different musical ideas are related; all of them derive from the opening ritornello; and vocal and instrumental layers are designed in a way that they can be combined simultaneously. What creates the image of a "battle scene" is the combination of the martial trumpet fanfares, the vivid, sometimes tumultuous accompaniment in the other instrumental voices, and the restless polyphony in the vocal sections. The "snarling (schnauben) of the enemies" is set with a long melismatic line in the first fugal section, while the "steadfast faith" is depicted with long notes in the second fugal section (mm. 76–88). The structure of the movement favors the first half of the text (lines 1–3), which is treated extensively in the A and A' sections, while the second half of the text is confined to the short B section. The result is an emphasis of the juxtaposition of the firm believe in God's strength and salvation in the conflict with the arrogant/insolent enemies. The trumpets fulfill a dual function as they are both royal instruments— thus referring back to the royal office of Christ that had been the topic of part I— and instruments of war, figuring prominently in the depiction of the battle against those enemies." Were these features that Bach changed after adding the new text or was the libretto shaped in a way that the words lined up with the music? This is impossible to discern without the original text. It is only possible to describe the overall character and effect of the movement. It is at once celebratory (as would be expected for the feast of the Epiphany) and highlights the martial subject of the libretto for the day.

The corrections Bach made in his score for the opening movement are symptomatic of a more or less mechanical copy of an already fully developed piece. The most frequent mistakes are skipped measures that then had to be inserted.[21] For the first time in m. 90 and several times after, Bach accidentally wrote "Gnade und Hülfe" (mercy and salvation) in tenor and bass, before he changed it to the correct "Macht und Hülfe" (strength and salvation). Could the word "Gnade" stem from the original composition? Or did this phrase, which frequently occurs in religious literature

---

[19]  See Dürr, *Weihnachts-Oratorium*, 37.

[20]  Several commentators have highlighted the balanced structure of the movement. The A section has 120 measures, the same length as the B and A' sections together; cf. Jena, *Brich an, o schönes Morgenlicht*, 209; Blankenburg, *Weihnachts-Oratorium*, 127–28; and Bossuyt, *Christmas Oratorio*, 159.

[21]  For instance, in mm. 85–87 Bach accidentally inserted the soprano part from mm. 86–88; he then erased the measures and entered the correct notes. Bach had to correct similar omissions in m. 91 (soprano; for example, Bach at first entered m. 92 a bar too early), mm. 127–28. (alto), and mm. 165– 66 (vocalists and bc), just to name a few.

from the eighteenth century, coincidently sneak into the score?[22] Whatever might be the case, Bach must have become aware of the mistake only after the parts had been copied because we find the mistake there as well.

Considering the clear and neat character of the manuscript, a correction of the final measures of the movement jumps off the page. In the soprano, the first note in m. 238 had been a *d''* followed in m. 239 by an eighth-note ligature *d''–a'*; this is the way Bach had previously set the text: the "und" appeared as an upbeat and the first syllable of "Hülfe" was sung to two eighth notes (see mm. 210 and 211). This was probably the way that final cadence had appeared in BWV 248a as well. In his version for the *Christmas Oratorio*, Bach replaced the *d''* in m. 238 with a rest and rearranged the text in the following measure so that the soprano (and the other voices) now declaimed the words syllabically, strongly marking each of the beats of the cadence: "und Hül-fe sehn!" The revised version gives a stronger sense of closure, and it also confidently proclaims the central idea of the movement, the divine support against the enemies.[23] Due to the loss of most of the parts from the model composition it is not possible to deduce what other changes Bach has made to BWV 248a. A rare exception to this are some measures in the trumpet and timpani parts.[24] Measures 20–22 originally had three short brass chords on the first beat of each measure. This earlier version is still present in the score, but the parts were revised in Bach's hand. The first trumpet now has a long note while the lower voices are confined to one single chord in m. 20 and then drop out for several measures. The same appears in mm. 116–18; again, the score represents the earlier version, while the parts were revised by Bach. The third time this short musical idea occurs (at mm. 212–14), the score has the revised version as well. These changes not only provide a small glimpse of the earlier version of the piece but also suggest that Bach's copyist did indeed use the score and some of the performance parts for BWV 248a when he worked on the parts for BWV 248/VI. This could also be a sign for the haste under which Bach completed the final part of the oratorio.

## The broken enemy (mvt. 64)

The massive opening chorus of part VI is balanced by an equally impressive final chorale setting. Like the first chorus, it was already part of the model composition BWV 248a. The melody was traditionally associated with "Herzlich tut mich

---

[22] The combination of "Gnade und Hilfe" appears, for instance, in Bach's cantata BWV 179/4.

[23] The final cadence in m. 239 follows a diminished seventh chord (vii of V) on "Macht" in m. 238, which for a moment has a destabilizing effect before the revised cadence affirms the stability that is given through the divine salvation.

[24] See the reconstruction in NBA II/6, KB, 319–21.

verlangen." The text is the fourth stanza of Georg Werner's Christmas hymn "Ihr Christen auserkoren," a hymn not found in any of the standard Leipzig hymnals.[25] The combination of these two hymns was somewhat unusual, but the meter and number of syllables goes well with the text. We have discussed earlier the perception of the melody as a "Passion chorale" and thus as an allusion to Christ's Passion and death. For Bach's contemporary listeners, though, the melody would not have evoked that specific association and it would be wrong to read too much into its use, especially because the chorale setting had already been part of the model composition BWV 248a. In fact, it might simply be a coincidence that the *Christmas Oratorio* is now framed by two settings of the same hymn melody, the chorale "Wie soll ich dich empfangen" (no. 5) and "Nun seid ihr wohl gerochen" (no. 64).

The movement combines an elaborate ritornello structure with the setting of the hymn stanza. The dimensions far transcend the earlier closing movements. In parts I and II, the final chorales had opened with the statement of the first line of the hymn, followed by an alternation between individual lines and short interludes. Both movements ended with two to three measures of instrumental postlude. In part IV, the chorale setting (based on a melody composed by Bach himself) began with four ritornello measures, before the voices entered in m. 5. Derivates of the four measures appeared between the lines of the hymn and also at the close of the movement. In the final chorale setting of part VI, the ritornello reaches an impressive length of twelve measures, a size that would be more appropriate for an elaborate opening movement than a final chorale. The ritornello is repeated before the A′ section of the melody and then returns at the very end of the movement. The sections A′ and B of the hymn in bar form are separated by a short interlude that is derived from the beginning of the ritornello. The chorale setting resembles some of the opening movements from Bach's chorale cantata cycle (1724/25)[26]:

| | |
|---|---|
| 1–12 | Ritornello |
| 13–18 | Vocal section A |
| 19–30 | Ritornello |
| 31–36 | Vocal section A′ |
| 37–40 | Short interlude |
| 41–57 | Vocal section B |
| 57–68 | Ritornello |

---

[25] Blankenburg, *Weihnachts-Oratorium*, 136.

[26] For instance: *Herr Jesu Christ, du höchstes Gut*, BWV 113, or *Ich freue mich in dir*, BWV 133; see Rathey, "Der zweite Leipziger Jahrgang—Choralkantaten," 374–75, and 410–11.

In addition to the large scale ritornello structure, the individual lines of the chorale are separated by short interludes, similar to the smaller sized chorale settings at the ends of parts I and II. The length of these interludes varies between one and three measures; the only exception appears before the final line where Bach delays the entrance of the vocalists and expands the interlude to five measures. Given the regular structure of the movement, the entrance of the voices feels "too late" and thus creates tension and anticipation, which is finally released in the closing line, "das menschliche Geschlecht" (the human family).

The chorale setting "modernizes" the modal melody (Phrygian) by setting it with modern harmonies. While Bach had maintained the Phrygian character of the melody in the first setting at no. 5 in part I of the oratorio, even ending with an archaic plagal cadence, he now surrounds the tune with modern major-minor tonalities. Bach created the chorale movement as a counterpart to the first movement of BWV 248a. As in the opening movement for part VI, the final chorale prominently features the trumpet; Meinrad Walter likened the setting to a trumpet concerto with a built-in chorale![27] Both movements also share the fanfare-like motif in the trumpet and extensive virtuosic figurations of the solo instrument (mm. 9–11). The semantic function of the trumpet fanfares in the final chorale movement is the same as in the opening movement. The battle with the enemies, which had been the subject of mvt. 54, is now interpreted as an apocalyptical battle against death, devil, sin, and hell. No. 54 leaves the enemies' identity ambiguous; the listener can hear it as a preparation for the Herod-narrative or as a description of his own afflictions. The final chorale now specifically names the source of all evil: it is general and concrete at the same time. The different types of enemies also correspond with the three-partite temporal structure of the *Christmas Oratorio*: the enemy in the time of the narrative (Herod), the time of the *first* coming of Christ; the enemies in the experience of the faithful, the time of Christ's *second* coming; and the victory against the archenemies at the end of times, the time of Christ's *third* coming. This final chorale brings the temporal structure of the entire oratorio to a joyous close. Within the musical structure of the oratorio, the chorale also balances the opening chorus "Jauchzet, frohlocket" (no. 1). Even though the correspondences between the two choruses are secondary as Bach combines two preexisting movements, they are still intentional and connect the movements on several levels: both are in D major and prominently feature the first trumpet with virtuosic fanfares. While the melody connects the final chorale with the first hymn setting (no. 5), the instrumentation connects it with the very beginning of the oratorio.

---

[27] Walter, *Weihnachtsoratorium*, 180; similarly Jena, *Brich an, o schönes Morgenlicht*, 231.

## Herod, the enemy (mvts. 55–57)

The opening movement freely plays with the aural associations of who the enemy is to the listeners. It would be wrong to narrow this down in a too-early interpretation. The liturgical context already provided a way of hearing the words: the gospel text for the day mentioned King Herod; and the gospel on the previous Sunday told the story of the killing of the children by that same king. In addition, Bach's audience might also have been reminded of the "altböse Feind," the archenemy, the devil, and his afflictions in daily life. And the movement is also open for a political way of listening. The prosperity of Saxony (or at least of its ruler) was threatened by Stanislaus Leszczynski, the claimant to the Polish throne, who had questioned the legitimacy of the kingship of August III. Since the king's authority rested on his authorization through God, questioning him meant questioning the divine order. The semantic ambivalence of the tumultuous battle scene in the opening movement is then narrowed down in the following gospel recit.

When inserting the recit into the model BWV 248a, Bach accidentally began to copy the beginning of the first recit from the model at the bottom of the first page of the score, directly underneath the beginning of the opening chorus. He entered the title "Recit. nach dem Chor," the soprano clef, the accidentals for a soprano line, and several notes. Bach must have quickly noticed the error. He erased the notes, changed the word "Recit." into "Evangel[ist]" and entered the correct notes for the tenor recit. The soprano recit should then follow as the third movement. Bach's mistake suggests that the soprano recit in its original version in BWV 248a was not accompanied by the strings (or any other instruments for that matter) because he did not make any provisions for accompanying instruments when he entered the beginning of the recit at the bottom of the first page of the score. The accompaniment is also missing from the surviving string parts from the older cantata. Bach added the accompaniment in the oratorio to underscore the sonic differentiation between the secco recits for the gospel text and accompagnati for the madrigalistic poetry.

The gospel recit (no. 55) begins with an introduction by the evangelist, followed by a statement from King Herod. Bach's primary goal in the recit is to highlight Herod's deceptive intentions in his dealings with the wise men. In m. 2, the text states that the king secretly ("heimlich") called the wise men; Bach sets the word with a rising seventh, which is also the tritone to the bc note $G\sharp$. The result is a truly deceptive sound. Bach had revised the measure during the composition. In an earlier version the second note in the tenor had been a $g\sharp$ instead of the $e$; the leap up to $d'$ would have been a tritone; still an interval that could have suggested insincerity, but less effective than the leap of a seventh into a different register. Bach also made a change to the transition from the section of the evangelist to the part of Herod. The bass line originally moved from $g\sharp$ (m. 5) to $a$ (m. 6). The leading tone would have evoked a sense of closure which would have severed the coherence of the recit. Bach changed the last note in m. 5 into a g♮ and the first note in the following measure into a quarter note f♯ at first before he finally extended the f♯ to two whole notes. The harmonic progression now lacks the cadential quality of the earlier version and organically connects the two halves of the gospel recit. When Herod enters, he states matter-of-factly that he wants to come and adore the child. Only small details hint at his deception: the chromatic ascent in the bc in m. 9/10, which obscures the harmonic progression,[28] and a small melismatic embellishment on the final syllable of "anbete." The little flourish reminds us of similar figures Bach commonly uses to highlight a state of devotion. We saw a similar instance at the end of mvt. 45, where the name "Jesus" received a similar treatment (m. 28). Now, however, the flourish sounds somehow wrong since it accentuates a weak syllable. Herod employs a gesture of devotion but uses it incorrectly, thus revealing his deception.

The following soprano recit (no. 56) picks up on this dishonesty: "Du Falscher" (you deceitful one). While this movement is one of the rare occasions where Bach parodied a recit, the bc parts for BWV 248a show that Bach made significant changes to the voice line, while he left the instrumental bass essentially intact. Alfred Dürr has reconstructed the original version (ex. 11.1).

*Example 11.1*  Reconstruction of BWV 248a/2 and final version in BWV 248/56

---

[28] Cf. Walter, *Weihnachtsoratorium*, 174, and Petzoldt, *Bach-Kommentar* II, 392.

The revised version now emphasizes the noun "Falscher" with an ascending fifth, while the high note in m. 3 is lowered to *c″*; the original text probably featured an important word, while the noun "List" (cunning) was better depicted by the use of a dissonant *c♯*. In m. 8 Bach leads the soprano down to *e′*, when the text mentions Herod's cunning. The descent prepares an ascent in m. 9 on "des Höchsten Sohn" (the Son of the Most High). It is evident that the original text, while it must have had a similar structure, set different thematic accents than the parody in the *Christmas Oratorio*. The recit was originally unaccompanied. In his parody, Bach added a simple string accompaniment to what had been a secco recit. The two violins and viola play extended chords but do not develop motivic independence as in other recits from the oratorio. The exception is the final measure where the strings echo a dotted motif from the soprano. The galant gesture sets the stage for the following soprano aria. Although the two movements are not motivically related, the aria has a similarly modern, galant character. The two movements are also textually connected. In the recit, it is Herod who wants to "bring down" ("fällen") the Lord, while in the aria it is the "most high" who "overthrows the feeble strength of humankind."

The enemy in the aria is not overthrown through the strength of arms but by a "signal from his hands" and by "one word" of the "Most High." The mention of the single word alludes to the biblical story of the centurion of Capernaum, who had asked Jesus to heal his servant: "only speak one word and my servant will be healed" (Mt 8:8). Listeners might also have been reminded of the first stanza of Luther's "A mighty fortress"; after this well-known hymn text has mentioned the "alt böse Feind," the archenemy, it warns that "ein Wörtlein kann ihn fällen" (a little word can bring him down). Finally, the power that is ascribed to the "word" echoes the centrality of the word (of God) in the doctrine of the threefold coming of Christ: the presence of Christ is mediated through the word, and it is the presence of Christ (in the human heart) that drives away fear, death, and the "enemy." The second aria of part VI (no. 62) will return to this thought, "how could [the enemies] arouse any fear in me? . . . my refuge is here with me . . . my Savior dwells here."

The "hands of God" is a metaphor that appears occasionally in the Old Testament.[29] Johann Olearius decodes God's hands in his interpretation of a phrase from Isaiah 49:16a, "Siehe, in die Hände hab ich dich gezeichnet" as symbol for divine omnipotence: "Die göttlichen Hände bedeuten seine Allmacht und Würckung / *palmae significant potentiam divinam & operationes divinas*" (The divine hands signify his omnipotence and efficacy / *the hands represent divine power and divine efficacy*).[30] Even closer to the wording in Bach's aria text is Olearius's exegesis of Psalm 68:2 (God's triumph over the wicked), when he alludes to the "Wink"

---

[29] Cf. Petzoldt, *Bach-Kommentar* II, 394.

[30] Johann Olearius, *Biblische Erklärung* IV (Leipzig: Tarnov, 1680, 248), quoted after Petzoldt, *Bach-Kommentar* II, 394.

(signal) of God's hands.[31] In general, God's hands are used in cantata texts set by Bach as a symbol for divine strength and might.[32] The image returns later when recit no. 63 asks, "what will world and sin intend to do to us, since we rest in Jesus's hands!"

The soprano aria for obbligato oboe d'amore, strings, and bc begins with an instrumental ritornello that resembles a polonaise. While the movement is not mentioned in the standard studies on Bach's use of dance movements in his vocal works,[33] both the phrase structure (4 + 4) and the rhythmic profile with its accentuated quarter notes on the second and third beat are typical for the stylized form of the Polish dance in the first half of the eighteenth century.[34] Alfred Dürr has suggested a simplified version of the opening ritornello that turns it into a regular polonaise (ex. 11.2).[35] While Dürr's "reconstruction" represents a more usual version of a polonaise, it sacrifices the characteristic accentuated quarter notes in m. 1. A reconstruction of a regular form is not necessary. In its original version, the melodic line resembles the main theme in the polonaise of Bach's French Suite No. 6, BWV 817 (ex. 11.3); a similar melodic line can be found in polonaises by Georg Philipp Telemann, the composer who was famous in his time for extensively employing Polish features in his music. The example shows an excerpt from his *Concerto for oboe and strings* in C minor (TWV 51:c1) (ex. 11.4).

*Example 11.2* J. S. Bach, BWV 248/57: aria ritornello (a) in reduction to traditional Polonaise (b)

[31] Johann Olearius, *Biblische Erklärung* III (Leipzig: Tarnov, 1679), 369; quoted after Petzoldt, *Bach-Kommentar* II, 394.

[32] Cf. Lucia Haselböck, *Bach Textlexikon: Ein Wörterbuch der religiösen Sprachbilder im Vokalwerk von Johann Sebastian Bach* (Kassel: Bärenreiter, 2004), 94.

[33] Finke-Hecklinger, *Tanzcharaktere*, and Little/Jenne, *Dance and the Music of J. S. Bach*.

[34] Cf. the description of the rhythmic features in Scheibe, *Critischer Musicus*, 118–19 and 149–50; see also Steven Zohn, *Music for a Mixed Taste: Style, Genre, and Meaning in Telemann's Instrumental Works* (Oxford: Oxford University Press, 2008), 493–94.

[35] Dürr, *Weihnachts-Oratorium*, 34

Example 11.3  J. S. Bach, *French Suite VI* BWV 817, Polonaise, mm. 1–5

Example 11.4  Georg Philipp Telemann, *Concerto in C minor* for oboe
and strings, TWV 51:c1/iv, mm. 1–5

Another detail that connects the aria with Bach's polonaises is the unusual performance instruction "Largo e staccato," which only appears in the performing parts
from BWV 248a. Bach uses a similar indication for the polonaise from his B-minor
orchestral suite BWV 1067. That movement is superscribed with "moderato e staccato" and "lentement." In both cases the tempo indication demands that the movement should be played slower than the notation in eighth and sixteenth notes might
suggest. While Bach clearly plays with allusions to the popular dance, the aria from
248a/248, part VI is not a standard polonaise. Bach abandons the regular structure
at the end of the ritornello; however, his listeners in Leipzig would have recognized
the allusion. This begs the question regarding what the original text for the aria
might have been and whether the movement was originally composed for a secular
cantata (where a dance movement would have been more common than in a sacred
work). The use of a Polish dance would have been appropriate in a cantata in honor
of the Saxon Elector, who had been crowned king of Poland on January 17, 1734.
Bach's *Collegium musicum* had, in fact, performed an unknown piece for this occasion in Zimmermann's coffee house.[36] The movement (maybe together with others
that have become part of BWV 248a) might have been composed for that occasion.
Even within part VI of the *Christmas Oratorio*, the aria "Nur ein Wink von seinen
Händen" retained a residual political message. As mentioned earlier, the memory of
the War of Polish Succession was still fresh. A piece in a recognizably Polish style—
that invoked the toppling of a proud enemy—must have evoked memories among

---

[36] *BachDok* II, 346; cf. NBA I/37, KB, 12.

Bach's audience; even more so because the performance took place only eleven days before the first anniversary of the contested coronation.

The structure of the aria is unusual. The complete ritornello only appears at the very end as a postlude. The instrumental prelude features the first twelve measures of the ritornello, while the second half of the ritornello separates the A and B sections of the bipartite aria:

| | | |
|---|---|---|
| 1–12 | Ritornello I | A–>E |
| 12–24 | Vocal section A | A–>E |
| 24–40 | Ritornello II | [b–>f♯]–>A |
| 40–68 | Vocal section B | [b–>f♯]–>A |
| 68–96 | Ritornello I+II | A–>E–>[b–>f♯]–>A |

As Dürr has already noted, the complete ritornello almost seems like an independent instrumental movement and could stand on its own.[37] Especially if we consider that the first and second half of the movement would have been repeated, the instrumental piece would have had a substantive length of fifty-six measures. Even though the thought is intriguing, there is no evidence that the movement had originally existed as an independent instrumental piece. Bach rather uses, as he does frequently, an instrumental form and turns it into an aria. Several earlier examples from his compositions from Cöthen employ the same technique.

The ritornello opens with the main motif of four measures, featuring the characteristic emphasis on beats two and three in the first measure, followed by two measures of syncopation that create rhythmic ambiguity. For a while it is not clear whether the opening motif stands in triple time or in $\frac{2}{4}$ meter. Only at the end of the first phrase (m. 4) will the listener have grasped that the movement is indeed in triple time. Consequently, when the opening measures are repeated in piano (mm. 5–8), one hears the measures with a clearer sense of metrical order.[38] The opening ritornello ends with a four-measure epilogue, which continues the play with syncopations and leads directly into the first vocal part. This first vocal section is a *vokaleinbau* with a twist. Starting with the upbeat of m. 17, the soprano voice is built into the instrumental fabric of the ritornello. For the most part, the singer follows the melodic line of the oboe d'amore, but occasionally it is led independently. At the beginning of the vocal section, Bach loosens the texture and accompanies the singer (who sings the notes from the opening motif) with a polyphonic stretto: the

---

[37] Dürr, *Weihnachts-Oratorium*, 216; see also Petzoldt, *Bach-Kommentar* II, 393.

[38] Bach does, in fact, give the listener a small hint at the very beginning of the movement: the upbeat before m. 1 begins with the tonic in first inversion, while the tonic in root position only appears on the first beat of the first measure, which gives this beat a stronger emphasis. This small hint is easy to overlook, and it is obscured by the rhythmic accents that are setup by the upper voices.

arch-like melody from the first measure is immediately echoed by the bc (first half m. 13), the oboe (second half m. 13), the viola (m. 14), and finally the second violin (m. 15). The fact that the vocal section is mostly a literal repetition of the opening ritornello is almost imperceptible. The staggered entrance of the voices suggests for a moment a polyphonic independence of the voices.

The first vocal section is followed by another extensive instrumental section (ritornello II), which will later return as the second half of the closing ritornello. The interlude freely develops the material from the opening measures, combining arch-like melodic gestures with sequences of syncopations. The second vocal section (mm. 40–68) is then again integrated into a repetition of material from ritornello II. Bach repeatedly expands the instrumental texture by inserting additional measures (for instance in mm. 43/44, 48/49, 52–54, 58–60). Like the stretto-opening of the first vocal section, the interpolations suggest a greater independence from the instrumental ritornello; they also give Bach the opportunity to pay closer attention to the meaning of the text. An instructive example of a compositional change to the material from the ritornello appears the end of the second vocal section (mm. 62–66). Bach gives the melodic line from the ritornello II to the soprano but adds an oboe d'amore part that imitates the vocal line with a delay of two quarter notes. The bc plays a pulsating pedal point on E (later F♯ and G♯), which creates a moment of nervous anticipation. The dialogue between the singer and the oboe is repeated a third higher (on g♯), before the two voices return to the original material from the ritornello II. In the *Christmas Oratorio* this dramatic moment in the music is combined with the announcement that the plans of the mortals had to be cut short immediately: it signals the defeat of the enemy. The movement closes with a combination of the two halves of the ritornello, giving the listener a long moment for meditation before the following recit returns to the gospel text.

Even though the combination of music and text in this aria is not original, some of the textual details line up well with features in the music. The arch-like figure in mm. 12/13 can be heard as a depiction of the gesture of the divine hand; the accentuated quarter notes in mm. 13/14 highlight the hands of God, and the melisma on "verlacht" (mm. 22/23) paints the mocking mentioned in the text. Ascending lines coincide with the word "Höchste" (highest, mm. 40–41 and 43), while an exposed high note in m. 44 accentuates the central theological term "Word." It is impossible to decide whether these details were already present in BWV 248a or if Bach changed the voice-leading when he reworked the aria for the *Christmas Oratorio*. In any case, the score for the aria does not show any signs of revision.

## Precious gifts (mvts. 58–59)

The following short scene from Matthew 2:9–11 narrates the departure of the wise men from the court of King Herod, their finding of the manger and child, and their delivery of the gifts. The scene stands a bit outside of the main subject of the final part of the *Christmas Oratorio*. The model composition did not provide movements that would have lent themselves to this scene that thematically departs from the topic of the enemies. Bach and his librettist therefore limited it to a setting of the gospel text followed by a single chorale stanza, which was added to the preexisting movements. Under other circumstances, the gospel text would have provided an opportunity to return to the subject of the star and its symbolism (as in part V); however, the librettist instead focuses on the final lines of the text in mvt. 58: the gifts the three wise men bring to the newborn child. Bach's recit setting takes advantage of several words of height: In m. 6 the text reports that the star settled over the manger in which the little child was lying. Bach's setting paints an arch by beginning at a low *e*, then rises sharply to *d'* and *f♯'* before it descends to *b*. The line then ascends even higher and reaches *a'* (m. 8) when the text notes that the wise men became exceedingly (highly, "hoch") glad. When the men bow down to worship the child, the tenor line drops down to *d♯*, the lowest pitch in the recit (m. 12), only to leap up immediately by a diminished seventh on the word "beteten" (prayed). Again, the final line of the recit enumerates the gifts brought by the wise men: gold, frankincense, and myrrh. Bach sets each of the words differently. "Gold" is reached by an ascending minor seventh, creating an *exclamatio* gesture[39]; "Weihrauch" is set with an ascending gesture, gliding into a tritone between tenor and bc, and finally a harsh diminished chord (vii of V) on the word "Myrrhen." The setting of the three words creates a climax, ascending chromatically from *f* to *g*. Bach creates a similar chromatic ascent (shifted by an eighth note) in the bc of m. 15, which rises from *c* to *c♯* and *d*. The latter chromatic ascent was the result of a revision in the score. The cancellation sign before the first note (*c*) was added after the sign for the note had been written. The dual chromatic ascent in the final measures highlights the subject that the libretto focuses on; the symbolic and allegorical meaning of the three precious gifts is then interpreted in the following chorale stanza.

In the exegetical tradition, the three gifts of the wise men have often been interpreted symbolically. Christoph Starke, in his *Synopsis Bibliothecae Exegeticae* (Leipzig, 3rd ed., 1745) relates the gifts freely to the three offices of Christ. The gold stands for his royal office; the bitter taste of myrrh is a symbol for Christ's sacrifice and thus stands for his high priestly office; and frankincense symbolizes prayer, which Starke reads as a symbol for the divine nature of Christ.[40] It is this third point, where Starcke stretches his interpretation. The third office of Christ is traditionally his prophetic office, which would not have fit in his symbolical interpretation. Later, Starke suggests an interpretation that decodes the three gifts as ways in which the individual could respond to Christ's birth: the gold of faith, the frankincense of prayer, and the myrrh of self-denial and sacrifice of carnal desires (Starke, col. 57).

---

[39] Walter already mentioned the exclamation (Walter, *Weihnachtsoratorium*, 175).
[40] Starcke, *Synopsis Bibliothecae Exegeticae*, col. 57.

This second interpretation had been an established way of reading the biblical passage. In fact, Olearius in his *Seelenparadies* from 1669 had already interpreted the gifts in an analogous way.[41]

The hymn stanza inserted after the gospel text ("Ich steh an deiner Krippen hier") suggests a similar reading of these gifts. Without equating specific gifts and their symbolic meaning, the list given in the first stanza of Paul Gerhard's famous Christmas hymn corresponds to the categories in Starke and Olearius: spirit, inclination, heart, soul, courage. The melody in the *Christmas Oratorio* is the tune commonly known as "Nun freut euch lieben Christen g'mein" that was usually associated with this text in the hymnals of his time. Probably around the time of the composition of the oratorio Bach also wrote his own melody, published in the *Schemelli Gesangbuch* from 1736, but he did not include this new melody in the oratorio. The use of a traditional chorale melody, however, does not prohibit Bach from highlighting some of the intimate and emotional qualities of the text. Frequently, two voices move in parallel thirds, and the lower voices often proceed in a smoothly flowing eighth-note motion. In addition to this, the instrumental bass voice moves continuously in eighth notes, only resting briefly at cadences. Small details again stand out: a syncopation in the alto in m. 3 on "Jesu" highlights the name of the newborn child, and short moments of rhythmic stagnation in the dotted quarter notes of the vocal bass line in m. 1 reflect the standing at the manger ("Ich steh . . .", I stand).

# New paths (mvts. 60–63)

After this short moment of repose the narrative returns again to King Herod and his plotting. The gospel recit, which opens the final sequence of movements in the *Christmas Oratorio*, is only loosely connected to the following movements. The accompagnato is antithetical to the gospel. While the recit states that the wise men returned to their land, the subsequent accompagnato recit replies that Jesus, the "treasure," will not leave but stay. This inversion is emblematic of the interpretation of external motion prevalent in the oratorio. The journeys of the shepherds as well as of the wise men to the manger had been interpreted as the journey into the human heart, the dwelling place of Jesus. The departure of the wise men, though, could not possibly have been interpreted as the departure of Jesus from the heart. Thus, the librettist had to establish an antithetical connection. The accompagnato recit reaffirms the *inhabitatio Christi*: he has come into the heart and he will stay and dwell there permanently. The text returns to motifs and images from earlier parts of the oratorio. He is expected with desire ("Trieb") and tenderness ("Zärtlichkeit")

---

[41] Olearius, *Seelenparadies*, 101–2.

and he shall remain the believer's bridegroom and friend. Breast and heart are entrusted to him as a dwelling place. As in earlier instances, the language of mystic unity with Jesus draws on images and phrases from the Song of Songs. The image of the bridegroom is the most prominent connection, but also the line "Ich will ihn auch nicht von mir lassen" (I will also not let him [free] from me) refers to the love poem from the Old Testament: "I hold him, and will not let him go" (Song 3:4).[42] Olearius, in his exegesis of this verse, interprets it as a symbol for the insepa-rable unity of love: "**Ich will ihn nicht lassen** / *amor est copula amantis & amati arctissima & unio indissolubilis* [die Liebe ist das festeste Band des Liebens und das Geliebtwerdens und eine unauflösliche Einheit" (**I will not let him go**, *love is the firmest connection between loving and being loved and an inseparable unity*). Later, in his exegetical remarks on Song of Songs 4:9 ("You have ravished my heart, my sister, my bride), Olearius employs the metaphor of "glue"—which is derived from the field of metaphors associated with the *inhabitatio Christi*—to describe this insepa-rable unity: "Du hast mein Hertz in dein Hertz eingeschlossen / zu dir gerissen / zu dir gezogen / mit deinem Hertzen vereiniget . . . *agglutinatur unus spiritus*, denn die liebe ist eine liebreiche Vereinigung" (You have embraced my heart with yours, seized it, pulled it towards you, unified it with your heart . . . *the one Spirit is glued [to it]*, because love is a loving unification).[43] The phrase "Sein Herz will mich . . . umfassen" (his heart will embrace me) also refers back to the beautiful soprano-bass duet in part IV (no. 38) in which the bass had pleaded, "Ich will dich mit Lust umfassen" (With delight I will embrace you). The text for the accompagnato recit is the final confirmation of the *inhabitatio Christi*, which formed the meta-narrative of the oratorio. In its final lines, the recit then returns to the central topic of part VI and calls on Jesus, the "friend," for help against "any enemy." The aria "Nun mögt ihr stol-zen Feinde schrecken" (no. 62) elaborates on this theme. The insolent enemies are powerless because "my savior dwells here." The term "wohnet" (dwells) is not used lightly but is theologically charged as it refers to the idea of the indwelling of Christ.

Bach's librettist constructs the two sections of the text for the *da capo* aria in a parallel structure. The first two lines ask what the enemies might do, while the final lines of the A and B sections reaffirm Christ's enduring presence. These lines are poetically linked through rhyme: "bei mir"—"wohnet hier." The following *Recitativo à 4* (no. 63) has the same structure. The first two lines ponder what hell, world, and sin might do to the faithful while the closing line reaffirms the sheltering presence of Jesus's hands. The mention of "Hände" (hands) ties back to the powerful hands of God in aria no. 57. The idea of protection seemingly departs far from the gospel text that stands at the beginning of this sequence. Interpretations of Matthew 2:12 from Bach's time, however, view the dream of the wise men as a protection of the wise

---

[42]  Cf. Marissen, *Bach's Oratorios*, 26, fn. 77.

[43]  Olearius, *Biblische Erklärung* III, 1112, 1128, quoted after Petzoldt, *Bach-Kommentar* II, 398.

men as well. Starke's *Synopsis Bibliothecae exegeticae* reads the verse as an example of
God's protection against the enemies:

| | |
|---|---|
| Gott sorget für die seinigen, und wendet die gefahr ab. Bewahret sie für der gotlosen tücken, und geleitet sie auch auf reisen durch seinen engel. . . . Gott macht zunichte die anschläge seiner feinde, und erhaschet die weltweisen in ihrer klugheit.[44] | God takes care of those who belong to him and he averts danger. He protects them from the malice of the godless and his angels guide them on their travels. . . . God ruins the attacks of his enemies, and he catches the world-wise in their cleverness. |

The divine command to take a different path comes in a dream. Bach alludes to the
otherness of the dream by beginning the recit no. 60 in a key that contrasts with the
previous chorale setting "Ich steh an deiner Krippen hier," which had ended in bright
G major; the recit now begins in E minor, on a V chord (B major) in first inversion. The mediant-relationship immediately indicates the shift: we are now in a different reality. This dreamworld is evoked at the beginning of m. 2. Bach sets the word
"Traum" (dream) with a diminished chord, creating a sound that recalls the haziness
of dream-images. The leap from $a'$ down to $c'$ in mm. 1/2 sounds like the leap into a
different reality. The revelation of the "other way" is a transcendental experience; its
otherness is audible. Toward the end of m. 2 Bach heavily revises the voice-leading
of the tenor. In the original version, the voice had descended in a triad on the words
"wieder zu." The revision maintains the triad but shifts it to the words "zu Herodes,"
thus moving the accent from "wieder" (again) to the name of the enemy.[45] Bach
made another change at the end of the recit. The second note in m. 4 of the bass line
originally had been a simple half note on E♯, similar to the preceding half notes in
the bc part. During the compositional process Bach changed the note into a quarter
note, followed by an eighth note and an ascending line that continued in the following measure and led up to $d$ on the second beat of m. 5.[46] The change allowed Bach
to compose an ascending (and descending) bc line that echoed the walking of the
wise men alluded to in the text. Bach had already used the ascending-line motif as a
symbol for "travel" earlier on similar occasions, such as the chorus of the shepherds
("Lasset uns nun gehen," no. 26) or the chorus of the wise men ("Wir haben seinen
Stern gesehen," no. 45). By introducing the *figura corta* (♫) in the final measures of
the recit, which departs from the slow movement of the bass voice in the previous

---

[44]  Starke, *Synopsis Bibliothecae exegeticae*, col. 58.

[45]  The printed libretto does skip the word "wieder" (cf. Petzoldt, *Bach-Kommentar* II, 389); however, this is probably only a typographical error.

[46]  The note on the third beat in m. 5 was also changed from a quarter note to an eighth note followed by two sixteenths.

measures, Bach also creates the impression of kinetic energy that reflects the urgency of the departure of the wise men and propels the listener into the next movement. It appears that Bach had originally planned to have an additional measure after m. 5. He wrote a whole rest with a fermata in the tenor voice but did not execute the bc. He then wiped away the ink that was still wet and wrote the time signature (**c**) for the following movement. The elimination of the additional measure and the acceleration in the bc line now tie the two movements—gospel setting and reflection—closer together.

In the earlier parts of the *Christmas Oratorio,* an accompagnato recit like no. 61 (with a text invoking the love for the friend and bridegroom Jesus Christ) would have been set for alto; but since Bach is using the recit from BWV 248a without transpositions, he gives the movement to the tenor instead. Conversely, it is possible that he added the two oboi d'amore, turning what originally had been a secco recit into a recitativo accompagnato.[47] The choice of the two "love oboes" underscores the topic of the recit and connects it with earlier accompangnati that dealt with the same subject, in particular the very first recit, "Nun wird mein liebster Bräutigam" (no. 3).[48] The recit is similar to the earlier movement in that the phrases of the text are separated by short instrumental interpolations by the oboes and the bc. It is important for the compositional process that these interludes do not show signs of significant revisions or corrections.[49] This means that either they were already part of the recit in BWV 248a or that Bach had a clear plan from the start regarding how to shape the interpolations. Because the sixteenth-note interpolations in the bc in mm. 8, 10, and 13 are already present in the parts from BWV 248a, it is clear that (at least) the instrumental bass line was expanded; it does not, however, prove beyond a doubt that the movement necessarily had an additional instrumental accompaniment as well.

The highly emotional and agitated affect of the text—the confession of love and trust for Jesus and the expression of contempt for the enemy—inspires Bach to an equally agitated setting. The first sixteenth-note interpolation by the oboes (mm. 4–5) and probably the following interpolations too have to be played *allegro,* while the tempo returns to a calmer *adagio* when the oboes accompany the singer in longer note values. The interpolations are further accentuated by the dynamic change to *forte* (in contrast to the *piano* accompaniment during the vocal sections). The result

---

[47]  Most of the rare corrections appear in the oboe parts while the tenor and the bc is almost without any revisions.

[48]  This has correspondence between the first and the last recit of the oratorio, and which has already been pointed out by Blankenburg, *Weihnachts-Oratorium,* 133, and Jena, *Brich an, o schönes Morgenlicht,* 223.

[49]  The only exceptions are m. 15, where Bach added a sixteenth note flourish in the bc (originally two half notes), and in m. 16, where he changed an extended half-note chord into four sixteenth notes (bc, beat 1) or two quarter notes (oboes, beat 3).

is a dynamically, rhythmically, and emotionally diverse movement. Bach pays further attention to details of the text. While the opening measure, bidding farewell to the wise men, has a descending trajectory, the following three phrases of the text are set as an ascending sequence. The tenor first climbs up to *d'* (m. 2), then to *e'* (m. 3) and finally climaxes on *a'* on the text "ich will ihn auch nicht von mir lassen." (m. 4, I will also not let him [free] from me). The agitated mood is picked up by the oboi d'amore in the first instrumental interpolation (mm. 4/5). In the next vocal section, Bach highlights the word "Zärtlichkeit" (m. 7, tenderness) with two smooth sixteenth-note appogiaturas before the voice leaps up excitedly by an octave on the final syllable of the word. Confidence and love are juxtaposed in mm. 11/12. The phrase "Ich weiß gewiss" (I know for certain) climbs up with a dotted eighth note over the very low sounding oboes, while the following "er liebet mich" (he loves me) descends again with a smooth sixteenth-note flourish on the verb "loves." The invocation of Jesus as the "Freund" (friend) inspires Bach to revise his composition. An earlier version with half notes in the oboes in m. 16 and a rhythmically and melodically different version in m. 17 is still visible in the score. The revised version now emphasizes the name of "Jesus" on the final beat of m. 16 and adds a calmer accompaniment in the following measure.[50] The calm note evoked by the long, extended note in oboe d'amore I beautifully mirrors the permanence of Jesus's friendship expressed by the text. The movement ends with a plea for Jesus's help, set expressively with sigh-like figures in both the voice and the accompanying instruments.

Like the accompagnato recit, the following aria "Nun mögt ihr stolzen Feinde" (no. 62) would probably have been sung by the alto had Bach not decided to use the music without alterations. The aria is accompanied by two obbligato oboi d'amore, maintaining the instrumentation from the previous accompagnato recit. Only one of the parts, the continuo part B 17, indicates "Vivace" as tempo for the aria. But the character of the music, as well as the text, demands a lively tempo throughout. Thus, the indication, even though not in Bach's own hand, seems appropriate. Like most of the arias in the second half of the oratorio, this one is in modified *da capo* form. We have already seen that the texts for the A and B sections are designed similarly, with a turn in the final line from the enemy toward the hope for Jesus. The three vocal sections are separated and framed by variations of the opening ritornello:

| | | |
|---|---|---|
| 1–16 | Rit. | b–> F♯ |
| 17–48 | Vocal section A | b–> f♯ |
| 49–64 | Modified rit. | f♯–> f♯ |
| 65–80 | Vocal section B₁ | b–> e |
| 80–88 | Rit. | e–> e |

[50] Cf. NBA II/6, KB, 73 and 331–32.

| 89–104 | Vocal section B$_2$ | e–> D |
| 105–20 | Modified rit. | b–> b |
| 121–60 | Vocal section A' | b–> b |
| 160–76 | Modified rit. | b–> b |

The structure of the ritornello resembles the first aria of part VI. Measures 1–4 present the main theme in *forte*, which is then repeated verbatim in *piano*. The second half introduces a new idea, a sigh-like figure, which will return throughout the aria repeatedly with the invocation of Jesus as the "treasure" and "refuge." In the vocal sections, Bach does not dwell long on individual phrases of the text; instead, he goes through each section of the text repeatedly and with only minor melismatic embellishments. In the A section, the first part of the text is treated in mm. 17–32 and then again in mm. 33–48. The two subsections are separated by an expressive fermata in m. 32 on a dissonant seventh-chord on "mir," creating a sigh-like cry for the help of Jesus. In the first subsection of section A, the tenor almost literally repeats the ritornello (with modified accompaniment by the oboes). Conversely, the second time Bach treats the material more freely. The melismatic expansions on "erwecken" (arouse) (mm. 39–40) and on the final phrase "mein Schatz, mein Hort, ist hier bei mir" (mm. 44–48) are especially significant. Only the concluding line, the plea to Jesus, is sung twice in a row in each of the subsections.

The B section exhibits an analogous structure. In two subsections, the text appears twice, with the final line again repeated. The B section ends in an *adagio* cadence (mm. 103–4.), descending low to *d*. A variant of the opening ritornello (now reduced to just one of the oboes, the second enters in mm. 108 and 109) leads to the modified *da capo*. The text is first presented in its entirety in a literal recapitulation of the opening of the A section (including the expressive fermata on "mir") in m. 136. But the fermata already indicates a change. Bach transposes the oboe parts down an octave, so that the high tenor note is exposed and stands out more clearly. The following second treatment of the text begins with a verbatim repetition of the second subsection from A, but from m. 140 on gradually departs from the model. The movement slowly reaches its climax with no less than four repetitions of the final line of the text; first with the main motif, then (mm. 148–51) accentuated with expansive octave leaps. The tenor, rather than simply singing the words, confidently proclaims them. The section reminds us of the confident proclamation of Jesus's presence by the alto in the terzet from part V (mm. 164–66), although via different melodic intervals. Even though the two movements might originate from different models, here in the *Christmas Oratorio* the similar compositional device creates an intertextual connection between the proclamation of the divine presence in the terzet and the assertion of the presence of the "treasure and refuge" in the final aria. The final statement of the text in the aria comes to a halt on a fermata. The halt, however, is premature. The final phrase of the text is still missing. Bach sets it as an expressive adagio before the closing ritornello returns to the previous tempo and closes the movement.

Like the first aria (no. 57) of part VI, this one has a very clear phrase structure. Segments of four measures are grouped into larger units of mostly eight or sixteen measures (occasionally expanded by an additional measure). The only exception is the second half of A' which is extended by eight measures to interpolate the additional repetitions of the culminating invocation of Jesus's presence. As in the first aria, the square structure and mostly syllabic presentation points toward a secular model. Still, the only model we possess are the fragmentary sources for the sacred aria from BWV 248a. Bach took the model, as far as we can tell from the surviving parts, without major changes. The only significant difference is the bc line in mm. 31/32. In the original version, m. 31 was a fourth higher than m. 30, a pattern started from m. 28 (see also in the score the bc revision at mm. 20–22). Bach changed the bass line at m. 31 into a smooth sixteenth-note motion, which sets up the fermata in m. 32 as an even greater surprise (ex. 11.5).

*Example 11.5* J. S. Bach, BWV 248/62, mm. 29–34 (revisions in mm. 31–32)

The aria is both a celebration of the victory over the enemy and an invocation of Jesus as the refuge. Walter Blankenburg has aptly described the character of the aria as "frohes Siegesbewußtsein" (joyful awareness of victory).[51] But it is that very awareness that repeatedly comes to a halt, contemplates, and then moves on. The celebration of victory has to wait until the final movement of part VI. Bach and his librettist inserted another moment of repose with the *Recitativo à 4* "Was will der Hölle schrecken nun" (no. 63). While recits like this are uncommon in Bach's sacred cantatas, they are quite common in secular cantatas, where they provide an opportunity for the protagonists to give a final statement before joining in the closing choral movement.[52] Bach had already used this type in a sacred context. In the final recit (no. 67) in the *St. Matthew Passion*, BWV 244, Bach juxtaposes recit statements by the four singers from chorus I with short choral statements by chorus II. We also find a similar closing statement of the singers toward the end of Stölzel's passion oratorio *Ein Lämmlein geht und trägt die Schuld*, which had in more than one way served as an inspiration for the *Christmas Oratorio*. It seems that this type of setting was more common in oratorios and secular contexts. It also seems to fit better here at the end of the oratorio than in BWV 248a. The older model had only featured three of the four singers as soloists, whereas in BWV 248 the four singers who had solo parts now come together for a final statement.[53]

The recit begins with an extended sequence. The four vocalists each sing a fanfare-like motif which comes to a halt in a long, extended note. The series of entrances is quite unusual, featuring triads of seventh chords in A major—F major—B minor—E major; the movement then returns more conventionally back to A major, D major, G, major, and finally reaches D major, which is also the key of the final movement of the oratorio (no. 64). This final tonic chord, however, is performed only by the bc. The voices end on the dominant A major with the rhetorical question about what the enemy could accomplish if man rests in the hands of Jesus. The question is not immediately answered, but the final D-major chord under a fermata depicts this resting and provides a moment of repose before the victorious fanfare of the trumpet in the last movement gives the answer.

The recit is full of harmonic tension. The vocal texture rests on an instrumental bass line with unstable sixth chords or dissonant seventh chords. Only the final chord provides a convincing and stable resolution. Bach's use of the four voices reflects their function within the rest of the oratorio. While the other voices participate in the questions, the alto only sings the last phrase of the text, "since we rest

[51] Blankenburg, *Weihnachts-Oratorium*, 134.

[52] I am grateful to Joshua Rifkin for pointing this out in an unpublished paper on part VI of the *Christmas Oratorio*.

[53] Rifkin has suggested that the recit, together with the other movements from BWV 248a and probably some other pieces came from an unknown secular cantata, in which the alto would have had a solo part as well. While this assumption is intriguing, we do not have any evidence to support this.

in Jesus's hands." As in earlier arias, and in particular in the terzet from part V, Bach uses the alto as the voice of the human heart that is aware of the *inhabitatio Christi*. Since only the bc part for the movement has survived, it is impossible to determine how much of the texture from BWV 248a Bach had borrowed and what he changed. He was, however, rather limited by the existing harmonic progression of the instrumental bass, and we can assume that the changes (if any) were only minor. The new text allowed Bach to use the music without significant revisions. The autograph score shows two smaller changes that the composer made during the composition of the BWV 248 version. In m. 3 the fourth beat in the soprano originally had an eighth note *d″* (on "wir") followed by two sixteenth notes. Bach changed this into a smooth falling chain of sixteenth notes, starting now on *f♯″*. He probably made the change before writing the alto voice, which now moves in parallel sixths with the soprano. A second change in the soprano voice occurred in the second half of m. 4. Bach had notated a leap of a seventh up to the high *e″*. But he then decided to lead the voice down to *e′* instead—probably the more appropriate direction for a text that talks about rest.

The fanfare-like motif that is treated sequentially by the four voices at the beginning of the recit is picked up again, now in a real fanfare, in the closing movement. The bright and stable D-major sound of the instrumental ritornello answers the question from the recit in the affirmative. The *inhabitatio Christi*, the dwelling of Jesus in the human heart and the resting of man in the hands of Jesus, leads to victory in the eschatological battle. As Johann Gerhard had explained, the Second Coming of Christ is the precondition for the salvation in his Third Coming.[54] But both are historically (and soteriologically) based on the manifestation of Jesus in a manger as a poor and helpless child. With the final chorale, the two "stories" of the *Christmas Oratorio* end. The story of the nativity of Christ from the gospels according to Luke and Matthew, and the story of the coming of Christ into the human heart are at a close. What the alto in part I had hoped for, the same singer had confirmed in part V, "he is already here;" and we hear it again in part VI: "my Savior dwells here."

[54] Gerhard, *Postille*, 11–12.

# 12

# Looking Ahead

## *An Epilogue*

Part VI of the *Christmas Oratorio* was performed on January 6, 1735 at the morning service in St. Thomas's Church and then reprised during the vespers service at St. Nicholas's Church. After the final movement had sounded, Bach and his musicians did not have much time to rest. On January 9, the first Sunday after Epiphany, another cantata had to be performed during the regular Sunday morning service. It was presumably not an entirely new composition. Bach had several pieces for this occasion already in his repertoire: *Mein liebster Jesus ist verloren*, BWV 154,[1] *Meinen Jesum laß ich nicht*, BWV 124,[2] and *Liebster Jesu, mein Verlangen*, BWV 32.[3] All three cantatas share the theme of loving desire for Jesus and thus would perpetuate one of the major themes of the *Christmas Oratorio*. The last cantata, BWV 32, would have been particularly fitting as it features a dialogue between Jesus and the Soul, represented by soprano and bass. The Soul searches for Jesus and finds him eventually, culminating in a typical love duet between the two soloists. If Bach had any interest in continuing a theme from the oratorio, this cantata would have been the best choice. It is also the cantata for that Sunday that uses the least number of soloists and thus gave Bach's singers some rest after the strenuous 1734/35 Christmas season. But, again, all of this must remain speculation.

Bach's first new composition of a cantata (as far as we know) is one for the fourth Sunday after Epiphany, *Wär Gott nicht mit uns diese Zeit*, BWV 14.[4] This particular work looks back to an earlier large-scale project, Bach's chorale cantata cycle from 1724/25. However, new cantata compositions like this one are rare in the 1730s.

---

[1] The cantata was composed in 1724, but sources suggest another performance around 1736/37. This, however, does not rule out that the cantata was performed with the original performance material in 1735; see KB NBA I/5, 67 and 78.

[2] The cantata was composed in 1725 and is part of Bach's chorale cantata cycle; cf. Rathey, "Der zweite Leipziger Jahrgang—Choralkantaten," 418f.

[3] Composed in 1726; corrections in the performance parts suggest later performances as well.

[4] As is the *Christmas Oratorio*, the score is dated by Bach himself after the last movement.

Bach mostly performed works he had composed in the first decade of his tenure in Leipzig (or even earlier), or he programmed pieces by other composers. Between the first Sunday after Trinity 1735 and Trinity Sunday 1736, Bach performed large parts of a cantata cycle by Gottfried Heinrich Stölzel, based on texts by Silesian theologian and poet Benjamin Schmolck (1672–1737).[5] Bach's choice is significant for several reasons. For one, Stölzel and his music already had had a considerable impact on the composition of the *Christmas Oratorio*. Second, Bach had performed Stölzel's Passion oratorio on Good Friday 1734 and at least one double-movement from BWV 248, the unusual chorale trope no. 38/40, was influenced by a movement from Stölzel's passion. The performance of Stölzel's cantata cycle betrays Bach's interest in the music by his contemporary that dates back at least to the Lenten season of 1734. It is also noteworthy that Bach chooses a cantata cycle based on libretti by Benjamin Schmolck. The idea of a mystical unity between Christ and the believer figures prominently in Schmolck's devotional poetry. Thus, the performance of the Stölzel cycle in 1735/36 not only musically connects to the oratorio but it is also theologically related.

Bach also continued to work on his oratorio project. His *Ascension Oratorio* BWV 11 was performed on Ascension Day 1735 (May 19). Like the *Christmas Oratorio*, this piece makes extensive use of parodies, combined with sections from the biblical narrative. It is a clear continuation of the pattern employed in the larger piece for Christmas, albeit now on a compressed scale, as the entire oratorio is not much longer than a regular church cantata and was performed in place of the cantata during the service. In the later 1730s Bach would again return to the genre of oratorio and transform an earlier Easter cantata into the *Easter Oratorio* BWV 249. We discussed this work briefly in chapter 4 as an example for Bach's oratorio concept.

Recycling earlier compositions—both from his own pen and works by Stölzel—left Bach time to work on another large-scale project, the publication of keyboard works in his *Clavierübung*. In 1725 Bach had begun to print his partitas for keyboard, with the six partitas appearing as *Clavierübung* Part I in 1731.[6] This was a significant step for Bach as it allowed the composer to raise his profile beyond the city of Leipzig and the middle German territories of Thuringia and Saxony, where he had spent most of his life. In 1735, just weeks after the completion of the *Christmas Oratorio*, Bach published the second part of the *Clavierübung*, containing the "Overtüre nach französischer Art," BWV 831, and the "Italienisches Konzert,"

---

[5] See Mark-Roderich Pfau, "Ein unbekanntes Leipziger Kantatentextheft aus dem Jahre 1735—Neues zum Thema Bach und Stölzel," *Bach-Jahrbuch* 94 (2008): 99–112; and Peter Wollny, "'Bekennen will ich seinen Namen'—Authentizität, Bestimmung und Kontext der Arie BWV 200: Anmerkungen zu Johann Sebastian Bachs Rezeption von Werken Gottfried Heinrich Stölzels," *Bach-Jahrbuch* 94 (2008): 123–58, esp. 137–47.

[6] For the complex genesis of *Clavierübung I*, see Richard D. P. Jones, "The History and Text of Bach's Clavierübung I." PhD diss., Oxford University, 1988.

BWV 971.[7] The prints appeared during the Leipzig Easter fair in 1735 and the pieces received good reviews. Johann Adolph Scheibe wrote about the "Italian Concerto": "There are some quite good concertos of this kind, particularly for clavier. But preeminent among published musical works is a clavier concerto of which the author is the famous Bach in Leipzig. . . . It would take a great master of music as Mr. Bach, who has almost alone taken possession of the clavier, and with whom we can certainly defy foreign nations, to provide us with such a piece in this form of composition—a piece that deserves emulation by all our great composers and that will be imitated all in vain by foreigners."[8]

The *Clavierübung* clearly contributed to Bach's prominence and fame. But what about the *Christmas Oratorio*? Regular performances of church music were neither advertised in newspapers nor were they reviewed. While there was a market for printed keyboard music, like the *Clavierübung*, sacred vocal music largely remained unprinted.[9] We lack any external references regarding the performances or reception of the *Christmas Oratorio*. All that exists from Bach's time are the immediate sources: the score, the parts, and the libretto print. It is not known whether Bach's listeners were aware of the special significance of the performance. In fact, it seems that the *Christmas Oratorio* only turned into a wider success story during the Bach revival in the nineteenth century.

The creation of the *Ascension* and *Easter Oratorio*s show that Bach was interested in this genre during the following years. It is likely that he also performed the *Christmas Oratorio* (or parts thereof) again. Some of the corrections in the performance parts seem to date from later years and thus correspond to later performances. Unfortunately, they cannot be dated with certainty, and we do not have a printed libretto for a subsequent performance. Even if he did not perform the complete oratorio, the first three parts could have been performed on the three days of Christmas. Similarly, part IV does not require the context of the larger piece and could have been used as an independent New Year's cantata. Complete performances of BWV 248, on the other hand, would have required a special alignment of feast days, with no Sunday after Christmas but a Sunday between New Year's and the feast of Epiphany. This was the case only three times between 1735 and 1750: 1739/40, 1744/45, and 1745/46 respectively.

---

[7] For the publication and print history of *Clavierübung II*, see Gregory Butler, "The Engravers of Bach's Clavier-Übung II," in *A Bach Tribute: Essays in Honor of William H. Scheide*, ed. Paul Brainard (Kassel: Bärenreiter, 1993), 57–69.

[8] David, Mendel, Wolff, *New Bach Reader*, 332.

[9] For the culture of music printing in the seventeenth and eighteenth centuries and especially the problems of selling vocal music, see Friedhelm Krummacher, *Die Überlieferung der Choralbearbeitungen in der frühen evangelischen Kantate. Untersuchungen zum Handschriftenrepertoire evangelischer Figuralmusik im späten 17. und beginnenden 18. Jahrhundert*, Berliner Studien zur Musikwissenschaft 10 (Berlin: Merseburger, 1965), 45–78.

The only time a single movement from the *Christmas Oratorio* was performed after Johann Sebastian Bach's death in 1750 was a performance of the opening movement. Carl Philipp Emanuel Bach had used it in his own Easter cantata, *Jauchzet, frohlocket,* H 804, from 1778.[10] Johann Sebastian Bach's second son also planned to borrow the chorale setting "Ich steh an deiner Krippen hier" (BWV 248, part VI/59) for his 1769 Passion (with the text "O Jesu hilf zur selben Zeit"). As C. P. E. Bach's compositional work progressed, he eliminated the chorale again.[11] Although C. P. E.'s main copyist, Johann Heinrich Michel, made a fair copy of the entire score of BWV 248,[12] there is no evidence that the whole oratorio was ever performed in Hamburg or anywhere else during the second half of the eighteenth century.

After the death of Carl Philipp Emanuel Bach in 1788, Georg Poelchau gained possession of the *Christmas Oratorio*'s original score and parts, and in turn gave them to Carl Friedrich Zelter and the Berlin Sing-Akademie in 1814. The sources were finally sold, together with other Bach autographs, to the Royal Prussian Library in 1854—later Deutsche Staatsbibliothek—where they are still housed.[13] At least theoretically, copies of the performance parts for the *Christmas Oratorio* had been available to the public in the early decades after Johann Sebastian Bach's death. In 1764 the music publisher Breitkopf offered copies of the performance parts of the oratorio in their catalogue for the Leipzig New Year's fair, but, yet again, it is uncertain (and rather unlikely) if the material was sold or whether it was ever used for a performance.

The performance history of the oratorio in the nineteenth century begins with the Berlin Sing-Akademie and C. F. Zelter around 1830. Zelter initiated the copying of additional vocal parts for all six parts. Some sections of the oratorio were studied during the rehearsals of the Sing-Akademie.[14] It was common for the Sing-Akademie to practice pieces that were not performed publicly, and this was also true for sections of the *B-Minor Mass* as well as for the *St. Matthew Passion* before Mendelssohn finally conducted a public performance of the Passion in 1729.[15] Some annotations

[10] See Stephen Lewis Clark, *The Occasional Choral Works of C. P. E. Bach* (PhD diss., Princeton University, 1984), 154–74; and Clemens Harasim, *Die Quartalsmusiken von Carl Philipp Emanuel Bach: Ihre Quellen, ihre Stilistik und die Bedeutung des Parodieverfahrens* (Marburg: Tectum, 2010), 177–83.

[11] Carl Philipp Emanuel Bach, *The Complete Works,* vol 4/4.1, *Passion According to St. Matthew 1769,* ed. Ulrich Leisinger (Los Altos: Packard Humanities Institute, 2008) xiv.

[12] Bibliothek Nationale in Paris, F-Pn D. 551 (1–6). A scan of this manuscript is available at: http://gallica.bnf.fr/ark:/12148/btv1b84511589.

[13] During World War II and the following decades, the score was temporarily housed in the Westdeutsche Bibliothek Marburg.

[14] See the description of the parts in NBA KB II/6, 161.

[15] For the context of Mendelssohn's performance see Martin Geck, *Die Wiederentdeckung der Matthäuspassion im 19. Jahrhundert: Die zeitgenössischen Dokumente und ihre ideengeschichtliche Deutung.* Studien zur Musikgeschichte des 19. Jahrhunderts 9 (Regensburg: Bosse, 1967); and Celia

by Zelter in the performance parts for part III of the oratorio could suggest that this part might have been performed in one of the semi-public Friday afternoon concerts; however, there is no external evidence to support this assumption.[16]

The Berlin Sing-Akademie was not the first ensemble to publicly perform parts of the oratorio. In 1844, the Breslau Sing-Akademie, under the direction of Carl Theodor Mosewius, had put on a performance of parts I and II of the *Christmas Oratorio* in the Silesian capital. Further performances in other German cities followed soon. Parts I–III were performed in Hamburg in November 1857, and parts IV–VI followed in 1859. In Dresden, parts of the oratorio were performed in 1858, interestingly enough in a concert on Palm Sunday.[17]

It would take until December 17, 1857, for the Sing-Akademie to perform the complete *Christmas Oratorio* for the public. The choir was conducted by Eduard Grell, the director of the Sing-Akademie at that time. A year earlier, in 1856, the score for the oratorio had appeared as volume 5.2 of the *Bach Gesellschaft Edition*, edited by Wilhelm Rust. That edition was based mostly on the score and performance material owned by the Sing-Akademie. The choir, in turn, used Rust's edition (as well as a piano reduction that had appeared in 1857 published by Bote und Bock, Berlin).

Grell—during his preparations for the performance by the Berlin Sing-Akademie—realistically discerned that a complete performance of the *Christmas Oratorio* was not feasible and that even a complete performance divided into two evenings would not have found an appreciative audience.[18] Thus, he decided to perform the piece with numerous cuts: nine of the twelve arias were cut, as well as several of the accompagnato recits and chorales. Cuts like this were common in early performances of Bach's large scale works; Mendelssohn had done the same when he performed the *St. Matthew Passion* in 1729. By streamlining the piece, Grell focused

Applegate, *Bach in Berlin: Nation and Culture in Mendelssohn's Revival of the St. Matthew Passion* (Ithaca, NY: Cornell University Press, 2005).

[16] Cf. Andreas Glöckner, "Bachs Weihnachts-Oratorium. Bemerkungen zur ersten Aufführung der Sing-Akademie zu Berlin (1857)," in *150 Jahre Weihnachts-Oratorium: ein musikalischer Festgottesdient [Programmheft]*, 2007, 23–29. Johann Nepomuk Schelble considered performing the piece in Frankfurt with his Caecilienverein in the 1830s but he died in 1837 before the project could be realized; cf. Schweitzer, *Bach I*, 245.

[17] Glöckner, "Bachs Weihnachts-Oratorium. Bemerkungen zur ersten Aufführung der Sing-Akademie zu Berlin (1857)," 23–29. The first performance of parts I and II of the *Christmas Oratorio* in England was mounted by the English Bach enthusiast and conductor William Sterndale Bennett in 1861. His interest in Bach had been sparked by Mendelssohn who he had visited in Leipzig in 1836/37; Sterndale Bennett was also friends with Robert Schumann, another important player in the Bach revival in the nineteenth century; see J. R. Sterndale Bennett, *The Life of William Sterndale Bennett*, (Cambridge: Cambridge University Press, 1907), 451.

[18] See Grell's remarks in Glöckner, "Bachs Weihnachts-Oratorium. Bemerkungen zur ersten Aufführung der Sing-Akademie zu Berlin (1857)," 27.

on the biblical narrative and eliminated most of the interpretative elements. The cuts, though, were neither random nor purely pragmatic. The movements Grell took out were those that represented the coming of Christ and the idea of mystic unity: the arias "Bereite dich, Zion" (no. 4) and "Schließe, mein Herze" (no. 31) as well as the terzet "Ach, wenn wird die Zeit erscheinen" (no. 51). What remained were primarily pieces that could fit an understanding of Christmas as a romantic family feast, as it was conventionally constructed by the nineteenth century. The sinfonia at the beginning of part II, the lullaby "Schlafe, mein Liebster" (no. 19), and even the chorale trope no. 38, "Immanuel, o süßes Wort," could easily be heard as praise of the sweet baby Jesus, instead of a symbolic enactment of *unio mystica*. What resulted was a piece that provided a lyrical and folk-like counterpoint to Bach's much more serious Passions and that fit squarely into the understanding of Christmas in the middle of the nineteenth century. An anonymous reviewer of the Sing-Akademie performance from 1857 articulates this perception of the oratorio in his review in the *Berliner Musik Zeitung Echo*:

> A contemporary rightly observes that this cyclus of cantatas, by its essentially cheerful and *naïve* character, forms a sharp contrast to the invariably serious and transcendental purpose of the *Passion of St. Matthew*. As in the latter, the material arrangement and treatment of the subject is partly epic and dramatic, partly lyric, only the last element greatly preponderates in the *Christmas Oratorio*. All is clear, flowing and transparent, both in form and expression. The same master to whom we are generally accustomed to look up as the most profound interpreter of God's word, and the boldest and most powerful tone-painter, here displays all the fulness [*sic!*] and poetry of a childlike pious spirit.[19]

And thus, Christmas—that feast of the family and of childlike naiveté—found its equivalent in Bach's simple and childlike Grell-edited *Christmas Oratorio*. The chorale settings in particular, according to the anonymous reviewer, were an expression of this simplicity. Regarding the final chorale of part I, "Ach mein herzliebes Jesulein," he adds, "the treatment is characterized by playful grace and smiling mildness. While, in the insipid text, we find only the cloying sentimentality of pietism, the music moves us by its childlike *naïveté*." It is of secondary relevance that the chorale text was not written by a Pietist but was in fact penned by Luther himself. Of paramount importance, however, is the way the movement is contextualized by

[19] The review originally appeared on December 27, 1857, in *Berliner Musik Zeitung Echo*, 414. An English translation, from which we are quoting here, was published just a few weeks later in the English journal *Musical World* (January 16, 1858, 38) with the title "Johann Sebastian Bach's Christmas Oratorio."

downplaying the text (which expresses the *inhabitatio Christi*) and by highlighting instead the childlike simplicity of the music. As Joe Perry has pointed out in *Christmas in Germany—A Cultural History*, in the nineteenth century, Christmas in Germany, as a "family celebration . . . became increasingly . . . sentimental as the century progressed."[20]

This sentimentality, combined with the ideal of family, is continued in the part II aria "Schlafe, mein Liebster," which, according to the reviewer, "is one of the most beautiful and feeling cradle-songs ever sung from the fulness of a mother's heart."[21] The reviewer hears what his cultural context has prompted him to hear. The lullaby, originally associated with the sphere of the shepherds, becomes a cradle-song from the mother to her child, manifesting the strongest bond within a bourgeois family. While the *Christmas Oratorio* could be heard as a sentimental piece, the cuts made by Grell for his first performance emphasized these elements by widely eliminating the "second narrative" of the text.

This, in part, is the basis of the success of the *Christmas Oratorio*, that it can be heard selectively as a simple and naïve piece. A paradigmatic reflection of this view is the assessment by the philosopher Wilhelm Dilthey in the first decade of the twentieth century:

Die Evangelienerzählung der Geburt Christi, die Hirten auf dem Felde, die Geburt selbst am armseligsten Ort auf der Reise, der Stern und die Huldigung der drei Könige—all das ist ein augenscheinlich legendarischer Stoff, konzipiert in der Phantasie, die hier volksmäßig, ohne Tendenz, ohne Verhältnis zu dogmatischen Fragen wirksam gewesen ist. Kein Teil der Evangelien steht dem nordisch-germanischen Gemüt näher als dieser, keiner ist schlichter, volksmäßiger, keiner hat denn auch die Kunst starker angeregt zu Schöpfungen von naivem, allgemeinverständlichem Charakter, in dem die heilige Schönheit des

The gospel narrative of the birth of Christ, the shepherds in the fields, the birth itself at the poorest place during the journey, the star and the adoration of the three kings—all of this obviously is legendary material, conceived by fantasy [and elaborated] here in a folk-like manner, without being tendentious and unrelated to dogmatic questions. No part of the gospels is closer to the Nordic-Germanic spirit than this one; none is simpler, more folk-like, none has more inspired art to create works of a similarly naïve character that were accessible

---

[20] Joe Perry, *Christmas in Germany. A Cultural History* (Chapel Hill: University of North Carolina Press, 2010), 39.

[21] "Johann Sebastian Bach's Christmas Oratorio," *Musical World*, 38.

Familienlebens zu bildlicher Darstellung gelangen konnte. Hierdurch ist nun zunächst der innere Zusammenhang des Weihnachtsoratoriums von Bach mit aller Weihnachtspoesie und zugleich mit allen weltlichen Glücksgefühlen gegeben. . . . Hierdurch ist nun auch der Charakter der Musik bedingt. Sie ist volkstümlicher, einfacher in der Form . . .[22]

for everybody, in which the holy beauty of family life was depicted visually. In this, Bach's oratorio is connected with all other Christmas poetry as well as with secular feelings of joy. . . . This also influences the character of the music: it is more folk-like, simpler in form . . .

The *Christmas Oratorio* has been converted into an un-theological work; an expression of joy, simplicity, and family values. By tuning out its theological profile, it was prone to become a representation of the same kind of religious and secular sentimentality that was then, and is now, associated with Christmas. Its simple and folk-like tunes made it accessible to the Volk, the people. Dilthey's nationalist Germanic views are obvious; but, more than a monument to Nordic identity, the oratorio for him is an example of emotionality and simplicity. This simplicity, combined with its esthetic blemish of being largely constructed from parodies, contributed to the lack of scholarly interest in the *Christmas Oratorio* during the twentieth century even though it became at the same time one of the most popular works by the composer.

Our study has shown that the *Christmas Oratorio* does indeed have a clear theological profile. A "second narrative" runs through the interpretative additions in the arias and accompagnato recits as well as it determines the selection of the hymn stanzas. The "threefold coming of Christ,"—as interpreted by seventeenth- and early eighteenth-century Lutheran theologians— included the historical event of Jesus's birth in Bethlehem and his return at the end of times, but its existential center was the presence of the divine Word (and the incarnation of the Word, Jesus Christ) in the believer's heart. In a teleological exegesis of the biblical narrative, the libretto transitions from expectation (aria no. 4) to fulfillment (terzet no. 51), with the "turning point" being the newly composed aria "Schließe, mein Herze" (no. 31). This temporal framework is reflected in the use of different aria forms throughout the oratorio, with a preference of circular *da capo* forms in the first half of the oratorio and a preponderance of modified and bipartite arias in the second half. Here again, the aria "Schließe, mein Herze" serves as a turning point.

The oratorio was the result of meticulous preliminary planning as well as major revisions during the composition phase. We have been able to see how musical ideas

---

[22] Wilhelm Dilthey, *Von deutscher Dichtung und Musik: Aus den Studien zur Geschichte des deutschen Geistes*, vol. 2, unveränderte Auflage (Stuttgart/Göttingen: Teubner/Vandenhoeck&Ruprecht, 1957), 232–33.

took shape and how Bach transformed parody movements to fit the context of the oratorio. Some of these revisions of older material were motivated by the text, others were triggered by Bach's aiming for continuous improvement of his compositions. Part of this integration of preexisting movements into the whole of the oratorio was the creation of motivic connections, as it is the case in the first recitative-aria pair, nos. 3 and 4, and also between movements that are farther apart, as the aria no. 31 and the terzet no. 51. It is immaterial whether Bach's listeners heard these connections. Since the composer establishes them, they must have been of importance to him. Some of these connections can be explained by exploring the theological landscape of Bach's time. Bach was not a theologian, but he lived and worked in a religious environment, and the theological and philosophical paradigms that ruled in that reality in turn provide pathways for understanding Bach.

An important musical inspiration for Bach was his contemporary, Gottfried Heinrich Stölzel. Bach was familiar with Stölzel's Passions and might even have known a Christmas oratorio by him. Bach, the Leipzig cantor, was clearly intrigued by the simpler style of the Gotha composer. Similarly, the Dresden composer Johann Adolph Hasse also influenced the composition of the oratorio, albeit indirectly. In the early 1730s, Bach's attention was captivated by the developments in the Saxon capital. The *Dresden Missa*, later expanded into the *Mass in B Minor*, is just one manifestation of this fascination. When Hasse began performing oratorios in Dresden, on Good Friday 1734, this must have sparked Bach's interest to try this genre as well. The situation in Leipzig was quite different and it would have been impossible to mount a performance of a large-scale oratorio outside of the liturgy. Still, multipart Passion performances had already been established for some time in central Germany. Accordingly, Bach and his librettist used this model to create an oratorio that could be performed on six subsequent feast days and Sundays. As a liturgical piece, BWV 248 consisted of six parts; as an oratorio, it formed a complete entity, unified both by the biblical narrative as well as by its theological concept.

The feast of Christmas has been in perpetual transition over the past three centuries. While it had retained much of its carnivalesque (and pagan) roots until after the Reformation, it was redefined during the second half of the seventeenth century, turning the external celebration into an expression of internal devotion. During Bach's early career, the sometimes riotous traditions were still very much alive, and some of the external, corporeal, and physical practices of celebrating Christmas were still in place during this transitional period. We might discover remnants of these traditions in some of the movements of the oratorio, like the "Kindelwiegen" (rocking of the cradle) in the lullaby "Schlafe, mein Liebster" or the tradition of shepherds' music in the opening sinfonia of part II. Overall, though, the corporeality of the Christmas celebrations had already been transformed into metaphors and images of speech. The metaphors of love, bride and bridegroom, and unification were very physical, and yet the celebration of the feast was not. This becomes very clear in the interpretation of those biblical texts that talk about movement: the journey of the shepherds and that of the three wise men are immediately turned inward. No external actions give access to the divine.

An image that epitomizes all these concepts is the symbol of the heart: ubiquitous in the devotional literature of Bach's time, both as a poetic metaphor and as a graphic image. When Bach drew the little hearts in several of the movements of part IV to save space, he had no intention of capturing the meaning of the entire oratorio. It was mainly a pragmatic decision. Nonetheless, this decision was motivated (regardless of consciously or subconsciously) by the devotional tradition in which Bach and his listeners lived.

Christmas underwent another shift in the early nineteenth century. The feast was now characterized by the idea of the family feast and the purity of the child in the manger. The famous Christmas carol *Silent Night*, written and composed in 1818, epitomizes this shift. At its center are the holy couple and the child, the model for the Christian (and bourgeois) family. The little boy is the epitome of a sweet little baby, complete with his curly hair:

1. Stille Nacht! Heilige Nacht! Alles schläft; einsam wacht nur das traute heilige Paar. Holder Knab im lockigten Haar, schlafe in himmlischer Ruh! Schlafe in himmlischer Ruh!

1. Silent night! Holy night! All are sleeping, alone wakes only the intimate holy couple, lovely boy with curly hair, sleep in heavenly peace! Sleep in heavenly peace!

Christmas images and texts in the nineteenth century increasingly focused on such idyllic and naïve scenes. Christmas was still a celebration of affections—but now it was the affections between members of the family. And while these feelings were to an increasing extent expressed through gift giving (leading to a growing commercialization of the feast), the children, in their naiveté and simplicity, could serve as models for the ideal of "true" Christmas. The Swiss reformer of education, Heinrich Pestalozzi (1746–1827), expressed this shift in the early nineteenth century: "And you, my beloved children, who celebrate this Christmas in the simplicity of your hearts, what shall I say to you? We wish to be partakers of your simplicity, of your childlike joy."[23] The "childlike joy" demanded by Pestalozzi as the true spirit of Christmas, is not far from the "childlike naïveté" that the reviewer of the Berlin performance of the *Christmas Oratorio* heard in Bach's music in 1857.

---

[23] Quoted after George Eduard Biber, *Henry Pestalozzi and his plan of education; being an account of his life and writings; with copious extracts from his works, and extensive details illustrative of the practical parts of his method* (London: J. Souter, 1831), 102; see also Nissenbaum, *Battle for Christmas*, 210.

It is not accidental that it is a child, Tiny Tim, who is at the center of Charles Dickens's *Christmas Carol* from 1843; and it is the affection toward his neighbors that Ebenezer Scrooge discovers when facing the spirits of Christmas past, present, and future. Christmas is still a feast of love; yet, not the vertical love relationship of the mystical love in the Song of Songs or in Bernard's sermons but rather the horizontal love toward one another in family and (in Dickens's case) society.

The adaptable interpretations of the *Christmas Oratorio*, the fact that it could play to these changing understandings of Christmas, contributed to its success.[24] Its simplicity, emotionality, and sentiments of love were easily integrated into the Christmas culture that emerged in the nineteenth century and still endures today. But this strength also produces one of the fundamental problems of the oratorio. Since it seems to "fit" in different contexts, we fail to see the circumstantial differences. It is these nuanced distinctions, woven around Bach's *Christmas Oratorio*, that this book has striven to bring into focus.

[24] For a modern perspective on the adaptability of Bach's "message" in the oratorio see Stefan Böntert, "Vom Himmel hoch, da kommt nichts her?—Erkundungen zu der Kunst, an Weihnachten Gottesdienst zu feiern," *Liturgisches Jahrbuch* 54 (2004): 223–48.

# BIBLIOGRAPHY

Alberts, Susanne. *Musik in Naumburg/Saale 1650–1720: Kirchliches und höfisches Musikleben in Naumburg an der Saale zur Zeit der Sekundogenitur.* Saarbrücken: VDM Verlag, 2008.

Altenburg, Detlef. *Untersuchungen zur Geschichte der Trompete im Zeitalter der Clarinblaskunst.* Kölner Beiträge zur Musikforschung 75. Regensburg: Bosse, 1973.

Applegate, Celia. *Bach in Berlin: Nation and Culture in Mendelssohn's Revival of the St. Matthew Passion.* Ithaca, NY: Cornell University Press, 2005.

Arndt, Johann. *Sechs Bücher vom Wahren Christenthum . . . Nebst dessen [Arndt's] Paradieß-Gärtlein.* Altdorff: Zobel, 1735.

Arnold, Jochen. *Von Gott poetisch-musikalisch reden: Gottes verborgenes und offenbares Handeln in Bachs Kantaten.* Göttingen: Vandenhoeck & Ruprecht, 2009.

Asendorf, Ulrich. *Heiliger Geist und Rechtfertigung.* Göttingen: Vandenhoeck & Ruprecht, 2004.

Axmacher, Elke. "Aus Liebe will mein Heiland leben: Zum Text des Weihnachts-Oratoriums BWV 248 von Johann Sebastian Bach." In *Im Klang der Wirklichkeit: Musik und Theologie,* edited by Norbert Bolin and Markus Franz, 108–21. Martin Petzoldt zum 65. Geburtstag. Leipzig: Evangelische Verlagsanstalt, 2011.

Axmacher, Elke. *"Aus Liebe will mein Heyland sterben": Untersuchungen zum Wandel des Passionsverständnisses im frühen 18. Jahrhundert.* Beiträge zur theologischen Bachforschung 2. Neuhausen-Stuttgart: Hänssler, 1984. Rev. ed. Stuttgart: Carus, 2005.

Axmacher, Elke. "Ein Quellenfund zum Text der Matthäus-Passion." *Bach-Jahrbuch* 64 (1978): 181–91.

*Bach-Dokumente (BachDok).* Leipzig and Kassel, 1963–72. Complete critical edition of the source material on Bach, with extensive commentaries. Edited under the auspices of the Bach-archiv Leipzig as a supplement to the *Neue Bach-Ausgabe.*

*Badersche Chronik. Die Mühlhäusischen Alterthümer in einer Chronica vorgestellet zum Nützlichen Gebrauch vor die Nachkommen aus vielen Alten Chronicken und einiger Erfahrung zusammen getragen, auch mit vielen Gemählden gezieret von George Andreas Sellmann.* Mühlhausen 1791 (manuscript), Stadtarchiv Mühlhausen 61/24.

Bach, Carl Philipp Emanuel. *The Complete Works, Vol. IV/4.1: Passion According to St. Matthew 1769.* Edited by Ulrich Leisinger. Los Altos, CA: Packard Humanities Institute, 2008.

Bach, Johann Christoph Friedrich. *Die Kindheit Jesu.* Edited by Hermann J. Dahmen. Heidelberg: Willy Müller, 1976.

Bach, Johann Sebastian. *Weihnachts-Oratorium* BWV 248, facsimile. Edited by Alfred Dürr. Leipzig: Deutscher Verlag für Musik, 1984.

Bach, Johann Sebastian. *Weihnachts-Oratorium BWV 248. Faksimile des originalen Textdruckes von 1734.* Faksimile-Reihe Bachscher Werke und Schriftstücke, Neue Folge 6. With an introduction by Christoph Wolff. Leipzig: Bach-Archiv, 2012.

Bakhtin, Mikhail. *Rabelais and his World.* Translated by Hélène Iswolsky. Bloomington: Indiana University Press, 1984.

Baselt, Bernd. "Actus Musicus und Historie um 1700 in Mitteldeutschland." *Hallesche Beiträge zur Musikwissenschaft,* Ser. G 1 (1978/69): 77–103.

Baselt, Bernd. "Der 'Actus Musicus auf Weyh-Nachten' des Leiziger Thomaskantors Johann Schelle." In *Wissenschaftliche Zeitschrift der Martin-Luther-Universität Halle-Wittenberg. Gesellschafts- und Sprachwissenschaftliche Reihe* XIV (1965): 331–44.

Bayreuther, Rainer. "Bachs Weimarer Wortgeber: Salomo Franck." In *Johann Sebastian Bach in Weimar (1708–1717),* edited by Helen Geyer, 41–61. Göttingen: Hainholz, 2008.

Becker, Hansjacob. "Es ist ein Ros' entsprungen." In *Geistliches Wunderhorn: Große deutsche Kirchenlieder,* edited by H. Becker et al. with cooperation from M. Rathey, 135–45. Munich: Beck, 2001.

Begbie, Jeremy. *Music, Modernity, and God: Essays in Listening.* Oxford: Oxford University Press, 2013, 41–72.

Bekuhrs, Gottlob Friedrich Wilhelm. *Ueber die Kirchen Melodien.* Halle: Johann Christian Hendel, 1796.

Bennett, J. R. Sterndale. *The Life of William Sterndale Bennett.* Cambridge: Cambridge University Press, 1907.

Berger, Karol. *Bach's Cycle, Mozart's Arrow: An Essay on the Origins of Musical Modernity.* Berkeley: University of California Press, 2007.

Bernard of Clairvaux. *Sermones super Cantica canticorum* sermon 19.7. In *S. Bernardi opera* 1, edited by J. Leclercq, C. H. Talbot, and H. M. Rochais. Rome: Editiones Cistercienses, 1957.

Biber, George Eduard. *Henry Pestalozzi and his plan of education; being an account of his life and writings; with copious extracts from his works, and extensive details illustrative of the practical parts of his method.* London: J. Souter, 1831.

Bitter, Karl Hermann. *Johann Sebastian Bach.* 4th ed. Berlin, 1881.

Blanken, Christine. "A Cantata-Text Cycle of 1728 from Nuremberg: A Preliminary Report on a Discovery Relating to J. S. Bach's so-called 'Third Annual Cantata Cycle.'" *Understanding Bach* 10 (2015): 9–30.

Blanken, Christine. Kritischer Bericht (Critical commentary). *Weihnachtsoratorium: Dialogus von der Geburt Christi.* By Reinhard Kaiser. Stuttgart: Carus, 2007.

Blankenburg, Walter. *Das Weihnachts-Oratorium von Johann Sebastian Bach.* Munich: Deutscher Taschenbuch-Verlag/Bärenreiter, 1982.

Böhme, Erdmann Werner. "Die frühdeutsche Oper in Thüringen." PhD diss., Greifswald, 1931.

Böntert, Stefan. "Vom Himmel hoch, da kommt nichts her?—Erkundungen zu der Kunst, an Weihnachten Gottesdienst zu feiern." *Liturgisches Jahrbuch* 54 (2004): 223–48.

Bossuyt, Ignace. *Johann Sebastian Bach: Christmas Oratorio (BWV 248).* Translated by Stratton Bull. Leuven: Leuven University Press, 2004.

Bovon, François. *Luke 1: A Commentary on the Gospel of Luke 1:1–9:50.* Edited by Helmut Koester. Translated by Christine M. Thomas. Minneapolis: Fortress Press, 2002.

Boyd, Malcolm. "Bach, Telemann und das Fanfarenthema." *Bach-Jahrbuch* 82 (1996): 147–50.

Braun, Werner. "Aspekte des Klingenden in lutherischen Universitätsschriften zwischen 1600 und 1750." In *Universität und Musik im Ostseeraum,* edited by Ekkehard Ochs et al., 11–22. Greifswalder Beiträge zur Musikwissenschaft 17. Berlin: Frank & Timme, 2009.

Braun, Werner. "Bachs Echoarie." In *Die Quellen Johann Sebastian Bachs: Bachs Musik im Gottesdienst,* edited by Renate Steiger, 119–31. Heidelberg: Manutius Verlag, 1998.

Braun, Werner. "Beiträge zu G. F. Händels Jugendzeit in Halle (1685–1703)." *Wissenschaftliche Zeitschrift der Universität Halle* VIII/4–5 (1959): 851–62.

Brecht, Martin. "Das Aufkommen der neuen Frömmigkeitsbewegung in Deutschland" In *Geschichte des Pietismus I: Der Pietismus vom siebzehnten bis zum frühen achtzehnten Jahrhundert,* edited by M. Brecht, 130–51. Göttingen: Vandenhoeck & Ruprecht, 1993.

Brockpähler, Renate. *Handbuch zur Geschichte der Barockoper in Deutschland.* Emsdetten: Lechte, 1964.

Burke, Peter. *Popular Culture in Early Modern Europe*. Revised reprint. Aldershot: Scholar Press 1994.

Butler, Gregory. "The Engravers of Bach's Clavier-Übung II." In *A Bach Tribute: Essays in Honor of William H. Scheide*, edited by Paul Brainard, 57–69. Kassel: Bärenreiter, 1993.

Butt, John. *Bach's Dialogue with Modernity: Perspectives on the Passions*. Cambridge: Cambridge University Press, 2012.

Butt, John. Review of *Johann Sebastian Bach: Christmas Oratorio (BWV 248)*, by Ignace Bossuyt. *Music and Letters* 87 (2006): 654–56.

Büttner, David Siegmund. *Christ-Larven oder Böß-benahmter Heiliger Christ / nach dem Ursprung und Häßlichkeit meist Historisch beschrieben*. Halle: Waisenhaus, 1702.

*BWV Kleine Ausgabe nach der von Wolfgang Schmieder vorgelegten 2. Ausgabe*, edited by Alfred Dürr and Yoshitake Kobayashi. Wiesbaden: Breitkopf & Härtel, 1998.

Calov, Abraham. *Das Neue Testament / verdeutschet durch D. Martin Luthern / Nach der eigentlichen Intention und Meinung des Heil. Geistes . . . fürgestellet*. Wittenberg: Schröder, 1682.

Carbach, Johann Jacob. *Nürnbergisches Zion: worinne. . . . Kirchen-Pflegere, Prediger, Capläne, Rectores und Collegae, sowohl vor als nach der Reformation . . . zu finden sind*. Nürnberg: [s.n.], 1733.

Carrier-McClimon, Carolyn. "Hearing the 'Töne eines Passionsliedes' in J. S. Bach's Christmas Oratorio: The Nineteenth-century Critical Reception of BWV 248." *Bach* 45 (2014): 34–67.

Chafe, Eric Thomas. *Analyzing Bach Cantatas*. Oxford: Oxford University Press, 2000.

Chafe, Eric Thomas. "*Anfang und Ende*: Cyclic Recurrence in Bach's Cantata *Jesu, nun sei gepreiset*, BWV 41." *Bach Perspectives* 1 (1995): 103–34.

Chafe, Eric Thomas. *Tears into Wine: J. S. Bach's Cantata 21 in its Musical and Theological Contexts*. New York: Oxford University Press, 2015.

Chafe, Eric Thomas. *Tonal Allegory in the Vocal Music of J. S. Bach*. Los Angeles: University of California Press, 1991.

Clark, Stephen Lewis. "The Occasional Choral Works of C. P. E. Bach." PhD diss., Princeton University, 1984.

Cook, Larry D. "The German Troped Polyphonic Magnificat." Vol. 1. PhD diss., University of Iowa, 1976.

Crist, Stephen A. "The Question of Parody in Bach's Cantata 'Preise dein Glücke, gesegnetes Sachsen,' BWV 215." In *Bach Perspectives* 1 (1995): 135–61.

Cuno, Johann. *Ein schön Christlich Action von der Geburt und Offenbarung unders Herrn und Heylandts Jhesu Christi, wie er zu Bethlehem im Stall geboren, den Hirten und Weysen offenbaret*. Magdeburgk: Duncker, 1595.

*Curieuses Natur-Kunst-Gewerk und Handlungs-Lexicon*. Leipzig, 1722.

Dammann, Rolf. *Der Musikbegriff im deutschen Barock*. Cologne, 1967. Reprint, Laaber: Laaber-Verlag, 1995.

Danckert, Werner. *Unehrliche Leute: Die verfemten Berufe*. Bern/Munich: Francke, 1963.

Dannhauer, Johann Conrad. *Hodomoria Spiritus Calviniani*. Straßburg: von der Heyden, 1654.

*Das versperrte und wieder eröffnete Paradeiß in einem Weinacht-Singe Spiel vorgestellet*. Goslar, 1695.

David, Hans T., Arthur Mendel, and Christoph Wolff, eds. *The New Bach Reader: A Life of Johann Sebastian Bach in Letters and Documents*. New York: Norton, 1998.

Deyling, Salomon. *Herrliche Dinge wurden in der Stadt Gottes geprediget, und in einem Jahrgange 1734 der Gemeine zu St. Nicholai in Leipzig auf jeden Sonn- und Festtag . . . vorgetragen*. Leipzig, 1734.

*Die heilige Christfart: das ist: ein holdseliges und gantz liebliches Gespräch wie sich der frommeheilige Christ mit seinen lieben Ertz-Engeln und andern Heiligen gegen itzt künfftigen heiligen Christ-Abend auf seinem himmlischen Kammer-Wagen und güldenen Schlitten herümmer zu fahren aufgemacht . . .—Der lieben Jugend zu Nutz u. Dienst aufs neue zum Druck befördert*. Leipzig, 1720.

Dillherr, Johann Michael. *Heilsame Beschneidung / und Tröstliche Benahmsung unsers liebsten Christkindleins. In der ordentlichen Neu-Jahrs-Predigt / Aus dem Evangelisten Luca 2. Cap. v. 21. Gezeiget*. Nürnberg: Endter, 1662.

Dilthey, Wilhelm. *Von deutscher Dichtung und Musik: Aus den Studien zur Geschichte des deutschen Geistes*, 2., unveränderte Auflage. Stuttgart/Göttingen: Teubner/Vandenhoeck & Ruprecht, 1957.

Drechssler, Johann Gabriel. *Christianorum Larvas Natalitias Sancti Christi nomine commendatas, post evolutam originem, confodit Stylo Theologico conscientiosus Christi cultor Chressulder*. Leipzig: Coler, 1674.

Drechssler, Johann Gabriel. *Christianorum larvas natalitias Sancti Christi nomine commendatas, post evolutam originem, confodit Stylo Theologico conscientiosus Christi cultor: auctius jam prodit, cum Apologia, quam Autor opposuit festinatio quorundam judiciis*. Leipzig: Coler, 1677.

Drechssler, Johann Gabriel. "Curiöser Bericht wegen der schändlichen Weyhnacht-Larven so man insgemein Heiligen Christ nennet herausgegeben," *Deliciarum Manipulus, das ist: Annehmliche und rare Discurse von mancherley nützlichen und curiosen Dingen*. Leipzig and Dresden: Mieth, 1703, no. 18.

Drechssler, Johann Gabriel. *De cithara musica*. Leipzig, 1670 (with subsequent editions in 1671 and 1712).

Drechssler, Johann Gabriel. *De Larvis Natalitiis, Earumque Usu & Fine, Tempore, ut vocant, Sancti Christi solitis Cum Apologia*. Leipzig: Weidmann, 1683.

Dremel, Erik. "Matthesons 'Behauptung der himmlischen Musik.'" In *Johann Mattheson als Vermittler und Initiator: Wissenstransfer und die Etablierung neuer Diskurse in der ersten Hälfte des 18. Jahrhunderts*, edited by Wolfgang Hirschmann and Bernhard Jahn, 443–61. Hildesheim: Olms, 2010.

Dreyfus, Laurence. *Bach and the Patterns of Invention*. Cambridge, MA: Harvard University Press, 1996.

Dürr, Alfred. *The Cantatas of J. S. Bach with Their Librettos in German-English Parallel Text*. Revised and translated by Richard D. P. Jones. Oxford: Oxford University Press, 2005.

Dürr, Alfred. *Johann Sebastian Bach: Weihnachts-Oratorium, BWV 248*. Meisterwerke der Musik 8. Munich: Fink, 1967.

Dürr, Alfred. "Zur Parodiefrage in Bachs h-Moll-Messe: Eine Bestandsaufnahme." *Musikforschung* 45 (1992): 117–38.

Eisenbart, Lieselotte Constanze. *Kleiderordnungen der deutschen Städte zwischen 1350 und 1700: Ein Beitrag zur Kulturgeschichte des deutschen Bürgertums*. Göttingen: Musterschmidt, 1962.

Eisler, Tobias. *Christlicher Unterricht von der dreifachen Zukunft Jesu Christi, insonderheit von der innern geistlichen Zukunft oder Geburt Christi in uns . . .* (n.p.), 1733.

Emans, Reinmar. "Zu den Arien mit einem obligaten Flöteninstrument." In *Vom Klang der Zeit: Besetzung, Bearbeitung und Aufführungspraxis bei Johann Sebastian Bach*, edited by Ulrich Bartels and Uwe Wolf, 73–85. Klaus Hofmann zum 65. Geburtstag. Wiesbaden: Breitkopf & Härtel, 2004.

Engel, Hans. "Echo." In *Die Musik in Geschichte und Gegenwart*. Vol. 3. Kassel: Bärenreiter, 1954, 1076–83.

Etzdorff, Lorenz. *Des Evangelisch-Lutherischen Zions erfreuliche Vorbereitung zum Andern Jubel-Fest der Augspurgischen Confession*. Jena: Bielcke, 1730.

Falck, Robert. "Parody and Contrafactum: A Terminological Clarification." *Musical Quarterly* 65 (1979): 1–21.

Finke-Hecklinger, Doris. *Tanzcharaktere in Johann Sebastian Bachs Vokalmusik*" Tübinger Bach-Studien 6. Trossingen: Hohner, 1970.

Finscher, Ludwig. "Zum Parodieproblem bei Bach." In *Bach-Interpretationen*, edited by Martin Geck, 94–105. FS Walter Blankenburg zum 65. Geburtstag. Göttingen: Vandenhoeck & Ruprecht, 1969.

Fischer, Albert, and Wilhelm Tümpel. *Das deutsche evangelische Kirchenlied des 17. Jahrhunderts*. Vol. 1. Gütersloh: Brockhaus, 1904. Reprint, Hildesheim: Olms, 1964.

Fitzmyer, Joseph A. *The Gospel According to Luke (I–IX)*. Anchor Bible Series. New York: Doubleday, 1981.

Fitzpatrick, Horace. *The Horn and Horn-Playing in the Austro-Bohemian Tradition from 1680 to 1830*. London: Oxford University Press, 1970.

Flügel, Axel. "'Gott mit uns'—Zur Festkultur im 17. Jahrhundert am Beispiel der Lob- und Dankfeste und Fastnachtsbräuche in Leipzig." In *Feste und Feiern: Zum Wandel städtischer Festkultur in Leipzig*, edited by Karin Keller, 49–68. Leipzig: Edition Leipzig, 1994.

Forchert, Arno. *Johann Sebastian Bach und seine Zeit*. Laaber: Laaber Verlag, 2000.

Franck, Salomo. *Evangelische Sonn- und Fest-Tages-Andachten . . . . in Geistlichen Arien erwecket*. Weimar/Jena: Bielcke, 1717.

Frandsen, Mary. *Crossing Confessional Boundaries: The Patronage of Italian Sacred Music in Seventeenth-Century Dresden*. Oxford: Oxford University Press, 2006.

Franke, August Hermann. *Erfreuung des Menschlichen Hertzens durch die Geburt Christi am 1. Christ-Tage A. 1717 in einer über den ordentlichen Evangelischen Text Luc. II, 1–14. in der Stadt-Kirchen zu Blaubeuren im Hertzogthum Würtemberg . . .* Halle: Waisenhaus, 1740.

Freiesleben, Gerhard. "Ein neuer Beitrag zur Entstehungsgeschichte von J. S. Bachs Weihnachtsoratorium." *Neue Zeitschrift für Musik* 83, nos. 29/30 (1916): 237–38, and Beilage (Supplement) 1–2.

Frick, Christoph. *Music-Büchlein oder Nützlicher Bericht von dem Uhrsprunge, Gebrauche und Erhaltung christlicher Music*. Lüneburg: Sternen 1631. Reprint, Leipzig: Zentralantiquariat d. DDR, 1976.

Friese, Friedrich. *Das Danckbarliche Andencken Der heiligen Christ-Nacht / Wolte auff Hohe Vergünstigung Und nach längst eingeführter Gewohnheit ohne Heydnische und Abgöttische Ceremonien Der zarten und in der Gottseeligkeit anzuführenden Jugend In schuldiger Auffwartung und hier entworffenen Action Zu Gemüthe führen die zu Altenburg Anno 1695. Studirende Jugend*. Altenburg: Richter, 1695.

Frohne, Johann Adolph. *Der Erleuchtete und in seiner Amts-Last Erleichterte Regent bey Auffuehrung Eines . . . Neuen Rahts der . . . Stadt Mühlhausen im Jahr Christi 1697 . . .* Mühlhausen: Pauli, 1697.

Gardner, Matthew. "Öffentlichkeit als Veranstaltungsform: Werkgestalt, Primärrezeption und Umstände der Aufführungen von Händels englischen Oratorien." In *Händels Oratorien, Oden und Serenaten*, edited by Michael Zywietz, 59–74. Das Händel-Handbuch 3. Laaber: Laaber Verlag 2010.

Geck, Martin. *"Denn alles findet bei Bach statt": Erforschtes und Erfahrenes*. Stuttgart: Metzler, 2000.

Geck, Martin. "Die *vox-Christi*-Sätze in Bachs Kantaten." In *Bach und die Stile*, edited by Martin Geck, 79–101. Bericht über das 2. Dortmunder Bach-Symposion 1998. Dortmund: Klangfarben Musikverlag, 1999.

Geck, Martin. *Die Wiederentdeckung der Matthäuspassion im 19. Jahrhundert: Die zeitgenössischen Dokumente und ihre ideengeschichtliche Deutung*. Studien zur Musikgeschichte des 19. Jahrhunderts 9. Regensburg: Bosse, 1967.

Geier, Martin. *Zeit und Ewigkeit nach Gelegenheit der ordentlichen Sonntags-Evangelien in des HErrn Furcht heibevor der Christlichen Gemeine in Leipzig Anno 1664 fürgestellet*. Leipzig: Friedrich Lanckischens Erben, 1715.

Gerhard, Johann. *Schola pietatis, das ist: Christliche und Heilsame Unterrichtung, was für Ursachen einen jeden wahren Christen zur Gottseligkeit bewegen sollen, auch welcher Gestalt er sich an derselben üben soll*: Nunmehr zum siebendemal aufgelegt. Nürnberg: Endter, 1691.

Gerhard, Johann. *Postille das ist die Auslegung und Erklärung der sonntäglichen und vornehmsten Fest-Evangelien über das ganze Jahr . . . Nach den Original-Ausgaben von 1613 und 1616. Vermehrt durch die Zusätze der Ausgabe von 1663*. 1st ed. Berlin: Schlawitz, 1870.

*Gesetze der Schule zu S. Thomae*. Leipzig: Breitkopf, 1733, 5–6.

Gill, Meredith J. *Angels and the Order of Heaven in Medieval and Renaissance Italy*. Cambridge: Cambridge University Press, 2014.

Glöckner, Andreas. "Alumnen und Externe in den Kantoreien der Thomasschule zur Zeit Bachs." *Bach-Jahrbuch* 92 (2006): 9–36.

Glöckner, Andreas. "Bachs Es-Dur-Magnificat BWV 243a—eine genuine Weihnachtsmusik?" *Bach Jahrbuch* 89 (2003): 37–45.

Glöckner, Andreas. "Bachs Weihnachts-Oratorium: Bemerkungen zur ersten Aufführung der Sing-Akademie zu Berlin (1857)." In *150 Jahre Weihnachts-Oratorium: ein musikalischer Festgottesdient [Programmheft]*, 2007, 23–29.

Glöckner, Andreas. "Bemerkungen zur vokalen und instrumentalen Besetzung von Bachs Leipziger Ensemblewerken." In *Vom Klang der Zeit: Besetzung, Bearbeitung und Aufführungspraxis bei Johann Sebastian Bach*, edited by Ulrich Bartel and Uwe Wolf, 86–96. Klaus Hofmann zum 65. Geburtstag, Wiesbaden: Breitkopf & Härtel, 2004.

Glöckner, Andreas. *Die Musikpflege an der Leipziger Neukirche zur Zeit Johann Sebastian Bachs.* Leipzig: Nationale Forschungs und Gedenkstätten J. S. Bach, 1990.

Glöckner, Andreas. "Eine Michaeliskantate als Parodievorlage für den sechsten Teil des Bachschen Weihnachts-Oratoriums?" *Bach-Jahrbuch* 86 (2000): 317–26.

Goetze, Gottfried Christian. *Kirchen-Buch Gläubiger Beter oder Zufällige Gedancken über einige Lieder-Seuffzer, welche in Denen Evangelisch-Lutherischen Kirchen öffentlich gebraucht werden.* Lübeck: Willers, 1728.

Gottsched, Johann Christoph. *Versuch einer Critischen Dichtkunst.* Leipzig 1751.

Grabow, Georg. *Danck-Opffer in welchem zugleich erwiesen / daß das so genante heilge Christ-Spiel / kein gut Werck / oder Mittelding; sondern ein sündliche Wesen / und schädlicher Greuel vor Gott sey.* Leipzig: Krüger, 1683.

Graun, Carl Heinrich. *Oratorium in festum nativitatis Christi für Soli (SATB), Chor (SATB), zwei Querflöten, zwei Oboen, zwei Fagotte (ad lib.), zwei Hörner, drei Trompeten, Pauken, zwei Violinen, Viola, Viola pomposa und Basso continuo.* Edited by Ekkehard Krüger and Tobias Schwinger. Beeskow: Ortus, 1998.

Greer, Mary Jewett. "The Sacred Duets and Terzets of Johann Sebastian Bach: A Study of Genre and Musical Text Interpretation." PhD diss., Harvard University, 1996.

Grosse, Bernhard. "Zwei Arnstädter 'Heilige Christ-Komödien.'" In *Programm des Fürstl. Gymnasiums zu Arnstadt*, 3–19. Arnstadt: Frotscher, 1899.

Haacke, Walter. "Die Organisten an St. Wenceslai zu Naumburg a.d. Saale im 17. und 18. Jahrhundert." In *Kerygma und Melos: Christhard Mahrenholz 70 Jahre*, edited by Walter Blankenburg, 291–93. Kassel: Bärenreiter, 1970.

Häfner, Klaus. *Aspekte des Parodieverfahrens bei Johann Sebastian Bach: Beträge zur Wiederentdeckung verschollener Vokalwerke.* Neue Heidelberger Studien zur Musikwissenschaft 12. Laaber: Laaber Verlag, 1987.

Häfner, Klaus. "Zum Problem der Entstehungsgeschichte von BWV 248a." *Musikforschung* 30 (1977): 304–8.

Hahn, Gerhard. *Evangelium als literarische Anweisung: Zu Luthers Stellung in der Geschichte des deutschen kirchlichen Liedes.* Münchener Texte und Untersuchungen zur deutschen Literatur des Mittelalters 73. Munich: Artemis, 1981.

Harasim, Clemens. *Die Quartalsmusiken von Carl Philipp Emanuel Bach: ihre Quellen, ihre Stilistik und die Bedeutung des Parodieverfahrens.* Marburg: Tectum, 2010.

Harrington, Joel F. *Reordering Marriage and Society in Reformation Germany.* Cambridge: Cambridge University Press, 1995.

Hase, Karl. *Das geistliche Schauspiel: Geschichtliche Übersicht.* Leipzig: Breitkopf & Härtel, 1858.

Haselböck, Lucia. *Bach-Textlexikon: Ein Wörterbuch der religiösen Sprachbilder im Vokalwerk von Johann Sebastian Bach.* Kassel: Bärenreiter, 2004.

Hauschildt, Karl. *Die Christusverkündigung im Weihnachtslied unserer Kirche: Eine theologische Studie zur Liedverkündigung.* Veröffentlichungen der Evangelischen Gesellschaft für Liturgieforschung 8. Göttingen: Vandenhoeck & Ruprecht, 1952.

Havsteen, Sven Rune. "Aspects of Musical Thought in the Seventeenth-Century Lutheran Tradition." In *The Arts and the Cultural Heritage of Martin Luther*, edited by Eyolf Østrem et al., 151–70. Copenhagen: Museum Tusculum Press, 2003.

Heidrich, Rudolf. *Christnachtsfeier und Christnachtsgesänge in der evangelischen Kirche.* Göttingen: Vandenhoeck & Ruprecht, 1907.

Hencke, Georg Johann. *Die Dreyfache Zukunft Unsers Herrn und Heylands Jesu Christi: Aus einigen auserlesenen Oertern Alten und Neuen Testaments Jn der Heil. Advents-Zeit betrachtet . . .* Halle: Hendel, 1720.

Hennenberg, Fritz. *Das Kantatenschaffen von Gottfried Heinrich Stölzel.* Leipzig: VEB Deutscher Verlag 1976.

Henrici, Christian Friedrich (Picander). *Ernst-Schertzhaffte und Satyrische Gedichte,* 5 parts. Leipzig: Friesen, 1727, 1729, 1732, 1737, and 1751.

Henrici, Christian Friedrich (Picander). *Sammlung Erbaulicher Gedancken über und auf die gewöhnlichen Sonn- und Fest-Tage in gebundner Schreib-Art entworffen.* Leipzig: Boetius, [1725].

Herbst, Wolfgang. "Johann Sebastian Bach und die Lutherische Mystik." PhD diss., Friedrich-Alexander-Universität Erlangen, 1958.

Herdt, Jennifer A. *Putting on Virtue: The Legacy of the Splendid Vices.* Chicago: University of Chicago Press, 2008.

Herz, Gerhard. "Lombard Rhythm in Bach's Vocal Music." In Herz, *Essays on J. S. Bach,* Studies in Musicology 71, 233–68. Ann Arbor, MI: UMI Press, 1985.

Hofmann, Klaus. "'Großer Herr, o starker König': Ein Fanfarenthema bei Johann Sebastian Bach." *Bach-Jahrbuch* 81 (1995): 31–46.

Hofmann, Klaus. *Johann Sebastian Bach: Die Motetten.* Kassel: Bärenreiter, 2003.

Hofmann, Klaus. "Nochmals: Bachs Fanfarenthema." *Bach-Jahrbuch* 83 (1997): 177–79.

Hunold, Friedrich Christian (Menantes). *Die Allerneueste Art, zur reinen und galanten Poesie zu gelangen.* Hamburg: Liebernickel, 1707.

Hurley, David R. *Handel's Muse: Patterns of Creation in his Oratorios and Musical Dramas, 1743–1751.* Oxford: Oxford University Press, 2001.

Irvin, Joyce L. *Foretastes of Heaven in Lutheran Church Music Tradition: Johann Mattheson and Christoph Raupach on Music in Time and Eternity.* Edited and translated by Joyce L. Irvin. Lanham: Rowman & Littlefield, 2015.

Irwin, Joyce L. "German Pietists and Church Music in the Baroque Age." *Church History* 54 (1985): 29–40.

Ittig, Thomas. "Dissertatio III. De Ritu festum nativitatis Christi d. 25. Decembr. celebrandi ejusque antiquitate." In Ittig, *Appendix dissertationis de Haeresiarchis . . .* Leipzig: Sumptibus haeredum Lanckisianorum, 1696.

Janz, Tobias. "Oratorien: Entstehungsgeschichtlicher Kontext." In *Das Bach-Handbuch 3: Bachs Passionen, Oratorien und Motetten,* edited by Reinmar Emans and Sven Hiemke, 313–24. Laaber: Laaber Verlag 2009.

Jena, Günter. *Brich an, o schönes Morgenlicht: Das Weihnachtsoratorium von Johann Sebastian Bach.* Freiburg, Herder, 1999.

Jerger, Wilhelm. "Ein unbekannter Brief Johann Gottfried Walthers an Heinrich Bokemeyer." *Musikforschung* 7 (1954): 205–7.

Jones, Richard D. P. *The Creative Development of Johann Sebastian Bach.* Vol. 2, *Music to Delight the Spirit.* Oxford: Oxford University Press, 2013.

Jones, Richard D. P. "The History and Text of Bach's Clavierübung I." PhD diss., Oxford University, 1988.

Jung, Hermann. *Die Pastorale: Studien zur Geschichte eines musikalischen Topos.* Neue Heidelberger Studien zur Musikwissenschaft 9, Bern: Francke, 1980.

*Kern geistlicher lieblicher Lieder.* Nuremberg, 1733.

Kevorkian, Tanya. *Baroque Piety: Religion, Society, and Music in Leipzig, 1650–1750.* Aldershot: Ashgate, 2007.

Kim, Jin-Ah. "Händel und Bach als Akteure ihrer musikalischen Produktion." *Archiv für Musikwissenschaft* 65 (2008): 289–308.

Kirkendale, Ursula. *Antonio Caldara: Life and Venetian-Roman Oratorios.* Revised and translated by Warren Kirkendale. Firenze: Olschki, 2007.

Kirsch, Adam Friedrich. *Neu-verfertigtes und in zwey Theil eingerichtetes Kunst-, Hauß-, Arzney- und Wunder-Buch.* Nuremberg: Buggel, 1720.

Klek, Konrad. "Die Mär mit der Maria: Zur Symbolik der Altstimme im Weihnachtsoratorium Johann Sebastian Bachs." *Concerto* 29 (2012): 14–15.

Knapp, J. Merrill. "The Luke 2 Portions of Bach's Christmas Oratorio and Handel's Messiah." In *A Bach Tribute: Essays in Honor of William H. Scheide*, edited by Paul Brainard and Ray Robinson, 155–61. Kassel: Bärenreiter, 1993.

Knöpf, Ulrich. *Religiöse Erfahrung in der Theologie Bernhards von Clairvaux*. Beiträge zur Historischen Theologie 61. Tübingen: J. C. B. Mohr (Paul Siebeck), 1980.

Knüpfer, Sebastian. *Vom Himmel hoch, da komm ich her: Ein Weihnachtskonzert*. Edited by Claudia Theis. Kassel: Bärenreiter, 1992.

Koch, Ernst. "Die Stimme des Heiligen Geistes: Theologische Hintergründe der solistischen Altpartien in der Kirchenmusik Johann Sebastian Bachs." *Bach-Jahrbuch* 81 (1995): 61–81.

Koch, Ernst. "Tröstendes Echo: Zur theologischen Deutung der Echo-Aria im IV. Teil des Weihnachts-Oratoriums von Johann Sebastian Bach." *Bach-Jahrbuch* 75 (1989): 203–11.

Koch, Michael. *Die Oratorien Johann Adolf Hasses: Überlieferung und Struktur. Erster Teilband: Wirkungsgeschichte, Überlieferung und Gestalt der Oratorien*. Pfaffenweiler: Centaurus, 1989.

Koczirz, Adolf. "Das Kollegium der sächsischen Stadt- und Kirchenmusikanten von 1653." *Archiv für Musikwissenschaft* 1 (1920/21): 280–88.

Kreitzer, Beth. *Reforming Mary: Changing Images of the Virgin Mary in Lutheran Sermons of the Sixteenth Century*. Oxford: Oxford University Press, 2004.

Kroker, Ernst. "Hans Pfriem im Märchen und im Weihnachtsspiel." In *Schriften des Vereins für die Geschichte Leipzigs* 7 (1904), 177–240.

Krummacher, Friedhelm. *Die Überlieferung der Choralbearbeitungen in der frühen evangelischen Kantate: Untersuchungen zum Handschriftenrepertoire evangelischer Figuralmusik im späten 17. und beginnenden 18. Jahrhundert*. Berliner Studien zur Musikwissenschaft 10. Berlin: Merseburger, 1965.

Küster, Konrad. "Die Vokalmusik." In Küster, *Bach Handbuch*. Kassel/Stuttgart: Bärenreiter/Metzler, 1999, 59–534.

Leahy, Anne. *J. S. Bach's "Leipzig" Chorale Preludes: Music, Text, Theology*. Lanham, MD: Scarecrow Press, 2011.

Leaver, Robin A. *Bach's Theological Library: A Critical Bibliography*. Beiträge zur theologischen Bachforschung 1. Neuhausen-Stuttgart: Hänssler, 1983.

Leaver, Robin A. "The Mature Vocal Works and Their Theological and Liturgical Context." In *Cambridge Compendium Bach*, 86–122. Cambridge: Cambridge University Press, 1997.

Leclercq, Jean. *St. Bernard et l'esprit cistercien*. Maîtres spirituels 36. Paris: Éditions du Seuil, 1975.

Lehmkühler, Karsten. *Inhabitatio: Die Einwohnung Gottes im Menschen*. Forschungen zur systematischen und ökumenischen Theologie 104. Göttingen: Vandenhoeck & Ruprecht, 2004.

Leipzig, Rat (Leipzig, City council). *E. E. Hochweisen Raths der Stadt Leipzig verbesserte Ordnung Wie ein jeder Stand bey Verlöbnissen / Hochzeiten / Gastereyen / Kindtäuffen und Leich-Begängnissen Ingleichen Kleidungen sich zuverhalten*. Leipzig, 1680.

*Leipziger Kirchen-Staat: das ist deutlicher Unterricht vom Gottes-Dienst in Leipzig . . . ; nebst darauff eingerichteten Andächtigen Gebeten und denen dazu verordneten Teutsch- und Lateinischen Gesängen; welchem zuletzt noch mit beygefüget Geistreiche Morgen- und Abend-Segen auf jeden Tag in der Woche*. Leipzig: Groschuff, 1710.

Lewalski, Barbara Kiefer. *Protestant Poetics and the Seventeenth-Century Religious Lyric*. Princeton: Princeton University Press, 1979.

Lindner, Andreas. *Leben im Spannungsfeld von Orthodoxie, Pietismus und Frühaufklärung: Johann Martin Schamelius, Oberpfarrer in Naumburg*. Kirchengeschichtliche Monographien 3. Giessen/Basel: Brunnen, 1998.

Little, Meredith, and Natalie Jenne. *Dance and the Music of J. S. Bach*. Exp. ed. Bloomington: Indiana University Press, 2009.

Lloyd, Rebecca Joanne. "Bach Among the Conservatives: The Quest for Theological Truth." PhD diss., King's College London, 2006.

Lloyd, Rebecca Joanne. "Luther's Musical Prophet?" *Current Musicology* 83 (2007): 5–32.

Loos, Helmut. *Weihnachten in der Musik. Grundzüge der Geschichte weihnachtlicher Musik.* Bonn: Gudrun Schöder, 1992.

Loos, Helmut. "Weihnachtsmusiken Leipziger Thomaskantoren des 17. Jahrhunderts." *Jahrbuch Ständige Konferenz Mitteldeutsche Barockmusik 2002,* 264–71. Hamburg: Wagner, 2004.

Lowack, Alfred. *Die Mundarten im hochdeutschen Drama bis gegen das Ende des Achtzehnten Jahrhunderts: Ein Beitrag zur Geschichte des deutschen Dramas und der deutschen Dialektdichtung.* Breslauer Beiträge zur Literaturgeschichte 7. Leipzig: Hesse und Becker, 1905

Lütgens, Franz Julius. *Geistreiche und erbauliche Evangelium-Predigten.* Leipzig: Campen, 1727.

Luther, Martin. *Basic Theological Writings.* Edited by Timothy F. Lull. Minneapolis: Fortress Press, 1989.

Luther, Martin. *Sämmtliche Schriften 13: Die Hauspostille nach Veit Dietrich.* Edited by Johann Georg Walch. St. Louis: Concordia, 1904.

Luther, Martin. *Works 53: Liturgy and Hymns.* Edited by Ulrich S. Leupold. Philadelphia: Fortress Press, 1965.

Mahlmann, Theodor. "Die Stellung der unio cum Christo in der lutherischen Theologie des 17. Jahrhunderts." In *Unio: Gott und Mensch in der nachreformatorischen Theologie,* edited by Matti Repo and Rainer Vinke, 72–199. Schriften der Luther-Agrikola-Gesellschaft 35. Helsinki: Luther-Agrikola-Gesellschaft, 1996.

Marissen, Michael. *Bach's Oratorios: The Parallel German-English Texts with Annotations.* Oxford: Oxford University Press, 2008.

Marissen, Michael. "Historically Informed Rendering of the Librettos from Bach's Church Cantatas." In *Music and Theology: Essays in Honor of Robin Leaver,* edited by Daniel Zager, 103–20. Lanham: MD: Scarecrow Press, 2007.

Marshall, Robert L. *The Compositional Process of J. S. Bach. A Study of the Autograph Scores of the Vocal Works.* 2 vols. Princeton: Princeton University Press, 1972.

Marshall, Robert L. "Bach at Mid-Life: The Christmas Oratorio and the Search for New Paths." *Bach* 43 (2012): 1–28.

Massenkeil, Günther. *Oratorium und Passion* I. Handbuch der musikalischen Gattungen 10/1. Laaber: Laaber Verlag, 1998.

Matter, E. Ann. *The Voice of my Beloved: The Song of Songs in Western Medieval Christianity.* Philadelphia: University of Pennsylvania Press, 1990.

Mattheson, Johann. *Der musicalische Patriot.* Hamburg: [s.n.] 1728.

Mattheson, Johann. *Behauptung der himmlischen Musik aus den Gründen der Vernunft, KirchenLehre und heiligen Schrift.* Hamburg: Herold, 1747.

Maul, Michael. "Neues zu Georg Balthasar Schott, seinem Collegium musicum und Bachs Zerbster Geburtstagskantate." *Bach-Jahrbuch* 93 (2007): 61–103.

Maul, Michael. *Barockoper in Leipzig (1693–1720).* Textband, Freiburger Beiträge zur Musikgeschichte 12/1. Freiburg: Rombach, 2009.

Maul, Michael. *"Dero berühmter Chor": Die Leipziger Thomasschule und ihre Kantoren (1212–1804).* Leipzig: Lehmstedt, 2012.

McClary, Susan. "The Blasphemy of Talking Politics During Bach Year." In *Music and Society: The Politics of Composition, Performance and Reception,* edited by Richard Leppert and Susan McClary, 13–62. Cambridge: Cambridge University Press, 1987.

McClary, Susan. *Desire and Pleasure in Seventeenth-Century Music.* Berkeley: University of California Press, 2012.

Melamed, Daniel R. "Bach's *Christmas Oratorio,* BWV 248, and the Jews." *Yale Journal of Music and Religion* 1/1 (2015): 81–102.

Melamed, Daniel R. *Hearing Bach's Passions.* Oxford: Oxford University Press 2005.

Melamed, Daniel R. "Multi-Day Passions and J. S. Bach's *Christmas Oratorio.*" *Eighteenth Century Music* 11 (2014): 215–34.

Mersmann. Hans. "Ein Weihnachtsspiel des Görlitzer Gymnasiums von 1668." *Archiv für Musikwissenschaft* 1 (1918/19): 244–66.

Meyer, Ulrich. "Liturgie und Kirchenjahr." In *Bachs Kantaten: Das Handbuch,* edited by Reinmar Emans and Sven Hiemke, 181–228. Das Bach-Handbuch 1/1. Laaber: Laaber-Verlag, 2012.

Miller, Daniel. "A Theory of Christmas." In *Unwrapping Christmas,* edited by Daniel Miller, 3–37. Oxford: Clarendon Press, 2001.

Millner, Frederick L. *The Operas of Johann Adolf Hasse.* Ann Arbor, MI: UMI Research Press, 1979.

Mizler von Koloff, Johann Lorenz. *Neu eröffnete Musicalische Bibliothek.* Vol 4. Leipzig, 1754.

Möller, Hans-Jürgen. "Das Wort-Ton-Verhältnis im Weihnachtsoratorium Johann Sebastian Bachs." *Neue Zeitschrift für Musik* 113/12 (1972): 686–91.

Moller, Martin. *Praxis Evangeliorum, Das ist: Einfältige Erklärung und nützliche Betrachtung der Evangelien . . . Erster Theil. Vom Advent biß auff Laetare.* Lüneburg: Johann Stern, 1651.

Müller, Heinrich. *Evangelische Schluß-Kette / und Krafft-Kern / oder Gründliche Außlegung der Sonn- und Fest-Tags-Evangelien . . . Festteil.* Frankfurt a.M.: Balthasar Christoph Wust, 1698.

Müller, Heinrich. *Göttliche Liebes-Flamme Oder Auffmunterung zur Liebe Gottes: Durch Vorstellung dessen undendlichen Liebe gegen uns. Mit vielen schönen Sinnebildern gezieret.* Frankfurt a.M.: Wust, 1676.

Münden, Christian. *Bey der Geburt Christi Gott lobende Stimme Der Himmlischen Heerschaaren.* Helmstädt: Schnorr, 1729.

Münnich, Richard. "Kuhnaus Leben." *Sammelbände der Internationalen Musikgesellschaft* 3 (1902): 524–25.

Neudorf, Johann Joachim. *Christlicher Unterricht, für die Jugend, wie die H. Advents-Zeit, das H. Christ-Fest und das Neue Jahr GOttgefällig zu feyren sey.* Nebst einer Vorrede von Erdmann Neumeistern. Hamburg: Kißner, [1727].

*Neue Bach-Ausgabe (NBA): Johann Sebastian Bach Complete Works.* Edited under the auspices of the Johann-Sebastian-Bach-Institute Göttingen and the Bach-Archiv Leipzig. Kassel and Leipzig, 1954–

Neumann, Werner. "Über Ausmaß und Wesen des Bachschen Parodieverfahrens." *Bach-Jahrbuch* 51 (1965): 63–85.

Neumeister, Erdmann. *Priesterliche Lippen in Bewahrung der Lehre; Das Ist: Sonn- und Festtags-Predigten durchs gantze Jahr.* Leipzig/Görlitz: Laurentius, 1714.

Nissenbaum, Stephen. *The Battle for Christmas.* New York: Vintage, 1996.

Olearius, Johann Gottfried. *Geistliches Seelen-Paradies und Lust-Garten, des allerheiligsten Lebens Jesu Christi unseres hochgelobten Herrn und Heylandes: Darinnen Die Geheimnüsse solches Lebens, in 24. Capiteln kürtzlich und erbaulich betrachtet, Wie auch vermittelst so viel schöner meistentheils Biblischer Gewächse und Blumen anmuthig fürgestellet und in schöne Kupfer abgebildet, Und zu Erweckung schuldiger Dancksagung mit Gebeten und Gesängen andächtig angewendet werden.* Nürnberg: Hoffmann, 1669.

Pelikan, Jaroslav. *Bach Among the Theologians.* Philadelphia: Fortress Press, 1986.

Perry, Joe. *Christmas in Germany: A Cultural History.* Chapel Hill: University of North Carolina Press, 2010.

Peters, Mark. "J. S. Bach's *Meine Seel' erhebt den Herren* (BWV 10) as Chorale Cantata and Magnificat Paraphrase." *Bach* 43 (2012): 29–64.

Petzoldt, Martin. "Auswahl und Gebrauch geistlicher Texte durch Bach, dargestellt am Himmelfahrtsoratorium (BWV 11)." In *Kirche als Kulturfaktor,* edited by Ulrich Kühn, 88–115. Festschrift Johannes Haupt. Hannover: Lutherisches Verlagshaus 1994.

Petzoldt, Martin. *Bach-Kommentar II: Die geistlichen Kantaten vom 1: Advent bis zum Trinitatisfest.* Schriftenreihe Internationale Bachakademie 14.2. Stuttgart/Kassel: Internationale Bachakademie/Bärenreiter, 2007.

Petzoldt, Martin. "Johann Sebastian Bach in theologischer Interaktion: Persönlichkeiten in seinem beruflichen Umfeld." In *Über Leben, Kunst, und Kunstwerke: Aspekte musikalischer Biographie. Johann Sebastian Bach im Zentrum*, edited by Christoph Wolff, 133–59. Leipzig: Evangelische Verlagsanstalt, 1999.

Petzoldt, Martin. *Texthefte zur Kirchenmusik aus Bachs Leipziger Zeit: Die 7 erhaltenen Drucke der Jahre 1724–1749 in faksimilierter Wiedergabe.* Stuttgart: Carus, 2000.

Pezold, Carl Friedrich. *Dissertatio Philosophica: De Sancti ut vocant Christi Larvis Et Munusculis . . .* Leipzig: Brandenburger, 1699.

Pfau, Mark-Roderich. "Ein unbekanntes Leipziger Kantatentextheft aus dem Jahre 1735—Neues zum Thema Bach und Stölzel." *Bach-Jahrbuch* 94 (2008): 99–112.

Pfeiffer, August. *Antimelanchcholicus oder Melancholey-Vertreiber.* Leipzig: Gleditsch, 1684.

Pirro, André. *J. S. Bach.* Paris: Librairie Félix Alcan, 1906 (German ed.: *Bach sein Leben und seine Werke*, autorisierte deutsche Ausgabe von Bernhard Engelke). Vols. 3–6. Berlin/Leipzig: Schuster & Loeffler, 1910. Reprint, 1920.

Poetzsch, Ute. "Ordentliche Kirchenmusiken, genannt Oratorium—Telemanns 'oratorische' Jahrgänge." In *Musikkonzepte—Konzepte der Musikwissenschaft*. Bericht über den Internationalen Kongreß der Gesellschaft für Musikforschung Halle (Saale) 1998, Bd. 2: Freie Referate, edited by by Kathrin Eberl and Wolfgang Ruf, 317–24. Kassel: Bärenreiter, 2001.

Poppe, Gerhard. "Ein Sohn des Thomaskantors in der kursächsischen Residenzstadt—Annotationen zum Thema 'Dresden und Wilhelm Friedemann Bach.'" In *Wilhelm Friedemann Bach und die protestantische Kirchenkantate nach 1750*, edited by Peter Wollny and Wolfgang Hirschmann, 69–78. Beeskow: Ortus, 2012.

Praetorius, Johannes. *Saturnalia, das ist, Eine Compagnie Weihnachts-Fratzen, oder Centner-Lügen und possierliche Positiones . . . Im Jahr: LIeber! antVVorte deM Narren naCh seIner Narrheit.* Leipzig: Joh. Wittigau, [1663].

Prinz, Ulrich. *Johann Sebastian Bachs Instrumentarium: Originalquellen, Besetzung, Verwendung.* Schriftenreihe der Internationalen Bachakademie Stuttgart 10. Stuttgart/Kassel: Bachakademie/Bärenreiter, 2005.

Quenstedt, Johannes Andreas. *Theologia didactico-polemica, sive systema theologicum, in duas seciones, didacticam et polemicam, divisum.* Wittenberg: Quenstedt, 1685.

Rambach, Johann Jacob. *Betrachtungen über das Evangelium Esaiä: von der Geburt Jesu Christi, Cap. IX, 6 wie auch über dessen trost-vollen Namen Immanuel.* Halle: Waisenhaus, 1729.

Rathey, Markus. *Bach's Major Vocal Works. Music, Drama, Liturgy.* New Haven: Yale University Press, 2016.

Rathey, Markus. "The Chorale Cantata in Leipzig: The Collaboration between Schelle and Carpzov in 1689–1690 and Bach's Chorale Cantata Cycle." *Bach* 43 (2012): 46–92.

Rathey, Markus. "Der zweite Leipziger Jahrgang—Choralkantaten." In *Bachs Kantaten: Das Handbuch* (Das Bach-Handbuch 1/1), edited by Reinmar Emans and Sven Hiemke, 331–450. Laaber: Laaber-Verlag, 2012.

Rathey, Markus. "Die Geistliche Hirten-Freude: Eine Leipziger Weihnachtsmusik im Jahre 1685 und die Transformation weihnachtlicher Bukolik im späten 17. Jahrhundert." *Daphnis: Zeitschrift für Mittlere Deutsche Literatur und Kultur der Frühen Neuzeit (1400–1750)* 40 (2011): 567–606.

Rathey, Markus. "Drama and Discourse: The Form and Function of Chorale Tropes and Bach's Oratorios." In *Bach Perspectives* 8 (2010): 59–62.

Rathey, Markus. "Instrumentaler Satz und Orchesterbehandlung in den Köthener Glückwunschkantaten." *Cöthener Bach Hefte* 11 (2003): 116–35.

Rathey, Markus. *Johann Rudolph Ahle, 1625–1673: Lebensweg und Schaffen.* Eisenach: Wagner, 1999.

Rathey, Markus. "Johann Sebastian Bach's *St. John Passion* from 1725: A Liturgical Interpretation." *Colloquium: Music, Worship, Arts* 4 (2007): 123–39.

Rathey, Markus. "Rehearsal for the Opera—Remarks on a Lost Composition by Johann Kuhnau from 1683." *Early Music* 42 (2014): 409–20.

Rathey, Markus. "Rezeption als Innovation: Zur Aktualisierung traditioneller geistlicher Texte durch die Musik im 17. und frühen 18. Jahrhundert." In *Aedificatio: Erbauung im interkulturellen Kontext der Frühen Neuzeit*, edited by Andreas Solbach, 42–52. Tübingen: Niemeyer, 2005.

Rathey, Markus. "'Singet dem Herrn ein neues Lied' (BWV 190): Johann Sebastian Bachs Auseinandersetzung mit dem Te Deum laudamus." In *Bachs 1. Leipziger Kantatenjahrgang*, edited by Martin Geck, 287–301. Dortmunder Bach Forschungen 3. Dortmund: Klangfarben Musikverlag, 2002.

Rathey, Markus. "Zur Entstehungsgeschichte und Datierung von Bachs Universitätsmusik *Gloria in Excelsis Deo* BWV 191." *Bach-Jahrbuch* 99 (2013): 319–28.

Raupach, Christoph. *Veritophili: Deutliche Beweis-Gründe / worauf der rechte Gebrauch der MUSIC, beydes in den Kirchen/als ausser denselben / beruhet*. Hamburg: Benjamin Schillers Erben, 1717.

Reipsch, Ralph-Jürgen. "Der Telemann Bestand des Notenarchivs der Sing-Akademie zu Berlin— ein Überblick." In *Telemann, der musikalische Maler / Telemann Kompositionen im Notenarchiv der Sing-Akademie zu Berlin*, edited by Carsten Lange and Brit Reipsch, 275–363. Telemann-Konferenzberichte 15. Hildesheim: Olms, 2010.

Rémi, Cornelia. *Philomela mediatrix: Friedrich Spees Trutznachtigal zwischen poetischer Theologie und geistlicher Poetik*. Mikrokosmos. Beiträge zur Literaturwissenschaft und Bedeutungsforschung 73. Frankfurt a.M.: Peter Lang, 2006.

Roll, Susan K. *Toward the Origins of Christmas*. Kampen: Kok Pharos, 1995.

Roper, Lyndal. *The Holy Household: Women and Morals in Reformation Augsburg*. Oxford: Oxford University Press, 1989.

Rose, Stephen. *The Musician in Literature in the Age of Bach*. Cambridge: Cambridge University Press, 2011.

Rosenwein, Barbara. *Emotional Communities in the Early Middle Ages*. Ithaca, NY: Cornell University Press, 2006.

Rössler, Martin. *Bibliographie der deutschen Liedpredigt*. Bibliotheca Humanistica & Reformatorica 19. Niewkoop: de Graaf, 1976.

Rössler, Martin. *Da Christus geboren ward: Texte, Typen und Themen des deutschen Weihnachtsliedes*, Stuttgart: Calwer, 1981.

Rust, Wilhelm. Preface to *Johann Sebastian Bachs Werke* V.2. Leipzig: Breitkopf & Härtel, 1856.

Sandberger, Wolfgang. *Das Bachbild Philipp Spittas: Ein Beitrag zur Geschichte der Bachrezeption im 19. Jahrhundert*. Beihefte zum Archiv für Musikwissenschaft 39. Stuttgart: Steiner, 1996.

Schabalina, Tatjana. "'Texte zur Music' in Sankt Petersburg: Neue Quellen zur Leipziger Musikgeschichte sowie zur Kompositions- und Aufführungstätigkeit Johann Sebastian Bachs." *Bach-Jahrbuch* 94 (2008): 33–98.

Schade, Johann Caspar. *Ein Herrliches Geschenck, oder schöne Christ-Bescherung in einem Einfältigen Gespräch Zwischen Lehrer und Kinder Von der Geburth des lieben Jesus-Kindleins . . . von Einem Kinder Freunde*. Leipzig: Heinichen/Richter, 1693.

Schamelius, Johann Martin. *Evangelischer Lieder-Comentarius, worinnen das glossirete Naumburgiche Gesang-Buch weiter ausgeführet und verbessert wird*. Vol. 1. Leipzig: Friedrich Lankischens Erben, 1724.

Scheibe, Johann Adolph. *Critischer Musicus*. Leipzig, 1745. Reprint, Hildesheim: Olms, 1970.

Scheibel, Gottfried Ephraim. *Poetische Andachten Uber alle gewöhnliche Sonn- und Fest-Tage, durch das ganze Jahr: Allen Herren Componisten und Liebhabern der Kirchen-Music zum Ergötzen*. Leipzig/Breßlau: Rohrlach, 1725.

Scheibel, Gottfried Ephraim. *Zufällige Gedanken von der Kirchenmusik*. Frankfurt and Leipzig, 1722.

Scheitler, Irmgard. *Deutschsprachige Oratorienlibretti: Von den Anfängen bis 1730*. Beiträge zur Kirchenmusik 12, Paderborn: Schönigh, 2005.

Scheitler, Irmgard. "Ein Oratorium in der Nürnberger Frauenkirche 1699 und seine Nachfolger." *Morgen-Glantz* 14 (2004): 179–211.

Schemelli, Georg Christian. *Musicalisches Gesang-Buch herausgegeben von George Christian Schemelli . . .* Leipzig: Breitkopf, 1736. Reprint, Hildesheim/New York 1975.

Schering, Arnold. *Musikgeschichte Leipzigs II*. Leipzig: Kistner, 1926.

Scherzer, Gottfried Heinrich. *Texte zur Kirchen-Music, So Mit Gott Aufs 1722. Jahr in Gera soll aufgeführet werden*. Leipzig: Tietze, [1721].

Schmidgen, Wolfram. *Exquisite Mixture: The Virtues of Impurity in Early Modern England*. Philadelphia: University of Pennsylvania Press, 2013.

Schmidt-Hensel, Roland Dieter. *La musica è del Signor Hasse detto il Sassone . . . Johann Adolf Hasses "Opere serie" der Jahre 1730 bis 1745: Quellen, Fassungen, Aufführungen*. Teil I: Darstellung. Abhandlungen zur Musikgeschichte 19.1. Göttingen: Vandenhoeck & Ruprecht, 2009.

Schneider, Matthias. "Bachs 'Arnstädter Choräle'—komponiert in Weimar?" In *Bachs Musik für Tasteninstrumente*, edited by Martin Geck, 287–308. Berich über das 4. Dortmunder Bach-Symposium 2002. Dortmund: Klangfarben Musikverlag, 2003.

Schubart, Tobias Heinrich. *Ruhe nach geschehener Arbeit: in unterschiedlichen Gedichten und Uebersetzungen, der Ehre Gottes und dem Dienste des Nächsten gewidmet*. Hamburg: Kißner, 1733.

Schulenberg, David. *The Music of Wilhelm Friedemann Bach*. Rochester, NY: University of Rochester Press, 2010.

Schulze, Hans-Joachim. "Bachs Parodieverfahren." In *Die Welt der Bach Kantaten II: Johann Sebastian Bachs weltliche Kantaten*, edited by Christoph Wolff, 167–87. Stuttgart/Kassel: Metzler/Bärenreiter, 1997.

Schulze, Hans-Joachim. *Die Bach-Kantaten. Einführungen zu sämtlichen Kantaten Johann Sebastian Bachs*. Leipzig: Evangelische Verlagsanstalt, 2007.

Schulze, Hans-Joachim. "Zum Themenbereich der neueren Bach-Forschung." In *Johann Sebastian Bach und Johann Joseph Fux*, edited by Johann Trummer and Rudolf Flotzinger, 25–37. Bericht über das Symposium anläßlich des 58. Bachfestes der Neuen Bachgesellschaft 24–29 Mai 1983 in Graz. Kassel: Bärenreiter, 1985.

Schütz, Heinrich. *Historia der Freuden- und Gnadenreichen Geburth Gottes und Marien Sohnes, Jesu Christi (Weihnachtshistorie)*, SWV 435/435a. Edited by Friedrich Schöneich. Kassel: Bärenreiter, 1976.

Schweitzer, Albert. *J. S. Bach*. Translated by Ernest Newman. New York: Dover, 1966.

Schwindt-Gross, Nicole. "Parodie um 1800: Zu den Quellen im deutschsprachigen Raum und ihrer Problematik im Zeitalter des künstlerischen Autonomie-Gedankens." *Die Musikforschung* 41 (1988): 16–45.

Scribner, Robert W. *Popular Culture and Popular Movements in Reformation Germany*. London: Hambledon Press, 1987.

Sent, Eleonore, ed. *Die Oper am Weißenfelser Hof*. Weißenfelser Kulturtraditionen 1. Rudolstadt: Hain Verlag, 1996.

Serpilius, Georg. *Gloria, Pax Et Alleluja. Das ist: Gott geheiligte Sing- Und Früh-Stunden: Welche auß dem Geistreichen Psalm / Lob-Gesang und Lieblichen Advents-Liede: Gott sey danck durch alle Welt . . . Nach der Dreyfachen Zukunfft Christi angestellet*. Regensburg: Seidel/Hanckwitz, 1697.

Siegele, Ulrich. "Das Parodieverfahren des Weihnachtsoratoriums von J. S. Bach als dispositionelles Problem." In *Studien zur Musikgeschichte: Eine Festschrift für Ludwig Finscher*, edited by Annegrit Laubenthal, 257–66. Kassel: Bärenreiter, 1995.

Siegert, Christine. "Genderaspekte in und um Johann Sebastian Bachs 'Weihnachtsoratorium.'" In *Frauen hör- und sichtbar machen. 20 Jahre "Frau und Musik" an der Universität für Musik und darstellende Kunst Wien*, edited by Sarah Chaker and Ann-Kathrin Erdélyi, 47–69. Vienna: Institut für Musiksoziologie, 2010.

Smend, Friedrich. *Joh. Seb. Bach: Kirchen Kantaten, Heft 5 (vom 1. Sonntag im Advent bis zum Epiphanias-Fest)*. 3rd ed. Berlin: Christlicher Zeitschriftenverlag, 1966.

Smend, Friedrich. "Neue Bach-Funde." *Archiv für Musikwissenschaft* 7 (1942): 1–16.

Smither, Howard E. *A History of the Oratorio 1: The Oratorio in the Baroque Era: Italy, Vienna, Paris*. Chapel Hill: University of North Carolina Press, 1977.

Smither, Howard E. *A History of the Oratorio 2: The Oratorio in the Baroque Era: Protestant Germany and England*. Chapel Hill: University of North Carolina Press, 1977.

Snyder, Kerala J. *Dieterich Buxtehude. Organist in Lübeck.* Rev. ed., Rochester, NY: University of Rochester Press, 2007.

Snyder, Kerala J. "Oratorio on Five Afternoons: From the Lübeck Abendmusiken to Bach's *Christmas Oratorio.*" In *Bach Perspectives 8* (2011): 69–95.

Speck, Christian. *Das Italienische Oratorium 1625–1665.* Musik und Dichtung. Turnhout: Brepols, 2003.

Spitta, Friedrich. "Die Melodie 'Herzlich tut mich verlangen' in J. S. Bachs Weihnachtsoratorium." *Monatsschrift für Gottesdienst und kirchliche Kunst* 13/1 (Jan. 1908): 25–27.

Spitta, Philipp. *Johann Sebastian Bach: His Work and Influence on the Music of Germany, 1685–1750.* 2 vols. Translated by Clara Bell and J. A. Fuller-Maitland. London: Novello, 1889. Reprint, New York: Dover, 1979.

Starke, Christoph. *Synopsis Bibliothecae Exegeticae in Novum Testamentum: Kurzgefaster Auszug Der gründlichsten und nutzbarsten Auslegungen über alle Bücher Neues Testaments, In Tabellen, Erklärungen, Anmerkungen und Nutzanwendungen* . . . Vol. 1. Biel: Heilmann, 1746.

Stauffer, George B. *The Mass in B Minor: The Great Catholic Mass.* New Haven: Yale University Press, 2003.

Stauffer, George B. "Music for 'Cavaliers et Dames': Bach and the Repertoire of His Collegium Musicum." In *About Bach*, edited by Gregory G. Butler et al., 135–56. Urbana-Champaign: University of Illinois Press, 2008.

Steiger, Renate. *Gnadengegenwart: Johann Sebastian Bach im Kontext lutherischer Orthodoxie und Frömmigkeit.* Doctrina et Pietas II/2. Stuttgart-Bad Canstatt: Frommann-Holzboog, 2002.

Stenger, Nicolaus. *Der Hochtröstliche Artickel Von der Einwohnung Gottes in den Gläubigen oder: Von der Gäubigen Vereinigung mit GOTT* . . . Erfurt: Birckner, [1642].

Stevens, Scott Manning. "Sacred Heart and Secular Brain." In *The Body in Parts. Fantasies of Corporeality in Early Modern Europe*, edited by David Hillmann and Carla Mazzio, 263–82. New York: Routledge, 1997.

Stickelbrock, Michael. *Mysterium Venerandum: Der trinitarische Gedanke im Werk des Bernhard von Claixvaux.* Münster: Aschendorf, 1994.

Stiller, Günther. *Johann Sebastian Bach and Liturgical Life in Leipzig.* Edited by Robin A. Leaver. Translated by H. J. A. Bouman et al., St. Louis, MO: Concordia, 1984.

Stinson, Russell. *The Orgelbüchlein*, Oxford: Oxford University Press, 1999.

Stock, Christian. *Homiletisches Real-Lexicon oder Reicher Vorrath zur geist- und weltlichen Beredtsamkeit: in sich haltend Der Sachen kurtzen Entwurff, die nöthigen Beweißthümer und Bewegungs-Gründe, die auserlesensten Gleichnüsse, schöne Historien, geschickte Exempel, vortreffliche Sinn-Bilder und nachdenckliche Zeugnisse So wohl Lehrer der Kirchen älterer, neuerer und neuesten Zeiten; als auch Heydnischer und anderer Profan-Skribenten, Deren sich ein Prediger und Redner bey Ausarbeitung einer erbaulichen Predigt; oder sonst geschickten Rede bedienen kan;* nebst einer Vorrede Johann Georg Walchs. 4th ed. Jena: Hartung, 1749.

Stockigt, Janice B. "Consideration of Bach's *Kyrie e Gloria* BWV 232I within the Context of Dresden Catholic Mass Settings, 1729–1733." *International Symposium: Understanding Bach's B-minor Mass. Discussion Book.* Vol. I, edited by Yo Tomita et al., 84–90. Belfast: School of Music & Sonic Arts, 2007.

Stölzel, Gottfried Heinrich. *Die höchst-tröstliche Fasten-Zeit Wurde nebst andern gottseligen Betrachtungen über das bittere Leiden und Sterben unsers HErrn und Heylandes JEsu Christi / auch mit Harmonischer Devotion, nach Anleitung der Vier Evangelisten zugebracht / Also / daß wöchentlich zweymal / nemlich Sonntags und Donnerstangs / von Invocavit an bis auf Palmarum des 1711ten Jahres / bey öffentlichem Gottesdienste / einen Theil davon musicalisch aufführete Ihr. Hochfl. Durchl / zu Sachsen-Eisenach Capelle.* Gotha: Reyher [1711].

Strauch, Aegidius. *Starcke und Milch-Speise, Hiebevor der Christlichen Gemeine daselbst in hundert sechs und siebentzig Sonn- und Fest-Tags-Predigten vorgetragen.* 1st ed. Danzig 1683; 2nd ed. Leipzig: Gleditsch, 1702.

Strohm, Reinhard. "Johann Adolph Hasse's Opera 'Cleofide' und ihre Vorgeschichte." In *Johann Sebastian Bachs Spätwerk und dessen Umfeld: Bericht über das wissenschaftliche Symposium anläßlich des 61. Bachfestes der Neuen Bachgesellschaft, Duisburg 1986*, edited by Christoph Wolff, 170–76. Kassel: Bärenreiter, 1988.

Stuart, Kathy. *Defiled Trades and Social Outcasts: Honor and Ritual Pollution in Early Modern Germany.* Cambridge: Cambridge University Press, 1999.

Tarr, Edward H. "Monteverdi, Bach und die Trompetenmusik ihrer Zeit." In *Bericht über den musikwissenschaftlichen Kongreß Bonn 1970*, 592–96. Kassel: Bärenreiter, 1971.

Telemann, Georg Philipp. *Harmonischer Gottesdienst* (1725/26), "Jauchzet, frohlocket, der Himmel ist offen" (TVWV 1:953). In *Telemann: Musikalische Werke V.* Kassel and Basel: Bärenreiter, 1967.

Telemann, Georg Philipp. *Hirten bei der Krippe* (1759). In *Telemann: Musikalische Werke XXX.* Edited by Wolf Hobohm. Kassel: Bärenreiter, 1997.

Teller, Romanus. *Der grosse Unterscheid zwischen den Gerechten und Gottlosen, zum theil aus denen ordentlichen Sonn- und Fest-Tags-Evangeliis, grösten theils aber aus hierzu auserlesenen . . . Sprüchen/Vorgetragen.* Leipzig: Braun, 1720.

Theis, Claudia. "'Vom Himmel hoch, da komm ich her'—Ein Weihnachtskonzert von Sebastian Knüpfer." *Musik und Kirche* 62 (1992): 264–69.

Thomasius, Jakob. *Acta Nicolaitana et Thomana: Aufzeichungen von Jakob Thomasius während seines Rektorates an der Nicolai- und Thomasschule zu Leipzig (1670–1684).* Edited by Richard Sachse. Leipzig: Wörner, 1912.

Tille, Alexander. *Die Geschichte der Deutschen Weihnacht.* Leipzig: Ernst Keil's Nachfolger, 1893.

Tinctoris. *On the Dignity & the Effects of Music: Two Fifteenth-Century Treatises.* Edited by J. Donald Cullington and Reinhard Strohm. Translated by J. Donald Cullington. London: Institute of Advanced Musical Studies, King's College, 1996.

Tlusty, B. Ann. *Bacchus and Civic Order: The Culture of Drink in Early Modern Germany.* Charlottesville: University Press of Virginia, 2001.

Trexler, Richard C. *The Journey of the Magi: Meanings in History of a Christian Story.* Princeton, NJ: Princeton University Press, 1997.

Turner, Denys. *Eros and Allegory: Medieval Exegesis of the Song of Songs.* Cistercian Studies Series 156. Kalamazoo, MI: Cistercian Publications, 1995.

van Boer, Bertil. "Observations on Bach's Use of the Horn, Part I." *Bach* 11 (1980): 21–28.

van Dülmen, Richard. "Volksfrömmigkeit und konfessionelles Christentum im 16. und 17. Jahrhundert." *Geschichte und Gesellschaft,* Sonderheft 11 (1986): 14–30.

van Elferen, Isabella. *Mystical Love in the German Baroque: Theology, Poetry, Music.* Contextual Bach Studies 2. Lanham, MD: Scarecrow Press, 2009.

van Ingen, Ferdinand. "Die Wiederaufnahme der Devotio Moderna bei Johann Arndt und Philipp von Zesen." In *Religion und Religiosität im Zeitalter des Barock*, edited by Dieter Breuer, 467–75. Wolfenbütteler Arbeiten zur Barockforschung 25. Wiesbaden: Harrassowitz, 1995.

van Ingen, Ferdinand. *Echo im 17. Jahrhundert: Ein literarisch-musikalisches Phänomen in der Frühen Neuzeit.* Amsterdam: Koninklijke Nederlandse Akademie van Wetenschappen, 2002.

Varwig, Bettina. "Metaphors of Time and Modernity in Bach." *Journal of Musicology* 29 (2012): 154–90.

Vogel, Johann Jacob. *Leipzigisches Geschicht-Buch, oder Annales, das ist: Jahr- und Tage-Bücher Der Weltberümten Königl. und Churfürstl. Sächsischen Kauff- und Handels-Stadt Leipzig in welchen die meisten merckwürdigsten Geschichte und geschehene Veränderungen . . . enthalten sind.* Leipzig: Lank, 1756.

von Holst, Ortwin. "Turba Chöre des Weihnachts-Oratoriums und der Markuspassion." *Musik und Kirche* 38 (1968): 229–33.

von Winterfeld, Carl. *Der evangelische Kirchengesang und sein Verhaltnis zur Kunst des Tonsatzes.* Leipzig, 1847. Reprint, Hildesheim: Olms, 1966.

Wade, Mara. *The German Baroque Pastoral "Singspiel."* Berner Beiträge zur Barockgermanistik 7. Bern: Peter Lang, 1990.

Wald, Melanie. "Kanon, Kombinatorik, Echokompositionen: Die musikalische Vermittlung zwischen Himmel und Erde in der Frühen Neuzeit." *Musiktheorie* 23 (2008): 51–70.

Wallmann, Walter. Review of *Gnadengegenwart: Johann Sebastian Bach im Kontext lutherischer Orthodoxie und Frömmigkeit,* by Renate Steiger. *Pietismus und Neuzeit* 29 (2003): 327–32.

Walther, Johann Gottfried. *Musikalisches Lexikon oder musikalische Bibliothek.* Leipzig: Deer, 1732.

Walter, Meinrad. *Johann Sebastian Bach: Johannespassion. Eine musikalisch-theologische Einführung.* Stuttgart: Carus Verlag and Reclam, 2011.

Walter, Meinrad. *Johann Sebastian Bach—Weihnachtsoratorium.* Kassel: Bärenreiter, 2006.

Weise, Christian. *Die drei ärgsten Erznarren in der ganzen Welt.* Abdruck der Ausgabe von 1673. Halle: Niemeyer, 1878.

Weise, Christian. *Reiffe Gedancken, das ist, Allerhand Ehren-Lust-Trauer- und Lehr-Gedichte . . . zu Verbesserung der überflüssigen Gedanken herausgegeben,* Leipzig: C. Weidmann, 1682.

Weiss, Ulman. "Nicolaus Stenger und Ezechiel Meth im Jahre 1640: Des Pfarrers Versehgang bei einem Verirrten." In *Nicolaus Stenger (1609–1680): Beiträge zu Leben, Werk und Wirken,* edited by Michael Ludscheidt, 65–77. Erfurt: Ulenspiegel-Verlag, 2011.

Wentzel, Johann Christoph. *Der unerkandte Jesus zu Christlicher Vorbereitung auf das Heilige Weyhnacht-Fest von der studierenden Jugend in Zittau den 21. Decembr. 1718 in einem kurtzen Dramate vorgestellet.* Budissin: David Richter, 1719.

Werner, Arno. *Städtische und fürstliche Musikpflege in Weißenfels.* Leipzig: Breitkopf und Härtel, 1911.

Werthemann, Helene. *Studien zu den Adventsliedern des 16. und 17. Jahrhunderts.* Basler Studien zur Historischen und Systematischen Theologie 4. Zürich: EVZ, 1963.

Werthemann, Helene. "Jesus Christus, vorgestellt zu einem Gnadenstuhl durch den Glauben in seinem Blut: Der alttestamentliche Sühnedeckel und seine Erfüllung in Christus," In *Das Blut Jesu und die Lehre von der Versöhnung im Werk Johann Sebastian Bachs,* edited by Albert A. Clement, 63–78. Amsterdam: Royal Netherlands Academy of Arts and Sciences, 1995.

Wheeler, Joe, and Jim Rosenthal. *St. Nicholas: A Closer Look at Christmas.* Nashville: Thomas Nelson, 2005.

Wiesend, Reinhard. "'Erbarme dich,' alla Siciliana." In *Bach und die italienische Musik / Bach e la musica italiana,* edited by Wolfgang Osthoff and Reinhard Wiesend, 19–41. Venice: Centro Tedesco di Studi Veneziani, 1987.

Wiesend, Reinhard. "Siciliana: Literarische und musikalische Traditionen." Habilitation, University of Würzburg, 1986.

Williams, Peter. *The Organ Music of J. S. Bach.* 2nd ed. Cambridge: Cambridge University Press, 2003.

Wolff, Christoph. "Anmerkungen zu Bach und 'Cleofide' (Dresden 1731)." In *Johann Sebastian Bachs Spätwerk und dessen Umfeld: Bericht über das wissenschaftliche Symposium anläßlich des 61. Bachfestes der Neuen Bachgesellschaft, Duisburg 1986,* edited by Christoph Wolff, 167–69. Kassel: Bärenreiter, 1988.

Wolff, Christoph. "Bachs weltliche Kantaten: Repertoire und Kontext." In *Die Welt der Bach Kantaten II: Johann Sebastian Bachs weltliche Kantaten,* edited by Christoph Wolff, 13–31. Stuttgart/ Kassel: Metzler/Bärenreiter 1997.

Wolff, Christoph. "Carl Philipp Emanuel Bachs Trio in d-Moll (BWV 1036/Wq 145)." *Bach-Jahrbuch* 95 (2009), 177–90.

Wolff, Christoph. *Johann Sebastian Bach: The Learned Musician.* New York: Norton, 2000.

Wolff, Christoph. *Johann Sebastian Bach: Messe in h-Moll.* Kassel: Bärenreiter, 2009.

Wolff, Christoph. "Under the Spell of Opera? Bach's Oratorio Trilogy." In *J. S. Bach and the Oratorio Tradition,* edited by Daniel R. Melamed, 1–12. *Bach Perspectives* 8. Urbana: University of Illinois Press, 2011.

Wollny, Peter. "'Bekennen will ich seinen Namen'–Authenzität, Bestimmung und Kontext der Arie BWV 200. Anmerkungen zu Johann Sebastian Bachs Rezeption von Werken Gottfried Heinrich Stölzels." *Bach-Jahrbuch* 94 (2008): 123–58.

Wollny, Peter. "Johann Christoph Friedrich Bach und die Teilung des väterlichen Erbes." *Bach-Jahrbuch* 87 (2001): 55–70.

Wolschke, Martin. *Von der Stadtpfeiferei zu Lehrlingskapelle und Sinfonieorchester: Wandlungen im 19. Jahrhundert*. Studien zur Musikgeschichte des 19. Jahrhunderts 59. Regensburg: Bosse, 1981.

Zahn, Johannes. *Die Melodien der deutschen evangelischen Kirchenlieder aus den Quellen geschöpft und mitgeteilt*. Vol. 3. Nachdr. d. Ausg. Gütersloh., 1889. Reprint, Hildesheim: Olms, 2006.

*Das Gott-lobende Zion, oder, Zeitzisches Kirch- Schul und Haus- Gesang-Buch*. Zeitz/Bohsögel, 1736

Zohn, Steven. *Music for a Mixed Taste: Style, Genre, and Meaning in Telemann's Instrumental Works*. Oxford: Oxford University Press, 2008.

# INDEX